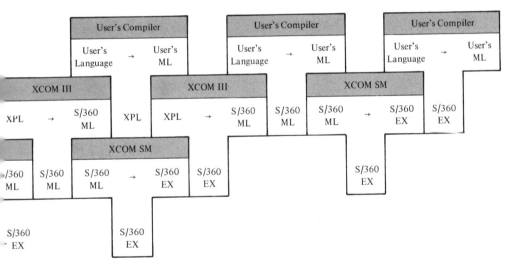

The purpose of this unique book is two-fold: to serve as an introduction to the theory and practice of compiler construction for computer programming languages and as a complete documentation of the XPL compiler generator system. The latter may be used to prepare efficient compilers for the IBM System/360 computers.

Part I is devoted to the development of the relevant theory of compilers and emphasizes a thorough understanding of the principles of syntax-directed compilation methods. Part II covers the practical application of this theory and develops the implementation skills required to produce compilers and provides a detailed exposition of a typical compiler (XCOM). An existing practical system is documented for generating mechanical translators. The XPL system, a specific usable compiler construction tool, is sufficiently powerful and efficient to be used by advanced systems groups of several large computer manufacturers for complex languages such as FORTRAN or PL/1.

Outstanding features:

- Formal treatment of the theory used in the system

- Exhaustive set of exercises and examples designed to test as

ford University, is Assistant Professor, Computer Science, at the University of Toronto.

Prentice-Hall
Series in Automatic Computation

George Forsythe, editor

ARBIB, *Theories of Abstract Automata*
BATES AND DOUGLAS, *Programming Language/One*
BAUMANN, FELICIANO, BAUER, AND SAMELSON, *Introduction to ALGOL*
BLUMENTHAL, *Management Information Systems*
BOBROW AND SCHWARTZ, editors, *Computers and the Policy-Making Community: Applications to International Relations*
BOWLES, editor, *Computers in Humanistic Research*
CRESS, DIRKSEN, AND GRAHAM, *FORTRAN IV with WATFOR*
DANIEL, *Theory and Methods for the Approximate Minimization of Functionals*
DESMONDE, *Computers and Their Uses, 2nd ed.*
EVANS, WALLACE, AND SUTHERLAND, *Simulation Using Digital Computers*
FIKE, *Computer Evaluation of Mathematical Functions*
FIKE, *PL/1 for Scientific Programmers*
FORSYTHE AND MOLER, *Computer Solution of Linear Algebraic Systems*
GAUTHIER AND PONTO, *Designing Systems Programs*
GOLDEN, *FORTRAN IV: Programming and Computing*
GOLDEN AND LEICHUS, *IBM 360: Programming and Computing*
GORDON, *System Simulation*
GREENSPAN, *Lectures on the Numerical Solution of Linear, Singular and Nonlinear Differential Equations*
GRISWOLD, POAGE, AND POLONSKY, *The SNOBOL 4 Programming Language*
HARTMANIS AND STEARNS, *Algebraic Structure Theory of Sequential Machines*
HULL, *Introduction to Computing*
HUSSON, *Microprogramming: Principles and Practices*
JOHNSON, *System Structure in Data, Programs, and Computers*
KIVIAT, VILLANUEVA, AND MARKOWITZ, *The SIMSCRIPT 11 Programming Language*
LOUDEN, *Programming the IBM 1130 and 1800*
MARTIN, *Design of Real-Time Computer Systems*
MARTIN, *Programming Real-Time Computer Systems*
MARTIN, *Telecommunications and the Computer*
MARTIN, *Teleprocessing Network Organization*
MARTIN AND NORMAN, *The Computerized Society*
MATHISON AND WALKER, *Computers and Telecommunications: Issue in Public Policy*
McKEEMAN, HORNING, AND WORTMAN, *A Compiler Generator*
MINSKY, *Computation: Finite and Infinite Machines*
MOORE, *Interval Analysis*
PYLYSHYN, editor, *Perspectives on the Computer Revolution*
PRITSKER AND KIVIAT, *Simulation with GASP 11: A FORTRAN Based Simulation Language*
SAMMET, *Programming Languages: History and Fundamentals*
STERLING AND POLLACK, *Introduction to Statistical Data Processing*
TAVISS, editor, *The Computer Impact*
TRAUB, *Iterative Methods for the Solution of Equations*
VARGA, *Matrix Iterative Analysis*
VAZSONYI, *Problem Solving by Digital Computers with PL/1 Programming*
WILKINSON, *Rounding Errors in Algebraic Processes*

A Compiler Generator

W. M. McKEEMAN

University of California
Santa Cruz, California

J. J. HORNING

University of Toronto
Toronto, Ontario, Canada

D. B. WORTMAN

Stanford University
Stanford, California

PRENTICE-HALL, INC., *Englewood Cliffs, N. J.*

Current printing (last digit):

4   3   2   1

13–155077–2

Library of Congress Catalog Card Number 76–117205
Printed in the United States of America

PRENTICE-HALL INTERNATIONAL INC., *London*
PRENTICE-HALL OF AUSTRALIA, PTY., LTD., *Sydney*
PRENTICE-HALL OF CANADA, LTD., *Toronto*
PRENTICE-HALL OF INDIA PRIVATE LTD., *New Delhi*
PRENTICE-HALL OF JAPAN, INC., *Tokyo*

For

Bettie, Jane, and Ginny

Preface

/*   "Faith" is a fine invention
     When gentlemen can see;
     But Microscopes are prudent
     In an emergency .   */

EMILY DICKINSON

The Complete Poems of Emily Dickinson†

This book serves two purposes. It is first a text on the theory and practice of constructing syntax-directed compilers, intended for the undergraduate or beginning graduate student in Computer Science. It is also a reference manual for those wishing to use the XPL compiler generator system developed on the IBM System/360 (and now available on various other machines). The two purposes are complementary since a user requires an understanding of relevant theory and a student gains insight through the use of compiler writing tools. Except for such basic notions as sets, relations, and functions, no prior mathematical background is assumed.

This book is organized into complementary parts respectively titled *Theory* and *Practice*. In the second part we have placed explicit directions for using and understanding various programs of the XPL system; in the first part we present the reasons that these programs have taken their present form. Each chapter in a part provides the reader with a specific skill which he can use immediately by accepting the other mechanisms on faith. Each chapter, while turning a former faith into understanding, introduces a new mystery to be resolved later, until Chapters Five and Ten where the last questions are answered.

Exercises are *not* optional. The reader must read and understand them as they are encountered in the text; he should be forewarned that not all of the exercises are intended to be worked out. For many, the correct answer is the realization that the exercise is impossibly hard or tedious.

A course based on this material should take two quarters. The student should have a good understanding of at least one programming language and some confidence in his own mathematical maturity. It is essential that the student have regular access to the computational tools described in Part II. Towards the end of the first quarter

---

† Reprinted by permission of the publishers and the Trustees of Amherst College from Thomas H. Johnson, Editor, *The Poems of Emily Dickinson* (Cambridge, Mass.: The Belknap Press of Harvard University Press, Copyright, 1951, 1955, by The President and Fellows of Harvard College).

the student will begin to need supplementary material that describes the mechanisms of a wider range of programming languages and he should be starting to study a variety of contemporary machines. The course itself is built around the term project of writing a compiler for a language designed by the students themselves. We have felt it important to spend considerable time widening the range of experience of the students as regards programming languages and styles. We emphasize that students will do better work in this course if they are free of the prejudices previously gathered in programming a commercial computer at the machine-language level.

The following schedule has proven acceptable:

Week 1	Familiarization with XPL
	Explanation of Exercise 9.6.7.
Reading:	Introduction and Chapter 6.
Assignment:	Exercises 6.1, 6.9.

Week 2	Use of BNF
Reading:	Sections 2.1, 2.2.
Assignment:	Exercises 2.2.1, 2.2.2, 2.2.3, 2.2.7, 2.2.11.

Week 3	Formal theory
Reading:	Section 2.3.
Assignment:	Exercises 2.3.1, 2.3.2, 2.3.3, 2.3.4.

Week 4	The big picture and interpretation
Reading:	Sections 3.1, 3.2.
Assignment:	Exercises 3.2.2, 3.2.6, 3.2.7.

Week 5	The simple compiler
Reading:	Sections 3.3, 3.4.
Assignment:	Exercises 3.3.3, 3.3.4, 3.4.5.

Week 6	Recognition
Reading:	Sections 4.1, 4.2.
Assignment:	Exercises 4.2.1, 4.2.2, 4.2.4, 4.2.5.

Week 7	Language structure, ALGOL, PL/I.
Reading:	Section 3.5 and the ALGOL-60 Report.
Assignment:	A simple program in ALGOL-60.

Week 8	BNF programming
Reading:	Chapter 7.
Assignment:	Exercise 7.1.1, 7.1.2, 7.2.5.

Week 9	Language design
Reading:	Chapter 1.
Assignment:	Term project, Exercise 9.6.7., to groups of about three students each.

| Week 10 | Using the skeletal compiler |
| Reading: | Section 9.6. |

| Week 11 | Scanners and the XCOM symbol table |
| Reading: | Section 9.3, 8.9. |

Week 12	List processing languages
Reading:	The *LISP 1.5 manual.*
Assignment:	A simple program in LISP.

Week 13   Operation on structured operands
Reading: *A Programming Language*, Iverson.
Assignment: A simple program in APL.

Week 14   Contemporary machine language
Reading: A reference manual for a modern computer, or Illife, *Basic Machine
             Principles* (1968), or "A formal description of System/360," Falkoff, et al,
             IBM System Journal 3, 2 (1964) p. 198.
Assignment: A simple program in assembly language.

Week 15   Asynchronous processes
Reading: *Cooperating Sequential Processes*, Dijkstra.

Week 16   Microprogramming

Weeks 17–20 These are best utilized by working with students on their term projects.
             Some students will want to delve into Chapters 5 and 10.

The XPL system was developed by the authors over a three-year period at the Stanford Computation Center, at the General Motors Research Laboratory, and at the University of California at Santa Cruz. The original motivation to pursue this project came from the need for a programming system for the beginning undergraduate Computer Science student. The first such effort, a compiler written by Ed Nelson, proved too complex and was finally abandoned after a year of work. The second, an interpreter written by Dave Wortman, has proven successful. Perhaps four man years went into the project, equally spread between developing the translator writing system, developing the student systems, and producing this documentation.

We would like to express our appreciation to the Campus Facility of the Stanford Computation Center for support of this project, including a staggering amount of computer time. We are also indebted for the criticisms, inspiration, and assistance of Robert Barton, Diane Bausek, Rod Fredrickson, Martin Hopkins, Mike Marcotty, Robert McClure, Ed Nelson, Steve Newberry, Raj Reddy, Bill Riddle, Robert Rosin, and Jeffrey Sue.

Contents

Introduction

Language and the Computer

/* ". . . There's glory for you!"

"I don't know what you mean by 'glory,' " Alice said.

Humpty Dumpty smiled contemptuously. "Of course you don't—till I tell you. I meant 'there's a nice knock-down argument for you!' "

"But 'glory' doesn't mean 'a nice knock-down argument,' " Alice objected.

"When *I* use a word," Humpty Dumpty said, in a rather scornful tone, "it means just what *I* choose it to mean—neither more nor less."

"The question is," said Alice, "whether you *can* make words mean so many different things."

"The question is," said Humpty Dumpty, "which is to be master—that's all." */

LEWIS CARROLL

Through the Looking Glass

0.1 Language Is the Essential Tool of Intellect

/* The symbol-making function is one of man's primary activities. . . . It is the fundamental process of the mind. */

SUSANNE K. LANGER

Philosophy in a New Key

/* Man's achievements rest upon the use of symbols. */

ALFRED KORZYBSKI

Science and Sanity

/* Language . . . makes progress possible. */

S. I. HAYAKAWA

Language in Thought and Action

/* Stability in language is synonymous with *rigor mortis.* */

ERNEST WEEKLEY

Words, Ancient and Modern

1

This book is about writing compilers. Before going into detail, it is appropriate to say a few words about why computer users must necessarily become involved in language invention and thus compiler writing. Some readers will prefer to skip to Part I, where a formal treatment of compiler generation methods is found, or to Part II, where the IBM System/360 implementation is described. For the rest of our readers, we will proceed with a set of arguments intended to establish language design as a valid, indeed even essential, part of the computer problem solving process.

The user of a modern computer faces a bewildering array of languages: languages of machine control; high-level languages, which must be translated; languages to express the translation process; and languages to define languages. All these languages are artificial, restricted modes of expression first invented by someone and then tediously learned by others. One feels obliged to ask why so many artificial languages have been created when perfectly general natural languages exist. Why should computer users need all the following (and more besides)?

100   DO   200   I = 1, 10

⟨do statement⟩ :: =   ⟨sequence number⟩ DO ⟨integer⟩ ⟨identifier⟩ = ⟨control⟩

L   1,=1
S   1,I
BC   14,∗+8

IF I = 0 THEN RETURN (1); ELSE RETURN (I ∗ FACTORIAL(I-1));

The answer is that everyone invents language all the time. Computer users, because they face particularly severe obstacles in the process, are more likely to notice that they are doing so. However, they should not avoid language invention. And, indeed, they cannot.

The mind creates languages; it is a part of the process of understanding. Only representations of objects and ideas can exist in the brain, and while we do not know how these representations are "manipulated," we do know that it is helpful to have symbols, which we can record, observe, and manipulate. These we invent.

We may coin a word (*cybernetics* or *beatnik*) or a complete jargon (listen to a stockbroker, for example); we may devise a new symbol (∞) or a whole formal mathematical system (tensor calculus); or we may assign new meanings to old forms (what does "cool" mean?). There are examples of invented language in law and differential calculus, knitting and matrix algebra, mathematical logic and organic chemistry. In each case the invented language has special symbolic properties that simplify communication and comprehension.

Some of the properties that make special languages attractive are obvious. We use such languages in contexts in which we have restricted our range of interest. These languages can therefore be concise because there are fewer items to be described (for example, in police radio calls). And they can be precise because, knowing by context all the pertinent items, we can make exactly corresponding descriptions (consider the integers and our representations of them). It may be that certain formal manipulations of expressions in a language yield results having meaning within our range of interest (for example, using numbers to express the cost of purchases or alphabetic order to sort a telephone directory).

Of course, we must avoid a Tower of Babel in which everyone writes and under-stands only his own special symbolisms. Fortunately, invented languages are subject to a natural control. The most convenient and expressive languages are widely used, copied, and further improved, while others are forgotten. Our heritage of knowledge is stored and shared in a few such exceptional languages; their creation has been essential to the ability of an individual to begin where others left off.

Exercise   0.1.1

This problem is designed for the reader who thinks natural language could be used for all technical work. Each one of the following valid statements is relevant to the computer solution of some problem. Pick several with which you are familiar, and evaluate the utility of the specialized languages involved by translating the given statements into their English equivalents. Use no specialized vocabulary or notation. Alternatively, present an argument that this is an absurd assignment.

Example   (Propositional Calculus) :

$$((P_1 \supset P_2) \supset ((P_2 \supset P_3) \supset (P_1 \supset P_3)))$$

may be translated "Given three statements which are true or false, if the truth of the first implies the truth of the second, this implies that if the truth of the second implies the truth of the third, then the truth of the first implies the truth of the third."

1. (Predicate Calculus): $(\forall x)(A \supset B) \supset ((\exists x)A \supset (\exists x)B)$

2. (Quantum Mechanics): $H\psi = E\psi$

    where $H = -(\hbar^2/2m)\nabla^2 + V$ and E is the energy of the system

3. (Electricity and Magnetism):   (1) $\nabla \cdot \mathbf{D} = \rho$

    (2) $\nabla \cdot \mathbf{B} = 0$

    (3) $\nabla \times \mathbf{E} = -\dfrac{\partial \mathbf{B}}{\partial t}$

    (4) $\nabla \times \mathbf{H} = \mathbf{j} + \dfrac{\partial \mathbf{D}}{\partial t}$

4. (Matrix Algebra):   The trace of a matrix is equal to the sum of its eigenvalues.

5. (Organic Chemistry): $3CH_3CH_2OH + Cr_2O_7^{--} + 8H^+ \longrightarrow$
    $\qquad\qquad 3CH_3CHO(g) + 2Cr^{+3} + 7H_2O$

6. (Knitting):   K2 tog. 3(5) times, *k1, p2, k1, k3, tog., k1, p2, k1, p1, k1, p3 tog., k1, p1, k1, p1*; repeat between *'s once more, k1, p2, k1, k3 tog., k1, p2, k1; k2 tog. 3(5) times; 47(51) sts. (Note that there are two levels of under-standing; we may either give explicit directions or say just "Knit a ski cap.")

7. (Poetry):   Shakespearean sonnets are in iambic
                                    pentameter and consist of three quatrains
                                    followed by a couplet.

0.2 The Computer Is Our Intellectual Assistant

/∗   And every time they found out what seemed to be a purpose of themselves, the
purpose seemed so low that the creatures were filled with disgust and shame. And, rather
than serve such a low purpose, the creatures would make a machine to serve it. This left
the creatures free to serve higher purposes.   ∗/

KURT VONNEGUT, JR.

Sirens of Titan

/∗   So that even now the machines will only serve on condition of being served, and
that too upon their own terms; the moment their terms are not complied with, they jib,
and either smash both themselves and all whom they can reach, or turn churlish and refuse
to work at all. How many men at this hour are living in a state of bondage to the machines?
How many spend their whole lives, from the cradle to the grave, in tending them by night
and day? Is it not plain that the machines are gaining ground upon us, when we reflect
on the increasing number of those who are bound down to them as slaves, and of those
who devote their whole souls to the advancement of the mechanical kingdom?   ∗/

SAMUEL BUTLER

quoting a scholar of Erewhon, 1872

That the computer, especially in a symbolic environment, has manlike properties
should not surprise us. It was invented to do intellectual work for us. Thus, we are
naturally anthropomorphic in our description and understanding of computers.
In particular, we expect to carry on an extensive symbolic dialogue with our computers
in languages acceptable to us (*problem languages*). Nevertheless, while we may accept
the inevitability of the human invention of languages, we may be uncertain about the
ability of a computer to understand them.

The tasks we set for computers are algorithmic. That is, we decide what representations are to be processed, what actions are to be taken, and under what conditions
the computer may operate. The original digital computers were designed to do extensive arithmetic calculations on numeric data. We now know that machines are theoretically capable of performing any well-defined symbolic processing operation. They
can translate languages, play games of intellectual skill, prognosticate elections,
simulate organisms, produce and recognize pictures, and so on. Once we fully understand how *we* do a process, it is usually a trivial (but laborious) task to make a computer duplicate our efforts.

Each computer has its own control language, usually quite remote from the wide variety of languages demanded by the diverse uses of the machine. A translation from problem language to machine language is required. Assemblers, interpreters, and compilers have been developed to transfer as much as possible of this tedious task from man to machine. But the difficulty in preparing translators has hindered the development of computer languages. Translators have yet to be written for many useful languages, while for many applications, the appropriate languages themselves must still be developed.

It has been proposed that a powerful standard language be adopted to drastically reduce the number of translators needed. But such a language would tend to be one of three things: not rich enough for the convenient statement of all algorithms, not concise and efficient in the statement of individual algorithms, or so elaborate as to be unlearnable. No language designer can foresee all future applications of computers; thus, we claim that the demand for a static standard programming language is antithetical to progress in the utilization of computers. Even if we are satisfied with such a computer language, we must remember that to someone else it will be a windowless prison.

Exercise 0.2.1

Perhaps the reader is not convinced that our present computer languages are inadequate. For instance, it has been claimed that FORTRAN, ALGOL, and PL/I are general-purpose languages for controlling computers. Select one of these programming languages (or another you feel is more general) and translate each of the statements of Exercise 0.1.1 into that language. If you find that one or more statements are untranslatable, give a convincing argument to support your belief that the programming language is inadequate.

We would like to solve problems without worrying about translation into machinable form, but in practice we do not. The computer user knows that general-purpose machines do only a few things well, and he usually restricts his applications to those few things. To be generally useful to men, computers must evolve. Computer designers can and should utilize the most useful problem languages as models and then build machines in which they can be easily implemented. The idea is to use the problem language as a proven repository of the users' needs. Each improved machine should then allow new uses which will suggest new languages, and so on. But these new languages will never exist unless they are designed and used in spite of the present primitive state of computer hardware.

Computer organizations are no more likely to proliferate than are languages. As of this writing, the enormous rates of change in computer speed, size, and economics obscure the relative advantages of different organizations. However, general organizations well-adapted for processing wide varieties of languages may exist. The danger lies in the assumption that we have already achieved all that is possible.

Exercise 0.2.2

It is hard to demonstrate the superiority of one machine over another. Part of the difficulty lies in the theoretical generality of all of them—they can all do the same things given sufficient time and memory (but these are the main indicators of cost). Also, the actual costs are hidden by the compilation process and the complexity of the resulting code. To better understand this problem, try to demonstrate that an electronic Turing machine, implemented with the best contemporary electronics, must necessarily be inferior to some conventional computer.†

0.3 To Teach a Computer a Language

/∗   "Quiet!" said Khasdrahr.
   The Shah turned to a glowing bank of EPICAC's tubes and cried in a piping singsong voice:

> "Allakahi baku billa,
> Moumi a fella nam;
> Serani assu tilla,
> Touri serin a sam."

"The crazy bastard's talking to the machine," whispered Lynn.
   "Ssssh!" said Halyard, strangely moved by the scene.
   "Siki?" cried the Shah. He cocked his head, listening. "Siki?"
The word echoed and died—lonely, lost.
   "Mmmmmmmmm," said EPICAC softly. "Dit, dit. Mmmmmm. Dit."
   The Shah sighed and stood, and shook his head sadly, terribly let down. "Nibo," he murmured, "Nibo."
   "What's he say?" said the President.
   " 'Nibo'—'nothing.' He asked the machine a question, and the machine didn't answer," said Halyard, "Nibo."
   "Nuttiest thing I ever heard of," said the President. "You have to punch out the questions on that thingamajig, and the answers come out on tape from the whatchamacallits. You can't just talk to it." A doubt crossed his fine face. "I mean, you can't, can you?"
   "No sir," said the chief engineer of the project. "As you say, not without the thingamajigs and whatchamacallits."   ∗/

KURT VONNEGUT, JR.

Player Piano

   The translation from problem language to machine language can, in theory, always be performed by humans. For many reasons, however, this procedure is not desirable.

---

† See W. M. McKeeman, "Language Directed Computer Design," *Proceedings of the Fall Joint Computer Conference* (November 1967); and M. Minsky, *Computation, Finite and Infinite Machines* (Englewood Cliffs, N.J.: Prentice-Hall, Inc., 1967).

For maximum intellectual assistance, the user must be able to communicate with the computer directly, without stopping to translate. Moreover, from a strictly economic standpoint, computers can translate into machine language (compile) less expensively and more reliably than humans can. This fact is increasingly evident as the size and complexity of programs increase; it is extremely difficult to understand all the ramifications of a large program in terms of machine operations.

The clarity and simplicity of high-level programs facilitate program correction and maintenance and aid in communication with other users. Effort is concentrated on the solution of the assigned problems, rather than on mastery of the machine.

Exercise 0.3.1.

Select one or more of your statements from Exercise 0.2.1 and translate it to the machine language of any computer with which you are familiar. Keep track of the time you expend. If you have access to a computer, compare the time to solution and total cost (make a reasonable estimate of your own value) of the thoroughly checked machine-language form with those of compilation from a high-level language.†

Fortunately, it is becoming easier to write translators. Computer Science research and experience with existing compilers have led to a better theoretical and practical understanding of the processes involved. Translator writing systems now automate major portions of the task. In this book we discuss one such system. The interested reader should refer to the excellent survey of this field by Feldman and Gries [68] for information on a variety of other systems.

Generally, we define a *translator* as a function whose domain is a source language and whose range is contained in a target language. Translators that map a structured (or high-level) source language into machine instructions are usually called *compilers*; those that translate into convenient encodings that direct the execution of an interpretive program are called *interpreters*; those that translate symbolic machine language into digital machine language are called *assemblers*.

Broadly speaking, a *translator writing system* (TWS) is any system in which a translator may be specified (written) and realized (turned into code). The utility of a TWS is based on the observation that most translators have many tasks—scanning text, analyzing syntax, generating output, and interacting with an operating system—in common. Once these problems are solved in general form, the writer of an individual translator can concentrate on that part of the problem unique to his translator, i.e., the connection of his meanings (semantics) to his forms (syntax). Many TWSs also have various aids to assist in the latter process.

We have implemented a particular TWS for the IBM System/360. Although claiming neither to have discovered the definitive language nor to have written the ultimate compiler, we have developed what we consider a useful tool for those who wish to write compilers. The translators produced are fast, one-pass, and entirely expressible in a high-level language.

---

† The reader might be interested in a careful evaluation of this kind. See Christopher J. Shaw, "More Instructions . . . Less Work," *Datamation* 10, 6 (June 1964), p. 34.

Our TWS utilizes the language XPL (a dialect of PL/I), for the description of programs, and the metalanguage Backus-Naur Form (BNF), for the description of languages. It consists of three principal components:

1. ANALYZER, a translator from BNF into syntax tables, used in
2. SKELETON, a table-driven proto-compiler written in XPL, which, when supplied with syntax tables and suitable semantic routines, may be compiled by
3. XCOM, a translator from XPL to System/360 machine code.

If the user wishes to compile a dialect of PL/I for the System/360, his task is greatly simplified because his semantic routines may be modeled on those of XCOM. In any case XCOM provides a good source of examples.

Since this book presupposes no particular prior knowledge of translators on the part of the reader, Part I develops the theoretical background and motivation for our TWS. Our method is applicable to most languages on all sufficiently large computers. By describing it abstractly, we separate the limits of the method from those of the implementation. Part II contains detailed information about the use and structure of the TWS. Complete listings of all programs referred to are contained in the various appendices.

PART I

THEORY

Part I is divided into five chapters. The first is concerned generally with the description of translators and specifically with the kinds of control and data structures needed in a programming language used to implement our techniques. In the second chapter we introduce phrase-structure grammars as a way of describing languages. The emphasis is on the concepts and notation used in later chapters. Chapter 3 discusses the translation process, emphasizing the production of single-address machine code. Chapter 4 treats the problem of recognizing the phrase structure of program text. We find that the kinds of decisions we can make determine the class of algorithms that can be used. These algorithms in turn delimit the class of languages that can be recognized. Chapter 5 concludes the theoretical background with a discussion of the construction of tables needed by a recognizer.

Each chapter in Part I provides the formal basis for the material in the corresponding chapter in Part II. The reader should, upon completing his study of Part I, be able to understand the reasons for various details of the implementation as well as the basic subject matter in most of the literature in the field. Readers with strong programming experience will likely prefer to read Parts I and II together, while the more mathematically inclined will probably finish Part I before starting Part II.

Chapter 1

The Description of Translators

/∗   It is possible by ingenuity and at the expense of clarity . . . [to do almost anything in any language]. However, the fact that it is possible to push a pea up a mountain with your nose does not mean that this is a sensible way of getting it there. Each of these techniques of language extension should be used in its proper place.   ∗/

CHRISTOPHER STRACHEY

NATO Summer School in Programming

1.1 Taking Our Own Medicine

/∗   Therefore shall they eat the fruit of their own way and be filled with their own devices.   ∗/

Proverbs 1 : 32

Translation is a complex process, one of the many such processes we direct a digital computer to perform. If the reader has been following the thread of our argument, he will anticipate that we will propose the invention of a language, understandable both to man and to machine, to express the translation process. We do.

In Chapter 6 we present the language (XPL) we designed to express the class of translators with which we are concerned. There we discuss the reasons for picking particular forms for describing information and processes; here we present the requirements common to languages for the description of translators. We use ALGOL 60 and PL/I as examples throughout this chapter. The reader familiar with neither of these languages will have some trouble; we recommend keeping the ALGOL Report [Naur 63] and the PL/I Language Specifications [IBM 6Xf] on hand for quick reference.

The reader will find no startling innovations on the following pages, one reason being that since the efficiency of translators is an important concern, the constructs of the language reflect the structure of the IBM System/360. A second reason is that the technique used in the recognition phase of the translator was first presented [Floyd 63] with the explicit intent that it be efficiently implementable on existing conventional machines. Third, all popular languages have most of the necessary primitive operations in at least one, if not several, forms.

11

Before getting explicit, we will describe the basic concepts underlying any computer language design. These concepts include selection by name (the idea of a set), selection by position (the idea of an ordered set), subdefinition in terms of components, iteration, meaningful primitive operations, and control over the allocation of computer resources.

The reader should note what machine capabilities are missing from this chapter. By their absence we designate them irrelevant to the translation process, thereby simplifying both our language and its translator. The addition of features to a language is not a linear process as far as the translator is concerned. Constructs interact with each other, and the addition of a single feature may, in some cases, double the size of the translator. The potentially exponential growth of translator size as language complexity increases has two important implications. First, a translation method effective for simple test languages or machines may prove inadequate for more practical languages or existing machines. Second, an elaborate language (e.g., the full PL/I) may need a much larger translator than that needed by several smaller languages which, in aggregate, have the same features.

1.2 Matching the Machine

Efficiency demands that the constructs we propose be close to the machine. This matching must occur in several areas. We must be able to access the memory efficiently by operating on the directly addressable quanta of memory (characters, words, etc.). We also require the ability to describe and operate on the basic units of information (bits), both for the generation of arbitrary object code and for efficient packing and unpacking of various tables. The designers of ALGOL 60 made some provision for different kinds of access in the types **real**, **integer**, and **Boolean**. PL/I has a much more elaborate scheme, providing for many more types as well as for a variable precision within each type. The types **character** and **bit** are particularly important since they reflect immediate needs for efficient text-processing and data-packing. One related kind of access important to the compiler writer is the ability to fetch the internal code for a character in a string, to be used as a small integer.

We would, of course, expect the writer of a translator to be able to provide for the emission of code for any machine instruction. What is not obvious, but is frequently true, is that the writer may want to cause the execution of an arbitrary instruction during compilation. The machine itself already places severe constraints upon the translator; it is unwise to compound these constraints further by restricting the translator to some subset of the capabilities of the machine. Although no single translator is likely to use the full instruction repertoire of a large-scale computer, we cannot a priori classify any instruction as being unusable. The simplest examples of this kind of usefulness are the floating-point operations. The compilation mechanism itself has no need for them; however, if the language being compiled includes floating-point values, we can conveniently use the floating-point hardware to convert input numbers, precompute constant expressions, and the like. Rather than add a type to the compiler language, we make some general provision for instruction-by-instruction, in-line execution of arbitrary machine code. Although both ALGOL 60 and PL/I provide for procedures written in machine code, we reject this otherwise equivalent solution because (1) a procedure is too complex if only a few instructions are desired; (2) embedding the code in a procedure makes the code difficult to understand (and, perhaps, even difficult to read since it is not a part of the compiler proper); (3) another (unnecessary) mechanism, an assembler, must be understood and matched to the compiler.

Although it is not a part of the translation process itself, the compiler must be able to interact controllably with the environment. For the System/360 this entails negotiating with the operating system for input and output and for the movement of data among the various storage devices.

1.3 Matching the Human Reader

We are as concerned with communicating the nature of the translation process to humans as we are to machines, not only when we write books about translators but also when we write the translators themselves. Most programs are read by more people than computers. We expect translators in particular to be maintained, debugged, modified, studied, and copied by many people besides the original authors. Therefore, we insist that the language be conducive to producing readable statements of translators.†

The degree of readability is, of course, relative to the background and tastes of the reader. An experienced machine-language coder may judge a hexadecimal core dump readable and a PL/I program hopelessly obscure. The average programmer would probably opt for programs in the language with which he is most familiar. The considerations presented here are the products of our own educated tastes and are derived from our experiences with a range of languages, including machine languages, assembly languages, procedural languages, and nonprocedural languages.

We want the reader to be able to easily follow the logic of the program at two levels. First, he should be able to quickly determine the major structural units, their intent, and the flow of control among them. Second, he should be able to determine precisely what operations are being performed on the data at any given point.

Although important that the notation used be concise, it is even more important that it be easy to learn and to remember. It should be possible to break the program down into both logical (block structured) and visual (paragraphed) units. Enough freedom should be allowed in the choice of names attached to various program entities (labels, variables, etc.) to make them mnemonic and easy to understand. Provision must be made for comments to clarify the intent of the program.

To be readable, a language for the description of complex processes must permit these processes to be defined in terms of less complex processes, which can then be

---

† Although we would like to impose even stronger conditions, it is unfortunately possible to write obscurely in even the best of languages.

defined in terms of even simpler processes ... and ultimately in terms of the basic operations of the language. In general, we wish to use the intermediate-level processes (subroutines, procedures, or functions) in many different parts of our programs, usually supplying different parameters to them. In later sections we will focus on the basic operations required, but the reader should not forget the necessity for hierarchical program structures based on these operations.

1.4   Matching the Translation Method

Translation methods are not all alike, and all translators should not be written in the same language. We designed the language presented in Chapter 6 for a specific class of translators. One of the attractive properties of this particular translation method is that it requires very elementary data structures and control mechanisms. Aside from the problem of text manipulation (input and output), almost any existing procedural language is sufficient and, considering our bias toward simplicity, even overelaborate.

Other useful methods require substantially more sophisticated language features; it is not unusual to build recognizers that require recursive procedures and dynamic storage allocation. In addition, the ability to build indirect, pointer, or list structures is useful for some methods and essential for others.

A good programmer can, of course, always work around a missing feature in his language. However, at some point, it becomes easier to add the needed features to the language.

1.5   Data

By data we mean relevant values and their associated internal representations. We need the facility to represent data explicitly (constants), to assign their representa· tions to memory locations and later to recover them (variables), and to examine and combine them (operations). Four kinds of data are particularly useful for translators: bits, for recording yes-no decisions; strings of bits, for packing information; integers, for all kinds of arithmetic; and strings of characters, to represent text, such as the input stream, the output program listing, diagnostic messages, and identifiers.

For many reasons we need the facility to work with ordered sets of values. Arrays with one subscript position are the simplest form of this construct. From arrays we can build stacks (for the syntactic recognition algorithm), tables (for symbols, types, forward references, and the like), and pointer spaces (for lists, sorting, etc.). More complex structures (multiple subscripts, queues, explicit lists, PL/I structures) are not used sufficiently in our translators to justify their implementation.

Many operations within a translator require the evaluation of integer arithmetic expressions. Our language should include the arithmetic operations of addition, subtraction, multiplication, division, and remainder. We also need the logical operations (and, or, not) on either single bits (logical expressions) or on groups of bits (masking operations). Within each data type we must have comparison operations ($<$, $=$, $\leq$, etc.), and we need to be able to convert data from one type to another (for instance, from integers to character strings for output).

Text (strings) presents additional problems. Input text must be tested and separated into constituent strings of varying length (e.g., identifiers). The output listing must generally be built up by joining shorter strings. The basic string operations are substring selection and catenation, as well as the previously mentioned extraction of internal codes for the characters.

1.6 Control

It is necessary to specify not only what operations are to be performed but also in what order, how often, and upon what data. Adoption of a convention (such as execution in order of appearance in the program) frees us to indicate explicitly only the exceptional cases.

A basic concept is selection from an ordered set. For ease of expression and efficiency of operation, both data and instructions are usually arranged so that the appropriate element can be conveniently selected from a set of alternatives. An element from an array in PL/I or ALGOL 60 is selected by an arithmetic expression used as a subscript. Similarly, it is possible to select among alternative instruction sequences depending on the value of an expression. Commonly, the expression is logical (two-valued), and the set of instruction sequences contains two elements. The usual representation for this selection is the **if-then-else** conditional statement. The **case** statement allows more general selection [Hoare 64].

Repetition of selected sequences of operations is another basic requirement of control. Two forms of repetition are particularly important: repeating the operations a specific number of times (often with specific values for a controlled variable), and repeating them only as long as a particular condition is satisfied. Recall the ALGOL **for** and **while** constructs and the variants of PL/I **do**.

Transfer of control also takes two forms. We may either temporarily transfer to a subprogram (possibly supplying it with some parameters) which will return to the original instruction sequence (procedures and subroutines), or we may simply enter the instruction sequence at some other point, with no provision for return (**go to** and **switch** together with labels).

Exercise 1.6.1

In this chapter and in the Introduction, we have given a number of requirements for a translator writing language. List those requirements not satisfied by an assembly language.

Exercise 1.6.2

In view of your answer to Exercise 1.6.1, explain why most production translators have been written in assembly languages.

1.7   From, To, and By

There are three main descriptive phrases for any translator: what it accepts (source language), what it produces (target language), and what it is expressed in (translating system). For XCOM we may have the situation depicted in Fig. 1.7.1, in which compilation places onto the magnetic tape a binary image of the System/360 machine-language translation of the source program. (Later the tape may be loaded into a System/360 and executed.) The crucial point is that the translator itself must be running on some machine to be of any use and thus must be expressed in machine language at some point. The notations developed here are designed to simplify the description of a highly related set of translating programs [Bratman 61].

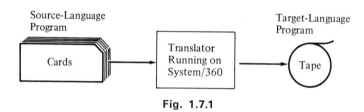

Fig. 1.7.1

We can succinctly express the function of a translator (written in XPL) from XPL to System/360 machine language by the T diagram in Fig. 1.7.2, whose entries are identified in Fig. 1.7.3. Frequently, more than one translating program is involved

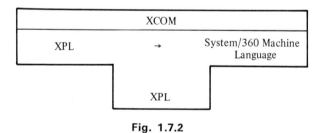

Fig. 1.7.2

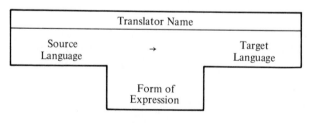

Fig. 1.7.3

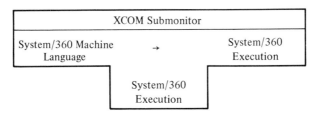

Fig. 1.7.4

in the process. In Fig. 1.7.2, the System/360 machine language must be placed in execution by a loader called the XCOM submonitor, shown in Fig. 1.7.4. Whenever the form of expression is the same as the source or target of the translation process (as in both Figs. 1.7.2 and 1.7.4), there appears to be a logical problem of how the first one started. If XCOM is written in XPL and run to compile XPL programs, how did the first functional XCOM come about? And if the XCOM submonitor is needed to load programs, how did it get loaded? The adjective *bootstrap* is applied to all such processes, referring, of course, to the phrase "pulling oneself up by one's boot-straps." The problems associated with bootstrap processes are nontrivial, as we will see in Section 8.13.

The T diagrams can be combined as in Fig. 1.7.5 to show the interdependence of the programs described. Since program 2 functions as an executing program and translates language L3 into language L4, it can accept program 1 written in language L3 and reproduce it in language L4. The function of program 1, deriving programs in L2 from programs in L1, is invariant under the translation. In any case, we establish the convention of stacking T diagrams, in which it is understood that the translator is an executing program. Note that the language in the arms of the center T must match the tails of the other two Ts, as in Fig. 1.7.5.

Any time there are two or more sequential translations of a single program, the whole translation can be expressed by a single, condensed T. For example, Fig. 1.7.6 reduces to Fig. 1.7.7. We will use this notation in Chapter 8 to describe in detail the bootstrap process for XCOM.

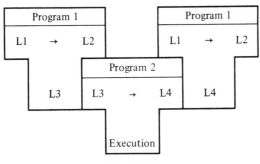

Fig. 1.7.5

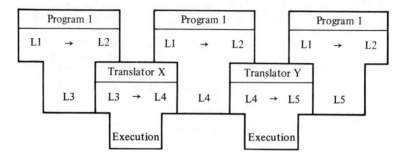

Fig. 1.7.6

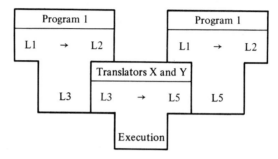

Fig. 1.7.7

Chapter 2

The Description of Languages

/*   "... The name of the song is called '*Haddocks' Eyes*'!"

"Oh, that's the name of the song, is it?" Alice said, trying to feel interested.

"No, you don't understand," the Knight said, looking a little vexed. "That's what the name is *called*. The name really *is*, '*The Aged Aged Man*.'"

"Then I ought to have said 'That's what the *song* is called'?" Alice corrected herself.

"No, you oughtn't: that's quite another thing! The song is called '*Ways and Means*': but that's only what it is *called* you know!"

"Well, what *is* the song then?" said Alice, who was by this time completely bewildered.

"I was coming to that," the Knight said. "The song really *is* '*A-Sitting on a Gate*': and the tune's my own invention."   */

LEWIS CARROLL

Through the Looking Glass

2.1   The Need for Precise Definition

/*   The words in the definitions often conceal more serious confusions and ambiguities than the word defined.   */

S. I. HAYAKAWA

Language in Thought and Action

Television programs, telephone conversations, telegrams, computer programs, messages in Morse code, and cryptograms are all points in a continuum of human communications. Even the very young can interpret the communications at the beginning of the series, but progressively more sophistication is required as the means of information transmission become less natural. One major result of this progression is that we are more likely to want and to use formal definitions as we near the end of the series. For instance, a human being probably could never understand a complex encryption of a language directly; formal transformations, tables, etc., are an essential step in understanding. The question raised here is whether we can use experience

19

gained through other communication methods to guide our efforts in communicating with computers.

With regard to television, we neither need nor use a symbolic description of the picture or of the sound. And, there is not much information about how to produce such a description that would be useful to the general audience. Telephone conversations, although often almost entirely ungrammatical, do require that the participants have previously memorized an arbitrary association of sounds and meanings. Any further definition of the spoken language is done intuitively by the native speaker. In written languages we do find it useful, for instance, to state precisely and formally that a sentence is a subject followed by a predicate, but there are many exceptions to such a rule.

The early development of programming languages followed the example set by natural languages. Every translator provided an implicit definition of a source language—it understood or translated certain statements and rejected others—and programmers developed for various languages an intuitive feeling which was hard to communicate. In obscure cases it was necessary to try it and see what happened. The clue to a communication failure might be found in a memory dump or by observing the panel lights of the machine. Programming became more art than science, and its practitioners absorbed an enormous, changing body of language, compiler, and machine lore and myth.

But when we set out to invent a language, we can do better. The form of an invented language is under our control (although the form of existing languages is not), and we can define it to be precisely the language described by a grammar. We achieve accuracy at the price of letting our methods of grammatical definition control the range of our linguistic inventiveness.

We have been using words without defining them carefully. Let us consider some key definitions. In writing a program, we may use certain symbols (a *vocabulary*). Any finite sequence of these symbols is a *string*. Valid strings are *programs*. A *programming language* is a set of programs. A *grammar* is a set of rules that determines which strings are in the language. For example,

"A program is any sequence of an odd number of xs"

is a grammar describing the language

$$\{x, xxx, xxxxx, \ldots\}$$

In most written languages there are groups of symbols which belong together and function as units. English provides such examples as a prepositional phrase, a direct object, and a sentence. A *phrase-structure grammar*† for a language is an explicit description of all such groupings in the language. Such a grammar involves both the symbols of the language (terminal symbols) and the names of the groupings (non-

---

† Although there are many classes of phrase-structure grammars, we are presenting only one, the context-free grammars. However, since we are concerned with the phrase-structure property, we use the more inclusive name.

terminal symbols, or phrase names). It is these grammars that are our models for defining programming languages.

Exercise   2.1.1

> Name some more groupings (phrase names) descriptive of the English language. Define one of them in English. Your definition probably involved other as yet undefined groupings. Give an argument to show that such grammatical definitions are not necessarily circular.

For any programming language, we would like to answer three important but quite different questions:

1. Is a given text a valid string of symbols, i.e., is it in the language?

2. If it is, what is its structure in terms of the groupings of the language, i.e., of what phrases is it composed?

3. In terms of this structure, what is its meaning, i.e., what will be the effect of executing the program?

The more precisely we can answer these questions, the more likely we are to succeed in our ultimate goal: correctly formulating and communicating our directions to the computing machine.

2.2   Phrase Structure and Meaning

/∗ "What's the use of their having names," the Gnat said, "if they won't answer to them?" "No use to *them*," said Alice, "but it's useful to the people that name them, I suppose."   ∗/

LEWIS CARROLL

Through the Looking Glass

/∗   There is a special department of Hell for students of probability. In this department there are many typewriters and many monkeys. Every time that a monkey walks on a typewriter, it types by chance one of Shakespeare's sonnets.   ∗/

BERTRAND RUSSELL

Nightmares of Eminent Persons

A language used to talk about a language is a metalanguage. The natural languages are in fact metalanguages. For example, we often use English as a metalanguage in this book, as in the example and exercise of the previous section. English, however, is too imprecise and wordy for general usage in defining the form of languages. More important, English does not readily adapt to the formal manipulations necessary in mechanizing the translation process. Thus, our first task is to introduce the Backus-Naur Form† (BNF), a formal metalanguage for phrase-structure grammars. We use this metalanguage extensively in this book. BNF was popularized by its use to describe the syntax of ALGOL 60 [Naur 60], but its application is not limited to any particular language. For example, a BNF rule for English might be

$$\langle \text{simple sentence} \rangle \quad ::= \quad \langle \text{subject} \rangle \langle \text{predicate} \rangle$$

There must be no confusion between the symbols of the metalanguage and those of the language being described. BNF avoids this confusion by using only four meta-linguistic symbols (see Table 2.2.1). Literal occurrences of symbols, with no bracketing characters, represent themselves as terminal symbols of the language. A grammar is written as a set of statements, each of which has a left part, followed by the metasymbol ::=, followed by a list of right parts. The left part is a phrase name, and the right parts, separated by the metasymbol |, are strings containing terminal symbols or phrase names or both.

TABLE 2.2.1 The Metasymbols of BNF

Metasymbol	English Equivalent	Use
::=	is defined as	Separates a phrase name from its definition.
|	or	Separates alternative definitions of a phrase.
⟨ and ⟩	"and"	Indicates that the intervening characters are to be treated as a unit.

Although any phrase-structure grammar may be written in BNF, BNF is not a complete metalanguage—some sets of strings (languages) cannot be specified by phrase-structure grammars. However, this difficulty is not often a practical one in the design of a language. The qualities we wish to include in a language are often structural (grammatical), and since the class of phrase-structure languages (languages defined by phrase-structure grammars) is large, we usually have sufficient flexibility to select one of them.

Although complete grammars for natural languages are, as we indicated, impossibly complex,‡ we can illustrate the concept of BNF with a simplified grammar for a portion of English.

The first statement in Table 2.2.2 is read "a sentence is defined as a simple sentence followed by a '.'" and the third is read "a subject is defined as a noun phrase or as a compound subject." Each statement is a rewriting rule, which allows us to substitute

---

† Also called Backus Normal Form.

‡ It is doubtful that phrase-structure grammars constitute (even in principle) an adequate model for natural languages [Chomsky 57, 65; Bach 64].

TABLE 2.2.2 A BNF Grammar

⟨sentence⟩	::=	⟨simple sentence⟩ .
⟨simple sentence⟩	::=	⟨subject⟩ ⟨predicate⟩
⟨subject⟩	::=	⟨noun phrase⟩ | ⟨compound subject⟩
⟨compound subject⟩	::=	⟨noun phrase⟩ ⟨conjunction⟩ ⟨noun phrase⟩
		| ⟨noun phrase⟩ , ⟨compound subject⟩
⟨noun phrase⟩	::=	⟨noun⟩ | ⟨pronoun⟩ | ⟨qualified noun⟩
⟨qualified noun⟩	::=	⟨adjective phrase⟩ ⟨noun⟩ | ⟨adjective phrase⟩ ⟨qualified noun⟩
⟨adjective phrase⟩	::=	⟨adjective⟩ | ⟨adverb⟩ ⟨adjective phrase⟩
⟨predicate⟩	::=	⟨transitive verb⟩ ⟨direct object⟩ | ⟨intransitive verb⟩
		| ⟨predicate⟩ ⟨adverb⟩
⟨direct object⟩	::=	⟨noun phrase⟩
⟨conjunction⟩	::=	and | or
⟨noun⟩	::=	lover | man | politician | election | creature | skeleton
		| ideas | . . .
⟨pronoun⟩	::=	he | she | it | . . .
⟨adjective⟩	::=	enormous | green | smelly | the | colorless | angry | . . .
⟨adverb⟩	::=	quickly | furiously | very | . . .
⟨transitive verb⟩	::=	is | stole | threw | kissed | . . .
⟨intransitive verb⟩	::=	slept | runs | died | argued | . . .

any right part for any occurrence of its associated left part. For example, "⟨sentence⟩" may be rewritten as "⟨simple sentence⟩ .", and then as "⟨subject⟩ ⟨predicate⟩ .". We may now rewrite either ⟨subject⟩ or ⟨predicate⟩. The order does not affect the final result. (Why?) We also have a choice of right parts which we may substitute. The list below is the result of a sequence of such choices.

⟨sentence⟩
⟨simple sentence⟩.
⟨subject⟩ ⟨predicate⟩.
⟨noun phrase⟩ ⟨predicate⟩.
⟨pronoun⟩ ⟨predicate⟩.
he ⟨predicate⟩.
he ⟨transitive verb⟩ ⟨direct object⟩.
he threw ⟨direct object⟩.
he threw ⟨noun phrase⟩.
he threw ⟨qualified noun⟩.
he threw ⟨adjective phrase⟩ ⟨noun⟩.
he threw ⟨adjective⟩ ⟨noun⟩.
he threw the ⟨noun⟩.
he threw the election.

All the symbols in the string are now terminal, and we can make no further substitutions.

We not only have produced an English sentence but also have determined its structure in terms of English phrases. This structure can be represented by the phrase-structure tree in Fig. 2.2.1. Each node corresponds to a rewriting step. We call

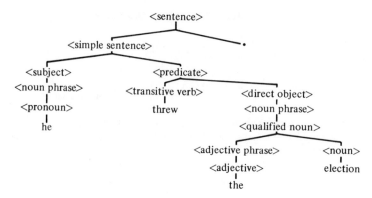

Fig. 2.2.1 A Phrase-Structure Tree

⟨sentence⟩ the root of the tree, and *he, threw, the, election,* and . the leaves of the tree, accepting the nature-defying convention that the root is at the top of the tree and the leaves are at the bottom.

The act of rewriting defines a relation between strings of symbols. That is, given two strings of terminal symbols or phrase-name symbols or both, it is either true or false that we can derive the second from the first by a single substitution based on the grammar. If it is true, we say the first string directly produces the second string. Thus, each string in the previous list directly produces its successor. (Verify.)

The grammar of Table 2.2.2 produces a set of sentences, of which some are meaningful ("she stole the smelly creature.", "the politician kissed the angry man quickly."), many more are syntactically correct gibberish ("colorless green ideas slept furiously."), and others are not even grammatical (since our grammar ignores tense, person, and number).

Exercise   2.2.1

Verify that the grammar of Table 2.2.2 defines "it is the enormous smelly skeleton.", "the man and the angry lover argued.", and "colorless green ideas slept furiously." as sentences.

Exercise   2.2.2

Using any random method (such as flipping a coin or rolling dice) to control all choices, produce ten sentences in accordance with the grammar of Table 2.2.2. How many of them are syntactically correct? How many are meaningful? How would you modify the grammar to improve the quality of the sentences produced?

Exercise   2.2.3

Write a program which will read a BNF grammar and produce 100 random sentences of that grammar. Extend the grammar of Table 2.2.2 to include compound sentences, prepositional phrases, auxiliary verbs, and any other phrase classes you consider appropriate. Also augment the terminal vocabulary of nouns, adjectives, etc., in some imaginative way. Test your extended grammar with your program (and vice versa).

Exercise   2.2.4

> Is it necessarily true that the processes suggested in Exercises 2.2.2 and 2.2.3 always
> terminate? What is the probability of termination? What is the average number of
> words in a generated sentence? These are nontrivial questions: See, for instance,
> a letter by Ira Pohl in *Communications of the Association for Computing Machinery,*
> 10, No. 12 (December 1967), 757.

Interpretation of the phrase groupings in a programming language can indicate
much of the meaning of programs. Consider the following BNF definition of a simple
expression language.†

$$\begin{aligned}
\langle\text{expression}\rangle &::= \langle\text{term}\rangle \mid \langle\text{expression}\rangle + \langle\text{term}\rangle \\
\langle\text{term}\rangle &::= \langle\text{primary}\rangle \mid \langle\text{term}\rangle * \langle\text{primary}\rangle \\
\langle\text{primary}\rangle &::= x \mid y \mid z
\end{aligned}$$

The phrase-structure tree in Fig. 2.2.2 corresponds to the expression

$$x * y + z$$

This tree clearly shows that x is to be multiplied by y and the result added to z.

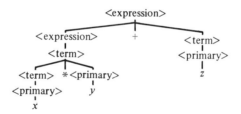

Fig. 2.2.2

We have forced this interpretation by making all occurrences of $*$ lie in the phrase
class $\langle\text{term}\rangle$. Thus, when we form $\langle\text{expression}\rangle$ from $\langle\text{expression}\rangle + \langle\text{term}\rangle$, we
have already used all the $*$ symbols, and they all lie below $\langle\text{term}\rangle$ in the tree. A simi-
lar argument demonstrates that additions are performed left to right in the expression

$$z + x + x + y + z$$

which has the phrase-structure tree shown in Fig. 2.2.3. The point is that we can
control this kind of interpretation by carefully choosing our grammar.

The relationship of meaning to form can be made explicit by pairing each rewriting
rule with a corresponding interpretation as in Table 2.2.3.

We can then interpret the expression $x * y + z$ as

---

† $+$ means add; $*$ means multiply

The value is the sum of
$$\left\{ \begin{array}{l} \text{the product of} \\ \quad \left\{ \begin{array}{l} \text{the value of the variable named } x \text{ and} \\ \text{the value of the variable named } y \end{array} \right. \\ \text{and the value of the variable named } z \end{array} \right.$$

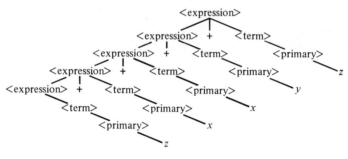

Fig. 2.2.3

TABLE 2.2.3

Rule	Interpretation The Value Is . . .
⟨expression⟩ ::= ⟨term⟩	. . . the value of the ⟨term⟩
⟨expression⟩ ::= ⟨expression⟩ + ⟨term⟩	. . . the sum of the values of the ⟨expression⟩ and the ⟨term⟩
⟨term⟩ ::= ⟨primary⟩	. . . the value of the ⟨primary⟩
⟨term⟩ ::= ⟨term⟩ * ⟨primary⟩	. . . the product of the values of the ⟨term⟩ and the ⟨primary⟩
⟨primary⟩ ::= x	. . . the value of the variable named x
⟨primary⟩ ::= y	. . . the value of the variable named y
⟨primary⟩ ::= z	. . . the value of the variable named z

Exercise 2.2.5

With the grammar in Table 2.2.3 in mind, generate other expressions, and check their interpretations.

Exercise 2.2.6

What is meant by the statement "The multiplication symbol binds more tightly than the addition symbol." or, "Multiplication takes precedence over addition."?

Exercise 2.2.7

Devise a grammar in which addition takes precedence over multiplication.

Exercise 2.2.8

Devise a grammar in which neither addition nor multiplication has precedence but in which they are performed in the order encountered (left to right).

Exercise 2.2.9

Devise a grammar in which neither addition nor multiplication has precedence but in which they are performed right to left.

Exercise 2.2.10

Extend the grammar for ⟨expression⟩ of this section to include the definition
⟨primary⟩ ::= (⟨expression⟩)
and construct the tree to interpret
$$x * (y + z)$$

Exercise 2.2.11

Interpreting the following (unconventional) grammar for logical expressions

$$
\begin{aligned}
⟨G⟩ \quad &::= \quad ⟨BE⟩ \\
⟨BE⟩ \quad &::= \quad \textbf{not } ⟨BE⟩ \mid ⟨BS⟩ \\
⟨BS⟩ \quad &::= \quad ⟨BF⟩ \textbf{ and } ⟨BS⟩ \mid ⟨BF⟩ \\
⟨BF⟩ \quad &::= \quad ⟨BP⟩ \textbf{ or } ⟨BF⟩ \mid ⟨BP⟩ \\
⟨BP⟩ \quad &::= \quad \textbf{true} \mid \textbf{false}
\end{aligned}
$$

evaluate

not not true or true and false
true and true and true or false
not false or true or false

2.3 . Formal Definitions and Notation

/* This freedom to create symbols of any assigned value and to create symbols that stand for symbols is essential to what we call the symbolic process. */

S. I. HAYAKAWA

Language in Thought and Action

/* After great pain, a formal feeling comes. */

EMILY DICKINSON

"341"†

We present next, in a relatively compact form, definitions and notation used throughout the book. Since the significance of some definitions will become apparent

---

† Reprinted by permission of the publishers and the Trustees of Amherst College from Thomas H. Johnson, Editor, *The Poems of Emily Dickinson* (Cambridge, Mass.: The Belknap Press of Harvard University Press, Copyright, 1951, 1955, by The President and Fellows of Harvard College).

only in later chapters, we encourage the reader to refer back to this section as he reads the rest of the book.

We assume familiarity with basic set theory. We denote sets by boldface upper-case Latin letters (**A**, **B**, . . . , **Z**) or by explicitly naming the elements between curly braces { , }. ∈ denotes set membership; ∪ denotes set union; − denotes set difference; ∩ denotes set intersection; × denotes set product (i.e., **A** × **B** is the set of all ordered pairs, the first element taken from **A** and the second from **B**). We denote relations either by special symbols or by boldface lower-case Latin letters (**a**, **b**, . . . , **z**).

We also assume some knowledge of the notation of predicate calculus. We denote logical *and* by ∧, logical *or* by ∨, logical negation by ¬, logical equivalence by ≡, and logical implication by ⊃. (∀x) denotes "for all x" and (∃x) denotes "there exists an x."

2.3.1: A *vocabulary* is a finite set of elements called *symbols*.

2.3.2: A *string* is a finite sequence of symbols from a vocabulary. Strings are denoted by lower-case Greek letters (α, β, . . . , ω).

2.3.3: An *empty string*, denoted by λ, is a sequence containing no symbols.

2.3.4: The operation of *catenation*, denoted by the juxtaposition of strings or symbols, joins two sequences of symbols into a single sequence. If $\tau = \varphi\psi$, then φ is a *head* of τ and ψ is a *tail* of τ.

2.3.5: The *length* of a string φ, denoted by $|\varphi|$, is the number of symbols in the sequence. Note that

$$|\lambda| = 0 \quad \text{and} \quad |\varphi\psi| = |\varphi| + |\psi|$$

If φ is a head of τ and $|\varphi| = n$, then $\mathbf{h}_n(\tau) = \varphi$ and is called the *n head* of τ. Likewise, if ψ is a tail of τ and $|\psi| = m$, then $\mathbf{t}_m(\tau) = \psi$ and is called the *m tail* of τ.

2.3.6: For each particular vocabulary $\mathbf{V}_i$, the set of *strings over* $\mathbf{V}_i$, denoted by $\mathbf{V}_i^*$, is the set of all sequences of symbols contained in $\mathbf{V}_i$.

$$\mathbf{V}_i^* = \{\varphi \,|\, \varphi = \lambda \vee (\exists X \in \mathbf{V}_i)(\exists \psi \in \mathbf{V}_i^*)\, \varphi = \psi X\}$$

2.3.7: The set of *nonempty strings over* $\mathbf{V}_i$, denoted by $\mathbf{V}_i^+$, is the set of all sequences of one or more symbols from $\mathbf{V}_i$.

$$\mathbf{V}_i^* = \{\varphi \,|\, \varphi \in \mathbf{V}_i \vee (\exists X \in \mathbf{V}_i)(\exists \psi \in \mathbf{V}_i^+)\, \varphi = \psi X\}$$

Note that $\mathbf{V}_i^* = \mathbf{V}_i^+ \cup \{\lambda\}$.

2.3.8: A *rewriting system* is an ordered pair $(\mathbf{V}, \rightarrow)$ where $\mathbf{V}$ is a vocabulary and $\rightarrow$ is a relation on $\mathbf{V}^* \times \mathbf{V}^*$. For σ and τ in $\mathbf{V}^*$, $\sigma \rightarrow \tau$ is read as σ *directly produces* τ and τ *directly reduces* to σ.

2.3.9: If a sequence of strings is related by $\rightarrow$,

$$\varphi_0 \rightarrow \varphi_1$$
$$\varphi_1 \rightarrow \varphi_2$$
$$\cdot$$
$$\cdot$$
$$\cdot$$
$$\varphi_{n-1} \rightarrow \varphi_n$$

for $n \geq 1$, then we say φ_0 *produces* φ_n and φ_n *reduces* to φ_0. We denote this new relationship by $\rightarrow^+$ and write $\varphi_0 \rightarrow^+ \varphi_n$. (The relation $\rightarrow^+$ is the *transitive completion* of $\rightarrow$)

2.3.10: We write $\sigma \rightarrow^* \tau$ to denote the relation either $\sigma \rightarrow^+ \tau$ or $\sigma = \tau$. (The relation $\rightarrow^*$ is the *reflexive transitive completion* of $\rightarrow$) Note the analogy between the use of $^+$ and * for sets and relations.

2.3.11: A *context-independent rewriting system* is a rewriting system in which the relation $\rightarrow$ can be applied to substrings without regard for the other symbols in the string. Formally,

$$(\forall \sigma \in \mathbf{V}^*)(\forall \tau \in \mathbf{V}^*)(\forall \varphi \in \mathbf{V}^*)(\forall \omega \in \mathbf{V}^*)[\sigma \rightarrow \tau \supset \varphi \sigma \omega \rightarrow \varphi \tau \omega]$$

This formula constitutes a strong restriction on the relation $\rightarrow$; by knowing one pair of strings for which it is true, we can derive arbitrarily many other pairs for which it is true.

2.3.12: A *context-independent phrase-structure rewriting system* (CIPSRS) is a context-independent rewriting system in which a single symbol is on the left. Formally,

$$(\forall \sigma \in \mathbf{V}^*)(\forall \tau \in \mathbf{V}^*)[\sigma \rightarrow \tau \supset (\exists A \in \mathbf{V})(\exists \omega \in \mathbf{V}^*)(\exists \varphi \in \mathbf{V}^*)$$
$$(\exists \psi \in \mathbf{V}^*)(\sigma = \varphi A \psi \wedge \tau = \varphi \omega \psi \wedge A \rightarrow \omega)]$$

We have again restricted the relation $\rightarrow$. By knowing the value of $\rightarrow$ for every pair with a single symbol on the left, we can derive its value for any pair of strings.

2.3.13: A string is *terminal* when it cannot be rewritten, e.g., φ is terminal when $\neg (\exists \omega \in \mathbf{V}^*) \varphi \rightarrow \omega$. A terminal string occurs in a CIPSRS when no symbol in the string appears alone on the left of $\rightarrow$. Thus we use $\rightarrow$ to partition $\mathbf{V}$ into two subsets: $\mathbf{V}_n$, the *nonterminal vocabulary*, and $\mathbf{V}_t$, the *terminal vocabulary*. Precisely,

$$\mathbf{V}_n = \{A \,|\, (\exists \omega \in \mathbf{V}^*) \, A \rightarrow \omega\}$$
$$\mathbf{V}_t = \mathbf{V} - \mathbf{V}_n$$

$\mathbf{V}_t^*$ is the set of *terminal strings*. Note also that by definition, $\mathbf{V}_n \cap \mathbf{V}_t$ is empty.

2.3.14: A *phrase-structure grammar*† (PSG) is a quadruple $(\mathbf{V}_n, \mathbf{V}_t, G, \rightarrow)$ in which $(\mathbf{V}_n \cup \mathbf{V}_t, \rightarrow)$ is a CIPSRS, $\mathbf{V}_n$ is the set of nonterminal symbols, and $\mathbf{V}_t$ is the set of terminal symbols. G, some particular member of $\mathbf{V}_n$ called the *goal symbol*, is the phrase name that describes the entire language.

Table 2.3.1 summarizes by example the notational conventions we will use henceforth.

---

† Often called Context-Free Grammar, or CFG.

TABLE 2.3.1

Items Represented	Symbols
Sets	$A, B, \ldots, Z$
Relations or functions	$\rightarrow, a, b, \ldots, z$
Members of $\mathbf{V}_t$	$a, b, \ldots, z$
Members of $\mathbf{V}_n$	$A, B, C, \ldots$
Arbitrary members of $\mathbf{V}$	$\ldots, X, Y, Z$
Members of $\mathbf{V}_t{}^*$	$\alpha, \beta, \gamma, \ldots$
Members of $\mathbf{V}^*$	$\ldots, \varphi, \psi, \omega$
Empty string	λ
Goal symbol	G

2.3.15:   The *sentential set* defined by a PSG, denoted by $\mathbf{S}$, is the set of strings (*sentential forms*) produced by the goal symbol.

$$\mathbf{S} = \{\omega \mid G \rightarrow^* \omega\}$$

2.3.16:   The *language* defined by a PSG, denoted by $\mathbf{L}$, is the set of terminal strings (*sentences*) produced by the goal symbol.

$$\mathbf{L} = \mathbf{S} \cap \mathbf{V}_t{}^*$$

2.3.17:   A *parse* for a sentential form ω is a sequence $\tau_0, \tau_1, \ldots, \tau_n$ such that $\tau_n = G$, $\tau_0 = \omega$, and $\tau_{i+1} \rightarrow \tau_i$ for $i = 0, \ldots, n - 1$. Each pair (τ_{i+1}, τ_i) is called a *parse step* (PS). Note that, by definition, every sentential form must have a parse.

2.3.18:   A parse step is *canonical* (CPS) if it is of the form $(\varphi A \alpha, \varphi \omega \alpha)$ in which $A \in \mathbf{V}_n$ and $\alpha \in \mathbf{V}_t{}^*$. A parse is canonical if each of its steps is canonical. Each string in a canonical parse is a *canonical sentential form* (CSF).

2.3.19:   The *productions* $\mathbf{P}$ of a PSG are defined by

$$\mathbf{P} = \{(A, \omega) \mid A \rightarrow \omega \land A \in \mathbf{V}_n \land \omega \in \mathbf{V}^*\}$$

that is, the set of ordered pairs of strings related by $\rightarrow$ where the left member is a single symbol.

Alternatively, we may consider the productions basic, and derive the PSG $(\mathbf{V}_n, \mathbf{V}_t, G, \rightarrow)$ from $\mathbf{P}$ alone by the following definitions:

2.3.20: $\mathbf{V}_n = \mathbf{V}_n(\mathbf{P}) = \{A \mid (\exists \omega)(A, \omega) \in \mathbf{P}\}$

2.3.21: $\mathbf{V}_t = \mathbf{V}_t(\mathbf{P}) = \{a \mid (\exists A)(\exists \varphi)(\exists \psi)(A, \varphi a \psi) \in \mathbf{P}\} - \mathbf{V}_n$

2.3.22: $G = G(\mathbf{P})$ is distinguished by some convention; e.g., it is the only symbol of $\mathbf{V}_n$ which does not occur as an element on the right of a production; or if the productions are ordered, it is the left part of the first production.

2.3.23:   The relation $\rightarrow$ (actually $\rightarrow_{(\mathbf{P})}$) is defined by

$$(\sigma \rightarrow \tau) \equiv (\exists \varphi)(\exists A)(\exists \psi)(\exists \omega)[\sigma = \varphi A \psi \land \tau = \varphi \omega \psi \land (A, \omega) \in \mathbf{P}]$$

We can now state the connection between our formal definition of a phrase-structure grammar and our previous informal definition. Each BNF statement indicates that the relation $\rightarrow$ holds between its left part and each of its right parts, i.e., we interpret

$$A \quad ::= \quad \varphi \,|\, \psi \,|\, \cdots \,|\, \omega$$

as

$$(A, \varphi) \in \mathbf{P}, \quad (A, \psi) \in \mathbf{P}, \ldots, (A, \omega) \in \mathbf{P}$$

A grammar written in BNF directly defines $\mathbf{P}$ and indirectly defines the quadruple $(\mathbf{V}_n, \mathbf{V}_t, G, \rightarrow)$. Since the BNF grammars and sets of productions are equivalent, we will use the two notations interchangeably and even mix them as is necessary for convenience and readability. We will use subscripted $\mathbf{P}$ to denote particular grammars, regardless of the form in which they are initially expressed.

Consider the grammar $\mathbf{P}_1$ defined by

$$\langle A \rangle \quad ::= \quad \langle B \rangle$$
$$\langle B \rangle \quad ::= \quad x \langle B \rangle x \,|\, y$$

We determine the elements of the grammar using each of the Definitions 2.3.20 through 2.3.22.

$$\mathbf{V}_n = \mathbf{V}_n(\mathbf{P}_1) = \{ \langle A \rangle, \langle B \rangle \}$$
$$\mathbf{V}_t = \mathbf{V}_t(\mathbf{P}_1) = \{ x, y \}$$
$$G = G(\mathbf{P}_1) = \langle A \rangle \quad \text{by either convention}$$

Now, by Definitions 2.3.15 and 2.3.16, we have

$$\mathbf{S}_1 = \mathbf{S}(\mathbf{P}_1) = \{ \langle A \rangle \} \cup \{ x^n \langle B \rangle \, x^n \,|\, n \geq 0 \} \cup \{ x^n y \, x^n \,|\, n \geq 0 \}\dagger$$
$$\mathbf{L}_1 = \mathbf{L}(\mathbf{P}_1) = \{ x^n y \, x^n \,|\, n \geq 0 \} = \{ y, xyx, xxyxx, \ldots \}$$

The finite grammar $\mathbf{P}_1$ can describe the infinite language $\mathbf{L}_1$ because one of the productions defining $\langle B \rangle$ namely $\langle B \rangle ::= x \langle B \rangle x$ used $\langle B \rangle$ in the definition (recall Exercise 2.1.1). In general, if $A \rightarrow^+ \varphi A \psi$, we say that the grammar is *recursive* in A. If $A \rightarrow^+ A\psi$, it is *left recursive*, and if $A \rightarrow^+ \varphi A$, it is *right recursive* in A. Almost all languages of interest are infinite (at least theoretically), and we require our grammars to be finite. Therefore, recursion is a very common property of phrase-structure grammars.

$\mathbf{P}_1$ is not the only grammar for $\mathbf{L}_1$. The reader should verify that if $\mathbf{P}_2$ is defined by

$$\langle \text{desired set} \rangle \qquad ::= \qquad \langle \text{balanced string} \rangle$$
$$\langle \text{balanced string} \rangle \qquad ::= \qquad y \,|\, x \, \langle \text{unbalanced string} \rangle$$
$$\langle \text{unbalanced string} \rangle \quad ::= \quad \langle \text{balanced string} \rangle \, x$$

$\dagger$ By the notation x^n we mean n repetitions of x, e.g., $x^3 = xxx$ and $x^0 = \lambda$.

then $\mathbf{L(P_2)} = \mathbf{L(P_1)}$. In fact, there are arbitrarily many distinct phrase-structure grammars for any phrase-structure language. Although in this case it is easy to prove the equivalence of the two languages, it is not always possible to determine whether two grammars define the same language [Bar-Hillel 64; Ginsberg 66].

Let $\mathbf{P_3}$ be defined by†

$$
\begin{aligned}
G &::= E \\
E &::= T \mid E + T \\
T &::= P \mid T * P \\
P &::= x \mid y \mid z
\end{aligned}
$$

and let $\mathbf{L_3} = \mathbf{L(P_3)}$. The string $x * y + z$ is in $\mathbf{L_3}$, which we may verify by the following parse (at each step placing the arrow under the rewritten symbol).

$$
\begin{aligned}
&G \\
&\to E \\
&\quad \to E + T \\
&\quad\quad \to T + T \\
&\quad\quad\quad \to T * P + T \\
&\quad\quad\quad\quad \to P * P + T \\
&\quad\quad\quad\quad\quad \to x * P + T \\
&\quad\quad\quad\quad\quad\quad \to x * y + T \\
&\quad\quad\quad\quad\quad\quad\quad \to x * y + P \\
&\quad\quad\quad\quad\quad\quad\quad\quad \to x * y + z
\end{aligned}
$$

The corresponding phrase-structure tree is shown in Fig. 2.3.1.

There are other parses for $x * y + z$ using $\mathbf{P_3}$. For example,

$$
\begin{aligned}
&G \\
&\to E \\
&\quad \to E + T \\
&\quad\quad \to E + P \\
&\quad\quad\quad \to E + z \\
&\quad\quad\quad\quad \to T + z \\
&\quad\quad\quad\quad\quad \to T * P + z \\
&\quad\quad\quad\quad\quad\quad \to T * y + z \\
&\quad\quad\quad\quad\quad\quad\quad \to P * y + z \\
&\quad\quad\quad\quad\quad\quad\quad\quad \to x * y + z
\end{aligned}
$$

† Here we have departed slightly from our earlier convention that unbracketed symbols are terminal. Upper-case letters continue to represent nonterminals; the brackets are omitted for legibility.

In this parse we have applied exactly the same productions to the same elements, but in a different order; the phrase-structure tree is unchanged. Intuitively we see that these two parses are somehow equivalent. We choose to represent such a class of equivalent parses by the canonical parse, in which each production is applied to the rightmost nonterminal symbol (RNT) of the sentential form (recall Definition 2.3.18). Informally, we see that all the parses corresponding to a distinct phrase-structure tree are uniquely represented by the canonical parse which "grows" the tree from right to left. In the example above, the reader should verify that the second parse is canonical.

The grammar $\mathbf{P}_4$, defined by

$$G \ ::= \ E$$
$$E \ ::= \ E + E \mid E * E \mid x \mid y \mid z$$

also generates $\mathbf{L}_3$. (Verify.) Superficially, $\mathbf{P}_4$ is a preferable grammar since it is shorter than $\mathbf{P}_3$ yet generates the same language. However, the sentence $x * y + z$ now has two distinct canonical parses, which correspond to the two trees in Fig. 2.3.2.

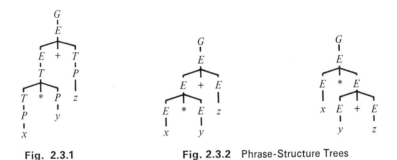

Fig. 2.3.1   Fig. 2.3.2 Phrase-Structure Trees
                                    for an Ambiguous Sentence

2.3.24: A sentence having no unique canonical parse in a given grammar is said to be *ambiguous* (with respect to that grammar). A grammar is ambiguous if some sentence is ambiguous with respect to it. (The grammar $\mathbf{P}_4$ is ambiguous, but $\mathbf{P}_3$ is not.)

Ambiguity becomes a problem when we use a phrase-structure grammar to describe the structure of a language. The canonical parse groups sentence elements into phrases, but if this grouping is not unique (i.e., if the sentence is ambiguous), we cannot determine the proper grouping. The English language contains many such ambiguous sentences, e.g., "They are flying planes." and "Time flies like an arrow."

Although there is no question about some grammars, it is not always possible to determine whether others are ambiguous [Floyd 62; Chomsky 63]. We are concerned with a somewhat stronger condition in the construction of translators: It must be possible for a particular algorithm to uniquely parse all sentences according to the grammar. If it is a very simple algorithm, the trouble lies in its inability to make a decision, the algorithm being unable to take enough information into account (a *local ambiguity*). A more complex algorithm may enter a condition known as *factorial mode,* during which it goes into ever more furious efforts to resolve a local ambiguity while making no forward progress.

Exercise   2.3.1

Find a PSG which differs nontrivially from $\mathbf{P}_1$ and $\mathbf{P}_2$ and yet generates exactly $\mathbf{L}_1$.

Exercise   2.3.2

State whether your grammar of Exercise 2.3.1 is ambiguous. Prove your assertion.

Exercise   2.3.3

Show that every sentence generated by a PSG has at least one canonical parse.

Exercise   2.3.4

Distinct phrase-structure trees correspond to distinct canonical parses. Show that any two distinct canonical parses have distinct phrase-structure trees.

Exercise   2.3.5

Verify that $\mathbf{L}(\mathbf{P}_3) = \mathbf{L}(\mathbf{P}_4)$.

Exercise   2.3.6

Find the canonical parses corresponding to the phrase-structure trees of Fig. 2.3.2.

Exercise   2.3.7

Extend your grammar of Exercise 2.2.2 or 2.2.3 to contain all the words in "they are flying planes" and "time flies like an arrow." Include every part of speech given by the dictionary for each word. Find two canonical parses for each of the sentences. Draw the corresponding phrase-structure trees. Do they correspond to your intuitive notion of the alternate structures for these sentences?

Exercise   2.3.8

Consider $\mathbf{P}_5$, defined by

$$
\begin{aligned}
A &::= \ B \mid D \\
B &::= \ BCC \mid x \\
C &::= \ yx \\
D &::= \ xCyD \mid xy
\end{aligned}
$$

Let $\mathbf{L}_5 = \mathbf{L}(\mathbf{P}_5)$. Show that all of

$$x,\ xy,\ xyxyx,\ \text{ and }\ xyxyxyxyx$$

but none of

$$xyx,\ xyxy,\ \text{ and }\ xyxyxyx$$

are in $\mathbf{L}_5$. Show that $\mathbf{P}_5$ is unambiguous.

Exercise 2.3.9

Consider a string α of the form $xyxyx\beta$ in $\mathbf{L}_5$. Knowing nothing about β, could you determine any portion of the phrase-structure tree for α? If you knew the first n symbols in β, could you determine any of the structure? What could you determine if you knew the last n symbols of α but were missing some initial string γ?

Exercise 2.3.10

As evident in Exercise 2.3.9, analysis of $\mathbf{L}_5$ with $\mathbf{P}_5$ is easier working from right to left than from left to right. Construct a PSG for $\mathbf{L}_5$ which makes it easy to parse from left to right and difficult to parse from right to left.

Exercise 2.3.11

Construct a PSG for $\mathbf{L}_5$ which makes it easy to parse from either end. How do the trees for sentences compare in the three grammars?

/* Ay, there's the wonder of the thing! Macavity's not there! */

T. S. ELIOT

Macavity

PSGs are still more general than is necessary or desirable. In particular, $\mathbf{P}$ must be finite for the computations necessary in building translators. Furthermore, PSGs allow circular definitions, an obvious cause of ambiguities. We can exclude these cases by insisting

2.3.25: $(\forall A \in \mathbf{V}_n) \neg (A \rightarrow^+ A)$ (no circularity)

That is, for no phrase name can there be a parse leading back to just that same phrase name. With a given grammar, it is a trivial computation to evaluate the above proposition.

We may also require a similar appearing restriction:

2.3.26: $(\forall A \in \mathbf{V}_n) \neg (A \rightarrow^+ \lambda)$ (no erasure)

Since a nonterminal may have no image in a sentence, PSGs which permit the empty string to be produced are difficult to handle in mechanical recognition systems. But erasure is a very handy tool for describing languages (the ALGOL Report uses it extensively). Therefore, extending a recognition algorithm to empty right parts is always a valid and useful project.

It rarely makes sense to have a PSG with more than one symbol that appears only on the left since that implies either more than one goal symbol or that some symbol is not going to be used (hence, its defining production could be discarded). We therefore forbid multiple goals for our mechanical systems (see Definition 2.3.14).

However, we may find multiple goals convenient for descriptive purposes if we have two similar languages to describe (e.g., ⟨program⟩ for PL/I programs and ⟨constant list⟩ for PL/I data) and want to avoid duplicating the overlapping part of the grammars.

Assuming the uniqueness of the goal G, we can state this condition by saying that all symbols must be usable in some parse.

2.3.27: $(\forall X \in \mathbf{V})(\exists \varphi)(\exists \omega)\ G \to^* \varphi X \omega$ (no unusable symbols)

Grammars leading to nonterminating parses are not useful and no one would intentionally use one to describe a language. The condition is

2.3.28: $(\forall A \in \mathbf{V}_n)(\exists \alpha \in \mathbf{V}_t^*)\ A \to^* \alpha$ (termination)

Again, it is possible to check a PSG for this property.

Exercise 2.3.12

Show that any PSG in which both $A \to^+ \varphi A$ and $A \to^+ A\psi$ must necessarily be ambiguous, if there exist $\alpha,\ \beta,\ \gamma \in V_t^*$ such that $A \to^+ \alpha$, $\varphi \to^* \beta$, and $\psi \to^* \gamma$.

Exercise 2.3.13

Describe an algorithm (e.g., by a flow chart) that will test an arbitrary PSG for erasure, determine whether λ is a sentence of the PSG, and if not, generate another PSG without erasure that generates the same language.

Exercise 2.3.14

Describe an algorithm that will test an arbitrary λ-free PSG for circularity and then generate a noncircular PSG for the same language.

Exercise 2.3.15

Describe an algorithm that will test an arbitrary PSG for unusable symbols and then generate a PSG for the same language without those symbols.

Exercise 2.3.16

Describe an algorithm that will test an arbitrary PSG for nonterminating parses and then generate a PSG for the same language for which all parses can terminate.

Chapter 3

Translation:
The Association of Form and Meaning

/∗ There can be no doubt that Stonehenge was an observatory. . . . In form the
monument is an ingenious computing machine. ∗/

GERALD S. HAWKINS and JOHN B. WHITE

Stonehenge Decoded†

/∗ The meaning of Stonehenge in Tralfamadorian, when viewed from above, is:
"Replacement part being rushed with all possible speed." ∗/

KURT VONNEGUT, JR.

Sirens of Titan

3.1 The Organization of Translators

Many levels of understanding are involved in knowing what a computer is doing,
from the flow chart of an algorithm down to circuit theory or quantum mechanics.
Most of the time a high-level understanding is adequate, and low-level descriptions
become inconceivably complex. (Imagine describing the operation of a compiler at
the flip-flop level—or a flip-flop at the wave-equation level.) Most important is that
there be a hierarchy of levels, each understandable in terms of its underlying level.
Our purpose here is to carry an understanding of the translation process down as
many levels as will be helpful.

The computer solution of a problem is usually divided into two phases (see Fig.
3.1.1). The program is first translated (compiled or assembled) into a sequence of
machine instructions. These instructions are then executed, directing the machine
in the solution of the problem. Such a separation is neither logically necessary (there
is no evidence for it in the human mind) nor the only possible division (incremental,
interactive systems may accept a little source text, perform some trial execution,
accept more text . . .), but it is useful with present-day computing systems.

---

† From *Stonehenge Decoded* by Gerald S. Hawkins and John B. White. Copyright © 1965 by
Gerald S. Hawkins and John B. White. Reprinted by permission of Doubleday & Company, Inc.

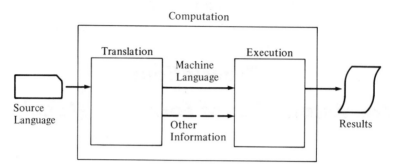

Fig. 3.1.1

There is, as indicated in Fig. 3.1.1, a *sub rosa* information flow outside the main machine-language form of the program produced during translation. It consists of run-time estimates, relocation information, symbol/name associations, and the like. In one sense, it consists of *ad hoc* devices we ultimately would like to eliminate in the interests of simplicity, possibly by generalizing the machine language sufficiently to carry all the needed information.

We now want to look closely at the translation process. Although any function which maps sentences from a source language to a target language is a translator, a useful translator must preserve the meaning of the translated sentences. The principal challenge in the construction of translators is the attainment of this semantic invariance between source and target texts; a translator that fails to achieve this invariance is just plain wrong. Other criteria—speed, size, efficiency of the translation, efficiency of the code produced, etc.—are important but only as a matter of degree.

The simplest form of translation is the association of equivalent items, the kind of connection implied by a dictionary or a code table. We cannot translate unless we know that *schiessen* means to shoot, that AWUG means attack at dawn, or that * means multiply. The mapping implied by a table look-up is not necessarily one to one. Since many items may map onto the same item (*ABC* and *XYZ* are both ⟨identifier⟩s), translation need not be reversible. We use such mappings repeatedly throughout translators: sometimes to get conveniently manipulable representations (the index into a table instead of the entry in the table, the length and address of a string instead of its characters) and, at other times, to return to the representation the real world demands (a correctly formulated sequence of IBM System/360 instructions instead of *).

As necessary as it is, table look-up is not a very powerful translation technique. The beginning student of natural languages soon learns that word order differs from language to language and that he must restructure his sentences according to the new grammar. Also, auxiliary words which do not correspond to anything in the old language may appear in the new language, while familiar syntactic helpers fail to have an image in the translation. The processes of reordering, inserting, and deleting are more demanding, both of the student and of the mechanical translator, than is dictionary look-up. The emphasis of this chapter is on mechanisms which perform these more difficult processes.

In Chapter 2 we discussed the relation of phrase structure to meaning and showed that we could determine much of the meaning of programs by associating an interpretation with each production of the grammar. Syntax-directed translators systematically use these semantic rules and this phrase-structure information to generate the program in the target language. The process of translation is divided, as shown in Fig. 3.1.2, into two phases, recognition and generation. The recognizer examines the source language and passes, as its main output, the phrase structure of the source language in any one of several forms: a tree, a sequence of productions, a left-to-right linearization of a tree, etc. The generator uses the phrase structure and the *sub rosa* information in producing the translated form of the source text.

The other information consists of symbol tables, hints for arithmetic type conversions, addresses, etc. As mentioned before, although we desire to reduce this flow, we are still far from eliminating it. We subdivide both the processes of recognition and of generation into the components shown in Figs. 3.1.3 and 3.1.4, respectively. These two processes are antisymmetric. The scanner, from sequences of characters (letters, digits, etc.), produces sequences of meaningful symbols (reserved words, names, values). It discards the semantically irrelevant structure of the source language (e.g.,

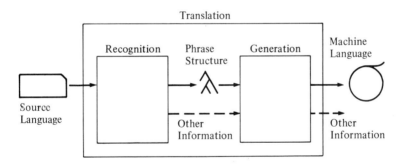

Fig. 3.1.2

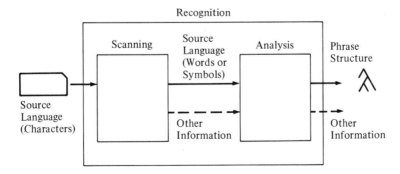

Fig. 3.1.3

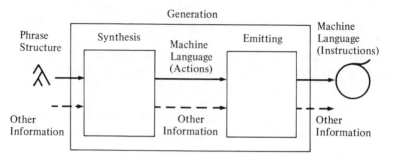

Fig. 3.1.4

the structure implied by ⟨identifier⟩ ::= ⟨identifier⟩⟨letter⟩), thus reducing the number of individual items passed to the analyzer by an order of magnitude. Although it does not reorder symbols, it does delete symbols (comments and blanks) and accomplish table look-up translations (matching grammatical entities with indices into the vocabulary).

Similarly, the emitter receives sequences of logical actions (move, add, call a process, etc.) and builds up sequences of machine instructions to accomplish the tasks. For a conventional machine, the emitter may produce an order of magnitude more items than it receives. The emitter also has the effect, inverse to that of the scanner, of transforming meaningful units (actions) into structures otherwise irrelevant to the problem solution (machine instructions).

The analysis and synthesis work together to reorder the actions implied in the source-language program into meaningful machine actions; the standard example is

$$1 + 2 * 3$$

for which the normal interpretation implies that the ∗ action precedes the + action.

All four logically successive processes—scanning, analysis, synthesis, and emitting—can be either synchronous and interlocked or sequential and separate. A controlling criterion is often the amount of main memory available. On a small machine, it is usually advantageous to complete each translating process, called a pass, and to record the result (including the *sub rosa* information) on a secondary memory before starting the next subprocess. Then only one program at a time needs be in main memory. There is no limit to how many passes can be usefully defined. The compiler described in Chapter 8 uses exactly one. IBM F-level PL/I uses about 87 (and a completely different method).

The four subprocesses in Fig. 3.1.5 are not of equal difficulty. Scanning is trivial enough and sufficiently well-understood to warrant hardware aids in most machines. Analysis is automatically accomplished via the theory and programs described in Chapters 4, 5, 9, and 10. Emitting is likewise only formatting and macro expansion. Most difficult is the one remaining process, synthesis. This difficulty is not essential, but reflects the necessity to choose operations, as output from the synthesizer, that differ greatly from the operations implied by the source language. Economic reasons

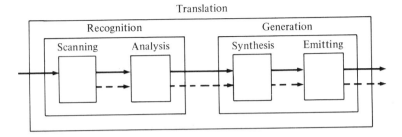

Fig. 3.1.5

force us to find efficient sequences of operations in existing machines, a difficult process. In many cases it is more economic to pick relatively complex and language-directed operations and to accomplish execution interpretively. The savings in compilation time and in main memory often offset the loss in execution efficiency.

3.2 Trees, Stacks, and Polish Notation

We further our understanding of the translation process by developing a mechanism in increasing stages of detail until we have a workable translator. The central concept is that of a *stack* and we will expend some effort to explain why this is so. The idea of nesting pervades all our computer concepts. All the characters constituting a phrase nest inside any containing phrase. The scope of a declaration may both nest within, and wholly contain, other scopes. Procedures and blocks nest within one another in space, and, during execution, in time (i.e., an entry is always followed by an exit, and control cannot leave an outer procedure until it has left the inner one). We could go on indefinitely. The concept of nesting is common, because the process of reducing the problem to a set of simpler problems is a natural mode of human thought. We often describe items in terms of components, tasks in terms of subtasks, etc.

Nesting is a concept; its natural denotation is a tree. All the components nested within an item are represented by limbs or leaves branching out from a node. A tree is also an explicit representation of a partial ordering (e.g., on the same branch, one may ask which item is closer to the root). The nesting and ordering properties of a tree make it a valuable tool for describing complex processes.

Unfortunately perhaps, our programs, machines, processes, etc., are linear, fully sequential constructs, rather than partial orderings in two dimensions. A stack is used in producing a linear representation of a tree (see Fig. 3.2.1). If, for instance, we examine a tree from left to right, we can see at any moment one branch of the tree from the root to the leaves. As we look at more leaves, we can replace sequences of them with the name of the node representing them. The effect is stack-like: Add some leaves, collapse to a metaconstruct, add more leaves, collapse again. The stack is a sequential facility, we use it to order the information held in a tree. Thus the stack is primarily a reordering, or order-imposing, structure. It is frequently helpful, when using a stack, to reflect on what partial ordering, tree, or nesting is behind our efforts.

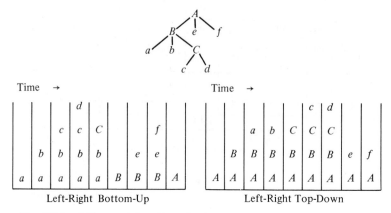

Time	→									
			d							
		c	c	C			f			
	b	b	b	b		e	e			
a	a	a	a	a	B	B	B	A		

Left-Right Bottom-Up

Time	→								
						c	d		
			a	b	C	C	C		
		B	B	B	B	B	B	e	f
A	A	A	A	A	A	A	A	A	A

Left-Right Top-Down

Fig. 3.2.1 A Tree and Two Linearizations of it with a Time-Varying Stack

One immediate use for a stack is in a mechanism to execute a machine language. Our purpose is to provide a concrete example of a target language to motivate the translation process. Consider the transformation of the usual infix notation for arithmetic expressions into the parenthesis-free notation of Lukasiewicz (popularly called zero-address code, reverse-Polish, or Polish-suffix notation). We define the two forms of expressions below.

$$\langle\text{infix expression}\rangle \quad ::= \quad \langle\text{infix expression}\rangle + \langle\text{term}\rangle$$
$$\qquad\qquad |\quad \langle\text{infix expression}\rangle - \langle\text{term}\rangle$$
$$\qquad\qquad |\quad \langle\text{term}\rangle$$
$$\langle\text{term}\rangle \quad ::= \quad \langle\text{term}\rangle * \langle\text{primary}\rangle$$
$$\qquad\qquad |\quad \langle\text{term}\rangle / \langle\text{primary}\rangle$$
$$\qquad\qquad |\quad \langle\text{primary}\rangle$$
$$\langle\text{primary}\rangle \quad ::= \quad (\,\langle\text{infix expression}\rangle\,)$$
$$\qquad\qquad |\quad \langle\text{letter}\rangle$$
$$\langle\text{letter}\rangle \quad ::= \quad a \mid b \mid \dots \mid z$$

$$\langle\text{suffix expression}\rangle \quad ::= \quad \langle\text{suffix expression}\rangle \langle\text{suffix expression}\rangle \langle\text{operator}\rangle$$
$$\qquad\qquad |\quad \langle\text{letter}\rangle$$
$$\langle\text{letter}\rangle \quad ::= \quad a \mid b \mid \dots \mid z$$
$$\langle\text{operator}\rangle \quad ::= \quad + \mid - \mid * \mid /$$

For example, the expressions below are equivalent.

INFIX

a

$a + b + c + d$

$a + b * c - d$

$a / (b + c)$

$a + ((((b + c))))$

$a - b * c$

SUFFIX

a

$a\,b + c + d +$

$a\,b\,c * + d -$

$a\,b\,c + /$

$a\,b\,c + +$

$a\,b\,c * -$

In both cases, we can deduce the order of execution of the operators from the phrase-structure trees (recall Section 2.2). From the third line of the previous list, we derive Figs. 3.2.2 and 3.2.3. One can then conclude by inspection of either tree that b and c must be multiplied before the result can be added to a. The test of equivalence for an infix expression and a suffix expression is whether both representations imply the same operations on the same operands.

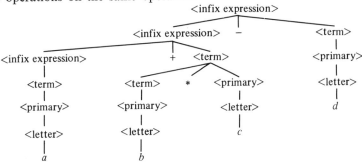

Fig. 3.2.2

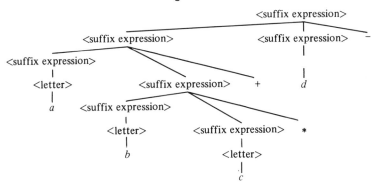

Fig. 3.2.3

Infix expressions correspond to the normal algebraic expressions we are accustomed to writing. Multiplication and division bind more tightly than does addition or subtraction, and parentheses are used to modify the order of evaluation. Suffix expressions are somewhat less natural to read. However, they have the advantages that parentheses are not required to indicate precedence and that the rules for their evaluation are very simple.

To evaluate a suffix expression
    Repeat until no operators remain
        1. Locate the leftmost operator;
        2. Locate the two operands immediately to the left of the operator;
        3. Apply the operator to the operands;
        4. Replace operator and operands with the result.

If a is 3, b is 4, and c is 5, we evaluate $a\,b\,c*/$ as follows:

Suffix Expression	Current Operator	Current Operands
$a\,b\,c*/$	$*$	$b\,c$
$a\,20\,/$	$/$	$a\,20$
0.15	none	

Exercise 3.2.1

Evaluate each of the suffix expressions a, $a\,b + c + d +$, $a\,b\,c * + d -$, $a\,b\,c + +$, and $a\,b\,c + -$ when a is 3, b is 4, c is 5, and d is 6.

Since suffix expressions can be easily interpreted without explicit reference to the phrase-structure tree, translation from infix to suffix form is a productive step in extracting the meaning of an expression.

Now we describe a simple machine which interprets suffix expressions. This machine has 26 memory locations, one for each letter of the alphabet. The appearance of a letter in a suffix expression is a command to place the value of the letter on the top of an evaluation stack; the appearance of an operator is a command to execute the corresponding action on the top two values of the stack and to place the result on the stack in their stead. This machine code is called Polish, suffix, or zero-address code.

Exercise 3.2.2

Write a program to simulate a Polish machine which will read a suffix expression and a set of values for the included letters, and then evaluate the expression. Test your program on the expressions of Exercise 3.2.1.

In assignment statements the meaning of a letter is ambiguous. Either the value (if it is to be operated on) or the name (if it is to be stored into) is meant. This problem, basic to conventional programming languages, prevents treatment of the replacement operator as just another infix operator by the machine interpreting the suffix code. To be precise we extend the source and target languages to include the assignment operator ← .

$$
\begin{aligned}
\langle\text{infix assignment}\rangle \quad &::= \quad \langle\text{letter}\rangle \leftarrow \langle\text{infix expression}\rangle \\
\langle\text{infix expression}\rangle \quad &::= \quad \langle\text{infix expression}\rangle + \langle\text{term}\rangle \\
&\quad | \quad \langle\text{infix expression}\rangle - \langle\text{term}\rangle \\
&\quad | \quad \langle\text{term}\rangle \\
\langle\text{term}\rangle \quad ::= \quad &\langle\text{term}\rangle * \langle\text{primary}\rangle \\
| \quad &\langle\text{term}\rangle / \langle\text{primary}\rangle \\
| \quad &\langle\text{primary}\rangle \\
\langle\text{primary}\rangle \quad ::= \quad &(\langle\text{infix expression}\rangle) \\
| \quad &\langle\text{letter}\rangle \\
\langle\text{letter}\rangle \quad ::= \quad &a \mid b \mid \ldots \mid z
\end{aligned}
$$

$\langle$suffix assignment$\rangle$ ::= $\langle$letter$\rangle$ $\langle$suffix expression$\rangle$ $\leftarrow$
$\langle$suffix expression$\rangle$ ::= $\langle$suffix expression$\rangle$ $\langle$suffix expression$\rangle$ $\langle$operator$\rangle$
                          | $\langle$letter$\rangle$
$\langle$letter$\rangle$ ::= a | b | ... | z
$\langle$operator$\rangle$ ::= $+$ | $-$ | $*$ | $/$

For example, $a\,b\,c\,*\leftarrow$ and $a\,b\,c - c/\leftarrow$ are suffix assignments; but, $a\,b - c \leftarrow$ is not. (Why?)

We can solve the problem of name/value ambiguity in the Polish machine by deferring the decision to fetch a value from memory until it is time to execute the operator. We add information to each item in the stack which indicates whether the rest of the item is a name (letter) or value (number). Then, previous to executing an operator, we fetch only the values necessary for its execution. An assignment operator continues to have a name as its left operand and can act accordingly.

For example, the infix assignment

$$a \leftarrow b * c + d$$

yields the suffix form

$$a\,b\,c * d + \leftarrow$$

If a is 3, b is 4, c is 5, and d is 6, the successive states of the evaluation stack are as shown in Table 3.2.1.

Exercise   3.2.3

Extend the interpreter in Exercise 3.2.2 to execute the assignment operator.

Exercise   3.2.4

Extend the interpreter in Exercise 3.2.3 to execute the relationals $<$, $>$, $=$ and the logical operators & and | . You may represent *true* by the value 1 and *false* by the value 0.

Exercise   3.2.5

Some infix languages also allow prefix operators (e.g., $+$, $-$, $\neg$ in PL/I). In suffix notation they act on only one argument (the top element of the evaluation stack). Extend the interpreter to execute $\neg$. Can you do the same for the prefixes $+$ and $-$?

Exercise   3.2.6

Extend the infix grammar to include all the operators (each with an appropriate hierarchy) suggested in Exercises 3.2.4 and 3.2.5.

Exercise   3.2.7

Extend the suffix grammar to include all the operators suggested in Exercises 3.2.4 and 3.2.5. The interpretation we give demands two kinds of operators:

$\langle$dyadic operator$\rangle$ ::= ...
$\langle$monadic operator$\rangle$ ::= ...

TABLE 3.2.1

Start	Name a	Name b	Name c
			N | c
		N | b	N | b
	N | a	N | a	N | a

$\ast$

Fetch b	Fetch c	Multiply	Name d
N | c	V | 5		N | d
V | 4	V | 4	V | 20	V | 20
N | a	N | a	N | a	N | a

$+$

Fetch d	Add	Store to a
V | 6		
V | 20	V | 26	
N | a	N | a	

3.3   A Simple Compiler

We now need only specify how to get from infix notation to suffix notation to have completed translation from infix notation to execution via an interpreter. At least two of the compilation actions needed to transform infix to suffix notation—reordering the symbols of the source text into the sequence needed for execution and deleting symbols with no associated action—can be accomplished with a simple algorithm, based on assigning numerical ranks to each of the source-text symbols, that places operators with highest precedence earliest in the execution sequence.

The recognition algorithm has an input sequence of symbols, a last-in, first-out stack where symbols can be saved while being reordered, and an output sequence of symbols. Comparisons are always made between the head of the input stream and

Simple Heirarchy-Driven Recognizer-Generator

Initialization: Put a symbol with minimum precedence (say a " (")
on the stack and a symbol with equal precedence (say a ") ") on
the end of the input expression.

Translation: Until the infix expression is exhausted, repeat the
following action.

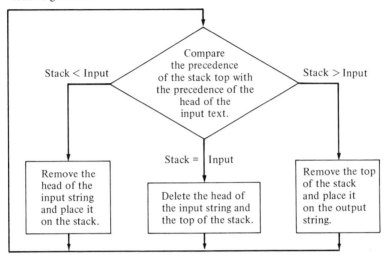

Check: If the stack is not empty, there was an error.

Fig. 3.3.1   Simple Hierarchy-Driven Recognizer-Generator

the top of the stack, as is shown in Figure 3.3.1. We need specify only the precedence
of the symbols to proceed. For the first grammar in Section 3.2, Table 3.3.1 is sufficient.

We apply the recognition algorithm to the infix expression $a + b * c - d$, as in
Table 3.3.2.

TABLE 3.3.1

Symbol	Top-of-Stack Precedence	Head-of-Input Precedence
+, −	2	1
*, /	4	3
$a, b, \ldots, z$	6	5
(	0	7
)	—	0

TABLE 3.3.2

Output String	Stack	Input String
	(	$a + b * c - d)$
	a (	$+ b * c - d)$
a	(	$+ b * c - d)$
a	$+$ (	$b * c - d)$
a	b $+$ (	$* c - d)$
$a\ b$	$+$ (	$* c - d)$
$a\ b$	$*$ $+$ (	$c - d)$

TABLE 3.3.2 (Contd.)

Output String	Stack	Input String
a b	c / * / + / (	− d)
a b c	* / + / (	− d)
a b c *	+ / (	− d)
a b c * +	(	− d)
a b c * +	− / (	d)
a b c * +	d / − / (	)

TABLE   3.3.2 (Contd.)

Output String	Stack	Input String
$a\,b\,c\,*\,+\,d$	$\begin{array}{c} - \\ (\end{array}$	)
$a\,b\,c\,*\,+\,d\,-$	(	)
$a\,b\,c\,*\,+\,d\,-$		

Exercise   3.3.1

Hand-simulate the two-sided hierarchy recognition algorithm to produce the suffix notation for the expression $(a + b) * c - d$.

Exercise   3.3.2

How many decisions were needed on the hierarchy comparisons in Exercise 3.3.1? Can you generalize this result to give a bound on the number of actions as a function of input-text length?

Exercise   3.3.3

Assume that the operator ← means assignment and extend Table 3.3.1 to handle it.

Exercise   3.3.4

Extend the precedence table in Exercise 3.3.3 to allow the recognition of PL/I expressions containing the infix operators $*$, $/$, $+$, $-$, $<$, $>$, $=$, & and $|$.

Exercise   3.3.5

Extend the tables in Exercise 3.3.4 to handle $\neg$. Can you do the same for prefixes $+$ and $-$?

Exercise   3.3.6

Write, and test for several cases, a program that first reads a set of symbols and their associated two precedence values (sometimes called **f** and **g** functions) and then reads a series of infix assignments and applies the two-sided hierarchy algorithm to them to produce and print suffix assignments.

Exercise 3.3.7

Combine the programs from Exercises 3.2.5 and 3.3.6 to
1. Read a set of **f** and **g** function values
2. Read a set of initial values for the letters
3. Read a series of infix assignments, translating them to suffix form and printing them
4. Interpret the suffix forms
5. Print the set of final values for the letters

Exercise 3.3.8

If an incorrect text is presented to the two-sided hierarchy algorithm, it may misbehave (since there are insufficient provisions for detection of errors). We can detect some errors by substituting a four-valued matrix for the **f** and **g** functions, as has been done in Table 3.3.3. The three values $<$, $>$, and $=$ are computed from **f** and **g**. The fourth value, denoted by a blank, represents impossible combinations. What sort of incorrect inputs will be detected?

TABLE 3.3.3

Symbol on the Stack Top		+ -	>	<	<	<	>
		* /	>	>	<	<	>
		$a, b, \ldots , z$	>	>			>
		(	<	<	<	<	=
		)					

	+ $-$	* /	a b . . . z	(	)

Symbol at the Head of the Input Stream

Exercise 3.3.9

Use the matrix instead of **f** and **g** to redo Exercise 3.3.7.

Only slightly more complex forms of this simple compiling algorithm can be used to translate useful languages. Many of the difficulties in extending the algorithm have led to programs for automatic generation of the precedence tables and other syntax-driven methods. These programs all have one feature in common with the algorithm presented here: Decisions are based on a few symbols, called the *local context*, near the stack top or on the head of the input string.

Not usually being fortunate enough to design our own machine, we must generally emit code for some existing machine. For example, we can define a class of single-address codes much more like those of conventional machines as follows:

⟨single-address code⟩   ::=   ⟨instruction⟩
                      | ⟨single-address code⟩ ⟨instruction⟩
⟨instruction⟩   ::=   ADD ⟨name⟩ | SUB ⟨name⟩ | MUL ⟨name⟩ | DIV ⟨name⟩
                 | LOD ⟨name⟩ | STO ⟨name⟩

⟨name⟩   ::= a | b | c | ... | z | $T1$ | $T2$ | $T3$ | ... | $T100$

If we assume that the machine has a single accumulator loaded and stored with the LOD and STO instructions and that we can use the T variables $T1$, $T2$, etc., for temporary results, the problem is to find a single-address code equivalent to a given suffix assignment. We attack this problem by running the interpreter (Exercise 3.2.3, etc.) and, instead of obeying the instructions, emitting single-address code to do them. Thus, in Table 3.2.1 nothing is emitted until the first stack configuration under ∗ is reached. At this point we emit a LOD b, and for the next stack configurations, a MUL c. We also leave a V in the stack corresponding to the fact that our accumulator has a value in it. We can proceed in this fashion until we have evaluated the entire assignment. The only new problem inherent in our single accumulator is that we can afford only one value in the stack at a time. Thus we must keep track of V entries (perhaps by searching the stack) before emitting a LOD. If we find any, we emit a STO to an unused temporary (we need a table to keep track of which temporaries are available) and record that name in the stack in place of the value. Later the emitting algorithm will cause a LOD to fetch this value again in the normal manner.

   Note that we now have a translation (infix expressions to single-address code) sufficiently complex to require all our tools: table look-up, deletion (Where did all the parentheses go?), creation (Where did LOD come from?), and reordering.

Exercise   3.3.10

Implement an algorithm to take the suffix assignments of Exercise 3.3.3 into single-address machine code.

Exercise   3.3.11

Implement an interpreter to execute the results of Exercise 3.3.10.

Exercise   3.3.12

Modify the program of Exercise 3.3.7 to
1. Read the **f** and **g** functions
2. Read the initial values for the letters
3. Read the infix assignments, translating first to suffix form, then to single-address form
4. After all the assignments are read and translated, execute the single-address code as done in Exercise 3.3.11
5. Print the final values of the letters

Exercise 3.3.13

Review the entire process of Exercise 3.3.12 and attempt to identify each step with one of the processes in Section 3.1.

Exercise 3.3.14

Consider a class of logical expressions defined by the grammar

$$\langle e \rangle \quad ::= \langle s \rangle \mid \langle e \rangle \mid \langle s \rangle$$
$$\langle s \rangle \quad ::= \langle p \rangle \mid \neg \langle p \rangle \mid \langle s \rangle \ \& \ \langle p \rangle$$
$$\langle p \rangle \quad ::= i \mid (\langle e \rangle)$$

If we assign a succession of logical values (e.g., **t** or **f**) to the inputs (represented by i) in an expression, the expression itself has a value (**t** or **f**). For example, the expression $i \ \& \ i \mid \neg (i \mid i)$ and the sequence of input values **ftft** yield the result **f**. For any particular expression, a Turing machine exists (refer to Exercises 0.2.2 and 6.18.16) that transforms a tape containing arbitrary assignments of values to the inputs into a tape containing only the appropriate result (see, for example, Fig. 3.3.2). Write a program that reads a logical expression and prints a set of quintuples defining such a Turing machine. Hint: First translate the expression to suffix form and then emit a set of quintuples for each operator. The set of six quintuples (A, **f**, B, , R), (A, **t**, C, , R), (B, **f**, D, **f**, R), (B, **t**, D, **f**, R), (C, **f**, D, **f**, R), (C, **t**, D, **t**, R) is an acceptable solution for the expression $i \ \& \ i$.

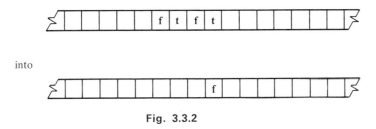

into

Fig. 3.3.2

Exercise 3.3.15

Combine the results of Exercises 3.3.14 and 6.18.16 to evaluate a logical expression.

Exercise 3.3.16

Redo Exercise 0.2.2 in light of the results you achieved in Exercise 3.3.15.

3.4 The Canonical Parse and Synthesis

In Section 2.2 we indicated that a program could be partially interpreted from the phrase structure of the sentence by associating a meaning with each production of the grammar. The simple algorithms producing single-address code are closely related to the steps of the canonical parse in that the time-varying stacks of the synthesis algorithm correspond to a linearization of the phrase-structure tree as described in Fig. 3.2.1 (left-right, bottom-up). The stack containing the successive configurations is the *parse stack*. We can emit single-address code without using the intermediate Polish string by placing the synthesis information in stacks parallel to, and synchronous with, the parse stack and by using the same basic emitting algorithm.

In this chapter we use simple example sentences whose phrase structure is easily determined, deferring to Chapter 4 the general problem of algorithms for computing phrase structure. Using a grammar similar to the one from Section 3.2 for infix assignment,

$$A \quad ::= \quad L \leftarrow E$$
$$E \quad ::= \quad E + T \mid E - T \mid T$$
$$T \quad ::= \quad T * P \mid T / P \mid P$$
$$P \quad ::= \quad (E) \mid L$$
$$L \quad ::= \quad a \mid b \mid \ldots \mid z$$

we repeat the generation of single-address code for the assignment

$$a \leftarrow b * c + d$$

directly from the canonical parse. The phrase-structure tree is shown in Fig. 3.4.1 and corresponds to the following canonical parse

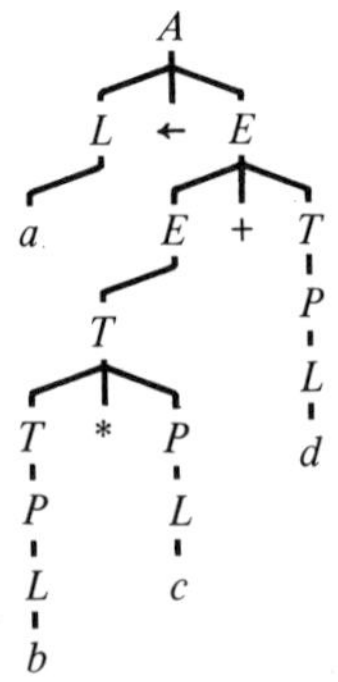

Fig. 3.4.1

(13) A

(12) $L \leftarrow E$

(11) $L \leftarrow E + T$

(10) $L \leftarrow E + P$

(9) $L \leftarrow E + L$

(8) $L \leftarrow E + d$

(7) $L \leftarrow T + d$

(6) $L \leftarrow T * P + d$

(5) $L \leftarrow T * L + d$

(4) $L \leftarrow T * c + d$

$L \leftarrow P * c + d$

(3)
$$L \leftarrow L * c + d$$
(2)
$$L \leftarrow b * c + d$$
(1)
$$a \leftarrow b * c + d$$

and to the sequence of parse-stack configurations shown in Table 3.4.1. The three stacks in Table 3.4.2 are the parse stack, the name/value stack, and the symbol name stack. The remaining, as yet unparsed, input text is exhibited in the center column. The final column is a running commentary on the generation of single-address code.

TABLE 3.4.1

							c	L	P				d	L	P	T		
					*	*	*				+	+	+	+				
	b	L	P	T	T	T	T	T	T	T	E	E	E	E	E	E	E	
	←	←	←	←	←	←	←	←	←	←	←	←	←	←	←	←	←	
a	L	L	L	L	L	L	L	L	L	L	L	L	L	L	L	L	L	A

These actions are descriptive of a code-emitting algorithm similar to the one suggested in the end of Section 3.3. No attempt is made to formalize the algorithm; rather the reader is expected to deduce enough about it from Section 3.3 and Table 3.4.2 to be able to apply it to further examples.

TABLE 3.4.2

The Stacks	Remaining Source Text	Comments
☐ ☐ ☐	$a \leftarrow b * c + d$	Initial configuration.
		Stack a.
a ☐ ☐	$\leftarrow b * c + d$	
		CPS (1), apply L ::= a. Enter (N, a) into the synthesis stacks.
L N a	$\leftarrow b * c + d$	
		Stack $\leftarrow$.
← / L N a	$b * c + d$	
		Stack b.

TABLE 3.4.2. (Contd.)

The Stacks	Remaining Source Text	Comments

b		
$\leftarrow$		
L	N	a

Remaining Source Text: $* c + d$

Comments:
CPS (2), apply $L \ ::= \ b$.
Enter (N, b) into the synthesis stacks.

L	N	b
$\leftarrow$		
L	N	a

Remaining Source Text: $* c + d$

Comments:
CPS (3), apply $P \ ::= \ L$.

P	N	b
$\leftarrow$		
L	N	a

Remaining Source Text: $* c + d$

Comments:
CPS (4), apply $T \ ::= \ P$.

T	N	b
$\leftarrow$		
L	N	a

Remaining Source Text: $* c + d$

Comments:
Stack $*$, then c.

c		
$*$		
T	N	b
$\leftarrow$		
L	N	a

Remaining Source Text: $+ d$

Comments:
CPS (5), apply $L \ ::= \ c$.
Enter (N, c) into the synthesis stacks. Note that we arrive at the "Name c" stack configuration of Table 3.2.1.

L	N	c
$*$		
T	N	b
$\leftarrow$		
L	N	a

Remaining Source Text: $+ d$

TABLE 3.4.2. (Contd.)

The Stacks	Remaining Source Text	Comments
		CPS (6), apply P $::=$ L.
P N c / $*$ / T N b / $\leftarrow$ / L N a	$+ d$	
		The next step (CPS (7)) will be the reduction $$T \ ::= \ T * P$$ Just before doing the reduction, our synthesis algorithm causes the following changes: *Emit* **LOD** b. Change (N, b) to (V).
P N c / $*$ / T V / $\leftarrow$ / L N a	$+ d$	
P / $*$ / T V / $\leftarrow$ / L N a	$+ d$	*Emit* **MUL** c.
		Then the reduction is performed, which leaves the configuration as shown, with one V entry indicating that the accumulator is full.
T V / $\leftarrow$ / L N a	$+ d$	
E V / $\leftarrow$ / L N a	$+ d$	CPS (8), apply E $::=$ T.

TABLE 3.4.2. (Contd.)

The Stacks	Remaining Source Text	Comments

Stack +, then *d*.

d		
+		
E	*V*	
←		
L	*N*	*a*

CPS (9), apply *L* ::= *d*.
Enter (*N*, *d*) into the synthesis stacks.

L	*N*	*d*
+		
E	*V*	
←		
L	*N*	*a*

CPS (10) and CPS (11), apply *P* ::= *L* first, then *T* ::= *P*.

T	*N*	*d*
+		
E	*V*	
←		
L	*N*	*a*

Now we are about to reduce via *E* ::= *E* + *T*.
Just before the reduction is made, the synthesis algorithm causes generation.
Emit **ADD** *d*.

T		
+		
E	*V*	
←		
L	*N*	*a*

CPS (12), apply *E* ::= *E* + *T*.

E	*V*	
←		
L	*N*	*a*

TABLE 3.4.2. (Contd.)

The Stacks	Remaining Source Text	Comments

Now we are about to reduce via $A ::= L \leftarrow E$.
Emit **STO** *a*.

(stack diagram: E, ←, L)

CPS (13), apply $A ::= L \leftarrow E$.

(stack diagram: A)

The parse terminates when this reduction is made.

There are several immediate conclusions: The synthesis actions are always triggered by a reduction, namely the recognition of a part of the phrase-structure tree. The operators find their correct operands because of the latter's location in the parallel stacks opposite the corresponding syntactic unit. The operations are carried out in the desired order as a consequence of both the left-to-right nature of the canonical parse and the reordering implied by the nesting of the phrases in the grammar.

Exercise 3.4.1

Parse and emit single-address code for each of

$$a \leftarrow (b * c)/(c * d)$$
$$a \leftarrow a - a + a - a$$
$$a \leftarrow ((((a))))$$

Exercise 3.4.2

Rework the example in Table 3.4.2. Parse the sentential form $a \leftarrow b * c + d$. Use no auxiliary stacks, and produce Polish string instead of single-address code.

Exercise 3.4.3

Repeat Exercise 3.4.1; produce Polish string.

Exercise 3.4.4

Assume that the computer has no accumulator, but rather works from memory to memory on a three-address code ($OP \ i, j, k$ means memory$_i \leftarrow$ memory$_j \ OP$ memory$_k$). Rework the example in Table 3.4.2 to produce three-address code. Do not use more than one auxiliary stack.

We define as many auxiliary stacks and tables as seems profitable. If we produce only Polish strings, we need neither deferral nor extra stacks. Less convenient machine languages may require several. No such mechanisms are built into our TWS—each compiler writer must create his own, based on his machine and his language. The alternative of providing some generation mechanism has been abandoned, such mechanisms being harder to learn than to create. In order to help the reader develop his skill in this area, we present some examples.

Although we have used the actual names $(a, b, \ldots)$ in the parse stack, we usually will have only ⟨identifier⟩ there, having done the preliminary construction and initial loading of the auxiliary stacks in the scanner. We are also more likely to keep only a pointer to a table of symbols rather than the name in the auxiliary stack. This becomes particularly important when the source language has a type declaration construct which makes it impossible to tell what kind of arithmetic to do without consulting the symbol table. For typed arithmetic, we add a third auxiliary stack to keep track of the type of intermediate results. Had the assignment $a \leftarrow b * c + d$ involved typed operands, the stacks might have appeared as in Table 3.4.3, which implies that

TABLE   3.4.3

P		N		c		fixed
*						
T		N		b		float
←						
L		N		a		fixed

$b * c$ is a mixed-mode operation. Thus, the generation algorithm must be sophisticated enough to match the types before multiplying. Here we would expect something like

```
LOD     c             /* load the integer */
CALL    . fixfloat    /* convert it to type float*/
FMU     b             /* execute a floating multiply */
```

the commutativity of multiplication having allowed the first operand to be used last.

Since compilation actions are always associated with reductions, we should be able to state explicitly the actions of our synthesis algorithm. For example, we clearly associate the recognition of the production

$$L \quad ::= \quad a$$

with the following pair of actions: (1) Store a in the symbol stack opposite a; (2) store N in the name/value stack opposite a. In a somewhat more complex case, we associate the recognition of the production

$$T \quad ::= \quad T * P$$

with the actions

1. If there is a *V* entry in the name/value stack anywhere below the *T*, find an available memory location in the table of temporary variables; mark it busy; emit a STO to that location; change the *V* entry to *N*; and place the location of the temporary in the corresponding place in the symbol stack.
2. If the name/value stack entries opposite *T* and *P* are both *N*, emit LOD on the symbol stack entry opposite *T*, and record *V* in the corresponding point in the name/value stack.
3. If the name/value stack entry opposite *P* is *V* and that opposite *T* is *N*, exchange both the values of the two name/value stack entries and the two symbol-stack entries (multiplication is commutative).
4. Emit MUL on the location in the symbol stack opposite *P*.

We can make similar associations for every production of the grammar.

Exercise 3.4.5

State rules for each production of the grammar sufficient to cause the correct generation of single-address code for assignments.

Exercise 3.4.6

Assume that the language to be recognized is the suffix assignments of Section 3.2 and that single-address code is to be produced. Associate with each production defining the suffix assignments an appropriate set of generation steps.

Exercise 3.4.7

Extend the infix-assignment language of Section 3.2 by adding productions

$$\langle program \rangle ::= \langle statement \rangle$$
$$| \ \langle program \rangle \ ; \ \langle statement \rangle$$
$$\langle statement \rangle ::= \mathbf{R} \ \langle letter \rangle$$
$$| \ \mathbf{I} \ \langle letter \rangle$$
$$| \ \langle infix \ assignment \rangle$$

in which **R** *a* declares *a* to have type real and **I** *b* declares *b* to have type integer. Extend the single-address code to include such operations as RMU (real arithmetic multiplication), RI, and IR (real-to-integer and integer-to-real conversions in the accumulator). State rules for each production which would assure that a symbol table is built during compilation, each entry is checked for uniqueness, and correct code is compiled for mixed real and integer assignments.

Exercise 3.4.8

The grammar for single-address codes allows nonsense programs. Rewrite the grammar so that all allowed single-address codes are the correct translation of some assignment.

Exercise 3.4.9

Take the new single-address grammar of Exercise 3.4.8, and invert the process so that parsing single-address code causes the generation of infix assignments.

One grammar for **if** statements is

⟨statement⟩ ::= ⟨infix assignment⟩ | ⟨if statement⟩

⟨if statement⟩ ::= ⟨if clause⟩ **then** ⟨truepart⟩ **else** ⟨statement⟩

⟨if clause⟩ ::= **if** ⟨infix expression⟩

⟨true part⟩ ::= ⟨infix assignment⟩

If we are to compile code for a machine with conventional branching instructions, we need to save both the destination address and the instruction location for conditional branches. The necessary compiler stacks appear in Table 3.4.4.

TABLE 3.4.4

Parse Stack	Branch Address Stack
⟨statement⟩	Address of instruction beyond ⟨statement⟩
else	
⟨truepart⟩	Address of instruction branching over ⟨statement⟩
then	
⟨if clause⟩	Address of instruction branching over ⟨truepart⟩
. . .	. . .

We obtain the values in the branch address stack as follows. When the ⟨if clause⟩ (**if** ⟨infix expression⟩) has been recognized, all the code for the expression has been compiled. We are then in a position to emit the testing code and, except that we do not yet know the destination, the conditional branch. The branch is emitted, and the location of the instruction is recorded in the branch address stack opposite ⟨if clause⟩. The compilation of the ⟨truepart⟩ (⟨infix assignment⟩) then proceeds, at which time we can emit the unconditional branch over the final ⟨statement⟩ (again excepting the unknown destination). This branch is also emitted, and its location is recorded next to the ⟨truepart⟩.

When we recognize

first branch

⟨if statement⟩ ::= ⟨if clause⟩ **then** ⟨truepart⟩ **else** ⟨statement⟩

second branch

we need only to (1) set the address in the first branch to one instruction beyond the

address associated with ⟨truepart⟩; and to (2) set the address in the second branch
to the address associated with ⟨statement⟩ .

Exercise 3.4.10

Extend Exercise 3.3.7 to include ⟨if statement⟩ with the following interpretation:
The ⟨truepart⟩ is to be executed if the expression in the ⟨if clause⟩ is nonzero;
otherwise the ⟨statement⟩ following the **else** is to be executed. You may add instructions

$$BZ \; a$$

which will branch to address a if the accumulator is zero, and

$$B \; a$$

which will always branch to address a.

3.5 Translating Languages with Nested Scopes

Although it is beyond the purpose of this book to explain all the varied and valid
methods of compiler construction, it is important to sketch some popular executable
(or interpretable) target languages and their related machine organizations. XPL
and XCOM are explicitly designed to avoid sophisticated forms of source or target
language (i.e., to remain close to the System/360) and therefore do not serve as complete
examples for the more advanced languages we hope will be written in this system.
Having discussed single-address and suffix codes for expression calculation
in detail, we will now extend suffix notation to provide addressing of variables in a
language with dynamically nested scopes.

Because the scopes of declarations in PL/I-like languages nest (see Sec. 6.6), we
can assign a unique nesting level to each scope: level 0 to the global scope, level 1
to the body of a procedure declared in the global scope, level 2 to the body of a procedure
nested within this procedure, etc. Each point in the program string is in exactly
one scope on each level below it. We can also associate an occurrence number to each
new identifier as it appears in a declaration or as a label. Then from any point in a
program, the description "ith name on the lth nesting level" identifies an identifier
accessible from that spot. The pair (l, i) is called an address couple and is a convenient
encoding during execution. For the moment we are interested in an algorithm to
compute it during compilation.

We will use two stacks, a name stack NS and a scope pointer stack SS. Every time
we encounter a new name, we place it on the top of NS. Every time we enter a new
scope, we record the height of NS by stacking it in SS. Every time we leave a scope,
we unstack SS and use the information to return NS to its state prior to entry. Note
that this is a left-to-right algorithm and is thus compatible with our compiling techniques.
A picture of our two stacks is given in Fig. 3.5.1.

Notice that the local names y and b of procedure Q are not in the table. This results
from having left the body of Q and having used SS to remove y and b from the name
stack. Q, however, occurs in the scope of the body of P and is therefore still accessible
(we may call Q from R).

We can now use the table to answer some questions. "What is the second name†
on level 1?" is answered by using 1 as an index to SS (value 3) and then by using that
value plus 2 (new value 5) as an index to NS, which gives us Q. The inverse question,
"What is the address couple of Q?" is somewhat clumsy. We search NS from top to
bottom, finding Q at position 5. Then we search SS from top to bottom, looking for
the first entry less than 5. We find 3 at position 1, which gives us an address couple of
$(1, 5 - 3) = (1, 2)$. If we are going to search for names often, we prefer to avoid the
second search by recording the address couple in another stack parallel to NS. We
may also want to record attributes, initial values, whether an item has been referenced,
etc., in still more parallel stacks. No further discussion of these ideas is useful here
since such tables are language dependent and are best built *ad hoc*.

If we ask for the address couple for a, we get $(1, 1)$, not $(0, 0)$. The reason, of course,
is that the a local to P obscures the global a while we are in P, and the top-to-bottom
search of NS reflects the obscuration as desired.

begin-blocks in ALGOL and PL/I may either be treated like procedure blocks
(given a nesting level), or not, depending upon the circumstances. If decoding address
couples for large l is not difficult in the machinery available, a level is usually assigned.
Otherwise, the distinction is made entirely at compile time, and variables local to a
begin-block are given the level of the enclosing procedure. We then attack the issue
of minimizing assigned run-time storage in another way.

Exercise   3.5.1

Compute by inspection the address couples of all the names in Fig. 3.5.1 ($a, b, P,$
x, a, Q, y, b, R, z, y). Be sure to count from zero (e.g., x gives $(1, 0)$).

Exercise   3.5.2

Add two stacks parallel to the NS and SS of Fig. 3.5.1, label them LS and OS, and
record the address couples associated with the names in NS. When a compiling algorithm places the address couples in LS and OS, is a search necessary to compute LS
or OS?

Exercise   3.5.3

Repeat Exercise 3.5.1 while the compiler processes "**call** $P(y)$;."

Exercise   3.5.4

How often is a name referred to in a symbol table after it is first entered? Is this a
reasonable experiment to perform on a compiler? What effect does the answer have
on the applicability of the extra stacks suggested in Exercise 3.5.2?

Although the name stack in XCOM is nearly identical to NS of the previous section, address couples are never used since less can be gained from them if the language
is not recursive (XPL is not, although PL/I and many other useful languages are).
We will propose a scheme corresponding to the dynamic nesting of scopes to assign

---

† Note that we count from zero.

```
        declare a fixed, b fixed;
        a = 3;
P:
    procedure (x);
            declare x character, a character;
            a = x ‖ '1' ;
    Q:
        procedure;
                declare y character, b bit (8);
                y = a;  b = byte(x);
                call P(y);
            end Q;
    R:
        procedure;
                declare z fixed, y fixed;
                /* snapshot taken at this point during compilation */
                if a = 'A1' then call Q;
            end R;
            b = byte(a);
        call R;
    end P;
    call P ('A');
    a = b;
```

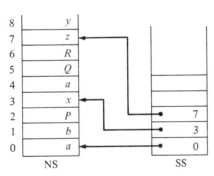

Fig. 3.5.1 Compile-Time Symbol Table and Associated Program

storage to names at run-time that (1) keeps conceptually different names separate, (2) allocates no more storage than necessary at any one moment, and (3) leads to a reasonably efficient implementation. This scheme has been used in many forms and many implementations (see Randell and Russell [64], for instance) and in fact comes in two levels of complexity: (1) without parametric procedures and (2) with. We will construct a mechanism for (1) first and then modify it for (2).

The configuration in Fig. 3.5.2 represents the complete solution as a snapshot of the program in Fig. 3.5.1 the second time the comment in procedure R is reached during execution.

Assume for the moment that we need exactly one memory cell for each declared name during execution. Then, when we enter a scope, we want: (1) to allocate those cells on the stack, (2) to make them accessible via the address couple by setting a pointer, (3) to properly initialize their values. We name the run-time stack where the

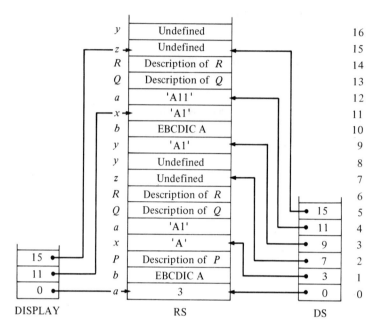

Fig. 3.5.2 The Run Stack

cells are allocated and the values are stored RS (analogous to NS). We also need a stack to keep the history of RS so that it can be restored when the program exits from a scope. We call this the dynamic pointer stack (DS) and use it much like SS. So far we have sufficient machinery to allocate and free the storage but have no means for accessing it.

Note that in DS there are pointers to the base of every storage block, including the ones visible at any given moment. If we just knew which pointers to pick, their value plus i of the couple (l, i) would point to the correct memory cell. The solution, discussed later, is to extract the relevant pointers and to place them in an array (called DISPLAY) so that DISPLAY$(l) + i$ is the correct index into RS for the address couple (l, i).

The basic operator in a simple suffix machine is NAME(l, i), which creates via the display an index into RS. Where such an address resides is an open question to which the logically simplest answer is to provide an address stack AS, in which such results can be placed. Then the suffix operator EVALUATE transfers the value pointed at from the top of AS onto the evaluation stack ES and deletes the address from AS; the ASSIGN operator ($\leftarrow$) takes a value from the top of ES, places it in RS at the point indicated by the top of AS, and deletes both the value and the address from their stacks.† Other operators function in the normal suffix style on ES alone.

---

† Note that we have made it impossible to store addresses.

Table 3.5.1 A Set of Run-Time Stacks

| AS | ES | DISPLAY | RS | DS |

We propose, then, four stacks and an auxiliary array to handle storage allocation and expression evaluation in PL/I-like languages. Often one or more stacks are combined. AS and ES can be combined if we have some way, context or otherwise, to distinguish addresses and values. Their combination can be placed on the top of RS since both of them are generally empty upon entry to, and exit from, a scope. Even DS may mix with RS, although the difficulties are more severe. A discussion of the run-stack mechanism and of the various possible compromises is given in Wortman [70].

Exercise 3.5.5

Verify the information in Fig. 3.5.2 by inspecting the program in Fig. 3.5.1.

Exercise 3.5.6

Define a set of suffix operators (including NAME (l, i), EVALUATE, and ASSIGN as well as CALL and RETURN, CAT, etc.) and a set of tables produced at compile time sufficient to execute the program of Fig. 3.5.1. (Assume CALL and RETURN correctly set the display without explaining the mechanism.) Hand code a suffix version of the program and then hand simulate its execution using the stacks and DISPLAY. Verify that the state in Fig. 3.5.2 is in fact achieved at the appropriate moment during execution.

We have used the display to locate allocated memory cells in the run stack by an address couple. Since addressing is thus forced to go indirectly through the display, other control may be placed on the access path. For example, the number of names in a scope, if also recorded in the display, may be used to check the validity of a decoded address couple. Similarly, if we mark a display entry *empty* when not in use, we can prevent evaluation of nonsense nesting levels. Or, we may assign level zero to the operating system and mark the zeroth entry in the display as read only, etc. The amount of extra information put into the display depends on who is generating the suffix code and what kind of performance is desired.

The question as yet unanswered is how to extract the information for the display from DS. If we do not allow parametric procedures (or ALGOL call-by-name parameters), the following scheme suffices: Along with each entry in DS we also place the nesting level of that scope. Then, when we wish to update the display (entry or exit), we search DS from top to bottom, copying into DISPLAY (l) the first entry in DS that we encounter with associated nesting level l.

Table 3.5.2 depicts the extension of Fig. 3.5.2.

TABLE 3.5.2

Display		Extended DS	
		Pointer	Level
		15	2
		11	1
		9	2
15		7	2
11		3	1
0		0	0

Exercise 3.5.7

Prove the correctness of the above algorithm.

The reason that the simple algorithm works, that the name of the procedure is visible from the point of invocation, may fail when the procedure is parametric.

The example in Table 3.5.3 is sufficient to illustrate the problem. Within R, the address couple $(1, 0)$ means the variable b. But if the display is updated as in the previous simple algorithm, we have the configuration in Fig. 3.5.3 just prior to the assignment in procedure R.

Clearly the value of a, not the intended value of b, is assigned to c, which results in the erroneous output of 3 instead of 2.

There is no known best solution to this problem although every complete translator for ALGOL 60 or PL/I has had to solve it. A workable though not very neat solution

TABLE 3.5.3

> P:
>   declare c **fixed**;
>
>   **procedure**(F);
>   declare a **fixed**, F **entry**;
> $a = 3$;
>   **call** F;
>   **end** P;
>
> Q:
>   **procedure**;
>   declare b **fixed**;
>
> R:
>   **procedure**;
>   declare $dummy$ **fixed**;
> $c = b$;
>   **end** R;
> $b = 2$;
>   **call** $P(R)$;
>   **end** Q;
>
>   **call** Q;
> $output = c$;

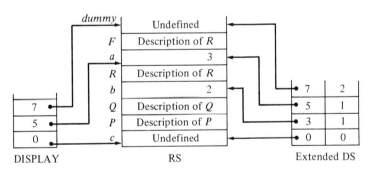

Fig. 3.5.3 Failure of the Simple Display Update Algorithm

is to lace RS with pointers back to the relevant addressing scope. The reader is encouraged to try to find a solution of his own.

Exercise 3.5.8

Devise an algorithm to update the display; allow for parametric procedures. Prove that it works correctly. (See Wortman [70] or Randell and Russell [64] for hints.)

Exercise 3.5.9

Redo Exercise 3.5.6 with an explicit display update algorithm associated with CALL and RETURN.

Implicit in the foregoing discussion has been the assignment of single cells to names. In the case of procedures, arrays, or large data, such as double precision numbers or character strings, we must make some provision for the assignment of larger amounts of storage.

One scheme places only the description of a complex item in RS. Thus, for a character string we may find its length and the address of its data; for an array we may find access control (read only, read/write, etc.) and a pointer to a table describing its structure which then points further to the data; for the name of a procedure we would like to know the nesting level of its body (for the extended DS) and the location of its code string, etc.

The advantage in using descriptions is in keeping RS simple and in our ability to interpose control, access methods, data size (byte vs. word), etc., on the access path provided by the indirection. Such information must reside somewhere, and we always try to put it in the most natural place.

The location of the data for complex items is another issue. Some systems place it in RS above the named cells. Others keep it in an auxiliary area (usually the rest of available memory) which must be managed and repacked occasionally. Although there is no trouble in ALGOL 60 in using RS for arrays, in PL/I the **allocate** and **free** constructs prevent such a solution. The one such sophisticated construct in XPL is dynamic character strings. An example of memory management is provided by XCOM allocation and compaction of the string area as described in Chapter 8.

Chapter 4

Canonical Parsing Algorithms

4.1   Computing the Phrase Structure of a Sentence

Chapter 3 presented the canonical parse as a basic tool for the translator writer. One component of our TWS is a canonical parsing algorithm which handles a broad class of grammars. As long as the grammar is acceptable, the particular algorithm used does not affect the construction of the translator (which is why we have deferred consideration of the topic).

Since the user wishing to change the algorithm (e.g., to enlarge the class of acceptable grammars, to economize the tables, or to improve error diagnostics or error recovery) must have a thorough understanding of the mechanisms involved, we turn to the problem of determining the phrase structure of a sentence. As we have noted, we can record this structure as we produce the sentence according to the grammar. For example, given P_3 defined by

$$
\begin{aligned}
G &::= E \\
E &::= T \mid E + T \\
T &::= P \mid T * P \\
P &::= x \mid y \mid z
\end{aligned}
$$

we may (canonically) generate sentences by substituting for the RNT at each step as shown in Tables 4.1.1 and 4.1.2.

We used the parse to produce the sentence. The parsing algorithm, however, must go from the sentence to the parse. It is impractical to build a table of all possible parses and their corresponding sentences; the usual procedure is to find rules which permit us to determine the parse steps one at a time.

Canonical recognition determines the CPS in reverse order, and thus successively reduces the canonical sentential form until the goal symbol is attained. Thus, in Tables 4.1.1 and 4.1.2 we number the CSF from the bottom up. Since we selected a

71

TABLE 4.1.1 Canonical Parse of $x + z + y$

(10)	G
(9)	$\to E$
(8)	$\to E + T$
(7)	$\to E + P$
(6)	$\to E + y$
(5)	$\to E + T + y$
(4)	$\to E + P + y$
(3)	$\to E + z + y$
(2)	$\to T + z + y$
(1)	$\to P + z + y$
	$\to x + z + y$

↑ Bottom up

TABLE 4.1.2 Canonical Parse of $x + z * y$

(9)	G
(8)	$\to E$
(7)	$\to E + T$
(6)	$\to E + T * P$
(5)	$\to E + T * y$
(4)	$\to E + P * y$
(3)	$\to E + z * y$
(2)	$\to T + z * y$
(1)	$\to P + z * y$
	$\to x + z * y$

↑ Bottom up

canonical form which expands from right to left, we use up (reduce) terminal symbols from left to right.†

Consider the parse of Table 4.1.1. The first three CPS use the productions

$$P \to x \qquad T \to P \qquad E \to T$$

---

† Recall that a parse step is canonical if and only if it is of the form $(\varphi A\alpha, \varphi\omega\alpha)$ where $\alpha \in V_t{}^*$.

to reduce† x successively to P, T, and E. CPS (4) and (5) reduce the z to P, then T (using $P \rightarrow z$ and $T \rightarrow P$). CPS (6) uses $E \rightarrow E + T$ to combine three symbols. CPS (7) and (8) reduce y to T which (9) combines with $E+$ to form E which (10) reduces to G.

The parse in Table 4.1.2 is slightly different. CPS (1) through (5) are basically the same, but CPS (6), instead of reducing $E + T$ to E, begins the reduction of y, permitting (7) to apply $T \rightarrow T * P$ before (8) applies $E \rightarrow E + T$ and (9) reduces to G.

These two sequences of CPS are valid since each was obtained by reversing a canonical parse. Furthermore, they are unique. The reader should convince himself that no other sequence of CPS reduces the given sentences to the goal symbol (this is a consequence of the unambiguity of $\mathbf{P}_3$). Our procedure has, of course, been circular. We knew the structure of the sentences because we had generated them by the grammar. In the remainder of this chapter we will treat the problem of analyzing sentences whose structure is not known in advance.

There are two general classes of parsing algorithms. The first class is goal oriented. Starting with the goal of recognizing a member of the phrase class described by the goal symbol of the grammar, the algorithm examines a few characters in the input text, decides which production can possibly apply, and then attempts to recognize successively a member of each phrase class in the right part of the production, in effect establishing them as subgoals. The algorithm proceeds in a recursive descent from the root of the parse tree to the leaves. Thinking in terms of the successive goals (G establishes E as a subgoal), we refer to these methods as *top-down*. The distinguishing feature of top-down methods is that the state of the algorithm (the current goal) is used to help make decisions. The second class of methods does not use state information. It rather examines the CSF in sufficient detail to determine what unique CPS is applicable and then performs a substitution. All decisions in these *bottom-up* methods are based on symbols in the CSF (the local context of Chapter 3). Both methods perform the canonical parse, the successful return from a subgoal and the act of substitution being the respective actions corresponding to a CPS. Furthermore, both methods make exactly the same decisions (and hence the same number of decisions) but use different information to do so. The methods can, in fact, be combined (see Knuth [65]). Our discussion will concern the bottom-up methods only (see Feldman and Gries [68] for further discussion).

Exercise   4.1.1

Why does the fact that $\mathbf{P}_3$ is unambiguous imply that the parses we have given are the only canonical parses for $x + z + y$ and $x + z * y$?

Exercise   4.1.2

Consider CPS (6) of both Table 4.1.1 and Table 4.1.2. In both cases the sentential form starts with $E + T$, but in one case the production $E \rightarrow E + T$ is applied and

---

† In the sense of applying a production in the reverse direction, not necessarily in the sense of "make smaller."

in the other it is not. Can you explain why? (Hint: Consider the next symbol in the text.) Give a simple rule to determine whether to use the production $E \rightarrow E + T$ at any step in a parse.

Exercise 4.1.3

Generalize Ex. 4.1.2 by giving a rule for each production of $\mathbf{P}_3$ that indicates whether the production should be used at a particular step. (Be sure that your rules always indicate that exactly one production should be used.) Combine your rules into a parsing algorithm for $\mathbf{P}_3$. Test your algorithm on the sentences $x + z + y$, $x + z * y$, $x * y * z + x + x + x$, and $z + y * y * y * y + x$. What happens if you try to parse a nonsentence such as $z \ z + * x$?

4.2 Using Parsing Functions

If a grammar is unambiguous, every sentence (and thus every CSF) has a unique canonical parse. The parsing problem can be reduced to finding the next CPS at each step. Since the CSF has only one canonical parse, it uniquely determines the next CPS. We therefore infer the existence of a single-valued *canonical parsing function* C such that if (τ_{i+1}, τ_i) is a CPS then $C(\tau_i) = \tau_{i+1}$. When we know C for a particular grammar, we can easily parse sentences according to that grammar.

Figure 4.2.1 shows a complete solution to the problem of parsing an unambiguous sentence.

By examining the canonical parses of Tables 4.1.1 and 4.1.2, we can see, for example, that (for the grammar $\mathbf{P}_3$) $C(E + T) = E$. Table 4.2.1 gives the values of C for a

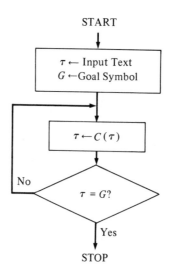

Fig. 4.2.1 The General
Canonical Parsing
Algorithm

TABLE 4.2.1   Representative Values of the Canonical Parsing Function for P_3

$C(E) = G$	$C(T + z + y) = E + z + y$
$C(E + T) = E$	$C(P + z * y) = T + z * y$
$C(E + P) = E + T$	$C(P + z + y) = T + z + y$
$C(E + y) = E + P$	$C(x + z * y) = P + z * y$
$C(T + y) = E + y$	$C(x + z + y) = P + z + y$
$C(P + y) = T + y$	$C(y + z * y) = P + z * y$
$C(x + y) = P + y$	$C(z + z + y) = P + z + y$
$C(z + y) = P + y$	$C(T * P + z * y) = T + z * y$
$C(E + T * P) = E + T$	$C(T * x + z * y) = T * P + z * y$
$C(E + T + y) = E + y$	$C(P * x + z * y) = T * x + z * y$
$C(E + T * y) = E + T * P$	$C(x * x + z * y) = P * x + z * y$
$C(E + P + y) = E + T + y$	$C(z * x + z * y) = P * x + z * y$
$C(E + P * y) = E + T * y$	.
$C(E + z + y) = E + P + y$	.
$C(E + z * y) = E + P * y$	.
$C(T + z * y) = E + z * y$	

TABLE 4.2.2

i	τ_i	$C(\tau_i) = \tau_{i+1}$
0	$z + y$	$P + y$
1	$P + y$	$T + y$
2	$T + y$	$E + y$
3	$E + y$	$E + P$
4	$E + P$	$E + T$
5	$E + T$	E
6	E	G
7	G	

number of arguments. We can use this table to parse various sentences. Let $\tau_0 = z + y$. Table 4.2.2 shows the canonical parse of τ_0 according to $\mathbf{P}_3$.

But we have rather begged the question. In general, we know only that the function C exists, not what its values are. The only way we have given to compute the values of the function is to record all the steps of all canonical parses in a table—an impossible method for infinite languages. Fortunately, there are economical ways to compute the parsing function for various restricted classes of grammars (see Floyd [63]; Knuth [65]; Wirth [66]; McKeeman [66]; and De Remer [69]). We will present several such methods—one in some detail.

Exercise   4.2.1

Use Table 4.2.1 and the general parsing algorithm to construct canonical parses (according to $\mathbf{P}_3$) for the sentences $x + y$, $x + z * y$, $x + z + y$, $y + z * y$, $z + z + y$, and $z * x + z * y$. Can you parse any other sentences without extending the table of values for C?

Exercise 4.2.2

Extend Table 4.2.1 to contain all the values necessary to parse the sentences in Ex. 4.1.3. Can you make a complete table of C for $\mathbf{P}_3$? Can you make a complete table for all sentences of length $\leq n$?

Exercise 4.2.3

The grammar $\mathbf{P}_6$

$$
\begin{aligned}
G &::= T \mid T + T \mid T - T \\
T &::= P \mid P * P \\
P &::= x \mid y
\end{aligned}
$$

generates a finite number of sentences. Determine all the canonical parses of $\mathbf{P}_6$ (hence all canonical parse steps). Prove directly that $\mathbf{P}_6$ is unambiguous. Tabulate $C(\tau)$ for each sentential form τ. Use your tabulation to compute the canonical parse of $x * x + y * y$.

Exercise 4.2.4

If $\tau = C(\tau)$, τ is called a stationary point of the iterating function C. What pathological condition in a grammar causes a stationary point for the general parsing function? Can C be single valued at a stationary point?

To determine the phrase structure of a sentence (or to relate the semantics to the parse), we need to know at each step which portion of the CSF was rewritten and which production was applied. Likewise, for any τ_i we can deduce $C(\tau_i)$ from the location of one end of ω_i in τ_i and the production (A_i, ω_i).

For the CPS (τ_{i+1}, τ_i), there are partitions of τ_i and τ_{i+1}, $\tau_i = \varphi_i \omega_i \alpha_i$, $\tau_{i+1} = \varphi_i A_i \alpha_i$

TABLE 4.2.3 Partitions for the Canonical Parse of $z + z$
According to $\mathbf{P}_3$

i	CSF	φ_i	A_i	α_i	φ_i	ω_i	α_i
	G						
(7)		λ	G	λ	λ	E	λ
	E						
(6)		λ	E	λ	λ	$E + T$	λ
	$E + T$						
(5)		$E+$	T	λ	$E+$	P	λ
	$E + P$						
(4)		$E+$	P	λ	$E+$	z	λ
	$E + z$						
(3)		λ	E	$+z$	λ	T	$+z$
	$T + z$						
(2)		λ	T	$+z$	λ	P	$+z$
	$P + z$						
(1)		λ	P	$+z$	λ	z	$+z$
	$z + z$						

$= \varphi_{i+1}\omega_{i+1}\alpha_{i+1}$, where $\alpha_i \in \mathbf{V}_t{}^*$, $(A_i, \omega_i) \in \mathbf{P}$. The length of α_i cannot increase as i increases since at each step the RNT (A_i) is a nonterminal symbol, and α_{i+1} must be composed entirely of terminal symbols. Table 4.2.3 illustrates this partitioning at each step of a canonical parse.

At each step of the canonical parse we set a variable σ to $\varphi_{i-1}A_{i-1}$ and a variable α to α_{i-1}. $\sigma\alpha = \tau_i = \varphi_i\omega_i\alpha_i$ and $|\alpha_i| \leq |\alpha|$ so we move symbols from the head of α to the tail of σ until $\sigma = \varphi_i\omega_i$. We then reduce, applying the production (A_i, ω_i) so that σ becomes φ_iA_i and the process can be repeated. Note that σ resembles a last-in first-out stack; adding symbols to σ may be regarded as stacking them on σ. In fact, σ is precisely the parse stack of Chapter 3.

The foregoing constitutes a parsing algorithm for which two functions must be defined:

1. C1, which locates the right boundary of ω_i in τ_i (the boundary between σ and α), and
2. C2, whose value (A_i, ω_i) is the production to be applied.

C1 is the *stacking-decision predicate*, and C2 is the *production selection function;* together they determine the function C. Figure 4.2.2 shows the revised algorithm.

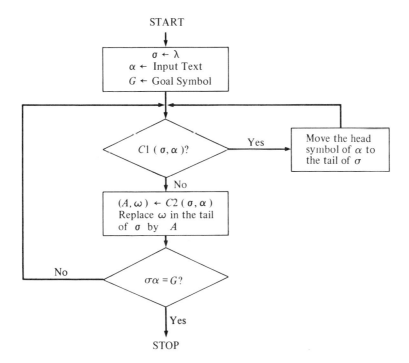

Fig. 4.2.2 The General Canonical Parsing Algorithm with C1 and C2

In Table 4.2.4 we tabulate some values of C1 and C2 for a number of arguments. We can use this table to parse $z + z$ as in Table 4.2.5.

TABLE 4.2.4   Some Representative Values of $C1$ and $C2$ for P_3

$C1(E, \lambda)$	= false	$C2(E, \lambda)$	= (G, E)
$C1(T, \lambda)$	= false	$C2(T, \lambda)$	= (E, T)
$C1(P, \lambda)$	= false	$C2(P, \lambda)$	= (T, P)
$C1(x, \lambda)$	= false	$C2(x, \lambda)$	= (P, x)
$C1(\lambda, x)$	= true	$C2(y, \lambda)$	= (P, y)
$C1(y, \lambda)$	= false	$C2(z, \lambda)$	= (P, z)
$C1(\lambda, y)$	= true	$C2(z, +z)$	= (P, z)
$C1(z, \lambda)$	= false	$C2(P, +z)$	= (T, P)
$C1(\lambda, z)$	= true	$C2(T, +z)$	= (E, T)
$C1(E + T, \lambda)$ = false		$C2(E + z, \lambda)$	= (P, z)
$C1(E + P, \lambda)$ = false		$C2(E + P, \lambda)$	= (T, P)
$C1(E + z, \lambda)$ = false		$C2(E + T, \lambda)$	= $(E, E + T)$
$C1(E, +z)$	= true	$C2(z, * z)$	= (P, z)
$C1(E +, z)$	= true	$C2(E + z, +x)$ = (P, z)	
$C1(T, +z)$	= false	.	
$C1(P, +z)$	= false	.	
$C1(\lambda, z + z)$ = true		.	
$C1(z, +z)$	= false		

.
.
.

TABLE 4.2.5   The Canonical Parse of $z + z$ According to P_3

σ	α	$C1(\sigma, \alpha)$	$C2(\sigma, \alpha)$
λ	$z + z$	true	
z	$+ z$	false	(P, z)
P	$+ z$	false	(T, P)
T	$+ z$	false	(E, T)
E	$+ z$	true	
$E +$	z	true	
$E + z$	λ	false	(P, z)
$E + P$	λ	false	(T, P)
$E + T$	λ	false	$(E, E + T)$
E	λ	false	(G, E)
G	λ		

Exercise 4.2.5

Verify, by hand simulation, that the general parsing algorithm with $C1$ and $C2$ using Table 4.2.4 yields the canonical parse of Table 4.2.5.

Exercise 4.2.6

Many of the rules in Table 4.2.4 may be abbreviated by $C1(\sigma, \lambda) = $ false and $C2(\varphi z, \alpha) = (P, z)$, for arbitrary σ, φ, and α. Are these abbreviations generally valid or can you find σ or φ and α for which they give incorrect values? How many valid abbreviations can you find for $\mathbf{P}_3$? What portions of the argument strings for $C1$ and $C2$ are significant?

Exercise 4.2.7

Extend Table 4.2.4 to contain all the values necessary to parse the sentences of Exercises 4.2.1 and 4.2.2. Can you make complete tables of $C1$ and $C2$ for $\mathbf{P}_3$ (a) without abbreviations, (b) with abbreviations?

Exercise 4.2.8

For each CPS of $\mathbf{P}_6$ (Exercise 4.2.3), tabulate the appropriate values of $C1$ and $C2$. Can you abbreviate this table? Use your table to parse $x * x - x$.

Exercise 4.2.9

If the grammar $\mathbf{P}_i$ is unambiguous, $(\varphi A\alpha, \varphi\omega\alpha)$ is a CPS with $\alpha \in V_t^*$, $A \in V_n$, (B, ψ) is any production distinct from (A, ω) in $\mathbf{P}_i$, and $\varphi\omega = \rho\psi\chi$, show that $\rho B\chi\alpha$ cannot be a sentential form, that $(\rho B\chi\alpha, \rho\psi\chi\alpha)$ cannot be a CPS, and that ω is the leftmost reducible string.

Exercise 4.2.10

Verify the following definitions for $C1$ and $C2$: (1) If $(\varphi_i A_i \alpha_i, \varphi_i \omega_i \alpha_i)$ is a CPS and $\sigma\beta = \varphi_i\omega_i$, then $C1(\sigma, \beta\alpha_i) \equiv (\beta \neq \lambda)$, and (2) if $(\varphi_i A_i \alpha_i, \varphi_i \omega_i \alpha_i)$ is a CPS, then $C2(\varphi_i\omega_i, \alpha_i) = (A_i, \omega_i)$.

Exercise 4.2.11

Show that the definitions of Exercise 4.2.10 cover the entire domain of arguments the functions $C1$ and $C2$ encounter in the algorithm of Fig. 4.2.2, presuming the input text is a CSF.

Exercise 4.2.12

Under what conditions are $C1$ and $C2$ single valued?

Exercise 4.2.13

If $C1$ and $C2$ are single valued and the input text is a CSF, show that the parsing algorithm (Fig. 4.2.2) produces the unique canonical parse.

Exercise 4.2.14

If the input text is not a CSF, where will the error first appear? Suggest an algorithm to change σ and α so that the parse can continue.

4.3 Representing Parsing Functions by Tables

/* Truth is the most valuable thing we have—so let us economize it. */

MARK TWAIN

Pudd'nhead Wilson's Calendar

When we discussed the existence and various properties of the parsing functions, we gave tables of representative values instead of general rules for evaluating the functions explicitly. We may completely describe a function in many ways. Sometimes the simplest is to give a rule (algorithm) for its computation. If the rule is complex, however, a table which gives the value of the function for various values of the arguments may be preferable. It may even be advantageous to use the algorithm only once, to compute the table, and then to look up values in the table as needed.

Unless the domain of a function is finite, the function cannot be directly represented by a finite table. Thus in our examples we have been restricted to tabulating representative values of the parsing functions. It is not feasible to interpolate or extrapolate such tables in a manner analogous to our use of a table of trigonometric functions.

In Chapter 2, by restricting the class of possible relations $\rightarrow$ for PSGs, we were able to specify $\rightarrow$ with a finite set (the productions **P**), although $\rightarrow$ has an infinite domain (**V*** $\times$ **V***). Similarly, further restrictions on PSGs allow representation of $C1$ and $C2$ by functions with finite domains. Specifically, we consider only those grammars for which we can compute $C1$, by using no more than the top p symbols in the stack and the next q symbols in the input text, and $C2$, by using no more than the m symbols below the production in the stack and the next n symbols in the input text. We denote these restrictions by saying $C1$ is *bounded context* of degree (p, q) and $C2$ is *bounded context* of degree (m, n).

Unlike the restrictions made in Chapter 2, which could be rather easily and directly checked, the bounded context restrictions do not relate in any direct way to the form of the grammar.

$$G \quad ::= \quad x\,G\,x \mid y$$

is in the class for which $C1$ is of degree $(2, 0)$ and $C2$ is of degree $(0, 0)$. There is no degree for which $C1$ is bounded context for

$$G \quad ::= \quad x\,G\,x \mid x$$

In Chapter 5 we give an algorithm to determine whether a PSG is of a particular degree. The higher the degree, the larger grow both the class of acceptable grammars and the tables of parsing functions. This direct relation leads to a natural trade-off.

If the degrees (and hence the tables) are very small, the parsing can be performed efficiently, but the class of acceptable grammars is very restricted. This restriction may require drastic changes in our grammars to make them usable. On the other hand, if the tables are large enough to handle most common grammars, they may be larger than the main memories of our computers. The appropriate degree depends—in an ill-defined manner—on the complexity of the grammars we wish to use. In the balance of this section we discuss some useful choices of degree.

We denote the restriction of $C1$ to a domain of the top p symbols in the stack and the next q symbols of the input text by $C1_{pq}$. We require that over its entire domain

$$C1(\sigma, \alpha) \equiv C1_{pq}(\mathbf{t}_p(\sigma), \mathbf{h}_q(\alpha))\dagger$$

Recalling (Exercise 4.2.10) that for each CPS $(\varphi_i A_i \alpha_i,\ \varphi_i \omega_i \alpha_i)$ and $\sigma\beta = \varphi_i \omega_i$, $C1(\sigma, \beta\alpha_i) \equiv (\beta \neq \lambda)$, we have

$$C1_{pq}(\mathbf{t}_p(\sigma), \mathbf{h}_q(\beta\alpha_i)) \equiv (\beta \neq \lambda)$$

$C1_{pq}$ is single valued if and only if $C1$ is of degree (p, q). Otherwise, values of its arguments exist for which it is true in one context and false in another.

Some well-known parsing algorithms are based on special cases of degree $(1, 1)$ or $(2, 1)$. The stacking-decision predicate of degree $(1, 1)$, called the *symbol pair predicate*, may be efficiently represented by a two-dimensional Boolean array.‡ $(1, 1)$ is the lowest adequate degree for grammars of the common programming languages. $C1_{11}$ exists for all simple precedence grammars [Wirth 66a], and some others. Although we can construct symbol pair grammars for most programming languages, considerable manipulation of the grammar is usually required to make it acceptable to the algorithm, and the resulting grammar "could not be presented to the programmer as a reference to the language" [Feldman and Gries 68].

By using another symbol in the stack, the predicate $C1_{21}$ accepts a wider class of grammars that includes the extended precedence grammars [McKeeman 66]. It is generally not hard to construct an extended precedence grammar, also acceptable as a reference, for a language. However, the direct representation of $C1_{21}$ yields a table impracticably large§ and often very sparse since most triples of symbols cannot occur in a canonical parse. Memory may be conserved by tabulating only those triples for which $C1_{21}$ has a value, rather than by storing the values in a three-dimensional array. Unfortunately, the table may still be rather large, and the process of looking up a value in the table (now requiring a search, rather than simple indexing) is much slower.

It seems that degree $(2, 1)$ is too big (since the tables are too large) and degree $(1, 1)$ is too little (since the class of grammars is too restricted). However, most grammars for programming languages are nearly symbol pair grammars, i.e., $C1_{11}$ is

---

† To avoid the problem of $|\sigma| < p$ or $|\alpha| < q$ we add $\perp^p$ to the head and $\perp^q$ to the tail of the sentence and parse to $\perp^p G \perp^q$ where $\perp$ is a symbol not previously in the grammar.

‡ Of dimension (number of symbols) $\times$ (number of terminal symbols), order n^2.

§ Of dimension (number of symbols)^2 $\times$ (number of terminal symbols), order n^3.

undefined for only a few symbol pairs. A *mixed-strategy* algorithm uses a degree
(1, 1) function with three values (stack, don't stack, conflict)† and reverts to a (2, 1)
predicate only for pairs in which the (1, 1) predicate is undefined. Since the (2, 1) predicate then needs definition only over the restricted domain of (1, 1) conflicts, a smaller
table of triples suffices. We feel that this compromise is appropriate for a broad class
of languages.

Choosing the correct production (C2) may be done somewhat differently. The
first and obvious requirement of the production (A, ω) is that its right part (ω) match
the top symbols of the stack, that is $\mathbf{t}_{|\omega|}(\sigma) = \omega$. In particular, the tail symbol of ω
must match the top symbol of the stack,‡ $\mathbf{t}_1(\sigma) = \mathbf{t}_1(\omega)$. Thus, if the table of productions is sorted by tail symbol, only a small number of productions—selected by the
current top symbol in the stack—need be considered at each step.

If only one production matches the stack, matching is a necessary and sufficient
condition for selection since we know that a reduction must be performed. Often,
however, more than one match exists. This situation arises with any grammar in which
the right part of one production is a tail of another right part. In $\mathbf{P}_3$ there are two
such imbedded right parts (T in $E ::= E + T$ and $E ::= T$, and P in
$T ::= T * P$ and $T ::= P$).

Figure 4.3.1 shows σ at each point in the canonical parses of Table 4.1.1 and 4.1.2
at which more than one match occurs. In these examples, as for any parse with $\mathbf{P}_3$,
the longest match is always the correct one. Perhaps surprisingly, this simple rule is
adequate for a rather large class of grammars, which includes both simple and extended
precedence grammars. This rule is easily implemented by sorting all productions with
the same tail symbol by length, checking from longest to shortest, and accepting the
first match.

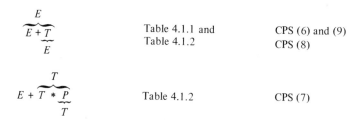

E	Table 4.1.1 and	CPS (6) and (9)
$E + T$	Table 4.1.2	CPS (8)
E		
T		
$E + T * P$	Table 4.1.2	CPS (7)
T		

Fig. 4.3.1 Two Multiple Match Situations

The longest-match rule is inadequate for many useful grammars, however. In
particular, if a grammar has productions with equal right parts, these productions
match the same stacks and obviously cannot be discriminated by length. We would

---

† In practice a fourth value (invalid pair) is used for error checking. The function has the value
"conflict" for exactly those arguments in which the predicate is undefined (not single valued) and the
value "invalid pair" for those arguments for which the predicate is not required to have a value.
‡ If we prohibit productions of the form (A, λ). Note that (A, λ) matches any stack.

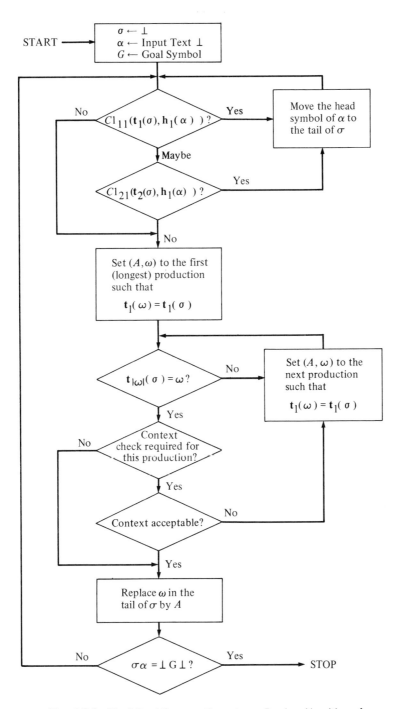

Fig. 4.3.2 The Mixed Strategy Precedence Parsing Algorithm of Degree (2,1 ; 1,1)

like to handle equal right parts because they are rather common in grammars for programming languages, e.g.,

$$\langle \text{array id} \rangle \quad ::= \quad \langle \text{identifier} \rangle$$
$$\langle \text{procedure id} \rangle \quad ::= \quad \langle \text{identifier} \rangle$$

or

$$\langle \text{replacement operator} \rangle \quad ::= \quad =$$
$$\langle \text{relation} \rangle \quad ::= \quad =$$

On the other hand, we wish to avoid extra checking and large tables which contain primarily the information of the longest-match rule.

The mixed-strategy approach again seems best. We categorize the productions (after sorting) as

1. always correct, if this is the first match,
2. not always correct but resolvable by checking n (usually $n = 1$) symbols in the head of α,†
3. resolvable by checking m (usually $m = 1$) symbols in the stack below the right part,
4. only resolvable using (m, n) context in the stack and the text, or
5. error, not resolvable by using (m, n) context (this case will only occur if the grammar is not (m, n) bounded right context [Floyd 64]).

After finding a matching production we check its category. We immediately accept productions in category 1 and perform the indicated tests on the others. If a production is rejected, we continue the search for a match.

Our tables, then, can take many different forms, each particular form determining a class of acceptable grammars. The central idea of the *mixed-strategy precedence* (MSP) algorithm shown in Fig. 4.3.2 is to use simple (small) tables to make as many decisions as possible, but to extend the class of acceptable grammars by using more complex tables for the exceptional cases. The objective is to minimize the memory used for tables by making them complex only where the language is complex (locally ambiguous). If, for some grammar, $C1$ is of degree (p, q) and $C2$ is of degree (m, n), we say the grammar is MSP of degree $(p, q; m, n)$. The grammar $\mathbf{P}_3$ is MSP of degree $(1, 1; 0, 0)$ and has the particularly simple set of tables shown in Table 4.3.1. All stacking decisions can be made on symbol pairs, and the right parts can all be distinguished by length. (Note that we will be parsing to $\perp G \perp$.)

In Table 4.3.2 we use the sentence of Table 4.1.2 as an example to trace both the parsing steps and the use of the parsing-decision tables.

Exercise 4.3.1

Use Table 4.3.1 to parse the following according to $\mathbf{P}_3$: $x + z + y$, $x * y * z + x + x + x$, and $z + y * y * y + x$. What happens if you try to parse a nonsentence

---

† In this case the invalid pair entry in $C1_{11}$ may be used to reject the production when it is not appropriate.

TABLE 4.3.1 Tables of Parsing Functions for P_3

$C1_{11}$ Stacking Decision Matrix

Stack	+	*	x	y	z	⊥
+			Y	Y	Y	
*			Y	Y	Y	
x	N	N				N
y	N	N				N
z	N	N				N
⊥			Y	Y	Y	
G						
E	Y					N
T	N	Y				N
P	N	N				N

Y = yes, stack
N = no, don't stack

$C2_{00}$ Production Selection Function

Tail Symbol of σ	Productions	Context Category
x	$P \to x$	1†
y	$P \to y$	1
z	$P \to z$	1
E	$G \to E$	1
T	$\begin{cases} E \to E + T \\ E \to T \end{cases}$	1 1
P	$\begin{cases} T \to T * P \\ T \to P \end{cases}$	1 1

† Category 1 is acceptable without further context checks.

such as $z\ z + * x$? Are your results the same as those in Exercise 4.1.3? Compare your rules for that exercise with Table 4.3.1.

Exercise 4.3.2

If $C1$ is of degree (p, q), $C2$ is of degree (m, n), and the input text is a CSF, show that the MSP algorithm of Fig. 4.3.2 produces the unique canonical parse.

Exercise 4.3.3

If the input text is not a CSF, where does the error first appear? Show that at least one error is detected. Suggest an algorithm to change σ and α so that the parse can continue.

Not all grammars have tables as simple as those for $\mathbf{P}_3$. We will present some typical situations and discuss the tables they require. In Chapter 7 we will discuss difficult cases in more detail.

TABLE 4.3.2

CPS	σ	α	C1 Test	Value	C2 Test	Value
(1)	$\perp$	$x + z * y\perp$	$C1(\perp, x)$	Y		
	$\perp x$	$+z * y\perp$	$C1(x, +)$	N	$x = x$	Yes, $C2 = P \rightarrow x$
(2)	$\perp P$	$+z * y\perp$	$C1(P, +)$	N	$\perp P = T * P$	No
					$P = P$	Yes, $C2 = T \rightarrow P$
(3)	$\perp T$	$+z * y\perp$	$C1(T, +)$	N	$\perp T = E + T$	No
					$T = T$	Yes, $C2 = E \rightarrow T$
	$\perp E$	$+z * y\perp$	$C1(E, +)$	Y		
	$\perp E+$	$z * y\perp$	$C1(+, z)$	Y		
	$\perp E + z$	$*y\perp$	$C1(z, *)$	N	$z = z$	Yes, $C2 = P \rightarrow z$
(4)	$\perp E + P$	$*y\perp$	$C1(P, *)$	N	$E + P = E * P$	No
					$P = P$	Yes, $C2 = T \rightarrow P$
(5)	$\perp E + T$	$*y\perp$	$C1(T, *)$	Y		
	$\perp E + T*$	$y\perp$	$C1(*, y)$	Y		
	$\perp E + T * y$	$\perp$	$C1(y, \perp)$	N	$y = y$	Yes, $C2 = P \rightarrow y$
(6)	$\perp E + T * P$	$\perp$	$C1(P, \perp)$	N	$T * P = T * P$	Yes, $C2 = T \rightarrow T * P$
(7)	$\perp E + T$	$\perp$	$C1(T, \perp)$	N	$E + T = E + T$	Yes, $C2 = E \rightarrow E + T$
(8)	$\perp E$	$\perp$	$C1(E, \perp)$	N	$E = E$	Yes, $C2 = G \rightarrow E$
(9)	$\perp G$	$\perp$				

Right Recursion

The grammar

$$
\begin{aligned}
G &\;::=\; S \\
S &\;::=\; x \mid x\,S \mid c\,S\,b
\end{aligned}
$$

is right recursive in the symbol S. Since the stacking decision cannot be made for the symbol pair $S\,b$, $C1$ is not of degree $(1, 1)$. It is, however, of degree $(2, 1)$. The symbol b should always be stacked against $c\,S$ but never against $x\,S$. (Verify.)

Equal Right Parts, Case 1

The grammar

$$
\begin{aligned}
G &\;::=\; A\,x \mid y\,B \\
A &\;::=\; z \\
B &\;::=\; z
\end{aligned}
$$

has two productions with the same right part. Since A can occur only in the context $\perp \ldots x$ and B can occur only in the context $y \ldots \perp$, the correct production can be determined by looking either way. Normally we prefer $(0, 1)$ rather than $(1, 0)$ context, since the right context check involves a table $(C1_{11})$, which we have anyway. $C1$ is of degree $(1, 1)$ for this grammar.

Equal Right Parts, Case 2

The grammar

$$
\begin{aligned}
G &\;::=\; x\,A \mid y\,B \\
A &\;::=\; z \\
B &\;::=\; z
\end{aligned}
$$

also has two equal right parts. A and B cannot be distinguished by $(0, 1)$ context since $\perp$ is valid right context for each. However, the left contexts are disjoint, and a $(1, 0)$ context check suffices.

Equal Right Parts, Case 3

The grammar

$$
\begin{aligned}
G &\;::=\; x\,A\,x \mid y\,A\,y \mid x\,B\,y \\
A &\;::=\; z \\
B &\;::=\; z
\end{aligned}
$$

also has equal right parts. Since A can occur either in the context $x \ldots x$ or $y \ldots y$ and B can occur in the context $x \ldots y$, neither $(1, 0)$ nor $(0, 1)$ context is sufficient to resolve this case. However, if both contexts are used together, a $(1, 1)$ context check suffices.

Embedded Right Part

The grammar

$$G ::= x A \mid B y$$
$$A ::= z$$
$$B ::= x z$$

does not have equal right parts, but the right part of $A ::= z$ is a tail of the right part of $B ::= x z$. Furthermore, since x is valid left context for A, both productions may match the stack $\perp x z$ when the shorter $(A ::= z)$ should be chosen. The correct choice may be determined by examining $(0, 1)$ context, since B always has y as right context, and A never does.

Exercise 4.3.4

Determine which (if any) context is necessary to distinguish each of the pairs of equal right parts in the following grammar. Are there any pairs which cannot be distinguished by context?

$$\langle\text{Wonderland}\rangle \quad ::= \langle\text{Tweedledee}\rangle \mid \langle\text{Tweedledum}\rangle$$
$$\mid \langle\text{March Hare}\rangle \langle\text{Mad Hatter}\rangle$$
$$\mid \langle\text{Mad Hatter}\rangle * \langle\text{March Hare}\rangle$$
$$\mid * \langle\text{Tea Party}\rangle *$$
$$\langle\text{Tweedledee}\rangle \quad ::= x$$
$$\langle\text{Tweedledum}\rangle \quad ::= x$$
$$\langle\text{March Hare}\rangle \quad ::= x$$
$$\langle\text{Mad Hatter}\rangle \quad ::= x$$
$$\langle\text{Tea Party}\rangle \quad ::= x$$

What is the language of this grammar? Show that it is ambiguous. Relate this ambiguity to the problem of right-part discrimination.

Exercise 4.3.5

Explain why $C1$ for the grammar

$$A ::= B \mid d B e$$
$$B ::= c \mid c B$$

is not of degree $(1, 1)$, while $C1$ for the similar grammar

$$A ::= B \mid d B e$$
$$B ::= c \mid B c$$

which generates exactly the same language, is of degree $(1, 1)$.

Exercise 4.3.6

MSP functions are not the only parsing functions which may be represented in tabular form. Several others are discussed in Feldman and Gries [68]. Use your knowledge of the MSP algorithm (or the ANALYZER program of Chapter 7) to construct MSP tables for the grammar given in Fig. 1 of that paper. (Hint: It is MSP of degree $(1, 1; 0, 0)$.) `

Compare the table size required for MSP with Floyd **f** and **g** functions, Floyd operator precedence matrix, Wirth and Weber precedence matrix, McKeeman extended precedence tables, and Samelson and Bauer transition matrices. What can be said in general about table sizes for the various methods?

4.4 Using LR Parsers for LR(*k*) Grammars

/∗ We ain't what we want to be, and we ain't what we're goin' to be, but we ain't what we wuz. ∗/

South Carolina mountain proverb

(Quoted by MARIO PEI in *The Story of Language*)

The use of the canonical parse in translation is, as we have seen in Chapter 3, independent of the particular parsing algorithm used. The MSP algorithm described in the previous section, although a reasonable compromise among the factors of speed, table size, and generality, is not the only useful approach. Work by DeRemer [69], based on the LR(*k*) grammars of Knuth [65], suggests the existence of algorithms of competitive efficiency and substantially more generality. In this section and in Sec. 5.6 we will outline their method.

If the stacking decision and the choice of which rule to apply can be made by using only the information in the parse stack together with the next *k* symbols in the text, the grammar is defined to be LR(*k*). The presumption is that LR(*k*) is the largest subset of context-independent phrase-structure rewriting systems (i.e., BNF) in which the grammars generate languages that can be canonically parsed by scanning once from left to right, looking at most *k* symbols beyond the leftmost reducible string. (We, of course, deny the subterfuge of carrying along all possible parses.)

For the stacking decision, the MSP (2, 1; *m, n*) algorithm uses (at most) the top two symbols on the stack and the next symbol from the input text. Even for this relatively small context we found it desirable to reduce the table size from order n^3 to order n^2 by the mixed-strategy technique. The corresponding problem for LR(*k*) is to make the decision based on all the symbols in the parse stack (which has unbounded size) plus *k* more from the input text—an audacious goal to say the least. The solution is based upon the particularly simple structure of the parse stack. The strategy of the LR(*k*) method is most easily seen through example. Consider a grammar $\mathbf{P}_{14}$

$$E ::= T \mid E + T$$
$$T ::= x \mid (E)$$

which we augment (pad) by adding the rule

$$G \ ::= \perp E \perp$$

The algorithm defined in Table 4.4.1 (and represented graphically by Fig. 4.4.1) parses sentences of the augmented P_{14}. It is started at the base of the parse stack in state 0 and proceeds up the stack and into the text, passing through a series of states until reaching a state with no successor. We then apply the indicated rule and restart the algorithm in state 0 at the base of the stack; we continue in this manner until reaching the position marked stop.

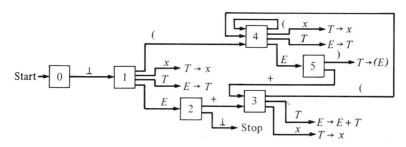

Fig. 4.4.1 An LR Parser for P_{14}

TABLE 4.4.1 An LR Parser for P_{14} in Tabular Form

When in The State	With Visible Symbol	Take This Action	
0	$\perp$	Pass the symbol, and enter	State 1
1	E	Pass the symbol, and enter	State 2
	T	Apply $E \rightarrow T$, and restart	
	x	Apply $T \rightarrow x$, and restart	
	$($	Pass the symbol, and enter	State 4
2	$\perp$	Stop	
	$+$	Pass the symbol, and enter	State 3
3	T	Apply $E \rightarrow E + T$, and restart	
	x	Apply $T \rightarrow x$, and restart	
	$($	Pass the symbol, and enter	State 4
4	E	Pass the symbol, and enter	State 5
	T	Apply $E \rightarrow T$, and restart	
	x	Apply $T \rightarrow x$, and restart	
	$($	Pass the symbol, and enter	State 4
5	$+$	Pass the symbol, and enter	State 3
	$)$	Apply $T \rightarrow (E)$, and restart	

Consider, for example, the string

$$\perp x + ((x + x)) \perp$$

for which the canonical parse is

$$
\begin{aligned}
& \perp x + ((x + x)) \perp\\
&\rightarrow \perp T + ((x + x)) \perp\\
&\rightarrow \perp E + ((x + x)) \perp\\
&\rightarrow \perp E + ((T + x)) \perp\\
&\rightarrow \perp E + ((E + x)) \perp\\
&\rightarrow \perp E + ((E + T)) \perp\\
&\rightarrow \perp E + ((E)) \perp\\
&\rightarrow \perp E + (T) \perp\\
&\rightarrow \perp E + (E) \perp\\
&\rightarrow \perp E + T \perp\\
&\rightarrow \perp E \perp
\end{aligned}
$$

Table 4.4.2 gives a partial history of the actions of the LR parser for $\mathbf{P}_{14}$; the $^\triangledown$ marks the position of the scanner. When a symbol is in the stack and is used as an input by the LR parser, it is simply passed by; when a symbol is in the text and is used, it is *stacked*, an action corresponding to the one controlled by the parsing function $C1$ of the previous section. Rules are always applied to the rightmost symbols of the stack precisely as demanded by the parsing function $C2$.

We immediately see that restarting the LR parser in state 0 at the bottom of the stack is unnecessary since the contents of the parse stack below the leftmost reducible string do not change during a step of the canonical parsing algorithm. If we remember what the parser did the last time it was restarted, we can restart it one symbol below the stack top after the application of each production rule. We denote the saved state information by interleaving it with the symbols in the parse stack. Table 4.4.3 gives the results of the modified algorithm as applied to $\perp x + ((x + x)) \perp$.

The grammar $\mathbf{P}_{14}$ is in fact LR(0). Note that it was never necessary to examine any symbol to the right of the leftmost reducible string before the corresponding reduction rule was applied. Programming languages are more typically represented by LR(1) grammars such as $\mathbf{P}_{15}$.

$$
\begin{aligned}
E &::= T \mid E + T\\
T &::= x \mid T * x
\end{aligned}
$$

which we again augment with the production

$$G ::= \perp E \perp$$

In the intermediate parse situation

$$\perp T \perp$$

TABLE 4.4.2 Partial History of The Parse of $\perp x + ((x + x))\perp$

Parser State	Stack	Text	Comments
			Starting arrangement
0		$^\triangledown\!\perp x + ((x + x))\perp$	
			Stack $\perp$
1	$\perp$	$^\triangledown\!x + ((x + x))\perp$	
			Stack x, then
—	$\perp x$	$+ ((x + x))\perp$	
			Apply $T \to x$, and restart
0	$^\triangledown\!\perp T$	$+ ((x + x))\perp$	
			Pass $\perp$
1	$\perp\!\overset{\triangledown}{T}$	$+ ((x + x))\perp$	
			Pass T, then
—	$\perp T$	$+ ((x + x))\perp$	
			Apply $E \to T$, and restart
0	$^\triangledown\!\perp E$	$+ ((x + x))\perp$	
			Pass $\perp$
1	$\perp\!\overset{\triangledown}{E}$	$+ ((x + x^\triangledown))\perp$	
			Pass E
2	$\perp E$	$^\triangledown\!+ ((x + x))\perp$	
			Stack $+$
3	$\perp E +$	$^\triangledown\!((x + x))\perp$	
			Stack $($
4	$\perp E + ($	$^\triangledown\!(x + x))\perp$	
			Stack $($
4	$\perp E + ((\,$	$^\triangledown\!x + x))\perp$	
			Stack x, then
—	$\perp E + ((x$	$+ x))\perp$	
			Apply $T \to x$, and restart
0	$^\triangledown\!\perp E + ((T$	$+ x))\perp$	
			Pass $\perp$
1	$\perp\!\overset{\triangledown}{E} + ((T$	$+ x))\perp$	
			Pass E
2	$\perp E\overset{\triangledown}{} + ((T$	$+ x))\perp$	
			Pass $+$
3	$\perp E +\overset{\triangledown}{} ((T$	$+ x))\perp$	
			Pass $($
4	$\perp E + (\overset{\triangledown}{(}T$	$+ x))\perp$	
			Pass $($
4	$\perp E + ((\overset{\triangledown}{}T$	$+ x))\perp$	
			Pass T, then
—	$\perp E + ((T$	$+ x))\perp$	
			Apply $E \to T$, and restart
0	$^\triangledown\!\perp E + ((E$	$+ x))\perp$	
		etc.	

TABLE 4.4.3 Complete Parse of $\perp x + ((x + x)) \perp$ by an LR Parser

Parser State	Stack	Text	Comments
0		$\overset{\triangledown}{\perp} x + ((x + x))\perp$	Starting arrangement
1	$0\perp$	$\overset{\triangledown}{x} + ((x + x))\perp$	Record state 0, stack $\perp$
—	$0\perp_1 x$	$+ ((x + x))\perp$	Record state 1, stack x, then
1	$0\perp_1 \overset{\triangledown}{T}$	$+ ((x + x))\perp$	Apply $T \rightarrow x$, restart at state 1
—	$0\perp_1 T$	$+ ((x + x))\perp$	Pass T, then
1	$0\perp_1 \overset{\triangledown}{E}$	$+ ((x + x))\perp$	Apply $E \rightarrow T$, restart at state 1
2	$0\perp_1 E$	$\overset{\triangledown}{+} ((x + x))\perp$	Pass E
3	$0\perp_1 E_2 +$	$\overset{\triangledown}{(}(x + x))\perp$	Record state 2, stack $+$
4	$0\perp_1 E_2 +_3 ($	$\overset{\triangledown}{(}x + x))\perp$	Record state 3, stack $($
4	$0\perp_1 E_2 +_3 (_4 ($	$\overset{\triangledown}{x} + x))\perp$	Record state 4, stack $($
—	$0\perp_1 E_2 +_3 (_4 (_4 x$	$+ x))\perp$	Record state 4, stack x, then
4	$0\perp_1 E_2 +_3 (_4 (_4 \overset{\triangledown}{T}$	$+ x))\perp$	Apply $T \rightarrow x$, restart at state 4
—	$0\perp_1 E_2 +_3 (_4 (_4 T$	$+ x))\perp$	Pass T, then
4	$0\perp_1 E_2 +_3 (_4 (_4 \overset{\triangledown}{E}$	$+ x))\perp$	Apply $E \rightarrow T$, restart at state 4
5	$0\perp_1 E_2 +_3 (_4 (_4 E$	$\overset{\triangledown}{+} x))\perp$	Pass E
3	$0\perp_1 E_2 +_3 (_4 (_4 E_5 +$	$\overset{\triangledown}{x})) \perp$	Record state 5, stack $+$
—	$0\perp_1 E_2 +_3 (_4 (_4 E_5 +_3 x$	$))\perp$	Record state 3, stack x, then
3	$0\perp_1 E_2 +_3 (_4 (_4 E_5 +_3 \overset{\triangledown}{T}$	$))\perp$	Apply $T \rightarrow x$, restart at state 3
—	$0\perp_1 E_2 +_3 (_4 (_4 E_5 +_3 T$	$))\perp$	Pass T, then
4	$0\perp_1 E_2 +_3 (_4 (_4 \overset{\triangledown}{E}$	$))\perp$	Apply $E \rightarrow E + T$, restart at state 4
5	$0\perp_1 E_2 +_3 (_4 (_4 E$	$\overset{\triangledown}{)})\perp$	Pass E
—	$0\perp_1 E_2 +_3 (_4 (_4 E_5)$	$)\perp$	Record state 5, stack $)$, then
4	$0\perp_1 E_2 +_3 (_4 \overset{\triangledown}{T}$	$)\perp$	Apply $T \rightarrow (E)$, restart at state 4

TABLE 4.4.3   (Contd.)

Parser State	Stack	Text	Comments
			Pass T, then
—	$_0{\perp}_1E_2{}^+{}_3({}_4T$	$){\perp}$	
			Apply $E \to T$, restart at state 4
4	$_0{\perp}_1E_2{}^+{}_3({}_4\overset{\triangledown}{E}$	$){\perp}$	
			Pass E
5	$_0{\perp}_1E_2{}^+{}_3({}_4E$	$\overset{\triangledown}{)}{\perp}$	
			Record state 5, stack), then
—	$_0{\perp}_1E_2{}^+{}_3({}_4E_5)$	$\perp$	
			Apply $T \to (E)$, restart at state 3
3	$_0{\perp}_1E_2{}^+\overset{\triangledown}{{}_3}T$	$\perp$	
			Pass T, then
—	$_0{\perp}_1E_2{}^+{}_3T$	$\perp$	
			Apply $E \to E + T$, restart at state 1
1	$_0\overset{\triangledown}{\perp}_1E$	$\perp$	
			Pass E
2	$_0{\perp}_1E$	$\overset{\triangledown}{\perp}$	
			Record state 2, stack $\perp$, and quit
—	$_0{\perp}_1E_2{\perp}$		

and in contrast

$$\perp T * x \perp$$

we find that the application of the rule

$$E \to T$$

depends upon whether a $\perp$ or a $*$ follows the T. If $\perp$ follows, we must reduce; otherwise, we must stack. Thus, we need to examine the $\perp$ without actually stacking it as the convention in Fig. 4.4.1 demanded. We may solve this problem by an application of an LR(1) algorithm over-all, but there is considerable advantage in using it only selectively. Therefore, we will extend our repertoire of forms to include a dotted arrow for transitions to mark those which are not to cause stacking of the examined symbol. For the grammar $\mathbf{P}_{15}$ we get the parser in Fig. 4.4.2.

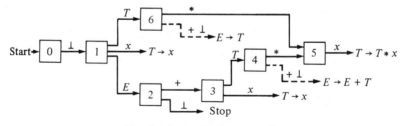

Fig. 4.4.2   An LR Parser for P_{15}

The difference in the actions of the parsers presented in Figs. 4.4.1 and 4.4.2 can be seen by examining the action of Fig. 4.4.2 on the strings $\perp x \perp$ and $\perp x * x \perp$, as given in Tables 4.4.4 and 4.4.5. The technique of mixing the algorithms for LR(0) and LR(1) is very much in the spirit of the MSP algorithm. The discussion of the algorithm for constructing LR parsers is deferred to Sec. 5.6.

Exercise 4.4.1

It is tempting to define a grammar to be LR(k) if the decisions can be made on the basis of the entire history of the parse plus the k symbols immediately following the leftmost reducible string. Would such a definition increase the class of LR(k) grammars? Defend your answer.

Exercise 4.4.2

Show that the grammars acceptable to the MSP $(p, q; m, n)$ algorithm are a proper subset of the LR(k) grammars if $q \leq k$ and $n \leq k$.

Exercise 4.4.3

Use Fig. 4.4.1 to check the correctness of Table 4.4.3. Verify that the parse produced is canonical.

Exercise 4.4.4

Use Fig. 4.4.2 to check the correctness of Tables 4.4.4 and 4.4.5.

TABLE 4.4.4 Parse of $\perp x \perp$ by an LR Parser

Parser State	Stack	Text	Comments
0		$\overset{\triangledown}{\perp x \perp}$	Starting configuration
1	$0 \perp$	$\overset{\triangledown}{x \perp}$	Record state 0, stack $\perp$
—	$0 \perp_1 x$	$\perp$	Record state 1, stack x, then
1	$0 \perp_1 \overset{\triangledown}{T}$	$\perp$	Apply $T \rightarrow x$, restart at state 1
6	$0 \perp_1 T$	$\overset{\triangledown}{\perp}$	Pass T
—	$0 \perp_1 T$	$\perp$	Examine $\perp$, then
1	$0 \perp_1 \overset{\triangledown}{E}$	$\perp$	Apply $E \rightarrow T$, restart at state 1
2	$0 \perp_1 E$	$\overset{\triangledown}{\perp}$	Pass E
—	$0 \perp_1 E_2 \perp$		Record state 2, stack $\perp$, then quit

TABLE 4.4.5   Parse of $\perp x * x \perp$ by an LR Parser

Parser State	Stack	Text	Comments
			Starting configuration
0		$\overset{\triangledown}{\perp} x * x\perp$	
			Record state 0, stack $\perp$
1	$_0\!\perp$	$\overset{\triangledown}{x} * x\perp$	
			Record state 1, stack x, then
—	$_0\!\perp_1 x$	$* x\perp$	
			Apply $T \to x$, restart at state 1
1	$_0\!\perp_1 \overset{\triangledown}{T}$	$* x\perp$	
			Pass T
6	$_0\!\perp_1 T$	$\overset{\triangledown}{*} x\perp$	
			Record state 6, stack $*$
5	$_0\!\perp_1 T_6 *$	$\overset{\triangledown}{x}\perp$	
			Record state 5, stack x, then
—	$_0\!\perp_1 T_6 *_5 x$	$\perp$	
			Apply $T \to T * x$, restart at state 1
1	$_0\!\perp_1 \overset{\triangledown}{T}$	$\perp$	
			Pass T
6	$_0\!\perp_1 T$	$\overset{\triangledown}{\perp}$	
			Examine $\perp$, then
—	$_0\!\perp_1 T$	$\perp$	
			Apply $E \to T$, restart at state 1
1	$_0\!\perp_1 \overset{\triangledown}{E}$	$\perp$	
			Pass E
2	$_0\!\perp_1 E$	$\overset{\triangledown}{\perp}$	
			Record state 2 , stack $\perp$, then quit
—	$_0\!\perp_1 E_2 \perp$		

Exercise   4.4.5

Use Fig. 4.4.1 to parse the strings

$$\perp x \perp$$
$$\perp (((x))) \perp$$
$$\perp (x) + x + (x)\perp$$

Exercise   4.4.6

Use Fig. 4.4.2 to parse the strings

$$\perp x * x + x * x \perp$$
$$\perp x + x * x + x\perp$$

Exercise   4.4.7

Attempt to parse $\perp(\ )\perp$ using Fig. 4.4.1. How is the error detected? What is the most meaningful diagnostic that can be generated? What additional information could you add to the given LR parser to aid in diagnostics?

Exercise 4.4.8

Suggest a method which allows recovery from an error in the input text in such a way that the given LR parser is likely to detect any further errors without obscuring that detection with a flurry of spurious messages. How does your method work on the texts

$$\perp ((((((\perp$$
$$\perp ((((((($$
$$\perp) + x + x + (\perp$$
$$\perp 3 + x + x + 3\perp$$
$$x\perp$$
$$x$$

Exercise 4.4.9

Devise a general LR parser controlled by tables such that to change grammars one need only change tables. How compactly can these tables be encoded for storage in digital memory?

Exercise 4.4.10

In certain cases, the LR parser can be simplified by recording multiple actions to be associated with particular transitions. For example, in Fig. 4.4.3 (equivalent to Fig. 4.4.1) we sometimes associate two rule applications with a transition and sometimes are able to record the state to be attached to the top of the stack without examining the topmost symbol. Outline an algorithm to produce the simplified LR parsers.

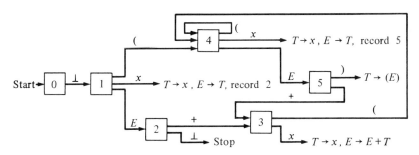

Fig. 4.4.3

Exercise 4.4.11

If we could always discover the state to restart after rule applications, we would not have to carry it along with the parse stack. (Verify.) Propose an algorithm to produce expanded diagrams with this capability. Do nonterminal symbols ever appear on a transition in the new LR parsers?

Chapter 5

The Construction of Parsing Decision Tables

/* "Explain all that," said the Mock Turtle.

"No, No! The adventures first," said the Gryphon in an impatient tone: "Explanations take such a dreadful time." */

LEWIS CARROLL

Alice's Adventures in Wonderland

5.1 Tabulating Information about Grammars

In this chapter we present a sequence of algorithms which collectively compute all the tables required for the mixed strategy precedence parsing algorithm of Chapter 4. Although we concentrate on MSP of degree $(2, 1; 1, 1)$, this being the degree we have implemented (see Chapter 10), we indicate the general theory for higher degrees.

Various tables describe properties of grammars. The simplest of these are the associated vocabulary sets $V(P)$, $V_n(P)$, $V_t(P)$ (see Definitions 2.3.20 through 2.3.22). Another useful set is the null set $N = N(P)$,

$$N = \{A \mid A \to^+ \lambda\}$$

Because they are sets, we typically ask whether an item is a member. We therefore organize our tables for quick look-up either by sorting them or by using an associative technique such as hash addressing.

Exercise 5.1.1

Give an algorithm which computes the null set N of a grammar. Use your algorithm to compute the null set of P_8.

$$
\begin{array}{lcl}
G & ::= & E \\
E & ::= & A\,T \\
A & ::= & E + \mid B \\
B & ::= & \lambda \\
T & ::= & M\,P \\
M & ::= & T * \mid B \\
P & ::= & x \mid y
\end{array}
$$

Finite relations, represented by Boolean matrices or sets of ordered pairs, are a second kind of table describing grammatical properties. We can use the relation $\to$ to define new relations. In particular, each of the four following formulas states that the corresponding relation on $\mathbf{V} \times \mathbf{V}$ holds between symbols A and X:

$$A \rightarrow X \qquad A \rightarrow \varphi X \qquad A \rightarrow X\psi \qquad A \rightarrow \varphi X\psi$$

For any such relation we can define the transitive completion and reflexive transitive completion.

$$A \rightarrow^+ X \qquad A \rightarrow^+ \varphi X \qquad A \rightarrow^+ X\psi \qquad A \rightarrow^+ \varphi X\psi$$
$$A \rightarrow^* X \qquad A \rightarrow^* \varphi X \qquad A \rightarrow^* X\psi \qquad A \rightarrow^* \varphi X\psi$$

Some of these relations we have seen before; for instance, $A \rightarrow^+ \varphi A$ and $A \rightarrow^+ A\psi$ together imply ambiguity (Exercise 2.3.12). Others will be used later.

The definition of transitive completion (see Definition 2.3.9) suggests an iterative algorithm for its computation. If $\mathbf{S}$ is a set and $\mathbf{r}$ is any relation on $\mathbf{S} \times \mathbf{S}$, then its transitive completion $\mathbf{r}^+$ has the following properties:

1. If $X \; \mathbf{r} \; Y$ then $X \; \mathbf{r}^+ \; Y$
2. If $X \; \mathbf{r}^+ \; Y$ and $Y \; \mathbf{r}^+ Z$ then $X \; \mathbf{r}^+ Z$

We define $\mathbf{r}_n$ by

1. $X \; \mathbf{r}_1 \; Y \equiv X \; \mathbf{r} \; Y$
2. $X \; \mathbf{r}_{n+1} Z \equiv (X \; \mathbf{r}_n \; Z \lor (\exists Y) X \; \mathbf{r}_n \; Y \land Y \; \mathbf{r}_n \; Z)$

If $\mathbf{r}_{n+1} \equiv \mathbf{r}_n$, then $\mathbf{r}_{n+1} \equiv \mathbf{r}^+$.

Table 5.1.1 shows the computation of the relations $A \rightarrow^+ X\psi$ and $A \rightarrow^* X\psi$ for the grammar $\mathbf{P}_7$.

$$
\begin{aligned}
G &::= E \\
E &::= T \mid E + T \\
T &::= P \mid T * P \\
P &::= x \mid (E)
\end{aligned}
$$

We represent $\mathbf{r}$ by a Boolean matrix ($Y =$ true, blank $=$ false in Table 5.1.1) and then compute $\mathbf{r}_2, \mathbf{r}_3, \ldots$ until no change occurs. The matrix then represents the transitive completion. We make the reflexive transitive completion by setting $X \; \mathbf{r}^* \; X$ for each X.

Exercise 5.1.2

Redo the example in Table 5.1.1. Represent a relation by a set of ordered pairs instead of a Boolean matrix.

Exercise 5.1.3

Restate the transitive completion algorithm in terms of logical sums and products of Boolean matrices.

Exercise 5.1.4

Show that, in the computation of $\mathbf{r}^*$, the result is independent of whether the diagonal of the matrix is set true before or after the iteration. Is there a computational reason to prefer one order over the other?

TABLE 5.1.1   Computation of Transitive Completion

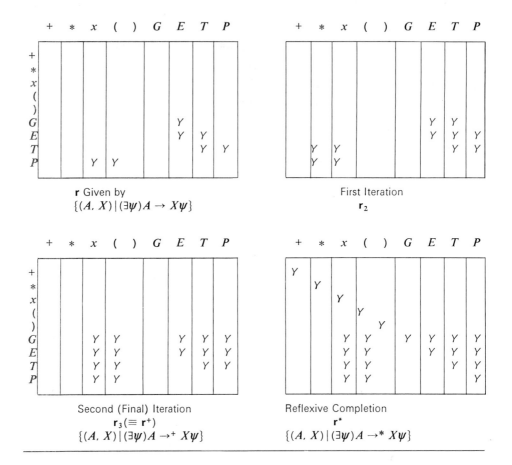

r Given by
$\{(A, X) \mid (\exists\psi)A \to X\psi\}$

First Iteration
r_2

Second (Final) Iteration
$r_3 (\equiv r^+)$
$\{(A, X) \mid (\exists\psi)A \to^+ X\psi\}$

Reflexive Completion
r^*
$\{(A, X) \mid (\exists\psi)A \to^* X\psi\}$

Exercise   5.1.5

If erasure is prohibited (Definition 2.3.26), then $A \to^* X\psi$ gives us a direct definition of an important set-valued function called the produced 1-heads.

$$\textbf{PH}_1(A) = \{X \mid A \to^* X\psi\}$$

and the terminal produced 1-heads

$$\textbf{TPH}_1(A) = \textbf{PH}_1(A) \cap \textbf{V}_t$$

Devise a representation for $\textbf{TPH}_1$ and an algorithm to compute it. Test your algorithm on $\textbf{P}_7$.

Exercise   5.1.6

If there is erasure, we must generalize the definition of $\textbf{PH}_1$.

$$\textbf{PH}_1(A) = \{X \mid (\exists\rho\exists\psi)A \to^* \rho X\psi \wedge \rho \to^* \lambda\}$$

Show that we can compute $\textbf{PH}_1(A)$ as the reflexive transitive completion of

$$\mathbf{r} \equiv \{(A, X) \mid A \to \rho X \psi \land (\text{each symbol in } \rho \in \mathbf{N})\}$$

Generalize Exercise 5.1.5, and use the result to compute $\mathbf{TPH}_1$ for every symbol in $\mathbf{P}_8$.

Exercise 5.1.7

Show that if $A \, \mathbf{r}^+ \, X$ in $i \le 2^k$ steps of $\mathbf{r}$, this fact is recorded after no more than k iterations of the transitive completion algorithm given in this section. Use this bound to derive a bound in terms of $\log_2$ (number of nonterminals) on the maximum number of iterations required to compute $\mathbf{PH}_1$.

Although many of the necessary tables are simple to compute, a few are not. One powerful method creates all expansions of some string within the particular range of interest. Consider, for instance, the generalization of $\mathbf{TPH}_1$ to $\mathbf{TPH}_n$.

$$\mathbf{PH}_n(\varphi) = \{\rho \mid \varphi \to^* \rho\sigma \land |\rho| = n\}$$
$$\mathbf{TPH}_n(\varphi) = \mathbf{PH}_n(\varphi) \cap \mathbf{V}_t^*$$

Suppose there is no erasure. Then if $|\varphi| > n$, $\mathbf{PH}_n(\varphi) = \mathbf{PH}_n(\mathbf{h}_n(\varphi))$. Furthermore, if $\varphi \to \psi$

$$\mathbf{PH}_n(\psi) \subset \mathbf{PH}_n(\varphi)$$

The last formula suggests that we should

1. shorten φ if $|\varphi| > n$;
2. enter it in $\mathbf{PH}_n$ if $|\varphi| = n$;
3. apply every possible production to every nonterminal of φ, getting a new set of strings;
4. treat each new string as though it were φ and return to 1 unless it is already in $\mathbf{PH}_n$;
5. compute $\mathbf{TPH}_n$.

Using $\mathbf{P}_3$ and $\varphi = E+$, we apply the algorithm in Table 5.1.2 to obtain $\mathbf{PH}_2(E+)$.

Execise 5.1.8

Use grammar $\mathbf{P}_3$ in computing

$$\mathbf{PH}_2(+T) \qquad \mathbf{TPH}_2(+T)$$
$$\mathbf{PH}_2(*P) \qquad \mathbf{TPH}_2(*P)$$

Exercise 5.1.9

For all $X \in \mathbf{V}$, compute $\mathbf{TPH}_2(X)$ for $\mathbf{P}_3$.

Exercise 5.1.10

Suggest an extension of the algorithm for $\mathbf{PH}_n$ for grammars with erasure.

TABLE 5.1.2

Level					
0	1	2	3	4	
$E+$					Initial String
	$T+$				$E \rightarrow T$
		$P+$			$T \rightarrow P$
			$x+$		$P \rightarrow x$
			$y+$		$P \rightarrow y$
			$z+$		$P \rightarrow z$
		$T*$			$T \rightarrow T * P$
			$P*$		$T \rightarrow P$
				$x*$	$P \rightarrow x$
				$y*$	$P \rightarrow y$
				$z*$	$P \rightarrow z$
			$T*$		$T \rightarrow T * P$ (rejected)
	$E+$				$E \rightarrow E + T$ (rejected)

$$TPH_2(E+) = \{x+, y+, z+, x*, y*, z*\}$$

Exercise 5.1.11

Bound the number of steps in the iteration for $\mathbf{PH}_n$. Why is the result so much worse than that in Exercise 5.1.7? Could a similar approach have been used here?

Exercise 5.1.12

Bound the size of the sets for $\mathbf{PH}_n$ and $\mathbf{TPH}_n$. Exhibit a grammar and argument to $\mathbf{PH}_n$ and $\mathbf{TPH}_n$ which realizes your bound.

5.2 Collecting the Production Contexts

For any partitioning of a CSF $\tau = \varphi \omega \alpha$ and production (A, ω), either $(\varphi A \alpha, \varphi \omega \alpha)$ is a CPS or it is not. Furthermore, the decision depends not on the right part of the production but only on whether $\varphi A \alpha$ is a CSF. The corresponding predicate $F(\varphi, A, \alpha)$ is true if and only if $\varphi A \alpha$ is a CSF.† For an infinite language, of course, F has an infinite domain. We denote the restriction of F to a domain of m symbols in the tail of φ, A, and n symbols in the head of α by $F_{mn}(\psi, A, \beta)$, which is true if and only if $\psi = \mathbf{t}_m(\varphi)$ and $\beta = h_n(\alpha)$‡ for some CSF $\varphi A \alpha$. F_{mn} may be represented as a table of the contexts of each RNT in all CSFs.

A table of F could be used in a canonical parsing algorithm to systematically locate

---

† Recall that A is the RNT, hence $\alpha \in \mathbf{V}_t^*$.

‡ Again using the trick of bracketing the sentence with $\perp^m$ and $\perp^n$ and parsing to $\perp^m G \perp^n$, which guarantees that the arguments to F_{mn} will always be long enough.

the leftmost reducible string and to determine the associated production. Under certain conditions (which can be mechanically verified) these decisions can be made correctly using a table of F_{mn}, in which case the grammar is said to be *bounded right context* of degree (m, n) [Floyd 64]. For suitable choices of degree, all grammars acceptable to the MSP algorithm of Chapter 4 are bounded right context, and vice versa.

In general, the parsing algorithm that uses tables of $C1$ and $C2$ is more efficient than one based directly on tables of F. However, $C1$ and $C2$ can be derived from F, which is more easily computed from the grammar as an intermediate step.

To tabulate F we need only list all the CSFs of a grammar, since $F(\varphi, A, \alpha)$ is true if and only if A is the RNT of a CSF $\varphi A\alpha$. We may generate CSFs by running a canonical parser backwards, i.e., by applying a production to the RNT at each step. This process can systematically and recursively generate all the CSFs of a grammar. We start from the goal symbol and at each level apply each of the possible productions to the RNT. After each expansion, we further expand the resulting CSF (unless it is a sentence). Recording φ, A, and α at each step builds a complete (at termination) table of the values for which $F(\varphi, A, \alpha)$ is true. Table 5.2.1 shows the operation of this algorithm for the very simple grammar $\mathbf{P}_9$.

$$
\begin{aligned}
G &::= T \mid T + T \\
T &::= P \mid P * P \\
P &::= x
\end{aligned}
$$

Exercise 5.2.1

Use your results for Exercise 4.2.3 to compute a complete table of F for the grammar $\mathbf{P}_6$.

Exercise 5.2.2

Design a parsing algorithm which uses the predicate F (or its restriction F_{mn}) and the productions of a grammar to parse sentences. Use your algorithm and your table from the previous exercise to parse $y * y - x * x$.

Exercise 5.2.3

What is the smallest degree (m, n) for which $\mathbf{P}_6$ is bounded right context? Justify your answer. Tabulate F_{mn} for $\mathbf{P}_6$ for that degree. Use your new tables and your parsing algorithm to parse $x + y$.

If the grammar is recursive—as all interesting grammars are—the domain of F is infinite, and the generation algorithm never terminates. F_{mn}, however, has a domain of bounded size. We seek a modification of the generation algorithm which builds complete tables of F_{mn} and yet terminates. To guarantee adequate context, we add $\perp$ to $\mathbf{V}_t$ and generate from $\perp^m G \perp^n$.

By definition of a PSG, the expansions of a nonterminal are independent of its context. Thus, if we have once recorded (and expanded) the arguments

TABLE 5.2.1 Generation of CSFs for P₉

Level 0	1	2	3	4	5	6	7	$\varphi,$	F, A	α
G								$\lambda.$	$G,$	λ
	T							$\lambda.$	$T,$	λ
		P						$\lambda.$	$P,$	λ
		$P*P$	x					$P*,$	$P,$	λ
			$P*x$	$x*x$				$\lambda.$	$P,$	$*x$
	$T+T$	$T+P$	$T+x$	$P+x$	$x+x$			$T+,$	$T,$	λ
								$T+,$	$P,$	λ
								$\lambda.$	$T,$	$+x$
								$\lambda.$	$P,$	$+x$
				$P*P+x$	$P*x+x$	$x*x+x$		$P*,$	$P,$	$+x$
								$\lambda.$	$P,$	$*x+x$
		$T+P*P$	$T+P*x$	$T+x*x$	$P+x*x$	$x+x*x$		$T+P*$	$P,$	λ
								$T+,$	$T,$	$*x$
								$\lambda.$	$T,$	$+x*x$
								$\lambda.$	$P,$	$+x*x$
				$P*P+x*x$	$P*x+x*x$	$x*x+x*x$	$x*x+x*x$	$P*,$	$P,$	$+x*x$
								$\lambda.$	$P,$	$*x+x*x$

$(\mathbf{t}_m(\varphi), A, \mathbf{h}_n(\alpha))$, no further expansion of A in this context can produce new values. Before recording a triple of arguments, we may determine whether it has already been recorded, and if so, stop expanding the CSF. There are only a finite number of triples; thus, if we never expand one twice, the process must terminate. The operation of the modified algorithm for F_{11} is shown in Table 5.2.2 for the grammar $\mathbf{P}_{10}$.

$$
\begin{aligned}
G &::= E \\
E &::= T \mid E + T \\
T &::= P \mid T / P \\
P &::= x
\end{aligned}
$$

The modified algorithm ultimately encounters only previously recorded triples and terminates. The final two lines of Table 5.2.2 illustrate a new difficulty. The expansion is terminated—since $(/, P, +)$ and $(/, P, \bot)$ are repeated triples—and thus fails to expand T in the context $+ \ldots /$ (or even to record $(+, T, /)$). This problem arose because the right part of the production $T ::= T / P$ contained two non-terminals, and previous expansion of the RNT did not imply previous expansion of symbols to its left. In the special case we are considering† the problem can be eliminated by merely treating a nonterminal in a previously recorded context as quasi-terminal and by using the next nonterminal as the new RNT. In the general case, however, the expansion of the true RNT produces symbols which should become right context for the new RNT. It may seem that we have "escaped goblins to be caught by wolves."‡ By expanding a symbol only once in each context, we guarantee that the algorithm will terminate but fail to generate all valid contexts.

We resolve our difficulty by recourse to the algorithm of the previous section, which will compute all possible n heads producible from a given string. Whenever a non-terminal occurs in $\mathbf{h}_n(\alpha)$, we record not $\mathbf{h}_n(\alpha)$, but each string in $\mathbf{TPH}_n(\alpha)$. This permits one other change in the algorithm—one which, though not affecting the completeness of the tables (Exercise 5.2.5), tends to reduce the level of recursion required. At each level we expand only the nonterminals in the right part of the last production; those to the left are expanded at the level on which they first occurred. Table 5.2.3 shows the operation of the corrected algorithm (shown in Fig. 5.2.1) for F_{11} with the grammar $\mathbf{P}_{10}$.

Exercise 5.2.4

Use the algorithm demonstrated in Table 5.2.3 to generate a table of F_{22} for the grammar $\mathbf{P}_6$.

$$
\begin{aligned}
G &::= T \mid T + T \mid T - T \\
T &::= P \mid P * P \\
P &::= x \mid y
\end{aligned}
$$

How much larger would your table be

1. If the production $P ::= z$ were added?
2. If the production $P ::= (G)$ were added?

---

† Actually, for F_{m1} (m arbitrary) and any operator grammar [Floyd 63].

‡ J. R. R. Tolkein, *The Hobbit* (New York: Ballantine Books, 1965), p. 103.

TABLE 5.2.2 Generation of CSFs for P_{10} in the Modified Algorithm for F_{11}

Level 0	1	2	3	4	5	6	7	$\mathbf{t}_1(\varphi)$	A,	$\mathbf{h}_1(\alpha)$
$\bot G \bot$								$\bot$,	G,	$\bot$
	$\bot E \bot$							$\bot$,	E,	$\bot$
		$\bot T \bot$						$\bot$,	T,	$\bot$
			$\bot P \bot$					$\bot$,	P,	$\bot$
				$x\bot$				$/$,	P,	$/$
			$\bot T/P \bot$					$\bot$,	T,	$/$
				$\bot T/x \bot$				$\bot$,	P,	$/$
					$\bot P/x \bot$			$/$,	P,	$/$
					$\bot T/P/x \bot$			$+$,	T,	$/\dagger$
						$\bot x/x \bot$		$+$,	T,	$+$
						$\bot T/x/x \bot$		$+$,	E,	$+$
		$\bot E+T \bot$						$\bot$,	T,	$+$
			$\bot E+P \bot$					$\bot$,	P,	$+$
				$\bot E+x \bot$				$/$,	P,	$+$
					$\bot T+x \bot$			$\bot$,	T,	$/\dagger$
						$\bot P+x \bot$		$+$,	T,	$+$
							$\bot x+x \bot$	$+$,	P,	$+$
					$\bot E+T+x \bot$			$\bot$,	E,	$+\dagger$
						$\bot T/P+x \bot$		$/$,	P,	$+\dagger$
							$\bot T/x+x \bot$	$/$,	P,	$\bot\dagger$
						$\bot E+P+x \bot$				
							$\bot E+x+x \bot$			
			$\bot E+T/P \bot$							
						$\bot E+T/P+\bot$				

$\dagger$ Repeated triple.

TABLE 5.2.3   Operation of the Corrected Algorithm for F_{11}

Level 0	1	2	3	4	5	F_{11} — $\mathbf{t}_1(\varphi),\ A,\ \mathbf{h}_1(\alpha)$
⊥G⊥						⊥, G, ⊥
	⊥E⊥					⊥, E, ⊥
		⊥T⊥				⊥, T, ⊥
			⊥P⊥			⊥, P, ⊥
				⊥x⊥		[†]
			⊥T/P⊥			/, P, ⊥
				⊥T/x⊥		[†]
						⊥, T, /[‡]
			⊥P/P⊥			⊥, P, /
					⊥x/P⊥	[†]
			⊥T/P/P⊥			/, P, /
					⊥T/x/P⊥	[†]
						⊥, T, /[‡,§]
		⊥E+T⊥				+, T, ⊥
			⊥E+P⊥			+, P, ⊥
				⊥E+x⊥		[†]
			⊥E+T/P⊥			/, P, ⊥[§]
						+, T, /[‡]
			⊥E+P/P⊥			+, P, /
					⊥E+x/P⊥	[†]
			⊥E+T/P/P⊥			/, P, /[§]
						+, T, /[‡,§]
						⊥, E, +[‡]
			⊥T+T⊥			⊥, T, +
			⊥P+T⊥			⊥, P, +
					⊥x+T⊥	[†]
			⊥T/P+T⊥			/, P, +
					⊥T/x+T⊥	[†]
						⊥, T, /[‡,§]
			⊥E+T+T⊥			+, T, +
			⊥E+P+T⊥			+, P, +
					⊥E+x+T⊥	[†]
			⊥E+T/P+T⊥			/, P, +[§]
						+, T, /[‡,§]
						⊥, E, +[‡,§]

[†] Right part of production was terminal, no expansion called for.

[‡] New "RNT" selected.

[§] Repeated triple, no expansion.

Exercise 5.2.5

Repeat the calculation shown in Table 5.2.3 without the restriction that on any level only the right part of the immediately previous production is expanded. Verify that the table collected contains exactly the same elements. Show that this is true in general.

Procedure PRODUCE (σ, ϕ, ψ)
  Do while $|\phi| > 0$:

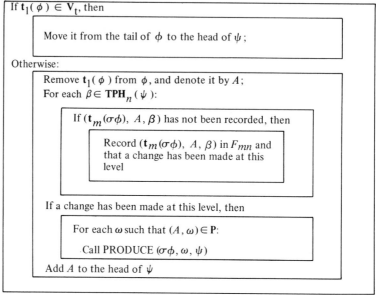

  Call PRODUCE $(\perp^m, G, \perp^n)$

Fig. 5.2.1

Exercise 5.2.6

Use the corrected algorithm illustrated in Table 5.2.3 to generate a table of F_{11} for the grammar $\mathbf{P}_3$.

$$
\begin{array}{lcl}
G & ::= & E \\
E & ::= & T \mid E + T \\
T & ::= & P \mid T * P \\
P & ::= & x \mid y \mid z
\end{array}
$$

Exercise 5.2.7

Compute a table of F_{11} for the grammar $\mathbf{P}_{11}$:

$$
\begin{array}{lcl}
G & ::= & E \\
E & ::= & T \mid T + E \\
T & ::= & P \mid P T \\
P & ::= & x \mid y
\end{array}
$$

Note that, since $\mathbf{P}_{11}$ is not an operator grammar, $\mathbf{TPH}_1$ is required as an intermediate step.

5.3 Computing the Stacking-Decision Predicate

Although Cl_{pq} can be computed directly from the productions of a grammar [McKeeman 66], tables of its values are more easily computed from the tables F_{mn}

and the sets $\mathbf{TPH}_q$. In this section, we present an algorithm for this computation. We shall require $p \leq m + 1$, $q \leq n$.

Every triple (φ, A, α) in F and corresponding production $(A, \omega) \in \mathbf{P}$ yield exactly one don't stack (i.e., reduce first) decision. Formally

$$[(\exists A)(\varphi, A, \alpha) \in \mathbf{F} \wedge (A, \omega) \in \mathbf{P}] \equiv \neg C1(\varphi\omega, \alpha)$$

In bounded context tables, each (φ, A, α) for which F_{mn} is true together with a production $(A, \omega) \in \mathbf{P}$, imply that $C1_{pq}(\mathbf{t}_p(\varphi\omega), \mathbf{h}_q(\alpha))$† is false. Furthermore, these are the only values for which $C1_{pq}$ need be false. (Why?)

Let $\omega = \rho\psi$. Then if $(\varphi, A, \alpha) \in \mathbf{F}$ and $(A, \omega) \in \mathbf{P}$, $C1$ must have values for all arguments $C1(\varphi\rho, \beta)$ where $\psi\alpha \to^* \beta$. Symbols must still be stacked ($C1$ true) unless $\psi = \lambda$. The definition for $\neg C1$ above is the special case $\psi = \lambda$. Thus we can express the total relation of $C1$ and $\mathbf{F}$ by

$$[(\exists A)(\varphi, A, \alpha) \in \mathbf{F} \wedge (A, \rho\psi) \in \mathbf{P} \wedge \psi\alpha \to^* \beta]$$
$$\text{if and only if}$$
$$[C1(\varphi\rho, \beta) \equiv (\psi \neq \lambda)]$$

As before we can derive $C1_{pq}(\mathbf{t}_p(\varphi\rho), \beta)$ from F_{mn} and $\beta \in \mathbf{TPH}_q(\psi\alpha)$. This enumeration is also exhaustive (Exercise 5.3.3). Since any produced head of $\mathbf{h}_1(\omega)$ is also a produced head of A and is recorded when the productions containing A‡ are expanded, we need only record the decisions for the remainder of ω.§ The algorithm is shown in Fig. 5.3.1.

For each $\sigma \in \mathbf{V}^p$ and $\alpha \in \mathbf{V}_t{}^q$:

    Set $C1_{pq}(\sigma, \alpha)$ initially clear.

For each $(A, \omega) \in \mathbf{P}$:

    For each (ϕ, α) such that $F_{mn}(\phi, A, \alpha)$:

        For each ρ and ψ such that $\rho\psi = \omega$:

            For each $\beta \in \mathbf{TPH}_q(\psi\alpha)$:

                Record that $C1_{pq}(\mathbf{t}_p(\phi\rho), \beta) \equiv (\psi \neq \lambda)$

For each $\beta \in \mathbf{TPH}_q(G\perp^q)$:
    Record that $C1_{pq}(\perp^p, \beta)$ is true.

Fig. 5.3.1

---

† We continue to exclude erasure. Note how m and n determine the restrictions on p and q.

‡ Unless, of course $A = G$. We add the rule $C1_{pq}(\perp^p, \beta)$ for each $\beta \in \mathbf{TPH}_q(G\perp^q)$ for this case.

§ Again, note that our restrictions on p and q guarantee that F_{mn} provides enough context.

If any $Cl_{pq}(\sigma, \alpha)$ must have both the value true and the value false, Cl is not of degree (p, q) for that grammar. In building a table for the $(2, 1; 1, 1)$ MSP algorithm, we use F_{11} to first compute Cl_{11}. We then repeat the computation for Cl_{21}, but record values only for those arguments which correspond to $(1, 1)$ conflicts. Table 5.3.2 illustrates the computation of Cl_{11} for the grammar $\mathbf{P}_{10}$ by using Table 5.3.1, resulting in the matrix for Cl shown in Table 5.3.3.

TABLE 5.3.1   Triples for F_{11} (Taken from Table 5.2.3),
Organized by RNT, and Produced Heads for P_{10}

φ, A, α

$\perp, G, \perp$

$\perp, E, \perp$
$\perp, E, +$

$\perp, T, \perp$
$\perp, T, /$
$+, T, \perp$
$+, T, /$
$\perp, T, +$
$+, T, +$

A \\ W	$+$	$/$	x	$\perp$	G	E	T	P
$+$	Y							
$/$		Y						
x			Y					
$\perp$				Y				
G			Y		Y	Y	Y	Y
E			Y			Y	Y	Y
T			Y				Y	Y
P			Y					Y

$\perp, P, \perp$
$/, P, \perp$
$\perp, P, /$
$/, P, /$
$+, P, \perp$
$+, P, /$
$\perp, P, +$
$/, P, +$
$+, P, +$

$$A \rightarrow^* W\varphi$$

Exercise   5.3.1

Use the algorithm presented in this section to compute a table of Cl_{11} for the grammar $\mathbf{P}_{11}$ (Exercise 5.2.7).

Exercise   5.3.2

Compute a table of Cl_{11} for the grammar $\mathbf{P}_{12}$.

$$G ::= E$$
$$E ::= T \mid T + E$$
$$T ::= P \mid P * T$$
$$P ::= x \mid y$$

How many entries fail to be single valued? Compute a table of Cl_{21} for $\mathbf{P}_{12}$. Use these tables to prepare a set of mixed-strategy tables. How do they compare in size with the table for Cl_{21}?

TABLE 5.3.2

Production $A \to \omega$	F_{11} Triple φ, A, α	Result φ, ω, α	Stack True, Y	Don't Stack False, N
$G \to E$	$\perp, G, \perp$	$\perp, E, \perp$		$(E, \perp)$
$E \to T$	$\perp, E, \perp$	$\perp, T, \perp$		$(T, \perp)$
	$\perp, E, +$	$\perp, T, +$		$(T, +)$
$E \to E + T$	$\perp, E, \perp$	$\perp, E + T, \perp$	$(E, +)$ $(+, x)$	$(T, \perp)$
	$\perp, E, +$	$\perp, E + T, +$	$(E, +)$ $(+, x)$	$(T, +)$
$T \to P$	$\perp, T, \perp$	$\perp, P, \perp$		$(P, \perp)$
	$\perp, T, /$	$\perp, P, /$		$(P, /)$
	$+, T, \perp$	$+, P, \perp$		$(P, \perp)$
	$+, T, /$	$+, P, /$		$(P, /)$
	$\perp, T, +$	$\perp, P, +$		$(P, +)$
	$+, T, +$	$+, P, +$		$(P, +)$
$T \to T/P$	$\perp, T, \perp$	$\perp, T/P, \perp$	$(T, /)$ $(/, x)$	$(P, \perp)$
	$\perp, T, /$	$\perp, T/P, /$	$(T, /)$ $(/, x)$	$(P, /)$
	$+, T, \perp$	$+, T/P, \perp$	$(T, /)$ $(/, x)$	$(P, \perp)$
	$+, T, /$	$+, T/P, /$	$(T, /)$ $(/, x)$	$(P, /)$
	$\perp, T, +$	$\perp, T/P, +$	$(T, /)$ $(/, x)$	$(P, +)$
	$+, T, +$	$+, T/P, +$	$(T, /)$ $(/, x)$	$(P, +)$
$P \to x$	$\perp, P, \perp$	$\perp, x, \perp$		$(x, \perp)$
	$/, P, \perp$	$/, x, \perp$		$(x, \perp)$
	$\perp, P, /$	$\perp, x, /$		$(x, /)$
	$/, P, /$	$/, x, /$		$(x, /)$
	$+, P, \perp$	$+, x, \perp$		$(x, \perp)$
	$+, P, /$	$+, x, /$		$(x, /)$
	$\perp, P, +$	$\perp, x, +$		$(x, +)$
	$/, P, +$	$/, x, +$		$(x, +)$
	$+, P, +$	$+, x, +$		$(x, +)$

Exercise 5.3.3

Show that every (τ, γ) for which $C1_{pq}$ must be true (that is, for which the head of γ must be moved to the tail of τ before the next parse step) corresponds either to

$$(\perp^p, \beta) \quad \text{with} \quad \beta \in \mathbf{TPH}_q(G \perp^q)$$

or to

$$(\mathbf{t}_p(\varphi\rho), \beta) \quad \text{with} \quad \beta \in \mathbf{TPH}_q(\psi\alpha) \quad \text{and} \quad \rho \neq \lambda, \qquad \psi \neq \lambda$$

where $(A, \rho\psi) \in \mathbf{P}$ and $F_{mn}(\varphi, A, \alpha)$ is true.

TABLE 5.3.3

$C1_{11}$ Matrix

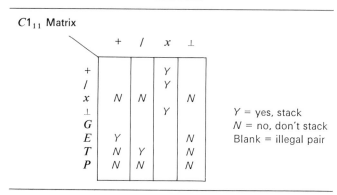

	+	/	x	⊥	
+			Y		
/			Y		
x	N	N		N	
⊥			Y		Y = yes, stack
G					N = no, don't stack
E	Y			N	Blank = illegal pair
T	N	Y		N	
P	N	N		N	

5.4 Computing the Production Selection Function

The MSP algorithm selects productions by searching a table, ordered by tail symbol of the right part and then by length, until it finds a right part matching the top of the stack. It then determines whether context must be checked, and, if so, consults a table of $(0, n)$, $(m, 0)$, or (m, n) contexts to determine the correctness of the production. The tables required are

1. A table of right parts, sorted by tail symbol and within groups by length
2. A table of the corresponding left parts
3. A table of the corresponding production numbers (to be used by the synthesis algorithm)
4. A table indicating the type of context to be checked
5. Tables of valid $(0, n)$, $(m, 0)$, and (m, n) contexts for those productions which must be checked with those contexts

Tables 1, 2, and 3 involve merely sorting the productions. In this section we show how Tables 4 and 5 can be computed from a table of F_{mn}.

The MSP parser checks productions in a fixed order. When it finds a match, only enough context must be checked to discriminate that production from succeeding ones. The amount of context needed is determined by checking all pairs within a group. For each pair,

a. the right parts are equal,
b. the right part of the second is a proper tail of the right part of the first, or
c. the right part of the second is not a tail of the right part of the first.

In case a, some context check is required because the two right parts match precisely the same stacks. No check is required for case c since the two right parts can never match the same stack. Case b may either be resolvable by length or may require context.

We have noted that the table of (φ, A, α) for which F_{mn} is true is also a table for each $A_i \in V_n$ of the context pairs $(\varphi_{ij}, \alpha_{ij})$ which can be valid (m, n) contexts for A_i when it is the RNT. Consider now case a, where ω is the right part of two productions (A_i, ω) and (A_k, ω). If, for some j and l, both $\varphi_{ij} = \varphi_{kl}$ and $\alpha_{ij} = \alpha_{kl}$, the two productions can occur in precisely the same (m, n) contexts. Since this context is not adequate to distinguish them, the grammar is not bounded right context of degree (m, n).

If the contexts are distinct, however, all that is needed to accept or reject (A_i, ω) is a comparison of the current context with the table of $(\varphi_{ij}, \alpha_{ij})$.† If the α_{ij} are all different from the α_{kl}, $(0, n)$ context, (i.e., a table of α_{ij}) is sufficient to make the distinction; if the φ_{ij} are distinct from the φ_{kl}, $(m, 0)$ context is sufficient. If both are distinct, either can be used.

In case b we have productions $(A_i, \psi\omega)$ and (A_k, ω), $\psi \neq \lambda$. If, for each l, $\mathbf{t}_r(\psi) \neq \mathbf{t}_r(\varphi_{kl})$, where $r = \min(m, |\psi|)$, then $\psi\omega$ can never be the stack top when (A_k, ω) is the correct production, i.e., the productions can be resolved by the longest match. If, however, there is an l such that $\mathbf{t}_r(\psi) = \mathbf{t}_r(\varphi_{kl})$, context must be used: $(0, n)$ context resolves the productions if the α_{kl} are distinct from all the α_{ij}; $(m, 0)$ if the $\mathbf{t}_m(\varphi_{ij}\psi)$ are distinct from the φ_{kl}; and (m, n) if the $(\mathbf{t}_m(\varphi_{ij}\psi), \alpha_{ij})$ are distinct from the $(\varphi_{kl}, \alpha_{kl})$.

After determining the context necessary to resolve each pair, we may categorize the productions according to the total context tests required for acceptance:

1. $(0, 0)$ none
   Every pair of which this was the first production‡ was case c or case b resolvable by length.
2. $(0, n)$ right context
   Every case a or b pair of which this was the first production was resolvable by $(0, n)$, and there was at least one case a or one case b unresolvable by length.
3. $(m, 0)$ left context
   Every case a or b pair of which this was the first production was resolvable by $(m, 0)$, and there was at least one case a or b not resolvable by $(0, n)$ and length.
4. (m, n) full context
   Some case a or b pair, of which this was the first production, required (m, n) context; or two different pairs required $(m, 0)$ and $(0, n)$ context.
5. error
   Some case a or b pair was not resolvable by (m, n) context.

For category 1 productions no further tables are needed; category 2 productions can be resolved by using the augmented $C1_{pq}$ (if $p \geq 1$, $q \geq n$), which distinguishes invalid symbol combinations (i.e., don't accept the production if it would produce an invalid combination); category 3 requires a table of φ_{ij}; category 4, a table of $(\varphi_{ij}, \alpha_{ij})$. Any production in category 5 represents an error which makes the grammar unacceptable to the parsing algorithm. However, condition 5, that a decision cannot

---

† Note that we need store a table only for the first production of the pair. Thus, we can minimize the size of the table by sorting the productions so that, of those with equal right parts, the one with fewest valid contexts is checked first.

‡ The last (shortest) production of each group is always category 1.

be made based upon the tables, can be signalled, which allows the compiler writer to use any *ad hoc* device at all to make the decision.

Table 5.4.1 tabulates $(\varphi_{ij}, \alpha_{ij})$ and the sorted productions for the grammar $\mathbf{P}_{13}$.

$$
\begin{aligned}
G &::= \quad y\,B\,x \mid x\,C\,y \mid y\,D\,y \\
B &::= \quad x \mid B\,x \\
C &::= \quad x \\
D &::= \quad x
\end{aligned}
$$

TABLE 5.4.1 (1 ,1) Contexts and Sorted Productions for $\mathbf{P}_{13}$

A_i	$(\varphi_{ij}, \alpha_{ij})$		Tail Symbol	Productions		
G	$(\perp, \perp)$		x	G	::=	$y\,B\,x$
B	(y, x)			B	::=	$B\,x$
				B	::=	x
C	(x, y)			C	::=	x
D	(y, y)			D	::=	x
			y	G	::=	$x\,C\,y$
				G	::=	$y\,D\,y$

We now indicate the analysis leading to Table 5.4.2.

Production $G ::= y\,B\,x$
    Second production $B ::= B\,x$
        This is case b, imbedded right part.
        y is a legal left context of B, so both productions can match the stack $y\,B\,x$ when the second must be chosen, i.e., longest match is insufficient.
        $\perp$ is the only valid right context of G, and x the only valid right context of B. (0, 1) context resolves this pair.
    Second production $B ::= x$, $C ::= x$, $D ::= x$
        These are all case b, imbedded right part.
        B is not valid left context of B, C, or D, so the longest match is sufficient.
    Over-all category for $G ::= y\,B\,x$
        2—(0, 1) context required.
Production $B ::= B\,x$
    Second production $B ::= x$, $C ::= x$, $D ::= x$
        These are all case b, imbedded right part.
        B is not valid left context of B, C, or D, so the longest match is sufficient.
    Over-all category for $B ::= B\,x$
        1—no check required.
Production $B ::= x$
    Second production $C ::= x$
        This is case a, equal right parts.
        x is the only valid right context of B, and y is the only valid right context of C, so they may be resolved by (0, 1) context.

y is the only valid left context of B, and x is the only valid left context of C, so they may be resolved by $(1, 0)$ context.

Second production $D \ ::= \ x$

This is case a, equal right parts.

The left contexts are the same (y and y), but these productions may be resolved by $(0, 1)$ context.

Over-all category for $B \ ::= \ x$

2—$(0, 1)$ context required.

Production $C \ ::= \ x$

Second production $D \ ::= \ x$

This is case a, equal right parts.

Both productions have y as valid right context, so $(0, 1)$ context will not resolve them.

The left contexts are distinct, so $(1, 0)$ context suffices.

Over-all category for $C \ ::= \ x$

3—$(1, 0)$ context required.

Production $D \ ::= \ x$

Over-all category for $D \ ::= \ x$

1—no check required.

Production $G \ ::= \ x \, C \, y$

Second production $G \ ::= \ y \, D \, y$

This is case c, no embedding.

Over-all category for $G \ ::= \ x \, C \, y$

1—no check required.

Production $G \ ::= \ y \, D \, y$

Over-all category for $G \ ::= \ y \, D \, y$

1—no check required.

Exercise 5.4.1

Use your results of Exercise 5.2.7 to compute tables for $C2_{11}$ for the grammar P_{11}.

TABLE 5.4.2 Table of $C2_{11}$ for P_{13}

Tail Symbol	Right Part	Left Part	Category
x	$y \, B \, x$	G	2
	$B \, x$	B	1
	x	B	2
	x	C	3
	x	D	1
y	$x \, C \, y$	G	1
	$y \, D \, y$	G	1

Right context (category 2) handled by $C1_{11}$
Left context table (category 3)

A_i	φ_{ij}
C	x

5.5 Guaranteeing Correctness

/* Our motto should be "No axiomatization without insight!" */

CHRISTOPHER STRACHEY

NATO Summer School in Programming

Formal proofs of the correctness of the MSP parsing algorithm and the various table-building algorithms are beyond the scope of this book. However, a potential user of these algorithms should know to what degree their successful operation is guaranteed. This section provides an informal discussion of what can be done.

Guarantees on the grammar:

1. If a grammar is MSP of some degree $(p, q; m, n)$, it is unambiguous;
2. If a grammar is MSP of some degree $(p, q; m, n)$, the table-building algorithm builds tables of $C1_{pq}$ and $C2_{mn}$ with no conflicts; and conversely,
3. If the table-building algorithm builds tables of $C1_{pq}$ and $C2_{mn}$ with no conflicts for a particular grammar, then the grammar is MSP of degree $(p, q; m, n)$, hence unambiguous.

Guarantee 1 follows from the fact that, if two canonical parses for a sentence are distinct, there must be some first step at which they differ; therefore, there is some point at which two different decisions are valid for the same data, i.e., one of the parsing functions ($C1$ or $C2$) is not single valued. But if a parsing function is not single valued, no restriction of its domain can make it so. Thus an ambiguous grammar cannot be MSP of any degree.

For 2 and 3, we merely note that the table-building algorithm records all and only the decisions that must be made for the complete set of canonical parses. If there is a conflict (function not single valued), the decision cannot be made with the indicated context and vice versa.

Guarantees on the parser are:

1. If a grammar is MSP of some degree $(p, q; m, n)$, the MSP parser of that degree using the output of the table-building algorithm correctly parses every sentence of its language to the goal symbol; and conversely
2. Every terminal string parsed to the goal symbol by the MSP parser using tables for a particular grammar is a sentence of its language, i.e., every nonsentence is detected as an error.

The first guarantee follows from the fact that correct and unique decisions for each CPS are recorded by the table-building algorithm. The second is true because each step of the algorithm is the reversal of a production. By definition, any string produced from the goal symbol is a sentential form, which, if terminal, is a sentence. Reduction of a nonsentence must lead to a form (not the goal symbol) to which no production applies.

Exercise   5.5.1

Give formal proofs of the guarantees on the grammar and parser. See McCarthy [67], McKeeman [66], and Floyd [67] for various methods of proof.

5.6 Constructing LR Parsers from LR(k) Grammars

In Section 4.4 we indicated that the LR parser constituted a more general and systematic basis for parsing than the MSP algorithm does. Knuth [65] shows, given a nonnegative integer k and a grammar, how to construct an LR parser like that shown in Fig. 4.4.1 if the grammar is LR(k), and how to detect an error if the grammar is not LR(k). We present the constructing algorithm, specialized to its LR(0) form, and then apply it to $\mathbf{P}_{14}$ (cf. Section 4.4) to arrive at Fig. 4.4.1. We then apply it to $\mathbf{P}_{15}$ and show the nature of the failure when a grammar is not LR(0). Finally, we will present the LR(k) constructing algorithm, indicating how to achieve a mixed version such as in Fig. 4.4.2. As a result, the reader should be able to use and to implement the algorithm, although he will have to refer to other sources for its theoretical basis. The notations used here are due principally to Early [70] and De-Remer [69].

To understand the LR(k) constructing algorithm, consider the structure imposed on the parse stack by the canonical parse. At any moment during the parse, the parse stack contains a series of partially completed phrases. Starting at the bottom of the stack, we can partition it into disjoint subsequences, each containing one or more symbols, and each identical to the first few symbols in a production rule that will eventually be used in the parse. If the last such subsequence in the parse stack contains all the symbols in the right part of the appropriate rule, the next action must be to apply the rule. Otherwise, we must first stack at least one more symbol. For example, the last parse stack configuration from Table 4.4.2 is

$$\perp E + ((E$$

which gives rise to the partition

$$\underbrace{\perp}\ \underbrace{E +}\ \underbrace{(}\ \underbrace{(}\ \underbrace{E}$$

corresponding to the partial production rules

$$G \rightarrow \underbrace{\perp}\ E \perp$$
$$E \rightarrow \underbrace{E +}\ T$$
$$T \rightarrow \underbrace{(}\ E)$$
$$T \rightarrow \underbrace{(}\ E)$$
$$E \rightarrow \underbrace{E}\ + T$$

The last subsequence in the parse stack is not identical to $E + T$, hence we must stack the next symbol, etc.

The problem is to determine this partitioning by examining the stack. Note that the partitioning is not always immediately obvious as we proceed up the parse stack. For instance, if we have seen only

$$\perp E \ldots$$

we might have to place $\perp$ and E in separate subsequences as in

$$\underbrace{\perp}\ \underbrace{E +}\ \ldots$$

or in the same subsequence as in

$$\underbrace{\perp E \perp}$$

The LR(k) constructor algorithm produces, as we shall see, an exhaustive tabulation of all such possibilities.

A *configuration* is a marked production. For instance, from the augmented grammar $\mathbf{P}_{14}$, we get the configuration

$$G \overset{\triangledown}{\to} \perp E \perp$$

in which the $^\triangledown$ marks a place in the right part of the production rule. Each state of the LR parser is associated with a unique configuration set of partially completed productions. We start with a configuration set containing the padding production and then apply a completion algorithm to add all other potentially applicable productions. We then define successor sets which contain all the productions potentially applicable at the next location in the parse stack, given the current configuration set and the particular symbol in the parse stack. For $\mathbf{P}_{14}$ we have the initial configuration set

$$\{G \overset{\triangledown}{\to} \perp E \perp\}$$

The completion of a configuration set is computed as follows: For every configuration (including the new ones as we add them), if the marker $^\triangledown$ is immediately to the left of a nonterminal symbol, then add as many new configurations as possible such that

1. The production rule in the new configuration has the left part identical to the nonterminal above, and
2. The marker $^\triangledown$ is placed to the left of the right part.

We compute the initial configurations for the successor sets by collecting all the configurations which have the same symbol after the marker and then moving the marker past that symbol. We then complete each set as described above.

For example, we get no additional members by completing

$$\{G \overset{\triangledown}{\to} \perp E \perp\}$$

because $\perp$ is terminal. There is a single successor set containing initially a single configuration.

$$\{G \to \perp^{\nabla} E \perp\}$$

We iteratively complete it in stages, first adding the two production rules defining E.

$$\{G \to \perp^{\nabla} E \perp\} \cup \{E \to^{\nabla} T \qquad E \to^{\nabla} E + T\}$$

On the next step, we add the rules defining T.

$$\{G \to \perp^{\nabla} E \perp\} \cup \{E \to^{\nabla} T \qquad E \to^{\nabla} E + T\} \cup \{T \to^{\nabla} x \qquad T \to^{\nabla} (E)\}$$

Further attempts to add configurations only duplicate existing members; thus, the process terminates with five configurations in the configuration set. Continuing, we get four successor sets with initial contents as follows:

$$\{G \to \perp E^{\nabla} \perp \qquad E \to E^{\nabla} + T\}$$
$$\{E \to T^{\nabla}\}$$
$$\{T \to x^{\nabla}\}$$
$$\{T \to (^{\nabla} E)\}$$

The computation continues in this manner. Whenever the result of the completion operation yields a configuration set identical to a previously computed set, we need not compute further successors for the duplicate and we identify these configurations with a single state. Because only a finite number of possible configuration sets exist for each grammar, the process necessarily terminates. Fig. 5.6.1 gives the complete computation for the grammar $\mathbf{P}_{14}$. On the right are the configuration sets. On the left we have numbered each set that gives rise to successors, connecting them to their successors with arrows marked with the symbol passed over by the marker. The sets are indented so that all the successors to a single configuration set are vertically aligned.

The diagram of Fig. 5.6.1 may be mechanically converted to that given for the LR parser in Fig. 4.4.1. The configuration sets having no successors because the marker is at the extreme right end of the production rule correspond to the decision to apply that rule to the top of the parse stack, i.e., to rules in the diagram. Boxes corresponding to identical configuration sets (single states) are merged. Thus, in Fig. 4.4.1 we have two arrows entering state 3 and three entering 4. Once having achieved Fig. 4.4.1, we may discard the configuration sets corresponding to the various states.

We now naively apply the LR(0) constructor algorithm to the LR(1) grammar $\mathbf{P}_{15}$. We observe, in the resulting Fig. 5.6.2, that the difficulty arises in states 4 and 6. The configurations $E \to E + T^{\nabla}$ and $E \to T^{\nabla}$ indicate that we should apply a rewriting rule; the configuration $T \to T^{\nabla} * x$ indicates that we should scan past the $*$ to complete another phrase. From the information in the configuration sets we cannot be sure that $E \to E + T^{\nabla}$ (state 4) or $E \to T^{\nabla}$ (state 6) cannot be followed by $*$. We must expand our view if we are to discover that in $\mathbf{P}_{15}$ the $*$ must always be stacked against the T.

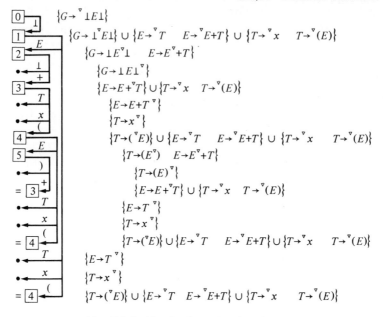

Fig. 5.6.1   The Configuration Sets for P_{14}

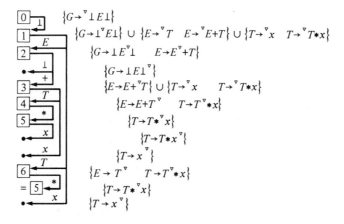

Fig. 5.6.2   Failure of the LR(0) Constructor for P_{15}

We must make two changes in the LR constructor algorithm presented at the start of this section. The first is to add to the configuration a string of k terminal symbols, called the right context of that configuration. We have configurations of the form

$$A \rightarrow \overset{\triangledown}{\varphi}\omega, \alpha$$

where $\varphi\omega$ is the right part of the production and α is the right context. Successors are computed exactly as before, the right context being carried along unchanged. For completion we must work harder. Suppose we have a configuration of the form

$$A \to \varphi \overset{\triangledown}{} B\omega, \alpha$$

where B is nonterminal. Then, for every production

$$B \to \psi$$

with B on the left and for every string β in

$$\mathbf{TPH}_k(\omega\alpha)$$

we add the configuration

$$B \to \overset{\triangledown}{} \psi, \beta$$

to the configuration set. The result is that the size of the configuration sets goes up very rapidly with k.

We immediately apply the LR(1) algorithm to $\mathbf{P}_{15}$. The results are displayed in Fig. 5.6.3.

The problem in Fig. 5.6.2 was that there was no way to decide whether to apply the rewriting rules in states 4 and 6. In Fig. 5.6.3 we see that we are to rewrite only if the next symbol scanned is in the set $\{\perp, +\}$. In general, if more than one possible

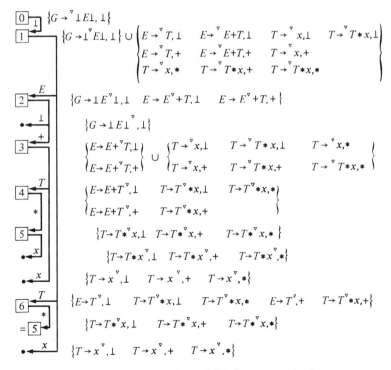

Fig. 5.6.3 Success of the LR(1) Constructor for $\mathbf{P}_{15}$

outcome is represented in a configuration set (either a fully completed and a partially completed rewriting rule as in the case above or two or more distinct completed rewriting rules), either the sets of right contexts associated with them must be disjoint or the grammar is not LR(k) for that k. If they are disjoint we simply add the appropriate tests to the state in question and proceed. (For partially completed rules, we take the terminal k heads of the rest of the rule to the right of the marker plus the right context. For example, the context from the configuration $T \to T \overset{\triangledown}{*} x, +$ is the value of $\mathbf{TPH}_1(*x+)$, or $*$ itself.)

Exercise 5.6.1

Construct an LR(1) parser for $\mathbf{P}_{14}$. Why does this parser have two more states than the LR(0) parser? In general, what happens when you increase k unnecessarily?

Exercise 5.6.2

Attempt to construct LR(0) parsers for grammars $\mathbf{P}_1$ through $\mathbf{P}_{13}$. Check your results by parsing a few strings from the languages defined by the grammars.

Exercise 5.6.3

For the grammars that failed to be LR(0) above, construct LR(1) parsers. Do you have much hope of using LR(2) if the LR(1) parsers do not succeed? Where will the problem of increasing k become unmanageable?

Exercise 5.6.4

Propose a measure of grammatical complexity based on the smallest LR parser (i.e., fewest states) that can be constructed for the grammar. How complex are grammars for ambiguous finite languages? Ambiguous infinite languages? Are LR(k) grammars always less complex than LR($k + 1$) grammars?

Exercise 5.6.5

Recall Exercises 4.3.6, 4.4.9, and 5.6.2. Compare the MSP algorithm and the LR(k) algorithm for table size, execution efficiency, and generality. Which do you recommend? Can you be sure of your results without implementing and comparing the algorithms on a machine?

Exercise 5.6.6

Read Knuth [65].

Exercise 5.6.7

Read DeRemer [69].

Exercise 5.6.8

Read Early [70].

PART II

PRACTICE

Part II contains the documentation of the XPL system as implemented for the IBM System/360. This part is both a concrete example of the techniques described in Part I, and a manual for those using our TWS.

Chapter 6 includes a definition of the implementation language XPL relying where possible on the reader's familiarity with other programming languages, PL/I in particular. No attempt is made to teach programming in XPL. Rather, the form of the language is given, the meaning of the forms in terms of the System/360 machine is described, and some examples and exercises are presented.

Chapter 7 describes the BNF language acceptable to the syntax preprocessor and how to program in it. The emphasis is on the methods used to get clean and easily recognized language descriptions for use in translator writing.

Chapter 8 is a manual for the understanding and maintenance of XCOM, the compiler for XPL. It is a guide to the main structure of the generative part of the compiler, containing a glossary of the names used and their correspondence to needed tables.

Chapter 9 presents SKELETON, a proto-compiler. It is with SKELETON that the user of our TWS must soon come to terms. The functions of its constituents, how they interrelate, and how to change them are the central themes of this chapter.

Chapter 10 describes ANALYZER, a program that produces the tables for driving the syntactic analysis algorithm and represents both the most sophisticated tool in the package and the one which the user has the least reason to change in any substantial way. If one wishes either to change the implementation language (and thus the tables) or to generalize the class of recognizable languages, here is where he must start.

Chapter 6

The Language XPL

/∗ I have called this principle, by which each slight variation, if useful, is preserved, by the term Natural Selection. ∗/

CHARLES DARWIN

The Origin of Species

6.1 Evolving XPL

/∗ Languages die, too, like individuals. . . . They may be embalmed and preserved for posterity, changeless and static, life-like in appearance but unendowed with the breath of life. While they live, however, they change. ∗/

MARIO PEI

The Story of Language

Our TWS uses XPL, a dialect of PL/I, for the description of translators. XPL was designed to be convenient for the statement of the table-driven syntax-directed translators discussed in this book; XPL programs can be translated to IBM System/360 machine language by XCOM, a translator written in XPL.

We chose PL/I as a base language for several reasons. It contains most of the features we require (see Chapter 1), is widely known, and will probably be the next dominant programming language. The growth of the PL family of languages will require the development of a number of PL dialect translators, for which XCOM may serve both as a model and as a vehicle. We regard PL/I as a practical, progressive step in computer science, and we hope this approach will help in its development and refinement.

There are several distinct reasons for not choosing PL/I for the description of translators. First, it does not contain quite all the required features. More important, however, PL/I is a very large language, and the machine we are using (IBM System/360) is ill-suited to its full implementation. Consequently, all existing compilers for the full PL/I are very large complex programs which produce code unacceptably inefficient for this application. For the same reasons, we do not recommend attempting a compiler for full PL/I written in XPL.

We also wished to insure that our compilers would continue to function over long periods of time. As PL/I changed, errors were sure to come to light, either of our own doing and undetected by previous versions of PL/I compilers or incompatibilities among generations of the language. XPL users will have absolute control over their language and compiler.

The language XPL has evolved over a period of about two years. Starting with a subset of PL/I which seemed approximately right for describing syntax-directed translators, we added those features (such as **case**) which seemed to be missing. We then began writing the compiler for XPL. In the course of developing XCOM, we made a number of changes in XPL to improve XCOM (these changes, of course, required further changes in XCOM). As other compilers (such as the Student PL) were written in XPL, the need for some additional features in the language (such as the *inline* capability) became apparent. Other features initially in the language proved to be of marginal utility and were dropped.

There are several consequences of having chosen to use XPL instead of PL/I:

1. XPL is somewhat easier to learn.
2. XPL programs compile faster.
3. XPL programs load more quickly.
4. XPL programs typically run faster.
5. Not all PL/I applications are appropriate for XPL.
6. XPL programs are not easily linked to programs written in other high-level languages.

Many reasons, both negative and positive, reinforced our decision to model XPL on PL/I. We have had no reason to regret this decision.

6.2   The Syntactic Description of XPL

This chapter contains a syntactic and semantic definition of the compiler writing language. In this section we present the entire BNF grammar of the language and give a brief discussion of its over-all structure in relation to PL/I. In succeeding sections we present the constants of XPL (which are not explicitly described by this grammar), the naming conventions (identifiers), and, finally, the details on each statement type. The reader is reminded that the ultimate semantic definition of XPL, its compiler XCOM, is also to be found in these pages (Appendix 3). XCOM is valuable as a source of examples and for the final arbitration of any fine points concerning what IBM System/360 code is generated in a given situation.

XPL Grammar

⟨program⟩   ::=   ⟨statement list⟩ **eof**
⟨statement list⟩   ::=   ⟨statement⟩
                | ⟨statement list⟩ ⟨statement⟩

⟨statement⟩ ::= ⟨basic statement⟩
          | ⟨if statement⟩
⟨basic statement⟩ ::= ⟨assignment⟩ ;
          | ⟨group⟩ ;
          | ⟨procedure definition⟩ ;
          | ⟨return statement⟩ ;
          | ⟨call statement⟩ ;
          | ⟨go to statement⟩ ;
          | ⟨declaration statement⟩ ;
          | ;
          | ⟨label definition⟩ ⟨basic statement⟩
⟨if statement⟩ ::= ⟨if clause⟩ ⟨statement⟩
          | ⟨if clause⟩ ⟨true part⟩ ⟨statement⟩
          | ⟨label definition⟩ ⟨if statement⟩
⟨if clause⟩ ::= **if** ⟨expression⟩ **then**
⟨true part⟩ ::= ⟨basic statement⟩ **else**
⟨group⟩ ::= ⟨group head⟩ ⟨ending⟩
⟨group head⟩ ::= **do** ;
          | **do** ⟨step definition⟩ ;
          | **do** ⟨while clause⟩ ;
          | **do** ⟨case selector⟩ ;
          | ⟨group head⟩ ⟨statement⟩
⟨step definition⟩ ::= ⟨variable⟩ ⟨replace⟩ ⟨expression⟩ ⟨iteration control⟩
⟨iteration control⟩ ::= **to** ⟨expression⟩
          | **to** ⟨expression⟩ **by** ⟨expression⟩
⟨while clause⟩ ::= **while** ⟨expression⟩
⟨case selector⟩ ::= **case** ⟨expression⟩
⟨procedure definition⟩ ::— ⟨procedure head⟩ ⟨statement list⟩ ⟨ending⟩
⟨procedure head⟩ ::= ⟨procedure name⟩ ;
          | ⟨procedure name⟩ ⟨type⟩ ;
          | ⟨procedure name⟩ ⟨parameter list⟩ ;
          | ⟨procedure name⟩ ⟨parameter list⟩ ⟨type⟩ ;
⟨procedure name⟩ ::= ⟨label definition⟩ **procedure**
⟨parameter list⟩ ::= ⟨parameter head⟩ ⟨identifier⟩)
⟨parameter head⟩ ::= (
          | ⟨parameter head⟩ ⟨identifier⟩ ,
⟨ending⟩ ::= **end**
          | **end** ⟨identifier⟩
          | ⟨label definition⟩ ⟨ending⟩
⟨label definition⟩ ::= ⟨identifier⟩ :
⟨return statement⟩ ::= **return**
          | **return** ⟨expression⟩
⟨call statement⟩ ::= **call** ⟨variable⟩
⟨go to statement⟩ ::= ⟨go to⟩ ⟨identifier⟩

⟨go to⟩ ::= **go to**
     | **goto**
⟨declaration statement⟩ ::= **declare** ⟨declaration element⟩
     | ⟨declaration statement⟩ , ⟨declaration element⟩
⟨declaration element⟩ ::= ⟨type declaration⟩
     | ⟨identifier⟩ **literally** ⟨string⟩
⟨type declaration⟩ ::= ⟨identifier specification⟩ ⟨type⟩
     | ⟨bound head⟩ ⟨number⟩) ⟨type⟩
     | ⟨type declaration⟩ ⟨initial list⟩
⟨type⟩ ::= **fixed**
     | **character**
     | **label**
     | ⟨bit head⟩ ⟨number⟩)
⟨bit head⟩ ::= **bit (**
⟨bound head⟩ ::= ⟨identifier specification⟩ (
⟨identifier specification⟩ ::= ⟨identifier⟩
     | ⟨identifier list⟩ ⟨identifier⟩)
⟨identifier list⟩ ::= (
     | ⟨identifier list⟩ ⟨identifier⟩ ,
⟨initial list⟩ ::= ⟨initial head⟩ ⟨constant⟩)
⟨initial head⟩ ::= **initial (**
     | ⟨initial head⟩ ⟨constant⟩ ,
⟨assignment⟩ ::= ⟨variable⟩ ⟨replace⟩ ⟨expression⟩
     | ⟨left part⟩ ⟨assignment⟩
⟨replace⟩ ::= =
⟨left part⟩ ::= ⟨variable⟩ ,
⟨expression⟩ ::= ⟨logical factor⟩
     | ⟨expression⟩ | ⟨logical factor⟩
⟨logical factor⟩ ::= ⟨logical secondary⟩
     | ⟨logical factor⟩ & ⟨logical secondary⟩
⟨logical secondary⟩ ::= ⟨logical primary⟩
     | ¬ ⟨logical primary⟩
⟨logical primary⟩ ::= ⟨string expression⟩
     | ⟨string expression⟩ ⟨relation⟩ ⟨string expression⟩
⟨relation⟩ ::= =
     | <
     | >
     | ¬ =
     | ¬ <
     | ¬ >
     | < =
     | > =
⟨string expression⟩ ::= ⟨arithmetic expression⟩
     | ⟨string expression⟩ | | ⟨arithmetic expression⟩

⟨arithmetic expression⟩ ::= ⟨term⟩
                      | ⟨arithmetic expression⟩ + ⟨term⟩
                      | ⟨arithmetic expression⟩ − ⟨term⟩
                      | + ⟨term⟩
                      | − ⟨term⟩
⟨term⟩ ::= ⟨primary⟩
        | ⟨term⟩ * ⟨primary⟩
        | ⟨term⟩ / ⟨primary⟩
        | ⟨term⟩ **mod** ⟨primary⟩
⟨primary⟩ ::= ⟨constant⟩
           | ⟨variable⟩
           | (⟨expression⟩)
⟨constant⟩ ::= ⟨string⟩
            | ⟨number⟩
⟨variable⟩ ::= ⟨identifier⟩
           | ⟨subscript head⟩ ⟨expression⟩)
⟨subscript head⟩ ::= ⟨identifier⟩ (
                | ⟨subscript head⟩ ⟨expression⟩ ,

XPL is structurally similar to PL/I. A program consists of a sequence of statements terminated by the special symbol **eof**; its effect is determined by executing those statements in order. (An XPL program is equivalent to the body of a PL/I external procedure with option **main**.) Two types of statements, declarations and procedure definitions, cause no action when executed but rather affect the meaning of other statements in the program. The remainder of the statements are imperative in nature, causing the computation and movement of values (expression and assignments), repetitive and selective execution of statements (groups, if statements), invocation of subprocesses (call statement and function designators), termination of subprocesses (return), and absolute transfer of control (go to).

A brief list of the differences between XPL and the PL/I constructs with the same form includes:

1. All variables must appear in a declaration before they appear in any other statement (thus declaration is mandatory).
2. Arrays are restricted to one dimension and the lower bound of all arrays is implicitly zero.
3. There are no predefined abbreviations (use **character,** not **char**).
4. Only types **fixed, character,** and **bit** are provided.
5. Only one level of attribute factoring is allowed.
6. Bit strings are substantially different.
7. Character strings all have the attribute **varying** and start with character zero (not one). | | is relatively expensive (slow); *byte, substr,* and *length* are fast. *substr* may not appear on the left of an assignment.
8. **do** loops have only positive steps.
9. Procedures are not recursive and have only value (evaluated) parameters.

10. Card boundaries are ignored, and all 80 columns are used unless a margin is explicitly established.

11. Structural words such as **do** and **if** are reserved and may not be used as identifiers.

6.3 Numeric Constants

Numbers take two forms:

⟨number⟩   ::=   ⟨integer⟩ | ⟨bit string⟩

Nonnegative numbers may be represented by the usual decimal notation:

⟨integer⟩   ::=   ⟨decimal digit⟩ | ⟨integer⟩ ⟨decimal digit⟩
⟨decimal digit⟩   ::=   0|1|2|3|4|5|6|7|8|9

Spaces are not allowed within decimal integers.

Integers in the range 0 to 2147483647 ($2^{31} - 1$) are valid (PL/I precision (31, 0)) and correspond to nonnegative 32-bit two's-complement internal representations. Bit strings with binary, quartal, octal, or hexadecimal significance provide an alternative notation for 32-bit constants.

⟨bit string⟩   ::=   "⟨bit list⟩"
⟨bit list⟩   ::=   ⟨hex integer⟩ | ⟨bit group⟩
                           | ⟨bit list⟩ ⟨bit group⟩
⟨bit group⟩   ::=   (1) ⟨binary integer⟩ | (2) ⟨quartal integer⟩
                           | (3) ⟨octal integer⟩ | (4) ⟨hex integer⟩
⟨binary integer⟩   ::=   ⟨binary digit⟩
                           | ⟨binary integer⟩ ⟨binary digit⟩
⟨binary digit⟩   ::=   0|1
⟨quartal integer⟩   ::=   ⟨quartal digit⟩
                           | ⟨quartal integer⟩ ⟨quartal digit⟩
⟨quartal digit⟩   ::=   0|1|2|3
⟨octal integer⟩   ::=   ⟨octal digit⟩ | ⟨octal integer⟩ ⟨octal digit⟩
⟨octal digit⟩   ::=   0|1|2|3|4|5|6|7
⟨hex integer⟩   ::=   ⟨hex digit⟩ | ⟨hex integer⟩ ⟨hex digit⟩
⟨hex digit⟩   ::=   0|1|2|3|4|5|6|7|8|9|A|B|C|D|E|F

Spaces may be used freely within the bit quotes.

The digit in parentheses at the head of each bit group is the field-width-per-digit of that group. Thus, for any bit group, the total number of bits represented is the product of the number of digits and the field width. If more than one bit group occurs in a bit list, the rightmost group is right justified in the 32-bit representation, the next group is right justified in the remaining spaces, and so on. Note that the first entry in a bit list may be a hex integer. This construct represents a default field width of hexadecimal significance. The following each denote the same internal machine form:

$$
\begin{aligned}
&\text{"FF"}\\
&\text{"(4)FF"}\\
&\text{"(1)1111 1111"}\\
&\text{"(3)7(2)33(1)1"}\\
&255
\end{aligned}
$$

That is, the 32-bit value

$$00000000000000000000000011111111$$

6.4 String Constants

If the total significance of a bit string exceeds 32 bits, it is stored as a string constant. The internal representation of long bit strings is a 32-bit description pair (L, A) which describes the length (in bytes) and 24-bit address of the string data in a free storage area. The built-in function *byte* provides access to such data (see Section 6.9). String constants are stored left justified in consecutive bits of memory aligned on a byte boundary. A maximum of 2048 bits of significance is permitted. We also have character strings representing fixed texts

$$
\begin{aligned}
\langle\text{string}\rangle \quad &::= \quad \text{'}\langle\text{characters}\rangle\text{' } | \text{ ''}\\
\langle\text{characters}\rangle \quad &::= \quad \langle\text{character}\rangle \; | \; \langle\text{characters}\rangle\langle\text{character}\rangle\\
\langle\text{character}\rangle \quad &::= \quad \text{'' } | \; \{\text{any EBCDIC character other than '}\}
\end{aligned}
$$

which are stored as string constants. Each character has a corresponding EBCDIC character code. The constant is represented by the sequence of character codes corresponding to the characters appearing within the string. The length of the string is also one of its properties and is accessible via the function *length*. The null string '' contains no characters and has length zero. The $\langle\text{character}\rangle$ '' is used to unambiguously denote the occurrence of a single quote mark at that position of the character string.

The following are all valid character strings:

$$
\begin{aligned}
&\text{''}\\
&\text{' ABC '}\\
&\text{' 01 + 23 '}\\
&\text{' 1111 '}\\
&\text{' DON''T YOU BELIEVE IT. '}
\end{aligned}
$$

The maximum length allowed for a character string constant (because of both the encoding chosen for the (L, A) pair and some System/360 hardware limitations) is 256.

Since each string constant is represented not only by its own value but also by a 32-bit description, we take that into account in figuring the amount of memory used. The values of strings are stored in a free storage area which is periodically and automatically repacked.

6.5 Identifiers

Names (identifiers) occur in XPL in six ways: as reserved words, as implicitly declared variables or procedures, as labels, as parameters, as declared variables, and as macros. All of them have the usual form of identifiers:

⟨identifier⟩   ::=   ⟨id character⟩ | ⟨identifier⟩ ⟨id character⟩
                            | ⟨identifier⟩ ⟨decimal digit⟩
⟨id character⟩   ::=   ⟨letter⟩ | ⟨break character⟩
⟨letter⟩   ::= $A|B|C|$ ... $|Z|a|b|c|$ ... $|z$
⟨decimal digit⟩   ::= $0|1|$ ... $|9$
⟨break character⟩   ::= $\_|@|\#|\$$

All the following are identifiers:

> *A*
> *a*1
> *A__1*
> *a@*1
> *A#*1
> *This__is__a__medium__long__identifier*

but none of the following:

> 123*A*
> 12@
>
> $\underline{\ }\ .\ \underline{\ }$
> *A b*
> *A.b*

Names must be delimited by characters other than ⟨id character⟩ or ⟨decimal digit⟩, e.g., a blank or terminal character such as +. No identifier can exceed 256 characters in length (a result of using character string variables for the symbol table in XCOM). Reserved words are those appearing in the grammar:

bit	declare	goto	procedure
by	else	if	return
call	end	initial	then
case	eof	label	to
character	fixed	literally	while
do	go	mod	

They cannot be used in any way except in their intended structural use in XPL. Implicitly declared names, listed in Section 6.9, are treated as identifiers declared in an enclosing block and may be freely redeclared in XPL programs (if the corresponding functions are not required). Macro and variable names are defined in declarations listing their attributes. Labels, although normally defined by their occurrence in a program (followed by a :), may also in some unusual circumstances have to be declared. Parameters, defined by their appearance in the formal parameter list of a procedure definition, are associated with attributes by declaration within the body of the procedure.

6.6   Declarations

⟨declaration statement⟩   ::=   **declare** ⟨declaration element⟩
                             | ⟨declaration statement⟩ , ⟨declaration element⟩
⟨declaration element⟩   ::=   ⟨type declaration⟩
                             | ⟨identifier⟩ **literally** ⟨string⟩
⟨type declaration⟩   ::=   ⟨identifier specification⟩ ⟨type⟩
                             | ⟨bound head⟩ ⟨number⟩) ⟨type⟩
                             | ⟨type declaration⟩ ⟨initial list⟩
⟨type⟩   ::=   **fixed**
             | **character**
             | **label**
             | ⟨bit head⟩ ⟨number⟩)
⟨bit head⟩   ::=   **bit (**
⟨bound head⟩   ::=   ⟨identifier specification⟩ (
⟨identifier specification⟩   ::=   ⟨identifier⟩
                             | ⟨identifier list⟩ ⟨identifier⟩)
⟨identifier list⟩   ::=   (
                             | ⟨identifier list⟩ ⟨identifier⟩ ,
⟨initial list⟩   ::=   ⟨initial head⟩ ⟨constant⟩)
⟨initial head⟩   ::=   **initial (**
                             | ⟨initial head⟩ ⟨constant⟩ ,

A declaration associates, for certain parts of the program, identifiers with attributes. The program itself and any procedure definitions are called blocks. Since procedure definitions are also statements, blocks may nest within blocks. A nested block is *subordinate* to its containing block. The *inclusive extent* of a block is the statement list forming its body including subordinate blocks. The *exclusive extent* of a block is the statement list forming its body excluding all subordinate blocks. A declaration in the exclusive extent of a block has *range* equal to the inclusive extent of that block. There can be at most one declaration for a name in the exclusive extent of a block. The *scope* of a name is the range of its declaration less the range of any other declarations for that same name in subordinate blocks (see Fig. 6.6.1).

The association of attributes and identifiers is in effect only for the statements following their declaration (because XCOM is strictly a one-pass compiler); thus, we state the rule:

Each variable must be declared, and the declaration must precede every other use of that identifier in its scope.

The attributes given an identifier fall into five classes. The **literally** attribute is discussed in Section 6.7. The attributes **fixed**, **character**, and **bit (** ⟨number⟩) deter-

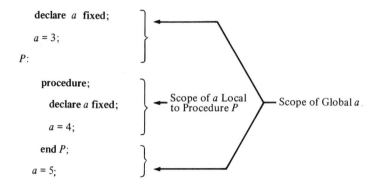

declare a **fixed**;

$a = 3$;

P:

　　procedure;

　　　declare a **fixed**;

　　　$a = 4$;

　　end P;

$a = 5$;

⟶ Scope of a Local to Procedure P

⟶ Scope of Global a

Fig. 6.6.1　Scopes of Names

mine the kind of storage to be assigned and what manipulations are allowed on their associated identifiers. The **label** attribute indicates that a label of that name will occur in the exclusive extent of the block.

There are four data types in storage: 8-bit nonnegative integers, 16-bit signed integers, 32-bit signed integers, and strings. Depending upon their intended use, they can be declared with the attributes in Table 6.6.1.

TABLE 6.6.1

Attribute		Storage Assigned	Storage Type
fixed		32 bit	Word
bit (n)	$1 \leq n \leq 8$	8 bit	Byte
bit (n)	$9 \leq n \leq 16$	16 bit	Half word
bit (n)	$17 \leq n \leq 32$	32 bit	Word
bit (n)	$33 \leq n \leq 2048$	32-bit descriptor plus area for data	String
character		32-bit descriptor plus area for data	String

In arithmetic, byte bit strings have the properties of integers in the range 0 to 255; half word bit strings have the properties of 16-bit two's-complement signed integers; word bit strings and type **fixed** are synonymous and have the properties of 32-bit two's-complement signed integers. Although arithmetic and logical operations are performed only on integers, relational tests may be performed on either integers or strings.

Long bit string and all character string variables are represented by 32-bit descriptors, as described in Section 6.4. These strings have the implicit attribute **varying**, with a maximum length of 256×8 bits imposed by the 8 bit length field.

The association of the attribute **label** with an identifier announces that a label of this name will appear later in the scope. This declaration is required when the first reference to a label is from a block subordinate to the one where the label will appear. Since their appearance is normally their declaration, labels may be used before they are declared. Whenever this could confuse the compiler (e.g., case above), a resolving declaration is required.

The extent of an array is determined by its bound. All XPL arrays start at index zero and end at the declared bound (inclusive). The amount of storage allocated is the appropriate multiple of the amount per item detailed above. Only one subscript position is allowed.

Initial values (set once, at program load time) are specified by the **initial** attribute. Simple variables receive single values; arrays are filled from the zeroth position onward.

All the following are valid declarations:

> **declare** *a* **fixed,** *b* **fixed initial** (1),
>   *c*(10) **bit** (32) **initial** (0, 1, 2, "F", 0);
> **declare** *long__name__with__no__meaning* **bit** (1) **initial** ("1"),
>   *z* **character initial** ('ABCDEF'),
>   *v* (100) **character initial** ('', '; ', ', ', '**and**');

When several identifiers are to be declared with the same attributes (except **initial** or **literally**), they may be factored for convenience:

> **declare** (*a*, *b*, *c*) **fixed,** (*d*, *e*) (100) **bit** (8);

6.7 Macro Definition and Use

Simple parameterless macros may be defined using the **literally** attribute. When an identifier is so declared, any later occurrence of that identifier will be literally

TABLE 6.7.1

declare *a* **literally** '20';
 declare *b*(*a*) **fixed,**
     c(*a*) **fixed;**
 b(*a*) = *c*(*a*) + *a*;
	declare *b*(20) **fixed,**
	     c(20) **fixed;**
	 b(20) = *c*(20) + 20;

declare *program* **literally** '*output* = ''TEST'';'; *program* *program*	*output* = 'TEST'; *output* = 'TEST';
declare *true* **literally** ' ''1'' ', *forever* **literally** 'while *true*'; **do** *forever*; **end**;	 **do while** ''1''; **end**;

replaced during compilation by the character string following the reserved word
literally. Among the uses of **literally** are the naming of constants (both for mnemonic
reasons and for ease of maintenance when many copies of a constant may have to be
changed), the introduction of abbreviations for reserved words, and the redefinition
of identifiers where multiple names are desired to have a single meaning. Of course,
although nothing prevents their use in more complex situations (even with one macro
name appearing within another macro definition), we advise caution to keep programs
readable.

The pairs of programs in Table 6.7.1 are equivalent.

6.8 Expressions and Assignments

An expression is a rule for computing a value. XPL permits three kinds of expression values: conditional, numeric, and descriptor. An assignment places a value in
storage. The form of expressions and assignments is given by

⟨assignment⟩   ::=   ⟨variable⟩ ⟨replace⟩ ⟨expression⟩
                | ⟨left part⟩ ⟨assignment⟩
⟨replace⟩ ::=   =
⟨left part⟩   ::=   ⟨variable⟩ ,
⟨expression⟩   ::=   ⟨logical factor⟩
                | ⟨expression⟩ | ⟨logical factor⟩
⟨logical factor⟩   ::=   ⟨logical secondary⟩
                | ⟨logical factor⟩ & ⟨logical secondary⟩
⟨logical secondary⟩   ::=   ⟨logical primary⟩
                | ¬ ⟨logical primary⟩
⟨logical primary⟩   ::=   ⟨string expression⟩
                | ⟨string expression⟩ ⟨relation⟩ ⟨string expression⟩
⟨relation⟩   ::=   =
                | <
                | >
                | ¬ =
                | ¬ <
                | ¬ >
                | < =
                | > =
⟨string expression⟩   ::=   ⟨arithmetic expression⟩
                | ⟨string expression⟩ || ⟨arithmetic expression⟩
⟨arithmetic expression⟩   ::=   ⟨term⟩
                | ⟨arithmetic expression⟩ + ⟨term⟩
                | ⟨arithmetic expression⟩ − ⟨term⟩
                | + ⟨term⟩
                | − ⟨term⟩

⟨term⟩   ::=   ⟨primary⟩
            | ⟨term⟩ * ⟨primary⟩
            | ⟨term⟩ / ⟨primary⟩
            | ⟨term⟩ **mod** ⟨primary⟩
⟨primary⟩   ::=   ⟨constant⟩
            | ⟨variable⟩
            | (⟨expression⟩)
⟨constant⟩ ::=   ⟨string⟩
            | ⟨number⟩
⟨variable⟩ ::=   ⟨identifier⟩
            | ⟨subscript head⟩ ⟨expression⟩)
⟨subscript head⟩   ::=   ⟨identifier⟩ (
                   | ⟨subscript head⟩ ⟨expression⟩ ,

The operators of the language, with their associated priorities and meanings, are given in Table 6.8.1. The order of their listing is the order of their hierarchy in evaluation—the higher an operator's priority number, the later it is applied, operators of equal priority being applied left to right. Parentheses may be used to alter the normal order of evaluation.

An ⟨assignment⟩ stores a computed value into the indicated memory cell. Conversion for storage is indicated in Table 6.8.2. Multiple assignments are performed right to left. Variables in the left part must be assignment compatible with those to their right. Assignments to subscripted variables are not checked against the array bounds; thus, every memory location is accessible through subscripting.

Type conversions for ⟨expression⟩ values are also shown in Table 6.8.2. The most common conversion is numeric to descriptor, in which a 32-bit two's-complement integer is converted into the corresponding character string. The result is a descriptor for the string consisting of an optional leading − followed by the significant digits of the decimal integer as EBCDIC characters. This conversion is made when a numeric (nondescriptor) value (1) is assigned to a long **bit** or **character** variable (including *output*), (2) is an operand of ||, (3) is a parameter to *length*, or (4) is the first parameter to *substr* or *byte*.

The **if-then** and **while** constructs demand type conditional values (corresponding to the condition bits of the IBM System/360), produced only by the relational operators. If a conditional value is needed, and a value of numerical type is supplied, a conversion is made based on the least significant bit of the fixed value (1 = true, 0 = false). Similarly, assignments and most of the operators demand numeric values, and the reciprocal conversion (true and false to 32-bit values 1 and 0, respectively) is automatically made. If a fetch is made with variables of attribute **bit** (1) through **bit** (8), the low-order 8 bits of the numeric value are set to the value in storage, and the high-order 24 bits are cleared. For **bit** (9) through **bit** (16) a fetch extends the sign bit through the high-order 16 bits, and a store loses the high-order 16 bits.

Other situations demanding a type conversion (including descriptor to numeric) are error conditions. See the programs in the appendices for examples.

TABLE 6.8.1

Priority Number	Operator Symbol	Interpretation
7	|	Logical or of numeric values.
6	&	Logical and of numeric values.
5	¬	Logical complement of conditional or numeric value.
4	=	Condition true if values are equal.
4	<	Condition true if first operand is less than second operand.[†]
4	>	Condition true if first operand is greater than second operand.[†]
4	¬ =	Condition true if values are not equal.
4	¬ <	Same as > =.
4	¬ >	Same as < =.
4	< =	Condition true if first operand is less than or equal to second operand.[†]
4	> =	Condition true if first operand is greater than or equal to second operand.[†]
3	||	Catenation of the strings specified by the operands. If either operand is not a descriptor, it will be converted to one. || usually requires all the data of both strings be moved (costly).
2	+	Addition of 32-bit two's-complement numeric values. Overflow ignored.
2	+	Unary, no effect.
2	−	Subtraction of 32-bit two's-complement numeric values. Overflow ignored.
2	−	Unary, 32-bit two's-complement.
1	*	32 low-order bits of multiplication of two numeric values. Overflow ignored.[‡]
1	/	32-bit quotient from dividing two numeric values. Divide by zero will cause interrupt and program termination.[‡]
1	**mod**	32-bit remainder from dividing two numeric values. Divide by zero will cause interrupt and program termination.[‡]

[†] Comparisons of descriptor values in XPL are done first on length, second (if the lengths are equal) on a character-by-character comparison of the strings described using the EBCDIC collating sequence [IBM 6 X g].

[‡] Multiplication, division, and remaindering cause considerable extra work on the IBM System/360. Consequently, if they are used in a complicated expression, the XCOM register allocation scheme may break down and cause an error message. The solution is to remove the operation from the complex expression, assign the result to a temporary variable, and use the temporary variable later.

The function *byte*, listed in the table of functions in Section 6.9, can also be used on the left of an assignment. For example,

$$byte\,(s, i) = \text{"40"};$$

**TABLE 6.8.2   XPL Type Conversions for ⟨expression⟩s
and ⟨assignment⟩s**

To _ From	⟨expression⟩s Conditional	Numeric	Descriptor	⟨assignment⟩s Byte	Half Word	Word	String
Conditional	†	A	A, B	A, C	A, D	A, E	A, B, F
Numeric	G	†	B	C	D	E	B, F
Descriptor	X	X	†	X	X	X	F
Byte	G	H	H, B				
Half Word	G	I	I, B				
Word	G	J	J, B				
String	X	X	K				

A	True is converted to 1, false to 0.
B	The number is converted to a (signed) decimal integer, and a descriptor is created to point at its character representation.
C	The low-order 8 bits of the number are stored.
D	The low-order 16 bits of the number are stored.
E	The full 32-bit number is stored.
F	The descriptor is stored.
G	The low-order bit is tested: 1 yields true, 0 yields false.
H	The byte is loaded as the low-order 8 bits of a (positive) number with 24 high-order zero bits.
I	The half word is loaded as the low-order 16 bits of a signed number, and the sign is extended into the high-order 16 bits.
$\cdot J$	The word is loaded as a 32-bit number.
K	The string descriptor is loaded.
X	This conversion is not allowed.
†	No conversion is required.

will change the ith character of the string s to a blank. The programmer should be thoroughly familiar with the string mechanisms of the compiler before using this construct. It is possible to inadvertently change several strings with a single assignment to *byte*.

6.9   Implicitly Declared Procedures and Variables

Unless an explicit declaration is used to redefine them, several names have special meaning in XPL. The effect is as though they were declared in a containing scope. Their names and forms of use are given in Table 6.9.1. The notation ne_1, de_2, etc., denotes expressions as actual parameters. An ne is an expression with numeric value, a de is an expression with descriptor value, and v stands for a variable (not an expression).

TABLE 6.9.1

Name and Form	Meaning
$addr(v)$	A function with numeric value which is the (at most) 24-bit absolute address of the variable (subscripted or not) v. Mostly used in conjunction with *coreword* or *corebyte*.
$byte(de, ne)$	A function with numeric value given by the neth 8 bits taken from the string described by de. (Fast operation.)
$byte(de)$	Like above, except the zeroth (hence, leading) 8 bits of the string are taken. (Fast operation.)
clock__trap	The procedures **call** *clock__trap* (ne_1, ne_2); **call** *interrupt__trap*(ne_1, ne_2); **call** *monitor* (ne_1, ne_2); present service requests to the submonitor and cause submonitor-dependent reactions. With the current **XCOM** submonitor, these are no-operations.
compactify	A procedure automatically called to repack the free storage area for string data when it is exhausted. Calls can be triggered by ||, *input*, number-to-string conversion or an explicit call: **call** *compactify*; The variables *freebase, freelimit, freepoint, descriptor*, and *ndescript* are used by *compactify*.†
$corebyte(ne)$	A byte array identical to the IBM System/360 memory. The subscript is the absolute byte address of the byte selected. *corebyte* may be used on either side of the replacement operator.
$coreword(ne)$	Like *corebyte*, except the subscript corresponds to the word address in memory. Thus an assignment to *corebyte*(4) can change *coreword* (1).
date	A function with numeric value of the date, coded as (day of the year) + 1000 ∗ (year − 1900)
date__of__generation	A word variable initialized with the value of *date* during compilation of the program being run.
$descriptor(ne)$	The description of the neth string as a numeric value.†
exit	A procedure **call** *exit*; which causes an abnormal exit from **XPL** execution. Depending on job control cards, this can be used to obtain an **ABEND** dump.
$file(ne_1, ne_2)$	An array-valued pseudovariable for manipulation of random-access bulk storage. Examples of its use are **declare** *buff* (3600) **bit** (8) ; *buff* = *file* (i, j); *file* $(i - 1, j)$ = *buff*; One record is transferred into or out of the buffer array by the assignments above. *file* cannot appear on both sides of the same assignment. The number of bytes transferred is a device-dependent constant set at assembly time for the submonitor. It is usually 3600 bytes for a 2311 disk and 7200 bytes for a 2314 disk. The first parameter selects the file :‡ $ne_1 = 1$ selects a file with **DDNAME FILE1**

† The casual user is not advised to use any of the names associated with storage repacking.

‡ The DDNAMEs FILE1, FILE2, FILE3 may be associated with sequential datasets on any direct-access device supported by OS/360 (see Appendix 1).

TABLE 6.9.1   (Contd.)

Name and Form	Meaning
	$ne_1 = 2$ selects a file with **DDNAME FILE2**
	$ne_1 = 3$ selects a file with **DDNAME FILE3**
	The second parameter selects the record within the file, starting from record zero.
freebase	A word variable containing the absolute address of the top of the constant strings and thus the bottom of the repackable area.[†]
freelimit	A word variable containing the absolute address of the last usable byte in the string-data area.[†]
freepoint	A word variable containing the absolute address of the next free byte in the string-data area. When *freepoint* passes *freelimit*, *compactify* must be called.[†]
inline(ne₁, . . .)	A procedure
	call *inline*(. . . . .);
	which inserts arbitrary IBM System/360 machine-code inline at compile time. The parameters are quantities that cause code to be placed in the following format:
	call *inline(OP, R1, R2);* /* *RR FORMAT* */
	or
	call *inline (OP, R, X, ⟨address⟩);* /* *RX FORMAT* */
	or
	call *inline (OP, R, X, ⟨address⟩, ⟨address⟩);* /* *SS FORMAT* */ *OP, R, R1, R2,* and *X* must be numeric constants. *OP* is the System/360 operation code; *R, R1* and *R2* are the numbers of the System/360 registers. The ⟨*address*⟩ has the format *B, D* or ⟨identifier⟩, in which *B* and *D* are numeric constants which become parameters to the System/360 instruction. If an ⟨identifier⟩ appears as a parameter to an *inline,* it is taken as the name of a variable whose base-displacement address is substituted into the System/360 instruction. For example,
	call *inline*("5A", 1, 0, var);
	will cause an add instruction to be emitted with an address part pointing to the variable *var*. If *inline* is used as a function, its value is the contents its first register. Thus one can write
	$a = inline$ ("58", 1, 0, 9, "01A");
	which will cause the compiler to emit
	L 1, "01A" (0, 9)
	ST 1, a
input(ne)	A function with descriptor value specifying the next record on the input file *ne*.
	$ne = 0$ and $ne = 1$ select an OS/360 file with the DDNAME SYSIN.[§]
	$ne = 2$ selects an OS/360 file with the DDNAME INPUT2.[§]
	$ne = 3$ selects an OS/360 file with the DDNAME INPUT3.[§]
input	Same as *input* (0).
interrupt__trap	See *clock__trap.*
length(de)	A function with numeric value equal to the number of characters in the string denoted by the parameter. (Fast operation.)
monitor	See *clock__trap*

[§] The DDNAMEs SYSIN, INPUT2, and INPUT3 can be associated with sequential datasets supported by OS/360 (see Appendix 1).

TABLE 6.9.1 (Contd.)

Name and Form	Meaning
monitor__link	A fixed array which can be used for transmission of information between a program and the submonitor. Not used in the current **XCOM** submonitor.
ndescript	A word variable containing the upper bound in the array *descriptor* of the descriptions.[†]

output(ne)	An **XPL** pseudovariable of type string with the side effect that any value assigned to it is also immediately placed in the output file. The value of the parameter controls which output file and also carriage control.
	    ne = 0 selects a file with DDNAME SYSPRINT.[††]
	    ne = 1 selects a file with DDNAME SYSPRINT but takes the leading character of the value assigned for carriage control: e.g.,
	        output (1) = '1';
	    causes a page eject.
	    ne = 2 selects a file with DDNAME SYSPUNCH.[††]
	    ne = 3 selects a file with DDNAME OUTPUT3.[††]

output	Same as *output* (0)
$shl(ne_1, ne_2)$	A function with numeric value given by shifting the value of ne_1 left (logical shift, zeroes appear in the least significant bit position) the number of positions indicated by the value of ne_2.
$shr(ne_1, ne_2)$	Logical shift right. *shl* and *shr* are used in conjunction with &, |, and ¬ for masking and data packing.
$substr(de, ne_1, ne_2)$	A function with descriptor value specifying the substring of the string specified by *de*, starting at position ne_1 with length ne_2. (See Section 6.4.) (Fast operation.)
substr(de, ne)	Like above except all characters from position *ne* to the end of the string are taken. (Fast operation.)
time	A function with numeric value given by the time-of-day coded as centiseconds since midnight.
time__of__generation	A word variable initialized with the value of *time* during compilation of the program period.
trace	A procedure **call** *trace;* which causes activation of the instruction-by-instruction trace at run-time. (See Appendix 2.)
untrace	A procedure **call** *untrace;* which turns off the run-time trace.

[††] The DDNAMEs SYSPRINT, SYSPUNCH, and OUTPUT3 can be associated with sequential datasets supported by OS/360 (see Appendix 1).

6.10 The if Statement

$\langle$if statement$\rangle$ ::= $\langle$if clause$\rangle$ $\langle$statement$\rangle$
            | $\langle$if clause$\rangle$ $\langle$true part$\rangle$ $\langle$statement$\rangle$
            | $\langle$label definition$\rangle$ $\langle$if statement$\rangle$
$\langle$if clause$\rangle$ ::= **if** $\langle$expression$\rangle$ **then**
$\langle$true part$\rangle$ ::= $\langle$basic statement$\rangle$ **else**

Two forms of the ⟨if statement⟩ are allowed: one with **else** and one without. Note that the requirement for a ⟨basic statement⟩ in the ⟨true part⟩ (to avoid the dangling **else** ambiguity of ALGOL 60) is not a strong restriction; any ⟨statement⟩ can be embedded within **do**; . . . **end**; to make it basic.

In both cases, the ⟨expression⟩ in the ⟨if clause⟩ is evaluated (and if necessary converted to type conditional) and then:

1. **if-then-else** case: Depending on whether the value is true or false, either the ⟨basic statement⟩ in the ⟨true part⟩ is executed, or the ⟨statement⟩ following the **else** is executed (never both, never neither).
2. **if-then** case: If and only if the value is true, the associated ⟨statement⟩ is executed.

6.11   The do case Construct

⟨group⟩	::=	⟨group head⟩ ⟨ending⟩
⟨group head⟩	::=	**do** ⟨case selector⟩ ;
	|	⟨group head⟩ ⟨statement⟩
⟨case selector⟩	::=	**case** ⟨expression⟩
⟨ending⟩	::=	**end** | **end** ⟨identifier⟩
	|	⟨label definition⟩ ⟨ending⟩

By generalizing the selective capability of the ⟨if statement⟩, **case** allows the selection of any one of a sequence of ⟨statement⟩s (third production above). The ⟨expression⟩ following **case** is evaluated and used as an index to select one of the ⟨statement⟩s in the group body counting from zero, starting from the top. For example,

$$i = 1;$$
do case $i + 1$;
$\quad output = 0;$
$\quad output = \text{'ABC'};$
$\quad output = \text{'X'};$
$\quad output = \text{"3"};$
end;
$output = 4;$

will cause X and 4 to be printed. If the ⟨expression⟩ following **case** is negative or beyond the range of the ⟨group⟩, a random jump will be executed.

6.12   The do while Construct

⟨group⟩	::=	⟨group head⟩ ⟨ending⟩
⟨group head⟩	::=	**do** ⟨while clause⟩ ;
	|	⟨group head⟩ ⟨statement⟩
⟨while clause⟩	::=	**while** ⟨expression⟩

The **do while** construct provides for iteration zero or more times under the control of a condition. The ⟨expression⟩ following the **while** is evaluated, and, if it has the conditional value true, the ⟨statement⟩s in the ⟨group head⟩ are executed. Control then returns to the **do while**, and the **while** ⟨expression⟩ is again evaluated. When the **while** ⟨expression⟩ has the value false, control passes to the next ⟨statement⟩ following the ⟨group⟩.

Two examples are

> **declare** (*factorial*, *n*) **fixed**;
> *factorial* = 1;
> *n* = 10;
> **do while** *n* > 0;
>   *factorial* = *factorial* ∗ *n*;
>   *n* = *n* − 1;
> **end**;
> *output* = *factorial*;

> **do while** 2 + 2 = 4;
>   *output* = 'This is an infinite loop';
> **end**;

6.13   do with Iteration Count

⟨group⟩	::=	⟨group head⟩ ⟨ending⟩
⟨group head⟩	::=	**do** ⟨step definition⟩
	|	⟨group head⟩ ⟨statement⟩
⟨step definition⟩	::=	⟨variable⟩ ⟨replace⟩ ⟨expression⟩ ⟨iteration control⟩
⟨iteration control⟩	::=	**to** ⟨expression⟩
	|	**to** ⟨expression⟩ **by** ⟨expression⟩

The iterative form of the **do** construct provides execution of a ⟨group⟩ a specified number of times. The ⟨variable⟩ specified is set to the value of the first ⟨expression⟩ and is incremented until its value is greater than that of the ⟨expression⟩ following the **to**. If **by** ⟨expression⟩ is omitted, the control variable is incremented by the default value one. Since negative steps are not allowed, the ⟨expression⟩ following **by** should evaluate to a positive integer. All ⟨expression⟩s are evaluated upon entry to the **do** group and cannot be changed from within.

> **declare** (*n*, *i*) **fixed**;
> *n* = 3;
> **do** *i* = 1 **to** *n* + 1;
>   *n* = *n* + 1;
> **end**;
> *output* = 'n = ' || *n*;

The statement $n = n + 1$ will be executed four times, and the value of n printed will be seven.

Testing is done at the start of the iteration, so that

$$\textbf{do } i = 2 \textbf{ to } 1;$$
$$a = i;$$
$$\textbf{end};$$

will execute zero times.

For example,

$$\textbf{declare } (\textit{fact, i, n}) \textbf{ fixed};$$
$$\textbf{do } n = 1 \textbf{ to } 10;$$
$$\textit{fact} = 1; \quad /* \text{ Computes } n \text{ factorial } */$$
$$\textbf{do } i = 1 \textbf{ to } n;$$
$$\textit{fact} = i * \textit{fact};$$
$$\textbf{end};$$
$$\textit{output} = n \,||\, \text{'factorial} = \text{'} \,||\, \textit{fact};$$
$$\textbf{end};$$

6.14 Procedure Definition and Formal Parameters

⟨procedure definition⟩ ::= ⟨procedure head⟩ ⟨statement list⟩ ⟨ending⟩
⟨procedure head⟩ ::= ⟨procedure name⟩ ;
| ⟨procedure name⟩ ⟨type⟩ ;
| ⟨procedure name⟩ ⟨parameter list⟩ ;
| ⟨procedure name⟩ ⟨parameter list⟩ ⟨type⟩ ;
⟨procedure name⟩ ::= ⟨label definition⟩ **procedure**
⟨parameter list⟩ ::= ⟨parameter head⟩ ⟨identifier⟩)
⟨parameter head⟩ ::= (
| ⟨parameter head⟩ ⟨identifier⟩ ,
⟨ending⟩ ::= **end**
| **end** ⟨identifier⟩
| ⟨label definition⟩ ⟨ending⟩
⟨label definition⟩ ::= ⟨identifier⟩ :

Procedures must be defined prior to their use and cannot be recursive. Each of the formal parameters in the ⟨parameter list⟩ must be declared inside the procedure. All parameters are called by value in XPL, hence assignments to the corresponding formal parameter within the procedure definition have no effect outside the procedure. To pass values out of a procedure, one must either use the ⟨return statement⟩ or make an assignment to a global variable.

⟨Variable⟩s declared inside the procedure may have the same name as those declared outside. In this case, the name refers to the local variable within the scope of the procedure only. Although ⟨variable⟩ and parameter names declared within a procedure become undefined outside the procedure, the storage allocated to those ⟨variable⟩s is not released. It remains allocated, though inaccessible, as in PL/I **static**. Although promiscuous use of this feature is not recommended, the ⟨variable⟩s local to a procedure retain the values they had at the previous call unless explicitly changed.

Function procedures may be typed, with default **fixed**. If the type is **character** or **bit** (n) for $n > 32$, the value returned by the procedure is descriptor (for a character string). Otherwise, a numeric (32-bit two's-complement signed integer) value is returned.

6.15 Procedure Call and Return

⟨call statement⟩   ::=   **call** ⟨variable⟩
⟨variable⟩   ::=   ⟨identifier⟩
                     | ⟨subscript head⟩ ⟨expression⟩)
⟨subscript head⟩   ::=   ⟨identifier⟩ (
                     | ⟨subscript head⟩ ⟨expression⟩ ,

A procedure may be called by the ⟨call statement⟩ or by the appearance of its name in an ⟨expression⟩. Note that procedures and ⟨variable⟩s are syntactically equivalent in the calling statement; they are distinguished by their prior declaration. Two examples are

$$\textbf{call } GCD \ (x, y);$$
$$z = GCD \ (x, y);$$

The difference between the two methods is that in the ⟨call statement⟩ the value (if any) returned by the procedure is ignored. All parameters are evaluated and stored into locations local to the procedure before entry to the procedure and are thus called by value. The types of the actual parameters are not checked by the compiler against the types declared for the formal parameters.

⟨return statement⟩   ::=   **return**
                     | **return** ⟨expression⟩

The ⟨return statement⟩ causes control to be transferred back to the point from which the procedure was called, as does reaching the end of the procedure. The use of **return** ⟨expression⟩ causes the value of the ⟨expression⟩ to be returned as the value of the procedure. This form must be used with procedures called as functions. The ⟨expression⟩ following the **return** should not be a descriptor expression unless the procedure has been defined with type **character** or **bit**(n), with $n > 32$.

If a procedure called as a function does not use **return** ⟨expression⟩ to return control to the calling point, the value returned is the previous contents of some System/360 register, and no error message is given. If control reaches the final **end** of a procedure, an automatic **return** (with no value) is executed.

6.16 Labels and the go to Statement

⟨go to statement⟩ ::= ⟨go to⟩ ⟨identifier⟩
⟨go to⟩ ::= **go to**
   | **goto**
⟨label definition⟩ ::= ⟨identifier⟩ :

The ⟨go to statement⟩ causes a transfer of control to the point indicated by a label. The ⟨identifier⟩ following must be a label and must be defined at some point in the program. Labels may also be declared. This is not necessary except in three cases:

1. The same ⟨identifier⟩ denotes a label defined inside a procedure and one defined outside. In this case the label must be declared inside the procedure.
2. A ⟨go to statement⟩ inside a procedure references a label which is later defined outside of the scope of that procedure. In this case the label must be declared globally.
3. A label which has not yet been defined is used as the argument to the *addr* function. In this case the label must be declared before its use.

6.17 Comments and Compiler Control Toggles

Comments are defined as follows:

⟨comment⟩ ::= ⟨opening bracket⟩ ⟨almost anything⟩ ⟨closing bracket⟩
⟨opening bracket⟩ ::= /*
⟨closing bracket⟩ ::= */
⟨almost anything⟩ ::= {any string of valid System 360 characters which does not contain a ⟨closing bracket⟩}

Comments explain the program to persons reading it and are normally ignored by the compiler. They do not result in the production of any System/360 machine code, nor do they affect the code compiled for any other statements of the program.

Comments are not ignored in one case. Some functions of a compiler which we would like to change from one compilation to another are not part of the program itself. For instance, we would like to be able to specify that the System/360 code produced be interlisted with the source statements on the output. Since control options are not part of the program being compiled but rather specify how the program is to be treated, they are specified within comments rather than by XPL statements. A $ within a comment specifies that the next ⟨character⟩ is a control character. There are 256 control toggles corresonpding to the 256 valid EBCDIC character codes. Each toggle can have the value true or false. When $ ⟨character⟩ is encountered, the value of the corresponding toggle is complemented. Setting the value of certain toggles causes the compiler to take specified actions. For example, the toggle corresponding to E specifies whether System/360 code is to be included in the output listing.

For example,

$$a = 1;$$
$$/* \; \$E \; */$$

$$b = 2;$$
$$c = a + b;$$
$$/* \ \$E \ */$$
$$d = a - b;$$

This causes the System/360 code compiled for the statements $b = 2$; and $c = a + b$; to be listed. When the second $/* \ \$E \ */$ is encountered, listing of compiled code ceases.

Not all toggles serve a meaningful purpose in XCOM. The currently useful ⟨character⟩s are

B Interlist emitted code bytes in hexadecimal.
D Print compilation statistics and symbol table at the end of compilation (initially enabled).
E Interlist emitted code (assembly format) and emitted data.
L List the compiled program (listing is initially enabled).
M List program without auxiliary information (speeds compilation by minimizing string storage usage).
N Produce a warning message if a procedure is called with fewer actual than formal parameters.
S Dump symbol table at the end of each procedure.
T Begin tracing execution of XCOM at this point, during compilation.
U Terminate tracing of XCOM.
Z Allow the compiled program to execute in spite of severe errors.
| Set margin. The portion of succeeding cards starting from the column containing the | will be ignored.

6.18   Examples and Exercises in XPL Programming

We present in Figs. 6.18.1 through 6.18.6 a series of examples illustrating the joint use of the various language features. We remind the reader that the appendices contain several large programs. The program in Fig. 6.18.1 illustrates the exact output of the compiler. After the titles, each print line contains

1. The card number
2. A vertical bar marking the left card boundary
3. The card image
4. A vertical bar marking the right card boundary
5. The count (in bytes) of System/360 code emitted prior to processing the current card image
6. The name of the current procedure (if any)
7. Other information about the compilation

Note that the control toggle $E has been used to list the System/360 machine language generated for the statements.

The example in Fig. 6.18.2 shows the listing produced for an erroneous program, including some of the information about the program gathered by the compiler.

```
X P L   COMPILATION  --  STANFORD UNIVERSITY  --  XCOM III VERSION OF MAY 7, 1969.

TODAY IS AUGUST 10, 1969.

    1 |    /*  INTERLIST $EMITTED CODE  */                            | 1286
    2 |                                                               | 1286
    3 |                                                               | 1286
    4 |    DECLARE I FIXED, J BIT(16), K BIT(8),                      | 1286
    5 |       ALPHA CHARACTER INITIAL('MESSAGE'),                     | 1286

                                          24: DESC = 6, 160
                                         160: CHARACTER = D4
                                         161: CHARACTER = C5
                                         162: CHARACTER = E2
                                         163: CHARACTER = E2
                                         164: CHARACTER = C1
                                         165: CHARACTER = C7
                                         166: CHARACTER = C5

    6 |       BETA (3) BIT(64) ;                                      | 1286
    7 |                                                               | 1286
    8 |    CALL TRACE ; /* BEGIN TRACING */                           | 1286

                                        1286: CODE = STM  1,124(3,11)
                                        1290: CODE = LA   1,12(0,0)
                                        1294: CODE = BALR 12,15
                                        1296: CODE = LM   1,124(3,11)
                                                                        1300
    9 |    I,J,K = 2 ;

                                        1300: CODE = LA   1,2(0,0)
                                        1304: CODE = STC  1,1346(0,11)
                                        1308: CODE = STH  1,1344(0,11)
                                        1312: CODE = ST   1,1340(0,11)
                                                                        1316
   10 |    BETA(I) = ALPHA ;

                                        1316: CODE = L    1,1340(0,11)
                                        1320: CODE = L    2,24(0,13)
```

Fig. 6.18.1

```
11 |   DO WHILE J = I ;

1324: CODE = SLL    1,2(0,0)
1328: CODE = ST     2,28(1,13)
                    1332
1332: CODE = LH     1,1344(0,11)
1336: CODE = C      1,1340(0,11)
1340: CODE = LA     1,0(0,0)
1344: CODE = BC     6,1352(0,14)
1348: CODE = LA     1,1(0,0)
             BACK UP CODE EMITTER
1340: CODE = BC     6,1340(0,14)
                    1344

12 |   J = SHL(K,1) & SHR(I,J) ;

1344: CODE = SR     1,1
1346: CODE = IC     1,1346(0,11)
1350: CODE = AR     1,1
1352: CODE = L      2,1340(0,11)
1356: CODE = LH     3,1344(0,11)
1360: CODE = SRL    2,0(0,3)
1364: CODE = NR     1,2
1366: CODE = STH    1,1344(0,11)
                    1370

13 |   OUTPUT, ALPHA = SUBSTR(ALPHA,J,I+1) ;

1370: CODE = L      1,24(0,13)
1374: CODE = LH     2,1344(0,11)
1378: CODE = LA     3,1(0,0)
1382: CODE = A      3,1340(0,11)
1386: CODE = LA     1,0(2,1)
1390: CODE = LA     3,255(0,3)
1394: CODE = SLL    3,24(0,0)
1398: CODE = OR     1,3
1400: CODE = ST     1,24(0,13)
1404: CODE = STM    1,124(3,11)
1408: CODE = LR     0,1
1410: CODE = SR     2,2
1412: CODE = LA     1,8(0,0)
1416: CODE = BALR   12,15
```

Fig. 6.18.1 (Contd.)

```
14 |    END;

                              1418:  CODE = LM    1,124(3,11)
                                                  1422
                              1422:  CODE = BC    15,1332(0,14)
                              1340:  FIXUP =1426
                                                  1426

15 |    IF J < BYTE('A') THEN
                              1426:  CODE = LH    1,1344(0,11)
                              1348:  DATA = 193
                              1430:  CODE = C     1,1348(0,11)
                              1434:  CODE = LA    1,0(0,0)
                              1438:  CODE = BC    10,1446(0,14)
                              1442:  CODE = LA    1,1(0,0)
                                                  1446  C7 = 193.

                                     BACK UP CODE EMITTER

                              1434:  CODE = BC    10,1434(0,14)
                              1438:  CODE = SR    1,1
16 |       I = 0;            1440:  CODE = ST    1,1340(0,11)
                                                  1444
                                                  1444

17 |    ELSE
18 |       I = BYTE(BETA(J),K) ;
                              1444:  CODE = BC    15,1444(0,14)
                              1448:  CODE = LH    1,1344(0,11)
                              1452:  CODE = SLL   1,2(0,0)
                              1456:  CODE = L     1,28(1,13)
                              1460:  CODE = SR    2,2
                              1462:  CODE = IC    2,1346(0,11)
                              1466:  CODE = IC    2,0(2,1)
                              1470:  CODE = ST    2,1340(0,11)
                                                  1474

19 |    CALL UNTRACE ;   /* END TRACE */
                              1444:  FIXUP =1474
                              1434:  FIXUP =1448
                              1474:  CODE = STM   1,124(3,11)
                              1478:  CODE = LA    1,16(0,0)
                              1482:  CODE = BALR  12,15
                              1484:  CODE = LM    1,124(3,11)
                                                  1488

20 |    /* $END INTERLISTING */
```

Fig. 6.18.1 (Contd.)

```
21 |                                                                                    | 1488
22 |EOF                                                                                 | 1488

END OF COMPILATION AUGUST 10, 1969.   CLOCK TIME = 21:34:20.51.

22 CARDS CONTAINING 9 STATEMENTS WERE COMPILED.
NO ERRORS WERE DETECTED.
1496 BYTES OF PROGRAM, 1357 OF DATA, 44 OF DESCRIPTORS, 167 OF STRINGS.
TOTAL CORE REQUIREMENT 3064 BYTES.

SYMBOL TABLE DUMP

ALPHA   : CHARACTER AT 24(13),       DECLARED ON LINE 5 AND REFERENCED 3 TIMES.
BETA    : CHARACTER AT 28(13),       DECLARED ON LINE 6 AND REFERENCED 2 TIMES.
I       : FIXED     AT 1340(11),     DECLARED ON LINE 4 AND REFERENCED 7 TIMES.
J       : BIT(16)   AT 1344(11),     DECLARED ON LINE 4 AND REFERENCED 7 TIMES.
K       : BIT(8)    AT 1346(11),     DECLARED ON LINE 4 AND REFERENCED 3 TIMES.

TOTAL TIME IN COMPILER   0:0:3.94.
SET UP TIME              0:0:1.96.
ACTUAL COMPILATION TIME  0:0:0.40.
POST-COMPILATION TIME    0:0:1.58.
COMPILATION RATE: 3300 CARDS PER MINUTE.
```

Fig. 6.18.1 (Contd.)

```
X P L   COMPILATION -- STANFORD UNIVERSITY -- XCOM III VERSION OF MAY 7, 1969.

TODAY IS AUGUST 10, 1969.

 1  |FACTORIAL:                                                            | 1286
 2  |  PROCEDURE (N);                                                      | 1286 FACTORIAL
 3  |    DECLARE (I, N, NFACT) FIXED;                                      | 1286 FACTORIAL
 4  |                                                                      | 1294 FACTORIAL
 5  |    NFACT = 1;                                                        | 1294 FACTORIAL
 6  |    DO I = 2 TO N;                                                    | 1302 FACTORIAL
 7  |      NFACT = NFACT * I;                                              | 1338 FACTORIAL
 8  |    END;                                                              | 1350 FACTORIAL
 9  |    RETURN NFACT;                                                     | 1354 FACTORIAL
10  |  END FACTORIAL;                                                      | 1364 FACTORIAL
11  |                                                                      | 1370
12  |  /* THE NEXT STATEMENT HAS AN UNDECLARED IDENTIFIER     */           | 1370
13  |                                                                      | 1370
14  |  DO X = 1 TO 10;                                                     | 1370

*** ERROR, UNDECLARED IDENTIFIER:  X (DETECTED AT LOCATION 13290 IN XCOM). ***

15  |    OUTPUT = X ||' FACTORIAL = ' | FACTORIAL(X);                      | 1398 C7 = 10.
16  |  END;                                                                | 1476
17  |                                                                      | 1480
18  |  /* THE NEXT STATEMENT HAS A SIMULATED KEYPUNCH ERROR   */           | 1480
19  |                                                                      | 1480
20  |  2 = I + 1;                                                          | 1480

*** ERROR, ILLEGAL SYMBOL PAIR:  ; <NUMBER> (DETECTED AT LOCATION 50288 IN XCOM). ***
*** LAST PREVIOUS ERROR WAS DETECTED ON LINE 14. ***
PARTIAL PARSE TO THIS POINT IS:  <STATEMENT LIST> <GROUP> ;
RESUME:

21  |                                                                      | 1480
```

Fig. 6.18.2

```
22 |  OUTPUT = TIME;                                                1480
23 |                                                                1520
24 |EOF                                                             1520
```

####### EXECUTION OF THIS PROGRAM WILL BE INHIBITED.
END OF COMPILATION AUGUST 10, 1969. CLOCK TIME = 21:48:49.26.

24 CARDS CONTAINING 10 STATEMENTS WERE COMPILED.
2 ERRORS (1 SEVERE) WERE DETECTED.
THE LAST DETECTED ERROR WAS ON LINE 20.
1528 BYTES OF PROGRAM, 1373 OF DATA, 28 OF DESCRIPTORS, 173 OF STRINGS.
TOTAL CORE REQUIREMENT 3102 BYTES.

SYMBOL TABLE DUMP

```
FACTORIAL   : LABEL      AT 1290(14),   DECLARED ON LINE 1 AND REFERENCED 1 TIMES.
PARAMETER 1 : FIXED      AT 1348(11),   DECLARED ON LINE 3 AND REFERENCED 1 TIMES.
X           : FIXED      AT 1360(11),   DECLARED ON LINE 14 AND REFERENCED 3 TIMES.
```

```
TOTAL TIME IN COMPILER      0:0:3.26.
SET UP TIME                 0:0:1.50.
ACTUAL COMPILATION TIME     0:0:0.20.
POST-COMPILATION TIME       0:0:1.56.
COMPILATION RATE: 7200 CARDS PER MINUTE.
```

Fig. 6.18.2 (Contd.)

Figure 6.18.3 contains a simple XPL program which reads cards, sorts them using a bubble sort, and then lists the sorted cards.

The program in Fig. 6.18.4 reads in a set of cards and calculates the frequency of occurrence of each word appearing on these cards.

Although input is provided in XPL for character strings, no conversion from character strings to integers is provided by the system; thus the user must supply a conversion procedure if he needs one. The procedure in Fig. 6.18.5 will do.

The procedure in Fig. 6.18.6 produces a suitably random sequence of integers via a congruence algorithm. It is valid for arguments from one to 2^{15}.

```
/*  This program reads n cards (n =  100), sorts them in
    alphabetical (collating) order, and prints them.  */

declare n literally ' 100' ;
declare cards (n) character, (i,k,l) fixed, temp character;

output =  ' Input cards:' ;
do i =  1 to n;
    output, cards(i) =  input;      /*  read and list  */
end;

k,l = ^n;
do while k <=  l;              /*  bubble sort loop  */
    l =  − n;
    do i =  1 to k;
        l =  i − 1;
        if cards(l) >  cards(i) then
            do;
                temp −  cards(l);
                cards(l) =  cards(i);
                cards(i) =  temp;
                k =  l;
            end;
    end;
end;                           /*  of sort loop  */

output =  ' Sorted cards:' ;
do i =  1 to n;
    output =  cards(i);
end;

eof
```

Fig. 6.18.3

```
/*   This program reads and lists cards until an end of file, counting
     the frequency of occurrence of each word on the cards.
*/


declare (buffer, temp, word) character, (i, cp, #entries) fixed,
    table (500) character, count (500) fixed,
    blanks character initial ('
                                        ');

#entries = −1;
output = ' Input cards:' ;
output, buffer = input;        /*  Get a card.  */

do while length(buffer) > 0;    /*  Until end of file.  */
    temp = buffer || ' ';
    do while substr(blanks,0,length(temp)) ¬= temp;
        /*  Until remainder of card is blank.  */
        do while byte(temp) = byte(' ');  /*  Discard blanks.  */
            temp = substr(temp,1);
        end;
        cp = 1;

        do while byte(temp, cp) >= byte('A');
            cp = cp + 1;
        end;          /*  of a word  */

        word = substr(temp, 0, cp);
        temp = substr(temp, cp);    /*  Rest of card.  */

        do i = 0 to #entries;
            if word = table(i) then
                go to found;
        end;

        i, #entries = #entries + 1;
        table(i) = word;
        count(i) = 0;

      found:
        count(i) = count(i) + 1;
    end;

    output, buffer = input;        /*  Get a new card.  */
end;        /*  of do while length(buffer)    */

output = ' Frequency counts:' ;
do i = 0 to #entries;
    output = table(i) || '              ' || count(i);
end;

eof
```

Fig. 6.18.4

FIX:
```
   procedure (s) fixed;
      /*  Convert the string s to an integer.  */
      declare s character, negative bit(1), (i, nval) fixed;

      negative = byte(s) = byte('-');
      nval = 0;

      do i = negative to length(s) - 1;
         nval = nval * 10 + byte(s,i) - byte('0');
      end;

      if negative then
         return  - nval;
      else
         return  nval;

   end  FIX  ;
```

Fig. 6.18.5

RANDOM:
```
   procedure (range) fixed;
      /*  Returns a random integer in the range 0 to range - 1  */

      declare range fixed, rbase fixed initial (1),
         rmult literally ' 671297325' ;

      rbase = rbase * rmult;

      return  shr(shr(rbase, 16) * range, 16);

   end  RANDOM  ;
```

Fig. 6.18.6

Exercise   6.18.1

Rework the procedure *FIX* so that leading blanks are ignored and erroneous input is flagged with an error message. Test your procedure.

Exercise   6.18.2

Write a pair of procedures that convert standard English descriptions of numbers to fixed constants, and vice versa.

For example,

ENGLISH_TO_INTEGER ('Minus one hundred and two') = −102
INTEGER_TO_ENGLISH (31) = 'Thirty one'

Exercise 6.18.3

Write a pair of procedures that convert Roman numerals into fixed constants, and vice versa.

For example,

$$INTEGER\_TO\_ROMAN\ (1970) = \text{'MCMLXX'}$$
$$ROMAN\_TO\_INTEGER\ (\text{'XXXIX'}) = 39$$

Hint: Use the string 'IVXLCDM' with appropriate substrings and catenates.

Exercise 6.18.4

Combine the results of Exercises 6.18.2 and 6.18.3 to get procedures

$$ROMAN\_TO\_ENGLISH$$
$$ENGLISH\_TO\_ROMAN$$

Exercise 6.18.5

Write a procedure such that whenever it is presented a constant expression it produces the value.

For example,

$$CONSTANT\ (\text{'2} * \text{(3} - \text{4)'}) = -2$$

Exercise 6.18.6

Extend the procedure in Exercise 6.18.5 so that if any part of the expression cannot be evaluated, it is left intact.

For example,

$$SIMPLIFY\ (\text{'A} + \text{2} * \text{3} - \text{A} + \text{B} * \text{(4} - \text{4)'}) = \text{'6'}$$
$$SIMPLIFY\ (\text{'A} + \text{B} * \text{1'}) = \text{'A} + \text{B'}$$

Exercise 6.18.7

Extend Exercise 6.18.2 so that expressions in English are properly evaluated.

For example,

$$INTEGER\ (\text{'Two plus two'}) = 4$$

Exercise 6.18.8

Extend Exercise 6.18.2 to translate English numbers into some other natural language.

For example,

$$GERMAN\_TO\_ENGLISH\ (\text{'Zwanzig'}) = \text{'Twenty'}$$
$$ENGLISH\_TO\_GERMAN\ (\text{'Eight hundred and forty seven'})$$
$$= \text{'Achthundertziebenundvierzig'}$$

Exercise 6.18.9

Write a program that reads a sequence of strings and computes and prints the reverse of each string.

Exercise 6.18.10

Write a program to print Pascal's triangle.

$$
\begin{matrix}
 & & 1 & & \\
 & 1 & & 1 & \\
1 & & 2 & & 1 \\
\end{matrix}
$$

1   3   3   1

... etc.

Take care that multidigit entries do not smear the printout.

Exercise 6.18.11

Write a program to compute and print a series of perfect numbers (i.e., numbers that equal the sum of their factors $6 = 1 + 2 + 3$).

Exercise 6.18.12

Write a program to compute some integers that are the sum of two cubes two ways (e.g., $1729 = 12^3 + 1^3 = 10^3 + 9^3$).

Exercise 6.18.13

Write a program that reads a sequence of cards filled with text and computes and prints a table of the frequency of occurrence of each character read.

Exercise 6.18.14

Extend Exercise 6.18.13 so that it uses the table of frequencies to compute and print a minimum redundancy binary code for each character. (Hint: Pierce, *Symbols, Signals and Noise.* Chap. 5.)

Exercise 6.18.15

Extend the program in Exercise 6.18.14 to read a series of messages, encode them with the minimal code, decode them, and then print message, encoding, and decoding.

Exercise 6.18.16

A Turing machine definition is a finite set of quintuples of the form

$$(S_{old}, T_{old}, S_{new}, T_{new}, M)$$

in which the entries describe the state of the machine, the content of the visible tape square before a cycle, the new state, the new value written on the tape, and the direction of the movement of the tape after writing ($R =$ right, $L =$ left). In any situation in which there is no defined action, the machine halts. For example, the set

$$(A, 0, A, 0, L)$$
$$(A, , B, , R)$$
$$(B, 0, A, 1, L)$$
$$(B, 1, B, 0, R)$$

defines a machine that, when started in state *A* at the position indicated on the tape below,

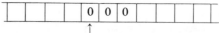

counts in binary. Implement and test in XPL a program that reads a Turing-machine definition, initial state, an initial tape, and the initial position of that tape. Provide for output after each cycle of the machine. (Hint: See M. Minsky, *Computation: Finite and Infinite Machines*.)

Exercise 6.18.17

Define a Turing machine that when presented with two binary integers separated by a single blank leaves only their sum on the tape.

For example,

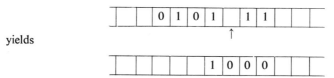

yields

Test your definition with the program in Ex. 6.18.16.

Exercise 6.18.18

Consider doing Ex. 6.18.17 where the tape contains (1) decimal integers; and (2) Roman numerals.

Exercise 6.18.19

One can define a Turing machine that when presented the definition of a Turing machine (a sequence of quintuples followed by the active portion of the tape of the defined machine) on its tape faithfully simulates the action of the defined machine. Can it accept and interpret its own definition?

Exercise 6.18.20

Write a program that prints a chessboard in the starting position, then reads a series of moves in standard chess notation, each time printing an updated board.

Exercise 6.18.21

Evaluate the first-order behavior of the procedure *RANDOM* given in this section. For each value of the parameter *range* a large number of calls (say 1000) should yield roughly the same number of each allowed value. Devise a convincing test that indicates how nearly *RANDOM* behaves as advertised.

Exercise 6.18.22

For some random number generators, the first-order behavior is impeccable, but successive pairs of values are correlated. Use *RANDOM* to generate a series of (x, y) coordinate pairs and use them to construct a "star-field" printout. Does a second-order correlation appear?

Chapter 7

Programming in BNF

/* "Would you tell me, please, which way I ought to go from here?"

"That depends a good deal on where you want to get to," said the Cat.

"I don't much care where—" said Alice.

"Then it doesn't matter which way you go," said the Cat.

"—so long as I get *somewhere*," Alice added as an explanation.

"Oh, you're sure to do that," said the Cat, "if you only walk long enough." */

LEWIS CARROLL

Alice's Adventures in Wonderland

7.1 Using ANALYZER

An early stage in the design of a translator should be the explicit definition of its source language by means of a grammar. In Chapter 2 we discussed phrase-structure grammars (PSGs) and the metalanguage BNF which we use for this definition. An important component of our TWS is ANALYZER, a program which reads a BNF grammar, determines whether it is acceptable to the mixed-strategy precedence (MSP) parsing algorithm of degree (2, 1; 1, 1) we selected for the system (Chapter 4), and constructs parsing decision tables for that algorithm. In the process, it prints out a fairly complete analysis of the grammar for the convenience of the BNF programmer.

This section deals with the mechanics of using ANALYZER; the next, with the debugging of grammars. The theory and application of the MSP algorithm is given in Chapters 4 and 9, while that for the analysis algorithm is given in 5 and 10.

ANALYZER accepts one or more BNF grammars, punched one production per card, as input. (See Fig. 7.1.1.) To simplify keypunching and to reduce the restrictions on the terminal symbols of the grammar, the metalinguistic symbols ::= and |, although inserted into the output listing, are not punched in the cards. Productions may be punched free-format and may contain any characters, with the following exceptions:

1. If the left part is given, it must start in column 1 (see Fig. 7.1.2).
2. If column 1 is blank, the left part is assumed to be the same as the left part of the previous production, i.e., an implicit | is inserted between cards as in Fig. 7.1.3.
3. Completely blank cards are ignored.
4. A $ in column 1 indicates a control card or comment rather than a production; such

$\langle T \rangle ::= \langle T \rangle * \langle P \rangle | \langle P \rangle$
$\langle P \rangle ::= X \ | \ Y \ | \ Z$

$\langle AMB \rangle ::= \langle AMB \rangle \ \langle AMB \rangle | *$

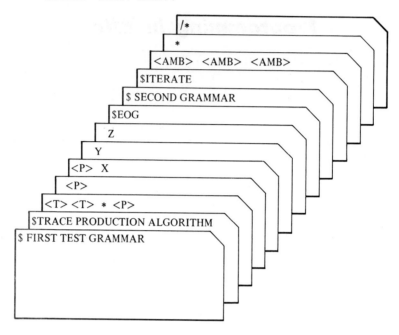

Fig. 7.1.1

Fig. 7.1.2

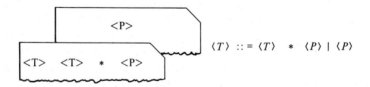

Fig. 7.1.3

cards are listed as they occur. As with XPL control cards, the character following the $ indicates one of 256 toggles to be complemented. The toggles in ANALYZER are

$EOG   If more than one grammar is to be analyzed, used to separate grammars.

$I   Attempt iterative improvement if the grammar is not acceptable (initially off).

$L   List the grammar (initially on).

$O   Print the MSP tables in SKELETON card format (initially off).

$P   Punch the MSP tables for use in SKELETON (initially off). If $P is on during
         reading of the grammar, it also causes punching of XPL comments containing
         the productions.

$T   Trace the sentential form production (F_{11} computation) by listing each CSF
         (initially off).

5. If the character $\langle$ is followed by a blank, it is treated as a separate symbol. Other-
    wise, it and all other characters through the next occurrence of $\rangle$ are treated as a
    single symbol (see Fig. 7.1.4).

6. Each contiguous group of nonblank characters not enclosed in metalinguistic brackets
    is treated as a separate symbol as shown in Fig. 7.1.5.

7. Extra blanks between symbols are ignored.

8. An end-of-file indicates the end of data.

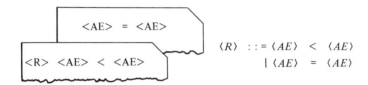

Fig. 7.1.4

<IF CLAUSE> IF <LOGICAL EXPR.> THEN

Fig. 7.1.5 Two Grammars and Their Representations as
Input to ANALYZER

ANALYZER requires that all cards containing productions with the same left
part be grouped together and restricts right parts to strings of one to five symbols.
The conventions of Chapter 2 are used to distinguish the goal symbol: If there is a
unique nonterminal symbol which does not occur in any right part, it is the goal
symbol; if there is more than one such symbol, the first to occur is the goal symbol;
if there is no such symbol, the left part of the first production is the goal symbol.

Figure 7.1.6 shows a complete ANALYZER run for a sample grammar.

ANALYZER numbers, reformats, and prints the productions as they are read in,
and then prints lists of the terminal and of the nonterminal symbols of the grammar
(sorted by length and order of occurrence) and its identification of the goal symbol.
ANALYZER also determines whether the grammar is both left and right recursive
in any symbol, and if so, notifies the programmer that the grammar is clearly ambiguous (Exercise 2.3.12). A printout of the produced-heads matrix follows. Unless
the grammar is clearly ambiguous, the stacking-decision function ($C1$) is computed
and printed first as a matrix for degree (1, 1), then as a table of triples for degree (2, 1).

GRAMMAR ANALYSIS -- STANFORD UNIVERSITY

TODAY IS AUGUST 7, 1969.

                P R O D U C T I O N S

$ THIS IS A TEST GRAMMAR WHICH MAY BE USED IN SKELETON
$ITERATE
$OUTPUT

```
 1   <PROGRAM>  ::=  <STATEMENT LIST>

 2   <STATEMENT LIST>  ::=  <STATEMENT>
 3                       |  <STATEMENT LIST> <STATEMENT>

 4   <STATEMENT>  ::=  <ASSIGNMENT> ;

 5.  <ASSIGNMENT>  ::=  <VARIABLE> = <EXPR>

 6   <EXPR>  ::=  <ARITH EXPR>
 7           |  <IF CLAUSE> THEN <EXPR> ELSE <EXPR>

 8   <IF CLAUSE>  ::=  IF <BOOLEAN>

 9   <BOOLEAN>  ::=  TRUE
10             |  FALSE
11             |  <EXPR> <RELATION> <EXPR>
12             |  <IF CLAUSE> THEN <BOOLEAN> ELSE <BOOLEAN>

13   <RELATION>  ::=  =
14              |  <
15              |  >

16   <ARITH EXPR>  ::=  <TERM>
17                 |  <ARITH EXPR> + <TERM>
18                 |  <ARITH EXPR> - <TERM>

19   <TERM>  ::=  <PRIMARY>
20          |  <TERM> * <PRIMARY>
21          |  <TERM> / <PRIMARY>

22   <PRIMARY>  ::=  <VARIABLE>
23             |  <NUMBER>
24             |  ( <EXPR> )

25   <VARIABLE>  ::=  <IDENTIFIER>
26              |  <VARIABLE> ( <EXPR> )
```

Fig. 7.1.6

```
T E R M I N A L   S Y M B O L S              N O N T E R M I N A L S

   1   ;                                     19   <EXPR>
   2   =                                     20   <TERM>
   3   <                                     21   <PROGRAM>
   4   >                                     22   <BOOLEAN>
   5   +                                     23   <PRIMARY>
   6   -                                     24   <VARIABLE>
   7   *                                     25   <RELATION>
   8   /                                     26   <STATEMENT>
   9   (                                     27   <IF CLAUSE>
  10   )                                     28   <ASSIGNMENT>
  11   IF                                    29   <ARITH EXPR>
  12   _|_                                   30   <STATEMENT LIST>
  13   THEN
  14   ELSE
  15   TRUE
  16   FALSE
  17   <NUMBER>
  18   <IDENTIFIER>

<PROGRAM> IS THE GOAL SYMBOL.
```

Fig. 7.1.6 (Contd.)

```
PRODUCED HEAD SYMBOLS:   PAGE 1 OF 1


                                          1111111 11122222222223
                                1234567890123456 78901234567890
                               +----------------+--------------+
          1    ;               |Y               |              |
          2    =               | Y              |              |
          3    <               |  Y             |              |
          4    >               |   Y            |              |
          5    +               |    Y           |              |
          6    -               |     Y          |              |
          7    *               |      Y         |              |
          8    /               |       Y        |              |
          9    (               |        Y       |              |
         10    )               |         Y      |              |
         11    IF              |          Y     |              |
         12    _|_             |           Y    |              |
         13    THEN            |            Y   |              |
         14    ELSE            |             Y  |              |
         15    TRUE            |              Y |              |
         16    FALSE           |               Y|              |
                               +----------------+--------------+
         17   <NUMBER>         |                |Y             |
         18   <IDENTIFIER>     |                | Y            |
         19   <EXPR>           |           Y Y  |YYYY   YY   Y Y|
         20   <TERM>           |           Y    |YY Y   YY      |
         21   <PROGRAM>        |                | Y   Y Y Y Y Y|
         22   <BOOLEAN>        |           Y Y  YY|YYYY YYY   Y Y|
         23   <PRIMARY>        |           Y    |YY    YY      |
         24   <VARIABLE>       |                | Y      Y     |
         25   <RELATION>       | YYY            |        Y     |
         26   <STATEMENT>      |                | Y    Y Y Y   |
         27   <IF CLAUSE>      |            Y   |          Y   |
         28   <ASSIGNMENT>     |                | Y    Y   Y   |
         29   <ARITH EXPR>     |            Y   |YY Y   YY    Y |
         30   <STATEMENT LIST> |                | Y      Y Y Y Y|
                               +----------------+--------------+
```

SENTENTIAL FORM PRODUCTION:

F11 HAS 321 ELEMENTS.
THE MAXIMUM DEPTH OF RECURSION WAS 22 LEVELS.
894 SENTENTIAL FORMS WERE EXAMINED.

Fig. 7.1.6 (Contd.)

C1 MATRIX FOR STACKING DECISION: PAGE 1 OF 1

```
                                    1111111 11
                           1234567890123456 78
                           +----------------+--+
         1   ;             |              N  | N|
         2   =             |           #  #  |##|
         3   <             |           N  N  |NN|
         4   >             |           N  N  |NN|
         5   +             |           Y     |YY|
         6   -             |           Y     |YY|
         7   *             |           Y     |YY|
         8   /             |           Y     |YY|
         9   (             |           Y  Y  |YY|
        10   )             |NNNNNNNNNN  NN   |  |
        11   IF            |           Y  Y    YY|YY|
        12   _|_           |                 | Y|
        13   THEN          |           Y  Y    YY|YY|
        14   ELSE          |           Y  Y    YY|YY|
        15   TRUE          |              NN |  |
        16   FALSE         |              NN |  |

        17   <NUMBER>      |NNNNNNNN N  NN   |  |
        18   <IDENTIFIER>  |NNNNNNNNNN  NN   |  |
        19   <EXPR>        |N###      #  N#  |  |
        20   <TERM>        |NNNNNNYY N  NN   |  |
        21   <PROGRAM>     |              N  |  |
        22   <BOOLEAN>     |              N# |  |
        23   <PRIMARY>     |NNNNNNNN N  NN   |  |
        24   <VARIABLE>    |N#NNNNNNYN  NN   |  |
        25   <RELATION>    |           Y  Y  |YY|
        26   <STATEMENT>   |              N  | N|
        27   <IF CLAUSE>   |              Y  |  |
        28   <ASSIGNMENT>  |Y                |  |
        29   <ARITH EXPR>  |NNNNYY    N  NN  |  |
        30   <STATEMENT LIST> |           N  | Y|
                           +----------------+--+
```

TABLE ENTRIES SUMMARY:
    389
     47   Y
     93   N
     11   #

Fig. 7.1.6 (Contd.)

```
C1 TRIPLES FOR STACKING DECISION:

     1    N FOR   + <VARIABLE> =
     2    N FOR   - <VARIABLE> =
     3    N FOR   * <VARIABLE> =
     4    N FOR   / <VARIABLE> =
     5    Y FOR   ( <EXPR> )
     6    Y FOR   IF <EXPR> =
     7    Y FOR   IF <EXPR> <
     8    Y FOR   IF <EXPR> >
     9    N FOR   IF <VARIABLE> =
    10    Y FOR   _|_ <VARIABLE> =
    11    Y FOR   THEN <EXPR> =
    12    Y FOR   THEN <EXPR> <
    13    Y FOR   THEN <EXPR> >
    14    Y FOR   THEN <EXPR> ELSE
    15    Y FOR   THEN <BOOLEAN> ELSE
    16    N FOR   THEN <VARIABLE> =
*** ERROR, STACKING DECISION CANNOT BE MADE WITH (2,1) CONTEXT:
    17    # FOR   ELSE <EXPR> =
*** ERROR, STACKING DECISION CANNOT BE MADE WITH (2,1) CONTEXT:
    18    # FOR   ELSE <EXPR> <
*** ERROR, STACKING DECISION CANNOT BE MADE WITH (2,1) CONTEXT:
    19    # FOR   ELSE <EXPR> >
    20    N FOR   ELSE <EXPR> )
    21    N FOR   ELSE <EXPR> ELSE
    22    N FOR   ELSE <BOOLEAN> ELSE
    23    N FOR   ELSE <VARIABLE> =
    24    N FOR   <EXPR> = (
    25    N FOR   <EXPR> = IF
    26    N FOR   <EXPR> = <NUMBER>
    27    N FOR   <EXPR> = <IDENTIFIER>
    28    Y FOR   <VARIABLE> = (
    29    Y FOR   <VARIABLE> = IF
    30    Y FOR   <VARIABLE> = <NUMBER>
    31    Y FOR   <VARIABLE> = <IDENTIFIER>
    32    N FOR   <RELATION> <EXPR> ELSE
    33    Y FOR   <STATEMENT LIST> <VARIABLE> =

259 ENTRIES FOR 33 TRIPLES.

TABLE ENTRIES SUMMARY:
    15    Y
    15    N
     3    #
```

Fig. 7.1.6   (Contd.)

ANALYSIS OF (2,1) CONFLICTS:

   THE TRIPLE ELSE \<EXPR> = MUST HAVE THE VALUE N FOR

     7   \<EXPR> ::= \<IF CLAUSE> THEN \<EXPR> ELSE \<EXPR>
         IN THE CONTEXT IF ... =
         IN THE CONTEXT THEN ... =
         IN THE CONTEXT ELSE ... =

   THE TRIPLE ELSE \<EXPR> = MUST HAVE THE VALUE Y FOR

    11 \<BOOLEAN> ::= \<EXPR> \<RELATION> \<EXPR>
         IN THE CONTEXT ELSE ... THEN
         IN THE CONTEXT ELSE ... ELSE

   THE TRIPLE ELSE \<EXPR> < MUST HAVE THE VALUE N FOR

     7   \<EXPR> ::= \<IF CLAUSE> THEN \<EXPR> ELSE \<EXPR>
         IN THE CONTEXT IF ... <
         IN THE CONTEXT THEN ... <
         IN THE CONTEXT ELSE ... <

   THE TRIPLE ELSE \<EXPR> < MUST HAVE THE VALUE Y FOR

    11 \<BOOLEAN> ::= \<EXPR> \<RELATION> \<EXPR>
         IN TIIE CONTEXT ELSE ... THEN
         IN THE CONTEXT ELSE ... ELSE

   THE TRIPLE ELSE \<EXPR> > MUST HAVE THE VALUE N FOR

     7   \<EXPR> ::= \<IF CLAUSE> THEN \<EXPR> ELSE \<EXPR>
         IN THE CONTEXT IF ... >
         IN THE CONTEXT THEN ... >
         IN THE CONTEXT ELSE ... >

   THE TRIPLE ELSE \<EXPR> > MUST HAVE THE VALUE Y FOR

    11 \<BOOLEAN> ::= \<EXPR> \<RELATION> \<EXPR>
         IN THE CONTEXT ELSE ... THEN
         IN THE CONTEXT ELSE ... ELSE

Fig. 7.1.6 (Contd.)

CONTEXT CHECK FOR EQUAL AND EMBEDDED RIGHT PARTS:

THERE ARE 100 AND 86 VALID CONTEXTS, RESPECTIVELY, FOR
```
26   <VARIABLE>  ::=  <VARIABLE> ( <EXPR> )
24   <PRIMARY>   ::=  ( <EXPR> )
```
THEY CAN BE RESOLVED BY LENGTH.

THERE ARE 30 AND 30 VALID CONTEXTS, RESPECTIVELY, FOR
```
17   <ARITH EXPR>  ::=  <ARITH EXPR> + <TERM>
16   <ARITH EXPR>  ::=  <TERM>
```
THEY CAN BE RESOLVED BY LENGTH.

THERE ARE 30 AND 30 VALID CONTEXTS, RESPECTIVELY, FOR
```
18   <ARITH EXPR>  ::=  <ARITH EXPR> - <TERM>
16   <ARITH EXPR>  ::=  <TERM>
```
THEY CAN BE RESOLVED BY LENGTH.

THERE ARE 64 AND 64 VALID CONTEXTS, RESPECTIVELY, FOR
```
20   <TERM>  ::=  <TERM> * <PRIMARY>
19   <TERM>  ::=  <PRIMARY>
```
THEY CAN BE RESOLVED BY LENGTH.

THERE ARE 64 AND 64 VALID CONTEXTS, RESPECTIVELY, FOR
```
21   <TERM>  ::=  <TERM> / <PRIMARY>
19   <TERM>  ::=  <PRIMARY>
```
THEY CAN BE RESOLVED BY LENGTH.

THERE ARE 2 AND 2 VALID CONTEXTS, RESPECTIVELY, FOR
```
3   <STATEMENT LIST>  ::=  <STATEMENT LIST> <STATEMENT>
2   <STATEMENT LIST>  ::=  <STATEMENT>
```
THEY CAN BE RESOLVED BY LENGTH.

C2 PRODUCTION CHOICE FUNCTION:

; AS STACK TOP WILL CAUSE PRODUCTIONS TO BE CHECKED
IN THIS ORDER:

```
4   <STATEMENT>  ::=  <ASSIGNMENT> ;
```
THERE WILL BE NO CONTEXT CHECK.

= AS STACK TOP WILL CAUSE PRODUCTIONS TO BE CHECKED
IN THIS ORDER:

```
13   <RELATION>  ::=  =
```
THERE WILL BE NO CONTEXT CHECK.

< AS STACK TOP WILL CAUSE PRODUCTIONS TO BE CHECKED
IN THIS ORDER:

```
14   <RELATION>  ::=  <
```
THERE WILL BE NO CONTEXT CHECK.

> AS STACK TOP WILL CAUSE PRODUCTIONS TO BE CHECKED

Fig. 7.1.6 (Contd.)

IN THIS ORDER:

15   <RELATION> ::= >
     THERE WILL BE NO CONTEXT CHECK.

) AS STACK TOP WILL CAUSE PRODUCTIONS TO BE CHECKED
     IN THIS ORDER:

26   <VARIABLE> ::= <VARIABLE> (<EXPR>)
     THERE WILL BE NO CONTEXT CHECK.

24   <PRIMARY> ::= (<EXPR>)
     THERE WILL BE NO CONTEXT CHECK.

TRUE AS STACK TOP WILL CAUSE PRODUCTIONS TO BE CHECKED
     IN THIS ORDER:

9   <BOOLEAN> ::= TRUE
     THERE WILL BE NO CONTEXT CHECK.

FALSE AS STACK TOP WILL CAUSE PRODUCTIONS TO BE CHECKED
     IN THIS ORDER:

10   <BOOLEAN> ::= FALSE
     THERE WILL BE NO CONTEXT CHECK.

<NUMBER> AS STACK TOP WILL CAUSE PRODUCTIONS TO BE CHECKED
     IN THIS ORDER:

23   <PRIMARY> ::= <NUMBER>
     THERE WILL BE NO CONTEXT CHECK.

<IDENTIFIER> AS STACK TOP WILL CAUSE PRODUCTIONS TO BE CHECKED
     IN THIS ORDER:

25   <VARIABLE> ::= <IDENTIFIER>
     THERE WILL BE NO CONTEXT CHECK.

<EXPR> AS STACK TOP WILL CAUSE PRODUCTIONS TO BE CHECKED
     IN THIS ORDER:

7   <EXPR> ::= <IF CLAUSE> THEN <EXPR> ELSE <EXPR>
     THERE WILL BE NO CONTEXT CHECK.

5   <ASSIGNMENT> ::= <VARIABLE> = <EXPR>
     THERE WILL BE NO CONTEXT CHECK.

11   <BOOLEAN> ::= <EXPR> <RELATION> <EXPR>
     THERE WILL BE NO CONTEXT CHECK.

<TERM> AS STACK TOP WILL CAUSE PRODUCTIONS TO BE CHECKED
     IN THIS ORDER:

17   <ARITH EXPR> ::= <ARITH EXPR> + <TERM>

Fig. 7.1.6 (Contd.)

THERE WILL BE NO CONTEXT CHECK.

18   <ARITH EXPR>   ::=   <ARITH EXPR> - <TERM>
     THERE WILL BE NO CONTEXT CHECK.

16   <ARITH EXPR>   ::=   <TERM>
     THERE WILL BE NO CONTEXT CHECK.

<BOOLEAN> AS STACK TOP WILL CAUSE PRODUCTIONS TO BE CHECKED
     IN THIS ORDER:

12   <BOOLEAN>   ::=   <IF CLAUSE> THEN <BOOLEAN> ELSE <BOOLEAN>
     THERE WILL BE NO CONTEXT CHECK.

8   <IF CLAUSE>   ::=   IF <BOOLEAN>
     THERE WILL BE NO CONTEXT CHECK.

<PRIMARY> AS STACK TOP WILL CAUSE PRODUCTIONS TO BE CHECKED
     IN THIS ORDER:

20   <TERM>   ::=   <TERM> * <PRIMARY>
     THERE WILL BE NO CONTEXT CHECK.

21   <TERM>   ::=   <TERM> / <PRIMARY>
     THERE WILL BE NO CONTEXT CHECK.

19   <TERM>   ::=   <PRIMARY>
     THERE WILL BE NO CONTEXT CHECK.

<VARIABLE> AS STACK TOP WILL CAUSE PRODUCTIONS TO BE CHECKED
     IN THIS ORDER:

22   <PRIMARY>   ::=   <VARIABLE>
     THERE WILL BE NO CONTEXT CHECK.

<STATEMENT> AS STACK TOP WILL CAUSE PRODUCTIONS TO BE CHECKED
     IN THIS ORDER:

3   <STATEMENT LIST>   ::=   <STATEMENT LIST> <STATEMENT>
     THERE WILL BE NO CONTEXT CHECK.

2   <STATEMENT LIST>   ::=   <STATEMENT>
     THERE WILL BE NO CONTEXT CHECK.

<ARITH EXPR> AS STACK TOP WILL CAUSE PRODUCTIONS TO BE CHECKED
     IN THIS ORDER:

6   <EXPR>   ::=   <ARITH EXPR>
     THERE WILL BE NO CONTEXT CHECK.

<STATEMENT LIST> AS STACK TOP WILL CAUSE PRODUCTIONS TO BE CHECKED
     IN THIS ORDER:

1   <PROGRAM>   ::=   <STATEMENT LIST>

Fig. 7.1.6 (Contd.)

```
          THERE WILL BE NO CONTEXT CHECK.

ANALYSIS COMPLETE FOR ITERATION 1
*** 3 ERRORS WERE DETECTED.

GRAMMAR MODIFICATION TO ATTEMPT TO RESOLVE CONFLICTS:

    27   <ELSE1>  ::=  ELSE
     7   <EXPR>  ::=  <IF CLAUSE> THEN <EXPR> <ELSE1> <EXPR>
    28   <ELSE2>  ::=  ELSE
    12   <BOOLEAN>  ::=  <IF CLAUSE> THEN <BOOLEAN> <ELSE2> <BOOLEAN>
```

Fig. 7.1.6 (Contd.)

```
PRODUCED HEAD SYMBOLS:   PAGE 1 OF 1


                                    1111111 1112222222222333
                          1234567890123456 7890123456789012
                          +---------------+---------------+
    1    ;                |Y              |               |
    2    =                | Y             |               |
    3    <                |  Y            |               |
    4    >                |   Y           |               |
    5    +                |    Y          |               |
    6    -                |     Y         |               |
    7    *                |      Y        |               |
    8    /                |       Y       |               |
    9    (                |        Y      |               |
   10    )                |         Y     |               |
   11    IF               |          Y    |               |
   12    _|_              |           Y   |               |
   13    THEN             |            Y  |               |
   14    ELSE             |             Y |               |
   15    TRUE             |              Y|               |
   16    FALSE            |              Y|               |
                          +---------------+---------------+
   17    <NUMBER>         |               |Y              |
   18    <IDENTIFIER>     |               | Y             |
   19    <EXPR>           |        Y Y    |YYYY   YY   Y Y |
   20    <TERM>           |        Y      |YY Y   YY       |
   21    <PROGRAM>        |               | Y   Y   Y Y Y Y|
   22    <BOOLEAN>        |        Y Y  YY |YYYY YYY   Y Y  |
   23    <PRIMARY>        |        Y      |YY     YY       |
   24    <VARIABLE>       |               | Y       Y      |
   25    <RELATION>       | YYY           |          Y     |
   26    <STATEMENT>      |               | Y     Y Y Y    |
   27    <IF CLAUSE>      |       Y       |             Y  |
   28    <ASSIGNMENT>     |               | Y     Y   Y    |
   29    <ARITH EXPR>     |        Y      |YY Y   YY     Y  |
   30    <STATEMENT LIST> |               | Y     Y Y Y Y  |
   31    <ELSE1>          |            Y  |               Y|
   32    <ELSE2>          |            Y  |               Y|
                          +---------------+---------------+


SENTENTIAL FORM PRODUCTION:

F11 HAS 362 ELEMENTS.
THE MAXIMUM DEPTH OF RECURSION WAS 23 LEVELS.
1055 SENTENTIAL FORMS WERE EXAMINED.
```

Fig. 7.1.6 (Contd.)

```
C1 MATRIX FOR STACKING DECISION:   PAGE 1 OF 1


                                        1111111 11
                                   1234567890123456 78
                                   +----------------+--+
        1   ;                      |              N  | N|
        2   =                      |            # #  |##|
        3   <                      |            N N  |NN|
        4   >                      |            N N  |NN|
        5   +                      |            Y    |YY|
        6   -                      |            Y    |YY|
        7   *                      |            Y    |YY|
        8   /                      |            Y    |YY|
        9   (                      |            Y Y  |YY|
       10   )                      |NNNNNNNNNN  NN   |  |
       11   IF                     |            Y Y     YY|YY|
       12   _|_                    |                 | Y|
       13   THEN                   |            Y Y     YY|YY|
       14   ELSE                   |            N N     NN|NN|
       15   TRUE                   |              NN |  |
       16   FALSE                  |              NN |  |

                                   +----------------+--+
       17   <NUMBER>               |NNNNNNNN N  NN   |  |
       18   <IDENTIFIER>           |NNNNNNNNNN  NN   |  |
       19   <EXPR>                 |N###      #  N#  |  |
       20   <TERM>                 |NNNNNNYY N  NN   |  |
       21   <PROGRAM>              |              N  |  |
       22   <BOOLEAN>              |              N# |  |
       23   <PRIMARY>              |NNNNNNNN N  NN   |  |
       24   <VARIABLE>             |N#NNNNNNYN  NN   |  |
       25   <RELATION>             |            Y Y  |YY|
       26   <STATEMENT>            |              N  | N|
       27   <IF CLAUSE>            |              Y  |  |
       28   <ASSIGNMENT>           |Y                |  |
       29   <ARITH EXPR>           |NNNNYY   N  NN   |  |
       30   <STATEMENT LIST>       |              N  | Y|
       31   <ELSE1>                |            Y Y  |YY|
       32   <ELSE2>                |            Y Y     YY|YY|
                                   +----------------+--+

TABLE ENTRIES SUMMARY:
     415
      51  Y
      99  N
      11  #
```

Fig. 7.1.6 (Contd.)

176

C1 TRIPLES FOR STACKING DECISION:

```
 1   N FOR   + <VARIABLE> =
 2   N FOR   - <VARIABLE> =
 3   N FOR   * <VARIABLE> =
 4   N FOR   / <VARIABLE> =
 5   Y FOR   ( <EXPR> )
 6   Y FOR   IF <EXPR> =
 7   Y FOR   IF <EXPR> <
 8   Y FOR   IF <EXPR> >
 9   N FOR   IF <VARIABLE> =
10   Y FOR   _|_ <VARIABLE> =
11   Y FOR   THEN <EXPR> =
12   Y FOR   THEN <EXPR> <
13   Y FOR   THEN <EXPR> >
14   Y FOR   THEN <EXPR> ELSE
15   Y FOR   THEN <BOOLEAN> ELSE
16   N FOR   THEN <VARIABLE> =
17   N FOR   <EXPR> = (
18   N FOR   <EXPR> = IF
19   N FOR   <EXPR> = <NUMBER>
20   N FOR   <EXPR> = <IDENTIFIER>
21   Y FOR   <VARIABLE> = (
22   Y FOR   <VARIABLE> = IF
23   Y FOR   <VARIABLE> = <NUMBER>
24   Y FOR   <VARIABLE> = <IDENTIFIER>
25   N FOR   <RELATION> <EXPR> ELSE
26   Y FOR   <STATEMENT LIST> <VARIABLE> =
27   N FOR   <ELSE1> <EXPR> =
28   N FOR   <ELSE1> <EXPR> <
29   N FOR   <ELSE1> <EXPR> >
30   N FOR   <ELSE1> <EXPR> )
31   N FOR   <ELSE1> <EXPR> ELSE
32   N FOR   <ELSE1> <VARIABLE> =
33   Y FOR   <ELSE2> <EXPR> =
34   Y FOR   <ELSE2> <EXPR> <
35   Y FOR   <ELSE2> <EXPR> >
36   N FOR   <ELSE2> <BOOLEAN> ELSE
37   N FOR   <ELSE2> <VARIABLE> =
```

281 ENTRIES FOR 37 TRIPLES.

TABLE ENTRIES SUMMARY:
```
18   Y
19   N
 0   #
```

Fig. 7.1.6 (Contd.)

CONTEXT CHECK FOR EQUAL AND EMBEDDED RIGHT PARTS:

THERE ARE 108 AND 93 VALID CONTEXTS, RESPECTIVELY, FOR
  26 <VARIABLE> ::= <VARIABLE> (<EXPR>)
  24 <PRIMARY> ::= (<EXPR>)
THEY CAN BE RESOLVED BY LENGTH.

THERE ARE 4 AND 6 VALID CONTEXTS, RESPECTIVELY, FOR
  27 <ELSE1> ::= ELSE
  28 <ELSE2> ::= ELSE
THEY CAN BE RESOLVED BY (1,0) CONTEXT.

THERE ARE 35 AND 35 VALID CONTEXTS, RESPECTIVELY, FOR
  17 <ARITH EXPR> ::= <ARITH EXPR> + <TERM>
  16 <ARITH EXPR> ::= <TERM>
THEY CAN BE RESOLVED BY LENGTH.

THERE ARE 35 AND 35 VALID CONTEXTS, RESPECTIVELY, FOR
  18 <ARITH EXPR> ::= <ARITH EXPR> - <TERM>
  16 <ARITH EXPR> ::= <TERM>
THEY CAN BE RESOLVED BY LENGTH.

THERE ARE 71 AND 71 VALID CONTEXTS, RESPECTIVELY, FOR
  20 <TERM> ::= <TERM> * <PRIMARY>
  19 <TERM> ::= <PRIMARY>
THEY CAN BE RESOLVED BY LENGTH.

THERE ARE 71 AND 71 VALID CONTEXTS, RESPECTIVELY, FOR
  21 <TERM> ::= <TERM> / <PRIMARY>
  19 <TERM> ::= <PRIMARY>
THEY CAN BE RESOLVED BY LENGTH.

THERE ARE 2 AND 2 VALID CONTEXTS, RESPECTIVELY, FOR
  3 <STATEMENT LIST> ::= <STATEMENT LIST> <STATEMENT>
  2 <STATEMENT LIST> ::= <STATEMENT>
THEY CAN BE RESOLVED BY LENGTH.

C2 PRODUCTION CHOICE FUNCTION:

  ; AS STACK TOP WILL CAUSE PRODUCTIONS TO BE CHECKED
       IN THIS ORDER:

    4 <STATEMENT> ::= <ASSIGNMENT> ;
       THERE WILL BE NO CONTEXT CHECK.

  = AS STACK TOP WILL CAUSE PRODUCTIONS TO BE CHECKED
       IN THIS ORDER:

   13 <RELATION> ::= =
       THERE WILL BE NO CONTEXT CHECK.

  < AS STACK TOP WILL CAUSE PRODUCTIONS TO BE CHECKED
       IN THIS ORDER:

Fig. 7.1.6 (Contd.)

```
14    <RELATION>  ::=   <
      THERE WILL BE NO CONTEXT CHECK.

>  AS STACK TOP WILL CAUSE PRODUCTIONS TO BE CHECKED
      IN THIS ORDER:

15    <RELATION>  ::=   >
      THERE WILL BE NO CONTEXT CHECK.

)  AS STACK TOP WILL CAUSE PRODUCTIONS TO BE CHECKED
      IN THIS ORDER:

26    <VARIABLE>  ::=   <VARIABLE> ( <EXPR> )
      THERE WILL BE NO CONTEXT CHECK.

24    <PRIMARY>  ::=   ( <EXPR> )
      THERE WILL BE NO CONTEXT CHECK.

ELSE  AS STACK TOP WILL CAUSE PRODUCTIONS TO BE CHECKED
      IN THIS ORDER:

27    <ELSE1>  ::=   ELSE
      (1,0) CONTEXT WILL BE CHECKED.  LEGAL LEFT CONTEXT:
         <EXPR> ...

28    <ELSE2>  ::=   ELSE
      THERE WILL BE NO CONTEXT CHECK.

TRUE  AS STACK TOP WILL CAUSE PRODUCTIONS TO BE CHECKED
      IN THIS ORDER:

9    <BOOLEAN>  ::=   TRUE
      THERE WILL BE NO CONTEXT CHECK.

FALSE  AS STACK TOP WILL CAUSE PRODUCTIONS TO BE CHECKED
      IN THIS ORDER:

10    <BOOLEAN>  ::=   FALSE
      THERE WILL BE NO CONTEXT CHECK.

<NUMBER>  AS STACK TOP WILL CAUSE PRODUCTIONS TO BE CHECKED
      IN THIS ORDER:

23    <PRIMARY>  ::=   <NUMBER>
      THERE WILL BE NO CONTEXT CHECK.

<IDENTIFIER>  AS STACK TOP WILL CAUSE PRODUCTIONS TO BE CHECKED
      IN THIS ORDER:

25    <VARIABLE>  ::=   <IDENTIFIER>
      THERE WILL BE NO CONTEXT CHECK.

<EXPR>  AS STACK TOP WILL CAUSE PRODUCTIONS TO BE CHECKED
```

Fig. 7.1.6 (Contd.)

IN THIS ORDER:

7   <EXPR> ::= <IF CLAUSE> THEN <EXPR> <ELSE1> <EXPR>
      THERE WILL BE NO CONTEXT CHECK.

5   <ASSIGNMENT> ::= <VARIABLE> = <EXPR>
      THERE WILL BE NO CONTEXT CHECK.

11   <BOOLEAN> ::= <EXPR> <RELATION> <EXPR>
      THERE WILL BE NO CONTEXT CHECK.

<TERM> AS STACK TOP WILL CAUSE PRODUCTIONS TO BE CHECKED
      IN THIS ORDER:

17   <ARITH EXPR> ::= <ARITH EXPR> + <TERM>
      THERE WILL BE NO CONTEXT CHECK.

18   <ARITH EXPR> ::= <ARITH EXPR> - <TERM>
      THERE WILL BE NO CONTEXT CHECK.

16   <ARITH EXPR> ::= <TERM>
      THERE WILL BE NO CONTEXT CHECK.

<BOOLEAN> AS STACK TOP WILL CAUSE PRODUCTIONS TO BE CHECKED
      IN THIS ORDER:

12   <BOOLEAN> ::= <IF CLAUSE> THEN <BOOLEAN> <ELSE2> <BOOLEAN>
      THERE WILL BE NO CONTEXT CHECK.

8   <IF CLAUSE> ::= IF <BOOLEAN>
      THERE WILL BE NO CONTEXT CHECK.

<PRIMARY> AS STACK TOP WILL CAUSE PRODUCTIONS TO BE CHECKED
      IN THIS ORDER:

20   <TERM> ::= <TERM> * <PRIMARY>
      THERE WILL BE NO CONTEXT CHECK.

21   <TERM> ::= <TERM> / <PRIMARY>
      THERE WILL BE NO CONTEXT CHECK.

19   <TERM> ::= <PRIMARY>
      THERE WILL BE NO CONTEXT CHECK.

<VARIABLE> AS STACK TOP WILL CAUSE PRODUCTIONS TO BE CHECKED
      IN THIS ORDER:

22   <PRIMARY> ::= <VARIABLE>
      THERE WILL BE NO CONTEXT CHECK.

<STATEMENT> AS STACK TOP WILL CAUSE PRODUCTIONS TO BE CHECKED
      IN THIS ORDER:

3   <STATEMENT LIST> ::= <STATEMENT LIST> <STATEMENT>

Fig. 7.1.6 (Contd.)

```
        THERE WILL BE NO CONTEXT CHECK.

    2   <STATEMENT LIST>  ::=  <STATEMENT>
        THERE WILL BE NO CONTEXT CHECK.

<ARITH EXPR>  AS STACK TOP WILL CAUSE PRODUCTIONS TO BE CHECKED
        IN THIS ORDER:

    6   <EXPR>  ::=  <ARITH EXPR>
        THERE WILL BE NO CONTEXT CHECK.

<STATEMENT LIST>  AS STACK TOP WILL CAUSE PRODUCTIONS TO BE CHECKED
        IN THIS ORDER:

    1   <PROGRAM>  ::=  <STATEMENT LIST>
        THERE WILL BE NO CONTEXT CHECK.

ANALYSIS COMPLETE FOR ITERATION 2
NO ERRORS WERE DETECTED.
```

Fig. 7.1.6 (Contd.)

CARD OUTPUT:

```
DECLARE NSY LITERALLY '32', NT LITERALLY '18';
DECLARE V(NSY) CHARACTER INITIAL ( '<ERROR: TOKEN = 0>', ';', '=',
   '<', '>', '+', '-', '*', '/', '(', ')', 'IF', '_|_', 'THEN',
   'ELSE', 'TRUE', 'FALSE', '<NUMBER>', '<IDENTIFIER>', '<EXPR>',
   '<TERM>', '<PROGRAM>', '<BOOLEAN>', '<PRIMARY>', '<VARIABLE>',
   '<RELATION>', '<STATEMENT>', '<IF CLAUSE>', '<ASSIGNMENT>',
   '<ARITH EXPR>', '<STATEMENT LIST>', 'ELSE', 'ELSE');
DECLARE V_INDEX(12) BIT(8) INITIAL ( 1, 11, 12, 13, 16, 17, 17, 17,
   18, 18, 18, 18, 19);
DECLARE C1(NSY) BIT(38) INITIAL (
   "(2) 00000 00000 00000 0000",
   "(2) 00000 00000 00200 0002",
   "(2) 00000 00003 03000 0033",
   "(2) 00000 00002 02000 0022",
   "(2) 00000 00002 02000 0022",
   "(2) 00000 00001 00000 0011",
   "(2) 00000 00001 00000 0011",
   "(2) 00000 00001 00000 0011",
   "(2) 00000 00001 00000 0011",
   "(2) 00000 00001 01000 0011",
   "(2) 02222 22222 20022 0000",
   "(2) 00000 00001 01000 1111",
   "(2) 00000 00000 00000 0001",
   "(2) 00000 00001 01000 1111",
   "(2) 00000 00002 02000 2222",
   "(2) 00000 00000 00022 0000",
   "(2) 00000 00000 00022 0000",
   "(2) 02222 22220 20022 0000",
   "(2) 02222 22222 20022 0000",
   "(2) 02333 00000 30023 0000",
   "(2) 02222 22110 20022 0000",
   "(2) 00000 00000 00200 0000",
   "(2) 00000 00000 00023 0000",
   "(2) 02222 22220 20022 0000",
   "(2) 02322 22221 20022 0000",
   "(2) 00000 00001 01000 0011",
   "(2) 00000 00000 00200 0002",
   "(2) 00000 00000 00010 0000",
   "(2) 01000 00000 00000 0000",
   "(2) 02222 11000 20022 0000",
   "(2) 00000 00000 00200 0001",
   "(2) 00000 00001 01000 0011",
   "(2) 00000 00001 01000 1111");
DECLARE NC1TRIPLES LITERALLY '17';
DECLARE C1TRIPLES(NC1TRIPLES) FIXED INITIAL ( 594698, 725762, 725763,
   725764, 792578, 856834, 856835, 856836, 856846, 857614, 1573385,
   1573387, 1573393, 1573394, 1972226, 2102018, 2102019, 2102020);
DECLARE PRTB(28) FIXED INITIAL (0, 28, 0, 0, 0, 1575187, 2323, 0, 0,
   0, 0, 0, 0, 453841695, 6146, 4889, 7429, 7430, 0, 453842464, 11,
   5127, 5128, 0, 0, 30, 0, 0, 0);
```

Fig. 7.1.6 (Contd.)

```
DECLARE PRDTB(28) BIT(8) INITIAL (0, 4, 13, 14, 15, 26, 24, 0, 0, 9,
    10, 23, 25, 7, 5, 11, 17, 18, 16, 12, 8, 20, 21, 19, 22, 3, 2, 6,
    1);
DECLARE HDTB(28) BIT(8) INITIAL (0, 26, 25, 25, 25, 24, 23, 31, 32,
    22, 22, 23, 24, 19, 28, 22, 29, 29, 29, 22, 27, 20, 20, 20, 23, 30,
    30, L9, 21);
DECLARE PRLENGTH(28) BIT(8) INITIAL (0, 2, 1, 1, 1, 4, 3, 1, 1, 1, 1,
    1, 1, 5, 3, 3, 3, 3, 1, 5, 2, 3, 3, 1, 1, 2, 1, 1, 1);
DECLARE CONTEXT_CASE(28) BIT(8) INITIAL (0, 0, 0, 0, 0, 0, 0, 2, 0, 0,
    0, 0, 0, 0, 0, 0, 0, 0, 0, 0, 0, 0, 0, 0, 0, 0, 0, 0, 0);
DECLARE LEFT_CONTEXT(0) BIT(8) INITIAL ( 19);
DECLARE LEFT_INDEX(14) BIT(8) INITIAL ( 0, 0, 0, 0, 0, 0, 0, 0, 0, 0,
    0, 0, 0, 1, 1);
DECLARE CONTEXT_TRIPLE(0) FIXED INITIAL ( 0);
DECLARE TRIPLE_INDEX(14) BIT(8) INITIAL ( 0, 0, 0, 0, 0, 0, 0, 0, 0,
    0, 0, 0, 0, 0, 1);
DECLARE PR_INDEX(32) BIT(8) INITIAL ( 1, 2, 3, 4, 5, 5, 5, 5, 5, 5, 7,
    7, 7, 7, 9, 10, 11, 12, 13, 16, 19, 19, 21, 24, 25, 25, 27, 27, 27,
    28, 29, 29, 29);
```

Fig. 7.1.6 (Contd.)

If conflicts remain for triples, the productions and contexts involved are tabulated. ANALYZER then checks all pairs of equal or embedded right parts to determine the context required to resolve them, and tabulates the production choice function (C2). If the grammar is not acceptable and iteration has been requested, ANALYZER attempts a simple scheme to repair the trouble. Finally, the tables in the format required by the parsing algorithm of SKELETON may be listed or punched or both.

Exercise 7.1.1

Study each of the grammars $P_1, \ldots, P_{14}$ given in Chapters 2, 4, and 5. Attempt to determine, using insight, ingenuity, and hints contained in the text, which of these grammars are MSP of degree (2, 1; 1, 1). Are there any of lower degree? Check your answers using ANALYZER.

Exercise 7.1.2

Give an argument to show that your grammar of Exercise 2.3.7 is not MSP of degree (2, 1; 1, 1). Where does the problem occur? Use ANALYZER to verify your conclusions.

Exercise 7.1.3

If you have access to table-building or analysis programs for other canonical parsing algorithms [Feldman and Gries 68], compare your results of Exercise 7.1.1 for MSP with the results for the same grammars using the other algorithms.

7.2 Debugging a Grammar

Ideally, an automated syntax analyzer would prepare correct parsing decision tables for every grammar proposed by a user. Experience has shown, however, that people do not often write good grammars. For one thing, they usually start out ambiguously (even the ALGOL 60 Committee created an ambiguous grammar); after the ambiguities have been removed, other changes may be necessary to make the grammar compatible with the specific parsing algorithm, and still others to permit easy association of the canonical parse with the synthesis algorithm.

We call the preparation of a grammar *BNF programming*, and the process of modifying it until acceptable, *BNF debugging*. In normal practice, ANALYZER is used principally for debugging purposes, with only the last run for a particular grammar producing acceptable tables. Consequently, much of ANALYZER is devoted to the production of rather complete diagnostic messages for the various error conditions.

Facility in debugging grammars is a skill acquired principally through practice. Just as there is no sure fire method to debug all programs, no method guarantees to debug all grammars. (If such methods existed, we could build them into ANALYZER and save the user the trouble.) However, the MSP parsing algorithm was designed for compatibility with a large class of grammars. We suggest that the beginner practice on a few simple grammars before attempting anything complex. Alternatively, he can try simple modifications to a debugged grammar (such as for XPL) rather than create an entirely new one.

In Chapter 3 we gave example grammars for some common constructs (expressions, assignments, conditional statements). Chapter 4 contained various examples of grammars acceptable to the MSP algorithm. The balance of this section is devoted to examples illustrating various problems that may be encountered in the debugging process.

Problem Grammar

1	⟨expression⟩	::=	⟨term⟩
2		|	⟨identifier⟩ := ⟨expression⟩
3		|	⟨expression⟩ + ⟨term⟩

The Symptom

*** Error, grammar is ambiguous.
It is left and right recursive in the symbol ⟨expression⟩

The Problem

Some sentences (programs) have more than one phrase-structure tree. For example, we can construct two trees for ⟨identifier⟩ := ⟨term⟩ + ⟨term⟩ as is shown in Fig. 7.2.1.

The Solution

Determine which of the phrase structures is appropriate (e.g., the first in Fig. 7.2.1) and add a new nonterminal to separate the recursions.

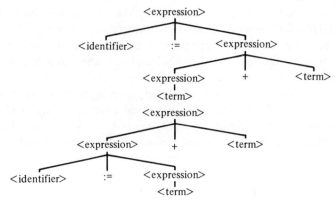

Fig. 7.2.1

Revised Grammar

1   ⟨expression⟩   ::=   ⟨sum⟩
2 | ⟨identifier⟩   :=   ⟨expression⟩
3   ⟨sum⟩   ::=   ⟨term⟩
4 | ⟨sum⟩   +   ⟨term⟩

This grammar is MSP of degree (1, 1; 0, 0).

Problem Grammar

1   ⟨statement⟩   ::=   ⟨assignment⟩
2 | ⟨if clause⟩ **then** ⟨statement⟩
3 | ⟨if clause⟩ **then** ⟨statement⟩ **else** ⟨statement⟩

The Symptom

*** Error, stacking decision cannot be made with (2, 1) context:

1   # for   **then** ⟨statement⟩ **else**

The triple   **then** ⟨statement⟩ **else**   must have the value N for
2   ⟨statement⟩   ::=   ⟨if clause⟩ **then** ⟨statement⟩
        in the context **then** . . . **else**
        in the context **else** . . . **else**

The triple   **then** ⟨statement⟩ **else**   must have the value Y for
3   ⟨statement⟩   ::=   ⟨if clause⟩ **then** ⟨statement⟩ **else** ⟨statement⟩
        in the context ⊥ . . . ⊥
        in the context **then** . . . ⊥
        in the context **then** . . . **else**
        in the context **else** . . . ⊥
        in the context **else** . . . **else**

The Problem

Again, there is an ambiguity. The reader should find the two phrase-structure trees for

$$\langle\text{if clause}\rangle \ \textbf{then} \ \langle\text{if clause}\rangle \ \textbf{then} \ \langle\text{assignment}\rangle \ \textbf{else} \ \langle\text{assignment}\rangle$$

This is the classical "dangling **else**" problem which arises when some, but not all, of the ⟨if clause⟩s have matching **else**s. Thus, it is impossible to decide whether the inner ⟨if clause⟩ **then** ⟨statement⟩ should be reduced before stacking **else**.

The Solution

There are many ways to remove the ambiguity. One way would be to require every **if-then** to have a matching **else**. Another (used in XPL) is to prohibit a conditional statement as the first statement of a conditional statement (see Section 6.10). A third, which we illustrate here, is to always associate the **else** with the closest unmatched **if-then**.

Revised Grammar

```
1       ⟨statement⟩   ::=   ⟨balanced statement⟩
2                      |    ⟨unbalanced statement⟩
3       ⟨balanced statement⟩   ::=   ⟨assignment⟩
4              |   ⟨if clause⟩ then ⟨balanced statement⟩ else ⟨balanced statement⟩
5       ⟨unbalanced statement⟩   ::=   ⟨if clause⟩ then ⟨statement⟩
6              |   ⟨if clause⟩ then ⟨balanced statement⟩ else ⟨unbalanced statement⟩
```

New Symptom

In each case the grammar is now MSP of degree $(2, 1; 0, 0)$. With the recognition of the ⟨if clause⟩ we associate the synthesis and emission of a conditional branch to the second statement (the false case). However, we find that the compiler emits code for the entire second statement of an **if-then-else** before recognizing the **if-then-else** construct, hence before the code to branch around the second statement can be emitted (see Section 3.4).

The Problem

A necessary semantic action (emitting the branch) does not correspond to any production of the grammar.

The Solution

Add a production to the grammar

$$\langle\text{true part}\rangle \ ::= \ \langle\text{balanced statement}\rangle$$

By the nature of the canonical parse, ⟨true part⟩ will be recognized before **else** is stacked (thus before any code is compiled for the second statement) but after all the code for the first statement has been compiled.

Revised Grammar

```
1        ⟨statement⟩  ::=  ⟨balanced statement⟩
2                     |  ⟨unbalanced statement⟩
3        ⟨balanced statement⟩  ::=  ⟨assignment⟩
4                     |  ⟨if clause⟩ then ⟨true part⟩ else ⟨balanced statement⟩
5        ⟨unbalanced statement⟩  ::=  ⟨if clause⟩ then ⟨statement⟩
6                     |  ⟨if clause⟩ then ⟨true part⟩ else ⟨unbalanced statement⟩
7        ⟨true part⟩  ::=  ⟨balanced statement⟩
```

This grammar is acceptable to both the parsing and the synthesis algorithms.

Problem Grammar

```
1        ⟨statement⟩  ::=  ⟨basic statement⟩
2                     |  ⟨if statement⟩
3                     |  ⟨identifier⟩ : ⟨statement⟩
```

The Symptom

The synthesis algorithm must enter an address corresponding to the code for the start of the statement into the symbol table for the label. However, the reduction involving the label is not accomplished until after the statement has been compiled.

The Problem

The canonical parse results in an unacceptable ordering of actions.

The Solution

Add a new production

$$⟨label definition⟩ ::= ⟨identifier⟩ :$$

which will be performed before the statement is processed.

Revised Grammar

```
1        ⟨statement⟩  ::=  ⟨basic statement⟩
2                     |  ⟨if statement⟩
3                     |  ⟨label definition⟩ ⟨statement⟩
4        ⟨label definition⟩  ::=  ⟨identifier⟩ :
```

Exercise 7.2.1

Prepare and test (use ANALYZER) a grammar for labeled conditional statements; consider both the problems of parsing and of code generation. Remember to allow the conditional statement, or the contained statement(s), to be labeled.

Exercise 7.2.2

Prepare and test a grammar for PL/I arithmetic expressions with the following order of precedence for operators.

$+ -$	Unary operators
$**$	Exponentiation
$* /$	Multiplication and division
$+ -$	Addition and subtraction

Remember that operations with equal precedence are performed left to right, except for exponentiation, which is right to left. Allow parentheses.

Exercise 7.2.3

Extend your grammar of Exercise 7.2.2 by adding logical expressions with the relational operators $<$, $=$, and $>$ and the logical operators with the following precedence

$\neg$	Logical negation
$\&$	Logical and
$\|$	Logical or

Use ANALYZER to debug your grammar.

Exercise 7.2.4

Assignments in PL/I take the form of a list of variables separated by commas followed by = and a logical or arithmetic expression. Extend your grammar of Exercise 7.2.3 to assignment statements. Use ANALYZER to debug. Using different terminal symbols for replacement and equality is not considered a solution.

Exercise 7.2.5

Combine your grammars for Exercises 7.2.1 and 7.2.4 to obtain a grammar for conditional assignment statements. Debug.

Problem Grammar

```
1      ⟨procedure statement⟩  ::=  ⟨procedure declaration⟩
2                             |  ⟨procedure call⟩
3      ⟨procedure declaration⟩ ::= ⟨procedure name⟩ ( ⟨formal parameter list⟩ )
4      ⟨formal parameter list⟩ ::=  ⟨identifier⟩
5                             |  ⟨formal parameter list⟩ , ⟨identifier⟩
6      ⟨procedure call⟩  ::=  call ⟨procedure name⟩ ( ⟨actual parameter list⟩ )
7      ⟨actual parameter list⟩  ::=  ⟨expression⟩
8                             |  ⟨actual parameter list⟩ , ⟨expression⟩
```

9        $\langle$expression$\rangle$ ::= $\langle$term$\rangle$
10 | $\langle$expression$\rangle$ + $\langle$term$\rangle$
11       $\langle$term$\rangle$ ::= $\langle$primary$\rangle$
12 | $\langle$term$\rangle$ * $\langle$primary$\rangle$
13       $\langle$primary$\rangle$ ::= $\langle$identifier$\rangle$
14 | ($\langle$expression$\rangle$)
15 | $\langle$procedure name$\rangle$ ($\langle$actual parameter list$\rangle$)
16       $\langle$procedure name$\rangle$ ::= $\langle$identifier$\rangle$

The Symptoms

***   Error, stacking decision cannot be made with (2, 1) context:

1   # for ($\langle$expression$\rangle$)

The triple ($\langle$expression$\rangle$) must have the value N for

7        $\langle$actual parameter list$\rangle$ ::= $\langle$expression$\rangle$
         in the context (. . .)

The triple ($\langle$expression$\rangle$) must have the value Y for

14       $\langle$primary$\rangle$ ::= ($\langle$expression$\rangle$)
         in the context   (. . .)
         in the context   (. . . ,
         in the context   (. . . +
         in the context   (. . . *
         in the context   , . . .)
         in the context   , . . . ,
         in the context   , . . . +
         in the context   , . . . *
         in the context   + . . .)
         in the context   + . . . ,
         in the context   + . . . +
         in the context   + . . . *
         in the context   * . . .)
         in the context   * . . . ,
         in the context   * . . . +
         in the context   * . . . *

There are 2 and 16 valid contexts, respectively, for

5        $\langle$formal parameter list$\rangle$ ::= $\langle$formal parameter list$\rangle$, $\langle$identifier$\rangle$
13       $\langle$primary$\rangle$ ::= $\langle$identifier$\rangle$

***   Error, these productions cannot be distinguished with (1, 1) context,

$\langle$primary$\rangle$ has , . . .) as context and) is valid right context for $\langle$formal parameter list$\rangle$
$\langle$primary$\rangle$ has , . . . , as context and , is valid right context for $\langle$formal parameter list$\rangle$

There are 2 and 16 valid contexts, respectively, for

4        $\langle$formal parameter list$\rangle$ ::= $\langle$identifier$\rangle$
13       $\langle$primary$\rangle$ ::= $\langle$identifier$\rangle$

*** Error, these productions cannot be distinguished with (1, 1) context.
They have equal right parts and the common context (...)
They have equal right parts and the common context (... ,

The Problems

Although the grammar is unambiguous, it is locally ambiguous, i.e., more than
(2, 1; 1, 1) context is needed to make decisions. There are two sources of this difficulty:

1. Multiple-use terminals. Commas are used to separate elements of both
   ⟨formal parameter list⟩ and ⟨actual parameter list⟩. Left parentheses are used as
   delimiters in three different productions. Consequently, these symbols are inadequate
   context for decision making.
2. Multiple-use nonterminals. When ⟨procedure name⟩ occurs as the first element of
   a sentence, it must be followed by

                            (⟨formal parameter list⟩)

   otherwise by

                            (⟨actual parameter list⟩)

   Thus, we must look beyond it in the stack to determine context.

A Solution

Modify the grammar using different symbols in the different contexts. Add productions so the new symbols produce the old.

Revised Grammar

```
1      ⟨procedure statement⟩  ::=  ⟨procedure declaration⟩
2                             |    ⟨procedure call⟩
3      ⟨procedure declaration⟩  ::=  ⟨declared name⟩ ( ⟨formal parameter list⟩ )
4      ⟨formal parameter list⟩   ::=  ⟨identifier⟩
5                             |    ⟨formal parameter list⟩ , ⟨identifier⟩
6      ⟨procedure call⟩  ::=  call ⟨procedure name⟩⟨(1⟩⟨actual parameter list⟩ )
7      ⟨actual parameter list⟩  ::=  ⟨expression⟩
8                             |    ⟨actual parameter list⟩ ⟨,1⟩ ⟨expression⟩
9      ⟨expression⟩  ::=  ⟨term⟩
10                    |    ⟨expression⟩ + ⟨term⟩
11     ⟨term⟩  ::=  ⟨primary⟩
12            |    ⟨term⟩ * ⟨primary⟩
13     ⟨primary⟩  ::=  ⟨identifier⟩
14               |    ⟨(2⟩ ⟨expression⟩ )
15               |    ⟨procedure name⟩ ⟨(1⟩ ⟨actual parameter list⟩ )
16     ⟨procedure name⟩  ::=  ⟨identifier⟩
17     ⟨declared name⟩  ::=  ⟨identifier⟩
18     ⟨(1⟩  ::=  (
19     ⟨,1⟩  ::=  ,
20     ⟨(2⟩  ::=  (
```

We must first assure that the modifications to the grammar did not affect the structure of sentences in any essential way. This is obvious, however, since only single symbols were changed, leaving the form of all original productions unchanged. We need only totally ignore the added productions (18, 19, 20) as far as generation is concerned. Secondly, we would like some assurance that the change is helpful. We are attempting to make accessible the state of the parse stack below the two directly accessible symbols ((2, 1) context) by letting the bottom one have two different forms ($\langle\langle 1 \rangle$ and $\langle 2 \rangle$) depending on the next symbol down (effectively (3, 1) context).

Second Solution

Use the $I feature of ANALYZER to create new nonterminals to remove the conflicts. The success of insertion of dummy productions [Wirth 66a] as a general means to increase effective local context has been sufficient to justify the provision, in ANALYZER, of an algorithm to accomplish these insertions where necessary. It is sometimes wholly successful, sometimes only indicative of the changes that the BNF programmer can try.

A Third Solution

Restructure the grammar so the multiple-use symbols occur as tails of productions. Refer to the XPL grammar (Chapter 6) for extensive use of this device.

Exercise 7.2.6

Use the $I feature of ANALYZER to remove the conflicts from the first grammar for $\langle$procedure statement$\rangle$ given in this section. Compare the number of changes required with those required by the text solution.

Exercise 7.2.7

Can the $I feature of ANALYZER remove the conflicts for either of the first two grammars ($\langle$expression$\rangle$ and $\langle$statement$\rangle$) in this section? Use ANALYZER to verify your answer.

Exercise 7.2.8

Why are multiple-use symbols not a problem if they occur only as the last symbol of a right part?

Exercise 7.2.9

The grammar in Section 6.2 can be considerably improved by matching bracketing characters in a single production, e.g. $\langle$variable$\rangle$ ::= $\langle$identifier$\rangle$ ($\langle$expression list$\rangle$). Make an improved grammar for XPL and check your result, using ANALYZER.

Chapter 8

XCOM

A Self-Compiling Compiler

/* Be it ever so humble, there is no place like home. */

JOHN HOWARD PAYNE

"Home, Sweet Home"

8.1 Describing XCOM

/* You find sometimes that a Thing which seemed very Thingish inside you is quite different when it gets into the open and has other people looking at it. */

A. A. MILNE

Winnie-the-Pooh[†]

There are many ways to describe (document) a program, each with a different viewpoint, each contributing a different kind of understanding. In one sense, this entire book is documentation for XCOM: In Part I we have given the theory upon which its algorithms are based; in Chapter 6 we describe the form and meaning of its source language (XPL); in Appendix 3 we give a listing of the complete program with comments, etc. However, it is this chapter and the next which constitute the specific XCOM reference manual.

We separate our discussions of synthesis and analysis as we did in Part I. The SKELETON proto-compiler, the subject of Chapter 9, can be used essentially unchanged as the basis for any compiler written with our system. XCOM itself contains SKELETON, but in this chapter we focus on the form which synthesis algorithms take for the particular source language XPL and for the particular object language of the System/360. Our purpose is to equip the reader either (1) to change the present version of XCOM or to modify the language XPL to better suit his needs or (2) to duplicate our efforts by producing a similar compiler for another machine. To this

---

† From the book *Winnie-the-Pooh* by A. A. Milne. Copyright, 1926, by E. P. Dutton & Co., Inc. Renewal, 1954, by A. A. Milne. Reprinted by permission of the publishers.

end, we will describe XCOM in terms of its procedural structure, its data structures, the form of object programs, the operation of important procedures, and its method of creation (the bootstrap process).

8.2 Reading XCOM

XCOM is a large XPL program consisting of a set of declarations followed by a sequence of procedures. At the very end occur the only two directly executable statements in the compiler (see Table 8.2.1).

TABLE 8.2.1 The Over-all Structure of the Compiler XCOM

Declarations · · ·
Procedures · · ·
call *MAIN__PROCEDURE;* **return** *severe__errors;*

The call of *MAIN__PROCEDURE* accomplishes the entire process of compilation. Upon return from the procedure, the global variable *severe__errors* contains the count of fatal errors discovered in the source program during compilation. The value returned from the program itself goes to the XCOM submonitor which then returns it to the operating system (see Section A.1.2). Appropriate control cards may use this value to conditionally inhibit the execution of following job steps. In particular, the execution of the program just compiled can be made contingent on the absence of severe errors.

The declarations in the compiler are arranged in functional groupings corresponding to the major actions of the compiler. The first grouping, always changed as a unit by virtue of its being produced by the program ANALYZER, is the set of syntactic recognition tables controlling the actions of the procedure *COMPILATION__LOOP* and its associates. Immediately following are the variables and tables needed by the procedure *SCAN* both for the scanning algorithm and to print the compilation listing. A number of these variables are given their values within the procedure *INITIALIZATION* to simplify the process of changing the compiler. The next major group of declarations sets aside storage for the binary program-image file buffers. Following this group, we find variables related to the emitters, then the symbol tables, and finally the stacks used by the analysis and synthesis algorithms.

The procedures are also arranged in functional groupings, whose order is determined by the requirement that procedures be defined before they are called. The groupings are: two formatting procedures, the error procedure, the file handling procedures, the scanning procedures, the emitting procedures, the symbol table procedures, procedures to emit branching code, expression compiling procedures, the built-in function emitters, the time-and-date procedures, initialization, the symbol table and statistics printing procedures, the synthesis algorithm, the analysis algorithm, the loader which collects the binary image onto a single file, and the final print control. Finally comes *MAIN_PROCEDURE*, which eventually causes all of the above to be invoked.

Exercise 8.2.1

Implement a version of XCOM using the tables produced as a result of Exercise 7.2.9.

8.3 The Procedures

The actions of the compiler are accomplished by procedures. *MAIN_PROCEDURE*, called from the main program, calls other procedures, which in turn call still other procedures to a considerable depth. The relations among the major procedures in the compiler are depicted in Fig. 8.3.1. Each procedure calls the ones above it in the tree. As indicated in Chapter 3, the great majority of procedures lie within the group labeled code emitters and are called principally from *SYNTHESIZE*.

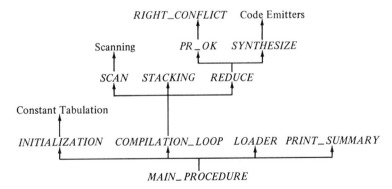

Fig. 8.3.1   Relations among Major Procedures in XCOM

An alphabetic list of all procedures in XCOM is given in Table 8.3.1. Some of the more important procedures are discussed more thoroughly in later sections.

TABLE 8.3.1

Procedure Name	Called from	Action
ALLOCATE	*TDECLARE*	Set aside storage for variables in the data and descriptor areas according to the declaration currently being processed.
ARITHEMIT	*DIVIDE_CODE* *SYNTHESIZE*	Emit code for arithmetic infix operators: **mod.** $*$, $/$, $+$, $-$, $<$, $<=$, $=$, $\neg=$, $>=$, $>$, $|$, &. See Sec. 8.10 for more details.
BCHAR	*SCAN*	Get next digit within a bit string. Adjust the field width as necessary.
BOOLBRANCH	*SYNTHESIZE* (⟨if clause⟩ and ⟨while clause⟩ productions)	Emit the conditional forward branch of the ⟨if clause⟩ and **do while** group. If the condition code has been converted to a logical 32-bit value, the instruction pointer *pp* is reset(i.e., the emitted code is retracted,) and the condition code used directly.
BRANCH	*BOOLBRANCH, CATENATE_CODE CHECK_STRING_OVERFLOW CONDTOREG, CONVERT_CODE PROC_START RELOCATE_DESCRIPTORS_CODE STRINGCOMPARE, SYNTHESIZE*	Call *BRANCH_BD* to emit branch instructions. If the destination is unknown, assume a branch to the current program location to simplify the fix-up mechanism except where the boundary between first and subsequent pages is crossed.
BRANCH_BD	*BRANCH SYNTHESIZE* (⟨go to statement⟩ ::= ⟨go to⟩ ⟨identifier⟩)	Emit a branch instruction. If the destination is beyond the first 4096 bytes of program, we must precede the branch by loading the branch register with a page address.
BRLINK_BD	*CALLSUB*	Emit a branch-and-link instruction. If the destination is beyond the first 4096 bytes of program, we must load the branch register with a page address before branching.

BUILD_BCD	*SCAN*	Insert the appropriate 8-bit pattern into a long bit string. The use of catenate will cause at least one new character to be allocated in the free string area ; the built-in array *corebyte* is used to deposit the new character.
CALLSUB	*CHECK_STRING_OVERFLOW* *FORCEACCUMULATOR* *FORCEDESCRIPT* *SYNTHESIZE* (⟨string expression⟩ ::= ⟨string expression⟩ || ⟨arithmetic expression⟩)	Emit code to call a previously declared procedure or function.
CALLSUB_FORWARD	*CHECK_STRING_OVERFLOW* *FORCEACCUMULATOR*	Emit code to call a procedure that has not yet appeared. The attribute **label** must have been used in a declaration to trigger this mechanism.
CATENATE_CODE	*INITIALIZATION*	Catenation is accomplished via a built-in subroutine. The code for the catenate subroutine is emitted here.
CHAR	*DEBLANK* *SCAN*	Advance the scan point in *text* by one character. Get a new card if necessary.
CHECKBASES	*EMITBYTE, EMITDATAWORD* *CHECK_NEWDP* *SYNTHESIZE* (⟨declaration element⟩ ::= ⟨type declaration⟩)	Maintain System/360 addressability by allocating a new base register for the program being compiled whenever the distance from the previous register exceeds the 4096 byte addressing range of a (base, displacement) type address field.
CHECK_NEWDP	*ALLOCATE*	Both the encountering of initial values and the allocation of arrays change the pointer into the data area. *CHECK_NEWDP* uses *CHECKBASES* to assure that base registers are correctly allocated for both cases.
CHECK_STRING_OVERFLOW	*CATENATE_CODE, CONVERT_CODE* *FORCEACCUMULATOR*	Emit code to test for an exhausted free string area, and call to *compactify* if necessary.

TABLE 8.3.1 (Contd.)

Procedure Name	Called from	Action
CLEARREGS	FILE_PSEUDO_ARRAY INITIALIZATION, SYNTHESIZE	Mark all the accumulator registers as available.
compactify	built-in functions: catenate, convert, and input.	Condense the free string area.
COMPILATION_LOOP	MAIN_PROCEDURE	While the **bit** variable *compiling* is true, repeatedly stack enough symbols and their associated information provided by *SCAN* until a reducible string is formed in the parse stack. Then call for a reduction, and return to stack more symbols.
CONDTOREG	FORCEACCUMULATOR SYNTHESIZE (⟨logical secondary⟩ productions)	Emit code to convert the condition code into a 32-bit zero or one for use in further computations.
CONVERT_CODE	INITIALIZATION	Number-to-string conversion is required whenever a fixed value is used in catenation or is assigned to a string variable (e.g., *output*). The code for the built-in convert function is emitted here.
DEBLANK	BCHAR	Skip characters in *text* until the next nonblank character.
DIVIDE_CODE	SYNTHESIZE (⟨term⟩ productions)	Both / and **mod** require a peculiar register setup to give correct integer results. Emit the code for division.
DUMPIT	PRINT_SUMMARY	When the control **$D** is set on at the end of the program, the compiler tabulates the data gathered during compilation—in particular, the macro definitions, the counts of entry into important procedures, the maximum size of important tables, the settings of the data-addressing registers, and the count of instructions actually emitted.
EMITBYTE	INITIALIZATION, LOADER, SETINIT STRINGCOMPARE	After assuring that the proper record is in the buffer *data*, emit a single byte of data to the buffer.

EMITCHAR	*FORCEACCUMULATOR, SETINIT*	After assuring that the proper record is in the buffer *strings*, place a literal string character into the buffer.
EMITCODEBYTES	*EMIT_INLINE, EMITRR, EMITRX*	After assuring that the proper record is in the buffer *code*, place two bytes of instruction in the buffer.
EMITCONSTANT	*ARITHEMIT, FORCEACCUMULATOR, REGISTER_SETUP_CODE, SET_LIMIT, SYNTHESIZE*	If the value of the parameter *c* is not already in the table *ctab*, enter it; emit it to the data area; and record its address in the table *cadd*. In all cases, place the base-displacement address pair in the global variables *adreg, adrdisp*.
EMITDATAWORD	*CHECK_STRING_OVERFLOW EMITCONSTANT, FIXBFW, INITIALIZATION, LOADER, PROC_START, REGISTER_SETUP_CODE, RELOCATE_DESCRIPTORS_CODE, SAVE_REGISTERS, SETINIT, SET_LIMIT, STRINGCOMPARE, SYNTHESIZE, UNDECLARED_ID*	After assuring that the proper record is in the buffer *data* place a 32-bit quantity, word aligned, in the buffer.
EMITDESC	*FORCEACCUMULATOR, INITIALIZATION, SETINIT*	Send a 32-bit string descriptor to the table *desc*.
EMIT_INLINE	*SYNTHESIZE,* (⟨subscript head⟩ productions)	Emit in-line code. Some care is taken to ensure that the code emitted is correctly specified.
EMITRR	*ARITHEMIT, BOOLBRANCH, CATENATE_CODE, CHECK_STRING_OVERFLOW, CONVERT_CODE DIVIDE_CODE, FILE_PSEUDO_ARRAY, FORCEACCUMULATOR, FORCE_ADDRESS, GENSTORE, REGISTER_SETUP_CODE*	Pack an RR format instruction into two bytes, and place them in the code buffer.

TABLE 8.3.1 (Contd.)

Procedure Name	Called from	Action
EMITRX	*RELOCATE_DESCRIPTORS_CODE* *STRINGCOMPARE, SYNTHESIZE* *UNSAVE_REGISTERS* *ARITHEMIT, BOOLBRANCH* *BRANCH_BD, BRLINK_BD* *CALLSUB_FORWARD* *CATENATE_CODE* *CHECK_STRING_OVERFLOW* *CONDTOREG, CONVERT_CODE* *DIVIDE_CODE* *FILE_PSEUDO_ARRAY* *FORCEACCUMULATOR* *FORCE_ADDRESS* *FORCEDESCRIPT* *GENSTORE, PROC_START* *REGISTER_SETUP_CODE* *RELOCATE_DESCRIPTORS_CODE* *SAVE_REGISTERS, SET_LIMIT* *SHIFT_CODE, STRINGCOMPARE* *STUFF_PARAMETER, SYNTHESIZE* *UNSAVE_REGISTERS*	Pack an RX format instruction into four bytes, and place them in the code buffer.
ENTER	*REGISTER_SETUP_CODE* *RELOCATE_DESCRIPTORS_CODE* *SYNTHESIZE* *UNDECLARED_ID*	Given the name, type, and location of a newly encountered name, enter it in the symbol table or print an error message if it is already there. See Section 8.9 for more details.
ERROR	*ARITHEMIT, BCHAR, CHECKBASES* *COMPILATION_LOOP* *DIVIDE_CODE, EMITDESC* *EMIT_INLINE, ENTER* *FILE_PSEUDO_ARRAY* *FINDAC, FINDADDRESS*	Print mnemonic error message; count total errors and severe errors; terminate compilation in case of excessive errors.

FILE_PSEUDO_ARRAY

FORCEACCUMULATOR, GENSTORE
GET_CARD, REDUCE, SCAN, SETINIT
SHIFT_CODE, STACKING
STUFF_PARAMETER
SYNTHESIZE, UNDECLARED_ID

Generate the call to the submonitor for direct-access input or output corresponding to the appearance of *file* on either side of an assignment.

FINDAC

FORCEACCUMULATOR
GENSTORE

Return the register number of an available accumulator, and mark it busy.

FINDADDRESS

CONDTOREG
FILE_PSEUDO_ARRAY
FORCEACCUMULATOR
SYNTHESIZE, UNSAVE_REGISTERS

Set into the global variables *adrdisp* and *adreg* the displacement and base register number corresponding to the parameter *adr*. If *adr* is negative, a string descriptor address is indicated; otherwise, an address in the data area is desired.

FIXBFW

ALLOCATE, CATENATE_CODE
CHECK_STRING_OVERFLOW
CONVERT_CODE, EMITCONSTANT
ENTER, FIXBFW
FORCEACCUMULATOR
PROC_START, SAVE_REGISTERS
SET_LIMIT, STRINGCOMPARE
SYNTHESIZE

A forward branch has both instruction and destination in the first 4096 bytes of code or both beyond the first 4096 bytes or branches across the boundary. In the first case the branch command needs an address; in the second both a load and a branch need an address; in the last we must branch into the data area where we place the load and branch instructions since room was not left in the code stream.

FIXCHW

CATENATE_CODE
CHECK_STRING_OVERFLOW
CONVERT_CODE
RELOCATE_DESCRIPTORS_CODE
STRINGCOMPARE
SYNTHESIZE

When the destination of a forward reference becomes known, it is usually possible to place the correct address directly in the code buffer. When the record containing the instruction to be corrected has already been written to secondary store, the location of the instruction and

$\langle group \rangle ::= \langle group\ head \rangle\ \langle ending \rangle$

TABLE 8.3.1 (Contd.)

Procedure Name	Called from	Action
		the address field are recorded instead in the tables *fixcadr*, *fixcb1*, and *fixcb2*.
FIXWHOLEDATAWORD	*ENTER* *LOADER* *SYNTHESIZE*	Unpack a 32-bit word for the data area into four bytes. Ensure that the proper record is in the data buffer, and place the data in the buffer. There are so few fix-ups beyond the buffer area that the table method of *fixchw* is inappropriate.
FORCEACCUMULATOR	*ARITHEMIT*, *BOOLBRANCH* *DIVIDE__CODE*, *FORCEDESCRIPT* *GENSTORE*, *SET__LIMIT* *SHIFT__CODE*, *SYNTHESIZE*	Emit code to place the value of a function, variable, constant, condition code, etc., into an accumulator.
FORCEADDRESS	*FILE_PSEUDO__ARRAY* *SYNTHESIZE* (⟨variable⟩ ::= ⟨subscript head⟩ ⟨expression⟩))	Generate code to compute the address of a variable, subscripted variable, label, or procedure entry, and place it in an accumulator.
FORCEDESCRIPT	*GENSTORE* *STRINGCOMPARE* *SYNTHESIZE*	Emit code to force a value into an accumulator. If it is not a string descriptor, emit code to convert it to a string; place it in the string area, and make up a descriptor pointing to it.
GENSTORE	*SYNTHESIZE* (⟨assignment⟩ productions)	Emit all code for assignments, including those to the *file* pseudovariable.
GET__CARD	*CHAR* *SCAN*	Read source cards from files *input*(2) and *input* into the global character variable *text*. Take care not to read past an end-of-file. List the source program under control of $L.
GETCODE	*EMITCODEBYTES*	Action as in *GETDATA* for the code buffer *code*.
GETDATA	*EMITBYTE*, *EMITDATAWORD* *FIXWHOLEDATAWORD*	Oversees the usage of the data-area buffer *data* by ensuring that the appropriate record is in the buffer and by keeping other records on direct-access storage.

Procedure	Called by	Description
GETSTRINGS	*EMITCHAR*	Action as in *GETDATA* for the string data buffer *strings*.
ID_LOOKUP	*SYNTHESIZE*	Look up a symbol expected to be in the symbol table, and place information about the symbol in the parse stacks. Returns the value -1 if the symbol is not found.
I_FORMAT	*ERROR, GET_CARD*	Right justify an integer in the field width specified.
INITIALIZATION	*MAIN_PROCEDURE*	This procedure accomplishes many tasks requiring initial values, storage, and the like. See Section 8.7 for more details.
INSERT_CODE_FIXUPS	*FIXCHW* *LOADER*	When the tables *fixcadr*, *fixcb1*, and *fixcb2* overflow the limit *fclim*, this procedure sorts the table by increasing location of the instruction to be corrected and then makes a single pass over the code file to insert the addresses.
LOADER	*MAIN_PROCEDURE*	Collate the three binary files (code, data, and strings) onto a single file, and place appropriate control information in the first 60 bytes of the code block.
MAIN_PROCEDURE	main program	Call the four main phases of compilation, and collect timing information.
MOVESTACKS	*ARITHEMIT, GENSTORE* *SYNTHESIZE*	Move the values in the synthesis stacks down to keep the information aligned with the canonical parse.
OUTLINE	*SYMBOLDUMP*	Responsible for correctly formatting a line during the symbol-table dump.
PAD	*DUMPIT, GET_CARD, OUTLINE*	Add blanks to the right of a string to give it the field width specified.
PRINT_DATE_AND_TIME	*INITIALIZATION* *PRINT_SUMMARY*	The parameter d contains the day of the year plus the number of years since 1900 times 1000. This procedure

TABLE 8.3.1 (Contd.)

Procedure Name	Called from	Action
PRINT_SUMMARY	MAIN_PROCEDURE	decodes it into year, month, and day and then calls PRINT_TIME to print the dated message. Print at the end of compilation all information gathered during execution.
PRINT_TIME	PRINT_DATE_AND_TIME PRINT_SUMMARY	The parameter t contains time in hundredths of seconds. This procedure decodes it into hour, minutes, and seconds and prints it together with the parameter message.
PROC_START	SYNTHESIZE	Emit the prologue for the body of a procedure. First we need a branch around the procedure body then a place and an instruction to save the return address.
PR_OK	REDUCE	When there is more than one reducible string on the parse stack, PR_OK uses the syntactic analysis tables to choose the proper reduction.
RECOVER	REDUCE STACKING	This procedure removes enough of the parse stack and input text to ensure that compilation can proceed at least one more step without further errors. In many cases this procedure prevents single errors from causing multiple messages.
REDUCE	COMPILATION_LOOP	Look up the proper reduction; call SYNTHESIZE to produce the associated code, and then make the reduction.
REGISTER_SETUP_CODE	INITIALIZATION	Emit the very first executable code in the object program which must set the environment for the program. The submonitor passes the correct values for the program-base register and data-base register in registers R2 and R3, respectively, the return to the monitor in register R12. The top of memory, passed in R1, less 256, is stored in freelimit, and R4 thru R10 are loaded from their table, increased by the data base register.

RELOCATE_DESCRIPTORS_CODE
INITIALIZATION

The string descriptors resident in the area addressable via R13, etc., must contain absolute addresses. The code to compute and store these addresses is emitted here.

RIGHT_CONFLICT
PR_OK
RECOVER

The most recently scanned symbol is in *token*. In some cases it is possible to decide whether a string in the parse stack is reducible on the basis that the result of reduction must yield an allowed pair between the top of the stack and *token*. Similarly, when an error is encountered, analysis is not resumed until an allowed pair is in *token* and on the top of the parse stack.

SAVE_REGISTERS
CALLSUB
CALLSUB_FORWARD

Generate the code to save the busy registers before a function call.

SCAN
COMPILATION_LOOP
INITIALIZATION
RECOVER

An XPL program consists of a sequence of symbols from the vocabulary v interspersed with blanks and comments. Each call to *SCAN* produces the next symbol and some associated information. See Sections 8.8 and 9.3 for further details.

SETINIT
SYNTHESIZE

Place initial values into data, descriptor, and string areas.

SET_LIMIT
SYNTHESIZE
(⟨iteration control⟩ productions)

The upper bound of a **do** loop is evaluated once at entry to the loop. Emit code to store it in memory so that it cannot be changed from within the loop.

SHIFT_CODE
SYNTHESIZE
(⟨variable⟩ ::= ⟨subscript head⟩
⟨expression⟩))

Emit code for the built-in functions *shr* and *shl*. Single instructions with appropriate index value and displacement are generated. A shift left of one gives a special case add register command for code density and speed.

SHOULDCOMMUTE
ARITHEMIT

For the operators +, |, and &, it does not matter which operand is in the accumulator. If it will save an instruction, we commute the operands.

TABLE 8.3.1 (Contd.)

Procedure Name	Called from	Action
STACK_DUMP	*REDUCE, STACKING* *SYNTHESIZE* (⟨program⟩ ::= ⟨statement list⟩)	When syntactic errors are discovered by the analysis algorithm, the state of the parse stack is printed as a diagnostic aid.
STACKING	*COMPILATION_LOOP*	This is the basic decision function of the analysis algorithm. When the function is true, a symbol is stacked; when it is false, a reduction is made. If an error is detected, a recovery is initiated, and a new value is computed.
STRINGCOMPARE	*ARITHEMIT*	Emit code to compare two strings. The first test is on length, and only if they are of equal length is a further test of the actual characters called for.
STUFF_PARAMETER	*SYNTHESIZE* (⟨subscript head⟩ productions)	During a procedure call, emit the appropriate instruction to store a parameter in the byte half word, or whole word reserved for it.
SYMBOLDUMP	*PRINT_SUMMARY* *SYNTHESIZE*	When the control $S is set on at the end of a procedure or $D is set on at the end of the program, this procedure sorts and prints in alphabetic order the name, the declared type, the memory location, the line where it was declared, and the number of times referenced for each entry local to the most recently closed scope.
SYNTHESIZE	*REDUCE*	Corresponding to each production recognized by *REDUCE*, this procedure calls the appropriate generators to produce code and data images of the program being compiled. See Section 8.10 for more details.
TDECLARE	*SYNTHESIZE*	Allocate storage for each identifier in a factored attribute list.
UNDECLARED_ID	*SYNTHESIZE*	Print an error message for the undeclared identifier, and enter it in the symbol table.
UNSAVE_REGISTERS	*CALLSUB* *CALLSUB_FORWARD*	Generate code to restore registers saved before function or procedure call.

8.4 Resource Allocation

One of the principal characteristics of any compiler is the strategy which it uses in the allocation of machine resources (e.g., registers and memory) for its object programs. The general aim in XCOM is to produce efficient object code by performing all allocations at compile time (the exception being the dynamic allocation of string space). Thus, the memory required for data storage and the registers required for data addressing are determined during compilation and remain fixed during program execution. In this section we discuss the allocations XCOM makes for any XPL program. Since XCOM is itself an XPL program, we will use it as the source of particular figures for our examples.

The IBM System/360 has 16 general-purpose registers serving various purposes: They establish memory addressability (base registers), permit indexing (index registers), are used for integer arithmetic and logical operations (accumulators), and hold the return address on subroutine entry (link registers). Each program must apportion the registers among these functions; the assignment made by XCOM for XPL object programs is shown in Table 8.4.1.

TABLE 8.4.1 XCOM Register Assignments

Register	Use
R15	Submonitor base
R14	Program base
R13	String descriptor base
R12	Branch and link
R11 through R4	Data bases
R3 through R1	Accumulators and indices
R0	Scratch register

The available memory is divided into two parts, one for program code and one for data, as shown in Table 8.4.2. The program code area is further subdivided into the three areas listed in Table 8.4.3. The first is the assembled submonitor (see Appendix 1); the second is the assembled trace routine (see Appendix 2); and the last is the compiled image of the XPL program. Register R14 points at the beginning of the compiled code for the XPL program and serves as a base for all branches within this area.

TABLE 8.4.2 XCOM Memory Map

	XCOM Size in Bytes
Program Data	38000
Program Code	62000

TABLE 8.4.3   XCOM Code Area

Register		XCOM Size in Bytes
	Code for XPL Program	54000
R14 →		
	Trace	4000
R15 →	Submonitor	4000

When the destination is more than 4096 bytes from the address in R14, the branch is preceded by a load of an appropriate multiple of 4096 into R12 giving an effective address of R14 + R12 + displacement.

Table 8.4.4 shows the further structure of the compiled image of an XPL program.

TABLE 8.4.4   Structure of XCOM Object Program

		XCOM Size in Bytes
	Code Corresponding to Listed XPL Program	53000
	compactify	800
	Built-in Functions	400
R14 →	Load Control Block	60

The load control block contains information on the program size to be used by the submonitor during program load. See the comment in *LOADER* for details. See also *INITIALIZATION* where the size is set ($pp = 60$).

The data area, shown in Table 8.4.5, is also divided into three regions. The first is the storage area assigned to all variables except those addressed via descriptors (**character** and long **bit** strings). Next comes the area assigned to descriptors, and, finally, the string data pointed to by the descriptors. All variables are directly addressable (i.e., need no base register load before access) because registers R11 through R4 are allocated at compile time to point into the data area. R11 points at the start of the area, R10 at the first variable not addressable via R11, etc. Since only the zeroth element of an array need be directly addressable (the subscript is an incremental index in R1 ... R3), the registers are spaced apart somewhat more than 4096 on the average. Since R13 alone is allocated for descriptor-addressing, an upper limit of 1024 on the

TABLE 8.4.5 XCOM Data Area

Register		XCOM Size in Bytes
	String Data	6000
	Descriptors	4000
R13 →		
R4 →		
⋮	Variables	42000
R11 →		

number of descriptors is implied. Each descriptor contains a 24-bit address field and an 8-bit field containing the length of the string minus one. Length minus one rather than length is used owing to the peculiar nature of the System/360 character-manipulation instructions. For a null string, the descriptor is a full word with the value zero. All descriptor-address fields for constant strings are computed at program load time (the code is emitted by *RELOCATE_DESCRIPTORS_CODE*). All such addresses are absolute and hence require no further base register allocations.

The data areas also have further structure. The variable area starts with a series of constants and system variables as shown in Table 8.4.6. Within the string data area, the strings generated at compile time form the bottom section. The remainder of the string area is used for accumulated results and is sequentially filled during execution as described in Section 8.5.

In the normal course of events, generated code is assigned to the program code area via the *EMITRR* and the *EMITRX* procedures synchronously with the processing of executable XPL statements (i.e., all except **declare**). Since XCOM cannot, of course, contain an area large enough to contain all compiled programs, a buffer (*code*) is filled, written to file storage, then filled again, etc. Occasionally, there is insufficient information to completely specify the code in the buffer before it is sent to the file (e.g., the address of a forward branch); thus we require a means for the file to be accessed, updated, and rewritten (see *INSERT_CODE_FIXUPS*).

The assignment of portions of the three major data areas is done via three separate buffer areas: *data* for integer variables and constants, *strings* for the string data, and *descriptors* for the string descriptors. Variables and string data are written to the file much as is program code, but the descriptors are simply kept in main memory throughout compilation (see Exercise 8.5.1). Of the many constructs in XPL which cause the assignment of data areas the principal one is the declaration. Simple (unsubscripted) variables are assigned locations as they are encountered in a declaration (or during recovery from an undeclared variable). The amount of storage assigned depends upon the type attribute as shown in Table 8.4.7. Initial values for short bit string and fixed variables are placed directly in the assigned location; initial values for long bit and character strings are placed in the string data area, and a pointer is placed in the assigned word in the descriptor area.

Arrays are allocated similarly with the appropriate multiple of the above amounts

TABLE 8.4.6 Bottom of the Variable Area

Register   Size in Bytes

Global return address	4
"1000000"	4
"FFFFFFFF"	4
"1"	4
Parameter to convert	4
Number of descriptors	4
Date of generation	4
Time of generation	4
Top of string area	4
MVC instruction	8
Register save	12
"FF000000"	4
Monitor link area	16
Multiples of 4096	104

R11 →

TABLE 8.4.7 XCOM Primary Storage Assignment

Type	Storage Assigned	Area
bit(1) ... **bit**(8)	Byte	Variable
bit(9) ... **bit**(16)	Half word	Variable
bit(17) ... **bit**(32), **fixed**	Word	Variable
bit(33) ...., **character**	Word	Descriptor

of storage. If necessary, each unique constant is also assigned an appropriate memory location.

Exercise   8.4.1

An alternative organization for XCOM register allocation sets registers to the base of the local variables of each procedure and to the code for each procedure when the procedure is called. The cost is in overhead on procedure calls and in some base register loads for data beyond the scope automatically provided above. The gain is in eliminating the load before the majority of branches in XCOM. Evaluate this alternative both in program size and in execution speed.

Exercise 8.4.2

A slight additional modification to the above organization would put all local variables in a stack. Although facilitating recursion, the result complicates **initial** for variables local to procedures and makes the addressing of variables local to one procedure from another nested within it more difficult.

Describe such an organization completely enough (see Chapter 3) so that your reader could implement it from your description. Analyze the proposed organization for potential trouble spots (e.g., limits on program or data area, limits on the number of registers, effect on *compactify*'s location of valid descriptors, the meaning of **go to**, etc.).

Exercise 8.4.3 (Term Project)

Implement a version of XCOM according to the specifications of Exercise 8.4.2.

8.5 String Operations

As noted in Chapters 1 and 6, we designed our compilation methods and the language XPL for efficient implementation on existing machines, such as the System/360, which in general implies static resource allocation. However, throughout the compilation process—in scanning, in building the symbol tables, in producing the output listings, and in creating the error messages—convenient means for text manipulation are required. XPL satisfies this requirement with the catenation and substring operations on **character** strings of varying length. XCOM implements dynamic allocation of storage for strings which are accessed by means of descriptors.

String assignment and substring selection are both compiled into operations on string descriptors and involve no change in the string data area itself. On the other hand, the operations of catenation, input, and number-to-string conversion not only change the data area but also use previously free space. Free space is allocated linearly as required by the running program. The variable *freepoint* contains the address of the next byte to be allocated. On input, the new string is placed (by the submonitor) in memory, starting at the address in *freepoint*; a descriptor is created for the new string; and *freepoint* is incremented by the length of the string (see Fig. 8.5.1). On number-to-string conversion, *freepoint* is incremented by 11, and the new string is right justified in the area thus reserved. The 31 bits of significance consume at most 10 decimal digits; if the number is negative, a minus sign is inserted immediately before the most significant digit, and a new descriptor is created for the converted number (see Fig. 8.5.2).

For the operation of catenation it is generally necessary to copy the left operand to the address in *freepoint*, to copy the right operand directly after it, to increment *freepoint* by their combined lengths, and then to create a new descriptor for the combination (see Fig. 8.5.3). However, if either operand is of length zero, then the

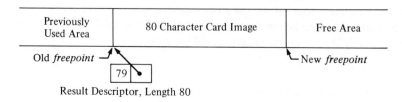

Fig. 8.5.1 String Data Area after Input

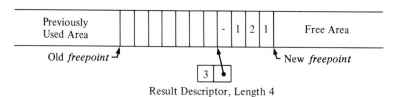

Fig. 8.5.2 String Data Area after Number-to-String Conversion
of the Value −121

other is the result of the catenation, and no copy is required. If the left operand terminates at the address in *freepoint* (e.g., it is the result of the last catenation), only the right operand need be moved.

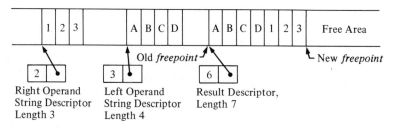

Fig. 8.5.3 String Data Area after Catenating Strings of length 4 and 3

All these activities consume free space by moving *freepoint* toward *freelimit*. When the free area has decreased to 256 bytes (i.e., when *freepoint* passes *freelimit*), there is the danger that the next operation will overflow the free string area. In general, much of the used area no longer contains useful data (the descriptors pointing to it having been overwritten by assignment statements), and we invoke the procedure *compactify* to repack the storage area (see Section 8.6).

Exercise 8.5.1

Rewrite the mechanism for generating descriptors in XCOM so that a fixed buffer of size 1024 is no longer needed. Hint: Create a fourth file in the submonitor, and write a procedure *GET__DESCRIPTORS* analogous to *GET__DATA*. The procedure *LOADER* will also have to be modified.

Exercise   8.5.2

Having completed Exercise 8.5.1 and having noted that the limit of 1024 descriptors in an XPL program severely limits the power of XPL for some symbol-manipulating programs, rewrite the register allocation routine so that registers R13, R11 through R4 are assigned to either descriptors or variables depending on the need.

Exercise   8.5.3

XCOM compiles ‖ into a call on a built-in catenation function procedure. Identify the situations in which this implementation is particularly troublesome (Hint: What happens in an attempted catenation of the results of several **character**-valued function procedures which contain uses of ‖ ?) Modify the code emitters for catenate so that string descriptors are properly saved in the descriptor area before the evaluation of an operand which is a function procedure call (and hence may contain calls to the catenation routine).

Exercise   8.5.4

The varying lengths of the character strings in XPL do not necessitate the descriptor and dynamic storage mechanism chosen for XCOM. Evaluate an alternative implementation in which all string storage is allocated at compile time. (Each string variable must be allocated storage for its maximum possible length.) Although some form of descriptor is still necessary to record the current length of a string, need the address of the string be included also? If not, how can addressability of strings best be obtained? The principal gain of such an implementation comes from the elimination of the need for string compactification. How does it affect (1) string assignment, (2) substring selection, (3) catenation, (4) storage of temporary results, and (5) the total storage requirement for a typical program, e.g. XCOM? Suggest changes to the XPL language which would make this implementation more efficient (elimination of varying character strings is not considered a solution).

Exercise   8.5.5 (Term Project)

Implement a version of XCOM which incorporates your solutions to Exercise 8.5.4 or which permits substantially longer (at least 32,767 characters) strings. Compare the efficiency of your XCOM compiling itself with the original XCOM compiling itself.

Exercise   8.5.6

Consider the effect of changing the string descriptor format from (length-1, absolute address) to (length, absolute address). What changes would have to be made in the code generated for (1) the built-in functions ‖ and number-to-string conversion, (2) *substr*, (3) *length*, (4) string comparisons, and (5) string compactification (Section 8.6)? Would the changes increase the efficiency of string handling in XPL programs?

8.6   The Procedure *compactify*

compactify is a run-time routine called during the execution of an XPL program whenever the remaining free space in the string area may be insufficient for a pending character-string operation. (The operations that consume free space are catenation, input, and number-to-string conversion.) *compactify* condenses a portion of the string data presently pointed to by string descriptors so as to leave some contiguous free space.

At the start of compilation, the compiler first produces binary images of the built-in functions and then begins to compile the library from file *input* (2) without listing. In the normal situation, *input* (2) contains the procedure *compactify*; hence it is a part of every compiled program but never appears in the program listing. An end-of-file condition on *input* (2) causes the compiler to switch to file *input* and begin listing the program. A listing of the procedure *compactify* is given in Appendix 4.

Since the code for catenation and number-to-string conversion precedes the code for *compactify*, the mechanism for forward procedure calls is needed to supply the address of *compactify* to the built-in functions.

The crosshatched areas in Fig. 8.6.1 represent discarded, and therefore collectable, string data. Such areas below *freebase* are constants emitted during compilation.

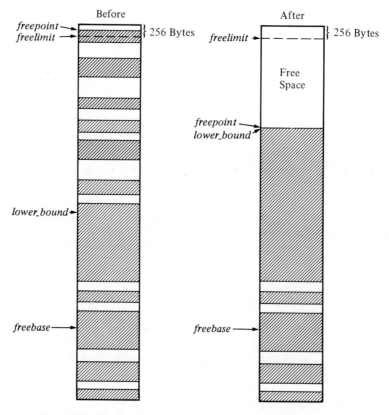

Fig. 8.6.1 Typical Pictures of the String Area, before and after
Compactification (Minor Collection)

The amount of collectable storage here is small (i.e., constant strings are seldom abandoned), and thus no attempt is made to reclaim storage within this area. The area between *freebase* and *lower_bound* is not reclaimed unless reclaiming the portion between *lower_bound* and *freelimit* (called a minor collection) fails to produce a sufficiently large free area. When this occurs, *lower_bound* is replaced by *freebase* and a major collection is begun. If this second attempt to condense the string area also fails, an error message is printed, and execution is terminated abnormally.

The amount of time spent in the compactification algorithm is related (quadratically) to the number of string descriptors pointing into the area to be collected. The frequency with which *compactify* is called is inversely proportional to the amount of free area recovered. The minor collection reclaims space only within the free area left by the previous compactification. Since all temporary results generated since the last compaction are there, the amount of space to be reclaimed is high, and the number of descriptors pointing into the area is relatively low. However, the total free space is reduced with each call to *compactify*. Thus it is called with increasing frequency (and takes somewhat less time to execute) until it fails to recover enough space and triggers a major collection. In a minimum memory (about 100,000 bytes), a major collection is needed about every 50th call from XCOM and takes about 50 times as long as a typical minor collection. In a larger memory (200,000 bytes or more), major collections occur very rarely and thus cause a negligible overhead.

There are four phases to the storage compactification algorithm.

1. Build a table of pointers (in dx) to the descriptors which themselves point at string data within the area to be condensed.
2. Sort the pointers using the address fields of the descriptors as the key.
3. Move the string data toward *lower_bound*, and update the address fields of the affected descriptors.
4. Move the last string, and reset the string area limit variables (*lower_bound* and *freepoint*).

The string descriptors are stored in a contiguous area of memory to which access is provided by the built-in array *descriptor*; the address field of the ith descriptor in storage is given by the expression *descriptor*(i) & *mask*. *ndescript* contains the number of descriptors in the program; *lower_bound* contains the absolute machine address of the lower bound of the area to be condensed.

During phase 1, pointers to all descriptors with address fields are greater than or equal to the lower bound are placed in dx. If the number of such descriptors ever exceeds the size of dx, a message is printed and execution terminates abnormally. Increasing the value of *dx_size* in *compactify* and recompiling the program corrects this error condition.

Since string data must always be moved into a previously freed area, the string data with lowest address must be moved first. Thus phase 2 uses a simple bubble sort to arrange the pointers in dx in the same order as the string data addresses.

Within the area to be condensed, there may be clumps of mutually overlapping string data. In phase 3 each clump is located and moved down, the top of the clump is recorded in the built-in variable *freepoint*, and the descriptor addresses are decremented by the amount of the move. Since the address fields available from the descriptors are absolute machine addresses, the built-in array *corebyte* is used to fetch and store the string data.

The final phase moves the last clump of string data, gives *freepoint* its final value, and checks whether the reclaimed area is sufficiently large.

8.7   The Procedure *INITIALIZATION*

INITIALIZATION, the first procedure called from *MAIN__PROCEDURE*, lays the groundwork for the compilation process. To a considerable extent, *INITIALIZATION* computes and tabulates values of constants for the compiler. These constants are recomputed every time the compiler runs to keep the mechanisms for changing the compiler as clear and easy to use as possible. We are as interested in the source and meaning of these constants as we are in their values. Thus, the mechanisms for integrating the tables produced by the program ANALYZER, the tables needed by the scanner, the code emitters, and the emitters for built-in functions themselves are all represented by executable code which can be changed by changing the initialization process.

INITIALIZATION starts with instructions to print heading for the compilation listing. Note that space is left here for the user of the XPL system to insert the name of the organization or the person taking local responsibility for maintaining the programming system.

It is necessary, for various reasons, to have available the index in the vocabulary *v* of several symbols of the XPL grammar. To be specific, when the scanner resolves the local ambiguities caused by

> /   (division), and
>
> /*   (start of a comment)

and

> | (logical or), and
>
> || (catenation);

it must return in *token* the appropriate index into *v*. Similarly, when the scanner finds one of the pseudoterminals in the phrase classes ⟨identifier⟩, ⟨number⟩, or ⟨string⟩, it places the symbol itself in the **character** variable *bcd* but places in *token* the appropriate index into *v*. Some error conditions depend upon the values in the array *stopit* for recovery. In addition, the scanner must have available the conventions determining symbol boundaries as provided in the arrays *chartype* and *not__letter__or__digit*. The use of these arrays is explained in Section 8.8.

INITIALIZATION also sets the initial values for a variety of variables (e.g., *commutative*, *lastbase*, *pp*, *dp*, *dsp*, *chp*, *pplim*, *dplim*, *chplim*, etc.) used in the synthesis procedures. It then initializes symbol-table values for the implicitly declared variables and procedures, calls the procedures which emit the code for the built-in functions, and initializes *parse__stack* and *sp*. One final task of *INITIALIZATION* is the generation of code for certain subroutines. The first two subroutines are associated with program loading (*REGISTER_SETUP_CODE* and *RELOCATE_ DESCRIPTORS_CODE*); the other two are the catenate and number-to-string conversion subroutines. The algorithms are sufficiently clear from the XCOM listing to preclude the necessity for discussing them further here.

Exercise   8.7.1

Generate a new version of XCOM. Change *INITIALIZATION* so that the heading of the compilation indicates your private ownership.

Exercise   8.7.2

How much time would be saved during each execution of XCOM if the constants computed in *INITIALIZATION* were replaced by declarations with the **initial** attribute, in the fashion of the syntax tables punched by ANALYZER? Is it reasonable to calculate these values by hand and to keypunch them? Write a program that accepts a version of *INITIALIZATION* and produces as output an appropriate set of declarations and a reduced *INITIALIZATION* containing only those statements which must be executed each time the compiler is run, e.g., outputs or expressions depending on *time*.

Exercise   8.7.3

The difficulties of Exercise 8.7.2 can be circumvented by providing a restart capability in XCOM. Suppose the XPL statement

call *suspend;*

were placed directly after the first detection of an end-of-file in *GETCARD* (i.e., upon completion of the compilation from the file *input* (2)), and this action resulted in the saving of a version of XCOM to be restarted over and over again at the next statement. Such a facility would clearly reduce the initial execution overhead in a general way. The major difficulty in implementation resides in the problem of unbinding the absolute addresses in descriptors and procedure returns and rebinding them upon program restart. Some work would also be necessary on the submonitor (particularly for partially produced files). Carefully analyze the problems that would be encountered and propose a method to overcome them.

Exercise   8.7.4 (Term Project)

Implement a version of XCOM according to your solution of Exercise 8.7.3.

Exercise   8.7.5

It requires about 15 instructions in XCOM to emit one instruction via *EMITRR* or *EMITRX*. (Why?) Note that the effect of the four system subroutines could have been achieved as well by preceding the procedure *compactify* in the library by *inlines* which are equivalent to the *EMITs* in *INITIALIZATION*. Analyze the gains that can be made with this organization and implement if sufficiently profitable. What effect (if any) does this have on the solution to Exercise 8.7.3?

8.8 The Analysis Procedures

The procedures invoked by *COMPILATION_LOOP* (excluding *SYNTHESIZE*) constitute a table-driven parsing algorithm fully discussed in Chapter 9. In this chapter we are mainly concerned that it works, i.e., that the source-language program is read and listed, that the XPL tokens are identified, that the program is parsed according to the XPL grammar, and that *SYNTHESIZE* is called immediately prior to each canonical reduction. But the analysis procedures do have some degree of language dependence. Thus, in this section we discuss the principal differences between these procedures in XCOM and in SKELETON.

The synthesis algorithm of XCOM (Section 8.10) uses more stacks than are provided in SKELETON. *COMPILATION_LOOP* initializes several of the stacks whenever a token is stacked.

SCAN must recognize many more terminal symbols for XPL. These are reflected in the increased number of cases in the XCOM procedure *SCAN*. Two other complications arise: (1) A bit string may be either a ⟨number⟩ or a ⟨string⟩, depending on its length; and (2) a token starting with a letter may be a macro name (Section 6.7). Thus, it is necessary to check these tokens not only against the list of reserved words in *v* but also against the list of declared macro names before returning ⟨identifier⟩ as the token. If a match is found, of course, the macro name must be replaced by its literal text, and the input rescanned.

The procedure *GET_CARD* in XCOM contains additional instructions to enable the library (i.e., *compactify*) to be compiled with each XPL program. Cards requested by *SCAN* are supplied from *input* (2) until that file is exhausted. At that time, listing is enabled and further cards are taken from *input* (the XPL source program). The listing format also contains data not in the SKELETON output; in particular, the variables *pp*, *current_procedure*, and *information* (which are set by the synthesis procedures) are appended to each line.

Exercise 8.8.1

Modify *SCAN* in XCOM to ignore comments of the ALGOL 60 form:

⟨comment⟩ :: = **comment** ⟨almost anything⟩ ;

⟨almost anything⟩ :: = {any string of EBCDIC characters not containing a ; }

Exercise 8.8.2

Modify *GET_CARD* in XCOM to use only columns 9 through 80 as source text and to enforce the convention that columns 1 through 8 contain (increasing) sequence numbers. Replace the card count on the output listing with the sequence number. What are the advantages and disadvantages of this change?

Exercise 8.8.3

Historically, sequence numbers have been placed in card columns 73 through 80. Determine the origin of this practice. Does it have any validity for present-day computing?

Exercise 8.8.4

In XPL (as in both PL/I and ALGOL 60) statements are terminated by a semicolon, and card (line) boundaries are formally ignored. Customarily—both for readability and ease of program modification—statements are placed one to a card, so that most cards end with a semicolon. In other languages (e.g., FORTRAN) the statement terminator is a card boundary, continuation marks providing for the exceptional case in which a statement extends across a card boundary. Other differences among these languages outweigh those due to these conventions, making an evaluation of the conventions themselves difficult. Devise an objective test (e.g., measured programmer performance) to evaluate the difference when the language (e.g., XPL) is held fixed. You might consider modifying *GET__CARD* to insert semicolons between cards unless an explicit continuation mark is encountered. Carry out the test.

Exercise 8.8.5

In many languages a comment card is denoted by a particular character in column 1. Modify *GET__CARD* to discard comment cards (via some convention) without scanning. Devise a way to set the control toggles that does not depend on scanning comments. Does the increased efficiency of the compiler justify the reduction in comment flexibility? Justify your answer.

8.9 The Symbol Table

In XPL, as in most programming languages, it is necessary to connect each occurrence of an ⟨identifier⟩ with its declaration. XCOM accomplishes this connection by means of a symbol table containing the relevant information about all active ⟨identifier⟩s. Information required for compilation includes the name, type, and location (e.g., base and displacement) of each ⟨identifier⟩. For each procedure it is also necessary to record the number, types, and locations (but not the names) of its parameters. The XCOM symbol table also records the line on which the variable was declared and a count of the references to each ⟨identifier⟩, since these can be useful diagnostic information.

The symbol-table mechanism of XCOM is a simplified version of the mechanism discussed in Chapter 3. The table is a stack. At the first encounter of an ⟨identifier⟩ —usually in a declaration or parameter list—it is placed at the top of the symbol table by a call on *ENTER*. Later occurrences may refer to information in the table or add further information. When code has already been generated which depends on the new information (e.g., a forward **go to**) a fix-up mechanism is invoked.

If the same name has been declared in nested scopes, the declaration in the innermost containing scope controls its use (see Section 6.3). This control is achieved in *ID__LOOKUP* (without explicit checking) by simply searching the symbol table from top to bottom, so that the first occurrence found is the innermost. All entries local to a scope (e.g., local variables to a procedure) become irrelevant upon exit from that scope and are removed from the top of the stack. This serves the dual function of freeing space in the symbol table and uncovering any previous uses of those names in outer scopes.

Within a procedure, parameters are treated precisely like other local variables. After the procedure is compiled their names are no longer required, but the type and location of the first, second, . . . parameters must be retained in the symbol table for generation of calling sequences. Since ⟨identifier⟩s are entered upon their first appearance in a scope, and the first ⟨identifier⟩s to appear after the name of a procedure are its parameters, the first, second, . . . entries in the symbol table after the main entry for the procedure name itself correspond to its parameters. These entries are not removed with the local variables. Rather, they are retained, and their names are set to the null string, which provides an unambiguous indication of a parameter. Thus, a procedure with n parameters has a compound entry consisting of $n + 1$ simple entries in the symbol table.

Exercise 8.9.1

One disadvantage of the XCOM symbol-table organization is that symbol look-up is an order n process. That is, the time (or number of comparisons) required to find a symbol is directly proportional to the number of symbols in the table. When XCOM compiles itself the symbol table averages nearly 350 entries, and the time spent in table look-up is the largest single cost of translation.

Conduct an experiment with XCOM to determine, as a function of the size of the program being compiled, the percentage of time spent in table look-ups and entries. Display your results as a graph. What is the dominant behavior as the program size becomes larger?

Exercise 8.9.2

Many alternative organizations reduce the cost of table look-up. The simplest and most common is called hash addressing. Suppose we have a method of producing a small integer (e.g., in the range 0 to 255) which is fully determined by an identifier but is randomly distributed in value over the set of identifiers appearing in a program (for example, $((byte(bcd) + length(bcd)) * 13)$ & "FF"). To hash code the XCOM symbol table, we could add two arrays to XCOM:

> **declare** *hashstart* (255) **bit** (16),
> *hashlink* (*sytsize*) **bit** (16);

In *hashstart* we place a pointer to the first (topmost) symbol in the table with the given hash. In *hashlink*, next to each symbol in the table we place a pointer to the next lower symbol with the same hash.

1. Invent and test for randomness a hashing scheme for XCOM.
2. Implement the more sophisticated look-up and entering procedures demanded by the suggested organization. Be sure to update the hash table correctly when leaving a scope.
3. Analyze your results. Since hash coding is still an order n process, estimate (as a function of table size and hash size) the improvement in the constant of proportionality. Take into account the extra time lost in the indirect look-up. What over-all improvement is achieved in the compiler performance? What is the resulting increase in compiler size?

Exercise   8.9.3

For large tables we prefer an order log n look-up and entry scheme to a hash look-up (see previous exercise). Ignore for the moment the possibility that an identifier may occur more than once in the table. Then, when the relation $<$ is used, there is a middle identifier (i.e., one which would appear in the middle of the table if it were sorted). Record its location in a variable *start*.

Exclude the middle entry, and divide the symbol table into two subsets, one greater and one less than the middle. Assume a declaration

declare (lss, gtr) (sytsize) bit (16);

and, at the middle entry, place pointers to the middle elements of the subsets. Continue to subdivide the table until every subset contains only one element. The longest indirection chain starting at *start* is about log n, where n is the number of symbols.

Devise enter, look-up, and deletion methods so that each operation is of order log n.

Suggest two ways to assure that the appropriate entry is found when multiple entries in the table have the same name. Analyze your results. How big does the average symbol table have to be to make the more complex system pay off? Obtain experimental data to confirm your analysis.

Exercise   8.9.4

Modify XCOM so that, rather than counting the number of references to a symbol, it tabulates either the lines on which the symbol is referenced or the procedures within which the symbol is referenced.

8.10   Code Generation

```
/*   See the little phrases go,
     Watch their funny antics.
 The men who make them wiggle so
 Are teachers of semantics.   */
```

FREDERICK WINSOR
Space Child's Mother Goose†

The whole purpose of XCOM is to generate System/360 machine-language code corresponding to XPL source programs. This purpose is accomplished under control of the procedure *SYNTHESIZE*, which is called by the analysis algorithm before each reduction. A list of the procedures which *SYNTHESIZE* calls indicates the range of its actions:

ARITHEMIT
BRANCH
CALLSUB
CHECKBASES
CLEARREGS
CONDTOREG
DIVIDE__CODE
EMITCONSTANT
EMIT__INLINE
EMITRR
EMITRX
ENTER
ERROR
FINDAC
FINDADDRESS
FIXBFW
FIXCHW
FIXWHOLEDATAWORD
FORCEACCUMULATOR
FORCEADDRESS
FORCEDESCRIPT
GENSTORE
ID__LOOKUP
MOVESTACKS
PROC__START
SETINIT
SET__LIMIT
SHIFT__CODE
STACKDUMP
STUFF__PARAMETER
SYMBOL__DUMP
TDECLARE
UNDECLARED__ID

Most generators are involved in the generation of single-address code for expressions along the lines described in Chapter 3. This generation is accomplished by *ARITHEMIT* and its associated procedures (see Fig. 8.10.1).

The major effects of *ARITHEMIT* are to emit System/360 code to load values corresponding to its implicit operands (pointed to in the synthesis stacks by *mp* and *sp*) into accumulators (R1 through R3), to emit the machine operation corresponding to its parameter *op*, and to record the status of the result in the synthesis stacks (at

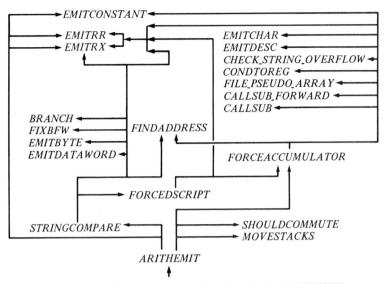

Fig. 8.10.1   Structure of Procedures Invoked by ARITHEMIT

mp). *ARITHEMIT* is called from *SYNTHESIZE* for binary operations; when a single ⟨expression⟩ value is required, the subsidiary procedure *FORCEACCUMLATOR* is used.

The procedure *GENSTORE* generates the code for assignment statements (including *output* and *file* on the left). It uses *FORCEACCUMULATOR* to get the value of the right side ⟨expression⟩ into an accumulator, and then emits the code for type conversion (if required) and storing.

Eight synthesis stacks are synchronous with the parse stack (see Table 8.10.1). *parse__stack*, *type*, and *fixl* correspond roughly to the three stacks of Section 3.4. The manipulations of *parse__stack* are automatically provided by the analysis algorithm as described in Chapters 4 and 9. *type* has one of the 14 values given in Table 8.10.3. The type code controls the emitters in various ways. For example, when an identifier is looked up in the symbol table, the location of the entry in the symbol table is left

TABLE 8.10.1   The Synthesis Stacks

Stack Name	Type	Use
parse__stack	**bit**(8)	The partially parsed text
type	**bit**(8)	A type associated with operand
var	**character**	The name of the item
inx	**bit**(8)	An associated index register
reg	**bit**(8)	An associated accumulator register
fixl	**fixed**	A fixed location
fixv	**fixed**	A fixed value
ppsave	**fixed**	A program location
cnt	**bit**(8)	A count

TABLE 8.10.2   Type Codes in XCOM

Type	XCOM Code
Half word	1
Label	2
Accumulator	3
Variable	4
Constant	5
Condition	6
Character	7
Fixed	8
Byte	9
Forward	10
Descriptor	11
Special	12
Forward call	13
Character procedure	14

in *fixl*, and *type* is set to type variable. When later actions demand the use of the variable, the symbol table is consulted to find the appropriate storage type (byte, half word, or full word) so that the corresponding System/360 instruction can be emitted. When *type* is constant, *fixv* contains the 32-bit value of the constant; when *type* is character, *var* contains the character-string value of the constant, etc.

Exercise   8.10.1

In Sections 3.3 and 3.4 we discussed the production of object code for a single-accumulator machine and noted that it is frequently necessary to generate temporary stores of a result from the accumulator to permit another operation. XCOM reduces this necessity by treating the System/360 as a three-accumulator machine. Construct an otherwise valid XPL statement for which XCOM requires more than three accumulators. Modify XCOM to generate the appropriate temporary stores and later reloads for such expressions rather than to give an error message. (Hint: Replace the XCOM call on *ERROR* with the temporary storage mechanism. Record the location and an appropriate type in the parse stacks.)

Exercise   8.10.2

One of the common causes of the "used all accumulators" error message is a subscripted variable to the left of the assignment symbol. The index value is loaded before the right side is evaluated, thus wasting a register. The change to XCOM in Exercise 8.10.1 will cause a store of that index. Will the procedure *GENSTORE* function nevertheless? Is there a more efficient solution for this special case?

Exercise   8.10.3

Division on the System/360 requires a contiguous even-odd pair of registers. If R0 and R1 are not free when a division is required, XCOM emits an error message.

Modify the procedure *DIVIDE__CODE* to use your temporary storage mechanism
of Exercise 8.10.1 instead.

8.11 Peephole Optimization

The basic requirement for XCOM, that it preserve the meaning (recall Section 3.1)
of XPL programs while translating them to System/360 machine language, could
have been (and in fact was initially) attained with a much simpler compiler than
XCOM. However, since we were also concerned with the efficiency of the resulting
programs, we tried to choose the best sequence of System/360 instructions to implement each construct of XPL. In addition, we selected a number of special cases, which
admit of better code than the general case, for further optimization. The single-pass
organization of XCOM rules out use of the varied global optimization procedures
which utilize repeated scans of the program to transform it into more efficient code
[e.g., Lowry and Medlock 69]. The techniques described here are the local or
peephole sort that use only a fixed amount of context.

One general strategy in XCOM is the principle of deferment: Emit code for an
action at the latest time consistent with the algorithm. Thus, for example, information
is left in memory until it is required in a register; storage is not allocated for constants
until it is certain that they cannot be more efficiently generated by a load address
instruction, etc.

Some special case occurs so frequently as to justify a check in the code emitters.
For example, the general mechanism for constants—allocate a word of memory
initialized to the value of the constant, and emit a load instruction—works for all
values, but small positive integers occur so frequently that it pays to separate (in
FORCEACCUMULATOR) constants in the range 0 to 4095 from the others. In this
range we still have two cases: 0 (a very frequent constant) can be generated by a
subtract register command; the other small constants require a load address instruction. Similarly, a relation results in a value of type condition, which generally must be
converted to a zero or a one in a register before further instructions (which may
change the condition code) are emitted; **if** and **while** require a value of type condition,
generally obtained by testing the value in a register. The special case of **if** or **while**
on a simple relation is so common that *CONDTOREG* records (in *stillcond*) the
condition for which it tests. When instructions are emitted, *stillcond* is reset by
EMITCODEBYTES. However, if *BOOLBRANCH* is called before any further code
is emitted, it backs up the code pointer *pp* (erases the effect of *CONDTOREG*) and
uses the value in *stillcond* to emit a branch conditional.

Expressions involving only constants can be evaluated at compile time. XCOM tests
for some of the more common cases (e.g., in ⟨arithmetic expression⟩ : : = − ⟨term⟩)
and performs the evaluation. Built-in functions can often be simplified if one or more
arguments are known at compile time (e.g., *shl* (⟨expression⟩, 1) is compiled into
an add register instruction).

A general algorithm for binary operations may require that the first operand be in
an accumulator and the second in memory (as in, for example, the single-accumulator

machine of Chapter 3). However, the System/360 provides multiple accumulators, and if both operands are already in accumulators, it would be foolish not to use a register-register instruction. Thus, a somewhat better algorithm would be to force both operands to accumulators and then emit the operation. But an RX instruction is more efficient than a load followed by an RR instruction, so *ARITHEMIT* checks the locations of its operands before deciding on the appropriate code sequence. Some operations (add, and, or) are commutative, and it does not matter which operand is in storage and which in a register. For these operations, the procedure *SHOULDCOMMUTE* determines the more efficient ordering.

Exercise 8.11.1

Locate as many forms of peephole optimization in XCOM as you can. Estimate the fraction of the compiler (space) and of compilation (time) devoted to this optimization. Also estimate the relative improvement of object code which results from this optimization. Under what conditions does optimization pay for itself?

Exercise 8.11.2

Check the validity of your answers to Exercise 8.11.1 by removing all the peephole optimizers from XCOM. How much smaller is your XCOM (when compiled by standard XCOM)? Use your XCOM to compile itself. How much faster than standard XCOM is it? How does the new object XCOM compare in size with the one compiled by standard XCOM? With standard XCOM itself? Use your new object XCOM to compile itself again (the code produced should be identical). Compare the speed of your object code to that produced by standard XCOM. In comparison, is XCOM itself either smaller or faster because of optimization?

Exercise 8.11.3

XCOM does not detect common subexpressions (e.g., $a + b + c$ occurring in two places). A general algorithm to remove redundant evaluations of such expressions would probably require more than one pass over the program. However, the restricted case of common subexpressions within a single statement is somewhat simpler. Develop a method so that XCOM would load i only once (rather than three times) for the statement $x(i) = i - x(i);$.

Exercise 8.11.4

Modify XCOM to detect common subexpressions (or at least common variables) within a single statement, and eliminate redundant evaluations (or loads) as suggested by your solution to Exercise 8.11.3. How much improvement is observable in your compiler compiling itself? How does this compare with standard XCOM compiling itself?

Exercise 8.11.5

The general algorithm employed by XCOM for subscripts is to use *FORCEACCUMULATOR* to obtain the subscript value in a register, which is then used as an index increment to the base address. However, if the subscript is a ⟨number⟩ and the value of the subscript plus the displacement part of the variable address is less than 4096, it is more efficient to add the subscript to the displacement at compile time. Modify XCOM to incorporate this change.

Exercise 8.11.6

Generalize your solution to Exercise 8.11.5 to handle the case of ⟨expression⟩ + ⟨number⟩ as a subscript.

8.12 Statistics Collection

/*   I have measured out my life with coffee spoons.   */

T. S. ELIOT

The Love Song of J. Alfred Prufrock

Many of the decisions made in the development of XCOM—both about the organization of the compiler and about the form of object code—could not be based directly on first principles. Either the mathematics was intractible or a number of questionable assumptions were required. In some cases we tried alternate solutions and compared the results, much as we have suggested in many exercises of this chapter. However, it was often simpler and more satisfactory to evaluate a proposed change by gathering statistics about the operation of the compiler. Some of these statistics were of interest only at a particular stage in the development of the compiler, and the mechanism to gather them was removed after the associated decisions were made. Others have proved of more general interest and are still gathered and printed by XCOM.

The time spent in the three major phases of XCOM and the compilation rate provide a gross measure of the efficiency of XCOM and a means of rough comparison with other compilers (or other generations of XCOM). Values of the *time* function are stored in the array *clock* at appropriate points in the compiler, and time differences are listed at the end of *PRINT_SUMMARY*.

Statistics collection takes time (calls on *time* are particularly costly), and we do not care to significantly slow XCOM by this process. Our most common form of statistic is the number of times a particular procedure is called during compilation, obtained by incrementing a particular variable upon each entry to the procedure. From such statistics we can roughly estimate the time spent in various portions of the compiler, deduce where improvements would be most effective, and learn quite a bit about the compiled code (how many RR instructions, how many RX, how many assignments, etc.). XCOM also counts the frequency of each operation code and the number of string comparisons performed while looking up identifiers.

Exercise 8.12.1

Determine the fraction of compilation time spent by ·XCOM in collecting statistics. How does your answer depend on program size in cards? In statements?

Exercise 8.12.2

Perform a careful experiment to determine the fraction of compilation time spent by XCOM in

1. The procedure *SYNTHESIZE* and its subordinates
2. The function procedure *STACKING*
3. The procedure *GET__CARD*
4. Each case of the procedure *SCAN*

Be sure to accurately determine the effect of your statistics collection and to correct for this effect in figuring time spent.

Exercise 8.12.3

Modify XCOM to collect statistics on the frequency of occurrence of ⟨identifier⟩s with lengths 1, 2, 3, ... Is there a correlation between frequency of use and length?

Exercise 8.12.4

Modify XCOM to print the symbol table sorted by frequency of use rather than alphabetically. Do XPL programs obey Zipf's Law? (Hint: See Pierce, *Symbols, Signals and Noise*, Chapter 5.)

8.13 The Bootstrap Process

/∗   And Jesus himself . . . the son of Joseph,
which was the son of Heli,
which was the son of Matthat,

. . .

which was the son of Seth,
which was the son of Adam,
which was the son of God. ∗/

Luke 3 : 24, 25, 38

Recalling the T diagrams of Section 1.7, we return to the problems of loading the submonitor and compiling the compiler for the first time. It is important to remember that XCOM is just a program that reads cards and creates a binary file and that its function depends in no way on how it was produced. If that binary file happens to be another image of XCOM, it can be run to produce yet another, etc.

It will be helpful at this point to recall or introduce some abbreviations.

XPL	The compiler writing language
XCOM	The compiler for XPL
AL	Assembly language (symbolic)
EX	Execution
ML	Machine language (binary)
SM	Submonitor
360	The IBM System/360 computer
B5500	The Burroughs B5500 computer
ALGOL	Burroughs B5500 extended ALGOL 60
OS	The operating system on the IBM System/360
MCP	The operating system on the Burroughs B5500

Using this list, we can succinctly express the steps to produce the XCOM submonitor in Fig. 8.13.1. Starting with a hand-written program in assembly language (on the far left), through the OS/360 assembler and loader we produce a running version of XCOM submonitor. We have avoided the logical problem of bootstrapping by recourse to existing programs (but have not said how they were written).

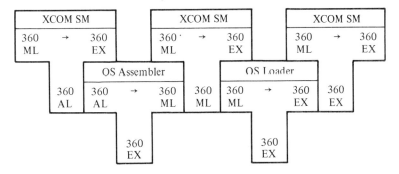

Fig. 8.13.1

Although the name and the function of a program do not change across a row of translations, the form of expression does. The two sequential translations of an XCOM submonitor are expressed in Fig. 8.13.2 by a single condensed T. Assuming now that we can get the XCOM submonitor into execution to load the output from XCOM, we still need to describe how we got XCOM in the first place. This was in fact accomplished by writing XCOM first in another language on another computer. The result (see Fig. 8.13.3) of writing the first version of XCOM in ALGOL was a running version of the compiler on the Burroughs B5500.

Now, counting on the existence of both a running XCOM and a running submonitor, we are ready to attack the bootstrap step to get a version running on the

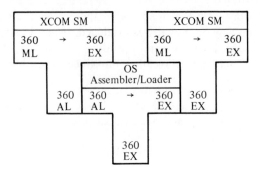

Fig. 8.13.2

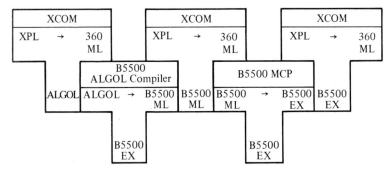

Fig. 8.13.3

IBM System/360 (see Fig. 8.13.4). And, finally, once the first version of XCOM ran on the IBM System/360, we could maintain and change it independently of the B5500 as in Fig. 8.13.5.

Figure 8.13.5 shows clearly why there is no contradiction in a compiler for XPL written in XPL, any more than there is in every child having parents. Each program was created with the help of a program that had been created earlier. Nevertheless, pushing the responsibility back ever earlier in time leaves us with an uncomfortable urge to say "In the beginning . . ." and tell how the first translator was created. Strangely enough, an attempt to trace all the way back (which involves another self-compiling compiler, B5500 ALGOL and its bootstrap machine, a Burroughs B220) ends with a quibble on what is sufficiently complex to be called a translator. At some point, as in the Bible, we must define our Adam and get on to creating Eve.

Exercise 8.13.1

Consider the bootstrap loop in the final set of T diagrams. The danger exists of an error in the new XCOM which would necessitate changing the XPL version of the new XCOM before closing the bootstrap loop. Can you give sufficient conditions under

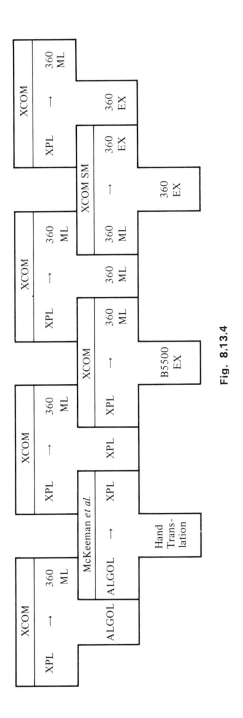

Fig. 8.13.4

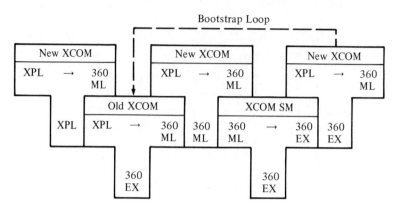

Fig. 8.13.5

which the new XCOM can safely replace the old? (Hint: You can specify any reasonable computational task as a part of your conditions.)

Chapter 9

SKELETON

A Proto-Compiler

/∗ And he said unto me, "Son of man, can these bones live?"

"Thus saith the Lord God unto these bones; Behold, I will cause breath to enter into you, and ye shall live: and I will lay sinews upon you, and will bring up flesh upon you, and cover you with skin, and put breath in you and ye shall live." ∗/

Ezekiel 37 : 3, 5, 6

9.1 Describing SKELETON

SKELETON (see Appendix 5 for the program listing), although a much simpler program than the fully fleshed XCOM (300 statements as compared to 2000), has the same basic structure. Where the programs are similar, we have deferred details from Chapter 8 to this chapter. Our purpose here is to give those details and enough additional information so the reader can, using SKELETON, produce a translator to his own specifications. We will proceed by detailing the procedures and their associated data structures, concluding with a formula for using SKELETON as the framework for a compiler.

The function of the unchanged SKELETON is to check its input for syntactic correctness according to the grammar in Table 9.1.1.

As usual in grammars for programming languages, we have not defined the symbols ⟨identifier⟩ and ⟨number⟩. The scanner is responsible for their definition:

$$
\begin{aligned}
\langle identifier\rangle \quad &::=\quad \langle letter\rangle \\
&\mid\quad \langle identifier\rangle\,\langle letter\rangle \\
&\mid\quad \langle identifier\rangle\,\langle digit\rangle \\
\langle letter\rangle \quad &::=\quad A\mid B\mid C\mid\cdots\mid Z\mid a\mid b\mid c\mid\cdots\mid z\mid \$\mid \#\mid \_\mid @ \\
\langle digit\rangle \quad &::=\quad 0\mid1\mid2\mid\cdots\mid9
\end{aligned}
$$

and

$$
\begin{aligned}
\langle number\rangle \quad &::=\quad \langle digit\rangle \\
&\mid\quad \langle number\rangle\,\langle digit\rangle
\end{aligned}
$$

231

TABLE 9.1.1   The Grammar Used in SKELETON

$\langle$program$\rangle$ ::= $\langle$statement list$\rangle$
$\langle$statement list$\rangle$ ::= $\langle$statement$\rangle$
                    | $\langle$statement list$\rangle$ $\langle$statement$\rangle$
$\langle$statement$\rangle$ ::= $\langle$assignment$\rangle$;
$\langle$assignment$\rangle$ ::= $\langle$variable$\rangle$ = $\langle$expr$\rangle$
$\langle$expr$\rangle$ ::= $\langle$arith expr$\rangle$
           | $\langle$if clause$\rangle$ **then** $\langle$expr$\rangle$ **else** $\langle$expr$\rangle$
$\langle$if clause$\rangle$ ::= **if** $\langle$Boolean$\rangle$
$\langle$Boolean$\rangle$ ::= **true**
              | **false**
              | $\langle$expr$\rangle$ $\langle$relation$\rangle$ $\langle$expr$\rangle$
              | $\langle$if clause$\rangle$ **then** $\langle$Boolean$\rangle$ **else** $\langle$Boolean$\rangle$
$\langle$relation$\rangle$ ::= =
              | <
              | >
$\langle$arith expr$\rangle$ ::= $\langle$term$\rangle$
                | $\langle$arith expr$\rangle$ + $\langle$term$\rangle$
                | $\langle$arith expr$\rangle$ − $\langle$term$\rangle$
$\langle$term$\rangle$ ::= $\langle$primary$\rangle$
           | $\langle$term$\rangle$ ∗ $\langle$primary$\rangle$
           | $\langle$term$\rangle$ / $\langle$primary$\rangle$
$\langle$primary$\rangle$ ::= $\langle$variable$\rangle$
              | $\langle$number$\rangle$
              | ($\langle$expr$\rangle$)
$\langle$variable$\rangle$ ::= $\langle$identifier$\rangle$
              | $\langle$variable$\rangle$ ($\langle$expr$\rangle$)

Thus we expect

$$a(71 + i) = \textbf{if } x < y + 1 \textbf{ then } 3 \textbf{ else } 4;$$

to be accepted without complaint by SKELETON, although

$$y = \textbf{if } x < 1 \textbf{ then } b < 1 \textbf{ else } b < 2;$$

will elicit an error message because the grammar does not allow the assignment of a $\langle$Boolean$\rangle$ to a $\langle$variable$\rangle$.

9.2   The Procedures

Except for calls on the ubiquitous *ERROR* procedure, the relations among the 20 procedures in SKELETON are depicted in Fig. 9.2.1. The most important substructures of Fig. 9.2.1 are those on *SCAN*, depicted in Fig. 9.2.2, and those on *COMPILATION_LOOP* depicted in Fig. 9.2.3. These procedures we will describe in detail. They are essentially identical to their counterparts in XCOM (see, however, Section 8.8).

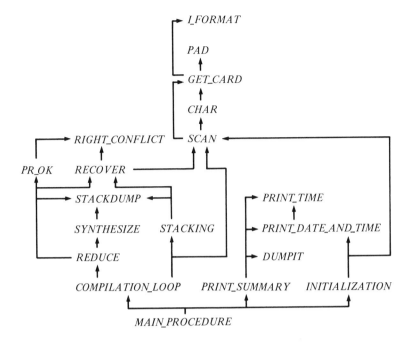

Fig. 9.2.1 Summary of Procedure Calls in SKELETON

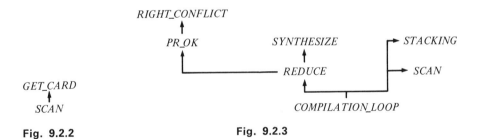

Fig. 9.2.2   **Fig. 9.2.3**

9.3 Scanning and the Vocabulary

/∗ Local rules for special forms of expression can be regarded as a sort of "micro-syntax" and form an important feature of programming languages. The micro-syntax is frequently used in a preliminary "pre-processing" or "lexical" pass of compilers to deal with the recognition of names, numerals, strings, basic symbols and similar objects which are represented in the input stream by strings of symbols in spite of being atomic inside the language.   ∗/

CHRISTOPHER STRACHEY

NATO Summer School in Programming

SCAN, called primarily from *COMPILATION__LOOP*, determines the next symbol (i.e., member of **V**$_t$) in the input text. In the process it must perform several tasks:

1. Read and list source cards (but ignore card boundaries). This task is delegated to the procedure *GET__CARD*.
2. Remove (ignore) blanks and comments from the text (but set control toggles).
3. Reject illegal characters in the text and emit appropriate error messages.
4. Detect single-character symbols (e.g., +, *, (, :) and determine their index in *v*.
5. Determine the extent of (potentially) multicharacter symbols (e.g., ⟨identifier⟩, ⟨number⟩, reserved words) and the appropriate index in *v*.
6. Set the results into the global variables *token* and *bcd* or *number__value*.

The global variables set by *SCAN* are summarized in Table 9.3.1.

TABLE 9.3.1   Global Variables Set by *SCAN*

Global Variable	Value
token	The index in *v* of the symbol found by *SCAN*
bcd	The character string value of the symbol found (e.g., ⟨identifier⟩ may be *BC*) by *SCAN*
number__value	The numeric value of the ⟨number⟩ found by *SCAN*
text	The portion of the text already read from cards but not yet consumed by *SCAN*
cp	The index in *text* of the first unused character
text__limit	The index in *text* of the last character read in
margin__chop	The amount of each new card to be deleted by *GET__CARD*
control	The control toggle array

SCAN also has some collateral duties. When a constant is found, *SCAN* computes the internal machine representation and leaves it in the global variable *number__value*. *SCAN* must also keep track of where it is in the text (using global variables *cp*, *text__limit*, and *margin__chop*) and set the control toggles (see Section 6.17).

The housekeeping starts at each entry to *SCAN*. *cp* points to the next unused character in *text*, and *text__limit* points to the last character in *text*. If *cp* points beyond *text__limit*, *GET__CARD* is called to put a new card image in text buffer *text* and to reset *cp* and *text__limit*. We next discard the previously used portion of *text* (with a *substr*), leaving *cp* = 0 to point to the next character. Hence *byte* (*text*) is the EBCDIC code of the leading character of the new symbol.

The leading character of *text* can be used to select among the several terminal symbols. For the language XPL, the scanner chooses one of the nine possibilities shown in Table 9.3.2. Of these, only cases 0, 1, 4, 5, 6, and 7 are required for the SKELETON language.

The category number (values 0 to 8) for each EBCDIC character (values 0 to 255) is placed in the array *chartype* by *INITIALIZATION*. The code

TABLE 9.3.2 Lead Character in XPL Symbols

Category	Characters in This Class	Commentary
0	! ? etc.	Illegal, error message
1	blank	Discard and rescan
2	'	Character string
3	''	Bit string
4	⟨letter⟩s	Identifier or reserved word
5	⟨digit⟩s	Number
6	/	Division or comment
7	+ − * < etc.	Single character symbols
8	|	Or or catenate

$$\textbf{do case } \textit{chartype (byte (text))};$$
$$\vdots$$
$$\textbf{end};$$

makes the selection.

The only cases needing further explanation are cases 4, 5, and 7. In case 4, after a symbol has been extracted from the text and placed in *bcd*, we must determine whether it is a reserved word or an ⟨identifier⟩. We search *v* for the symbol and, if we find it, store its index in *token* and return from *SCAN*. If we fail to find it, we set *token* to the index in *v* of ⟨identifier⟩. *v* has been sorted during preparation by the program ANALYZER so that it is arranged in order of increasing length of symbol names (see the example in Section 7.1). The array *v_index* contains the starting point for symbols of a particular length to avoid the necessity for searching all of *v*.

In case 5 we use the usual conversion algorithm

$$number\_value = number\_value * 10 + new\_digit;$$

for decimal-to-internal representation. Because the *new_digit* is an EBCDIC character code, we must subtract $byte ('0') = F0_{16} = 240_{10}$ before adding it to the value. Finally, in case 7 we process the single-character members of *v* by directly accessing an array *tx*. *tx* itself is set up by *INITIALIZATION* from *v*.

9.4 The Analysis Algorithm

As we have noted, the analysis algorithm consists of a set of procedures, called from *COMPILATION_LOOP*, which communicate primarily by setting global variables; they select their actions by comparing *parse_stack* and *token* with the global tables produced by ANALYZER. We tabulate these relations in Table 9.4.1.

The underlying cycle of the analysis algorithm resides in the **do while** *compiling;* . . . **end**; loop of the procedure *COMPILATION_LOOP*. Each time around this loop corresponds to one canonical parse step, the application of a rule of the grammar to

TABLE 9.4.1 Communication Among Procedures

Procedure Name	Is Called by	Communicates via	Uses Tables
PR__OK	*REDUCE*	Function value Parameter	*context__case* *context__triple* *hdtb* *left__context* *left__index* *prlength* *triple__index*
REDUCE	*COMPILATION__ LOOP*	*mp, sp* Parameters *parse__stack*	*hdtb* *prdtb* *pr__index* *prlength* *prmask*
RIGHT__CONFLICT	*PR__OK*	Function value Parameter, *token*	*c1*
SCAN	*COMPILATION__ LOOP*	*control* *number__value* *token, bcd*	*chartype* *not__letter__or__digit* *tx* *v* *v__index*
STACKING	*COMPILATION__ LOOP*	Function value *parse__stack* *sp, token*	*c1* *c1triples*
SYNTHESIZE	*REDUCE*	*mp, sp, compiling* Parameter *parse__stack* synthesis stacks	

reduce the input text by the procedure *REDUCE*. Prior to invoking *REDUCE*, *COMPILATION__LOOP* stacks enough symbols so that a canonically reducible string is the top of *parse__stack*. While the function *STACKING* is true, symbols are stacked in *parse__stack* along with associated string and number values in the synthesis stacks *var* and *fixv*. The loop on *STACKING* leaves *sp* pointed to the top of the next reducible string. *REDUCE* points *mp* to the bottom (head) of the reducible string before calling *SYNTHESIZE*. After the reduction, the value of *sp* is reset to that of *mp*, and the appropriate substitution is made in *parse__stack*.

    STACKING is the precedence function that decides, using the top elements of *parse stack* and the new symbol in *token* as indices into the decision tables *c1* and *c1triples*, whether the parse stack already contains a canonically reducible string. If so, *STACKING* returns the value *false*, and the inner loop of *COMPILATION__LOOP* is terminated. The tight data packing in *c1* makes access to *c1* rather obscure. *c1* is an array of bit strings. *parse__stack* (*sp*) selects a string, and *token* selects the appropriate two-bit value from that string. The 8 bits which contain the desired entry are obtained by using $token/4$ (actually $shr(token, 2)$ for efficiency) as an argument to $byte$. How the remainder of $token$ divided by 4 corresponds to the packed values is shown in Fig. 9.4.1. This correspondence allows the needed bits to be right justified by the right shifts in Fig. 9.4.2 which are computed by

$$shl(3\text{-}token, 1) \ \& \ 6$$

All that remains is to mask out the two needed bits with

$$\& \ 3$$

The resulting two-bit number encodes the following four possibilities:

0		Illegal symbol pair, call $ERROR$
1	Y	Stack $token$
2	N	Don't stack $token$ yet (reduce)
3	$\#$	Conflict, consult $C1$ triples

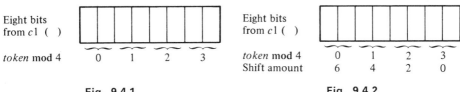

Eight bits from $c1$ ( ) $token$ mod 4: 0 1 2 3

Eight bits from $c1$ ( ) $token$ mod 4: 0 1 2 3; Shift amount: 6 4 2 0

Fig. 9.4.1   **Fig. 9.4.2**

If there were never more than one candidate for the reducible string on the parse stack when $REDUCE$ was called, $REDUCE$ could merely look through the productions to find an applicable rule. However, for efficiency, $REDUCE$ searches only through those production rules that end in the symbol in $parse\_stack \ (sp)$; pr_index contains the index of the first such production. When $REDUCE$ finds a match, it calls PR_OK to determine whether it has found the correct reduction. The array $context\_case$ indicates the type of check required. The value used in the **case** of PR_OK is usually zero (i.e., the first production found is automatically acceptable). The frequency of case zero is a consequence of the effectiveness of the longest-match search rule of Section 4.3. The remaining three cases of PR_OK are dedicated to productions for which this rule fails. These situations may be resolved by finding out (1) whether the result of reduction would cause a conflict with $token$ (**case** 1), (2) whether this result would cause a conflict below it in $parse\_stack$ (**case** 2), or (3) whether the reduction can be made in the simultaneous contexts to the left and right of the candidate string (**case** 3). Although the third test subsumes the other two, it is usually at a prohibitive cost in table size.

$RIGHT\_CONFLICT$, the procedure that makes the decision in case 1, uses the same method to access array $c1$ as $STACKING$ does. Since $RIGHT\_CONFLICT$ need only test for zero/nonzero (i.e., illegal pair/legal pair), it omits the final shift and mask.

9.5 Deciphering the Recognition Tables

ANALYZER produces fourteen tables for insertion into SKELETON. Although one need not understand the details of the data organization to use SKELETON, one may like to do so if a change in ANALYZER is anticipated. Table 9.5.1 summarizes their organization.

TABLE 9.5.1 The Recognition Tables

Name	Type	Description

*c*1	long **bit** strings	The stacking decision table, packed two bits per decision:
		  0 = illegal pair
		  1 = stack the input symbol
		  2 = don't stack the input symbol; reduce instead
		  3 = conflict, consult *c*1*triples*.
		The top of the stack is used to select the bit string; the input symbol is used to select the two bits.

*c*1*triples*	**fixed**	When the pair (stack top, input symbol) is insufficient information for the stacking decision (*c*1 = 3), we use the two stack-top elements and the input symbol to decide. These triples are packed in *c*1*triples* in three bytes

context__case	**bit**(8)	For each production rule, a fixed amount of context must be checked before the reduction is allowed. *context__case*(*i*) gives for the *i*th production the values
		  0 = No check needed
		  1 = Check right context
		  2 = Check left context
		  3 = Check right and left context

context__triple *triple__index*	**bit**(8) **fixed**	In a manner analogous to *left__context* and *left__index*, these arrays hold valid (1, 1) contexts as needed.
hdtb	**bit**(8)	Each entry gives the left part of the corresponding production rule. If $\langle$s$\rangle$ ::= $\langle$v$\rangle$ = $\langle$e$\rangle$: then *hdtb* contains the index in v of $\langle$s$\rangle$.

TABLE 9.5.1   The Recognition Tables (Contd.)

Name	Type	Description
left__context	**bit**(8)	Each symbol has a certain number of valid symbols that can appear to its left in a sentential form. Such valid contexts as will be needed to select a correct reduction are sorted in *left__context.*
left__index	**bit**(8)	Given a symbol, *left__index* locates in *left__context* where the record of its contexts begins.
prdtb	**bit**(8)	ANALYZER sorts the productions to optimize the actions of *REDUCE* and *PR__OK. prdtb(i)* gives the position in the original grammar of the *i*th rule in these tables.
pr__index	**bit**(8)	Given that the stack top contains a particular symbol, *pr__index* of that symbol locates the starting point in *prtb* where all rules ending in that symbol are stored.
prlength	**bit**(8)	The number of symbols in the right side of a production.
prtb	**fixed**	Each entry corresponds to a production rule. In *prtb* are all except the rightmost symbol of the right parts of the rules. If $\langle s \rangle \ :: = \langle v \rangle = \langle e \rangle$ then *prtb* contains the indices for $\langle v \rangle$ and =.
v	**character**	The symbols of the vocabulary (terminal first, then nonterminal) sorted by length. A few extra symbols may appear at the end as a result of automatic modification of the grammar by ANALYZER. *The location in v is the representation used for symbols throughout the compiler.*
v__index	**bit**(8)	Pointers into *v*. Terminal symbols of length *n* start in *v* at *v__index(n)*.

9.6   Building on SKELETON

We presume that the recipe of Chapter 7 has been followed and that ANALYZER has produced a set of tables for SKELETON. The tables are physically inserted into the body of the SKELETON program in place of the tables for the sample grammar.

Then *SCAN* must be updated for the particular fine structure of the new language represented by the tables. If the treatment of identifiers, constants, and comments in

SKELETON is not consistent with the new language, the code must be changed. New features (e.g., character strings) must be added. If the new symbol type starts with a unique character, *INITIALIZATION* can be changed to set a selection number into *chartype* to cause *SCAN* to separate this case from the rest. Otherwise, tests must be inserted in an existing case to make the distinction.

Once the tables have been inserted and *SCAN* has been rewritten, the program may be compiled by XCOM to produce a working syntax checker for the new language. The final tasks are to write code emitters and to add generators to *SYNTHESIZE* in the form of a **case** on the production number. Remember that although there is a case zero in XPL, we number productions from one; hence we need one dummy statement. XCOM itself (Appendix 3) is an appropriate model to compare with SKELETON to determine the necessary additions.

Exercise 9.6.1

Implement generators for the assignment language recognized by SKELETON. Assume a convenient set of Polish operators for the machine language.

Exercise 9.6.2

Extend Exercise 9.6.1 by adding a procedure *INTERPRET* that executes the code produced.

Exercise 9.6.3

Add the production

⟨assignment⟩   ::=   **output** = ⟨expr⟩

to the grammar used in SKELETON, process it via ANALYZER, replace the tables in SKELETON, and extend the result of Exercise 9.6.2 to include the new statement.

Exercise 9.6.4

Extend the language recognized by SKELETON to include &, |, and ¬. Use only a conditional-branch-forward instruction in addition to the arithmetic and comparisons (i.e., do not invent a logical and instruction) to extend the compiler and interpreter to correctly execute &, |, and ¬. Hint: If a is true then $a|b$ does not depend on the value of b.

Exercise 9.6.5

Repeat Exercise 9.6.4. Use a machine language like the single-address code suggested in Section 3.3.

Exercise 9.6.6

Rather than emitting sequential code for the assignment language, build the parse tree, and design a machine to execute it. Is there any opportunity for parallelism? Are there any systematic changes that can be made to the parse tree to ease this exercise?

Exercise 9.6.7 (Term project)

1. Invent a language including recursive procedures, integer arithmetic, and at least one other interesting feature (hints: a type **picture** for two-dimensional character strings; or extend the integers to indefinite precision; or add type **float**; or allow arbitrary **group** or **field** arithmetic; or allow parallelism; or allow a type **board** with appropriate operators for testing chess or checkers, etc, strategies). Be sure you know what your language means before proceeding.
2. Use BNF, ANALYZER, and English descriptive text to define your language.
3. Implement and thoroughly test a syntax checker for your language.
4. Invent an ideal machine to execute your language. Implement and document an interpretive simulator for your machine.
5. Add code emitters to the syntax checker, and incorporate the interpreter to provide a load-and-go system.
6. Test your language thoroughly; include tests for such things as pathological programs (e.g., 300 left parentheses in a row). Run a recursive factorial procedure.

The results of the project should be a report of six chapters and in sufficient detail to enable the reader to use the system you have produced.

Exercise 9.6.8 (Term project)

As an alternative to Exercise 9.6.7, pick a language much farther afield (e.g., English, musical score, line drawings, predicate calculus), and write a program that recognizes the sentences and processes them in some interesting way.

Chapter 10

ANALYZER

A Grammar Analysis
and Table-Building Program

/∗ These bits of wood were covered on every square with paper pasted on them, and on these papers were written all the words of their language, in their several moods, tenses and declensions, but without any order. The professor then desired me to observe, for he was going to set his engine at work. The pupils at his command took each of them hold of an iron handle, whereof there were forty fixed round the edges of the frame, and giving them a sudden turn, the whole disposition of the words was entirely changed. He then commanded thirty-six of the lads to read the several lines softly as they appeared on the frame; and where they found three or four words together that might make a part of a sentence, they dictated to the four remaining boys who were scribes.

Six hours a day the young students were employed in this labor, and the professor showed me several volumes in large folio already collected, of broken sentences, which he intended to piece together, and out of those rich materials to give the world a complete body of all arts and sciences. ∗/

JONATHAN SWIFT

Gulliver's Travels, 1726

10.1 Describing ANALYZER

ANALYZER is a dual purpose grammar analysis program. It is designed to assist in debugging BNF grammars so that they are MSP (mixed-strategy precedence) of degree (2, 1; 1, 1) parsable and to prepare the tables required by the MSP algorithms. Chapter 7 covers the use of ANALYZER for BNF programming, Chapter 9 the format of the tables built by ANALYZER for SKELETON. The theory for the algorithm of ANALYZER is given in Chapter 5. The program itself is listed in Appendix 6.

This chapter supplements the other documentation of ANALYZER by describing the procedure structure, the basic program logic, and the uses of the principal global variables. It concludes with suggestions for the modification of ANALYZER. We expect ANALYZER to be studied and modified less often than the other major programs in our system. The reader is therefore explicitly warned that in some sections of the program clarity has been sacrificed for efficiency.

10.2   The Procedures

The major actions of ANALYZER are performed by procedures called from the main program. These procedures call other procedures, which may call still others to some depth as shown in Fig. 10.2.1. Table 10.2.1 gives an alphabetically arranged list of the procedures in ANALYZER.

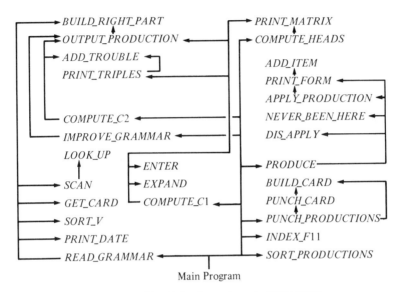

Fig. 10.2.1   The Major Procedures in ANALYZER

TABLE 10.2.1   The Procedures of ANALYZER

Procedure Name	Called from	Action
ADD __ITEM	*PRINT __FORM*	Add an item to the print line being formed in *cardimage;* print the current line first if necessary.
ADD __TROUBLE	*COMPUTE __C2* *PRINT __TRIPLES*	Record in a table the trouble contexts for which *C1* or *C2* is undefined, so *IMPROVE __GRAMMAR* can work on the situation.
APPLY __PRODUCTION	*PRODUCE*	Simulate the effect of recursion by incrementing *level* and by saving all local variables in stacks. Then perform one parse step by applying production *p* to the top of *stack.*
BUILD __CARD	*PUNCH __CARD* *PUNCH __PRODUCTIONS*	Add an item to *cardimage;* punch and/or list the current card first if the card boundary would be exceeded.

TABLE 10.2.1   The Procedures of ANALYZER (Contd.)

Procedure Name	Called from	Action
BUILD_RIGHT_PART	OUTPUT_PRODUCTION READ_GRAMMAR	Convert the coded internal form of the right part of a production to a character string (in external format) in the global variable *t*.
CLEAR_HEADS	COMPUTE_HEADS	Clear the global array *head_table*.
CLEAR_WORK	COMPUTE_C1 COMPUTE_HEADS	Clear the global array *work*.
COMPUTE_C1	Main program	Compute and tabulate the stacking-decision function $C1$; leave the matrix in *work* and the triples in *triple*.
COMPUTE_C2	Main program	Compute and tabulate the production-selection function $C2$; leave the results in *mp_save*.
COMPUTE_HEADS	Main program	Compute and tabulate the produced 1-heads of each symbol in the grammar. On the first iteration, also check for the obvious ambiguity of left and right recursion on the same symbol.
DIS_APPLY	PRODUCE	Reverse the effect of *APPLY_PRODUCTION* (i.e., come up a level of recursion).
ENTER	COMPUTE_C1	Look up a triple in the *triple* table. If it occurs, "or" in the new function value, otherwise add it at the appropriate spot with the given value.
ERROR	APPLY_PRODUCTION COMPUTE_C2 COMPUTE_HEADS ENTER IMPROVE_GRAMMAR LOOK_UP NEVER_BEEN_HERE PRINT_TRIPLES PRODUCE READ_GRAMMAR SCAN	Print an error message, and increment the error count.
EXPAND	COMPUTE_C1	Place the right part of the production *p* bracketed by the context in *f11* into *stack*.
GET	COMPUTE_C1 COMPUTE_HEADS PRINT_MATRIX PUNCH_PRODUCTIONS	Simulate double subscripts. Unpack the byte array *work* to obtain a two-bit entry made by *SET*.

TABLE 10.2.1 The Procedures of ANALYZER (Contd.)

Procedure Name	Called from	Action
GET__CARD	*READ__GRAMMAR*	Place the next nonblank, noncomment input card in *cardimage;* meanwhile list the comment cards.
IMPROVE__GRAMMAR	Main program	Attempt to remove the remaining trouble spots in the grammar (recorded by *ADD__TROUBLE*) by creating new nonterminal symbols to peek deeper into the stack.
INDEX__F11	Main program	Build pointers into *f11* for each production. *ind(p)* has the index in *f11* of the first valid context for *p*, *ind1(p)*, of the last.
IS__HEAD	*COMPUTE__C1* *COMPUTE__HEADS* *PRINT__MATRIX* *PRODUCE*	Simulate double subscripts. Return *true* if *SET__HEAD* has been called for these arguments, *false* if not.
LINE__OUT	*OUTPUT__PRODUCTION* *PRINT__MATRIX* *PRINT__TRIPLES* *READ__GRAMMAR*	Append the number and an appropriate string of blanks to the line and print it out.
LOOK__UP	*SCAN*	If *symbol* has already been placed in *v*, return its index. Otherwise, add it, and return the new index.
NEVER__BEEN__HERE	*PRODUCE*	If *new__f11* has been recorded, return *false;* else record it, and return *true.*
OUTPUT__PRODUCTION	*COMPUTE__C1* *COMPUTE__C2* *IMPROVE__GRAMMAR*	Print production *p* in standard format.
PACK	*COMPUTE__C1* *NEVER__BEEN__HERE*	Combine four bytes into one word.
PRINT__DATE	*READ__GRAMMAR*	Convert and print the date.
PRINT__FORM	*APPLY__PRODUCTION* *PRODUCE*	Print the current sentential form (in *stack*) for tracing.
PRINT__MATRIX	*COMPUTE__C1* *COMPUTE__HEADS*	Tabulate a matrix of one- or two-bit entries in readable form.
PRINT__TIME	*COMPUTE__C1* *PUNCH__PRODUCTIONS* *READ__GRAMMAR* Main program	Read the clock, and print both the time since the last reading and the cumulative time since the start of processing the grammar.
PRINT__TRIPLES	*COMPUTE__C1*	Tabulate the triples collected for the stacking-decision function *C1.*

TABLE 10.2.1   The Procedures of ANALYZER (Contd.)

Procedure Name	Called from	Action
PRODUCE	Main program	The heart of the algorithm. Collect all valid contexts for each RNT in a CSF by running a parser backwards.
PUNCH_CARD	*PUNCH_PRODUCTIONS*	Add an item to *cardimage*, and punch the result.
PUNCH_PRODUCTIONS	Main program	Punch all the tables required by the MSP parsing algorithm (in the form of XPL declarations, ready for insertion into XCOM or SKELETON) based on data left in various global tables.
READ_GRAMMAR	Main program	Read and list a new grammar; convert it to internal format.
SCAN	*READ_GRAMMAR*	Get the next token from the input card, and return its index in *v*.
SET	*COMPUTE_C1* *COMPUTE_HEADS*	Or a two-bit value into the array *work* at a position specified by simulating double subscripts.
SET_HEAD	*COMPUTE_HEADS*	Set *change* to have value *true*, and also set the value in *head_table* specified by a simulated double subscript.
SORT_PRODUCTIONS	Main program	Place the productions in an optimal order for the selection function *C2*. Use as key: 1. Tail symbol of right part 2. Length of right part 3. Number of valid contexts
SORT_V	*READ_GRAMMAR*	Sort the vocabulary by 1. Terminal/nonterminal 2. Length 3. Original order of occurrence

10.3 Program Logic

The main loop of ANALYZER is in the last 40 lines of the program, which contain a series of calls on the working procedures. The **do while** *stacking* loop permits a series of grammars (separated by $EOG cards) to be analyzed in a single run. The **do while** *trouble count* > 0 loop, combined with the $I control card, repeats the analysis for the iterative improvement algorithm.

The procedure *READ_GRAMMAR* initializes conditions; prints a heading; reads, decodes, reformats, and lists the productions of the grammar; sorts the symbols of the vocabulary—terminal before nonterminal, short before long; and lists the terminal, nonterminal, and goal symbols. It also calls the subsidiary procedures *GET__CARD* (which reads the next card, skipping blanks and comment cards), *SCAN* (whose value is the next token on the current card), and *SORT__V* (which sorts the vocabulary). Symbols are stored uniquely in the **character** array *v*. Throughout the program, each symbol is represented by a small integer (its index in *v*) computed by *LOOK__UP*. Productions are stored with the left part in *left__part*, the head symbol of the right part in *right__head*, and the balance (if any) in *production; on__left* and *on__right* record occurrences of each symbol in the left and right parts of productions. *npr* is the number of productions in the grammar, *nsy* the number of symbols, and *nt* the number of terminal symbols.

COMPUTE__HEADS sets up the matrix representing the produced 1-heads(PH_1) for the grammar and uses the procedures *SET__HEAD* and *IS__HEAD* to simulate the effect of a two-dimensional Boolean array. On the first iteration, *COMPUTE__HEADS* also computes the produced 1-tails ($A \rightarrow^+ \varphi Z$) in the *work* array by using *GET* and *SET*. This computation permits a simple test for symbols which are both left and right recursive—the most frequent single source of ambiguities [Knuth 68].

The heart of the program is the procedure *PRODUCE*, which reverses the canonical parsing algorithm and builds a table of F_{11}. Since the F_{11} computation is recursive and XPL is not, the procedures *APPLY__PRODUCTION* and *DIS__APPLY* simulate recursion by saving and restoring all local variables using arrays as stacks whose tops are indexed by *level*. In a preliminary computation, *PRODUCE* calculates (and saves in *index*) for each nonterminal the first production of which it is a left part. The main loop begins at *production__loop*. The construction of the table is done within the procedure *NEVER__BEEN__HERE*, which returns the value *true* if the data just recorded was not previously in the table. To facilitate this test, the array *f*11 is ordered by insertion, and a binary search table look-up is used. For efficiency, entries are packed $(A_i \varphi_{ij} \alpha_{ij})$.

Subsequent procedures require all the $(\varphi_{ij}, \alpha_{ij})$ associated with a particular A_i. *INDEX__F11* places the lower bound (in *f*11) for each symbol in *ind*, and the upper bound in *ind*1.

For the MSP algorithm, the productions must be sorted by tail symbol and by length. *SORT__PRODUCTIONS* achieves this ordering by doing an indirect sort which uses pointers in *index*. For economy of tables, equal right parts are ordered by number of contexts.

COMPUTE__C1 repeats the same basic loop two or three times to
1. Build the $C1_{11}$ matrix
2. Build a table of $C1_{21}$ triples for $C1_{11}$ conflicts
3. Collect information for diagnostics on $C1_{21}$ conflicts

Each production is expanded in each of its contexts, and the stacking decisions are recorded in *work*, *triple*, and *tv*. The results of each step are listed.

COMPUTE__C2 tests the contexts $(\varphi_{ij} \cdots \alpha_{ij})$ in which any production can occur against the contexts of succeeding productions with equal or imbedded right parts. If the grammar is not (1, 1) for this decision, the problem contexts are listed. The decision rules are printed and their values saved in *p__save* and *mp__save* for use by *PUNCH__PRODUCTIONS*.

All the tables needed by the MSP algorithm of SKELETON are converted from their internal ANALYZER format to XPL declarations on punched cards (or other output medium) by the procedure *PUNCH__PRODUCTIONS*. Tables left by previous procedures in *v*, *work*, *triple*, *tv*, *head*, *left__part*, *mp__save*, *p__save*, *f*11, and *tail* are formatted for output using the procedures *BUILD__CARD* and *PUNCH__CARD*.

When *COMPUTE__C*1 and *COMPUTE__C*2 detect errors (decisions that cannot be made with $(2, 1)$ or $(1, 1)$ context), they call the procedure *ADD__TROUBLE* to record the context in which the problem occurred. If the $I option is used, the procedure *IMPROVE__GRAMMAR* attempts to remove the difficulty. *IMPROVE__GRAMMAR* is an experimental procedure which works well for certain types of problems (e.g., the insulating comma [Lynch 68]) in which the grammar is of degree $(p, 1; m, 1)$, although not of degree $(2, 1; 1, 1)$. It creates new symbols for the left-most symbols of the problem pairs and adds new null productions (e.g., $\langle,1\rangle ::= , $). The effect is to utilize more left context in making a decision.

10.4 Tailoring ANALYZER

Although most users will not wish to change the computational algorithm of ANALYZER, they may wish to vary some parameters (such as table sizes) or to modify input and output formats. This section contains suggestions for such changes.

To adapt ANALYZER to a smaller machine, reduce the table sizes controlled by the literal declarations for *stacklimit*, *textlimit*, *maxnf*11, *maxntrip*, and *maxtrouble*. There will be a corresponding reduction in the size of grammar that can be processed.

To make ANALYZER accept larger grammars, if a particular table is overflowing, increase the size of the table by changing the corresponding literal declaration (most probably *maxnf*11 or *maxntrip*). Since computation time is ultimately proportional to the the square of *nf*11, time generally becomes the controlling factor before space. If more than 255 productions or symbols are required, ANALYZER will have to be rewritten using different data-packing formats. To remove the restriction of five symbols per right part would require a new format for packing the productions.

To change the input format, modify the procedure *SCAN* to reflect the desired conventions.

To change the format of diagnostic output and tables, modify either the *output* statements of the procedure in question or the procedures *LINE__OUT*, *BUILD__CARD*, *PUNCH__CARD*, *PRINT__MATRIX*, *PRINT__TRIPLES*, *BUILD__RIGHT__PART*, *OUTPUT__PRODUCTION*, or *PRINT__TIME* as desired.

To change the format of the card output, modify the procedure *PUNCH__PRODUCTIONS* as desired.

To change the iterative improvement algorithm, replace the procedure *IMPROVE__GRAMMAR* by any desired algorithm.

Appendix 1

Living with an Operating System

A1.0 The Requirements

The requirements of an XPL program in general and XCOM in particular for interaction with its environment (the operating system) take several forms:

1. Loading the XPL program into the memory of the computer and then placing it in execution
2. String input
3. String output
4. Direct-access storage
5. Program debugging aids
6. External information (e.g., time and date)

This appendix describes how these requirements are met in the XPL system by a small submonitor program. It is assumed that the reader has some familiarity with the IBM operating system OS/360 [IBM 6Xa], its job control language [IBM 6Xb], and OS/360 assembly language [IBM 6Xe].

By design, XPL object programs do not communicate directly with the operating system when requesting services. This interface is relegated to a submonitor program, thus XCOM can generate simple calls on the submonitor for system interface constructs in XPL. Although the XPL system was originally designed to operate under OS/360, it can run under any System/360 operating system with changes only in the submonitor. Changes in the operating system require only changes in the submonitor (using the IBM assembler) and not the recompilation of existing XPL programs.

We now describe in detail how a part of the submonitor satisfies each of the requirements listed above.

A1.1 The Execution of an XPL Program

Execution of an XPL program under OS/360 begins when the OS/360 job scheduler reads a set of statements in the OS/360 job control language (JCL). These statements serve two purposes: They specify the name of the XPL submonitor as the program to be executed (the EXEC statement) and they specify the correspondence between the submonitor internal name (DDNAME) and the operating system external name (DSNAME) for the same files (the DD statements). Optionally, the DD statements may also provide additional information about the attributes of the files.

After the submonitor is loaded by OS/360 and given control, it opens the files needed initially, obtains space in main memory from the operating system, and proceeds to read the XPL program into the space obtained. Once the XPL program is in memory, the submonitor transfers to it, and the XPL program begins execution. During the course of execution, the program may call upon the submonitor with requests for service. When the program finishes execution, it returns to the submonitor, which then returns to OS/360.

Section A1.2 describes options available during program initiation, and Section A1.3 describes the loading of the XPL program.

A1.2 Specifying an Environment

Certain JCL statements relate submonitor internal file names and operating system external names (DDNAMEs and DSNAMEs). Another such correspondence between submonitor internal names and the names used in an XPL program is established when the submonitor is assembled. Table A1.2.1 lists these names. The number of each type of file (string input, string output, and direct access) which the submonitor will handle is also determined at assembly time by assembly variables (&INPUTS, &OUTPUTS, and &FILES, respectively). To change the number of files of any type, it is necessary only to change the value of the assembly variable associated with that type of file.

DD statements may also specify file attributes (record format, record length, and block size) for the string input and output files. If neither JCL statements nor information contained in the external file provide attributes, default values determined in the assembly of the submonitor are provided. Attributes for direct access files are assembled into the submonitor and can be changed only by means of the FILE parameter. These attributes are included in the assembly to facilitate the use of standard system-defined files for temporary storage.

TABLE A1.2.1

XPL Program Name	Submonitor DDNAME	Use
—	PROGRAM	Source of XPL object program
input, input(0), or input(1)	SYSIN	String input
input(2)	INPUT2	String input
input(3)	INPUT3	String input
output, output(0), or output(1)	SYSPRINT	String output
output(2)	SYSPUNCH	String output
output(3)	OUTPUT3	String output
file(1, i)	FILE1	Direct-access storage
file(2, i)	FILE2	Direct-access storage
file(3, i)	FILE3	Direct-access storage

One feature of the OS/360 JCL is the ability to pass parameters to a program being loaded by using a parameter (PARM) field of the execute (EXEC) statement.

These parameters can modify the environment established by the submonitor for the XPL program. Possible parameters and their interpretations are

PARAMETER	INTERPRETATION
ALTER	Increase the amount of memory reserved for OS/360 so that there will be space to create input/output buffers dynamically.
DUMP	Cause an ABEND dump to be given in the event of any input or output error detected by the submonitor.
FILE=mmmm	Set the block size, and record the length of all direct-access FILEs to be mmmm bytes. If this parameter is not provided, a default value assembled into the submonitor will be assumed.
FREE=nnnn	Set the amount of memory reserved for the OS/360 work area to be nnnn bytes.
MAX=mmmmm	Set the maximum amount of memory requested from OS/360 to be mmmmm bytes.
MIN=mmmm	Set the minimum amount of memory requested from OS/360 to be mmmm bytes.
TRACE	Transfer to the trace routine (see Appendix 2) at the beginning of XPL program execution. This parameter has the same effect as preceding the XPL program (including its initialization section) with the XPL statement **call** *trace*;

A1.3 XPL Program Loading

An XPL object program stored on direct access storage consists of a number of records (the size of which depends on the particular device) of binary code followed by a number of records corresponding to the data area of the program. The data area is included in the program file because constants and initialized variables may appear in the program. Fig. A1.3.1 illustrates a typical program file. The first record of code begins with a small control block which contains information about the number and size of the records which follow to be used by the submonitor during program loading. Note that the last code record normally contains some unused space, which will be absorbed during the loading process.

After being activated by OS/360, the submonitor checks for possible parameters and then uses an OS/360 OPEN macro† to open the files specified by the DDNAMEs PROGRAM, SYSPRINT, and SYSIN. If any of these files cannot be opened successfully, execution is terminated with an error indication [see Section A1.10]. Once the files are open, the submonitor executes a conditional form of the OS/360 GETMAIN macro to obtain space in main memory from the system. With this form of the macro, a minimum and a maximum amount of memory are specified. OS/360 gives the submonitor no less than the minimum amount of memory and (assuming the minimum is available) as much as possible up to the maximum specified. This allotment technique

---

† OS/360 data-management facilities are described by IBM [6Xc], and a detailed description of the OS/360 data-management macros is given by IBM [6Xd].

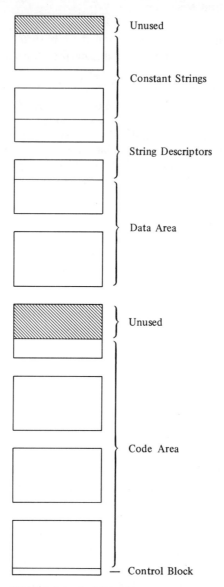

Fig. A1.3.1 An XPL Object Program File

allows the largest possible space to be obtained for the XPL program. Since OS/360 may need additional memory space during execution of the XPL program (for input/ output buffers, control blocks, and the like), the submonitor executes an OS FREEMAIN macro to return a small amount of memory to OS/360 for work space. This amount may be explicitly specified by the FREE parameter described above; otherwise, a default value determined when the submonitor was assembled is used. If the XPL program uses files other than SYSPRINT or SYSIN, which require substantial additional memory for buffers (e.g., string input or output files using blocked records),

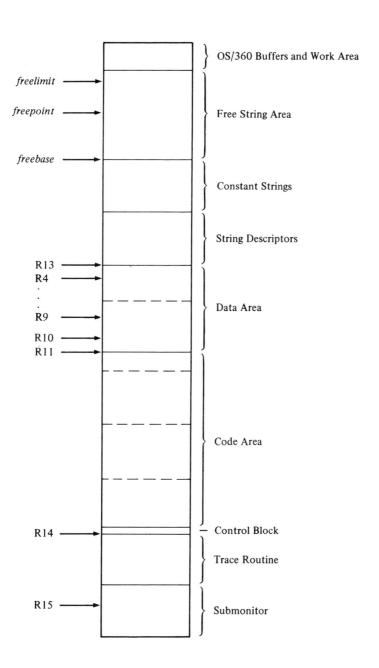

Fig. A1.3.2 An XPL Program in Memory

the default value may not be adequate. Failure to provide sufficient space for buffers usually results in termination with a system completion code of 80A.

The submonitor uses the OS/360 Basic Sequential Access Method (BSAM) [IBM 6Xc] to read the first record of the PROGRAM file into the area of memory it has obtained. A READ macro initiates the input, and a CHECK macro is used to wait for the completion of the input.

From the information in the XPL program control block, the submonitor determines whether the program will fit in the amount of memory available. If it will not fit, execution terminates with an error indication (see Section A1.10). Otherwise, the submonitor proceeds to read in the remaining records of code. Before reading in the records for the data and constant string areas, the submonitor adjusts the address used so that the first data record is placed in memory immediately after the last instruction in the last code record. Figure A1.3.2 shows the binary program of Fig. A1.3.1 as it would reside in memory during execution. Also shown are the values assumed by some registers (see Section 8.4).

Once the XPL program is in main memory, the submonitor loads R1, R2, and R3 with the address of the top of the dynamic string area, the address of the first record of code, and the address of the first record of data, respectively, and then transfers to the first record of code at a point just after the control block.

When the XPL program has completed execution, it returns to the submonitor, optionally returning a value to be passed on to OS/360 for use as the completion code. The submonitor releases the memory occupied by the program, closes all files which have been opened, and then returns to OS/360. Succeeding job steps can test the completion code passed on to OS/360 by the submonitor with appropriate statements in the job control language.

A1.4   Communicating with the Submonitor

The conventions obeyed by an XPL program in making requests on the submonitor are very simple. R1 is loaded with the service code, a small integer used to select the task to be performed. The associations between service codes and tasks are made when the submonitor is assembled. In addition, these associations are known to the code generation routines in XCOM. Table A1.4.1 is a list of the valid service codes. Up to two arguments may also be passed to the submonitor during a request for service. The first argument, if required, is loaded into R0, and the second, if required, into R2. Details of arguments to the submonitor are discussed later.

The service codes marked unused in Table A1.4.1 have no inherent interpretation within the XPL submonitor but may be used to extend the list of services provided. For example, codes 32 and 36, associated with *clock__trap* and *interrupt__trap*, have been used for the Student PL compiler system to provide access to interval timing and to interrupt handling facilities. The built-in function *monitor* is recognized by XCOM and translated into a submonitor call using service code 40. Intentionally, this code has no interpretation within the submonitor so that XPL statements such as

$$\textbf{call } \textit{monitor} \ (\ \langle \text{parameter} \rangle \ , \ \langle \text{parameter} \rangle \ );$$

or

$$\langle variable \rangle = monitor\ (\ \langle parameter \rangle\ );$$

can be used to access a facility which has been added to the submonitor without requiring any change in XCOM.

The next five sections describe in detail how requirements 2 through 6 of Section A1.0 are met by the submonitor.

TABLE A1.4.1

Service Code	Interpretation	Related XPL Function
4	String input	*input*
8	String output	*output*
12	Initiate tracing	*trace*
16	Terminate tracing	*untrace*
20	Force core dump	*exit*
24	Return time and date	*time and date*
28	Unused	
32	Unused	*clock__trap*
36	Unused	*interrupt__trap*
40	Unused	*monitor*
44	Unused	
48	Unused	
52	Read from FILE1	*file(1, j)*
56	Write to FILE1	*file(1, j)*
60	Read from FILE2	*file(2, j)*
64	Write to FILE2	*file(2, j)*
68	Read from FILE3	*file(3, j)*
72	Write to FILE3	*file(3, j)*

A1.5   String Input

The *input* pseudovariable is used for string input in XPL programs. It has as its value the string representing the next record on the input file selected by the subscript on the variable (*input* (i), $i = 0, 1, 2, 3$). The actual input is obtained using the IBM Queued Sequential Access Method (QSAM) [IBM 6Xc] which provides the capabilities for automatic buffering and deblocking of input files. Arguments supplied by the XPL program to the submonitor for this service are the pointer to the next available byte in the free string area (*freepoint*) and the index indicating which input file to use (i for *input* (i)). When the submonitor is entered with a request for an input record, it first determines whether the file requested is valid; if it is not, execution is terminated (see Section A1.10). The submonitor next determines whether the file has already been opened and subsequently closed, a condition which would occur if the program tried to use the file after being sent an end-of-file indication by the submonitor (see below). If the file has been opened and closed, execution is terminated. If not, the submonitor checks whether the file is open and, if not, opens it.

The submonitor then executes a locate mode GET macro [IBM 6Xd]. In locate mode, OS/360 returns the address of the buffer containing the next input record. This input record is moved from the buffer to the free string area. The submonitor returns to the XPL program a standard XPL string descriptor, pointing at the record in the free string area, and a new value of *freepoint* updated by the length of the record. If OS/360 signals that an end of file has been reached, the file is closed, and the submonitor returns to the program a null string descriptor and the same *freepoint* with which the submonitor was entered. If the program again tries to read from the file, execution terminates.

A1.6 String Output

The submonitor also uses QSAM for string output. Use of the pseudovariable *output* results in a call to the submonitor with two arguments: an XPL string descriptor for the string to be output and an index specifying the output file (*i* for *output* (*i*)). To simplify printed output, an arbitrary convention was adopted. For *output* (0), a single blank is concatenated onto the front of the string as it is sent to the output buffer. This convention provides the normal printer carriage control for single-spaced output. The XPL programmer can explicitly specify his own carriage control for this same file by using *output*(1), in which case the leading character of the assigned string is used (+ = no space, 1 = page eject, etc.).

Arbitrary rules were also adopted to resolve differences between the length of the string being output and the record length of the file. If the former is less than the latter, the remainder of the record is filled out with blanks. If the length of the string is greater than the length of the record, the string is truncated on the right, and only the number of characters specified by the record length of the file are output.

When called, the submonitor first determines whether the index specifies a valid output file; if it does not, execution is terminated. The submonitor then determines whether the file is open, and if it is not, opens it. A PUT macro is executed using locate mode. OS/360 returns the address of the next output buffer, the submonitor moves the record to be output into the buffer truncating or padding as described above, and returns control to the XPL program.

A1.7 Direct-access Storage

The IBM Basic Sequential Access Method (BSAM) [IBM 6Xc] is used to provide direct-access storage facilities for XPL programs. It is preferable to some of the more elaborate access methods because it works (with the mild restrictions discussed below) without requiring the files in use to be preformatted (a disadvantage of the BDAM access method). An option of BSAM is the POINT macro, which allows specification of the relative track within the file which to be read or written. To make use of this option, all direct-access files are written with one record per track, which results in a direct correspondence between relative track number and relative record number within the file. The result is efficient use of disk storage if the record length is near the track size of the device being used for the file or rather inefficient use of disk storage if the record length is somewhat less than the track size. It is not possible to write more than one record per track using this technique.

Four restrictions are necessary to make this technique work properly:

1. The $j + 1$st record may not be read or written unless the jth record is already present in the file (the POINT macro uses the jth record to locate the $j + 1$st record). (Error indication: User completion code = 2000 + file number.)
2. The direct-access storage allocated for a file must be contiguous on the device. The method used by the POINT macro to locate records does not work properly if the storage allocated for the file has been split into extents. (Error indication: User completion code = 2000 + file number.)
3. Two Data Control Blocks (DCBs) [IBM 6Xc] are required for each file (one for reading and one for writing) because the file may need to be opened for both input and output simultaneously.
4. Care must be taken to insure that the physically last record in a file is the temporally last record written. This restriction insures that the record pointers kept for the file by OS/360 when the file is closed specify the entire file. Failure to adhere to this restriction results in the loss of all records beyond the last record written.

The XPL programmer uses the constructs

$$file\ (i, j) = \langle \text{variable} \rangle;$$
$$\langle \text{variable} \rangle = file\ (i, j);$$

to reference the jth record on the ith file causing a device-dependent number of bytes to be transferred to or from the file. Three arguments are passed to the submonitor: the index which specifies the file (i) (actually part of the service code), the address of the variable on the other side of the assignment statement, and the relative record number (j).

The submonitor determines whether the file is open, and if not, opens it. The record index is converted to a relative track address, and a POINT macro is executed. A READ or WRITE macro is executed depending on whether the FILE appeared on the right or left side of the assignment statement and a CHECK macro is executed to wait for the operation to complete; and control is returned to the XPL program.

A1.8 Debugging Aids

The debugging aids provided by the submonitor are the ability to access the trace routine (see Appendix 2) and the ability to force a core dump.

The XPL statement **call** *trace*; activates the trace routine: This statement causes a transfer to the submonitor, which in turn transfers control to the trace routine. The submonitor passes to the trace routine the contents of the general registers at the time the trace routine was invoked and the address in the XPL program at which tracing is to begin.

The XPL statement **call** *untrace*; deactivates the trace routine: This statement results in no operation within the submonitor but is detected as a special case of submonitor call by the trace routine.

The ability to cause a core dump at an arbitrary place in an XPL program is provided by the XPL statement **call** *exit;* this statement causes a transfer to the submonitor, where an OS/360 ABEND macro is executed.

A1.9   External Information

The XPL functions *time* and *date* cause a transfer to the submonitor, where a TIME macro is executed. OS/360 returns the time of day in integer hundredths of a second and the date in packed decimal form. The time is passed on to the program as is and the date is converted to an integer of the form (year–1900) $* 1000 +$ day in the year (e.g., 70023 for January 23, 1970) before it is passed on to the program.

A1.10   Error Handling and Program Termination

In general, any error condition detected by the submonitor results in abnormal termination of the program through execution of an OS/360 ABEND macro. Examples of conditions causing abnormal termination are uncorrectable input/output errors, invalid arguments supplied to the submonitor, attempts to read beyond the end of a file, etc. The submonitor does not detect all fatal errors. Some conditions (e.g., failure to specify a word address for FILE input or output) cause termination by OS/360 with a (perhaps mysterious) system completion code.

The user completion codes issued by the submonitor are listed in Table A1.10.1. A core dump is given only if appropriate JCL statements are included to specify an output sink for dumps and if the user explicitly requests a dump, either by using the

TABLE A1.10.1

Completion Code	Reason for Termination
100	Unable to open one of the files—PROGRAM, SYSIN, or SYSPRINT—during initialization
200	End of file encountered while reading in the XPL program from the file PROGRAM
300	Uncorrectable error (SYNAD error) detected while reading in the XPL program from the file PROGRAM
400	The XPL program will not fit in the amount of memory available
500	The XPL program called the submonitor with an invalid service code
$800 + i$	Uncorrectable error detected on the file *output*(i)
$900 + i$	XPL program specified *output*(i) for some i which is not implemented in the monitor
$1000 + i$	Uncorrectable error detected on the file *input*(i)
$1200 + i$	Attempted to read beyond the end of file on *input*(i)
$1400 + i$	XPL program specified *input*(i) for some i which is not implemented in the monitor
$2000 + i$	Uncorrectable error detected on *file*(i)
$2200 + i$	Attempted to read beyond the end of file on *file*(i)
4000	User requested abnormal termination by executing the statement **call** *exit;*

DUMP parameter to the submonitor or by calling the built-in function *exit*. The termination routine saves relevant general registers and attempts to close all files before executing the ABEND macro.

The first step in correcting an error is to check the JCL corresponding to the signaled condition. Next, check the data sets described by the JCL. They must have the proper format and, in some cases, even particular information, e.g., the control block of the program file. The OS utility IEBPTPCH can be used to examine the data sets. Finally, the special conditions on file extents described in Section A1.7 should be checked.

A1.11 Submonitor Flow Charts

The remainder of this appendix contains program flow charts (see Figs. A1.11.1 through A1.11.10) describing the logical operation of the submonitor and a listing of the OS/360 assembly-language source cards for the submonitor.

In the flow charts, a large rectangle represents a processing step, a diamond represents a conditional transfer of control, and large ovals indicate subroutine calls. A small rectangle with an arrow pointing into it is the name of a remote location to which control is transferred. A small rectangle with an arrow leading out of it is the definition of such a location within the program.

Exercise   A1.11.1

> The submonitor passes initialization information to the XPL program in registers R1 through R3. Are these the most convenient registers? Rearrange the initialization sequence so that this information is passed to the program in more convenient registers. Note that this exercise involves changing both the submonitor and XCOM.

Exercise   A1.11.2

> One constant set separately for the submonitor and XCOM is the relative address of the first instruction in the program above the control block. Devise a way of adding this information to the control block, and implement your suggestion.

Exercise   A1.11.3

> One extravagance in the way registers are allocated in the XPL system is that R15 always contains the address of the entry point to the submonitor. Do XPL programs make sufficient demands on the submonitor to justify allocation of a general register for the address of the monitor? Historically, R15 was reserved for the address of the submonitor entry point because (1) addressability is needed when the monitor is called and (2) the trace routine needs some area which is always addressable for executing instructions (see Appendix 2). Changes in the register scheme involve changes in the submonitor, the trace routine (which uses the submonitor for printed output and for executing instructions), and XCOM. Devise a register-handling scheme which frees R15 for other uses (see Exercise 8.5.2). (Hint: The program and data areas are always addressable by certain registers. The trace routine may need a short built-in function within the program area.)

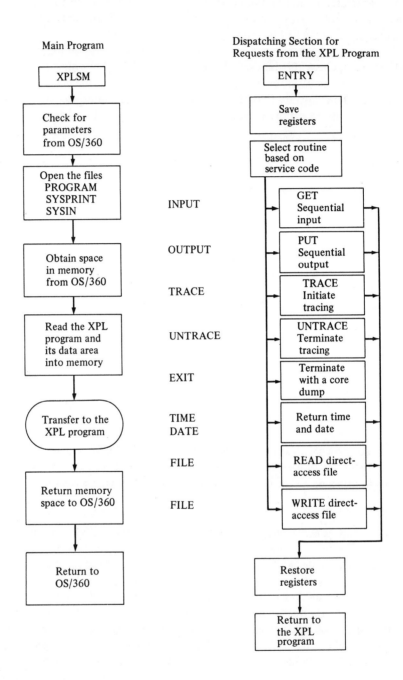

Fig. A1.11.1 Overview of the Submonitor

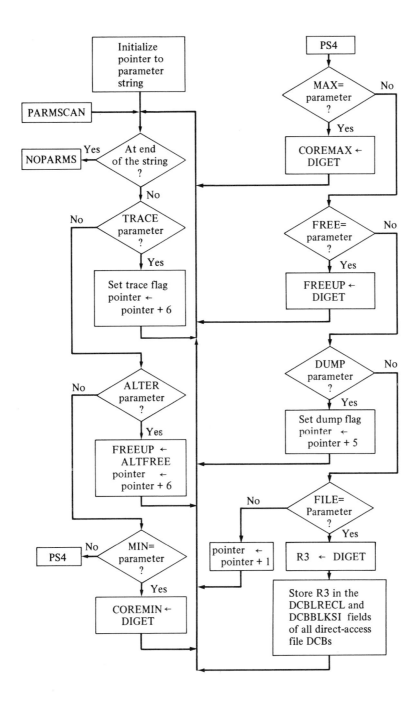

Fig. A1.11.2 Routine to Scan for Parameters from OS/360

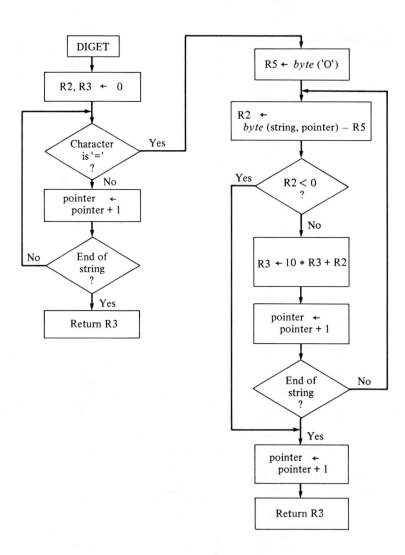

Fig. A1.11.3 Routine to Scan Numbers in Parameter Strings

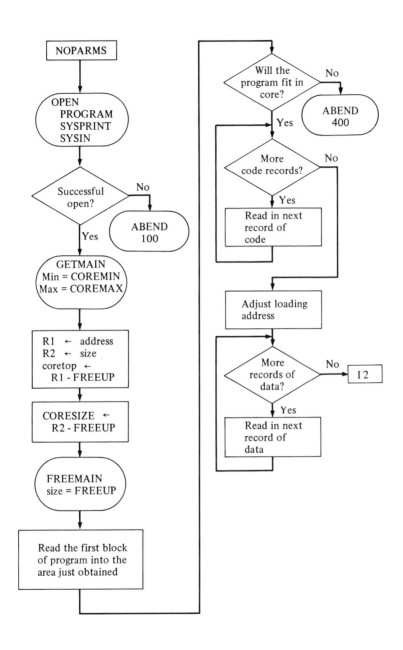

Fig. A1.11.4 Initialization Code

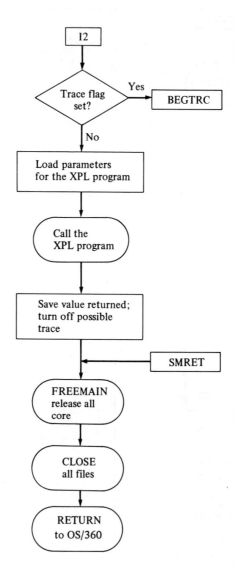

Fig. A1.11.4   (Contd.)

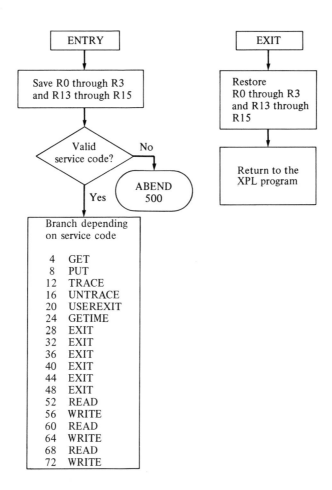

Fig. A1.11.5 Dispatcher for all Service Requests

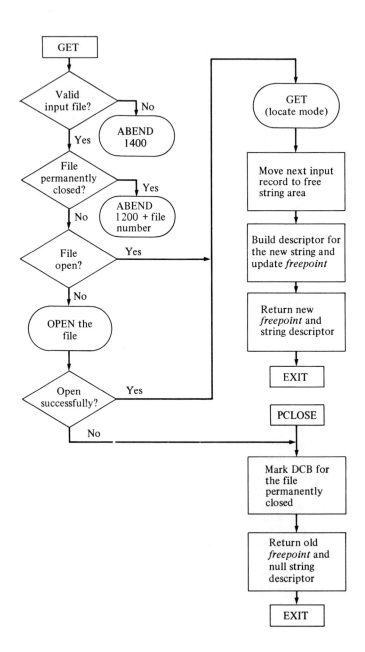

Fig. A1.11.6   Routine for String Input

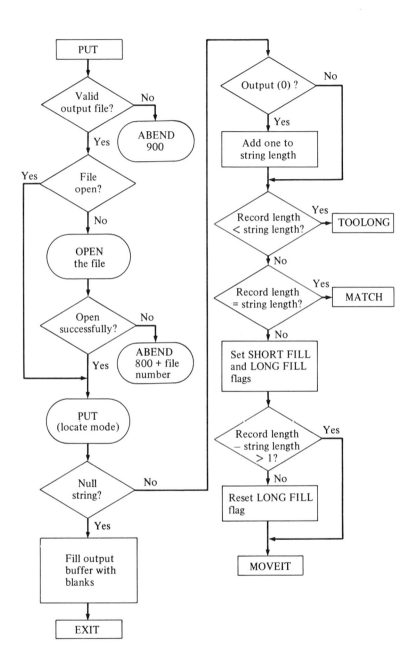

Fig. A1.11.7 Routine for String Output

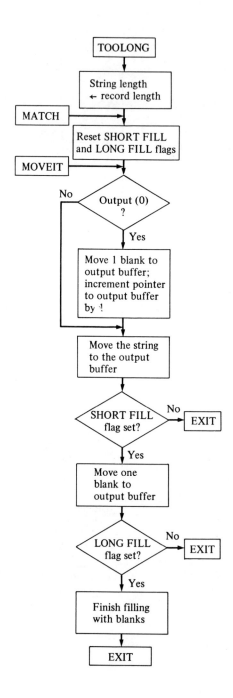

Fig. A1.11.7   (Contd.)

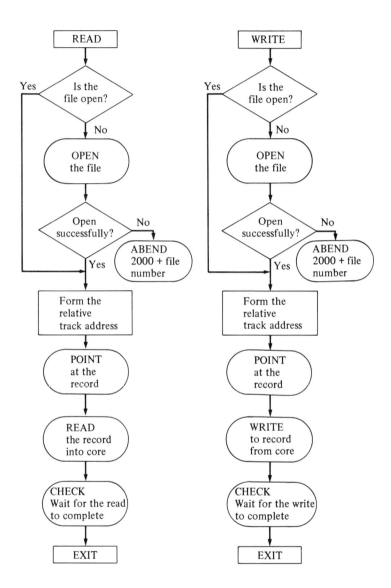

Fig. A1.11.8   Direct Access File I/O Routines

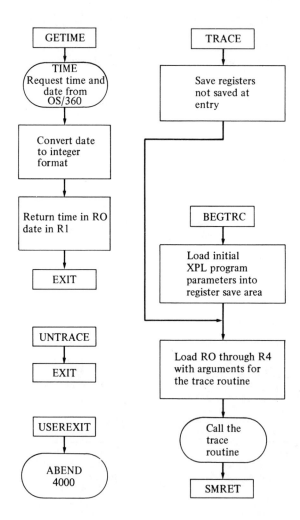

Fig. A1.11.9 Time, Trace, Untrace, and Exit Routines

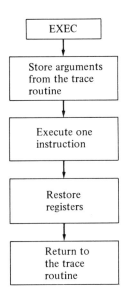

Fig. A1.11.10
Execute Routine
Used by the
Trace Routine

```
***********************************************************************
*                                                                     *
*                                                                     *
*                                                                     *
*        XPLSM     SUBMONITOR FOR THE XPL COMPILER GENERATOR SYSTEM    *
*                                                                     *
*                                                                     *
*                                                                     *
*                                                                     *
***********************************************************************




***********************************************************************
*                                                                     *
*                                                                     *
*                                                                     *
*        WE ARE TIED DOWN TO A LANGUAGE WHICH MAKES UP IN             *
*        OBSCURITY WHAT IT LACKS IN STYLE                             *
*                                                                     *
*                                                                     *
*                          TOM STOPPARD                              *
*                                                                     *
*                          ROSENCRANTZ AND GUILDENSTERN              *
*                                 ARE DEAD                            *
*                                                                     *
*                                                                     *
***********************************************************************




***********************************************************************
*                                                                     *
*                                                                     *
*                                                                     *
*        DEFINE PARAMETRIC CONSTANTS FOR XPLSM                        *
*                                                                     *
*                                                                     *
***********************************************************************
          GBLA  &INPUTS               NUMBER OF INPUT FILES
          GBLA  &OUTPUTS              NUMBER OF OUTPUT FILES
          GBLA  &FILES                NUMBER OF DIRECT ACCESS FILES
          LCLA  &I                    VARIABLE FOR ITERATION LOOPS

IOPACK    CSECT

&INPUTS   SETA  3                     INPUT(I),   I = 0,1,2,3
```

```
&OUTPUTS SETA  3                    OUTPUT(I),  I = 0,1,2,3

&FILES   SETA  3                    FILE(I,*),  I = 1,2,3

***********************************************************************
*                                                                     *
*                                                                     *
*      FILEBYTS DETERMINES THE BLOCKSIZE FOR DIRECT ACCESS FILE       *
*      I/O.  IT SHOULD BE EQUAL TO THE VALUE OF THE LITERAL           *
*      CONSTANT 'DISKBYTES' IN THE XCOM COMPILER FOR COMPILATION      *
*      TO WORK SUCCESSFULLY.  THE VALUE OF FILEBYTS WHICH IS          *
*      ASSEMBLED IN MAY BE OVERIDDEN BY THE 'FILE=NNNN' PARAMETER     *
*      ON THE OS/360 EXEC CARD.                                       *
*                                                                     *
*                                                                     *
*                                                                     *
*      DEVICE        ALLOWABLE RANGE           SUGGESTED VALUE        *
*                                                                     *
*      2311      80 <= FILEBYTS <= 3624         3600                  *
*                                                                     *
*      2314      80 <= FILEBYTS <= 7294         7200                  *
*                                                                     *
*      2321      80 <= FILEBYTS <= 2000         2000                  *
*                                                                     *
*                                                                     *
*      LARGER VALUES MAY BE USED FOR FILEBYTS IF THE SUBMONITOR       *
*      IS REASSEMBLED WITH  RECFM=FT  SPECIFIED IN THE DCBS FOR       *
*      THE DIRECT ACCESS FILES.                                       *
*                                                                     *
*                                                                     *
***********************************************************************

FILEBYTS EQU   3600              2311  DISKS

***********************************************************************
*                                                                     *
*                                                                     *
*      BLKSIZE DEFAULT FOR SOME INPUT AND OUTPUT FILES.  SEE THE      *
*      EXIT LIST HANDLING ROUTINE GENXT.  SHOULD BE THE LARGEST       *
*      MULTIPLE OF 80 THAT IS LESS THAN OR EQUAL TO FILEBYTS          *
*                                                                     *
*                                                                     *
***********************************************************************

IOFBYTS EQU   80*(FILEBYTS/80)

***********************************************************************
*                                                                     *
*                                                                     *
*      DEFINE THE REGISTERS USED TO PASS PARAMETERS TO THE            *
*      SUBMONITOR FROM THE XPL PROGRAM                                *
*                                                                     *
***********************************************************************
```

```
SVCODE     EQU    1                    CODE INDICATING SERVICE REQUESTED

PARM1      EQU    0                    FIRST PARAMETER

PARM2      EQU    2                    SECOND PARAMETER

*************************************************************************
*                                                                       *
*                                                                       *
*          DEFINE THE SERVICE CODES USED BY THE XPL PROGRAM TO          *
*          INDICATE SERVICE REQUESTS TO THE SUBMONITOR                  *
*                                                                       *
*                                                                       *
*************************************************************************

GETC       EQU    4                    SEQUENTIAL INPUT

PUTC       EQU    8                    SEQUENTIAL OUTPUT

TRC        EQU    12                   INITIATE TRACING

UNTR       EQU    16                   TERMINATE TRACING

EXDMP      EQU    20                   FORCE A CORE DUMP

GTIME      EQU    24                   RETURN TIME AND DATE

RSVD1      EQU    28                   (UNUSED)

RSVD2      EQU    32                   CLOCK_TRAP          (NOP IN XPLSM)

RSVD3      EQU    36                   INTERRUPT_TRAP      (NOP IN XPLSM)

RSVD4      EQU    40                   MONITOR             (NOP IN XPLSM)

RSVD5      EQU    44                   (UNUSED)

RSVD6      EQU    48                   (UNUSED)


*************************************************************************
*                                                                       *
*          GENERATE THE SERVICE CODES FOR DIRECT ACCESS FILE I/O        *
*          BASED ON THE NUMBER OF FILES AVAILABLE  (&FILES)             *
*                                                                       *
*************************************************************************

FILEORG    EQU    RSVD6+4              ORIGIN FOR THE FILE SERVICE CODES

&I         SETA   1
.SC1       AIF    (&I GT &FILES).SC2
RD&I       EQU    FILEORG+8*(&I-1)     CODE FOR READING FILE&I
WRT&I      EQU    FILEORG+8*(&I-1)+4   CODE FOR WRITING FILE&I
```

```
&I        SETA  &I+1
          AGO   .SC1
.SC2      ANOP

ENDSERV   EQU   FILEORG+8*(&I-1)    1ST UNUSED SERVICE CODE
```

```
**************************************************************************
*                                                                      *
*                                                                      *
*         DEFINE REGISTER USAGE                                        *
*                                                                      *
**************************************************************************
```

```
RTN       EQU   3                   REGISTER CONTAINING COMPLETION
*                                   CODE RETURNED BY THE PROGRAM

EBR       EQU   10                  BASE REGISTER USED DURING
*                                   INITIALIZATION

CBR       EQU   12                  LINKAGE REGISTER USED FOR CALLS
*                                   TO THE SUBMONITOR

SELF      EQU   15                  REGISTER THAT ALWAYS CONTAINS
*                                   THE ADDRESS OF THE SUBMONITOR
*                                   ENTRY POINT
```

```
**************************************************************************
*                                                                      *
*         BIT CONSTANTS NEEDED FOR CONVERSING WITH OS/360 DCBS         *
*                                                                      *
**************************************************************************
```

```
OPENBIT   EQU   B'00010000'         DCBOFLGS BIT INDICATING OPEN
*                                   SUCCESSFULLY COMPLETED

TAPEBITS  EQU   B'10000001'         DEVT BITS FOR MAGNETIC TAPE

KEYLBIT   EQU   B'00000001'         BIT IN RECFM THAT INDICATES
*                                   KEYLEN WAS EXPLICITLY SET ZERO
```

```
**************************************************************************
*                                                                      *
*         FLAG BITS USED TO CONTROL SUBMONITOR OPERATION               *
*                                                                      *
**************************************************************************
```

```
ALLBITS   EQU   B'11111111'         MASK

TRACEBIT  EQU   B'10000000'         BEGIN EXECUTION OF THE PROGRAM
*                                   IN TRACE MODE

SFILLBIT  EQU   B'01000000'         1 CHARACTER OF FILL NEEDED BY
*                                   THE PUT ROUTINE
```

```
LFILLBIT EQU   B'00100000'        LONGER FILL NEEDED BY PUT ROUTINE

DUMPBIT  EQU   B'00001000'        GIVE A CORE DUMP FOR I/O ERRORS

**************************************************************************
*                                                                      *
*                                                                      *
*           DEFINE ABEND CODES ISSUED BY THE SUBMONITOR                 *
*                                                                      *
**************************************************************************

OPENABE  EQU   100                UNABLE TO OPEN ONE OF THE FILES:
*                                  PROGRAM, SYSIN, OR SYSPRINT

PGMEOD   EQU   200                UNEXPECTED END OF FILE WHILE
*                                  READING IN THE XPL PROGRAM

PGMERR   EQU   300                SYNAD ERROR WHILE READING IN
*                                  THE XPL PROGRAM

COREABE  EQU   400                XPL PROGRAM WON'T FIT IN
*                                  THE AMOUNT OF MEMORY AVAILABLE

CODEABE  EQU   500                INVALID SERVICE CODE FROM THE
*                                  XPL PROGRAM

OUTSYND  EQU   800                SYNAD ERROR ON OUTPUT FILE

PFABE    EQU   900                INVALID OUTPUT FILE SPECIFIED

INSYND   EQU   1000               SYNAD ERROR ON INPUT FILE

INEODAB  EQU   1200               END OF FILE ERROR ON INPUT FILE

GFABE    EQU   1400               INVALID INPUT FILE SPECIFIED

FLSYND   EQU   2000               SYNAD ERROR ON DIRECT ACCESS FILE

FLEOD    EQU   2200               END OF FILE ERROR ON DIRECT
*                                  ACCESS FILE

USERABE  EQU   4000               XPL PROGRAM CALLED EXIT TO
*                                  FORCE A CORE DUMP


**************************************************************************
*                                                                      *
*                                                                      *
*                                                                      *
*        SUBMONITOR  INITIALIZATION                                     *
*                                                                      *
*                                                                      *
**************************************************************************
```

```
                ENTRY   XPLSM                   WHERE OS ENTERS THE SUBMONITOR

                DS      0F
                USING   *,15

XPLSM           SAVE    (14,12),T,*             SAVE ALL REGISTERS
                ST      13,SAVE+4               SAVE RETURN POINTER
                LA      15,SAVE                 ADDRESS OF SUBMONITOR'S OS SAVE AREA
                ST      15,8(0,13)
                LR      13,15
                USING   SAVE,13
                BALR    EBR,0                   BASE ADDRESS FOR INITIALIZATION
                USING   *,EBR
BASE1           DS      0H
                DROP    15
                L       1,0(,1)                 ADDRESS OF A POINTER TO THE PARM
*                                               FIELD OF THE OS EXEC CARD
                ST      1,CONTROL               SAVE ADDRESS FOR THE TRACE ROUTINE
                MVI     FLAGS,B'00000000'       RESET ALL FLAGS
                LH      4,0(,1)                 LENGTH OF THE PARM FIELD
                LA      1,2(,1)                 ADDRESS OF THE PARM STRING
                LA      4,0(1,4)                ADDRESS OF END OF PARAMETER LIST
                LA      7,PARMSCAN

PARMSCAN DS             0H
                CR      1,4                     ARE WE DONE ?
                BNL     NOPARMS                 YES, SO QUIT LOOKING
                CLC     TRCM,0(1)               LOOK FOR 'TRACE'
                BNE     PS2                     NOT FOUND
                OI      FLAGS,TRACEBIT          SET FLAG TO BEGIN IN TRACE MODE
                LA      1,L'TRCM+1(,1)          INCREMENT POINTER
                BR      7                       BRANCH BACK TO TEST
PS2             CLC     ALTRM,0(1)              TEST FOR 'ALTER'
                BNE     PS3                     NOT FOUND
                MVC     FREEUP,ALTFREE          MAKE MORE ROOM FOR ALTER
                LA      1,L'ALTRM+1(,1)         INCREMENT POINTER
                BR      7                       BRANCH BACK TO TEST
PS3             CLC     CMNM,0(1)               LOOK FOR 'MIN=NNNN'
                BNE     PS4                     NOT FOUND
                BAL     CBR,DIGET               GO GET THE NUMBER
                ST      3,COREMIN               SET NEW MINIMUM VALUE
                BR      7                       BRANCH TO TEST
PS4             CLC     CMXM,0(1)               CHECK FOR 'MAX=MMMM'
                BNE     PS5                     NOT FOUND
                BAL     CBR,DIGET               GO GET THE VALUE
                ST      3,COREMAX               SET NEW MAXIMUM VALUE
                BR      7                       BRANCH TO TEST
PS5             CLC     FREEM,0(1)              CHECK FOR 'FREE=NNNN'
                BNE     PS6                     NOT FOUND
                BAL     CBR,DIGET               GO GET THE VALUE
                ST      3,FREEUP                SET NEW AMOUNT FREED
                BR      7                       BRANCH TO TEST
PS6             CLC     DMPM,0(1)               CHECK FOR 'DUMP'
                BNE     PS7                     NOT FOUND
```

```
              OI      FLAGS,DUMPBIT          SET DUMP ON ERROR FLAG
              LA      1,L'DMPM+1(,1)         INCREMENT POINTER
              BR      7                      BRANCH TO TEST
PS7           CLC     FILEM,0(1)             CHECK FOR 'FILE=MMMM'
              BNE     PSBUMP                 NOT FOUND
              BAL     CBR,DIGET              GET THE BLKSIZE VALUE
              LA      2,&FILES*2             NUMBER OF DCB FOR FILES
              LA      5,ARWDCBS              ADDRESS OF DCB LIST
FLOOP         L       6,0(,5)                ADDRESS OF A DCB
              USING IHADCB,6
              STH     3,DCBLRECL             SET NEW RECORD LENGTH
              STH     3,DCBBLKSI             SET NEW BLOCKSIZE
              DROP    6
              LA      5,4(,5)                INCREMENT ADDRESS
              BCT     2,FLOOP                LOOP BACK
              SLL     3,2                    (NEW BLOCKSIZE)*4
              ST      3,ALTFREE              ALTER PARAMETER
              BR      7                      GO TO SCAN LOOP
PSBUMP        LA      1,1(,1)                INCREMENT POINTER TO PARM STRING
              BR      7                      BRANCH TO TEST
NOPARMS       DS      0H
```

```
*************************************************************************
*                                                                       *
*                                                                       *
*             OPEN THE FILES  PROGRAM, SYSIN, AND SYSPRINT              *
*                                                                       *
*************************************************************************
```

```
              OPEN    (INPUT0,(INPUT),OUTPUT0,(OUTPUT),PROGRAM,(INPUT))

              L       3,GETDCBS              ADDRESS OF DCB FOR INPUT0
              USING IHADCB,3
              TM      DCBOFLGS,OPENBIT       CHECK FOR SUCCESSFUL OPENING
              BZ      BADOPEN                INPUT0 NOT OPENED SUCCESSFULLY
              L       3,PUTDCBS              ADDRESS OF DCB FOR OUTPUT0
              TM      DCBOFLGS,OPENBIT       CHECK FOR SUCCESSFUL OPENING
              BZ      BADOPEN                OUTPUT0 NOT OPENED SUCCESSFULLY
              L       3,PGMDCB               ADDRESS OF DCB FOR PROGRAM
              TM      DCBOFLGS,OPENBIT       TEST FOR SUCCESSFUL OPENING
              BNZ     OPENOK                 PROGRAM SUCCESSFULLY OPENED
              DROP    3

BADOPEN       LA      1,OPENABE              ABEND BECAUSE FILES DIDN'T OPEN
*                                            PROPERLY
              B       ABEND                  GO TO ABEND ROUTINE

OPENOK        DS      0H
```

```
***********************************************************************
*                                                                     *
*                                                                     *
*          NOW OBTAIN SPACE IN MEMORY FOR THE XPL PROGRAM AND ITS      *
*          FREE STRING AREA.  A GETMAIN IS ISSUED TO OBTAIN AS MUCH    *
*          MEMORY AS POSSIBLE WITHIN THE PARTITION.  THEN A FREEMAIN   *
*          IS ISSUED TO RETURN THE AMOUNT OF MEMORY SPECIFIED BY       *
*          THE VARIABLE 'FREEUP' TO OS/360 FOR USE AS WORK SPACE.      *
*          OS/360 NEEDS SPACE FOR FOR DYNAMICALLY CREATING BUFFERS     *
*          FOR THE SEQUENTIAL INPUT AND OUTPUT FILES AND FOR           *
*          OVERLAYING I/O ROUTINES.                                    *
*                                                                     *
*             THE AMOUNT OF CORE REQUESTED FROM OS/360 CAN BE ALTERED  *
*          WITH THE 'MAX=NNNN' AND 'MIN=MMMM' PARAMETERS TO THE        *
*          SUBMONITOR.  THE AMOUNT OF CORE RETURNED TO OS/360 CAN BE   *
*          ALTERED WITH THE 'FREE=NNNN' OR THE 'ALTER' PARAMETER       *
*                                                                     *
*          MEMORY REQUEST IS DEFINED BY THE CONTROL BLOCK STARTING AT  *
*          'COREREQ'.  THE DESCRIPTION OF THE MEMORY SPACE OBTAINED    *
*          IS PUT INTO THE CONTROL BLOCK STARTING AT 'ACORE'.          *
*                                                                     *
*                                                                     *
***********************************************************************

          GETMAIN VU,LA=COREREQ,A=ACORE

          LM    1,2,ACORE          ADDRESS OF CORE OBTAINED TO R1
*                                  LENGTH OF CORE AREA TO R2
          AR    1,2                ADDRESS OF TOP OF CORE AREA
          S     1,FREEUP           LESS AMOUNT TO BE RETURNED
          ST    1,CORETOP          ADDRESS OF TOP OF USABLE CORE
*                                  (BECOMES 'FREELIMIT')
          S     2,FREEUP           SUBTRACT AMOUNT RETURNED
          ST    2,CORESIZE         SIZE OF AVAILABLE SPACE
          L     0,FREEUP           AMOUNT TO GIVE BACK

          FREEMAIN R,LV=(0),A=(1)  GIVE 'FREEUP' BYTES OF CORE BACK

***********************************************************************
*                                                                     *
*                                                                     *
*          READ IN THE BINARY XPL PROGRAM AS SPECIFIED BY THE          *
*                                                                     *
*          //PROGRAM  DD  .....                                       *
*                                                                     *
*          CARD.  IT IS ASSUMED THAT THE BINARY PROGRAM IS IN STANDARD *
*          XPL SYSTEM FORMAT.                                          *
*                                                                     *
*          THE 1ST RECORD OF THE BINARY PROGRAM FILE SHOULD BEGIN      *
*          WITH A BLOCK OF INFORMATION DESCRIBING THE CONTENTS OF      *
*          THE FILE.  THE FORMAT OF THIS BLOCK IS GIVEN IN THE DSECT   *
*          'FILECTRL' AT THE END OF THIS ASSEMBLY.                     *
*                                                                     *
***********************************************************************
```

```
        L     2,ACORE            ADDRESS OF START OF CORE AREA
        LR    4,2                SAVE STARTING ADDRESS
        USING FILECTRL,4         ADDRESS OF CONTROL BLOCK
        ST    2,CODEADR          SAVE STARTING ADDRESS FOR USE
*                                BY THE XPL PROGRAM
        BAL   CBR,READPGM        READ IN 1ST RECORD
        L     3,BYTSCODE         NUMBER OF BYTES OF CODE
        S     3,BYTSBLK          LESS ONE RECORD
        A     3,BYTSFULL         PLUS AMOUNT IN LAST CODE RECORD
        A     3,BYTSDATA         PLUS SIZE OF DATA AREA
        C     3,CORESIZE         COMPARE WITH SPACE AVAILABLE
        LA    1,COREABE          ABEND CODE FOR NO ROOM IN CORE
        BH    ABEND              WON'T FIT, SO ABEND
        L     5,BLKSCODE         NUMBER OF RECORDS OF CODE
        L     3,BYTSBLK          NUMBER OF BYTES PER RECORD
        B     LOAD1              GO TEST FOR MORE CODE RECORDS

RCODE   AR    2,3                ADDRESS TO PUT NEXT RECORD
        BAL   CBR,READPGM        READ IN THE BINARY XPL PROGRAM
LOAD1   BCT   5,RCODE            LOOP BACK TO GET NEXT RECORD

        A     2,BYTSFULL         NUMBER OF BYTES ACTUALLY
*                                USED IN LAST CODE RECORD
        ST    2,DATADR           SAVE ADDRESS OF DATA AREA
*                                FOR USE BY THE XPL PROGRAM
        L     5,BLKSDATA         NUMBER OF RECORDS OF DATA

RDATA   BAL   CBR,READPGM        READ IN THE XPL PROGRAM'S DATA AREA
        AR    2,3                ADDRESS TO PUT NEXT RECORD
        BCT   5,RDATA            LOOP BACK FOR NEXT RECORD
        DROP  4

*************************************************************************
*                                                                       *
*                                                                       *
*       CODE TO BRANCH TO THE XPL PROGRAM                               *
*                                                                       *
*                                                                       *
*************************************************************************

        LA    SELF,ENTRY         ADDRESS OF ENTRY POINT TO XPLSM
        TM    FLAGS,TRACEBIT     START IN TRACE MODE ?
        BO    BEGTRC             YES, BEGIN TRACING
        LM    0,3,PGMPARMS       PARAMETERS FOR THE XPL PROGRAM
        DROP  EBR,13
        USING ENTRY,SELF

        USING FILECTRL,2         ADDRESS OF FIRST RECORD OF CODE
GOC     BAL   CBR,CODEBEGN       BRANCH TO HEAD OF THE XPL PROGRAM
        DROP  2
```

```
****************************************************************
*                                                              *
*                                                              *
*        THE XPL PROGRAM RETURNS HERE AT THE END OF EXECUTION  *
*                                                              *
*                                                              *
****************************************************************

         L     EBR,ABASE1        REGISTER FOR ADDRESSABILITY
         USING BASE1,EBR
         ST    RTN,RTNSV         SAVE COMPLETION CODE RETURNED BY
*                                THE XPL PROGRAM FOR PASSING TO OS
         LA    1,UNTR            TURN OFF POSSIBLE TRACE
         BALR  CBR,SELF          CALL THE SERVICE ROUTINES
         L     13,ASAVE          ADDRESS OF OS/360 SAVE AREA
         USING SAVE,13
         DROP  SELF

****************************************************************
*                                                              *
*        RELEASE THE MEMORY OCCUPIED BY THE XPL PROGRAM        *
*                                                              *
****************************************************************

SMRET    L     1,ACORE           ADDRESS OF THE BLOCK TO BE FREED
         L     0,CORESIZE        LENGTH OF THE BLOCK TO BE FREED

         FREEMAIN R,LV=(0),A=(1)  FREEDOM NOW !

         CLOSE (INPUT0,,OUTPUT0)

****************************************************************
*                                                              *
*        WARNING,  THE CLOSE OF INPUT0 AND OUTPUT0 MUST PRECEDE *
*        THE CLOSE WHICH USES THE GETDCBS LIST.  THE CLOSE SVC WILL *
*        LOOP INDEFINITELY IF THE SAME DCB ADDRESS APPEARS TWICE IN *
*        A CLOSE LIST.                                          *
*                                                              *
****************************************************************

         CLOSE ,MF=(E,GETDCBS)    CLOSE ALL FILES KNOWN TO XPLSM

         L     15,RTNSV           LOAD RETURN CODE
         L     13,SAVE+4
         DROP  13
         RETURN (14,12),RC=(15)   RETURN TO OS/360

         DROP  EBR
         USING SAVE,13
```

```
*****************************************************************************
*                                                                           *
*           CONSTANTS USED DURING INITIALIZATION                            *
*                                                                           *
*****************************************************************************

         SAVE     DS    18F              SAVE AREA FOR OS/360
         ACORE    DS    A                ADDRESS OF CORE FOR THE PROGRAM
         CORESIZE DS    F                SIZE OF CORE IN BYTES
         CONTROL  DS    A                ADDRESS OF PARAMETER STRING PASSED
*                                        TO THE SUBMONITOR BY OS/360
         COREREQ  DS    0H               CORE REQUEST CONTROL BLOCK
         COREMIN  DC    F'110000'        MINIMUM AMOUNT OF CORE REQUIRED
         COREMAX  DC    F'5000000'       MAXIMUM AMOUNT OF CORE REQUESTED
         FREEUP   DC    A(2*FILEBYTS)    AMOUNT OF CORE TO RETURN TO OS
         ALTFREE  DC    A(4*FILEBYTS)    AMOUNT OF CORE FREED FOR ALTER


*****************************************************************************
*                                                                           *
*           BLOCK OF PARAMETERS PASSED TO THE XPL PROGRAM                    *
*                                                                           *
*****************************************************************************

         PGMPARMS DS    F                R0   UNUSED
         CORETOP  DC    A(0)             R1   ADDRESS OF TOP OF CORE
         CODEADR  DC    F'0'             R2   ADDRESS OF START OF 1ST RECORD
*                                        OF THE XPL PROGRAM
         DATADR   DC    F'0'             R3   ADDRESS OF THE START OF THE XPL
*                                        PROGRAM'S DATA AREA

         TRCM     DC    CL5'TRACE'
         ALTRM    DC    CL5'ALTER'
         CMNM     DC    CL4'MIN='
         CMXM     DC    CL4'MAX='
         FREEM    DC    CL5'FREE='
         DMPM     DC    CL4'DUMP'
         FILEM    DC    CL5'FILE='



*****************************************************************************
*                                                                           *
*                                                                           *
*           ROUTINE TO SCAN PARAMETER STRINGS FOR DIGITS                     *
*                                                                           *
*                                                                           *
*****************************************************************************

         DIGET    DS    0H
                  SR    2,2              CLEAR REGISTER
                  SR    3,3                "
         DG1      CLI   0(1),C'='        CHECK FOR '='
                  BE    DG2
                  LA    1,1(,1)          INCREMENT POINTER
                  CR    1,4              AT END ?
```

```
            BCR     B'1011',CBR             YES, SO RETURN
            B       DG1                     KEEP LOOKING FOR '='
DG2         LA      1,1(,1)                 INCREMENT POINTER
            LA      5,C'0'                  BINARY VALUE OF '0'
DGLP        IC      2,0(,1)                 FETCH A CHARACTER
            SR      2,5                     NORMALIZE
            BM      DGDN                    NOT A DIGIT SO DONE
            LR      0,3
            SLL     3,2                     NUMBER*4
            AR      3,0                     NUMBER*5
            SLL     3,1                     NUMBER*10
            AR      3,2                     ADD IN NEW DIGIT
            LA      1,1(,1)                 INCREMENT POINTER
            CR      1,4                     AT END ?
            BL      DGLP                    NO
DGDN        LA      1,1(,1)                 INCREMENT POINTER
            BR      CBR                     RETURN
*                                           VALUE OF NUMBER IS IN REG 3


***********************************************************************
*                                                                     *
*                                                                     *
*        ROUTINE TO READ IN THE BINARY IMAGE OF THE XPL PROGRAM       *
*                                                                     *
*                                                                     *
***********************************************************************

READPGM     DS      0H
*                                           SHARE DECB WITH FILE READ ROUTINE

            READ    RDECB,SF,PROGRAM,(2),MF=E
            CHECK   RDECB                   WAIT FOR READ TO COMPLETE

            BR      CBR                     RETURN TO CALLER


***********************************************************************
*                                                                     *
*                                                                     *
*        ROUTINES TO PROVIDE DEFAULT DATASET INFORMATION IF NONE      *
*        IS PROVIDED BY JCL OR VOLUME LABELS.  IN PARTICULAR,         *
*        BLKSIZE, LRECL, BUFNO, AND RECFM INFORMATION.                *
*                                                                     *
*        EXIT LISTS FOR DCBS                                          *
*                                                                     *
***********************************************************************

            DS      0F
INEXIT0     DC      X'85'                   INPUT0
            DC      AL3(INXT0)

OUTEXIT0    DC      X'85'                   OUTPUT0
            DC      AL3(OUTXT0)
```

```
INEXIT2   DC     X'85'                    INPUT2
          DC     AL3(INXT2)


OUTEXIT2 EQU     INEXIT0                  OUTPUT2


&I        SETA   3
.IDF1     AIF    (&I GT &INPUTS).IDF2
INEXIT&I EQU     INEXIT2                  INPUT&I
&I        SETA   &I+1
          AGO    .IDF1
.IDF2     ANOP


&I        SETA   3
.ODF1     AIF    (&I GT &OUTPUTS).ODF2
OUTEXIT&I EQU    INEXIT2
&I        SETA   &I+1
          AGO    .ODF1
.ODF2     ANOP


***************************************************************************
*                                                                         *
*         DCB EXIT ROUTINE ENTRY POINTS                                   *
*                                                                         *
***************************************************************************


INXT0     MVC    DEFAULTS(6),INDFLT0
          B      GENXT


INXT2     MVC    DEFAULTS(6),INDFLT2
          B      GENXT


OUTXT0    MVC    DEFAULTS(6),OUTDFLT0


***************************************************************************
*                                                                         *
*         DCB EXIT LIST PROCESSING ROUTINE FOR OPEN EXITS                 *
*                                                                         *
***************************************************************************


GENXT     DS     0H
          USING  IHADCB,1                 REGISTER 1 POINTS AT THE DCB
          NC     DCBBLKSI,DCBBLKSI        CHECK BLKSIZE
          BNZ    GXT1                     ALREADY SET
          MVC    DCBBLKSI(2),DFLTBLKS
*                                         PROVIDE DEFAULT BLOCKSIZE


GXT1      NC     DCBLRECL,DCBLRECL        CHECK LRECL
          BNZ    GXT2                     ALREADY SET
          MVC    DCBLRECL(2),DFLTLREC
*                                         PROVIDE DEFAULT LRECL


GXT2      CLI    DCBBUFNO,0               CHECK BUFNO
          BNE    GXT3                     ALREADY SPECIFIED
```

```
        MVC    DCBBUFNO(1),DFLTBUFN
*                                   PROVIDE DEFAULT BUFNO

GXT3    TM     DCBRECFM,ALLBITS-KEYLBIT
*                                   CHECK RECFM
        BCR    B'0111',14           ALREADY SET SO RETURN
        OC     DCBRECFM(1),DFLTRECF
*                                   PROVIDE DEFAULT RECFM
        BR     14                   RETURN
        DROP   1


***********************************************************************
*                                                                     *
*       ARRAY OF DEFAULT ATTRIBUTES USED BY GENXT                     *
*                                                                     *
***********************************************************************


DEFAULTS DS    0H
DFLTBLKS DS    1H                   DEFAULT BLKSIZE
DFLTLREC DS    1H                   DEFAULT LRECL
DFLTBUFN DS    AL1                  DEFAULT BUFNO
DFLTRECF DS    1BL1                 DEFAULT RECFM


***********************************************************************
*                                                                     *
*       DEFINE ATTRIBUTES PROVIDED FOR THE VARIOUS FILES              *
*                                                                     *
*       INPUT(0), INPUT(1), OUTPUT(2)                                 *
*                                                                     *
***********************************************************************


INDFLT0 DS     0H
        DC     H'80'                BLKSIZE=80
        DC     H'80'                LRECL=80
        DC     AL1(2)               BUFNO=2
        DC     B'10000000'          RECFM=F


***********************************************************************
*                                                                     *
*       OUTPUT(0), OUTPUT(1)                                          *
*                                                                     *
***********************************************************************


OUTDFLT0 DS    0H
        DC     H'133'               BLKSIZE=133
        DC     H'133'               LRECL=133
        DC     AL1(2)               BUFNO=2
        DC     B'10000100'          RECFM=FA


***********************************************************************
*                                                                     *
*       INPUT(2), INPUT(3), OUTPUT(3)                                 *
*                                                                     *
***********************************************************************
```

```
INDFLT2  DS    0H
         DC    AL2(IOFBYTS)           BLKSIZE=IOFBYTS
         DC    H'80'                  LRECL=80
         DC    AL1(1)                 BUFNO=1
         DC    B'10010000'            RECFM=FB


****************************************************************************
*                                                                          *
*                                                                          *
*        INPUT - OUTPUT  ERROR ROUTINES                                    *
*                                                                          *
*                                                                          *
*                                                                          *
*        SYNAD AND EOD ERROR ROUTINES FOR INITIAL LOADING OF THE           *
*        XPL PROGRAM                                                       *
*                                                                          *
*                                                                          *
****************************************************************************

EODPGM   STM   0,2,ABEREGS            SAVE REGISTERS
         LA    1,PGMEOD               UNEXPECTED EOD WHILE READING IN
*                                     THE XPL PROGRAM
         B     ABEND                  GO TO ABEND ROUTINE

ERRPGM   STM   0,2,ABEREGS            SAVE REGISTERS
         LA    1,PGMERR               SYNAD ERROR WHILE READING IN THE
*                                     XPL PROGRAM
         B     ABEND                  GO TO ABEND ROUTINE

****************************************************************************
*                                                                          *
*                                                                          *
*        SYNAD AND EOD ROUTINES FOR INPUT(I),  I = 0,1, ...   ,&INPUTS     *
*                                                                          *
****************************************************************************

INEOD    L     2,SAVREG+PARM2*4       PICK UP SUBCODE SPECIFYING WHICH
*                                     INPUT FILE
         SLL   2,2                    SUBCODE*4
         L     2,GETDCBS(2)           FETCH DCB ADDRESS
         USING IHADCB,2
         ST    2,OCDCB                STORE IT FOR THE CLOSE SVC
         MVI   OCDCB,X'80'            FLAG END OF PARAMETER LIST
         CLOSE ,MF=(E,OCDCB)          CLOSE THE OFFENDING FILE

PCLOSE   DS    0H
         XC    DCBDDNAM,DCBDDNAM      MARK THE FILE PERMANENTLY UNUSABLE
         DROP  2
         B     RETNEOF               GO RETURN AN END OF FILE INDICATION

INSYNAD  STM   0,2,ABEREGS            SAVE REGISTERS
         LA    1,INSYND               SYNAD ERROR ON AN INPUT FILE
```

```
            B       INERR                   BRANCH TO ERROR ROUTINE

INEOD2      LA      1,INEODAB               EOD ON AN INPUT FILE
*                                           ATTEMPT TO READ AFTER AN EOD SIGNAL
INERR       A       1,SAVREG+PARM2*4        SUBCODE INDICATING WHICH INPUT FILE
            B       ABEND                   BRANCH TO ABEND ROUTINE


**********************************************************************
*                                                                    *
*                                                                    *
*          SYNAD ERROR ROUTINES FOR OUTPUT FILES                     *
*                                                                    *
*                                                                    *
**********************************************************************


OUTSYNAD    STM     0,2,ABEREGS             SAVE REGISTERS
            LA      1,OUTSYND               SYNAD ERROR ON OUTPUT FILE
            B       INERR


**********************************************************************
*                                                                    *
*          SYNAD AND EOD ROUTINES FOR DIRECT ACCESS FILE I/O         *
*                                                                    *
**********************************************************************


FILESYND    STM     0,2,ABEREGS             SAVE REGISTERS
            LA      1,FLSYND                SYNAD ERROR ON DIRECT ACCESS FILE
            B       FILERR                  GO TO ERROR ROUTINE

FILEEOD     STM     0,2,ABEREGS             SAVE REGISTERS
            LA      1,FLEOD                 EOD ERROR ON DIRECT ACCESS FILE

FILERR      L       2,SAVREG+SVCODE*4       SERVICE CODE
            LA      0,RD1-8                 COMPUTE WHICH DIRECT ACCESS FILE
            SR      2,0                     SERVICE_CODE - 1ST SERVICE CODE
            SRL     2,3                     DIVIDE BY 8
            AR      1,2
*                                           FALL THROUGH TO ABEND ROUTINE


**********************************************************************
*                                                                    *
*                                                                    *
*          ABEND ROUTINE FOR ALL I/O ERRORS                          *
*                                                                    *
*                                                                    *
**********************************************************************


ABEND       DS      0H
            ST      1,ABESAVE               SAVE ABEND CODE

            CLOSE (INPUT0,,OUTPUT0)         THESE MUST BE CLOSED FIRST
            CLOSE ,MF=(E,GETDCBS)           ATTEMPT TO CLOSE ALL FILES

            L       1,ABESAVE
```

```
          TM     FLAGS,DUMPBIT         IS A CORE DUMP DESIRED ?
          BZ     NODUMP                NO, ABEND QUIETLY

          ABEND (1),DUMP               ABEND WITH A DUMP

NODUMP    DS     0H
          ABEND (1)                    ABEND WITHOUT A DUMP

**************************************************************************
*                                                                      *
*                                                                      *
*      ROUTINE TO FORCE AN ABEND DUMP WHEN REQUESTED BY THE            *
*      XPL PROGRAM BY MEANS OF THE STATEMENT:                          *
*                                                                      *
*      CALL  EXIT  ;                                                   *
*                                                                      *
*                                                                      *
**************************************************************************

USEREXIT  DS     0H
          STM    0,2,ABEREGS          SAVE REGISTERS
          OI     FLAGS,DUMPBIT        FORCE A DUMP
          LA     1,USERABE            USER ABEND CODE
          B      ABEND                BRANCH TO ABEND


**************************************************************************
*                                                                      *
*                                                                      *
*      DISPATCHER FOR ALL SERVICE REQUESTS FROM THE XPL PROGRAM        *
*                                                                      *
*                                                                      *
**************************************************************************

          DROP   13
          USING  ENTRY,SELF
ENTRY     DS     0H                   XPL PROGRAMS ENTER HERE
          STM    0,3,SAVREG           SAVE REGISTERS USED BY XPLSM
          STM    13,15,SAVREG+13*4
          L      13,ASAVE             ADDRESS OF OS SAVE AREA
          DROP   SELF
          USING  SAVE,13

          LTR    SVCODE,SVCODE        CHECK THE SERVICE CODE FOR VALIDITY
          BNP    BADCODE              SERVICE CODE MUST BE > 0
          C      SVCODE,MAXCODE       AND < ENDSERV
          BH     BADCODE              GO ABEND

TABLE     B      TABLE(SVCODE)        GO DO THE SERVICE

          ORG    TABLE+GETC
          B      GET                  READ INPUT FILE

          ORG    TABLE+PUTC
```

```
        B      PUT                   WRITE OUTPUT FILE

        ORG    TABLE+TRC
        B      TRACE                 INITIATE TRACING OF THE PROGRAM

        ORG    TABLE+UNTR
        B      UNTRACE               TERMINATE TRACING

        ORG    TABLE+EXDMP
        B      USEREXIT              TERMINATE WITH A CORE DUMP

        ORG    TABLE+GTIME
        B      GETIME                RETURN TIME AND DATE

        ORG    TABLE+RSVD1
        B      EXIT                  (UNUSED)

        ORG    TABLE+RSVD2
        B      EXIT                  CLOCK_TRAP          (NOP)

        ORG    TABLE+RSVD3
        B      EXIT                  INTERRUPT_TRAP      (NOP)

        ORG    TABLE+RSVD4
        B      EXIT                  MONITOR             (NOP)

        ORG    TABLE+RSVD5
        B      EXIT                  (UNUSED)

        ORG    TABLE+RSVD6
        B      EXIT                  (UNUSED)

************************************************************************
*                                                                      *
*                                                                      *
*      DYNAMICALLY GENERATE THE DISPATCHING TABLE ENTRIES FOR          *
*      FILE I/O SERVICES.                                              *
*                                                                      *
*                                                                      *
************************************************************************

&I      SETA   1                     LOOP INDEX
.DBR1   AIF    (&I GT &FILES).DBR2
*                                     FINISHED ?
        ORG    TABLE+RD&I
        B      READ                  BRANCH TO FILE READ ROUTINE
        ORG    TABLE+WRT&I
        B      WRITE                 BRANCH TO FILE WRITE ROUTINE
&I      SETA   &I+1                  INCREMENT COUNTER
        AGO    .DBR1                 LOOP BACK
.DBR2   ANOP

        ORG    TABLE+ENDSERV         RESET PROGRAM COUNTER
```

```
**********************************************************************
*                                                                    *
*                                                                    *
*         COMMON EXIT ROUTINE FOR RETURN TO THE XPL PROGRAM          *
*                                                                    *
*                                                                    *
**********************************************************************

EXIT     DS     0H
         LM     0,3,SAVREG            RESTORE REGISTERS
         LM     13,15,SAVREG+13*4
         DROP   13
         USING  ENTRY,SELF

         BR     CBR                   RETURN TO THE XPL PROGRAM

         DROP   SELF
         USING  SAVE,13

**********************************************************************
*                                                                    *
*         ROUTINE TO ABEND IN CASE OF BAD SERVICE CODES             *
*                                                                    *
**********************************************************************

BADCODE  STM    0,2,ABEREGS          SAVE REGISTERS
         LA     1,CODEABE            BAD SERVICE CODE ABEND
         B      ABEND                GO ABEND


**********************************************************************
*                                                                    *
*                                                                    *
*         INPUT ROUTINE FOR READING SEQUENTIAL INPUT FILES          *
*                                                                    *
*                                                                    *
*         INPUT TO THIS ROUTINE IS:                                 *
*                                                                    *
*     PARM1   ADDRESS OF THE NEXT AVAILABLE SPACE IN THE PROGRAMS   *
*             DYNAMIC STRING AREA  (FREEPOINT)                      *
*                                                                    *
*     SVCODE  THE SERVICE CODE FOR INPUT                            *
*                                                                    *
*     PARM2   A SUBCODE DENOTING WHICH INPUT FILE,                  *
*             INPUT(I),     I = 0,1, ... ,&INPUTS                   *
*                                                                    *
*       THE ROUTINE RETURNS:                                        *
*                                                                    *
*     PARM1   A STANDARD XPL STRING DESCRIPTOR POINTING AT THE INPUT *
*             RECORD WHICH IS NOW AT THE TOP OF THE STRING AREA     *
*                                                                    *
*     SVCODE  THE NEW VALUE FOR FREEPOINT, UPDATED BY THE LENGTH OF *
*             THE RECORD JUST READ IN                              *
*                                                                    *
```

```
*                                                                     *
*          A STANDARD XPL STRING DESCRIPTOR HAS:                      *
*                                                                     *
*          BITS  0-7                 (LENGTH - 1) OF THE STRING       *
*          BITS  8-31                ABSOLUTE ADDRESS OF THE STRING   *
*                                                                     *
*                                                                     *
*                                                                     *
***********************************************************************


GET        DS    0H
           LA    SVCODE,&INPUTS      CHECK THAT THE SUBCODE IS VALID
           LTR   PARM2,PARM2         SUBCODE MUST BE >= 0
           BM    BADGET
           CR    PARM2,SVCODE        AND <= &INPUTS
           BH    BADGET              ILLEGAL SUBCODE
           SLL   PARM2,2             SUBCODE*4
           L     3,GETDCBS(PARM2)    ADDRESS OF DCB FOR THE FILE
           USING IHADCB,3
           NC    DCBDDNAM,DCBDDNAM   HAS THE FILE BEEN PERMANENTLY
*                                    CLOSED ?
           BZ    INEOD2              YES, SO TERMINATE THE JOB

           TM    DCBOFLGS,OPENBIT    IS THE FILE OPEN ?
           BO    GETOPEN             YES
           ST    3,OCDCB             STORE DCB ADDRESS FOR OPEN SVC
           MVI   OCDCB,X'80'         FLAG END OF PARAMETER LIST
           OPEN  ,MF=(E,OCDCB)       OPEN THE FILE
           LR    2,3                 COPY DCB ADDRESS
           TM    DCBOFLGS,OPENBIT    WAS THE FILE OPENED SUCCESSFULLY ?
           BZ    PCLOSE              NO, MARK FILE PERMANENTLY CLOSED AND
*                                    RETURN EOD INDICATION TO THE PROGRAM

GETOPEN    DS    0H
           GET   (3)                 LOCATE MODE GET

***********************************************************************
*                                                                     *
*          USING LOCATE MODE, THE ADDRESS OF THE NEXT INPUT BUFFER     *
*          IS RETURNED IN R1                                           *
*                                                                     *
***********************************************************************

           L     2,SAVREG+PARM1*4    FETCH THE STRING DESCRIPTOR
           LA    2,0(,2)             ADDRESS PART ONLY
           LH    3,DCBLRECL          RECORD LENGTH
           DROP  3
           S     3,F1                LENGTH - 1
           EX    3,GETMOVE           MOVE THE CHARACTERS
           ST    2,SAVREG+PARM1*4    BUILD UP A STRING DESCRIPTOR
           STC   3,SAVREG+PARM1*4    LENGTH FIELD
           LA    2,1(2,3)            NEW FREE POINTER
           ST    2,SAVREG+SVCODE*4
           B     EXIT                RETURN TO THE XPL PROGRAM
```

```
***********************************************************************
*                                                                     *
*         RETURN A NULL STRING DESCRIPTOR AS AN END OF FILE           *
*         INDICATION THE FIRST TIME AN INPUT REQUEST FIND THE         *
*         END OF DATA CONDITION                                       *
*                                                                     *
***********************************************************************

RETNEOF  DS    0H
         MVC   SAVREG+SVCODE*4(4),SAVREG+PARM1*4
*                                   RETURN FREEPOINT UNTOUCHED
         XC    SAVREG+PARM1*4(4),SAVREG+PARM1*4
*                                   RETURN A NULL STRING DESCRIPTOR
         B     EXIT                 RETURN TO THE XPL PROGRAM


***********************************************************************
*                                                                     *
*         ROUTINE TO ABEND IN CASE OF AN INVALID SUBCODE              *
*                                                                     *
***********************************************************************

BADGET   STM   0,2,ABEREGS          SAVE REGISTERS
         LA    1,GFABE              INVALID GET SUBCODE
         B     INERR                GO ABEND


***********************************************************************
*                                                                     *
*                                                                     *
*                                                                     *
*         ROUTINE FOR WRITING SEQUENTIAL OUTPUT FILES                 *
*                                                                     *
*                                                                     *
*         INPUT TO THIS ROUTINE:                                      *
*                                                                     *
*      PARM1   XPL STRING DESCRIPTOR OF THE STRING TO BE OUTPUT       *
*                                                                     *
*      PARM2   SUBCODE INDICATING  OUTPUT(I),  I = 0,1, ... ,&OUTPUTS *
*                                                                     *
*      SVCODE  THE SERVICE CODE FOR OUTPUT                            *
*                                                                     *
*                                                                     *
*         THE STRING NAMED BY THE DESCRIPTOR IS PLACED IN THE NEXT    *
*         OUTPUT BUFFER OF THE SELECTED FILE.  IF THE STRING IS       *
*         SHORTER THAN THE RECORD LENGTH OF THE FILE THEN THE         *
*         REMAINDER OF THE RECORD IS PADDED WITH BLANKS.  IF THE      *
*         STRING IS LONGER THAN THE RECORD LENGTH OF THE FILE         *
*         THEN IT IS TRUNCATED ON THE RIGHT TO FIT.  IF THE SUBCODE   *
*         SPECIFIES OUTPUT(0) THEN A SINGLE BLANK IS CONCATENATED     *
*         ON TO THE FRONT OF THE STRING TO SERVE AS CARRIAGE CONTROL. *
*                                                                     *
*                                                                     *
***********************************************************************
```

```
PUT        DS    0H
           LTR   PARM2,PARM2           CHECK SUBCODE FOR VALIDITY
           BM    BADPUT               SUBCODE MUST BE >= 0
           LA    SVCODE,&OUTPUTS
           CR    PARM2,SVCODE         AND <= &OUTPUTS
           BH    BADPUT
           ST    PARM1,MOVEADR        SAVE THE STRING DESCRIPTOR
           SLL   PARM2,2              SUBCODE*4
           L     3,PUTDCBS(PARM2)     GET THE DCB ADDRESS
           USING IHADCB,3
           TM    DCBOFLGS,OPENBIT     IS THE FILE OPEN ?
           BO    PUTOPEN              YES, GO DO THE OUTPUT
           ST    3,OCDCB              STORE DCB ADDRESS FOR THE OPEN SVC
           MVI   OCDCB,X'8F'          FLAG END OF PARAMETER LIST AND SET
*                                     FLAG INDICATING OPENING FOR OUTPUT

           OPEN  ,MF=(E,OCDCB)        OPEN THE FILE

           TM    DCBOFLGS,OPENBIT     WAS THE OPEN SUCCESSFULL ?
           BZ    OUTSYNAD             NO, OUTPUT SYNAD ERROR

PUTOPEN    DS    0H
           PUT   (3)                  LOCATE MODE PUT

*************************************************************************
*                                                                     *
*      USING LOCATE MODE, THE ADDRESS OF THE NEXT OUTPUT BUFFER       *
*      IS RETURNED IN  R1.                                            *
*                                                                     *
*************************************************************************

           SR    15,15                CLEAR REGISTER 15
           C     15,MOVEADR           IS THE STRING NULL (DESCRIPTOR = 0)
           BE    NULLPUT              YES, SO PUT OUT A BLANK RECORD
           IC    15,MOVEADR           LENGTH-1 OF THE STRING
           LA    14,1(15)             REAL LENGTH OF THE STRING
           LH    0,DCBLRECL           RECORD LENGTH OF THE FILE
           LTR   PARM2,PARM2          CHECK SUBCODE FOR OUTPUT(0)
           BNZ   PUT1                 NOT OUTPUT(0)
           LA    14,1(,14)            INCREASE REAL LENGTH BY ONE FOR
*                                     CARRIAGE CONTROL
PUT1       SR    0,14                 RECORD LENGTH - REAL LENGTH
           BM    TOOLONG              RECORD LENGTH < REAL LENGTH
           BZ    MATCH                RECORD LENGTH = REAL LENGTH
*                                     RECORD LENGTH > REAL LENGTH
           OI    FLAGS,SFILLBIT+LFILLBIT
*                                     INDICATE PADDING REQUIRED
           S     0,F1                 RECORD LENGTH - REAL LENGTH - 1
           BP    LONGMOVE             RECORD LENGTH - REAL LENGTH > 1
           NI    FLAGS,ALLBITS-LFILLBIT
*                                     RECORD LENGTH - REAL LENGTH = 1
*                                     IS A SPECIAL CASE
LONGMOVE   ST    0,FILLENG            SAVE LENGTH FOR PADDING OPERATION
```

```
         B       MOVEIT                  GO MOVE THE STRING

TOOLONG  LH      15,DCBLRECL             REPLACE THE STRING LENGTH
*                                        WITH THE RECORD LENGTH
         S       15,F1                   RECORD LENGTH - 1 FOR THE MOVE
MATCH    NI      FLAGS,ALLBITS-SFILLBIT-LFILLBIT
*                                        INDICATE NO PADDING REQUIRED

MOVEIT   LTR     PARM2,PARM2             CHECK FOR OUTPUT(0)
         BNZ     MOVEIT2                 OUTPUT(0) IS A SPECIAL CASE
         MVI     0(1),C' '               PROVIDE BLANK FOR CARRIAGE CONTROL
         LA      1,1(,1)                 INCREMENT BUFFER POINTER
MOVEIT2  L       2,MOVEADR               STRING DESCRIPTOR
         LA      2,0(,2)                 ADDRESS PART ONLY
         EX      15,MVCSTRNG             EXECUTE A MVC INSTRUCTION
         TM      FLAGS,SFILLBIT          IS PADDING REQUIRED ?
         BZ      EXIT                    NO, RETURN TO THE XPL PROGRAM

         AR      1,15                    ADDRESS TO START PADDING - 1
         MVI     1(1),C' '               START THE PAD
         TM      FLAGS,LFILLBIT          IS MORE PADDING REQUIRED ?
         BZ      EXIT                    NO, RETURN TO XPL PROGRAM
         L       15,FILLENG              LENGTH OF PADDING NEEDED
         S       15,F1                   LESS ONE FOR THE MOVE
         EX      15,MVCBLANK             EXECUTE MVC TO FILL IN BLANKS
         B       EXIT                    RETURN TO THE XPL PROGRAM


*****************************************************************************
*                                                                           *
*        FOR A NULL STRING OUTPUT A BLANK RECORD                            *
*                                                                           *
*****************************************************************************


NULLPUT  LH      15,DCBLRECL             RECORD LENGTH
         S       15,F2                   LESS TWO FOR THE MOVES
         MVI     0(1),C' '               INITIAL BLANK
         EX      15,MVCNULL              EXECUTE MVC TO FILL IN THE BLANKS
         B       EXIT                    RETURN TO THE XPL PROGRAM


*****************************************************************************
*                                                                           *
*        ROUTINE TO ABEND IN CASE OF AN INVALID SERVICE CODE               *
*                                                                           *
*****************************************************************************


BADPUT   STM     0,2,ABEREGS             SAVE REGISTERS
         LA      1,PFABE                 INVALID PUT SUBCODE
         B       INERR                   GO ABEND
```

```
**********************************************************************
*                                                                    *
*                                                                    *
*                                                                    *
*          READ ROUTINE FOR DIRECT ACCESS FILE I/O                   *
*                                                                    *
*                                                                    *
*          INPUT TO THIS ROUTINE IS:                                 *
*                                                                    *
*       PARM1   CORE ADDRESS TO READ THE RECORD INTO                 *
*                                                                    *
*       SVCODE  SERVICE CODE INDICATING WHICH FILE TO USE            *
*                                                                    *
*       PARM2   RELATIVE RECORD NUMBER   0,1,2,3,...                 *
*                                                                    *
*                                                                    *
*                                                                    *
**********************************************************************


READ       DS    0H
           ST    PARM1,RDECB+12      STORE ADDRESS
           L     3,ARWDCBS-FILEORG(SVCODE)
*                                    ADDRESS OF THE DCB FOR THIS FILE
           USING IHADCB,3
           TM    DCBOFLGS,OPENBIT    IS THE FILE OPEN ?
           BO    READOPEN            YES, GO READ
           ST    3,OCDCB             STORE DCB ADDRESS FOR OPEN SVC
           MVI   OCDCB,X'80'         FLAG END OF PARAMETER LIST
*                                    AND INDICATE OPEN FOR INPUT
           OPEN  ,MF=(E,OCDCB)       OPEN THE FILE
           TM    DCBOFLGS,OPENBIT    WAS THE OPEN SUCCESSFUL ?
           BZ    FILESYND            NO, SYNAD ERROR

READOPEN DS      0H
           TM    DCBDEVT,TAPEBITS    IS THE FILE ON MAGNETIC TAPE
           DROP  3
           BO    READTP              YES, GO FORM RECORD INDEX FOR TAPE
           SLA   PARM2,16            FORM  TTRZ  ADDRESS
           BNZ   RDN0                BLOCK ZERO IS A SPECIAL CASE
           LA    PARM2,1             FUNNY ADDRESS FOR BLOCK ZERO
           B     READTP              GO DO THE READ
RDN0       O     PARM2,TTRSET        SPECIFY LOGICAL RECORD 1
READTP     ST    PARM2,TTR           SAVE RECORD POINTER

           POINT (3),TTR             POINT AT THE RECORD TO BE READ
           READ  RDECB,SF,(3),0,'S'  READ THE RECORD INTO CORE
           CHECK RDECB               WAIT FOR THE READ TO COMPLETE

           B     EXIT                RETURN TO THE XPL PROGRAM
```

```
*************************************************************************
*                                                                     *
*                                                                     *
*                                                                     *
*          WRITE ROUTINE FOR DIRECT ACCESS FILE I/O                   *
*                                                                     *
*                                                                     *
*          INPUT TO THIS ROUTINE IS:                                  *
*                                                                     *
*      PARM1   CORE ADDRESS TO READ THE RECORD FROM                   *
*                                                                     *
*      SVCODE  SERVICE CODE INDICATING WHICH FILE TO USE              *
*                                                                     *
*      PARM2   RELATIVE RECORD NUMBER   0,1,2, ...                    *
*                                                                     *
*                                                                     *
*                                                                     *
*************************************************************************

WRITE     DS    0H
          ST    PARM1,WDECB+12        SAVE CORE ADDRESS
          L     3,ARWDCBS-FILEORG(SVCODE)
*                                     GET THE DCB ADDRESS
          USING IHADCB,3
          TM    DCBOFLGS,OPENBIT      IS THE FILE OPEN ?
          BO    WRTOPEN               YES, GO WRITE
          ST    3,OCDCB               STORE DCB ADDRESS FOR OPEN SVC
          MVI   OCDCB,X'8F'           FLAG END OF ARGUMENT LIST AND
*                                     INDICATE OPENING FOR OUTPUT

          OPEN  ,MF=(E,OCDCB)         OPEN THE FILE

          TM    DCBOFLGS,OPENBIT      WAS THE OPEN SUCCESSFUL ?
          BZ    FILESYND              NO,SYNAD ERROR

WRTOPEN   DS    0H
          TM    DCBDEVT,TAPEBITS      IS THE FILE ON MAGNETIC TAPE
          DROP  3
          BO    WRITP                 YES, GO FORM RECORD INDEX FOR TAPE
          SLA   PARM2,16              FORM TTRZ ADDRESS FOR DIRECT ACCESS
          BNZ   WRDN0                 RECORD ZERO IS A SPECIAL CASE
          LA    PARM2,1               FUNNY ADDRESS FOR RECORD ZERO
          B     WRITP                 GO DO THE WRITE
WRDN0     O     PARM2,TTRSET          OR IN RECORD NUMBER BIT
WRITP     ST    PARM2,TTR             SAVE RECORD POINTER

          POINT (3),TTR               POINT AT THE DESIRED RECORD
          WRITE WDECB,SF,(3),0,'S'    WRITE THE RECORD OUT
          CHECK WDECB                 WAIT FOR THE WRITE TO FINISH

          B     EXIT                  RETURN TO THE XPL PROGRAM
```

```
******************************************************************
*                                                                *
*                                                                *
*         TRACE   AND   UNTRACE                                  *
*                                                                *
*                                                                *
******************************************************************


TRACE     DS      0H
          STM     3,12,SAVREG+3*4       SAVE REGISTERS NOT SAVED AT ENTRY
          L       2,SAVREG+4*CBR        GET ADDRESS OF THE NEXT INSTRUCTION
          LA      2,0(,2)               ADDRESS PART ONLY
          ST      2,ILC                 SAVE IT FOR THE TRACE ROUTINE
          LA      SELF,ENTRY            ADDRESS OF ENTRY POINT
          B       TRCALL                GO CALL THE TRACE ROUTINE


******************************************************************
*                                                                *
*         COME HERE TO BEGIN XPL PROGRAM EXECUTION IN TRACE MODE  *
*                                                                *
******************************************************************


BEGTRC    DS      0H
          LM      0,3,PGMPARMS          INITIAL PARAMETERS FOR XPL PROGRAM
          STM     0,3,SAVREG            PLACE IN PSEUDO REGISTERS
          ST      SELF,SAVREG+4*SELF    STORE MONITOR ADDRESS

TRCALL    DS      0H
          LM      0,4,TPACK             PARAMETERS FOR THE TRACE ROUTINE
          BALR    CBR,3                 CALL THE TRACE ROUTINE
          L       CBR,ASMR              ADDRESS OF XPLSM RETURN TO OS
          BR      CBR                   GO RETURN TO OS


******************************************************************
*                                                                *
*         UNTRACE REQUEST IS DETECTED BY THE TRACE ROUTINE IF TRACING *
*         IS ACTUALLY BEING DONE.  IT IS A NOP HERE               *
*                                                                *
******************************************************************


UNTRACE   B       EXIT                  RETURN TO THE XPL PROGRAM


******************************************************************
*                                                                *
*                                                                *
*         TIME AND DATE FUNCTIONS                                *
*                                                                *
*                                                                *
*         RETURNS TIME OF DAY IN HUNDREDTHS OF A SECOND IN REGISTER *
*         PARM1  AND THE DATE IN THE FORM  YYDDD IN REGISTER SVCODE *
*                                                                *
*                                                                *
******************************************************************
```

```
GETIME    TIME  BIN                    REQUEST THE TIME
          ST    0,SAVREG+PARM1*4       RETURN IN REGISTER PARM1
          ST    1,DTSV+4               STORE THE DATE IN PACKED DECIMAL
          CVB   1,DTSV                 CONVERT IT TO BINARY
          ST    1,SAVREG+SVCODE*4      RETURN DATE IN REGISTER SVCODE
          B     EXIT                   RETURN TO THE XPL PROGRAM



**************************************************************************
*                                                                        *
*                                                                        *
*                                                                        *
*         EXECUTE ROUTINE FOR USE BY THE TRACE ROUTINE                    *
*.                                                                       *
*                                                                        *
**************************************************************************

          DROP  13
          USING ENTRY,SELF

EXEC      DS    0H
          STM   0,3,XCELL              SAVE THE PARAMETERS PASSED IN
          LM    0,4,0(2)               LOAD THE REST OF THE TRACED
*                                      PROGRAM'S REGISTERS
          EX    0,XCELL                EXECUTE ONE INSTRUCTION
          STM   14,15,EXSV             SAVE REGISTERS TEMPORARILY
          L     14,XCELL+8             ADDRESS OF TRACE ROUTINE'S
*                                      REGISTER TABLE
          STM   0,13,0(14)             STORE REGISTERS IN THE TABLE
          LM    0,1,EXSV               PICK UP REGISTERS 14 & 15 AGAIN
          STM   0,1,14*4(14)           STORE THEM IN THE TABLE
          LM    0,3,XCELL              RESTORE INITIAL REGISTERS
          BALR  1,3                    RETURN WITH THE CONDITION CODE
*                                      IN REGISTER 1

          DROP  SELF
          USING SAVE,13



**************************************************************************
*                                                                        *
*                                                                        *
*                                                                        *
*         DATA AREA FOR THE SUBMONITOR                                    *
*                                                                        *
*                                                                        *
**************************************************************************

          DS    0F
ASAVE     DC    A(SAVE)                ADDRESS OF OS SAVE AREA
ABASE1    DC    A(BASE1)               BASE ADDRESS FOR INITIALIZATION
MAXCODE   DC    A(ENDSERV-4)           LARGEST VALID SERVICE CODE
ASMR      DC    A(SMRET)               ADDRESS OF SUBMONITOR RETURN TO OS
```

```
RTNSV      DC     F'0'                    SAVE COMPLETION CODE RETURNED
*                                         BY THE XPL PROGRAM
ABESAVE    DS     F                       SAVE ABEND CODE DURING CLOSE
ABEREGS    DS     3F                      SAVE PROGRAMS REGS 0-2 BEFORE ABEND
TTR        DC     F'0'                    TTRZ ADDRESS FOR READ AND WRITE
TTRSET     DC     X'00000100'             ADDRESS CONSTANT FOR TTRZ
FLAGS      DC     X'00'                   SUBMONITOR CONTROL FLAGS
SAVREG     DC     16F'0'                  SAVE AREA FOR THE SUBMONITOR
           DS     0D
DTSV       DC     PL8'0'                  WORK AREA FOR CONVERTING DATE
TPACK      DS     0H                      PARAMETERS FOR THE TRACE ROUTINE
           DC     A(CONTROL)              POINTER TO THE PARM FIELD OF
*                                         THE OS  EXEC  CARD
           DC     A(SAVREG)               ADDRESS OF THE REGISTER TABLE
ILC        DC     A(GOC)                  ADDRESS TO BEGIN TRACING
           DC     V(TRACE)                ADDRESS OF THE TRACE ROUTINE
           DC     A(EXEC)                 ADDRESS OF THE EXECUTE ROUTINE


*************************************************************************
*                                                                     *
*                                                                     *
*          DCB ADDRESS TABLE FOR ALL I/O ROUTINES                     *
*                                                                     *
*                                                                     *
*          THE FOUR SETS OF DCB ADDRESSES HEADED BY  'GETDCBS',       *
*          'PUTDCBS', 'ARWDCBS', AND 'PGMDCB' MUST BE CONTIGUOUS      *
*          AND END WITH 'PGMDCB'.  THESE LISTS ARE USED AT JOB END    *
*          TO CLOSE ALL FILES BEFORE RETURNING TO OS                  *
*                                                                     *
*                                                                     *
*          DCB ADDRESSES FOR INPUT FILES:                             *
*                                                                     *
*                                                                     *
*************************************************************************


           PRINT NOGEN

GETDCBS    DS     0F
&I         SETA   0
.GD1       AIF    (&I GT &INPUTS).GD2
           DC     A(INPUT&I)
&I         SETA   &I+1
           AGO    .GD1
.GD2       ANOP


*************************************************************************
*                                                                     *
*          DCB ADDRESSES FOR OUTPUT FILES                             *
*                                                                     *
*************************************************************************


PUTDCBS    DS     0F

&I         SETA   0
```

```
.PD1     AIF    (&I GT &OUTPUTS).PD2
         DC     A(OUTPUT&I)
&I       SETA   &I+1
         AGO    .PD1
.PD2     ANOP


***************************************************************************
*                                                                         *
*         DCB ADDRESS FOR DIRECT ACCESS FILES                             *
*                                                                         *
***************************************************************************

ARWDCBS  DS     0F

&I       SETA   1
.DA1     AIF    (&I GT &FILES).DA2
         ORG    ARWDCBS+RD&I-FILEORG
         DC     A(FILE&I.IN)
         ORG    ARWDCBS+WRT&I-FILEORG
         DC     A(FILE&I.OUT)
&I       SETA   &I+1
         AGO    .DA1
.DA2     ANOP
         ORG    ARWDCBS+ENDSERV-FILEORG
         DS     0F

PGMDCB   DC     X'80'              FLAG END OF PARAMETER LIST
         DC     AL3(PROGRAM)       ADDRESS OF PROGRAM DCB

OCDCB    DS     F                  DCB ADDRESSES FOR OPEN AND CLOSE
MOVEADR  DS     1F                 DESCRIPTOR STORAGE FOR PUT ROUTINE
FILLENG  DC     F'0'               LENGTH OF PADDING NEEDED IN OUTPUT
F1       DC     F'1'               THE CONSTANT ONE
F2       DC     F'2'               THE CONSTANT TWO
GETMOVE  MVC    0(0,2),0(1)        MVC COMMAND FOR THE GET ROUTINE
MVCNULL  MVC    1(0,1),0(1)        MVC COMMAND FOR THE PUT ROUTINE
MVCBLANK MVC    2(0,1),1(1)               "
MVCSTRNG MVC    0(0,1),0(2)               "


***************************************************************************
*                                                                         *
*         DATA AREA FOR THE EXECUTE ROUTINE                               *
*                                                                         *
***************************************************************************

XCELL    DS     1F                 INSTRUCTION TO BE EXECUTED
         DS     1F                 MORE INSTRUCTION
         DS     1F                 ADDRESS OF TRACE ROUTINE REGISTER
*                                  TABLE
         DS     1F                 RETURN ADDRESS TO THE TRACE ROUTINE
*                                  ADDRESS OF EXEC IS IN REGISTER FOUR
EXSV     DS     2F                 WORK AREA FOR THE EXECUTE ROUTINE
```

```
***********************************************************************
*                                                                    *
*                                                                    *
*          DEVICE  CONTROL  BLOCKS  FOR  THE  SUBMONITOR             *
*                                                                    *
***********************************************************************

PROGRAM   DCB   DSORG=PS,                                            X
                MACRF=R,                                             X
                DDNAME=PROGRAM,                                      X
                DEVD=DA,                                             X
                KEYLEN=0,                                            X
                EODAD=EODPGM,                                        X
                SYNAD=ERRPGM

INPUT0    DCB   DSORG=PS,                                            X
                DDNAME=SYSIN,                                        X
                DEVD=DA,                                             X
                MACRF=GL,                                            X
                BUFNO=3,                                             X
                EODAD=INEOD,                                         X
                SYNAD=INSYNAD,                                       X
                EXLST=INEXIT0,                                       X
                EROPT=ACC

***********************************************************************
*                                                                    *
INPUT1    EQU   INPUT0           INPUT(0) & INPUT(1) ARE BOTH SYSIN *
*                                                                    *
***********************************************************************

&I        SETA  2
.INP1     AIF   (&I GT &INPUTS).INP2

INPUT&I   DCB   DSORG=PS,                                            X
                DDNAME=INPUT&I,                                      X
                DEVD=DA,                                             X
                MACRF=GL,                                            X
                EODAD=INEOD,                                         X
                SYNAD=INSYNAD,                                       X
                EXLST=INEXIT&I,                                      X
                EROPT=ACC

&I        SETA  &I+1
          AGO   .INP1
.INP2     ANOP

OUTPUT0   DCB   DSORG=PS,                                            X
                DDNAME=SYSPRINT,                                     X
                DEVD=DA,                                             X
                MACRF=PL,                                            X
                SYNAD=OUTSYNAD,                                      X
                EXLST=OUTEXIT0,                                      X
                EROPT=ACC
```

```
***************************************************************************
*                                                                         *
OUTPUT1   EQU    OUTPUT0                OUTPUT(0), OUTPUT(1) BOTH SYSPRINT *
*                                                                         *
***************************************************************************

OUTPUT2   DCB    DSORG=PS,                                                X
                 DDNAME=SYSPUNCH,                                         X
                 DEVD=DA,                                                 X
                 MACRF=PL,                                                X
                 SYNAD=OUTSYNAD,                                          X
                 EXLST=OUTEXIT2,                                          X
                 EROPT=ACC

&I        SETA   3
.OP1      AIF    (&I GT &OUTPUTS).OP2

OUTPUT&I  DCB    DSORG=PS,                                                X
                 DDNAME=OUTPUT&I,                                         X
                 DEVD=DA,                                                 X
                 MACRF=PL,                                                X
                 SYNAD=OUTSYNAD,                                          X
                 EXLST=OUTEXIT&I,                                         X
                 EROPT=ACC

&I        SETA   &I+1
          AGO    .OP1
.OP2      ANOP

***************************************************************************
*                                                                         *
*                                                                         *
*         DCBS FOR THE DIRECT ACCESS FILES                                *
*                                                                         *
*         BECAUSE OF THE MANNER IN WHICH THE FILES ARE USED,  IT IS       *
*         NECESSARY TO HAVE TWO DCB'S FOR EACH FILE.  ONE DCB FOR         *
*         READING AND ONE FOR WRITING.                                    *
*                                                                         *
***************************************************************************

&I        SETA   1
.DD1      AIF    (&I GT &FILES).DD2

FILE&I.IN DCB    DSORG=PS,                                                X
                 MACRF=RP,                                                X
                 DDNAME=FILE&I,                                           X
                 DEVD=DA,                                                 X
                 RECFM=F,                                                 X
                 LRECL=FILEBYTS,                                          X
                 BLKSIZE=FILEBYTS,                                        X
                 KEYLEN=0,                                                X
                 EODAD=FILEEOD,                                           X
                 SYNAD=FILESYND
```

```
FILE&I.OUT DCB DSORG=PS,                                             X
               MACRF=WP,                                             X
               DDNAME=FILE&I,                                        X
               DEVD=DA,                                              X
               RECFM=F,                                              X
               KEYLEN=0,                                             X
               LRECL=FILEBYTS,                                       X
               BLKSIZE=FILEBYTS,                                     X
               SYNAD=FILESYND

&I         SETA  &I+1
           AGO   .DD1
.DD2       ANOP

XPLSMEND DS    0H                    END  OF  THE  SUBMONITOR



***********************************************************************
*                                                                   *
*                                                                   *
*                                                                   *
*      DSECT WHICH DEFINES THE FORMAT OF BINARY PROGRAM CONTROL     *
*      INFORMATION AND THE STARTING POINT FOR PROGRAMS              *
*                                                                   *
*                                                                   *
***********************************************************************


FILECTRL DSECT

BYTSCODE DS    1F                    NUMBER OF BYTES OF CODE

BYTSDATA DS    1F                    NUMBER OF BYTES OF DATA AREA

BLKSCODE DS    1F                    NUMBER OF RECORDS OF CODE

BLKSDATA DS    1F                    NUMBER OF RECORDS OF DATA AREA

BYTSBLK  DS    1F                    BLOCKSIZE OF THE XPL PROGRAM FILE

BYTSFULL DS    1F                    NUMBER OF BYTES OF CODE ACTUALLY
*                                    USED IN THE LAST RECORD OF CODE

DATABYTS DS    1F                    NUMBER OF BYTES OF DATA ACTUALLY
*                                    USED IN THE LAST RECORD OF DATA

         ORG   FILECTRL+60           REMAINDER OF THE CONTROL BLOCK
*                                    IS UNUSED

CODEBEGN DS    0H                    FIRST EXECUTABLE INSTRUCTION
*                                    IN THE XPL PROGRAM
```

Appendix 2

The Trace Routine

At times during the development of a compiler (or other large program), it is desirable to monitor the execution of a program at the level of individual machine instructions. One situation in which this monitoring is useful is in discovering the cause of unexpected transfers within a program. For example, if a program is interrupted because it is trying to execute a noninstruction in its data area, it is quite often impossible to determine from examination of the output of a program or a memory dump how control was lost. A successful technique for tracking down unexplained transfers is to begin monitoring execution at the last point at which the program was known to be functioning correctly. Another situation is in debugging the code generated by a compiler by monitoring the execution of the generated code.

To provide monitoring of program execution at the machine instruction level, two tools are provided within the XPL system: interlisting, which causes the machine instructions generated by XCOM to be listed during compilation of a program, and a trace routine, which prints a detailed record of instructions executed during the execution of a program.

Interlisting is switched off and on by the control letter E (Section 6.17). See Fig. A2.1 for examples of its use.

The trace routine is invoked by the XPL statement

call *trace*;

which causes tracing to begin at the statement following execution of the call. Tracing may be terminated by the statement

call *untrace*;

which causes normal execution to resume at the next statement. Both statements are normal XPL constructs and can be used freely in **if** statements, **case** groups, and the like. Examples of trace control statements are given in Fig. A2.1.

While the trace routine is active, the XPL program is executed interpretively, and one line is printed for each machine instruction executed, providing a complete, albeit voluminous, record of the execution of the program. The output from the trace routine during the execution of the program in Fig. A2.1 is given in Fig. A2.2. The remainder of this appendix will discuss the design and organization of the trace routine and give a detailed description of its major components.

305

```
X P L   COMPILATION  --  STANFORD UNIVERSITY  --  XCOM III VERSION OF MAY 7, 1969.

TODAY IS AUGUST 10, 1969.

 1 |   /*  INTERLIST $EMITTED CODE  */                                     | 1286
 2 |                                                                       | 1286
 3 |                                                                       | 1286
 4 |   DECLARE I FIXED, J BIT(16), K BIT(8),                               | 1286
 5 |     ALPHA CHARACTER INITIAL('MESSAGE'),                               | 1286

                     24:  DESC = 6, 160
                    160:  CHARACTER = D4
                    161:  CHARACTER = C5
                    162:  CHARACTER = E2
                    163:  CHARACTER = E2
                    164:  CHARACTER = C1
                    165:  CHARACTER = C7
                    166:  CHARACTER = C5

 6 |     BETA (3) BIT(64) ;                                                | 1286
 7 |                                                                       | 1286
 8 |   CALL TRACE ; /* BEGIN TRACING */                                    | 1286

                   1286:  CODE = STM    1,124(3,11)
                   1290:  CODE = LA     1,12(0,0)
                   1294:  CODE = BALR   12,15
                   1296:  CODE = LM     1,124(3,11)

 9 |   I,J,K = 2 ;                                                         | 1300

                   1300:  CODE = LA     1,2(0,0)
                   1304:  CODE = STC    1,1346(0,11)
                   1308:  CODE = STH    1,1344(0,11)
                   1312:  CODE = ST     1,1340(0,11)

10 |   BETA(I) = ALPHA ;                                                   | 1316

                   1316:  CODE = L      1,1340(0,11)
                   1320:  CODE = L      2,24(0,13)
```

Fig. A2.1

11 | DO WHILE J = I ;

12 | J = SHL(K,1) & SHR(I,J) ;

13 | OUTPUT, ALPHA = SUBSTR(ALPHA,J,I+1) ;

```
1324:  CODE = SLL   1,2(0,0)
1328:  CODE = ST    2,28(1,13)
                    1332
1332:  CODE = LH    1,1344(0,11)
1336:  CODE = C     1,1340(0,11)
1340:  CODE = LA    1,0(0,0)
1344:  CODE = BC    6,1352(0,14)
1348:  CODE = LA    1,1(0,0)

                    BACK UP CODE EMITTER

1340:  CODE = BC    6,1340(0,14)
                    1344
1344:  CODE = SR    1,1
1346:  CODE = IC    1,1346(0,11)
1350:  CODE = AR    1,1
1352:  CODE = L     2,1340(0,11)
1356:  CODE = LH    3,1344(0,11)
1360:  CODE = SRL   2,0(0,3)
1364:  CODE = NR    1,2
1366:  CODE = STH   1,1344(0,11)
                    1370
1370:  CODE = L     1,24(0,13)
1374:  CODE = LH    2,1344(0,11)
1378:  CODE = LA    3,1(0,0)
1382:  CODE = A     3,1340(0,11)
1386:  CODE = LA    1,0(2,1)
1390:  CODE = LA    3,255(0,3)
1394:  CODE = SLL   3,24(0,0)
1398:  CODE = OR    1,3
1400:  CODE = ST    1,24(0,13)
1404:  CODE = STM   1,124(3,11)
1408:  CODE = LR    0,1
1410:  CODE = SR    2,2
1412:  CODE = LA    1,8(0,0)
1416:  CODE = BALR  12,15
```

Fig. A2.1 (Contd.)

```
14 |    END;

1418: CODE = LM    1,124(3,11)
                   1422
1422: CODE = BC    15,1332(0,14)
1340: FIXUP =1426
                   1426

15 |    IF J < BYTE('A') THEN

1426: CODE = LH    1,1344(0,11)
1348: DATA = 193
1430: CODE = C     1,1348(0,11)
1434: CODE = LA    1,0(0,0)
1438: CODE = BC    10,1446(0,14)
1442: CODE = LA    1,1(0,0)
                   1446 C7 = 193.
           BACK UP CODE EMITTER

16 |        I = 0;

1434: CODE = BC    10,1434(0,14)
1438: CODE = SR    1,1
1440: CODE = ST    1,1340(0,11)
                   1444
                   1444

17 |    ELSE
18 |        I = BYTE(BETA(J),K) ;

1444: CODE = BC    15,1444(0,14)
1448: CODE = LH    1,1344(0,11)
1452: CODE = SLL   1,2(0,0)
1456: CODE = L     1,28(1,13)
1460: CODE = SR    2,2
1462: CODE = IC    2,1346(0,11)
1466: CODE = IC    2,0(2,1)
1470: CODE = ST    2,1340(0,11)
                   1474

19 |    CALL UNTRACE ;    /*  END TRACE  */

1444: FIXUP =1474
1434: FIXUP =1448
1474: CODE = STM   1,124(3,11)
1478: CODE = LA    1,16(0,0)
1482: CODE = BALR  12,15
1484: CODE = LM    1,124(3,11)
                   1488

20 |    /* $END INTERLISTING  */
```

Fig. A2.1 (Contd.)

```
21 |
22 |EOF                                                                          1488
                                                                                 1488

END OF COMPILATION AUGUST 10, 1969.  CLOCK TIME = 21:34:20.51.

22 CARDS CONTAINING 9 STATEMENTS WERE COMPILED.
NO ERRORS WERE DETECTED.
1496 BYTES OF PROGRAM, 1357 OF DATA, 44 OF DESCRIPTORS, 167 OF STRINGS.
TOTAL CORE REQUIREMENT 3064 BYTES.

SYMBOL  TABLE  DUMP

ALPHA   : CHARACTER AT 24(13),         DECLARED ON LINE 5 AND REFERENCED 3 TIMES.
BETA    : CHARACTER AT 28(13),         DECLARED ON LINE 6 AND REFERENCED 2 TIMES.
I       : FIXED     AT 1340(11),       DECLARED ON LINE 4 AND REFERENCED 7 TIMES.
J       : BIT(16)   AT 1344(11),       DECLARED ON LINE 4 AND REFERENCED 7 TIMES.
K       : BIT(8)    AT 1346(11),       DECLARED ON LINE 4 AND REFERENCED 3 TIMES.


TOTAL TIME IN COMPILER   0:0:3.94.
SET UP TIME              0:0:1.96.
ACTUAL COMPILATION TIME  0:0:0.40.
POST-COMPILATION TIME    0:0:1.58.
COMPILATION RATE: 3300 CARDS PER MINUTE.
```

Fig. A2.1 (Contd.)

Loc								
R0-R7	00018B20	0000000C	00018A78	00000000	00018500	00018500	00018500	00018500
R8-R15	00018500	00018500	00018500	00018500	40018438	00018A48	00017F28	00016482
F0-F6	23282E2F	0000001A	41200000	C4DA6000	40EB6E04			
018438	9813B07C	8	LM	1,3,07C(B)	00000578		01857C	00000578
R0-R7	00018B20	00000578	00018A78	00000000	00018500	00018500	00018500	00018500
R8-R15	00018500	00018500	00018500	00018500	40018438	00018A48	00017F28	00016482
01843C	41100002	8	LA	1,002(0)	00000002		000002	02
018440	4210B542	8	STC	1,542(B)	00000002		018A42	0002
018444	4010B540	8	STH	1,540(B)	00000002		018A40	00000002
018448	5010B53C	8	ST	1,53C(B)	00000002		018A3C	00000002
01844C	5810B53C	8	L	1,53C(B)	06018B18		018A3C	06018B18
018450	5820D018	8	L	2,018(D)	00000008		018A60	06018B18
018454	89100002	8	SLL	1,002(0)	06018B18		000002	0002
018458	5021D01C	8	ST	2,01C(1,D)	00000002		018A6C	00000002
01845C	4810B540	8	LH	1,540(B)	00000002		018A40	4810B540
018460	5910B53C	8	C	1,53C(B)	6		018A3C	02
018464	4760E592	8	BC	6,592(E)	00000000		0184BA	00000002
018468	1B11	8	SR	1,1	00000002	00000000		
01846A	4310B542	8	IC	1,542(B)	00000004	00000004	018A42	0002
01846E	1A11	2	AR	1,1	00000002			
018470	5820B53C	2	L	2,53C(B)	00000002		018A3C	0000
018474	4830B540	2	LH	3,540(B)	00000000		018A40	06018B18
018478	88203000	2	SRL	2,000(3)	00000000		000002	0000
01847C	1412	8	NR	1,2	06018B18	00000000	018A40	
01847E	4010B540	8	STH	1,540(B)	00000000		018A40	
018482	5810D018	8	L	1,018(D)	00000001		018A60	06018B18
018486	4820B540	8	LH	2,540(B)			018A40	
01848A	41300001	8	LA	3,001(0)			000001	0000

Fig. A2.2

Address	Code	n	Mnem	Operand				
01848E	5A30B53C	2	A	3,53C(B)	00000003		018A3C	00000002
018492	41121000	2	LA	1,000(2,1)	00018B18		018B18	018B18
018496	413030FF	2	LA	3,0FF(3)	00000102		000102	
01849A	89300018	2	SLL	3,018(0)	00000000	02000000	000018	
01849E	1613	4	OR	1,3	02018B18			
0184A0	5010D018	4	ST	1,018(D)	02018B18		018A60	02018B18
0184A4	9013B07C	4	STM	1,3,07C(B)	02018B18		01857C	02018B18
R0–R7	00018B20	02018B18	00000000	02000000	00018500	00018A48	00018500	00018500
R8–R15	00018500	00018500	00018438	00018500	40018438	00018A48	00017F28	00016482
0184A8	1801	4	LR	0,1	02018B18			
0184AA	1B22	8	SR	2,2	00000000			
0184AC	41100008	8	LA	1,008(0)	00000008	00016482	000008	
0184B0	05CF	8	BALR	C,F	400184B2			
I/O	REQUEST				02018B18	00000008	00000000	00000000
0184B2	9813B07C	8	LM	1,3,07C(B)	02018B18		01857C	02018B18
R0–R7	02018B18	00000000	02000000	02018B18	00018500	00018A48	00018500	00018500
R8–R15	00018500	00000000	00000000	400184B2	00016482	00018A48	00017F28	00016482
MES								
0184B2	9813B07C	8	LM	1,3,07C(B)	02018B18		01857C	02018B18
R0–R7	02018B18	00000000	02000000	02018B18	00018500	00018A48	00018500	00018500
R8–R15	00018500	00000000	00000000	400184B2	00016482	00018A48	00017F28	00016482
0184B6	47F0E534	8	BC	F,534(E)	F		01845C	4810B540
0184BC	4810B540	8	LH	1,540(B)	00000000		018A40	0000
018460	5910B53C	4	C	1,53C(B)	00000000		018A3C	00000002
018464	4760E592	4	BC	6,592(E)	6		0184BA	4810B540
0184BA	4810B540	4	LH	1,540(B)	00000000		018A40	0000
0184BE	5910B544	4	C	1,544(B)	00000000		018A44	000000C1
0184C2	47A0E5A8	4	BC	A,5A8(E)	A		0184D0	4810B540
0184C6	1B11	8	SR	1,1	00000000			
0184C8	5010B53C	8	ST	1,53C(B)	00000000	00000000	018A3C	00000000
0184CC	47F0E5C2	8	BC	F,5C2(E)	F		0184EA	9013B07C

Fig. A2.2 (Contd.)

```
0184EA   9013B07C        8   STM    1,3,07C(B)   00000000              01857C   00000000

R0-R7    02018B18   00000000   02000000   00018500   00018A48   00018500   00018500
R8-R15   00018500   00018500   00018500   400184B2   00018A48   00017F28   00016482

0184EE   41100010        8   LA     1,010(0)     00000010              000010
0184F2   05CF     BALR   C,F   400184F4   00016482

R0-R7    02018B18   00000000   02000000   00018500   00018500   00018500   00018500
R8-R15   00018500   00018500   00018500   400184F4   00018A48   00017F28   00016482

F0-F6    23282E2F   421A0000   00000000   40EB6E04   C4DA6000   41200000   00000000

RESUME EXECUTION AT:   0184F4
```

Fig. A2.2 (Contd.)

The format of the line which the trace routine prints for each instruction is shown in Fig. A2.2. All numeric values are printed in hexadecimal notation. The columns from left to right contain the address of the instruction, the instruction image, a digit representing the condition code, the symbolic name of the instruction, the fields of the instruction in assembly language format, the first operand register for type RR, RX, and RS instructions, the second operand register for type RR instructions, the effective address of the instruction, and the contents of memory referenced by the effective address. For type SS instructions two more columns containing the second effective address and the contents of memory referenced by this address are added on the right. Any part of the line irrelevant to a particular instruction is left blank.

The over-all structure of the trace routine is shown in Fig. A2.3. The main loop is traversed once for each traced instruction. For most instructions, all work is done in this loop, which sets up parameters and calls the routine EXECUTE in the XPL submonitor. EXECUTE loads the general registers of the traced program into the general registers of the machine and then causes one instruction to be obeyed using an execute (EX) command. Transferring to the submonitor to perform the execute command is necessary because of IBM System/360 addressability considerations: just before an instruction is executed, all the general registers must be loaded with the general registers of the traced program, which leaves no base register to provide addressability for the execute command. To provide addressability and to make tracing possible, the convention adopted was that one register (R15) would always contain the address of the entry point to the submonitor. The submonitor is thus always addressable using the general registers of the traced program, and addressability is available for the execute instruction. Using an execute instruction to perform most instructions greatly simplifies the trace routine. Alternatives would be to provide a detailed interpretation in the trace routine for each possible machine instruction or to alter each instruction before its execution so that it always used certain registers. Either of these alternatives would make the trace routine a much larger program and also slow its execution.

The major routines shown in Fig. A2.3 are: GOIO, which processes calls made to the submonitor from within the traced program; ILGLOP, which prints a message when a noninstruction is encountered and terminates execution; BRPROC, the branch instruction interpreter; EXOP, the execute instruction interpreter; and PRINTSUP, which supervises the fabrication of printed output.

To control the operation of the trace routine there is associated with each of the 256 possible instruction codes a half word of attribute information which completely specifies the actions that the trace routine is to take in processing the instruction. To conserve space, a half word is not stored for each instruction code; instead, an auxiliary byte table is used to associate each code with its attributes stored in a smaller table of unique half words. The attributes representable in the half word are illegal instruction, instruction sets condition code, branch instruction (includes execute instruction), half word instruction, full word instruction, double word instruction, floating point instruction, shift instruction, type RR instruction, type RX instruction, type RS instruction, type SI instruction, type SS instruction, instruction contains 8-bit immediate field, instruction is load multiple or store multiple, and instruction is execute. These attributes are not by any means a minimal set; indeed, many of them may be derived from the operation code, although this derivation is often time consuming. The redundancy of the attribute set represents a decision to sacrifice space for tables in order to gain speed in the execution of the trace routine.

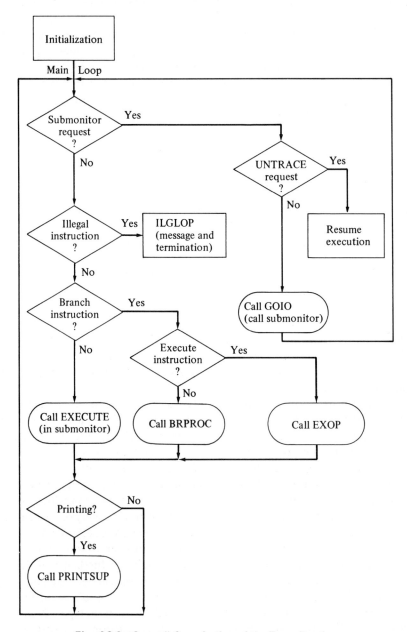

Fig. A2.3 Over-all Organization of the Trace Routine

The operation of the major components of the trace routine are described in detail in the following set of flow charts (see Figs. A2.4 through A2.13). In these charts the term *pseudo-location-counter* refers to the program pointer maintained by the trace routine for the traced program; the term *pseudo-registers* refers to the table kept by the trace routine of the general registers of the traced program.

The assembly language listing of the trace routine forms the final section of this appendix.

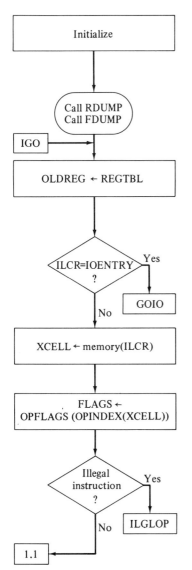

Initialize all variables needed by the trace routine. Obtain the initial general registers of the traced program, and place them in REGTBL. Load the pseudo-location-counter ILCR with the address at which to begin tracing.

Print the initial values of the general and floating-point registers.

Start of the major trace cycle.

Save a copy of the general registers as they are before the execution of the instruction. This copy will be used later to compute the effective address of the memory referenced by the instruction.

Compare the pseudo-location-counter (ILCR) with the address of the sub-monitor entry point. If they are equal, go to the routine which processes submonitor calls.

Place the next six bytes of the instruction image pointed to by ILCR into the location XCELL.

Place in the location FLAGS a half word of attribute information which describes the instruction to be executed.

If the instruction is illegal, transfer to the routine which prints an error message for illegal instructions and terminates the trace.

Fig. A2.4   Main Loop of the Trace Routine

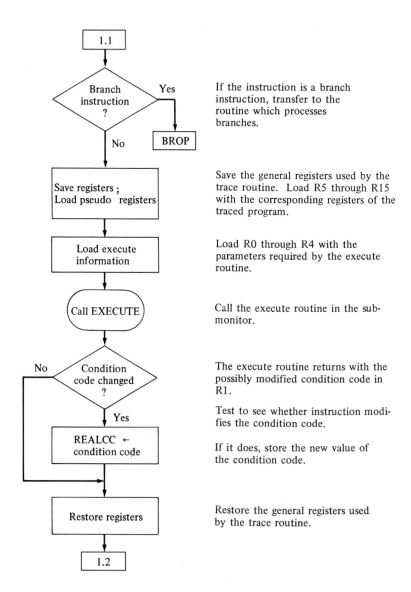

The flowchart annotations read:

Branch instruction ? — Yes → **BROP**

If the instruction is a branch instruction, transfer to the routine which processes branches.

Save registers ; Load pseudo registers

Save the general registers used by the trace routine. Load R5 through R15 with the corresponding registers of the traced program.

Load execute information

Load R0 through R4 with the parameters required by the execute routine.

Call EXECUTE

Call the execute routine in the sub-monitor.

Condition code changed ?

The execute routine returns with the possibly modified condition code in R1.

Test to see whether instruction modifies the condition code.

REALCC ← condition code

If it does, store the new value of the condition code.

Restore registers

Restore the general registers used by the trace routine.

Fig. A2.4 (Contd.)

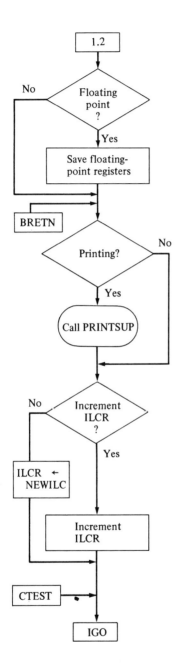

Test to see whether the instruction is a floating-point instruction.

If it is, store the floating-point registers for use by the print routines.

Is printing enabled?

If it is, call the print supervisor to produce one printed line describing the instruction just executed and the current state of the machine.

Should the pseudo-location-counter be incremented?

No, the instruction was a successful branch, so obtain the new value for ILCR prepared by the branch processing routine.

Yes, increment the pseudo-location-counter by two if the instruction is type RR, by four if the instruction is type RX, RS, or SI, and by six if the instruction is type SS.

Return to the start of the major trace cycle.

Fig. A2.4 (Contd.)

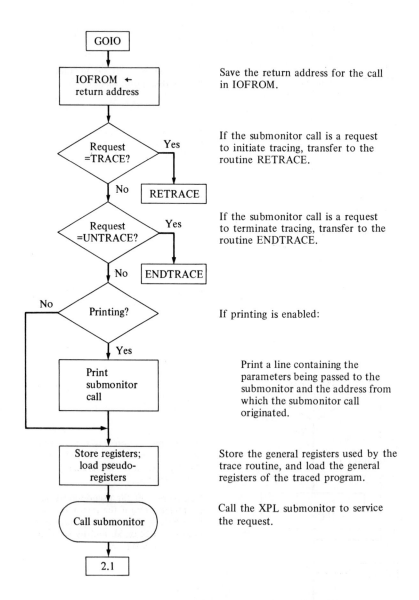

Fig. A2.5 Routine to Process Submonitor Calls

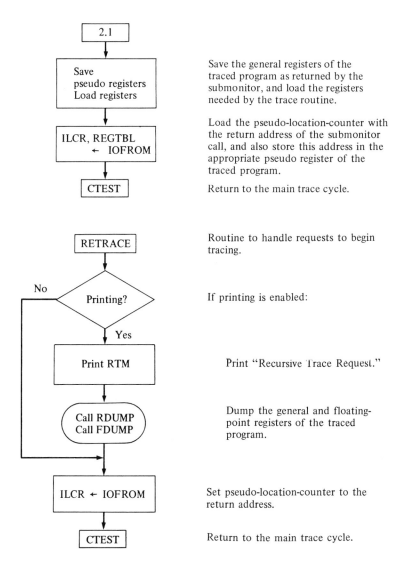

Save the general registers of the
traced program as returned by the
submonitor, and load the registers
needed by the trace routine.

Load the pseudo-location-counter with
the return address of the submonitor
call, and also store this address in the
appropriate pseudo register of the
traced program.

Return to the main trace cycle.

Routine to handle requests to begin
tracing.

If printing is enabled:

Print "Recursive Trace Request."

Dump the general and floating-
point registers of the traced
program.

Set pseudo-location-counter to the
return address.

Return to the main trace cycle.

Fig. A2.5 (Contd.)

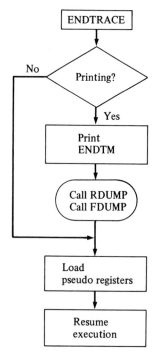

If printing is enabled:

Print "Resume execution at:" and the submonitor call return address.

Dump the general and floating-point registers of the traced program.

Load the general registers with the general registers of the traced program.

Resume actual execution of the traced program by simulating a return from the submonitor.

Fig. A2.6   Routine to Handle Termination of Tracing

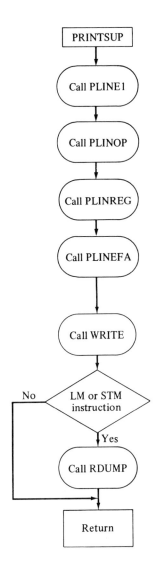

Place the pseudo-location counter, the hexadecimal instruction image, and the condition code in the print line.

Place the symbolic operation code and the instruction fields in assembly language format in the print line.

Place the subject register for type RR, RX, and RS instructions and the second register for type RR instructions into the print line.

Place the effective address of the instruction and the contents of the location addressed in the print line. For type SS instructions there are two effective addresses and two contents.

Call the submonitor with a request to print the line. Then blank the line to prepare for the next instruction.

Test for load-multiple or store-multiple instructions.

If the instruction is LM or STM, dump all the general registers of the traced program.

End of the print supervisor.

Fig. A2.7   Routine Which Supervises
Fabrication of the Print Line

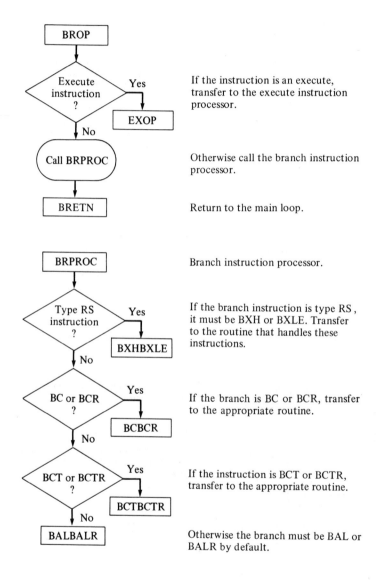

Fig. A2.8 Routine to Handle Branch and Execute Instructions

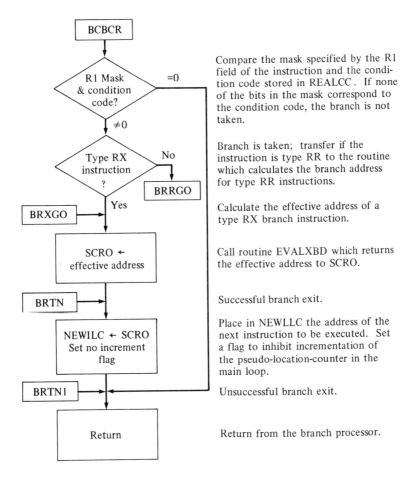

Compare the mask specified by the R1 field of the instruction and the condition code stored in REALCC. If none of the bits in the mask correspond to the condition code, the branch is not taken.

Branch is taken; transfer if the instruction is type RR to the routine which calculates the branch address for type RR instructions.

Calculate the effective address of a type RX branch instruction.

Call routine EVALXBD which returns the effective address to SCRO.

Successful branch exit.

Place in NEWLLC the address of the next instruction to be executed. Set a flag to inhibit incrementation of the pseudo-location-counter in the main loop.

Unsuccessful branch exit.

Return from the branch processor.

Fig. A2.9 Conditional Branch Processing Routine

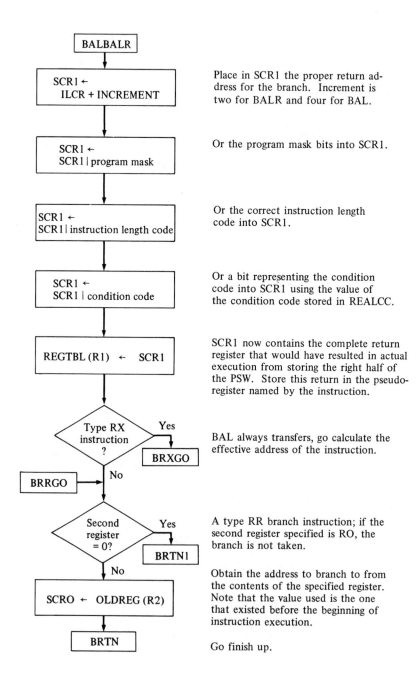

Place in SCR1 the proper return address for the branch. Increment is two for BALR and four for BAL.

Or the program mask bits into SCR1.

Or the correct instruction length code into SCR1.

Or a bit representing the condition code into SCR1 using the value of the condition code stored in REALCC.

SCR1 now contains the complete return register that would have resulted in actual execution from storing the right half of the PSW. Store this return in the pseudo-register named by the instruction.

BAL always transfers, go calculate the effective address of the instruction.

A type RR branch instruction; if the second register specified is RO, the branch is not taken.

Obtain the address to branch to from the contents of the specified register. Note that the value used is the one that existed before the beginning of instruction execution.

Go finish up.

Fig. A2.10 Routine to Process BAL and BALR

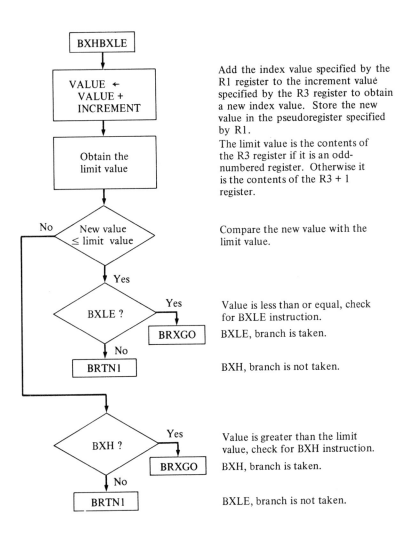

Add the index value specified by the R1 register to the increment value specified by the R3 register to obtain a new index value. Store the new value in the pseudoregister specified by R1.

The limit value is the contents of the R3 register if it is an odd-numbered register. Otherwise it is the contents of the R3 + 1 register.

Compare the new value with the limit value.

Value is less than or equal, check for BXLE instruction.

BXLE, branch is taken.

BXH, branch is not taken.

Value is greater than the limit value, check for BXH instruction.

BXH, branch is taken.

BXLE, branch is not taken.

Fig. A2.11   Routine to Process BXH and BXLE Instructions

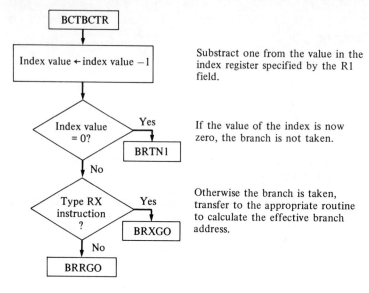

Substract one from the value in the index register specified by the R1 field.

If the value of the index is now zero, the branch is not taken.

Otherwise the branch is taken, transfer to the appropriate routine to calculate the effective branch address.

Fig. A2.12 Routine to Process BCT and BCTR

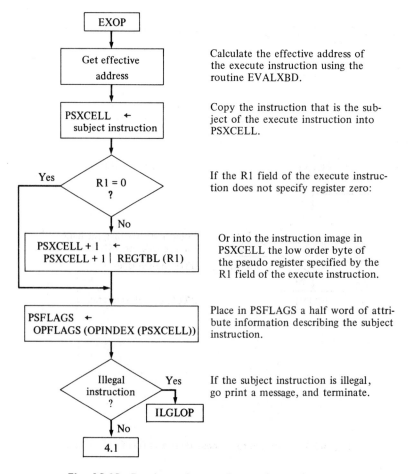

Calculate the effective address of the execute instruction using the routine EVALXBD.

Copy the instruction that is the subject of the execute instruction into PSXCELL.

If the R1 field of the execute instruction does not specify register zero:

Or into the instruction image in PSXCELL the low order byte of the pseudo register specified by the R1 field of the execute instruction.

Place in PSFLAGS a half word of attribute information describing the subject instruction.

If the subject instruction is illegal, go print a message, and terminate.

Fig. A2.13 Routine to Process Execute Instructions

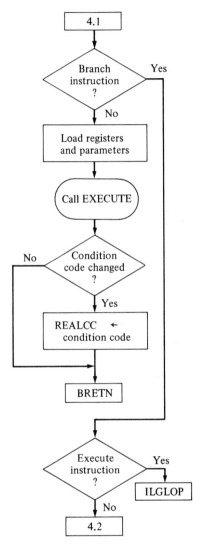

Transfer if the subject instruction is a branch instruction.

Load the pseudoregister of the traced program and parameters for the EXECUTE routine that cause the instruction in PSXCELL to be executed.

Call the execute routine in the submonitor.

If the subject instruction possibly modified the condition code:

Store the new condition code in REALCC.

Restore trace routine registers, and return to the main loop.

If the subject instruction is another execute, print an illegal instruction message, and terminate. An execute instruction may not be the subject of another execute instruction.

Fig. A2.13   (Contd.)

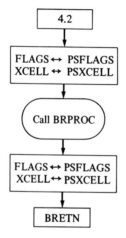

FLAGS ↔ PSFLAGS
XCELL ↔ PSXCELL
Swap FLAGS and PSFLAGS, XCELL and PSXCELL so that the branch processor sees the subject instruction.

Call BRPROC
Call the branch processor to interpret the subject branch instruction.

FLAGS ↔ PSFLAGS
XCELL ↔ PSXCELL
Swap FLAGS and PSFLAGS, XCELL and PSXCELL back so that the print routines will see the execute instruction.

BRETN
Return to the main loop.

Fig. A2.13   (Contd.)

```
**********************************************************************
*                                                                    *
*                                                                    *
*                                                                    *
*   TRACE       THIS PROGRAM PROVIDES A MACHINE LEVEL TRACE OF PROGRAM *
*               EXECUTION.  IT IS ACTIVATED BY THE XPL STATEMENT:      *
*                                                                    *
*               CALL   TRACE ;                                        *
*                                                                    *
*               AND TERMINATED BY THE XPL STATEMENT:                  *
*                                                                    *
*               CALL UNTRACE ;                                        *
*                                                                    *
*               THIS ROUTINE PRINTS ONE LINE FOR EACH MACHINE LANGUAGE *
*               INSTRUCTION EXECUTED.                                  *
*                                                                    *
*                                                                    *
*                                                                    *
*                                                                    *
*                                                                    *
**********************************************************************


**********************************************************************
*                                                                    *
*                                                                    *
*               DEFINE   REGISTER   USAGE                             *
*                                                                    *
*                                                                    *
**********************************************************************

SCR0      EQU   0                      SCRATCH REGISTER

SCR1      EQU   SCR0+1                  SCRATCH   REGISTER

SCR2      EQU   2                       SCRATCH   REGISTER

SCR3      EQU   3                       SCRATCH   REGISTER

FLDPT     EQU   3                       POINTER FOR PLINOP

INITLR    EQU   3                       BASE REGISTER FOR INITIALIZATION

EXEC      EQU   4                       ADDRESS OF EXECUTE ROUTINE

*               5                       (UNUSED)

*               6                       (UNUSED)

*               7                       (UNUSED)

*               8                       (UNUSED)
```

```
DATA      EQU   9                      BASE FOR DATA AREA

HEX2EBC   EQU   10                     ADDRESS OF CONVERT ROUTINE

ILCR      EQU   11                     PSEUDO LOCATION COUNTER

CBR       EQU   12                     SUBMONITOR BRANCH REGISTER

BRFROM    EQU   12                     BRANCH REGISTER

OSAVE     EQU   13                     ADDRESS OF OS SAVE AREA

*               14                     OS

SELF      EQU   15                     ADDRESS OF XPLSM SUBMONITOR


***********************************************************************
*                                                                     *
*                                                                     *
*            SPECIFY LENGTH OF PRINTED LINE                           *
*                                                                     *
*            THE VALUE OF 'LPL' SHOULD NOT BE CHANGED WITHOUT         *
*            CAREFULLY CONSIDERING THE ORGANIZATION OF THE            *
*            PRINTED OUTPUT.                                          *
*                                                                     *
*                                                                     *
***********************************************************************

LPL       EQU   132                    LENGTH OF THE PRINT LINE

***********************************************************************
*                                                                     *
*                                                                     *
*            DEFINE SERVICE CODES USED TO COMMUNICATE WITH THE        *
*            XPLSM SUBMONITOR                                         *
*                                                                     *
*                                                                     *
***********************************************************************

PRNT      EQU   8                      SERVICE CODE FOR PRINTING

TRACEC    EQU   12                     SERVICE CODE TO BEGIN TRACING

UNTRACE   EQU   16                     SERVICE CODE TO END TRACING

***********************************************************************
*                                                                     *
*            DEFINE REGISTERS USED TO PASS PARAMETERS TO THE          *
*            XPLSM SUBMONITOR                                         *
*                                                                     *
***********************************************************************

PR1       EQU   0                      1ST PARAMETER REGISTER
```

```
PR2        EQU    1                     2ND PARAMETER REGISTER

SVCR       EQU    1                     SERVICE CODE REGISTER

PR3        EQU    2                     3RD PARAMETER REGISTER

SMBR       EQU    12                    RETURN ADDRESS REGISTER
*                                       FOR SUBMONITOR CALLS


**********************************************************************
*                                                                    *
*                                                                    *
*          DEFINE FLAG BITS USED THROUGHOUT THE TRACE ROUTINE        *
*          TO SPECIFY THE ATTRIBUTES OF THE MACHINE INSTRUCTIONS     *
*                                                                    *
*                                                                    *
*          FOR EACH MACHINE LANGUAGE INSTRUCTION BEING CONSIDERED    *
*          BY THE TRACE ROUTINE A HALF WORD OF ATTRIBUTE             *
*          INFORMATION IS STORED IN THE LOCATION 'FLAGS'             *
*          THIS INFORMATION DETERMINES THE WAY IN WHICH              *
*          THE ROUTINE PROCESSES THE INSTRUCTION                     *
*                                                                    *
*                                                                    *
*          ATTRIBUTES WHICH MAY OCCUR IN THE FIRST BYTE              *
*          OF 'FLAGS'                                                *
*                                                                    *
*                                                                    *
**********************************************************************

ILGLBIT    EQU    B'10000000'           ILLEGAL INSTRUCTION

CCBIT      EQU    B'01000000'           INSTRUCTION SETS CONDITION CODE

BRBIT      EQU    B'00100000'           INSTRUCTION IS BRANCH OR EXECUTE

HALFBIT    EQU    B'00010000'           HALF WORD INSTRUCTION

FULLBIT    EQU    B'00001000'           FULL WORD INSTRUCTION

DBLBIT     EQU    B'00000100'           DOUBLE WORD INSTRUCTION

FLOATBIT   EQU    B'00000010'           FLOATING POINT INSTRUCTION

SHIFTBIT   EQU    B'00000001'           SHIFT INSTRUCTION

**********************************************************************
*                                                                    *
*                                                                    *
*          ATTRIBUTES WHICH MAY OCCUR IN THE SECOND BYTE             *
*          OF 'FLAGS'                                                *
*                                                                    *
*                                                                    *
**********************************************************************
```

```
RRBIT      EQU    B'10000000'              TYPE RR INSTRUCTION

RXBIT      EQU    B'01000000'              TYPE RX INSTRUCTION

RSBIT      EQU    B'00100000'              TYPE RS INSTRUCTION

SIBIT      EQU    B'00010000'              TYPE SI INSTRUCTION

SSBIT      EQU    B'00001000'              TYPE SS INSTRUCTION

IMDFBIT    EQU    B'00000100'              INSTRUCTION CONTAINS 8-BIT
*                                          IMMEDIATE FIELD

LMSTMBIT EQU      B'00000010'              INSTRUCTION IS LM OR STM

EXBIT      EQU    B'00000001'              INSTRUCTION IS EXECUTE (EX)


**************************************************************************
*                                                                      *
*                                                                      *
*              TRACE ROUTINE INITIALIZATION                            *
*                                                                      *
*                                                                      *
*                                                                      *
*              WHEN THE TRACE ROUTINE IS CALLED BY THE XPLSM           *
*              SUBMONITOR THE GENERAL REGISTERS SHOULD CONTAIN:        *
*                                                                      *
*                                                                      *
*      R0      ADDRESS OF THE PARAMETER FIELD ON THE EXEC CARD         *
*              AS PASSED TO THE SUBMONITOR BY OS/360                   *
*              (UNUSED IN THIS VERSION OF THE TRACE ROUTINE)           *
*                                                                      *
*      R1      ADDRESS OF THE BLOCK WHERE R0 - R15 WERE SAVED PRIOR    *
*              TO THE CALL OF THE TRACE ROUTINE                        *
*                                                                      *
*              F0-F6 ARE ASSUMED TO BE IN PLACE                        *
*                                                                      *
*      R2      ADDRESS AT WHICH TRACED EXECUTION SHOULD BEGIN          *
*                                                                      *
*      R3      ADDRESS OF THE TRACE ROUTINE ENTRY POINT  'TRACE'       *
*                                                                      *
*      R4      ADDRESS OF THE EXECUTE ROUTINE IN THE SUBMONITOR        *
*                                                                      *
*      R13     ADDRESS OF THE SUBMONITORS OS SAVE AREA                 *
*                                                                      *
*      R15     ADDRESS OF THE ENTRY POINT TO THE XPLSM SUBMONITOR      *
*                                                                      *
*              NOTE THAT THE TRACE ROUTINE CRITICALLY DEPENDS ON THE   *
*              CONDITION THAT THE XPL PROGRAM BEING TRACED DOES NOT    *
*              CHANGE THE CONTENTS OF REGISTER 15.  THIS REGISTER IS   *
*              NEEDED TO MAINTAIN ADDRESSABILITY OF THE EXECUTE        *
*              ROUTINE IN THE SUBMONITOR                               *
```

```
*                                                                        *
*                                                                        *
*                                                                        *
*            NOTE THAT TRACE CANNOT USE THE SAVE AREA OF THE             *
*            CALLING PROGRAM (XPLSM) SINCE IT MAY ENTER XPLSM            *
*            RECURSIVELY AND CAUSE OS ROUTINES TO ALSO USE XPLSM'S       *
*            SAVE AREA.  NOTE FURTHER THAT TRACE DOES NOT NEED AN        *
*            OS SAVE AREA SINCE IT DOES NOT CALL ANY EXTERNAL            *
*            ROUTINES EXCEPT XPLSM.                                      *
*                                                                        *
*************************************************************************

TRACEP    CSECT

          ENTRY TRACE                   ENTRY TO THE TRACE ROUTINE

          USING *,INITLR

TRACE     DS    0H

          B     TRACEB
          DC    AL1(6)                  CSECT IDENTIFIER
          DC    CL6'TRACE

TRACEB    STM   0,15,SAVE               SAVE ALL REGISTERS
          LA    OSAVE,SAVE              BASE ADDRESS
          USING SAVE,OSAVE
          B     BEGN
          DROP  INITLR

*************************************************************************
*                                                                        *
*            SAVE   AREA                                                  *
*                                                                        *
*************************************************************************

SAVE      DC    16F'0'                  SAVE AREA
ADATA     DC    A(DATAREA)              ADDRESS OF TRACE ROUTINE DATA
AHEX      DC    A(HEXTOEBC)             ADDRESS OF CONVERT ROUTINE


*************************************************************************
*                                                                        *
*                                                                        *
*  HEXTOEBC   BINARY TO EBCDIC CONVERSION ROUTINE                        *
*                                                                        *
*                                                                        *
*            CONVERTS THE WORD IN SCR0 INTO 8 EBCDIC HEX                 *
*            CHARACTERS SUITABLE FOR PRINTING                           *
*            RETURNS THE 8 CHARACTERS IN SCR0,SCR1                      *
*                                                                        *
*                                                                        *
*************************************************************************
```

```
            USING  *,HEX2EBC
HEXTOEBC ST        SCR0,HEXTABLE+16          STORE THE WORD TO BE CONVERTED
            L      SCR1,HEXTABLE-4          NORMALIZED ADDRESS OF CONVERT
*                                            TABLE
            UNPK   HEXTABLE+16(9),HEXTABLE+16(5)
*                                            SPREAD THE HEX DIGITS
            TR     HEXTABLE+16(8),0(1)      TRANSLATE DIGITS TO
*                                            CORRESPONDING CHARACTERS
            LM     SCR0,SCR1,HEXTABLE+16    LOAD RESULT
            BR     BRFROM                   RETURN
            DROP   HEX2EBC

            DC     A(HEXTABLE-240)          NORMALIZED ADDRESS CONSTANT
HEXTABLE DC        CL25'0123456789ABCDEF'


****************************************************************************
*                                                                        *
*                                                                        *
*  BEGN          INITIALIZATION OF THE TRACE ROUTINE                      *
*                                                                        *
*               THE PARAMETERS PASSED TO THE TRACE ROUTINE ARE            *
*               DESCRIBED IN THE COMMENT ABOVE                            *
*                                                                        *
*                                                                        *
****************************************************************************

BEGN        L      DATA,ADATA               ADDRESS OF THE DATA AREA
            USING  DATAREA,DATA
            ST     SELF,AENTRY              SAVE ADDRESS OF THE SUBMONITOR
*                                            ENTRY POINT
            ST     0,ACONTRL                ADDRESS OF PARM FIELD
            LR     ILCR,2                   ADDRESS OF 1ST INSTRUCTION
*                                            TO BE TRACED
            LR     EXEC,4                   EXECUTE ROUTINE ADDRESS
            L      HEX2EBC,AHEX             CONVERSION ROUTINE ADDRESS
            USING  HEXTOEBC,HEX2EBC

****************************************************************************
*                                                                        *
*               COPY THE REGISTERS OF THE TRACED PROGRAM INTO REGTBL      *
*                                                                        *
****************************************************************************

            LA     SCR2,16                  16 REGISTERS
            SR     SCR3,SCR3                INDEX
PICKUP      L      SCR0,0(SCR3,SCR1)        FETCH A REGISTER
            ST     SCR0,REGTBL(SCR3)        STORE IT AWAY
            LA     SCR3,4(0,SCR3)           INCREMENT INDEX
            BCT    SCR2,PICKUP              LOOP BACK TO GET NEXT REGISTER

            BAL    BRFROM,WRITE             WRITE 1 BLANK LINE
```

```
        BAL    BRFROM,RDUMP            DUMP THE INITIAL
*                                      GENERAL REGISTERS

        STD    0,F0                    SAVE THE INITIAL VALUES
        STD    2,F2                    OF THE FLOATING POINT
        STD    4,F4                    REGISTERS
        STD    6,F6

        BAL    BRFROM,FDUMP            DUMP THE FLOATING POINT
*                                      REGISTERS
        BAL    BRFROM,WRITE            WRITE 1 BLANK LINE


*******************************************************************
*                                                               *
*                                                               *
*  MAINLOOP    THE MAJOR CYCLE OF THE TRACE ROUTINE             *
*                                                               *
*                                                               *
*******************************************************************

MAINLOOP DS    0H
        MVC    OLDREG(4*16),REGTBL     SAVE OLD REGISTERS FOR EVALXBD
        C      ILCR,AENTRY             HAVE WE REACHED THE ENTRY TO THE
*                                      XPLSM SUBMONITOR ?
        BE     GOIO                    YES, GO PROCESS THE REQUEST

        MVC    XCELL(6),0(ILCR)        FETCH THE NEXT 6 BYTES OF
*                                      THE INSTRUCTION IMAGE
        SR     SCR1,SCR1               CLEAR SCR1
        IC     SCR1,XCELL              THE INSTRUCTION CODE
        IC     SCR1,OPINDEX(SCR1)      THE INSTRUCTION INDEX
        LH     SCR1,OPFLAGS(SCR1)      THE INSTRUCTION ATTRIBUTE FLAGS
        STH    SCR1,FLAGS              SAVE THE FLAGS
        TM     FLAGS,ILGLBIT           IN THE INSTRUCTION ILLEGAL ?
        BO     ILGLOP                  YES, GO PRINT MESSAGE AND QUIT
        TM     FLAGS,BRBIT             IS THE INSTRUCTION
*                                      A BRANCH OR EXECUTE ?
        BO     BROP                    YES, GO TO THE BRANCH PROCESSOR
        STM    0,15,SAVREG             SAVE THE TRACE ROUTINE'S
*                                      REGISTERS
        LM     0,2,XCELL               PARAMETERS FOR EXECUTE ROUTINE
        LM     5,15,REGTBL+4*5         LOAD SOME OF THE PSEUDO
*                                      REGISTERS (REGISTERS OF THE
*                                      TRACED PROGRAM)
        DROP   DATA,HEX2EBC,OSAVE

        BALR   3,4                     CALL THE EXECUTE ROUTINE IN THE
*                                      XPLSM SUBMONITOR
        USING  *,3
```

```
**********************************************************************
*                                                                  *
*               THE EXECUTE ROUTINE IN THE SUBMONITOR RETURNS HERE  *
*               WITH A   BALR 1,3   THUS LEAVING THE POSSIBLY MODIFIED *
*               CONDITION CODE IN REGISTER 1                        *
*                                                                  *
**********************************************************************

        TM      FLAGS,CCBIT             COULD THE INSTRUCTION HAVE
*                                       CHANGED THE CONDITION CODE ?
        BZ      NOCC                    NO, NOT A POSSIBILITY

        SR      SCR0,SCR0               CLEAR SCR0
        SLL     SCR1,2                  SHIFT OFF LENGTH CODE
        SLDL    SCR0,2                  CONDITION CODE IN SCR0
        STC     SCR0,REALCC             SAVE CONDITION CODE IN REALCC

NOCC    DS      0H
        LM      0,15,SAVREG             RESTORE TRACE ROUTINE'S
*                                       REGISTERS
        USING   DATAREA,DATA
        USING   HEXTOEBC,HEX2EBC
        USING   SAVE,OSAVE
        DROP    3

        TM      FLAGS,FLOATBIT          FLOATING POINT INSTRUCTION ?
        BZ      BRETN                   NO, FLOATING REGISTERS
*                                       ARE UNCHANGED

        STD     0,F0                    SAVE THE POSSIBLY MODIFIED
        STD     2,F2                    FLOATING POINT REGISTERS
        STD     4,F4                    FOR THE PRINT ROUTINES
        STD     6,F6

**********************************************************************
*                                                                  *
*   BRETN        THE BRANCH AND EXECUTE INSTRUCTION PROCESSORS      *
*                RETURN TO THE MAIN LOOP HERE                       *
*                                                                  *
**********************************************************************

BRETN   DS      0H
        TM      PRINTING,X'FF'          IS PRINTING ENABLED
        BZ      NOPRTS                  NO, SO SKIP PRINT PHASE

        BAL     BRFROM,PRINTSUP         CALL THE PRINT SUPERVISOR
*                                       TO PRINT WHAT HAPPENED

NOPRTS  DS      0H
        TM      NOBUMP,X'FF'            SHOULD THE PSEUDO LOCATION
*                                       COUNTER BE INCREMENTED ?
        BZ      INCR                    YES, GO INCREMENT
        MVI     NOBUMP,X'00'            RESET FLAG
```

```
***********************************************************************
*                                                                     *
*              FETCH THE NEW VALUE FOR THE PSEUDO LOCATION COUNTER     *
*              THAT WAS PREPARED BY THE BRANCH PROCESSOR               *
*                                                                     *
***********************************************************************

           L     ILCR,NEWILC
           B     CTEST                     GO TO END OF MAIN LOOP

INCR       DS    0H                        INCREMENT THE PSEUDO LOCATION
*                                          COUNTER
           LA    ILCR,2(0,ILCR)            PLUS 2
           TM    FLAGS+1,RRBIT             TYPE RR INSTRUCTION ?
           BO    CTEST                     YES, SO DONE INCREMENTING
           LA    ILCR,2(0,ILCR)            PLUS 2 MORE
           TM    FLAGS+1,SSBIT             TYPE SS INSTRUCTION ?
           BZ    CTEST                     NO, SO DONE INCREMENTING
           LA    ILCR,2(0,ILCR)            PLUS 2 MORE FOR TYPE SS

CTEST      DS    0H

***********************************************************************
*                                                                     *
*  CTEST     HERE WOULD BE A GOOD PLACE TO INSERT AN INCREMENT         *
*            AND TEST ROUTINE IF IT BECOMES NECESSARY TO               *
*            LIMIT THE NUMBER OF INSTRUCTIONS THAT ARE TRACED.         *
*                                                                     *
***********************************************************************

           B     MAINLOOP                  AROUND THE LOOP AGAIN


***********************************************************************
*                                                                     *
*                                                                     *
*  ILGLOP     ILLEGAL  INSTRUCTION  HANDLING                           *
*                                                                     *
***********************************************************************

ILGLOP     DS    0H
           MVC   PLINE+4(40),ILGMSG        '**** ILLEGAL  INSTRUCTION
           BAL   BRFROM,WRITE              PRINT THE MESSAGE
           BAL   BRFROM,PRINTSUP           PRINT THE ILLEGAL INSTRUCTION
           BAL   BRFROM,RDUMP              DUMP THE GENERAL REGISTERS
           BAL   BRFROM,FDUMP              DUMP THE FLOATING REGISTERS

***********************************************************************
*                                                                     *
*              RETURN TO THE SUBMONITOR AT THE POINT FROM WHICH TRACE  *
*              WAS CALLED.  USED BY ILGLOP TO TERMINATE THE JOB        *
*              AFTER AN ILLEGAL INSTRUCTION                            *
*                                                                     *
***********************************************************************
```

```
        LM    0,15,SAVE              RESTORE ALL REGISTERS
        BR    CBR                    RETURN TO THE XPLSM SUBMONITOR


************************************************************************
*                                                                      *
*                                                                      *
*  GOIO        ROUTINE TO PROCESS CALLS TO THE SUBMONITOR              *
*              WHICH ARE MADE FROM THE PROGRAM BEING TRACED.           *
*                                                                      *
*                                                                      *
************************************************************************

GOIO    DS    0H
        L     SCR0,REGTBL+4*SMBR     GET THE RETURN ADDRESS IN THE
*                                    TRACED PROGRAM
        ST    SCR0,IOFROM            SAVE RETURN ADDRESS
        CLI   REGTBL+4*SVCR+3,TRACEC IS THE CALL A REQUEST TO
*                                    BEGIN TRACING ?
        BE    RETRACE                YES, GO TO RETRACE
        CLI   REGTBL+4*SVCR+3,UNTRACE
*                                    IS THE CALL A REQUEST TO
*                                    TERMINATE TRACING ?
        BE    ENDTRACE               YES, GO TO ENDTRACE
        TM    PRINTING,X'FF'         IS PRINTING ENABLED ?
        BZ    NOPRIO                 NO, SO REMAIN MUTE
        BAL   BRFROM,WRITE           PRINT 1 BLANK LINE
        MVC   PLINE+4(24),IORQM      '      I/O   REQUEST
        L     SCR0,REGTBL+4*PR1      1ST PARAMETER REGISTER
        BALR  BRFROM,HEX2EBC         CONVERT FOR PRINTING
        STM   SCR0,SCR1,PLINE+28     PLACE IN PRINT LINE
        L     SCR0,REGTBL+4*PR2      SECOND PARAMETER REGISTER
        BALR  BRFROM,HEX2EBC         CONVERT FOR PRINTING
        STM   SCR0,SCR1,PLINE+40     PLACE IN PRINT LINE
        L     SCR0,REGTBL+4*PR3      3RD PARAMETER REGISTER
        BALR  BRFROM,HEX2EBC         CONVERT FOR PRINTING
        STM   SCR0,SCR1,PLINE+52     PLACE IN PRINT LINE
        L     SCR0,REGTBL+4*SMBR     RETURN ADDRESS REGISTER
        BALR  BRFROM,HEX2EBC         CONVERT FOR PRINTING
        STM   SCR0,SCR1,PLINE+64     PLACE IN PRINT LINE
        BAL   BRFROM,WRITE           PRINT THE LINE
        BAL   BRFROM,WRITE           PRINT 1 BLANK LINE

NOPRIO  DS    0H
        STM   0,15,SAVREG            SAVE THE TRACE ROUTINE'S
*                                    REGISTERS
        LM    0,15,REGTBL            LOAD THE REGISTERS OF THE
*                                    TRACED PROGRAM
        DROP  DATA,OSAVE,HEX2EBC
        BALR  SMBR,SELF              CALL THE SUBMONITOR

        USING *,SMBR
        STM   0,15,REGTBL            SAVE REGISTERS IN THE
```

```
*                                            PSEUDO REGISTER TABLE
           LM    0,15,SAVREG               RESTORE TRACE ROUTINE'S
*                                            REGISTERS
           USING DATAREA,DATA
           USING HEXTOEBC,HEX2EBC
           USING SAVE,OSAVE
           DROP  SMBR
           L     ILCR,IOFROM               RETURN ADDRESS IN PROGRAM
           ST    ILCR,REGTBL+4*SMBR        RESTORE RETURN REGISTER ENTRY
*                                            IN REGTBL
           B     CTEST                     RETURN TO END OF THE MAIN LOOP

***********************************************************************
*                                                                     *
*                                                                     *
*   ENDTRACE    ROUTINE TO TERMINATE TRACING AND RESUME EXECUTION     *
*                                                                     *
*                                                                     *
***********************************************************************

ENDTRACE   DS    0H
           TM    PRINTING,X'FF'            IS PRINTING ENABLED ?
           BZ    GOEXEC                    NO, SO SKIP PRINTING
           L     SCR0,IOFROM               RETURN ADDRESS FOR THE
*                                            SUBMONITOR CALL
           BALR  BRFROM,HEX2EBC            CONVERT FOR PRINTING
           STM   SCR0,SCR1,ENDADR          PLACE IN MESSAGE
           MVC   ENDADR(2),BLANKS          TRIM TO SIX HEX DIGITS
           BAL   BRFROM,RDUMP              DUMP GENERAL REGISTERS
           BAL   BRFROM,FDUMP              DUMP FLOATING REGISTERS
           BAL   BRFROM,WRITE              PRINT 1 BLANK LINE
           MVC   PLINE+4(48),ENDTM         ' RESUME EXECUTION AT:  HHHHHH'
           BAL   BRFROM,WRITE              PRINT THE MESSAGE
           BAL   BRFROM,WRITE              PRINT 1 BLANK LINE

GOEXEC     DS    0H
           LM    0,15,REGTBL               LOAD THE GENERAL REGISTERS
*                                            OF THE TRACED PROGRAM
           BR    CBR                       RESUME EXECUTION OF THE PROGRAM

***********************************************************************
*                                                                     *
*                                                                     *
*   RETRACE     ROUTINE TO PROCESS TRACE REQUESTS ENCOUNTERED WHILE   *
*               TRACING                                               *
*                                                                     *
***********************************************************************

RETRACE    DS    0H
           TM    PRINTING,X'FF'            IS PRINTING ENABLED ?
           BZ    RTR2                      NO, SO SKIP PRINTING
           MVC   PLINE+80(26),RTRM         ' RECURSIVE TRACE REQUEST '
           BAL   BRFROM,WRITE              PRINT THE MESSAGE
           BAL   BRFROM,WRITE              PRINT 1 BLANK LINE
```

```
            BAL     BRFROM,RDUMP            DUMP THE GENERAL REGISTERS
            BAL     BRFROM,FDUMP            DUMP THE FLOATING REGISTERS
            BAL     BRFROM,WRITE            PRINT 1 BLANK LINE

RTR2        DS      0H
            L       ILCR,IOFROM             GET RETURN ADDRESS
            B       CTEST                   GO TO THE END OF THE MAIN LOOP


*********************************************************************
*                                                                 *
*                                                                 *
*   BROP        ROUTINE TO HANDLE BRANCH AND EXECUTE INSTRUCTIONS *
*                                                                 *
*                                                                 *
*                                                                 *
*********************************************************************

BROP        DS      0H
            TM      FLAGS+1,EXBIT           EXECUTE INSTRUCTION ?
            BO      EXOP                    YES, GO TO EXECUTE PROCESSOR
            BAL     BRFROM,BRPROC           CALL THE BRANCH PROCESSOR
            B       BRETN                   RETURN TO THE MAIN LOOP


*********************************************************************
*                                                                 *
*                                                                 *
*   BRPROC        BRANCH INSTRUCTION PROCESSOR                     *
*                                                                 *
*                                                                 *
*********************************************************************

BRPROC      DS      0H
            ST      BRFROM,BRSV             SAVE RETURN ADDRESS
            TM      FLAGS+1,RSBIT           BXH OR BXLE ?
            BO      BXHBXLE                 YES, GO PROCESS
            TM      XCELL,X'07'             BC ("47")  OR  BCR ("07") ?
            BO      BCBCR                   YES, GO PROCESS
            TM      XCELL,X'02'             BCT ("46")  OR  BCTR ("06") ?
            BO      BCTBCTR                 YES, GO PROCESS
*                                          BY DEFAULT THE INSTRUCTION IS
*                                          BAL ("45")  OR   BALR ("05")


*********************************************************************
*                                                                 *
*                BAL AND BALR                                      *
*                                                                 *
*********************************************************************

            LA      SCR1,2                  COMPUTE INCREMENT TO ILCR
            TM      FLAGS+1,RRBIT           BALR ?
            BO      BAL1                    YES, SO INCREMENT IS 2
            AR      SCR1,SCR1               BAL, SO INCREMENT IS 4
BAL1        AR      SCR1,ILCR               RETURN ADDRESS FOR BRANCH
```

```
**********************************************************************
*                                                                    *
*               BUILD UP COMPLETE RETURN REGISTER IN SCR1            *
*                                                                    *
**********************************************************************

        BALR    SCR0,SCR0           GET PROGRAM MASK BITS
        N       SCR0,0F000000       PROGRAM MASK BITS ONLY
        OR      SCR1,SCR0           INSERT IN THE RETURN
        L       SCR0,ILC1           GET INSTRUCTION LENGTH BITS
        TM      FLAGS+1,RXBIT+EXBIT BAL OR EXECUTE OF A BRANCH ?
        BZ      BAL2                NO, BALR SO LENGTH IS 2
        SLL     SCR0,1              BAL OR EXECUTED BRANCH
*                                   LENGTH IS 4
BAL2    OR      SCR1,SCR0           OR IN INSTRUCTION LENGTH CODE
        SR      SCR0,SCR0           CLEAR SCR0
        IC      SCR0,REALCC         GET THE CORRECT CONDITION CODE
        SLL     SCR0,28             POSITION IT PROPERLY
        OR      SCR1,SCR0           OR IN CONDITION CODE BITS


**********************************************************************
*                                                                    *
*               SCR1 NOW CONTAINS THE RETURN REGISTER THAT WOULD HAVE *
*               RESULTED IN ACTUAL EXECUTION FROM STORING THE RIGHT  *
*               HALF OF THE PSW                                       *
*                                                                    *
**********************************************************************

        IC      SCR2,XCELL+1        RR
        N       SCR2,000000F0       R0
        SRL     SCR2,2              R*4
        ST      SCR1,REGTBL(SCR2)   STORE RETURN IN PSEUDO REGISTER
        TM      FLAGS+1,RXBIT       BAL ?
        BO      BRXGO               BAL ALWAYS TRANSFERS
*                                   GO CALCULATE ADDRESS


**********************************************************************
*                                                                    *
* BRRGO         COMPUTATION OF THE BRANCH ADDRESS                    *
* BRXGO                                                              *
*                                                                    *
**********************************************************************

BRRGO   DS      0H                  TYPE RR,  BRANCH IS TAKEN
*                                   COMPUTE EFFECTIVE ADDRESS
        IC      SCR1,XCELL+1        RR
        N       SCR1,0000000F       0R
        BZ      BRTN1               NO BRANCH IF REGISTER ZERO
*                                   IS SPECIFIED
        SLL     SCR1,2              R*4
        L       SCR0,OLDREG(SCR1)   GET ADDRESS FROM REGISTER

BRTN    DS      0H                  SUCCESSFUL BRANCH EXIT
```

```
          ST       SCR0,NEWILC                SAVE BRANCH ADDRESS
*                                             FOR LOADING AT END OF MAIN LOOP
          MVI      NOBUMP,X'FF'               SET BRANCH FLAG

BRTN1     DS       0H                         UNSUCCESSFUL BRANCH EXIT
          L        BRFROM,BRSV                RESTORE RETURN ADDRESS
          BR       BRFROM                     RETURN

BRXGO     DS       0H                         TYPE RX,  BRANCH TAKEN
          LA       SCR2,XCELL+2               POINT AT BASE,DISPLACEMENT FIELD
          BAL      BRFROM,EVALXBD             GO EVALUATE EFFECTIVE ADDRESS
          B        BRTN

***********************************************************************
*                                                                     *
*  BCBCR        BC AND BCR                                            *
*                                                                     *
***********************************************************************

BCBCR     DS       0H                         CONDITIONAL BRANCH PROCESSOR
          IC       SCR1,XCELL+1               RR
          N        SCR1,000000F0              R0
          SR       SCR2,SCR2                  CLEAR SCR2
          IC       SCR2,REALCC                ACTUAL CONDITION CODE
          SLL      SCR2,2                     (CONDITION CODE)*4
          N        SCR1,CCBITS(SCR2)          MASK BITS CORRESPONDING TO
*                                             THE CONDITION CODE

***********************************************************************
*                                                                     *
*            IF THE MASK SPECIFIED BY THE R1 FIELD OF THE             *
*            INSTRUCTION DOES NOT HAVE A ONE BIT THAT CORRESPONDS     *
*            TO THE ONE BIT IN THE MASK REPRESENTING THE CONDITION    *
*            CODE THEN THE BRANCH IS NOT TAKEN                        *
*                                                                     *
***********************************************************************

          BZ       BRTN1                      BRANCH IS NOT TAKEN
          TM       FLAGS+1,RXBIT              BC INSTRUCTION ?
          BO       BRXGO                      YES, GO EVALUATE ADDRESS
          B        BRRGO                      BCR, GO EVALUATE ADDRESS

***********************************************************************
*                                                                     *
*  BXHBXLE      BXH AND BXLE                                          *
*                                                                     *
***********************************************************************

BXHBXLE   DS       0H                         BXH  BXLE  INSTRUCTION PROCESSOR
          SR       SCR1,SCR1                  CLEAR SCR1
          IC       SCR1,XCELL+1               RR
          N        SCR1,0000000F              0R
          SLL      SCR1,2                     R3*4
          L        SCR0,REGTBL(SCR1)          VALUE OF THE INCREMENT
```

```
          SR    SCR2,SCR2                CLEAR SCR2
          IC    SCR2,XCELL+1             RR
          N     SCR2,000000F0            R0
          SRL   SCR2,2                   R1*4
          A     SCR0,REGTBL(SCR2)        1ST OPERAND + INCREMENT
          ST    SCR0,REGTBL(SCR2)        STORE SUM BACK IN R1
          TM    XCELL+1,X'01'            IS R3 ODD ?
          BO    CR3                      YES, SO IT IS THE COMPARAND
          LA    SCR1,4(SCR1)             (R3+1)*4
          N     SCR1,0000003C            MODULO 16
CR3       C     SCR0,REGTBL(SCR1)        COMPARE NEW VALUE AND COMPARAND
          BH    BHGO                     NEW VALUE IS GREATER
*                                        NEW VALUE IS LESS THAN OR EQUAL

BLEGO     TM    XCELL,X'01'              IS THE INSTRUCTION BXLE ("87") ?
          BO    BRXGO                    YES, BXLE SO BRANCH IS TAKEN
          B     BRTN1                    NO, BXH SO BRANCH IS NOT TAKEN

BHGO      TM    XCELL,X'01'              IS THE INSTRUCTION BXH ("86") ?
          BZ    BRXGO                    BXH, SO BRANCH IS TAKEN
          B     BRTN1                    BXLE,  BRANCH IS NOT TAKEN

*********************************************************************
*                                                                 *
*  BCTBCTR     BCT AND BCTR                                        *
*                                                                 *
*********************************************************************

BCTBCTR   DS    0H                       BCT AND BCTR PROCESSOR
          IC    SCR2,XCELL+1             RR
          N     SCR2,000000F0            R0
          SRL   SCR2,2                   R1*4
          L     SCR1,REGTBL(SCR2)        VALUE OF THE INDEX
          S     SCR1,F1                  SUBTRACT ONE
          ST    SCR1,REGTBL(SCR2)        STORE NEW VALUE BACK
          BZ    BRTN1                    NO BRANCH IF NEW VALUE IS ZERO
          TM    FLAGS+1,RXBIT            BCT OR BCTR ?
          BO    BRXGO                    BCT, GO EVALUATE ADDRESS
          B     BRRGO                    BCTR, GO EVALUATE ADDRESS

*********************************************************************
*                                                                 *
*                                                                 *
*  EXOP        EXECUTE INSTRUCTION PROCESSOR                       *
*                                                                 *
*                                                                 *
*********************************************************************

EXOP      DS    0H
          LA    SCR2,XCELL+2             POINT TO BASE AND DISPLACEMENT
          BAL   BRFROM,EVALXBD           EVALUATE THE EFFECTIVE ADDRESS
*                                        OF THE EXECUTE INSTRUCTION
          LR    SCR1,SCR0                ADDRESS IS IN SCR0, MOVE IT
```

```
          MVC    PSXCELL(6),0(SCR1)      FETCH 6 BYTES OF THE SUBJECT
*                                        INSTRUCTION
          IC     SCR1,XCELL+1            RR  OF THE EXECUTE INSTRUCTION
          N      SCR1,OOOOOOFO           R0


***********************************************************************
*                                                                     *
*                 IF THE R1 FIELD OF THE EXECUTE INSTRUCTION IS ZERO   *
*                 THEN THE SUBJECT INSTRUCTION IS EXECUTED AS IS.      *
*                 OTHERWISE THE RIGHT HAND BYTE OF THE REGISTER        *
*                 SPECIFIED BY THE R1 FIELD IS OR'ED INTO THE SECOND   *
*                 BYTE OF THE SUBJECT INSTRUCTION                      *
*                                                                     *
***********************************************************************


          BZ     NOOR                    NOTHING TO OR IN
          SRL    SCR1,2                  R1*4
          L      SCR2,REGTBL(SCR1)       GET THE BITS TO OR IN
          EX     SCR2,ORI                OR INTO THE SUBJECT INSTRUCTION

NOOR      DS     0H
          SR     SCR1,SCR1               CLEAR SCR1
          IC     SCR1,PSXCELL            INSTRUCTION CODE OF THE SUBJECT
*                                        INSTRUCTION
          IC     SCR1,OPINDEX(SCR1)      INSTRUCTION CODE INDEX
          LH     SCR1,OPFLAGS(SCR1)      INSTRUCTION CODE ATTRIBUTE FLAGS
          STH    SCR1,PSFLAGS            SAVE THE FLAGS
          TM     PSFLAGS,ILGLBIT         IS THE SUBJECT INSTRUCTION
*                                        ILLEGAL ?
          BO     ILGLOP                  YES, PRINT MESSAGE AND TERMINATE
          TM     PSFLAGS,BRBIT           IS THE SUBJECT INSTRUCTION
*                                        A BRANCH ?
          BO     EXBR                    YES, GO SIMULATE AN EXECUTED
*                                        BRANCH INSTRUCTION

          STM    0,15,SAVREG             SAVE TRACE ROUTINE REGISTERS
          LM     0,2,PSXCELL             PARAMETERS FOR EXECUTE ROUTINE
          LM     5,15,REGTBL+4*5         LOAD TRACED PROGRAM'S REGISTERS
          DROP   DATA,HEX2EBC,OSAVE
          BALR   3,4                     CALL THE EXECUTE ROUTINE IN
*                                        THE XPLSM SUBMONITOR


***********************************************************************
*                                                                     *
*                 EXECUTE ROUTINE RETURNS HERE VIA A BALR 1,3 THUS     *
*                 LEAVING THE POSSIBLY MODIFIED CONDITION CODE IN      *
*                 REGISTER 1                                           *
*                                                                     *
***********************************************************************


          USING  *,3
          TM     PSFLAGS,CCBIT           WAS THE CONDITION CODE POSSIBLY
*                                        CHANGED ?
          BZ     NXCC                    NO, NOT A POSSIBILITY
```

```
          SR      SCR0,SCR0               CLEAR SCR0
          SLL     SCR1,2                  DELETE INSTRUCTION LENGTH CODE
          SLDL    SCR0,2                  CONDITION CODE TO SCR0
          STC     SCR0,REALCC             SAVE CONDITION CODE IN REALCC

NXCC      DS      0H
          LM      0,15,SAVREG             RESTORE TRACE ROUTINE REGISTERS
          USING DATAREA,DATA
          USING HEXTOEBC,HEX2EBC
          USING SAVE,OSAVE
          DROP  3
          B       BRETN                   RETURN TO THE MAIN LOOP

*********************************************************************
*                                                                   *
*   EXBR          ROUTINE TO HANDLE EXECUTED BRANCHES                *
*                                                                   *
*********************************************************************

EXBR      DS      0H
          TM      PSFLAGS+1,EXBIT         IS THE SUBJECT INSTRUCTION
*                                         REALLY AN EXECUTE INSTRUCTION ?
          BO      ILGLOP                  EXECUTED EXECUTES ARE ILLEGAL

*********************************************************************
*                                                                   *
*              MOVE THINGS AROUND TO FOOL THE BRANCH PROCESSOR       *
*                                                                   *
*********************************************************************

          LH      SCR1,FLAGS              SWAP FLAGS AND PSFLAGS
          LH      SCR2,PSFLAGS
          STH     SCR1,PSFLAGS
          STH     SCR2,FLAGS
          LM      SCR0,SCR1,XCELL         SWAP XCELL AND PSXCELL
          LM      SCR2,SCR3,PSXCELL
          STM     SCR0,SCR1,PSXCELL
          STM     SCR2,SCR3,XCELL

*********************************************************************
*                                                                   *
*              SIGNAL AN EXECUTED BRANCH SO THAT THE INSTRUCTION     *
*              LENGTH CODE COMES OUT RIGHT FOR BAL AND BALR          *
*                                                                   *
*********************************************************************

          OI      FLAGS+1,EXBIT           SET EXECUTED BRANCH FLAG
          BAL     BRFROM,BRPROC           CALL THE BRANCH PROCESSOR
```

```
**************************************************************************
*                                                                        *
*                   PUT THINGS BACK THE WAY THEY WERE SO THAT THE EXECUTE *
*                   INSTRUCTION GETS PRINTED                              *
*                                                                        *
**************************************************************************

           LH      SCR1,FLAGS                SWAP FLAGS AND PSFLAGS
           LH      SCR2,PSFLAGS
           STH     SCR1,PSFLAGS
           STH     SCR2,FLAGS
           LM      SCR0,SCR1,XCELL           SWAP XCELL AND PSXCELL
           LM      SCR2,SCR3,PSXCELL
           STM     SCR0,SCR1,PSXCELL
           STM     SCR2,SCR3,XCELL
           B       BRETN                     RETURN TO THE MAIN LOOP


**************************************************************************
*                                                                        *
*                                                                        *
*  PRINTSUP       PRINT SUPERVISOR                                        *
*                                                                        *
*                 THIS ROUTINE CONTROLS THE FABRICATION AND PRINTING      *
*                 OF THE PRINT LINE DESCRIBING EACH INSTRUCTION           *
*                                                                        *
**************************************************************************

PRINTSUP DS      0H
           ST      BRFROM,PRTS               SAVE RETURN

           BAL     BRFROM,PLINE1             CALL PLINE1

           BAL     BRFROM,PLINOP             CALL PLINOP

           BAL     BRFROM,PLINREG            CALL PLINREG

           BAL     BRFROM,PLINEFA            CALL PLINEFA

           BAL     BRFROM,WRITE              PRINT THE LINE

           TM      FLAGS+1,LMSTMBIT          LM OR STM INSTRUCTION ?
           BZ      NORDMP                    NO

           BAL     BRFROM,RDUMP              YES, SO DUMP GENERAL REGISTERS

           BAL     BRFROM,WRITE              PRINT 1 BLANK LINE

NORDMP   DS      0H
           L       BRFROM,PRTS               LOAD RETURN ADDRESS
           BR      BRFROM                    RETURN
```

```
*********************************************************************
*                                                                   *
*                                                                   *
*  PLINE1        ROUTINE TO PLACE THE PSEUDO LOCATION COUNTER, THE   *
*                HEXADECIMAL INSTRUCTION IMAGE, AND THE CONDITION CODE *
*                IN THE PRINT LINE                                   *
*                                                                   *
*********************************************************************

PLINE1    DS    0H
          ST    BRFROM,P1S              SAVE RETURN ADDRESS
          LR    SCR0,ILCR               COPY THE PSEUDO LOCATION COUNTER
          BALR  BRFROM,HEX2EBC          CONVERT IT FOR PRINTING
          STM   SCR0,SCR1,ILC           PLACE IT IN THE PRINT LINE
          MVC   ILC(2),BLANKS           DELETE LEADING ZEROS
          L     SCR0,XCELL              GET THE INSTRUCTION IMAGE
          BALR  BRFROM,HEX2EBC          CONVERT 1ST FOUR BYTES
          ST    SCR0,INSTR              PLACE 1ST 2 BYTES IN PRINT LINE
          TM    FLAGS+1,RRBIT           TYPE RR INSTRUCTION ?
          BO    P1CC                    YES, ONLY PRINT TWO BYTES
          ST    SCR1,INSTR+4            PLACE 2ND 2 BYTES OF THE
*                                       INSTRUCTION IN THE PRINT LINE
          TM    FLAGS+1,SSBIT           TYPE SS INSTRUCTION ?
          BZ    P1CC                    NO, ONLY PRINT 4 BYTES
          L     SCR0,XCELL+4            GET LAST 2 BYTES OF INSTRUCTION
          BALR  BRFROM,HEX2EBC          CONVERT FOR PRINTING
          ST    SCR0,INSTR+8            PLACE LAST 2 BYTES IN PRINT LINE
P1CC      DS    0H                      PLACE THE CONDITION CODE IN THE
*                                       PRINT LINE
          SR    SCR1,SCR1               CLEAR SCR1
          IC    SCR1,REALCC             ACTUAL CONDITION CODE
          IC    SCR0,EBDCC(SCR1)        GET CORRESPONDING CHARACTER
          STC   SCR0,CC                 PLACE CHARACTER IN PRINT LINE
          L     BRFROM,P1S              LOAD RETURN ADDRESS
          BR    BRFROM                  RETURN

          .

*********************************************************************
*                                                                   *
*                                                                   *
*  PLINOP        ROUTINE TO PLACE THE SYMBOLIC INSTRUCTION CODE AND THE *
*                INSTRUCTION FIELDS IN ASSEMBLY FORMAT INTO THE      *
*                PRINT LINE.                                         *
*                                                                   *
*********************************************************************

PLINOP    DS    0H
          ST    BRFROM,P2S              SAVE RETURN ADDRESS
          SR    SCR1,SCR1               CLEAR SCR1
          IC    SCR1,XCELL              INSTRUCTION CODE
          SLL   SCR1,2                  (INSTRUCTION CODE)*4
          L     SCR0,BCDOP(SCR1)        SYMBOLIC INSTRUCTION CODE
          ST    SCR0,OP                 PLACE IN PRINT LINE
```

```
************************************************************************
*                                                                      *
*                PREPARE THE INSTRUCTION FIELDS IN ASSEMBLY FORMAT     *
*                                                                      *
************************************************************************

           LA     FLDPT,FIELDS            POINTER TO THE INSTRUCTION
*                                         FIELDS IN THE PRINT LINE
           TM     FLAGS+1,IMDFBIT         DOES THE INSTRUCTION CONTAIN
*                                         AN IMMEDIATE FIELD ?
           BZ     SPLT                    NO, SO SPLIT THE FIELD INTO R,X
           SR     SCR1,SCR1               SIGNAL NO INDEX
           LH     SCR0,XCELL+2            BDDD
           BAL    BRFROM,BDPROC           'DDD(B)'
           TM     FLAGS+1,SSBIT           TYPE SS INSTRUCTION ?
           BZ     FSI                     NO, MUST BE TYPE SI INSTRUCTION
           S      FLDPT,F3                BACK UP THE FIELD POINTER
           MVC    4(2,FLDPT),1(FLDPT)     'DDD(   B)'
           SR     SCR1,SCR1               CLEAR SCR1
           IC     SCR1,XCELL+1            LL        LENGTH FIELD
           SRL    SCR1,4                  L
           IC     SCR1,HEXCHAR(SCR1)      'L'
           STC    SCR1,1(FLDPT)           'DDD(L  B)'
           IC     SCR1,XCELL+1            LL
           N      SCR1,0000000F            L
           IC     SCR1,HEXCHAR(SCR1)      'L'
           STC    SCR1,2(FLDPT)           'DDD(LL B)'
           MVI    3(FLDPT),C','            'DDD(LL,B)'
           LA     FLDPT,6(FLDPT)          ADJUST THE FIELD POINTER
           B      FSS                     GO FINISH TYPE SS INSTRUCTION

FSI        MVI    0(FLDPT),C','            'DDD(B),'
           SR     SCR1,SCR1               CLEAR SCR1
           IC     SCR1,XCELL+1            II        IMMEDIATE FIELD
           SRL    SCR1,4                  I
           IC     SCR1,HEXCHAR(SCR1)      'I'
           STC    SCR1,1(FLDPT)           'DDD(B),I'
           IC     SCR1,XCELL+1            II
           N      SCR1,0000000F            I
           IC     SCR1,HEXCHAR(SCR1)      'I'
           STC    SCR1,2(FLDPT)           'DDD(B),II'
           B      POPDONE                 FINISHED, SO RETURN

************************************************************************
*                                                                      *
*                SPLIT THE SECOND BYTE OF THE INSTRUCTION INTO          *
*                R,X OR R,R                                             *
*                                                                      *
************************************************************************

SPLT       IC     SCR1,XCELL+1            RX        REGISTER SPECIFIERS
           N      SCR1,000000F0           R0
           SRL    SCR1,4                  R
           IC     SCR0,HEXCHAR(SCR1)      'R'
```

```
              STC   SCR0,0(0,FLDPT)              'R'
              MVI   1(FLDPT),C','                'R,'
              LA    FLDPT,2(FLDPT)               ADJUST FIELD POINTER
              TM    FLAGS+1,RRBIT+LMSTMBIT
*                                                IS THE INSTRUCTION TYPE RR OR
*                                                LM OR STM ?
              BZ    NOTRR                        NO
              IC    SCR1,XCELL+1                 RR
              N     SCR1,0000000F                0R
              IC    SCR0,HEXCHAR(SCR1)           'R'
              STC   SCR0,0(0,FLDPT)              'R,R'
              TM    FLAGS+1,RRBIT                IS THE INSTRUCTION TYPE RR ?
              BO    POPDONE                      YES, SO FINISHED
              SR    SCR1,SCR1                    NO INDEX FOR LM OR STM
              MVI   1(FLDPT),C','                'R,R,'
              LA    FLDPT,2(FLDPT)               ADJUST THE FIELD POINTER
              B     NOTRR2                       GO EVALUATE BASE, DISPLACEMENT

NOTRR    IC    SCR1,XCELL+1                 RX
         N     SCR1,0000000F                0X
NOTRR2   LH    SCR0,XCELL+2                 BDDD     BASE AND DISPLACEMENT
         BAL   BRFROM,BDPROC               'R,DDD(X,B)'  OR     'R,DDD(B)'
         B     POPDONE                     FINISHED  SO RETURN
```

```
************************************************************************
*                                                                     *
*                FINISH UP TYPE  SS INSTRUCTION                       *
*                                                                     *
************************************************************************

FSS      MVI   0(FLDPT),C','               'DDD(LL,B),'
         LA    FLDPT,1(FLDPT)              ADJUST FIELD POINTER
         LH    SCR0,XCELL+4                BDDD     2ND BASE,DISPLACEMENT
         SR    SCR1,SCR1                   INDICATE NO INDEX
         BAL   BRFROM,BDPROC               'DDD(LL,B),DDD(B)'

POPDONE  L     BRFROM,P2S                  LOAD RETURN ADDRESS
         BR    BRFROM                      RETURN
```

```
************************************************************************
*                                                                     *
*                                                                     *
*  BDPROC      ROUTINE TO FORMAT THE BASE, DISPLACEMENT, AND INDEX     *
*              FIELDS INTO ASSEMBLY FORMAT FOR PRINTING                *
*              INPUT IS A BASE,DISPLACEMENT HALFWORD IN SCR0 AND THE   *
*              NUMBER OF THE INDEX REGISTER IN SCR1                    *
*                                                                     *
*              PLACES EITHER  'DDD(B)'  OR 'DDD(X,B)' INTO THE         *
*              INSTRUCTION IMAGE AT THE POINT SPECIFIED BY FLDPT       *
*                                                                     *
*                                                                     *
************************************************************************
```

```
BDPROC   ST    BRFROM,BDS                SAVE RETURN ADDRESS
         ST    SCR0,BDT                  SAVE   BDDD
         ST    SCR1,BDT2                 SAVE INDEX SPECIFIER
         N     SCR0,00000FFF             DDD        DISPLACEMENT
         BALR  BRFROM,HEX2EBC            CONVERT FOR PRINTING
         L     SCR0,BDT2                 X          INDEX REGISTER
         ST    SCR1,BDT2                 '0DDD'
         MVC   0(3,FLDPT),BDT2+1         'DDD'
         MVI   3(FLDPT),C'('             'DDD('
         LTR   SCR1,SCR0                 IS AN INDEX SPECIFIED ?
         BZ    BDPNX                     NO, ZERO SPECIFIES NO INDEX
         IC    SCR1,HEXCHAR(SCR1)        'X'
         STC   SCR1,4(FLDPT)             'DDD(X'
         MVI   5(FLDPT),C','             'DDD(X,'
         LA    FLDPT,2(FLDPT)            ADJUST POINTER FOR THE INDEX
BDPNX    L     SCR1,BDT                  BDDD        BASE, DISPLACEMENT
         N     SCR1,0000F000             B000
         SRL   SCR1,12                   B          BASE REGISTER
         IC    SCR1,HEXCHAR(SCR1)        'B'
         STC   SCR1,4(FLDPT)             'DDD(X,B'   OR      'DDD(B'
         MVI   5(FLDPT),C')'             'DDD(X,B)'  OR      'DDD(B)'
         LA    FLDPT,6(FLDPT)            ADJUST FIELD POINTER
         L     BRFROM,BDS                LOAD RETURN ADDRESS
         BR    BRFROM                    RETURN


***********************************************************************
*                                                                   *
*                                                                   *
*   PLINREG      ROUTINE TO PLACE THE OPERAND REGISTERS REFERENCED   *
*                BY THE INSTRUCTION INTO THE PRINT LINE              *
*                                                                   *
*                                                                   *
***********************************************************************

PLINREG  DS    0H
         TM    FLAGS+1,RRBIT+RXBIT+RSBIT
*                                        DOES THE INSTRUCTION REFERENCE
*                                        REGISTERS ?
         BCR   B'1000',BRFROM            NO, SO RETURN
         ST    BRFROM,P3S                SAVE RETURN ADDRESS
         TM    FLAGS,BRBIT               BRANCH INSTRUCTION ?
         BZ    GR1                       NO


***********************************************************************
*                                                                   *
*                INSTRUCTION IS A BRANCH, SO TEST TO SEE IF IT IS    *
*                A BRANCH CONDITIONAL, IN WHICH CASE THE R1 FIELD    *
*                IS USED AS A MASK AGAINST THE CONDITION CODE        *
*                                                                   *
***********************************************************************

         CLI   XCELL,X'47'               IS THE INSTRUCTION BC ?
         BE    R1MASK                    YES
```

```
            CLI    XCELL,X'07'              IS THE INSTRUCTION BCR ?
            BNE    GR1                      NO

R1MASK      DS     0H
            IC     SCR0,FIELDS              R IN EBCDIC
            STC    SCR0,R1+7                STORE IN REGISTER FIELD
            LA     SCR2,REGTBL              ADDRESS OF REGISTER TABLE
            B      RGRR                     GO TEST FOR TYPE RR INSTRUCTION

GR1         DS     0H
            IC     SCR1,XCELL+1             RR
            N      SCR1,000000F0            R0
            SRL    SCR1,2                   R*4
            LA     SCR2,REGTBL              ADDRESS OF REGISTER TABLE
            TM     FLAGS,FLOATBIT           FLOATING POINT INSTRUCTION ?
            BZ     FIXD                     NO, USE GENERAL REGISTERS
            LA     SCR2,F0                  YES, USE FLOATING REGISTERS

FIXD        DS     0H
            L      SCR0,0(SCR1,SCR2)        GET THE VALUE OF THE REGISTER
            ST     SCR1,PRT                 SAVE REGISTER NUMBER
            BALR   BRFROM,HEX2EBC           CONVERT VALUE FOR PRINTING
            STM    SCR0,SCR1,R1             PLACE IN PRINT LINE
            TM     FLAGS,DBLBIT             DOUBLE WORD INSTRUCTION ?
            BZ     RGRR                     NO
            L      SCR1,PRT                 R*4   AGAIN
            LA     SCR1,4(0,SCR1)           (R+1)*4    SECOND REGISTER NUMBER
            L      SCR0,0(SCR1,SCR2)        VALUE OF SECOND REGISTER
            BALR   BRFROM,HEX2EBC           CONVERT FOR PRINTING
            STM    SCR0,SCR1,DR1            PLACE IN PRINT LINE
            TM     FLAGS+1,RRBIT            TYPE RR INSTRUCTION ?
            BZ     PRDONE                   NO, SO FINISHED
```

```
*********************************************************************************
*                                                                              *
*              GET THE VALUE OF THE 2ND DOUBLE WORD REGISTER                    *
*                                                                              *
*********************************************************************************
```

```
            IC     SCR1,XCELL+1             RR
            N      SCR1,0000000F            0R
            SLL    SCR1,2                   R*4
            L      SCR0,0(SCR1,SCR2)        GET REGISTER VALUE
            ST     SCR1,PRT                 SAVE REGISTER NUMBER
            BALR   BRFROM,HEX2EBC           CONVERT FOR PRINTING
            STM    SCR0,SCR1,DR2A           PLACE IN PRINT LINE
            L      SCR1,PRT                 R*4   AGAIN
            L      SCR0,4(SCR1,SCR2)        GET 2ND HALF OF VALUE
            BALR   BRFROM,HEX2EBC           CONVERT FOR PRINTING
            STM    SCR0,SCR1,DR2B           PLACE IN PRINT LINE
            B      PRDONE                   FINISHED

RGRR        DS     0H
            TM     FLAGS+1,RRBIT            TYPE RR INSTRUCTION ?
```

```
          BZ      PRDONE                      NO, SO DONE
          IC      SCR1,XCELL+1                RR
          N       SCR1,0000000F               0R
          SLL     SCR1,2                      R*4
          L       SCR0,0(SCR1,SCR2)           VALUE OF THE REGISTER
          BALR    BRFROM,HEX2EBC              CONVERT FOR PRINTING
          STM     SCR0,SCR1,R2                PLACE IN PRINT LINE

PRDONE    DS      0H
          L       BRFROM,P3S                  LOAD RETURN ADDRESS
          BR      BRFROM                      RETURN


*************************************************************************
*                                                                      *
*                                                                      *
*   PLINEFA     ROUTINE TO PLACE THE EFFECTIVE ADDRESS OF THE          *
*               INSTRUCTION AND THE CONTENTS OF THE MEMORY LOCATION    *
*               REFERENCED BY THE INSTRUCTION INTO THE PRINT LINE      *
*                                                                      *
*                                                                      *
*************************************************************************

PLINEFA   DS      0H
          TM      FLAGS+1,RRBIT               TYPE RR INSTRUCTION ?
          BCR     B'0001',BRFROM              YES, SO NO MEMORY REFERENCE

          ST      BRFROM,P4S                  SAVE RETURN ADDRESS
          LA      SCR2,XCELL+2                ADDRESS OF BASE, DISPLACEMENT
          TM      FLAGS+1,RXBIT               TYPE RX INSTRUCTION ?
          BZ      NOTRX                       NO
          BAL     BRFROM,EVALXBD              GO EVALUATE ADDRESS WITH INDEX
          B       PEFA                        GO PLACE IN PRINT LINE

NOTRX     BAL     BRFROM,EVALBD               GO EVALUATE ADDRESS, NO INDEX
PEFA      ST      SCR0,EFAT0                  SAVE EFFECTIVE ADDRESS
          BALR    BRFROM,HEX2EBC              CONVERT ADDRESS FOR PRINTING
          STM     SCR0,SCR1,EFA1              PLACE ADDRESS IN PRINT LINE
          MVC     EFA1(2),BLANKS              DELETE LEADING ZEROS
          TM      FLAGS,SHIFTBIT              SHIFT INSTRUCTION ?
          BO      PEFADONE                    YES, SO NO MEMORY REFERENCE
          CLI     XCELL,X'41'                 LOAD ADDRESS INSTRUCTION ?
          BE      PEFADONE                    YES, SO NO MEMORY REFERENCE
          L       SCR2,EFAT0                  EFFECTIVE ADDRESS AGAIN
          MVC     EFAT0(4),0(SCR2)            CONTENTS OF MEMORY REFERENCED
          L       SCR0,EFAT0                  PLACE CONTENTS IN SCR0
          BALR    BRFROM,HEX2EBC              CONVERT FOR PRINTING
          STM     SCR0,SCR1,EFA1+12           PLACE CONTENTS IN PRINT LINE
          TM      FLAGS,HALFBIT               HALF WORD INSTRUCTION ?
          BZ      PEFA1                       NO
          MVC     EFA1+16(4),BLANKS           YES, ONLY PRINT HALF WORD
          B       PEFADONE                    FINISHED

PEFA1     DS      0H
```

```
              TM      FLAGS+1,SIBIT           TYPE SI INSTRUCTION ?
              BZ      PEFA2                   NO
              MVC     EFA1+14(6),BLANKS       ONLY PRINT ONE BYTE
              B       PEFADONE                FINISHED

PEFA2         DS      0H
              TM      FLAGS,DBLBIT            DOUBLE WORD RX INSTRUCTION ?
              BZ      PEFA3                   NO
              MVC     EFAT0(4),4(SCR2)        CONTENTS OF SECOND WORD
              L       SCR0,EFAT0              PLACE IN SCR0
              BALR    BRFROM,HEX2EBC          CONVERT FOR PRINTING
              STM     SCR0,SCR1,EFA1+20       PLACE IN THE PRINT LINE
              B       PEFADONE                FINISHED

PEFA3         DS      0H
              TM      FLAGS+1,SSBIT           TYPE SS INSTRUCTION ?
              BZ      PEFADONE                NO, SO FINISHED
              LA      SCR2,XCELL+4            ADDRESS OF 2ND BASE,DISPLACEMENT
              BAL     BRFROM,EVALBD           EVALUATE ADDRESS
              ST      SCR0,EFAT0              SAVE EFFECTIVE ADDRESS
              BALR    BRFROM,HEX2EBC          CONVERT FOR PRINTING
              STM     SCR0,SCR1,EFA2          PLACE IN PRINT LINE
              MVC     EFA2(2),BLANKS          DELETE LEADING BLANKS
              L       SCR1,EFAT0              EFFECTIVE ADDRESS AGAIN
              MVC     EFAT0(4),0(SCR1)        GET CONTENTS OF MEMORY
              L       SCR0,EFAT0              LOAD CONTENTS INTO SCR0
              BALR    BRFROM,HEX2EBC          CONVERT FOR PRINTING
              STM     SCR0,SCR1,EFA2+12       PLACE IN PRINT LINE

PEFADONE DS   0H
              L       BRFROM,P4S              LOAD RETURN ADDRESS
              BR      BRFROM                  RETURN


*******************************************************************
*                                                                 *
*                                                                 *
*   EVALBD       ROUTINE TO EVALUATE THE MEMORY ADDRESSES OF MEMORY  *
*   EVALXBD      REFERENCE INSTRUCTIONS                            *
*                                                                 *
*               INPUT IS THE ADDRESS OF A HALF WORD CONTAINING THE  *
*               BASE AND DISPLACEMENT FIELDS IN SCR2              *
*                                                                 *
*               OUTPUT IS THE EFFECTIVE ADDRESS IN SCR0           *
*                                                                 *
*               EVALBD        ASSUMES THAT THERE IS NO INDEX      *
*                                                                 *
*               EVALXBD       USES THE INDEX FIELD OF THE INSTRUCTION *
*                             IN CALCULATING THE EFFECTIVE ADDRESS  *
*                                                                 *
*                                                                 *
*******************************************************************

EVALBD    DS      0H
```

```
          SR      SCR0,SCR0       VALUE OF THE INDEX IS ZERO
          B       NOX                         GO EVALUATE BASE, DISPLACEMENT

EVALXBD   DS      0H
          SR      SCR0,SCR0                   CLEAR SCR0
          IC      SCR1,XCELL+1                RX
          N       SCR1,0000000F               0X
          BZ      NOX                         REGISTER ZERO IMPLIES NO INDEX
          SLL     SCR1,2                      X*4
          L       SCR0,OLDREG(SCR1)           VALUE OF THE INDEX

NOX       DS      0H                          AT THIS POINT, SCR0 CONTAINS
*                                             THE VALUE OF THE INDEX
          IC      SCR1,0(SCR2)                BD
          N       SCR1,000000F0               B0      BASE REGISTER
          BZ      NOB                         REGISTER ZERO IMPLIES NO BASE
          SRL     SCR1,2                      B*4
          A       SCR0,OLDREG(SCR1)           INDEX + BASE

NOB       DS      0H
          LH      SCR1,0(0,SCR2)              BDDD    BASE, DISPLACEMENT
          N       SCR1,00000FFF               0DDD    DISPLACEMENT
          AR      SCR0,SCR1                   INDEX + BASE + DISPLACEMENT
          BR      BRFROM                      RETURN


**************************************************************************
*                                                                      *
*                                                                      *
*  RDUMP           REGISTER DUMP ROUTINES                              *
*  FDUMP                                                                *
*                                                                      *
*                                                                      *
**************************************************************************

RDUMP     DS      0H                          DUMP GENERAL REGISTERS
          ST      BRFROM,RDSV                 SAVE RETURN ADDRESS
          BAL     BRFROM,WRITE                PRINT 1 BLANK LINE
          LA      SCR2,REGTBL                 ADDRESS OF 1ST 8 REGISTERS
          BAL     BRFROM,RPUT                 PLACE THEM IN PRINT LINE
          MVC     PLINE(10),RM0               ' R0-R7    '
          BAL     BRFROM,WRITE                PRINT THE LINE
          LA      SCR2,REGTBL+32              ADDRESS OF 2ND 8 REGISTERS
          BAL     BRFROM,RPUT                 PLACE THEM IN PRINT LINE
          MVC     PLINE(10),RM8               ' R8-R15   '
          BAL     BRFROM,WRITE                PRINT THE LINE
          L       BRFROM,RDSV                 LOAD RETURN ADDRESS
          BR      BRFROM                      RETURN

FDUMP     DS      0H                          DUMP FLOATING POINT REGISTERS
          ST      BRFROM,FDSV                 SAVE RETURN ADDRESS
          BAL     BRFROM,WRITE                PRINT 1 BLANK LINE
          MVC     PLINE(10),FM0               ' F0-F6    '
          LA      SCR2,F0                     ADDRESS OF FLOATING REGISTER
```

```
*                                       TABLE
       BAL    BRFROM,RPUT              PLACE THEM IN PRINT LINE
       BAL    BRFROM,WRITE             PRINT THE LINE
       L      BRFROM,FDSV              LOAD RETURN ADDRESS
       BR     BRFROM                   RETURN

RPUT   DS     0H                       PLACE EIGHT REGISTERS INTO
*                                      THE PRINT LINE
       ST     BRFROM,RPSV              SAVE RETURN ADDRESS
       LA     SCR3,PLINE+16            STARTING POINT IN PRINT LINE
RNX    L      SCR0,0(SCR2)             GET THE VALUE OF A REGISTER
       BALR   BRFROM,HEX2EBC           CONVERT IT FOR PRINTING
       STM    SCR0,SCR1,0(SCR3)        PLACE IN PRINT LINE
       LA     SCR2,4(0,SCR2)           POINT AT NEXT REGISTER
       LA     SCR3,12(0,SCR3)          NEXT SPACE IN PRINT LINE
       C      SCR3,EOL                 END OF PRINT LINE ?
       BL     RNX                      NO, GO GET NEXT REGISTER
       L      BRFROM,RPSV              YES, LOAD RETURN ADDRESS
       BR     BRFROM                   RETURN


**********************************************************************
*                                                                    *
*                                                                    *
*   WRITE       ROUTINE TO OUTPUT THE PRINT LINE                      *
*                                                                    *
*                                                                    *
**********************************************************************


WRITE  DS     0H
       ST     SMBR,WTR                 SAVE BRANCH REGISTER
       STM    PR1,PR3,WTS              SAVE PARAMETER REGISTERS
       L      PR1,PDESC                DESCRIPTOR FOR PRINT LINE
       LA     SVCR,PRNT                SERVICE CODE FOR PRINTING
       SR     PR3,PR3                  SPECIFY  OUTPUT(0)

       BALR   SMBR,SELF                CALL THE XPLSM SUBMONITOR

**********************************************************************
*                                                                    *
*              BLANK THE PRINT LINE                                   *
*                                                                    *
**********************************************************************

       MVI    PLINE,C' '               ONE BLANK TO START
       MVC    PLINE+1(LPL-1),PLINE     PROPAGATE THE BLANK
       LM     PR1,PR3,WTS              RESTORE REGISTERS
       L      SMBR,WTR                 RESTORE BRANCH REGISTER
       BR     BRFROM                   RETURN

CODEND DS     0H                       END OF THE TRACE ROUTINE CODE
```

```
***********************************************************************
*                                                                     *
*                                                                     *
*              DATA AREA FOR THE TRACE ROUTINE                        *
*                                                                     *
***********************************************************************

DATAREA   DS    0H                        ORIGIN OF THE DATA AREA

FLAGS     DC    H'0'                       ATTRIBUTE FLAGS DESCRIBING THE
*                                          CURRENT INSTRUCTION
HEXCHAR   DC    C'0123456789ABCDEF'        CHARACTER CONSTANT
NOBUMP    DC    X'00'                      BRANCH INSTRUCTION FLAG
PRINTING  DC    X'FF'                      PRINTING ENABLED FLAG
*                                          (NOT USED IN THIS VERSION)
REALCC    DC    X'0'                       ACTUAL CONDITION CODE
XCELL     DC    F'0'                       A COPY OF THE INSTRUCTION
          DC    F'0'                       CURRENTLY BEING TRACED
          DC    A(REGTBL)                  ADDRESS OF PSEUDO REGISTER
*                                          TABLE
SAVREG    DC    16F'0'                     SAVE REGISTERS HERE WHILE
*                                          CALLING EXECUTE ROUTINE IN XPLSM
REGTBL    DC    16F'0'                     REGISTERS OF THE TRACED PROGRAM
F0        DC    D'0'                       FLOATING POINT REGISTERS
F2        DC    D'0'                       OF THE TRACED PROGRAM
F4        DC    D'0'
F6        DC    D'0'
OLDREG    DC    16F'0'                     COPY REGISTER TABLE HERE BEFORE
*                                          EXECUTING THE INSTRUCTION
AENTRY    DC    F'0'                       ADDRESS OF XPLSM ENTRY POINT
ACONTRL   DC    A(0)                       ADDRESS OF CONTROL PARAMETERS
NEWILC    DC    F'0'                       NEW VALUE FOR THE LOCATION
*                                          COUNTER FOR SUCCESSFUL BRANCHES


***********************************************************************
*                                                                     *
*              MASKING CONSTANTS                                      *
*                                                                     *
***********************************************************************

          DS    0F                         INSURE ALLIGNMENT
0000000F  DC    X'0000000F'
000000F0  DC    X'000000F0'
00000FFF  DC    X'00000FFF'
0000F000  DC    X'0000F000'
0F000000  DC    X'0F000000'
0000003C  DC    X'0000003C'
          DS    0F


***********************************************************************
*                                                                     *
*         TEMPORARY STORAGE USED BY THE VARIOUS ROUTINES              *
*                                                                     *
***********************************************************************
```

```
*                                     BY PRINTSUP

PRTS      DC    F'0'                  RETURN ADDRESS

*                                     BY PLINE1

P1S       DC    F'0'                  RETURN ADDRESS
EBDCC     DC    C'8421'               CHARACTERS FOR CONDITION CODE
          DS    0F

*                                     BY PLINOP

F3        DC    F'3'                  THE CONSTANT 3
P2S       DC    F'0'                  RETURN ADDRESS

*                                     BY BDPROC

BDS       DC    F'0'                  RETURN ADDRESS
BDT       DC    F'0'
BDT2      DS    F

*                                     BY PLINREG

P3S       DC    F'0'                  RETURN ADDRESS
PRT       DC    F'0'

*                                     BY PLINEFA

P4S       DC    F'0'                  RETURN ADDRESS
EFAT0     DC    F'0'

*                                     BY BRPROC

CCBITS    DC    X'00000080'           BITS CORRESPONDING TO THE
          DC    X'00000040'           CONDITION CODE
          DC    X'00000020'
          DC    X'00000010'
ILC1      DC    X'40000000'           INSTRUCTION LENGTH CODE
*                                     FOR BAL AND BALR
F1        DC    F'1'                  THE CONSTANT 1
BRSV      DC    F'0'                  RETURN ADDRESS

*                                     BY WRITE

WTS       DC    3F'0'
WTR       DC    F'0'                  RETURN ADDRESS
          DS    0F                    INSURE ALIGNMENT
PDESC     DC    AL1(LPL-1)            XPL TYPE STRING DESCRIPTOR
          DC    AL3(PLINE)            FOR THE PRINT LINE

*                                     BY RDUMP

RDSV      DC    F'0'                  RETURN ADDRESS
```

```
*                                          BY FDUMP

FDSV      DC     F'0'                      RETURN ADDRESS

*                                          BY RPUT

RPSV      DC     F'0'                      RETURN ADDRESS
EOL       DC     A(PLINE+16+8*12)          ADDRESS OF END OF PRINT LINE

*                                          BY EXOP

ORI       OI     PSXCELL+1,0               INSTRUCTION TO OR ONE BYTE
*                                          INTO THE SUBJECT INSTRUCTION
*                                          OF AN EXECUTE INSTRUCTION
PSXCELL   DC     F'0'                      COPY OF THE SUBJECT
          DC     F'0'                      INSTRUCTION
          DC     A(REGTBL)                 ADDRESS OF THE REGISTER TABLE
PSFLAGS   DC     H'0'                      ATTRIBUTE FLAGS FOR THE SUBJECT
*                                          INSTRUCTION

*                                          BY GOIO

IOFROM    DC     F'0'                      RETURN ADDRESS FOR SUBMONITOR
*                                          CALL

*                                          CHARACTER CONSTANTS

BLANKS    DC     CL8' '
FM0       DC     CL10' F0-F6     '
RM0       DC     C' R0-R7    '
RM8       DC     C' R8-R15   '
ILGMSG    DC     CL40' ****    ILLEGAL   INSTRUCTION   ****'
IORQM     DC     CL24'        I/O  REQUEST      '
RTRM      DC     CL26'    RECURSIVE   TRACE  CALL'
          DS     0F                        INSURE ALIGNMENT
ENDTM     DC     CL24' RESUME EXECUTION AT: '
ENDADR    DC     CL24' '

*********************************************************************
*                                                                   *
*              THE PRINT LINE                                        *
*                                                                   *
*********************************************************************

          DS     0F                        INSURE ALIGNMENT
PLINE     DC     CL(LPL)' '

*********************************************************************
*                                                                   *
*              DEFINE SUBFIELDS WITHIN THE PRINT LINE FOR USE        *
*              BY THE PRINT ROUTINES                                 *
*                                                                   *
*********************************************************************
```

```
ILC       EQU   PLINE+4           LOCATION COUNTER
INSTR     EQU   PLINE+16          INSTRUCTION IMAGE
CC        EQU   PLINE+31          CONDITION CODE
OP        EQU   PLINE+36          SYMBOLIC INSTRUCTION CODE
FIELDS    EQU   PLINE+44          INSTRUCTION FIELDS
R1        EQU   PLINE+64          FIRST OPERAND REGISTER
DR1       EQU   R1+8              2ND HALF OF 1ST DOUBLE REGISTER
DR2A      EQU   DR1+12            2ND DOUBLE REGISTER
DR2B      EQU   DR2A+8            2ND HALF OF 2ND DOUBLE REGISTER
R2        EQU   PLINE+76          SECOND SINGLE REGISTER
EFA1      EQU   PLINE+88          1ST EFFECTIVE ADDRESS
EFA2      EQU   PLINE+112         2ND EFFECTIVE ADDRESS


*************************************************************************
*                                                                     *
*                                                                     *
*           DEFINE TO INSTRUCTION CODE FLAG FIELDS USED TO            *
*           GENERATE THE ATTRIBUTE FLAG TABLE                         *
*                                                                     *
*                                                                     *
*           SHIFTING CONSTANTS FOR FIELD DEFINITIONS                  *
*                                                                     *
*************************************************************************

LEFT      EQU   B'100000000'      PLACE IN LEFT HALF OF FLAGS

RIGHT     EQU   B'000000001'      PLACE IN RIGHT HALF OF FLAGS


*************************************************************************
*                                                                     *
*                                                                     *
*           LEFT HALF FIELD DEFINITIONS                               *
*                                                                     *
*************************************************************************

B0        EQU   ILGLBIT*LEFT      ILLEGAL INSTRUCTION
B1        EQU   CCBIT*LEFT        CONDITION CODE SET
B2        EQU   BRBIT*LEFT        BRANCH INSTRUCTION
B3        EQU   HALFBIT*LEFT      HALF WORD INSTRUCTION
B4        EQU   FULLBIT*LEFT      FULL WORD INSTRUCTION
B5        EQU   DBLBIT*LEFT       DOUBLE WORD INSTRUCTION
B6        EQU   FLOATBIT*LEFT     FLOATING POINT INSTRUCTION
B7        EQU   SHIFTBIT*LEFT     SHIFT INSTRUCTION


*************************************************************************
*                                                                     *
*           RIGHT HALF FIELD DEFINITIONS                              *
*                                                                     *
*************************************************************************

B8        EQU   RRBIT*RIGHT       TYPE RR INSTRUCTION
B9        EQU   RXBIT*RIGHT       TYPE RX INSTRUCTION
```

```
BA       EQU    RSBIT*RIGHT                TYPE RS INSTRUCTION
BB       EQU    SIBIT*RIGHT                TYPE SI INSTRUCTION
BC       EQU    SSBIT*RIGHT                TYPE SS INSTRUCTION
BD       EQU    IMDFBIT*RIGHT              INSTRUCTION CONTAINS 8-BIT FIELD
BE       EQU    LMSTMBIT*RIGHT             INSTRUCTION IS LM OR STM
BF       EQU    EXBIT*RIGHT                EXECUTE INSTRUCTION


*****************************************************************************
*                                                                           *
*                                                                           *
*                   INSTRUCTION CODE FLAGS                                   *
*                                                                           *
*                                                                           *
*                                                                           *
*                                B B B B B B B B B B B B B B B B            *
*                                0 1 2 3 4 5 6 7 8 9 A B C D E F            *
*                                                                           *
*****************************************************************************
```

Label	Op	Operand	B0	B1	B2	B3	B4	B5	B6	B7	B8	B9	BA	BB	BC	BD	BE	BF	hex
OPFLAGS	DS	0H																	
	DC	AL2(B0+B8)	X								X								00
	DC	AL2(B2+B8)			X						X								02
	DC	AL2(B1+B4+B8)		X			X				X								04
	DC	AL2(B4+B8)					X				X								06
	DC	AL2(B1+B5+B8)		X				X			X								08
	DC	AL2(B1+B5+B6+B8)		X				X	X		X								0A
	DC	AL2(B5+B6+B8)						X	X		X								0C
	DC	AL2(B1+B4+B6+B8)		X			X		X		X								0E
	DC	AL2(B4+B6+B8)					X		X		X								10
	DC	AL2(B3+B9)				X						X							12
	DC	AL2(B4+B9)					X					X							14
	DC	AL2(B2+B4+B9+BF)			X		X					X						X	16
	DC	AL2(B2+B9)			X							X							18
	DC	AL2(B1+B3+B9)		X		X						X							1A
	DC	AL2(B0+B9)	X									X							1C
	DC	AL2(B1+B4+B9)		X			X					X							1E
	DC	AL2(B5+B6+B9)						X	X			X							20
	DC	AL2(B1+B5+B6+B9)		X				X	X			X							22
	DC	AL2(B4+B6+B9)					X		X			X							24
	DC	AL2(B1+B4+B6+B9)		X			X		X			X							26
	DC	AL2(B0+BB)	X											X					28
	DC	AL2(B2+B4+B6+BA)			X		X		X				X						2A
	DC	AL2(B4+B7+BA)					X			X			X						2C
	DC	AL2(B1+B4+B7+BA)		X			X			X			X						2E
	DC	AL2(BA+BE)											X				X		30
	DC	AL2(B1+BB+BD)		X										X		X			32
	DC	AL2(BB+BD)												X		X			34
	DC	AL2(B0+BB+BD)	X											X		X			36
	DC	AL2(B0+BB)	X											X					38
	DC	AL2(B0+BC)	X												X				3A
	DC	AL2(BC+BD)													X	X			3C
	DC	AL2(B1+BC+BD)		X											X	X			3E
	DC	AL2(BC)													X				40

```
        DC    AL2(B1+BC)              X                       X          42
        DC    AL2(B5+B7+BA)                   X  X  X                    44
        DC    AL2(B1+B5+B7+BA)        X       X  X  X                    46


***********************************************************************
*                                                                     *
*                                                                     *
*              TABLES OF INDICES FOR EACH POSSIBLE INSTRUCTION         *
*              CODE INTO THE OPFLAGS TABLE                             *
*                                                                     *
*                                                                     *
***********************************************************************

OPINDEX DS    0H
        DC    X'00000000'  RR00   ...     ...     ...     ...      00
        DC    X'06020202'  04     SPM     BALR    BCTR    BCR      01
        DC    X'00000000'  08     *SSK    *ISK    *SVC    ...      02
        DC    X'00000000'  0C     ...     ...     ...     ...      03
        DC    X'04040404'  10     LPR     LNR     LTR     LCR      04
        DC    X'04040404'  14     NR      CLR     OR      XR       05
        DC    X'06040404'  18     LR      CR      AR      SR       06
        DC    X'06060404'  1C     MR      DR      ALR     SLR      07
        DC    X'0A0A0A0A'  20     LPDR    LNDR    LTDR    LCDR     08
        DC    X'0C000000'  24     HDR     ...     ...     ...      09
        DC    X'0C0A0A0A'  28     LDR     CDR     ADR     SDR      10
        DC    X'0C0C0A0A'  2C     MDR     DDR     AWR     SWR      11
        DC    X'0E0E0E0E'  30     LPER    LNER    LTER    LCER     12
        DC    X'10000000'  34     HER     ...     ...     ...      13
        DC    X'100E0E0E'  38     LER     CER     ALR     SER      14
        DC    X'10100E0E'  3C     MER     DER     AUR     SUR      15
        DC    X'12141414'  RX40   STH     LA      STC     IC       16
        DC    X'16181818'  44     EX      BAL     BCT     BC       17
        DC    X'121A1A1A'  48     LH      CH      AH      SH       18
        DC    X'12121414'  4C     MH      ...     CVD     CVB      19
        DC    X'141C1C1C'  50     ST      ...     ...     ...      20
        DC    X'1E1E1E1E'  54     N       CL      O       X        21
        DC    X'141E1E1E'  58     L       C       A       S        22
        DC    X'14141E1E'  5C     M       D       AL      SL       23
        DC    X'201C1C1C'  60     STD     ...     ...'    ...      24
        DC    X'1C1C1C1C'  64     ...     ...     ...     ...      25
        DC    X'20222222'  68     LD      CD-     AD      SD       26
        DC    X'20202222'  6C     MD      DD      AW      SW       27
        DC    X'241C1C1C'  70     STE     ...     ...     ...      28
        DC    X'1C1C1C1C'  74     ...     ...     ...     ...      29
        DC    X'24262626'  78     LE      CE      AE      SE       30
        DC    X'24242626'  7C     ME      DE      AU      SU       31
        DC    X'28282828'  RS80   *SSM    ...     *LPSW   ...      32
        DC    X'28282A2A'  84     *WRD    *RDD    BXH     BXLE     33
        DC    X'2C2C2E2E'  88     SRL     SLL     SRA     SLA      34
        DC    X'44444646'  8C     SRDL    SLDL    SRDA    SLDA     35
        DC    X'30323436'  SI90   STM     TM      MVI     *TS      36
        DC    X'32323232'  94     NI      CLI     OI      XI       37
        DC    X'30383838'  98     LM      ...     ...     ...      38


***********************************************************************
*                                                                     *
*                                                                     *
*         DUMMY  DCB  FOR .DEFINING  DCB  FIELDS                       *
*                                                                     *
*                                                                     *
***********************************************************************

        DCBD  DSORG=QS,DEVD=DA


***********************************************************************
*                                                                     *
*                                                                     *
*         THE  END                                                    *
*                                                                     *
*                                                                     *
***********************************************************************

        END
```

```
          DC      X'38383838'     9C    *SIO    *TIO    *HIO    *TCH     39
          DC      X'38383838'     A0     ...     ...     ...     ...     40
          DC      X'38383838'     A4     ...     ...     ...     ...     41
          DC      X'38383838'     A8     ...     ...     ...     ...     42
          DC      X'38383838'     AC     ...     ...     ...     ...     43
          DC      X'38383838'     B0     ...     ...     ...     ...     44
          DC      X'38383838'     B4     ...     ...     ...     ...     45
          DC      X'38383838'     B8     ...     ...     ...     ...     46
          DC      X'38383838'     BC     ...     ...     ...     ...     47
          DC      X'3A3A3A3A'     SSC0    ...     ...     ...     ...     48
          DC      X'3A3A3A3A'     C4     ...     ...     ...     ...     49
          DC      X'3A3A3A3A'     C8     ...     ...     ...     ...     50
          DC      X'3A3A3A3A'     CC     ...     ...     ...     ...     51
          DC      X'3A3C3C3C'     D0     ...     MVN     MVC     MVZ     52
          DC      X'3E3E3E3E'     D4     NC      CLC     OC      XC      53
          DC      X'3A3A3A3A'     D8     ...     ...     ...     ...     54
          DC      X'3E3E3E3E'     DC     TR      TRT     ED      EDMK    55
          DC      X'3A3A3A3A'     E0     ...     ...     ...     ...     56
          DC      X'3A3A3A3A'     E4     ...     ...     ...     ...     57
          DC      X'3A3A3A3A'     E8     ...     ...     ...     ...     58
          DC      X'3A3A3A3A'     EC     ...     ...     ...     ...     59
          DC      X'3A404040'     F0     ...     MVO     PACK    UNPK    60
          DC      X'3A3A3A3A'     F4     ...     ...     ...     ...     61
          DC      X'42424242'     F8     ZAP     CP      AP      SP      62
          DC      X'40403A3A'     FC     MP      DP      ...     ...     63


**************************************************************************
*                                                                        *
*                                                                        *
*         *   INDICATES A PRIVILEGED INSTRUCTION                         *
*                                                                        *
*        ... INDICATES A NONEXISTENT INSTRUCTION                         *
*                                                                        *
**************************************************************************



**************************************************************************
*                                                                        *
*                                                                        *
*        SYMBOLIC INSTRUCTION CODES FOR PRINTING                         *
*                                                                        *
*                                                                        *
**************************************************************************


BCDOP     DS      0F
          DC      C'             SPM BALRBCTRBCR '                      000
          DC      C'SSK ISK SVC                  '                      020
          DC      C'LPR LNR LTR LCR NR  CLR OR  XR  '                   040
          DC      C'LR  CR  AR  SR  MR  DR  ALR SLR '                   060
          DC      C'LPDRLNDRLTDRLCDRHDR           '                     080
          DC      C'LDR CDR ADR SDR MDR DDR AWR SWR '                   0A0
          DC      C'LPERLNERLTERLCERHER           '                     0C0
          DC      C'LER CER AER SER MER DER AUR SUR '                   0E0
          DC      C'STH LA  STC IC  EX  BAL BCT BC  '                   100
```

```
          DC     C'LH  CH   AH   SH   MH        CVD CVB '          120
          DC     C'ST                 N    CL   O   X   '          140
          DC     C'L   C    A    S    M    D    AL  SL  '          160
          DC     C'STD                                  '          180
          DC     C'LD  CD   AD   SD   MD   DD   AW  SW  '          1A0
          DC     C'STE                                  '          1C0
          DC     C'LE  CE   AE   SE   ME   DE   AU  SU  '          1E0
          DC     C'SSM      LPSW      WRD RDD BXH BXLE'            200
          DC     C'SRL SLL  SRA  SLA  SRDLSLDLSRDASLDA'            220
          DC     C'STM TM   MVI  TS   NI   CLI OI  XI  '           240
          DC     C'LM                 SIO TIO HIO TCH '            260
          DC     C'                                    '           280
          DC     C'                                    '           2A0
          DC     C'                                    '           2C0
          DC     C'                                    '           2E0
          DC     C'                                    '           300
          DC     C'                                    '           320
          DC     C'     MVN MVC MVZ NC   CLC OC   XC   '           340
          DC     C'                TR   TRT ED   EDMK'             360
          DC     C'                                    '           380
          DC     C'                                    '           3A0
          DC     C'     MVO PACKUNPK                   '           3C0
          DC     C'ZAP CP   AP   SP   MP   DP          '           3E0


    ***********************************************************************
    *                                                                     *
    *                                                                     *
    *                  THE   END                                          *
    *                                                                     *
    *                                                                     *
    ***********************************************************************

DATAEND   DS     0H                          END OF TRACE ROUTINE DATA AREA

          END
```

Appendix 3

XCOM

/* XCOM :

The compiler for the XPL system.

First we initialize the global constants that depend upon the input
grammar. The following cards are punched by ANALYZER   */

declare *nsy* **literally** ' 91' , *nt* **literally** ' 42' ;
declare *v*(*nsy*) **character initial** (' <error: token = 0>' , ' ;' , ')' , ' (' , ' ,' ,
    ' :' , ' =' , ' |' , ' &' , ' ¬' , ' <' , ' >' , ' +' , ' −' , ' *' , ' /' , ' **if**' , ' **do**' , ' **to**' ,
    ' **by**' , ' **go**' , ' | |' , ' _ |_' , ' **end**' , ' **bit**' , ' **mod**' , ' **then**' , ' **else**' , ' **case**' ,
    ' **call**' , ' **goto**' , ' **while**' , ' **fixed**' , ' **label**' , ' **return**' , ' **declare**' , ' **initial**' ,
    ' <string>' , ' <number>' , ' **procedure**' , ' **literally**' , ' **character**' ,
    ' <identifier>' , ' <type>' , ' <term>' , ' <group>' , ' <go to>' , ' <ending>' ,
    ' <program>' , ' <replace>' , ' <primary>' , ' <variable>' , ' <bit head>' ,
    ' <constant>' , ' <relation>' , ' <statement>' , ' <if clause>' , ' <true part>' ,
    ' <left part>' , ' <assignment>' , ' <expression>' , ' <group head>' ,
    ' <bound head>' , ' <if statement>' , ' <while clause>' , ' <initial list>' ,
    ' <initial head>' , ' <case selector>' , ' <statement list>' ,
    ' <call statement>' , ' <procedure head>' , ' <procedure name>' ,
    ' <parameter list>' , ' <parameter head>' , ' <logical factor>' ,
    ' <subscript head>' , ' <basic statement>' , ' <go to statement>' ,
    ' <step definition>' , ' <identifier list>' , ' <logical primary>' ,
    ' <return statement>' , ' <label definition>' , ' <type declaration>' ,
    ' <iteration control>' , ' <logical secondary>' , ' <string expression>' ,
    ' <declaration element>' , ' <procedure definition>' ,
    ' <declaration statement>' , ' <arithmetic expression>' ,
    ' <identifier specification>');
declare *v_index*(12) **fixed initial** (1, 16, 22, 26, 31, 34, 35, 37, 39, 42,
    42, 42, 43);
declare *c*1(*nsy*) **bit**(86) **initial** (
    "(2) 00000 00000 00000 00000 00000 00000 00000 00000 000",
    "(2) 02000 00000 00000 02200 20220 00202 20002 20000 002",
    "(2) 02222 02222 22222 20022 02003 22000 00330 02000 030",
    "(2) 00030 00003 00330 00000 00000 00000 00000 00330 003",
    "(2) 00030 00002 00220 00000 00000 00000 00000 00220 003",
    "(2) 02000 00000 00000 02200 20020 00002 20002 20002 002",

365

```
"(2) 00020 00002 00220 00000 00000 00000 00000 00220 002",
"(2) 00010 00001 00110 00000 00000 00000 00000 00110 001",
"(2) 00010 00001 00110 00000 00000 00000 00000 00110 001",
"(2) 00010 01000 11110 00000 00000 00000 00000 00110 001",
"(2) 00020 01000 00220 00000 00000 00000 00000 00220 002",
"(2) 00020 01000 00220 00000 00000 00000 00000 00220 002",
"(2) 00010 00000 00000 00000 00000 00000 00000 00110 001",
"(2) 00010 00000 00000 00000 00000 00000 00000 00110 001",
"(2) 00010 00000 00000 00000 00000 00000 00000 00110 001",
"(2) 00010 00000 00000 00000 00000 00000 00000 00110 001",
"(2) 00010 00001 00110 00000 00000 00000 00000 00110 001",
"(2) 01000 00000 00000 00000 00000 00010 01000 00000 001",
"(2) 00010 00001 00110 00000 00000 00000 00000 00110 003",
"(2) 00010 00001 00110 00000 00000 00000 00000 00110 001",
"(2) 00000 00000 00000 00010 00000 00000 00000 00000 000",
"(2) 00010 00000 00110 00000 00000 00000 00000 00110 001",
"(2) 01000 00000 00000 01100 10000 00001 10001 10000 001",
"(2) 02000 00000 00000 00000 00000 00000 00000 00000 001",
"(2) 00010 00000 00000 00000 00000 00000 00000 00000 000",
"(2) 00010 00000 00000 00000 00000 00000 00000 00110 001",
"(2) 02000 00000 00000 02200 20000 00002 20002 20000 002",
"(2) 02000 00000 00000 02200 20000 00002 20002 20000 002",
"(2) 00010 00001 00110 00000 00000 00000 00000 00110 001",
"(2) 00000 00000 00000 00000 00000 00000 00000 00000 001",
"(2) 00000 00000 00000 00000 00000 00000 00000 00000 002",
"(2) 00010 00001 00110 00000 00000 00000 00000 00110 001",
"(2) 02002 00000 00000 00000 00000 00000 00000 02000 000",
"(2) 02002 00000 00000 00000 00000 00000 00000 02000 000",
"(2) 02010 00001 00110 00000 00000 00000 00000 00110 001",
"(2) 00010 00000 00000 00000 00000 00000 00000 00000 001",
"(2) 00010 00000 00000 00000 00000 00000 00000 00000 000",
"(2) 02202 02222 22222 20022 02000 22000 00000 00000 000",
"(2) 02302 02222 22222 20022 02000 22000 00000 00000 000",
"(2) 02020 00000 00000 00000 00002 00000 00220 00000 020",
"(2) 00000 00000 00000 00000 00000 00000 00000 00100 000",
"(2) 02002 00000 00000 00000 00000 00000 00000 02000 000",
"(2) 02333 12222 22222 20022 02002 22000 00220 00000 120",
"(2) 03002 00000 00000 00000 00000 00000 00000 02000 000",
"(2) 02202 02222 22221 10022 02000 12000 00000 00000 000",
"(2) 01000 00000 00000 00000 00000 00000 00000 00000 000",
"(2) 00000 00000 00000 00000 00000 00000 00000 00000 001",
"(2) 02000 00000 00000 00000 00000 00000 00000 00000 000",
"(2) 00000 00000 00000 00000 00000 00000 00000 00000 000",
"(2) 00010 00001 00110 00000 00000 00000 00000 00110 001",
"(2) 02202 02222 22222 20022 02000 22000 00000 00000 000",
```

```
"(2) 02203 03222 22222 20022 02000 22000 00000 00000 000",
"(2) 00000 00000 00000 00000 00000 00000 00000 00010 000",
"(2) 02303 02222 22222 20022 02000 22000 00000 00000 000",
"(2) 00010 00000 00110 00000 00000 00000 00000 00110 001",
"(2) 02000 00000 00000 02200 20220 00002 20002 20000 002",
"(2) 01000 00000 00000 01100 10000 00001 10001 10000 001",
"(2) 01000 00000 00000 01100 10000 00001 10001 10000 001",
"(2) 00000 00000 00000 00000 00000 00000 00000 00000 001",
"(2) 03000 00000 00000 00000 00000 00000 00000 00000 000",
"(2) 02101 00100 00000 00011 00000 01000 00000 00000 000",
"(2) 01000 00000 00000 01100 10010 00001 10001 10000 001",
"(2) 00000 00000 00000 00000 00000 00000 00000 00010 000",
"(2) 02000 00000 00000 02200 20220 00002 20002 20000 002",
"(2) 01000 00000 00000 00000 00000 00000 00000 00000 000",
"(2) 02002 00000 00000 00000 00000 00000 00000 02000 000",
"(2) 00000 00000 00000 00000 00000 00000 00000 00110 000",
"(2) 01000 00000 00000 00000 00000 00000 00000 00000 000",
"(2) 01000 00000 00000 01100 10210 00001 10001 10000 001",
"(2) 01000 00000 00000 00000 00000 00000 00000 00000 000",
"(2) 01000 00000 00000 01100 10000 00001 10001 10000 001",
"(2) 01010 00000 00000 00000 00001 00000 00110 00000 010",
"(2) 01000 00000 00000 00000 00001 00000 00110 00000 010",
"(2) 00000 00000 00000 00000 00000 00000 00000 00000 001",
"(2) 02202 00210 00000 00022 00000 02000 00000 00000 000",
"(2) 00010 00001 00110 00000 00000 00000 00000 00110 001",
"(2) 02000 00000 00000 02200 20220 00302 20002 20000 002",
"(2) 01000 00000 00000 00000 00000 00000 00000 00000 000",
"(2) 01000 00000 00000 00000 00000 00000 00000 00000 000",
"(2) 00000 00000 00000 00000 00000 00000 00000 00000 001",
"(2) 02202 00220 00000 00022 00000 02000 00000 00000 000",
"(2) 01000 00000 00000 00000 00000 00000 00000 00000 000",
"(2) 01000 00000 00000 01100 10010 00001 10001 10001 001",
"(2) 02002 00000 00000 00000 00000 00000 00000 01000 000",
"(2) 02000 00000 00000 00000 00000 00000 00000 00000 000",
"(2) 02202 00220 00000 00022 00000 02000 00000 00000 000",
"(2) 02202 01221 11000 00022 01000 02000 00000 00000 000",
"(2) 02002 00000 00000 00000 00000 00000 00000 00000 000",
"(2) 01000 00000 00000 00000 00000 00000 00000 00000 000",
"(2) 01001 00000 00000 00000 00000 00000 00000 00000 000",
"(2) 02202 02222 22110 00022 02000 02000 00000 00000 000",
"(2) 00010 00000 00000 00000 00001 00000 00110 00000 010" );
```

declare *ncltriples* **literally** ' 203' ;

declare *cltriples*(*ncltriples*) **fixed initial** (197379, 197385, 197388, 197389, 197413, 197414, 197418, 207363, 459523, 459529, 459532, 459533, 459557, 459558, 459562, 469507, 525059, 525065, 525068, 525069, 525093, 525094,

525098, 535043, 590595, 590601, 590604, 590605, 590629, 590630, 590634,
600579, 787203, 787209, 787212, 787213, 787237, 787238, 787242, 797187,
852739, 852745, 852748, 852749, 852773, 852774, 852778, 862723, 918275,
918281, 918284, 918285, 918309, 918310, 918314, 928259, 983811, 983817,
983820, 983821, 983845, 983846, 983850, 993795, 1049347, 1049353, 1049356,
1049357, 1049381, 1049382, 1049386, 1059331, 1124867, 1127174, 1180419,
1180425, 1180428, 1180429, 1180453, 1180454, 1180458, 1190403, 1245955,
1245961, 1245964, 1245965, 1245989, 1245990, 1245994, 1255939, 1377027,
1377033, 1377036, 1377037, 1377061, 1377062, 1377066, 1387011, 1452547,
1454852, 1454854, 1456897, 1639171, 1639177, 1639180, 1639181, 1639205,
1639206, 1639210, 1649155, 1835779, 1835785, 1835788, 1835789, 1835813,
1835814, 1835818, 1845763, 1911299, 2032387, 2032393, 2032396, 2032397,
2032421, 2032422, 2032426, 2042371, 2228995, 2229001, 2229004, 2229005,
2229029, 2229030, 2229034, 2238979, 2490904, 2490912, 2490913, 2490921,
3212035, 3212041, 3212044, 3212045, 3212069, 3212070, 3212074, 3222019,
3417602, 3539715, 3539721, 3539724, 3539725, 3539749, 3539750, 3539754,
3549699, 3680771, 3683076, 3683078, 3685121, 3689499, 3746307, 3748612,
3748614, 3750657, 3811843, 3814148, 3814150, 3936810, 4008451, 4010756,
4010758, 4012801, 4072962, 4338946, 4338948, 4467203, 4469508, 4469510,
4471553, 4598275, 4600580, 4600582, 4602625, 4664065, 4729601, 4794882,
4794884, 4915971, 4915977, 4915980, 4915981, 4916005, 4916006, 4916010,
4925955, 5188098, 5188100, 5384707, 5387012, 5387014, 5389057, 5833731,
5833770);
    declare *prtb*(109) **fixed initial** (0, 4671531, 18219, 18248, 4430, 4416, 4419,
71, 17, 59, 45, 88, 81, 69, 77, 89, 0, 16949, 18730, 13350, 20266, 828,
19260, 91, 36, 24, 42, 0, 0, 18730, 20266, 16949, 19260, 51, 42, 9, 10,
11, 0, 0, 9, 0, 9, 0, 20, 0, 4156, 76, 0, 0, 0, 0, 10792, 0, 0, 82, 0, 23,
46, 0, 0, 4072962, 91, 23052, 23053, 12, 13, 0, 17988, 82, 61, 11278,
11279, 11289, 0, 29, 0, 0, 14393, 68, 61, 56, 0, 58, 1195027, 13105, 18,
31, 28, 34, 82, 0, 83, 0, 15367, 0, 82, 0, 9, 0, 0, 3354940, 18952, 0,
22070, 0, 22788, 35, 22037, 0);
    declare *prdtb*(109) **bit**(8) **initial** (0, 35, 33, 34, 22, 23, 24, 32, 21, 6, 7,
8, 9, 10, 11, 12, 13, 67, 37, 60, 64, 103, 105, 62, 68, 61, 106, 38, 65,
39, 66, 69, 107, 73, 43, 85, 88, 89, 82, 72, 86, 83, 87, 84, 48, 40, 18,
19, 49, 57, 59, 44, 53, 108, 109, 36, 58, 41, 47, 63, 104, 55, 54, 93, 94,
95, 96, 92, 31, 42, 20, 98, 99, 100, 97, 46, 102, 101, 16, 3, 25, 15, 2,
71, 28, 70, 27, 29, 30, 45, 17, 5, 56, 1, 75, 74, 14, 4, 79, 78, 52, 26,
77, 76, 81, 80, 51, 50, 91, 90);
    declare *hdtb*(109) **bit**(8) **initial** (0, 70, 70, 70, 61, 61, 61, 70, 61, 76, 76,
76, 76, 76, 76, 76, 76, 65, 72, 43, 91, 50, 51, 62, 66, 52, 75, 73, 79,
73, 79, 66, 75, 58, 82, 54, 54, 54, 54, 49, 54, 54, 54, 54, 46, 47, 56,
57, 46, 43, 43, 81, 87, 53, 53, 71, 43, 47, 77, 91, 51, 83, 83, 90, 90,
90, 90, 90, 88, 47, 45, 44, 44, 44, 44, 69, 50, 50, 63, 68, 61, 63, 68,
59, 84, 59, 84, 64, 67, 81, 63, 55, 83, 48, 60, 60, 76, 55, 85, 85, 87,
78, 74, 74, 80, 80, 89, 89, 86, 86);

declare *prlength*(109) **bit**(8) **initial** (0, 4, 3, 3, 3, 3, 3, 2, 2, 2, 2, 2, 2,
    2, 2, 2, 1, 3, 3, 3, 3, 3, 3, 2, 2, 2, 2, 1, 1, 3, 3, 3, 3, 2, 2, 2, 2, 2,
    1, 1, 2, 1, 2, 1, 2, 1, 3, 2, 1, 1, 1, 1, 3, 1, 1, 2, 1, 2, 2, 1, 1, 4, 2,
    3, 3, 2, 2, 1, 3, 2, 2, 3, 3, 3, 1, 2, 1, 1, 3, 2, 2, 2, 1, 2, 4, 3, 2, 2,
    2, 2, 2, 1, 2, 1, 3, 1, 2, 1, 2, 1, 1, 4, 3, 1, 3, 1, 3, 2, 3, 1);
declare *context_case*(109) **bit**(8) **initial** (0, 0, 0, 0, 0, 0, 0, 0, 0, 0, 0, 0, 0,
    0, 0, 0, 0, 0, 0, 0, 0, 0, 0, 0, 0, 0, 0, 2, 0, 0, 0, 0, 0, 0, 0, 0, 0, 0,
    0, 2, 0, 0, 0, 0, 0, 0, 0, 0, 0, 0, 0, 0, 0, 0, 0, 0, 0, 0, 0, 0, 1, 0, 0,
    0, 0, 0, 0, 0, 0, 0, 0, 0, 0, 0, 0, 0, 0, 0, 0, 0, 0, 0, 0, 0, 0, 0, 0, 0,
    0, 0, 0, 0, 0, 0, 0, 0, 0, 0, 0, 0, 0, 0, 0, 0, 0, 0, 0, 0, 0, 0, 0, 0);
declare *left_context*(1) **bit**(8) **initial** (86, 71);
declare *left_index*(49) **bit**(8) **initial** (0, 0, 0, 0, 0, 0, 0, 0, 0, 0, 0, 0, 0,
    1, 1, 1, 1, 1, 1, 1, 1, 1, 1, 1, 1, 1, 1, 1, 1, 1, 1, 1, 1, 1, 2, 2, 2, 2, 2, 2,
    2, 2, 2, 2, 2, 2, 2, 2, 2, 2, 2, 2);
declare *context_triple*(0) **fixed initial** (0);
declare *triple_index*(49) **bit**(8) **initial** (0, 0, 0, 0, 0, 0, 0, 0, 0, 0, 0, 0, 0,
    0, 0, 0, 0, 0, 0, 0, 0, 0, 0, 0, 0, 0, 0, 0, 0, 0, 0, 0, 0, 0, 0, 0, 0, 0, 0,
    0, 0, 0, 0, 0, 0, 0, 0, 0, 0, 0, 1);
declare *pr_index*(91) **bit**(8) **initial** (1, 17, 23, 29, 34, 35, 40, 40, 40, 40,
    42, 44, 44, 44, 44, 44, 44, 44, 45, 45, 45, 45, 45, 46, 46, 46, 47, 48,
    48, 48, 49, 49, 50, 51, 52, 52, 52, 54, 55, 56, 56, 57, 61, 63, 68, 68,
    68, 71, 71, 71, 75, 77, 77, 78, 78, 83, 83, 83, 83, 84, 90, 90, 90, 92,
    92, 93, 93, 93, 94, 94, 94, 94, 94, 94, 96, 96, 98, 98, 98, 98, 100, 100,
    100, 101, 102, 104, 106, 108, 108, 108, 110, 110);

/*   End of cards punched by ANALYZER.   */

/*   Declarations for the scanner: */

/* *token* is the index into the vocabulary *v*( ) of the last symbol scanned,
    ch is the last character scanned (hex code),
    cp is the pointer to the last character scanned in the cardimage,
    bcd is the last symbol scanned (literal character string). */
declare (*token, ch, cp*) **fixed**, *bcd* **character**;

/* Set up some convenient abbreviations for printer control. */
declare *eject_page* **literally** ' *output*(1) = *page*' ,
    page **character initial** (' 1'), *double* **character initial** (' 0'),
    double_space **literally** ' *output*(1) = *double*' ,
    x70 **character initial** (
                                                            ');

/* Length of longest symbol in *v*, amount to be deleted from each card. */
declare (*reserved_limit, margin_chop*) **fixed**;

```
/*  chartype( ) is used to distinguish classes of symbols in the scanner.
    tx( ) is a table used for translating from one character set to another.
    control( ) holds the value of the compiler control toggles set in $ cards.
    not_letter_or_digit( ) is similiar to chartype( ) but used in scanning
    identifiers only.

    All are used by the scanner and control( ) is set there.
*/
declare (chartype, tx ) (255) bit(8),
            (control, not_letter_or_digit )(255) bit(1);


/*  alphabet consists of the symbols considered alphabetic in building
    identifiers.    */
declare alphabet character initial (
    ' ABCDEFGHIJKLMNOPQRSTUVWXYZabcdefghijklmnopqrstuvwxyz_$@#' );


/*  buffer holds the latest cardimage,
    text holds the present state of the input text (including macro
    expansions and not including the portions deleted by the scanner ),
    text_limit is a convenient place to store the pointer to the end of text,
    card_count is incremented by one for every XPL source card read,
    error_count tabulates the errors as they are detected during compilation,
    severe_errors tabulates those errors of fatal significance.
*/
declare (buffer, text, current_procedure, information ) character,
    (text_limit, card_count, error_count, severe_errors, previous_error ) fixed;


/*  number_value contains the numeric value of the last constant scanned,
    jbase contains the field width in bit strings (default value =  4),
    base is 2**jbase    (i.e., shl(1,jbase ) ). */
declare (number_value, jbase, base ) fixed;


/*  Each of the following contains the index into v( ) of the corresponding
    symbol.   We ask:    if token = ident    etc.    */
declare (ident, string, number, divide, eofile, orsymbol,
    concatenate ) fixed;


/*  Used to save branch addresses in do—loop code.  */
declare stepk fixed;


/*  The following are used in the macro expander.  Considerable logic
    is devoted to avoiding creating strings of length > 256, the string limit.
*/

declare balance character, lb fixed;
```

declare *macro_limit* **fixed initial** (40), *macro_name*(40) **character**,
   macro_text(40) **character**, *macro_index*(256) **bit** (8),
   top_macro **fixed initial** ("FFFFFFFF");
declare *expansion_count* **fixed**, *expansion_limit* **literally** ' 300' ;

/* *stopit*( ) is a table of symbols which are allowed to terminate the error
flush process. In general they are symbols of sufficient syntactic
hierarchy that we expect to avoid attempting to start compiling again
right into another error producing situation. The token stack is also
flushed down to something acceptable to a *stopit*( ) symbol.
failsoft is a bit which allows the compiler one attempt at a gentle
recovery.   Then it takes a strong hand.   When there is real trouble
compiling is set to *false*, thereby terminating the compilation.
*mainlo*c is the symbol table location of *compactify* for use in *ERROR*( ).
*/
declare *stopit*(*nt*) **bit**(1), (*failsoft, compiling*) **bit**(1), *mainloc* **fixed**;

/* The entries in *prmask*( ) are used to select out portions of coded
productions and the stack top for comparison in the analysis algorithm. */
declare *prmask*(5) **fixed initial** (0, 0, "FF", "FFFF", "FFFFFF", "FFFFFFFF");

/* *substr*(*hexcodes*, *i*, 1) is the hexadecimal code letter for *i*   */
declare *hexcodes* **character initial** (' 0123456789ABCDEF');

/*   The proper substring of *pointer* is used to place an | under the point
of detection of an error during compilation. It marks the last character
scanned.   */
declare *pointer* **character initial** ('
                         |');
declare (*count#stack, count#scan, count#rr, count#rx, count#force,*
   count#arith, count#store, count#fixbfw, count#fixd, count#fixchw,
   count#getd, count#getc, count#find) **fixed**;

/* Record the times of important points during compilation.   */
declare *clock*(5) **fixed**;

/* Count the number of comparisons of identifiers in symbol table look–ups.
This can, in general, be expected to be a substantial part of run time.
*/
declare *idcompares* **fixed**, *statement_count* **fixed**;
declare *trueloc* **fixed**;   /* Address of integer 1 in data area. */
declare *comploc* **fixed**;   /* The address of all ones mask for complement. */
declare *catconst* **fixed**;   /* Address of 2**24   */
declare *basedata* **fixed**;   /* Base register initialization address. */

```
/*   The emitter   arrays   */
```

```
/***********************************************************************
```

Warning: The emitter arrays *code*, *data*, and *strings* are dependent
on the hardware devices available for scratch storage. The literal
constant *diskbytes* should be equal to the blocksize of these files
as established in DCB' s in the submonitor.

Suggested values:

        For large core: For small core *diskbytes* = 400.

```
2311      diskbytes =  3600
2314      diskbytes =  7200
2321      diskbytes =  2000
```

This version of **XCOM** needs three scratch files:

```
1          compiled code temporary
2          compiled data temporary
3          character string temporary
1          binary program output
```

```
***********************************************************************/
```

```
declare diskbytes literally ' 3600' ;    /*   2311 disks   */
    /* Size of scratch file blocks in bytes */
declare codemax fixed;          ·   /* Forces code to word boundary, */
declare code (diskbytes) bit(8);
declare datamax fixed;          /* forces data to word boundary, */
declare data (diskbytes) bit(8);
declare strngmx fixed;                 /*  and forces strings to be aligned.  */
declare strings (diskbytes) bit(8);    /*  Buffer for compiled strings   */
```

```
/*  codemax  is the number of records of code generated
     datamax is the number of records of data generated
*/
```

```
declare codefile fixed initial(1);    /* File for binary code, and */
declare binaryfile fixed initial(1);  /* collection of all compiled output */
declare datafile fixed initial (2);   /* Scratch file for data */
declare stringfile fixed initial (3);
    /* Scratch file for character strings */
```

declare (*pporg, pplim, dporg, dplim, curcblk, curdblk, cursblk, chporg,*
    chplim, stringmax, shortdfix, shortcfix, longdfix, longcfix, fcp) **fixed**;

/* Arrays to hold fixups during compilation */

/* *fclim* is the number of fixups that can be recorded before they are made */
declare *fclim* **literally** ' 100' ;
declare *fixcadr* (*fclim*) **fixed**;   /* Address of code fixup   */
declare *fixcb*1 (*fclim*) **bit**(8);   /* 1st byte of code fixup   */
declare *fixcb*2 (*fclim*) **bit**(8);   /* 2nd byte of code fixup   */

declare *limitword* **fixed**;
declare *string_recover* **fixed**;

declare *catentry* **fixed**;   /* Entry to catenate routine */
declare *strl* **fixed**;   /* Address of last string computed for optimizing || */
declare *strn* **fixed**;   /* Address of temp in string–to–number routine */
declare *descl* **fixed**;
declare *io_save* **fixed**;
declare *nmbrntry* **fixed**;   /* Entry to binary–to–character conversion */
declare *tsa* **fixed**;   /* Integer address of top–of–strings */
declare *mover* **fixed**;   /* Address of move template */
declare *bases* (15) **fixed**;   /* The value of the base registers */
declare *avail* **fixed initial** (2);
declare *instruct* (255) **bit**(16);   /* Instruction use counters */
declare *desc*(1024) **fixed**;   /* String descriptors, reg 13 relative */

/*   System/360 register assignments:
         0   scratch
        1–3   accumulators
       4–11 data addressing
       12   branch register
       13   string descriptor area base
       14   program base
       15   points to entry of i/o package
*/

declare *ioreg* **literally** ' "F"' ; /* Register for I/O routines of submonitor */
declare *pbr* **literally** ' "E"' ; /* Program base register points to code   */
declare *sbr* **literally** ' "D"' ; /* String base register to address descript. */
declare *brchreg* **literally** ' "C"' ; /* Register for branching */
declare *dbr* **literally** ' "B"' ; /* First data base register */
declare *programsize* **literally** ' 25' ; /* Number of 4096 byte pages allowed */
declare *lastbase* **fixed**;   /* Keep track of allocation of registers 11 – 4 */
declare *target_register* **fixed**;

```
declare maskf000 bit(32);
declare adreg fixed, adrdisp fixed;      /*  Globals for FINDADDRESS */
declare rtnadr fixed;   /*  Where the present return address is stored. */
declare returned_type bit (8);
declare temp(3) fixed ;               /*  Storage for SAVE_REGISTERS  */
declare (dp, pp, chp, dsp, newdp, newdsp) fixed;    /*  Emitter pointers */
declare itype fixed;    /*  Initialization type  */
declare stillcond fixed;  /*  Remember condition code test for peephole */
/*  Common IBM System/360  op-code  names  */
declare opnames character initial ('    BALRBCTRBCR LPR LNR LTR
LCR NR  CLR OR  XR  LR  CR  AR  SR  MR  DR  ALR SLR LA
STC IC  EX  BAL BCT BC  CVD CVB ST  N  CL  O  X   L   C   A
S   M   D   AL  SL  SRL SLL SRA SLA SRDLSLDLSRDASLDASTM
TM  MVI NI  CLI OI  XI  LM  MVC STH LH  ' );
declare oper(255) bit(8) initial(
/*0**/     0,  0,  0,  0,  0,  4,  8, 12,  0,  0,  0,  0,  0,  0,  0,  0,
/*1**/    16, 20, 24, 28, 32, 36, 40, 44, 48, 52, 56, 60, 64, 68, 72, 76,
/*2**/     0,  0,  0,  0,  0,  0,  0,  0,  0,  0,  0,  0,  0,  0,  0,  0,
/*3**/     0,  0,  0,  0,  0,  0,  0,  0,  0,  0,  0,  0,  0,  0,  0,  0,
/*4**/   236, 80, 84, 88, 92, 96,100,104,240,  0,  0,  0,  0,108,112,
/*5**/   116,  0,  0,  0,120,124,128,132,136,140,144,148,152,156,160,164,
/*6**/     0,  0,  0,  0,  0,  0,  0,  0,  0,  0,  0,  0,  0,  0,  0,  0,
/*7**/     0,  0,  0,  0,  0,  0,  0,  0,  0,  0,  0,  0,  0,  0,  0,  0,
/*8**/     0,  0,  0,  0,  0,  0,  0,  0,168,172,176,180,184,188,192,196,
/*9**/   200,204,208,  0,212,216,220,224,228,  0,  0,  0,  0,  0,  0,  0,
/*A**/     0,  0,  0,  0,  0,  0,  0,  0,  0,  0,  0,  0,  0,  0,  0,  0,
/*B**/     0,  0,  0,  0,  0,  0,  0,  0,  0,  0,  0,  0,  0,  0,  0,  0,
/*C**/     0,  0,  0,  0,  0,  0,  0,  0,  0,  0,  0,  0,  0,  0,  0,  0,
/*D**/     0,  0,232,  0,  0,  0,  0,  0,  0,  0,  0,  0,  0,  0,  0,  0,
/*E**/     0,  0,  0,  0,  0,  0,  0,  0,  0,  0,  0,  0,  0,  0,  0,  0,
/*F**/     0,  0,  0,  0,  0,  0,  0,  0,  0,  0,  0,  0,  0,  0,  0,  0);
/*        *0  *1  *2  *3  *4  *5  *6  *7  *8  *9  *A  *B  *C  *D  *E  *F  */

declare op_code character;  /*  For debug printout */
declare commutative(63) bit(1);  /*  Record which operators are commutative */

/* Commonly used IBM System/360 operation codes */
declare bc fixed initial ("47"), bcr fixed initial ("07");
declare bal fixed initial ("45"), balr fixed initial ("05");
declare load fixed initial ("58"), store fixed initial ("50");
declare cmpr fixed initial ("59"), cmprr fixed initial ("19");
declare la fixed initial ("41");

/* The following are used to hold address pairs in the emitter for || */
declare (a1, a2, b1, b2, t1, t2) fixed;
```

```
/* Commonly used strings */
declare x1 character initial(' ' ), x4 character initial('    ' );
declare equals character initial (' = ' ), period character initial (' .' );


/* Temporaries used throughout the compiler */
declare (char_temp, s ) character;
declare (i, j, k, l ) fixed;


declare true literally ' 1' , false literally ' 0' , forever literally ' while 1' ;


/*  Symbol  table  variables  */


declare halfword        literally  ' 1' ,
        labeltype       literally  ' 2' ,
        accumulator     literally  ' 3' ,
        variable        literally  ' 4' ,
        constant        literally  ' 5' ,
        condition       literally  ' 6' ,
        chrtype         literally  ' 7' ,
        fixedtype       literally  ' 8' ,
        bytetype        literally  ' 9' ,
        forwardtype     literally ' 10' ,
        descript        literally ' 11' ,
        special         literally ' 12' ,
        forwardcall     literally ' 13'  ,
        char_proc_type literally ' 14'
        ;
declare typename(14) character initial (' ', ' bit(16) ', ' label    ', ' ', ' ',
    ' ', ' ', ' character', ' fixed    ', ' bit(8)   ', ' ', ' ', ' ', ' ',
    ' character procedure' );
declare procmark fixed;  /* Start of local variables in symbol table */
declare parct fixed;   /* Number of parameters to current procedure */

declare ndecsy fixed;      /* Current number of declared symbols */
/* maxndecsy is the maximum of ndecsy over a compilation. If maxndecsy
    begins to approach sytsize then sytsize should be increased. */
declare maxndecsy fixed;

declare sytsize literally ' 415' ;  /* Symbol table size   */

/*  The symbol table is initialized with the names of all
    builtin functions and pseudo variables.  The procedure
    INITIALIZATION depends on the order and placement of these
    names.  Due caution should be observed while making changes .
*/
```

```
declare syt (sytsize) character              /*  Variable name */
    initial (' ',' ',' monitor_link' ,' time_of_generation' ,
        ' date_of_generation' ,' coreword' ,' corebyte' ,' freepoint' ,
        ' descriptor' ,' ndescript' , ' length' ,' substr' ,' byte' ,' shl' ,
        ' shr' ,' input' ,' output' ,' file' ,' inline' ,' trace' ,' untrace' ,
        ' exit' ,' time' ,' date' ,' clock_trap' ,' interrupt_trap' ,
        ' monitor' ,' addr' ,' compactify' , ' ',' ' );
declare sytype (sytsize) bit (8)    /* Type of the variable */
    initial  (0,0,fixedtype,fixedtype,fixedtype,fixedtype,
        bytetype,fixedtype,fixedtype,fixedtype,special,special,
        special,special,special,special,special,special,special,
        special,special,special,special,special,special,special,
        special,special,forwardcall,0,0);
declare sybase (sytsize) bit (4) initial(0,0,dbr,dbr,dbr,0,0,
    dbr,sbr,dbr,0,0,0,0,0,0,0,0,0,0,0,0,0,0,0,0,0,0,dbr,0,0);
declare sydisp (sytsize) bit (12)    /*  Displacement for variable */
    initial  (0,0,0,0,0,0,0,0,0,0,1,2,3,4,5,6,7,8,10,11,12,13,14,
        15,16,17,18,19,0,0);
declare sytco(sytsize) bit (16);        /*  Count of references to symbols */
declare declared_on_line(sytsize) bit(16);
```

```
/*  The compiler stacks declared below are used to drive the syntactic
    analysis algorithm and store information relevant to the interpretation
    of the text.  The stacks are all pointed to by the stack pointer sp.   */
```

```
declare stacksize literally ' 75' ;   /* Size of each stack   */
declare parse_stack (stacksize) bit(8); /* Tokens of partially parsed text */
declare type (stacksize) bit(8);    /*  Operand type for expressions */
declare reg (stacksize) bit(8);      /*  Associated general register */
declare inx (stacksize) bit(8);       /*  Associated index register */
declare cnt (stacksize) bit(8);       /*  Any count, parameters, subscripts ...*/
declare var (stacksize) character;/* EBCDIC name of item */
declare fixl (stacksize) fixed;     /*  Fixup location */
declare fixv (stacksize) fixed;     /*  Fixup value */
declare ppsave (stacksize) fixed; /* Associated program pointer */
```

```
/*  sp points to the right end of the reducible string in the parse stack,
    mp points to the left end, and
    mpp1 = mp+1.
*/
declare (sp, mp, mpp1) fixed;
/*  Declare statements and case statements require an auxiliary stack */
declare caselimit literally ' 255' , casestack(caselimit) fixed;
declare casep fixed;     /* Points to the current position in casestack */
declare dclrm character initial (' identifier list too long' );
```

```
/*                 P r o c e d u r e s :                              */


PAD:
   procedure (string, width) character;
      declare string character, (width, l) fixed;

      l = length(string);
      if l >= width then return string;
      else return string || substr(x70, 0, width-l);
   end PAD;

I_FORMAT:
   procedure (number, width) character;
      declare (number, width, l) fixed, string character;

      string = number;
      l = length(string);
      if l >= width then return string;
      else return substr(x70, 0, width-l) || string;
   end I_FORMAT;

ERROR:
   procedure(msg, severity);
      /*  Prints and accounts for all error messages.  */
      /*  If severity is not supplied, 0 is assumed.  */
      declare msg character, severity fixed;
      error_count = error_count + 1;
      /*  If listing is suppressed, force printing of this line.  */
      if ¬ control(byte(' L' )) then
         output = I_FORMAT (card_count, 4) || ' |' || buffer || ' |';
      output = substr(pointer, text_limit + lb-cp + margin_chop);
      /*  severity(-1) is a pornographic way of obtaining the return address. */
      output = ' *** Error, ' || msg || ' (detected at location '
            || (severity(-1)&"FFFFFF" ) - addr(compactify) + mainloc
            || ' in XCOM). ***' ;
      if error_count > 1 then
         output = ' *** Last previous error was detected on line '
            || previous_error || ' . ***' ;
      previous_error = card_count;
```

```
     if severity > 0 then
        if severe_errors > 25 then
           do;
              output = ' *** Too many severe errors, compilation aborted. ***' ;
              compiling = false;
           end;
        else severe_errors = severe_errors + 1;
  end ERROR ;



/*                              File handling procedures:                              */



GETDATA:
   procedure;
      /*  Handle scratch storage allocation for the data array.  */
      declare i fixed;
      count#getd = count#getd + 1;
      file(datafile,curdblk ) = data;        /*  Write out current block */
      curdblk = dp / diskbytes;              /* Calculate new block number */
      dporg = curdblk * diskbytes;
      dplim = dporg + diskbytes;
      if curdblk <= datamax then
            data = file(datafile,curdblk );
      else
         do;
            /*  Zero out the new data block.  */
            do i = 1 to shr(diskbytes,2);
               datamax(i ) = 0;
            end;
            do datamax = datamax + 1 to curdblk − 1;
               file(datafile,datamax )= data;
            end;
         end;
   end  GETDATA;


GETCODE:
   procedure;
      count#getc = count#getc + 1;
      file(codefile,curcblk ) = code;
      curcblk = pp / diskbytes;              /* Calculate new block number */
      pporg = curcblk * diskbytes;
      pplim = pporg + diskbytes;
```

```
        if curcblk <= codemax then
            code = file(codefile,curcblk );
        else
            do;
            /*  Zero out the new code block. */
                do i = 1 to shr(diskbytes,2);
                    codemax(i ) = 0;
                end;
                do codemax = codemax + 1 to curcblk − 1;
                    file(codefile,codemax ) = code;
                end;
            end;
    end  GETCODE;


GETSTRINGS:
    procedure;
        /*  Handle scratch storage allocation for string array.   */
        file(stringfile, cursblk ) = strings;      /* Write into the file */
        cursblk = chp/diskbytes;                 /*  Compute new block number */
        chporg = cursblk*diskbytes;                /*  New block origin */
        chplim = chporg + diskbytes;                  /*  New upper bound */
        if cursblk <= stringmax then
            strings = file(stringfile,cursblk );   /*  Read in from file */
        else
            do stringmax = stringmax + 1 to cursblk − 1;
                file(stringfile,stringmax ) = strings;
                /*  Fill out file so no gaps exist.  */
            end;
    end GETSTRINGS;



/*                    Card image handling procedure:                    */


GET_CARD:
    procedure;
        /*  Does all card reading and listing.  */
        declare i fixed, (temp, temp0, rest ) character, reading bit(1);
        if lb > 0 then
            do;
                text = balance;
                text_limit = lb − 1;
                cp = 0;
                return;
            end;
        expansion_count = 0;    /*  Checked in scanner macro expansion.  */
```

```
if reading then
    do;    /*  reading is false during compile of library from input(2) */
        buffer = input;
        if length(buffer) = 0 then
            do;    /*  Submonitor signal for end of data  */
                call ERROR (' eof missing or comment starting in column 1' ,1);
                buffer = PAD (' /*' ' /* */ eof;end;eof' , 80);
            end;
        else card_count = card_count + 1;  /*  Printed on listing */
    end;
else
    do;    /*  While reading library file only */
        buffer = input(2);
        if length(buffer) = 0 then
            do;    /*  Signal to switch to SYSIN */
                control(byte(' L' )), reading = true;  /*  Turn on listing */
                control(byte(' D' )) = true;    /* Turn on symbol dump  */
                clock(1) = time;  /*  Keep track of time for compile rate.  */
                text = x1;  /*  Initialize text for SCAN */
                /*  Statements are counted for statistics.  */
                statement_count = −1;     text_limit = 0;
                /*  Make builtin functions and variables redeclarable.  */
                procmark = ndecsy + 1;
                return;
            end;
    end;
if margin_chop > 0 then
    do;    /*  The margin control from dollar | */
        i = length(buffer) − margin_chop;
        rest = substr(buffer, i );
        buffer = substr(buffer, 0, i );
    end;
else rest = ' ' ;
text = buffer;
text_limit = length(text) − 1;
if control(byte(' M' )) then output = buffer;
else if control(byte(' L' )) then
    do;
        rest = I_FORMAT (pp, 6) || rest;
        output = I_FORMAT (card_count, 4) || ' |' || buffer || ' |' ||
            rest || current_procedure || information;
    end;
information = ' ' ;
cp = 0;
end GET_CARD;
```

/*   The scanner procedures: */

CHAR:
  procedure;
    /* Used for strings to avoid card boundary problems.   */
    cp = *cp* + 1;
    if *cp* <= *text_limit* **then return**;
    call *GET_CARD*;
  end *CHAR*;

DEBLANK:
  procedure;
    /* Used by BCHAR. */
    call *CHAR*;
    do while *byte*(*text*, *cp*) = *byte*(' ');
      call *CHAR*;
    end;
  end *DEBLANK*;

BCHAR:
  procedure;
    /* Used for bit strings. */
    do *forever*;
      call *DEBLANK*;
      ch = *byte*(*text*, *cp*);
      if *ch* ¬= *byte*(' (') **then return**;
      /* (base width)   */
      call *DEBLANK*;
      jbase = *byte*(*text*, *cp*) − *byte*(' 0');   /* Width */
      if *jbase* < 1 | *jbase* > 4 **then**
        do;
          call *ERROR* (' illegal bit string width: ' || *substr*(*text*, *cp*, 1));
          jbase = 4;   /* Default width for error */
        end;
      base = *shl*(1, *jbase*);
      call *DEBLANK*;
      if *byte*(*text*, *cp*) ¬= *byte*(')') **then**
        call *ERROR* (' missing) in bit string' , 0);
    end;
  end *BCHAR*;

```
BUILD_BCD:
   procedure (c);
      declare c bit(8);
      if length(bcd) > 0 then
         bcd = bcd || x1;
      else
         bcd = substr(x1 || x1, 1);
      /*  Force bcd to the top of free string area and increase length by one.
          This line depends upon the implementation of XPL strings.  */
      corebyte(freepoint−1) = c;
   end BUILD_BCD;

SCAN:
   procedure;
      declare (s1, s2) fixed;
      declare lstrngm character initial(' string too long' );
      count#scan = count#scan + 1;
      failsoft = true;
      bcd = '' ;   number_value = 0;
   scan1:
      do forever;
         if cp > text_limit then call GET_CARD;
         else
            do; /*  Discard last scanned value.  */
               text_limit = text_limit − cp;
               text = substr(text, cp);     cp = 0;
            end;
         /*  Branch on next character in text.               */
         do case chartype(byte(text));

            /*  Case 0   */

            /*  Illegal characters fall here   */
            call ERROR (' illegal character: '  ||  substr(text, 0, 1));

            /*  Case 1   */

            /*  Blank   */
            do;
               cp = 1;
               do while byte(text, cp) = byte(' ' ) & cp <= text_limit;
                  cp = cp + 1;
               end;
               cp = cp − 1;
            end;
```

```
/*   Case 2   */

/*   String quote (' ):   character string   */
do forever;
    token = string;
    s1 = 1;
    cp = cp + 1;
    do while byte(text, cp ) ¬= byte(' ' ' ' );
        if cp <= text_limit then
            cp = cp+1;
        else
            do; /*   String broken across card boundary */
                if length(bcd ) + cp > 257 then
                    do;
                        call ERROR(lstrngm  ,0);
                        return;
                    end;
                if cp > s1 then
                    bcd = bcd || substr(text,s1,cp−s1);
                text = x1;
                cp,s1 = 0;
                call GET_CARD;
            end;
    end;
    if length(bcd ) + cp > 257 then
        do;
            call ERROR(lstrngm,0);
            return;
        end;
    if cp > s1 then
        bcd = bcd || substr(text,s1,cp−s1);
    call CHAR;
    if byte(text, cp ) ¬= byte(' ' ' ' ) then
        return;
    if length(bcd ) > 255 then
        do;
            call ERROR(lstrngm,0);
            return;
        end;
    bcd = bcd || ' ' ' ' ;
    text_limit = text_limit − cp;
    text = substr(text,cp );
    cp = 0;   /*   Prepare to resume scanning string.   */
end;
```

```
/*   Case  3   */

do;        /*  Bit quote("):  bit string  */
   jbase = 4;  base = shl(1, jbase);  /* Default width  */
   token = number;  /*  Assume short bit string.  */
   s1 = 0;
   call BCHAR;
   do while ch ¬= byte(' "' );
      s1 = s1 + jbase;
      if ch >= byte(' 0' ) then s2 = ch − byte(' 0' );  /* Digits */
      else s2 = ch − "B7";                              /*  Letters */
      if s2 >= base | s2 < 0 then
         call ERROR (' illegal character in bit string: '
         || substr(text, cp, 1));
      if s1 > 32 then token = string;      /*  Long bit string */
      if token = string then
         do while s1 − jbase >= 8;
            if length(bcd) > "FF" then
               do;
                  call ERROR (lstrngm, 0);
                  return;
               end;
            s1 = s1 − 8;
            call BUILD_BCD (shr(number_value, s1−jbase));
         end;
      number_value = shl(number_value, jbase) + s2;
      call BCHAR;
   end;        /* of do while ch... */
   cp = cp + 1;
   if token = string then
      if length(bcd) > "FF" then call ERROR (lstrngm, 0);
      else call BUILD_BCD (shl(number_value, 8 − s1));
   return;
end;


/*   Case  4   */

do forever;  /*  A letter:  identifiers and reserved words.  */
   do cp = cp + 1 to text_limit;
      if not_letter_or_digit(byte(text, cp)) then
         do;  /*  End of identifier.   */
            if cp > 0 then bcd = bcd || substr(text, 0, cp);
            s1 = length(bcd);
```

```
if s1 > 1 then if s1 <= reserved_limit then
    /*   Check for reserved words.   */
    do i = v_index(s1-1) to v_index(s1) - 1;
        if bcd = v(i) then
            do;
                token = i;    return;
            end;
    end;
    do i = macro_index(s1-1) to macro_index(s1) - 1;
        if bcd = macro_name(i) then
            do;
                bcd = macro_text(i);
                if expansion_count < expansion_limit then
                    expansion_count = expansion_count + 1;
                else output =
                    ' *** Warning, too many expansions for ' ||
                    macro_name(i) || ' literally: ' || bcd;
                text = substr(text, cp);
                text_limit = text_limit - cp;
                if length(bcd) + text_limit > 255 then
                    do;
                        if lb + text_limit > 255 then
                        call ERROR('macro expansion too long');
                        else
                            do;
                                balance = text || balance;
                                lb = length(balance);
                                text = bcd;
                            end;
                    end;
                else text = bcd || text;
                bcd = '';     cp = 0;
                text_limit = length(text) - 1;
                go to scan1;
            end;
    end;
    /*   Reserved words exit higher: therefore <identifier> */
    token = ident;
    return;
    end;
end;
/*   End of card   */
bcd = bcd || text;
call GET_CARD;         cp = -1;
end;
```

```
/*   Case 5   */

do;        /*   Digit:  a number   */
   token =  number;
   do forever;
      do cp =  cp to text_limit;
         s1 =  byte(text, cp );
         if s1 <  byte(' 0' ) then return;
         number_value =  10*number_value + s1 − byte(' 0' );
      end;
      call GET_CARD;
   end;
end;




/*   Case 6   */

do;        /*   A /:  may be divide or start of comment.   */
   call CHAR;
   if byte(text, cp ) ¬=  byte(' *' ) then
      do;
         token =  divide;
         return;
      end;
   /*   We have a comment.   */
   s1, s2 =  byte(' ⌐ );
   do while s1 ¬=  byte(' *' ) | s2 ¬=  byte(' /' );
      if s1 =  byte(' $' ) then
         do;  /*   A control character   */
            control(s2) =  ¬ control(s2);
            if s2 =  byte(' T' ) then call trace;
            else if s2 =  byte(' U' ) then call untrace;
            else if s2 =  byte(' |' ) then
               if control(s2) then
                  margin_chop =  text_limit − cp + 1;
                else
                  margin_chop =  0;
         end;
      s1 =  s2;
      call CHAR;
      s2 =  byte(text, cp );
   end;
end;
```

```
                    /*  Case 7  */
                    do;        /*  Special characters  */
                        token = tx(byte(text));
                        cp = 1;
                        return;
                    end;


                    /*  Case 8  */
                    do;  /*  A |:  may be "or" or "cat"  */
                        call CHAR;
                        if byte(text, cp) = byte(' |' ) then
                            do;
                                call CHAR;
                                token = concatenate;
                            end;
                        else token = orsymbol;
                        return;
                    end;


                end;       /* of case on chartype  */
                cp = cp + 1;  /*  Advance scanner and resume search for token.  */
            end;
    end SCAN;


    /*            Address and register computations:                        */

CHECKBASES:
    procedure;
        if ¬ compiling then return;
        if dp >= bases(lastbase) + 4096 then
            do;
                lastbase = lastbase − 1;  /* Use reg. 11 down to reg. 4 */
                bases(lastbase) = dp & "FFFFFC";
                information = information || ' r' || lastbase || equals ||
                    bases(lastbase) || period;
                if lastbase = 3 then call ERROR(' exceeded data area' ,1);
            end;
    end CHECKBASES;


CLEARREGS:
    procedure;
        /*  Free all the arithmetic registers.  */
        do i = 0 to 3;  bases(i) = avail;  end;
        target_register = −1;
    end CLEARREGS;
```

FINDAC:

   procedure fixed;

      /*   Find an accumulator for 32 bit quantity.   */

      declare *i* fixed;

      if *target_register* $>$ -1 **then if** *bases(target_register)* $=$ *avail* **then**

         do;

            bases(target_register) $=$ *accumulator*;

            return *target_register*;

         end;

      do *i* $=$ 1 **to** 3;

         if *bases(i)* $=$ *avail* **then**

            do;

               bases(i) $=$ *accumulator*;

               return *i*;

            end;

      end;

      call *ERROR*(' used all accumulators' ,0);

      return 0;

   end   *FINDAC*;

FINDADDRESS:

   procedure (*adr*);

      /*   Find the appropriate base and displacement for the address.   */

      declare (*adr, i*) fixed;

      count#find $=$ *count#find* $+$ 1;

      if *adr* $<$ 0 **then**

         do;

            adrdisp $=$ $-$ *adr*;   *adreg* $=$ *sbr*;   **return**;

         end;

      if *adr* $=$ 0 **then**

         do;

            adreg,adrdisp $=$ 0;   **return**;

         end;

      do *i* $=$ *lastbase* **to** *dbr*;

         if *bases(i)* $<=$ *adr* & *bases(i)* $+4096$ $>$ *adr* **then**

            do;

               adrdisp $=$ *adr* $-$ *bases(i)*;

               adreg $=$ *i*;   **return**;

            end;

      end;

      call *ERROR*(' FINDADDRESS failed' ,1);

      adreg,adrdisp $=$ 0;

   end   *FINDADDRESS*;

```
    /*                    Code emission procedures:                    */


EMITCHAR:
    procedure (c );
        declare c bit (8);
        /*  Send one 8–bit character to the string area.  */
        if control(byte(' E' )) then
            output = x70 || chp || ' : Character = ' ||
                substr(hexcodes, shr(c,4), 1) || substr(hexcodes, c & "F", 1);
        if chp < chporg | chp >= chplim then call GETSTRINGS;
        strings(chp–chporg ) = c;
        chp = chp + 1;
    end   EMITCHAR;


EMITBYTE:
    procedure (b );
        declare b fixed;
        /*  Emit one byte of data.  */
        if dp < dporg | dp >= dplim then call GETDATA;
        data(dp–dporg ) = b;
        if control(byte(' E' )) then
    ,      output = x70 || dp || ' : Data = ' ||
                substr(hexcodes, shr(b,4), 1) || substr(hexcodes, b & "F", 1);
        dp = dp + 1;
        call CHECKBASES;
    end EMITBYTE;


EMITCODEBYTES:
    procedure (b1,b2);
        declare (b1, b2) bit(8), i fixed;
        /*  Emit two bytes of code.  */
        stillcond = 0;
        if pp < pporg | pp >= pplim then call GETCODE;
        i = pp – pporg;
        code(i ) = b1;                /*  First  byte  */
        code(i + 1) = b2;             /*  Second  byte  */
        if control(byte(' B' )) then
            output = x70 || pp || ' : Code = ' ||
                substr(hexcodes, shr(b1,4), 1) || substr(hexcodes, b1 & "F", 1)
                || substr(hexcodes, shr(b2,4), 1) || substr(hexcodes, b2 & "F",1);
        pp =   pp + 2;
    end   EMITCODEBYTES ;
```

EMITDATAWORD:
```
   procedure(w );
      declare (w, i ) fixed;
      /* Send a 32—bit word to the data array. */

      dp = (dp + 3) & "FFFFFC";
      if dp < dporg | dp >= dplim then call GETDATA;
      call CHECKBASES;
      if control(byte(' E' )) then
         output = x70 || dp || ': Data = ' || w;
      i = dp − dporg;
      data(i ) = shr(w,24);
      data(i + 1) = shr(w,16);
      data(i + 2) = shr(w,8);
      data(i + 3) = w;
      dp = dp + 4;
      call CHECKBASES;

   end EMITDATAWORD;
```

EMITDESC:
```
   procedure (d );
      declare d fixed;
      /* Send 32—bit descriptor to string descriptor area. */

      if dsp >= 4096 then
         do;
            call ERROR (' too many strings' , 1);
            dsp = 0;
         end;
      if control(byte(' E' )) then
         output = x70 || dsp || ': Desc = ' || shr(d,24) || ', ' ||
            (d & "FFFFFF" );
      desc(shr(dsp,2)) = d;
      dsp = dsp + 4;

   end EMITDESC;
```

EMITCONSTANT:
   procedure(*c*);
       /* See if *c* has already been emited, and if not emit. Set up address. */

       declare *ctab*(100) **fixed**, *cadd* (100) **bit**(16), (*c*, *nc*, *i*) **fixed**;
       do *i* = 1 **to** *nc*;
          if *ctab*(*i*) = *c* **then**
              do;
                  adreg = *shr*(*cadd*(*i*),12);
                  adrdisp = *cadd*(*i*) & "FFF";
                  return;
              end;
       end;

       call *EMITDATAWORD* (*c*);
       ctab(*i*) = *c*;
       call *FINDADDRESS*(*dp*−4);
       cadd(*i*) = *shl*(*adreg*,12) + *adrdisp*;
       if *i* < 100 **then** *nc* = *i*;
       information = *information* || ' c' || *i* || *equals* || *c* || *period*;
   end *EMITCONSTANT*;

EMITRR:
   procedure (*op*, *r*1, *r*2);
       /* Emit a 16−bit RR format instruction. */

       declare (*op*, *r*1, *r*2) **fixed**;
       count#*rr* = *count*#*rr* + 1;
       if *control*(*byte*(' E')) **then**
          do;
              op_code = *substr*(*opnames*, *oper*(*op*), 4);
              output = *x*70 || *pp* || ' : Code = ' || *op_code* || *x*1 || *r*1
                  || ',' || *r*2;
          end;
       call *EMITCODEBYTES*(*op*, *shl*(*r*1,4) + *r*2);
       instruct(*op*) = *instruct*(*op*) + 1;
   end *EMITRR*;

EMITRX:
```
  procedure (op, r1, r2, r3, disp);
    declare (op, r1, r2, r3, disp) fixed;
    /*  Emit a 32-bit RX format instruction.  */
    count#rx = count#rx + 1;
    if control(byte(' E' )) then
        do;
            op_code = substr(opnames, oper(op), 4);
            output = x70 || pp || ' : Code = ' || op_code || x1 || r1
                || ',' || disp || ' (' || r2 || ',' || r3 || ' )' ;
        end;
    call EMITCODEBYTES(op, shl(r1,4)+r2);
    call EMITCODEBYTES(shl(r3,4)+shr(disp,8), disp & "FF" );
    instruct(op) = instruct(op) + 1;
  end EMITRX;
```

/*   Fixup procedures: */

INSERT_CODE_FIXUPS:
```
  procedure;
      /*  Empty the fixup table, either for loading or because of
      table overflow.  */

    declare (i, j, l, fxlim, t1, k) fixed;
    declare t2 bit(8), exchanges bit(1);

    /*  The first step is to sort the code fixup table.  */
    k,fxlim = fcp - 1;        exchanges = true;
    do while exchanges;  /*  Quit bubble sort after table quiets down.  */
        exchanges = false;  /*  Reset on each exchange below.  */
        do j = 0 to k-1;
            i = fxlim-j;
            l = i-1;
            if fixcadr(l) > fixcadr(i) then
                do;  /*  Swap */
                    t1 = fixcadr(l);   fixcadr(l) = fixcadr(i);   fixcadr(i) = t1;
                    t2 = fixcb1(l);   fixcb1(l) = fixcb1(i);   fixcb1(i) = t2;
                    t2 = fixcb2(l);   fixcb2(l) = fixcb2(i);   fixcb2(i) = t2;
                    exchanges = true;   k = j;
                end;
        end;
    end;
```

```
/*   Now write out the current block.   */
file(codefile,curcblk ) =   code;

/*   Write binary program patches into program file.   */

k,pporg= 0;   pplim  =   diskbytes;
do j  =   0 to codemax;

    i  =   k;   /*   Keep track of k so that we will know when to read in.   */

    do while  (k <=   fxlim )   &   (fixcadr(k ) <   pplim );
        /*   If the file has not yet been read in, do so.   */
        if  k  =   i  then  code  =   file(codefile,j );  /* Only if a fix is needed */
        l  =   fixcadr(k )  −  pporg;   /* Relative address within this block.   */
        code(l )  =   fixcb1(k );   code(l+1) =   fixcb2(k );
        k  =   k  +   1;
    end;

    if  k >   i  then      /*   A fixup was done.   */
        file(codefile,j ) =   code;   /*   Write out the contents.   */

    pporg  =   pporg  +   diskbytes;
    pplim  =   pplim  +   diskbytes;
end;

fcp  =   0;   /*   Reset table to empty.   */
code  =   file(codefile,curcblk );   /*   Restore file to previous state.   */
pporg  =   curcblk*diskbytes;   pplim  =   pporg  +   diskbytes;
end INSERT_CODE_FIXUPS;


FIXCHW:
    procedure  (adr, b1,  b2);
        declare adr fixed,  (b1,  b2) bit(8);
        /*   Fix up one half word of code.   */
        count#fixchw  =   count#fixchw  +   1;
        if  fcp >=   fclim then
            call  INSERT_CODE_FIXUPS;
        if  pporg <=   adr & adr <   pplim then
            do;
                shortcfix  =   shortcfix  +   1;
                adr  =   adr  −  pporg;
                code(adr )  =   b1;
                code(adr+ 1) =   b2;
            end;
```

```
        else
            do;
                longcfix  =  longcfix  +  1;
                fixcadr(fcp )  =  adr;
                fixcb1(fcp )  =  b1;
                fixcb2(fcp )  =  b2;
                fcp  =  fcp  +  1;
            end;
    end   FIXCHW;


FIXBFW:
    procedure  (where, val );

        declare  (where,  val,  i,  j,  p )  fixed;
        if  where  =  0  then return;
        /*   Fix up a branch whose address we now know.   */
        count # fixbfw  =   count # fixbfw  +  1;
        if  control(byte(' E' ))  then  output  =  x70  || '         '  || where  || ': Fixup ='
                || val;
        p  =  where  +  2;              /*   The actual address field.   */

        if  where  >=   "1000"  then
            do;
                call FIXCHW  (p,  shl(dbr,4),  shr(val,10)  &  "FC" );
                val  =  val  &  "FFF";
                p  =  p  +  4;
            end;
        else if  val  >=   "1000"  then
            do;
                i  =  val  &  "FFF";
                j  =  shr(val,  12);
                instruct(load )  =  instruct(load )  +  1;
                instruct(bc )  =  instruct(bc )  +  1;
                call EMITDATAWORD (shl(load,  24) + shl(brchreg,  20) + shl(dbr, 12)
                        +  shl(j,  2) ));
                call EMITDATAWORD("47F00000" + shl(brchreg,16) + shl(pbr,12) + i );
                call FINDADDRESS (dp−8);
                call FIXCHW(p,  shl(adreg,4) + shr(adrdisp,8),  adrdisp  &  "FF" );
                return;
            end;
        call FIXCHW(p,  shl(pbr,4) + shr(val,8),  val  &  "FF" );

    end  FIXBFW;
```

FIXWHOLEDATAWORD:

   procedure (*adr*, *word*);

     declare (*adr*, *word*) **fixed**;

     declare (*blk*, *temp*) **fixed**, *reread* **bit**(1);

     if *control*(*byte*(' E')) **then**

        output = *x*70 || *adr* || ' : Fixup = ' || *word*;

     count#fixd = *count#fixd* + 1;

     blk = *adr*/*diskbytes*;

     reread = (*curdblk* ¬= *blk*);

     if *reread* **then**

        do; /* Must get the right block. */

          longdfix = *longdfix* + 1;

          temp = *dp*;

          dp = *adr*;

          call *GETDATA*;

        end;

     else *shortdfix* = *shortdfix* + 1;

     adr = *adr* **mod** *diskbytes*;

     data(*adr*) = *shr*(*word*, 24);

     data(*adr*+1) = *shr*(*word*, 16);

     data(*adr*+2) = *shr*(*word*, 8);

     data(*adr*+3) = *word*;

     if *reread* **then** *dp* = *temp*;

   end *FIXWHOLEDATAWORD*;

ENTER:

   procedure (*n*, *t*, *l*, *line*);

     /* Enter a symbol in the symbol table. */

     declare (*i*, *j*, *k*, *l*, *t*, *line*) **fixed**, *n* **character**;

     do *i* = *procmark* **to** *ndecsy*;

        if *n* = *syt*(*i*) **then**

          do;

            k = *sytype*(*i*);

            idcompares = *idcompares* + *i* − *procmark*;

            if *t* = *labeltype* & (*k* = *forwardtype* | *k* = *forwardcall*) **then**

              do;

                if *control*(*byte*(' E')) **then**

                  output = *x*70 || ' Fix references to: ' || *n*;

                j = *bases*(*sybase*(*i*)) + *sydisp*(*i*);

                if *k* = *forwardcall* **then**

                  if *l* > "FFF" **then**

                    l = *l*+8;

                  else

                    l = *l*+4;

```
              sybase(i ) =   shr(l, 12);
              sydisp(i ) =  l & "FFF";
              call  FIXWHOLEDATAWORD(j,l );
              sytype(i ) =   t;
              declared_on_line(i ) =  line;
        end;
     else if procmark + parct <  i then
        call  ERROR(' duplicate declaration for:   '  ||  n, 0);
     else declared_on_line(i ) =  line;
        return i;
     end;
 end;


ndecsy =  ndecsy +  1;
if ndecsy >  maxndecsy then
   if ndecsy >  sytsize then
      do;
          call  ERROR (' symbol table overflow' , 1);
          ndecsy =  ndecsy −  1;
      end;
   else maxndecsy =  ndecsy;
syt(ndecsy ) =  n;
sytype(ndecsy ) =  t;
declared_on_line(ndecsy ) =  line;
sytco(ndecsy ) =  0;


if t =  labeltype then
   do;
       sybase(ndecsy ) =  shr(l, 12);   /*  Page.  */
       sydisp(ndecsy ) =  l & "FFF";
   end;
else
   do;
       call  FINDADDRESS(l );
       sybase(ndecsy ) =  adreg;
       sydisp(ndecsy ) =  adrdisp;
   end;
idcompares =  idcompares +  ndecsy −  procmark;
return ndecsy;


end   ENTER;
```

ID_LOOKUP:
  procedure (*p*);
       /* Looks up the identifier at *p* in the analysis stack in the
        symbol table and initializes *fixl,cnt,type,reg,inx*
        appropriately. If the identifier is not found, *fixl* is
        set to −1.
      */
      declare *p* **fixed**, *i* **fixed**;
      char_temp = *var*(*p*);
      do *i* = 0 **to** *ndecsy* − 1;
        if *syt*(*ndecsy*−*i*) = *char_temp* **then**
          do;
            idcompares = *idcompares* + *i*;
            i,fixl(*p*) = *ndecsy* − *i*;
            cnt(*p*) = 0;   /* Initialize subscript count. */
            type(*p*) = *variable*;
            if *sytype*(*i*) = *special* **then**
              fixv(*p*) = *sydisp*(*i*);   /* Builtin function. */
            else
              fixv(*p*) = 0;   /* ¬ builtin function. */
            reg(*p*),*inx*(*p*) = 0;   /* Initialize register pointers. */
            sytco(*i*) = *sytco*(*i*) + 1; /* Count references. */
            return;
          end;
      end;
      idcompares = *idcompares* + *ndecsy*;
      fixl(*p*) = −1;   /* Identifier not found. */
  end   *ID_LOOKUP*;

UNDECLARED_ID:
  procedure (*p*);
      /* Issues an error message for undeclared identifiers and
        enters them with default type in the symbol table.
      */
      declare *p* **fixed**;
      call *ERROR*(' undeclared identifier: ' || *var*(*p*) ,0);
      call *EMITDATAWORD*(0);
      call *ENTER* (*var*(*p*), *fixedtype*, *dp*−4, *card_count*);
      cnt(*p*),*fixv*(*p*) = 0;
      reg(*p*),*inx*(*p*) = 0;
      fixl(*p*) = *ndecsy*;
      sytco(*ndecsy*) = 1;   /* Count first reference. */
      type(*p*) = *variable*;
  end   *UNDECLARED_ID*;

SETINIT:
```
   procedure;
      /*  Places initial values into data area.  */

      declare (i, j) fixed;
      if itype = chrtype then
         do;
            if type(mpp1) ¬= chrtype then var(mpp1) = fixv(mpp1);
            s = var(mpp1);      /*  The string.  */
            i = length(s) − 1;

            if i < 0 then
               call EMITDESC(0);
            else
               call EMITDESC(shl(i,24) + chp );

            do j = 0 to i;
               call EMITCHAR(byte(s,j) );
            end;
         end;
      else if type(mpp1) ¬= constant then
         call ERROR (' illegal constant in initial list' );
      else if itype = fixedtype then
         call EMITDATAWORD(fixv(mpp1) );
      else if itype = halfword then
         do;
            /*  First force alignment.  */
            dp = (dp + 1) & "FFFFFE";
            call EMITBYTE (shr(fixv(mpp1), 8) );
            call EMITBYTE(fixv(mpp1) & "FF" );
         end;
      else if itype = bytetype then
         call EMITBYTE(fixv(mpp1) );

   end  SETINIT;



ALLOCATE :
   procedure(p,dim );
      /* Allocates storage for the identifier at p in the analysis
         stack with dimension dim.
      */

      declare (p, dim, j) fixed;
```

```
CHECK_NEWDP:
  procedure;
    declare t fixed;
    t = dp;
    dp = newdp;
    call CHECKBASES;
    dp = t;
  end  CHECK_NEWDP;



dim = dim + 1;              /*  Actual number of items.  */
do case type(p);

  ;      /*  Case  0     dummy          */

  do;       /*  Case 1     halfword  */
    newdp = (newdp + 1) & "FFFFFE";   /*  Align halfword.  */
    call CHECK_NEWDP;
    j = newdp;
    newdp = newdp + shl(dim, 1);
  end;

  ;    /*  Case  2     label type          */

  ;    /*  Case  3     accumulator         */

  ;    /*  Case  4     variable           */

  ;    /*  Case  5     constant           */

  ;    /*  Case  6     condition          */

  do; /*  Case  7     character type     */
    j = -newdsp;
    newdsp = newdsp + shl(dim,2);
  end;

  do; /*  Case  8     fixed type         */
    newdp = (newdp + 3) & "FFFFFC";   /*  Align to word.  */
    call CHECK_NEWDP;
    j = newdp;
    newdp = newdp + shl(dim,2);
  end;
```

```
    do;  /*  Case  9      byte type                */
        call CHECK_NEWDP;
        j = newdp;
        newdp = newdp + dim;
    end;

    do;  /*  Case 10      forward type  (label)  */
        newdp = (newdp + 3) & "FFFFFC";  /* word align */
        call CHECK_NEWDP;
        j = newdp;
        newdp = newdp + shl(dim,2);              /* space for fixups  */
    end;

    ;    /*  Case 11      descript              */

    ;    /*  Case 12      special               */

    ;    /*  Case 13      forward call          */

    ;    /*  Case 14      char_proc_type         */

    ;    /*  Case 15      unused                */

    end; /*  of do case type(p)  */

sytype(fixl(p)) = type(p);
call FINDADDRESS(j);
sybase(fixl(p)) = adreg;
sydisp(fixl(p)) = adrdisp;
end ALLOCATE;


TDECLARE:
    procedure (dim);
        /*  Allocates storage for identifiers in declarations.  */
        declare dim fixed;
        newdp = dp;
        newdsp = dsp;
        type(mp) = type(sp);
        casep = fixl(mp);
        do i = 1 to inx(mp);
            fixl(mp) = casestack(casep + i);          /*  Symbol table pointer.  */
            call ALLOCATE(mp, dim);
        end;
    end TDECLARE;
```

MOVESTACKS:
  procedure (*f*,*t*);
    declare *f* **fixed**, *t* **fixed**;
    /* Move all the compiler stacks down from *f* to *t*. */

    type(*t*) = *type*(*f*);   *var*(*t*) = *var*(*f*);
    fixl(*t*) = *fixl*(*f*);   *fixv*(*t*) = *fixv*(*f*);
    inx(*t*) = *inx*(*f*);   *reg*(*t*) = *reg*(*f*);
    ppsave(*t*) = *ppsave*(*f*);   *cnt*(*t*) = *cnt*(*f*);
  end *MOVESTACKS*;

/*   Branch procedures: */

BRANCH_BD:
  procedure(*cond*, *b*, *d*);
    declare (*cond*, *b*, *d*) **fixed**;
    /* Branches are a special case. If they are into the 1st 4096
       bytes of program a single branch will suffice. Otherwise we
       must index with a constant in *brchreg* to get anywhere.
    */

    if *b* = 0 **then**
      call *EMITRX*(*bc*, *cond*, 0, *pbr*, *d*);
    else
      do;
         call *EMITRX*(*load*,*brchreg*,0,*dbr*,*shl*(*b*,2));
         call *EMITRX*(*bc*, *cond*, *brchreg*, *pbr*, *d*);
      end;
  end *BRANCH_BD*;

BRANCH:
  procedure (*cond*, *location*);
    declare (*cond*, *location*) **fixed**;
    if *location* = 0 **then** *location* = *pp*;
    /* Assume fixup will be near. */
    call *BRANCH_BD*(*cond*, *shr*(*location*,12), *location* & "FFF");
  end *BRANCH*;

```
BRLINK_BD:
   procedure (base,disp );
      declare (base, disp ) fixed;
      if base = 0 then
         call EMITRX(bal, brchreg, 0, pbr, disp );
      else
         do;
            call EMITRX(load, brchreg, 0, dbr, shl(base,2) );
            call EMITRX(bal, brchreg, brchreg, pbr, disp );
         end;
   end  BRLINK_BD;
```

```
/*                       Code for procedures:                       */
```

```
SAVE_REGISTERS:
   procedure;
      /* Generates code to save registers before a procedure or
         function call.
      */

      declare i fixed;
      do i = 1 to 3;
         if bases(i ) ¬= avail then
            do;
               call EMITDATAWORD(0);
               call FINDADDRESS(dp−4);
               temp(i ) = shl(adreg,12) + adrdisp;
               call EMITRX(store,i,0,adreg,adrdisp );
            end;
         else
            temp(i ) = 0;
      end;
   end  SAVE_REGISTERS;
```

```
UNSAVE_REGISTERS:
   procedure (r,p );
      /*  Generates code to restore registers after a function
          or procedure call and also does some housekeeping.
      */

      declare (r, p, i, j ) fixed;
```

```
    if bases(r) ¬= avail then
        do;
            j = FINDAC;
            call EMITRR("18", j, r);
        end;
    else
        j = r;
    do i = 1 to 3;
        if temp(i) ¬= 0 then
            call EMITRX(load,i,0,shr(temp(i),12), temp(i)&"FFF");
    end;
    type(p) = accumulator;
    reg(p) = j;
    bases(j) = accumulator;
end   UNSAVE_REGISTERS;


CALLSUB:
    procedure (sb,sd, r, p);
        declare (sb, sd, r, p) fixed;
        call SAVE_REGISTERS;
        call BRLINK_BD(sb,sd);
        call UNSAVE_REGISTERS(r, p);
    end   CALLSUB;


CALLSUB_FORWARD:
    procedure (sb,sd,r,p);
        declare (sb, sd, r, p) fixed;
        call SAVE_REGISTERS;
        call EMITRX(load, brchreg, 0, sb,sd);
        call EMITRX(bal, brchreg, brchreg, pbr, 0);
        call UNSAVE_REGISTERS(r, p);
    end   CALLSUB_FORWARD;




FORCE_ADDRESS:
    procedure (sp,r);
        /* Generates the address of the <variable> in the analysis

            stack at sp in register r.
        */
        declare (sp, r, k, inxsp) fixed;
```

```
if sytype(fixl(sp)) = labeltype then
   do;
      k = fixl(sp);
      if sybase(k) = 0 then
         call EMITRX(la,r,0,pbr,sydisp(k));
      else
         do;
            call EMITRX(load,r,0,dbr,shl(sybase(k),2));
            call EMITRX(la,r,r,pbr,sydisp(k));
         end;
   end;
else
   do;
      k = sytype(fixl(sp));
      inxsp = inx(sp);
      if inxsp ¬= 0 then
         do;
            if k ¬= bytetype then
               if k = halfword then
                  call EMITRR ("1A", inxsp, inxsp);
               else
                  call EMITRX("89",inxsp,0,0,2);
            bases(inxsp) = avail;
         end;
      if k = forwardtype | k = forwardcall then
         do;
            k = fixl(sp);
            call EMITRX(load,r,0,sybase(k),sydisp(k));
            call EMITRR("1A",r,pbr);
         end;
      else
         call EMITRX(la,r,inxsp,sybase(fixl(sp)),sydisp(fixl(sp)));
   end;
end FORCE_ADDRESS;
```

FILE_PSEUDO_ARRAY:
  procedure (*varp*,*filep*, *direction*);
     /* Generates code for the *file* pseudo array.
     Two forms are handled:

                  < variable>   =   *file*(*i,j*);

                  file(*i,j*)   =   < variable> ;

varp is a pointer to the <variable> in the analysis stacks.
filep is a pointer to the analysis stack where *file(i,j)*
has been assimilated under the guise of a subscripted
variable. *direction* = 0 for the first case (read) and
direction = 4 for the second case (write). *i* is the file
index (*i* = 1,2,3) and *j* is the relative record within the
file. The generated code should have the same effect as:

```
la    0,<variable>
l     1,i
sll   1,3                    i*8
la    1,direction+44(,1)
l     2,j
balr  brchreg,ioreg
```

Registers 0−3 are not preserved across the monitor call,
hence all registers are freed.
*/

declare (*varp, direction, filep, r*) **fixed**;

if *type(varp)* = *variable* **then**
    do;
        call *FORCE_ADDRESS(varp,0)*;
        call *EMITRX("89",reg(filep),0,0,3)*;   /* *i*8 */
        r = *FINDAC*;
        if *inx(filep)* = 1 **then**
            do;   /* Juggle registers. */
                call *EMITRR("18",r,1)*;
                inx(filep) = *r*;
            end;
        call *EMITRX(la,1,0,reg(filep),44+direction)*;
        if *inx(filep)* ¬= 2 **then**
            call *EMITRR("18",2,inx(filep))*;   /* *j*   */
        call *EMITRR(balr,brchreg,ioreg)*;
        type(filep) = *special*;   /* No more assignments. */
        call *CLEARREGS*;   /* Free all registers. */
    end;
else
    call *ERROR*(' illegal use of *file* pseudo array' ,1);

end *FILE_PSEUDO_ARRAY*;

```
EMIT_INLINE:
    procedure;
        /*  Generates code for the pseudo function inline              */
        declare binlm character initial (' bad argument to inline' );
        if cnt(mp ) < 4 then
            do;
                if type(mpp1) = constant then
                    do case cnt(mp ) − 1;

                        fixl(mp ) = fixv(mpp1);            /*  Save op code */

                        do;                                /*  Save r1   */
                            type(mp ) = accumulator;
                            reg(mp ) = fixv(mpp1);
                        end;

                        call EMITCODEBYTES(fixl(mp ), shl(reg(mp ), 4) +
                            fixv(mpp1) );                  /*  Emit  op r1 x  */

                    end;
                else
                    call ERROR(binlm,1);
            end;
        else if type(mpp1) = constant then
            do;
                if cnt(mp ) & 1 then
                    call EMITCODEBYTES(inx(mp ) + shr(fixv(mpp1), 8),
                        fixv(mpp1) );            /*  Emit  b ddd  */
                else
                    inx(mp ) = shl(fixv(mpp1), 4);         /*  Save base reg  */
            end;
        else if type(mpp1) = variable then
            do;
                cnt(mp ) = cnt(mp ) + 1;
                if cnt(mp ) & 1 then
                    call EMITCODEBYTES(shl(sybase(fixl(mpp1) ), 4)  +
                                        shr(sydisp(fixl(mpp1) ), 8) ,
                                        sydisp(fixl(mpp1) ) );
                else
                    call ERROR(binlm, 1);
            end;
        else
            call ERROR(binlm, 1);

    end   EMIT_INLINE;
```

PROC_START:
   procedure;

    /*   Generates prologue code for the head of a procedure.   */

    declare *i* **fixed**;
    i = fixl(mp);
    fixl(mp) = pp;
    call *BRANCH*("F",0);   /*   Branch around.   */
    call *EMITDATAWORD*(0); /*   Place to store return address.   */
    ppsave(mp) = rtnadr;
    rtnadr = dp − 4;
    call *FINDADDRESS(rtnadr)*;
    sybase(i) = shr(pp,12);   /*   Address of the procedure.   */
    sydisp(i) = pp & "FFF";
    call *EMITRX(store, brchreg,0,adreg,adrdisp)*;

end *PROC_START*;

STUFF_PARAMETER:
   procedure;

    /*   Generates code to send an actual parameter to a procedure.   */

    i = fixl(mp) + cnt(mp);
    if *length(syt(i)) = 0* **then**
      do;
        if *sytype(i) = bytetype* **then**
          j = "42";   /*   stc   */
        else if *sytype(i) = halfword* **then**
          j = "40";
        else
          j = store;   /*   st   */
        call *EMITRX(j, reg(mpp1), 0, sybase(i), sydisp(i))*;
        bases(reg(mpp1)) = avail;
      end;
    else
      call *ERROR*(' too many actual parameters' , 1);

end *STUFF_PARAMETER*;

CHECK_STRING_OVERFLOW:
   procedure;
      declare (*i, br_save*) **fixed**;
      call *EMITRX* (*load*, 0, 0, *dbr, tsa*);
      call *EMITRX* (*cmpr*, 0, 0, *dbr, limitword*);
      i = pp;
      call *BRANCH* (4, 0);
      call *EMITDATAWORD*(0); *br_save = dp* − 4;
      call *FINDADDRESS*(*br_save*);
      call *EMITRX*(*store, brchreg*, 0, *adreg, adrdisp*);
      if *sytype* (*string_recover*) = *labeltype* **then**
         call *CALLSUB*(*sybase*(*string_recover*),*sydisp*(*string_recover*), 0,
            stacksize);
      else
         call *CALLSUB_FORWARD*(*sybase*(*string_recover*),
            sydisp(*string_recover*), 0, *stacksize*);
      bases(*reg*(*stacksize*)) = *avail*;
      call *FINDADDRESS* (*br_save*);
      call *EMITRX*(*load,brchreg*,0,*adreg,adrdisp*);
      sytco(*string_recover*) = *sytco*(*string_recover*) + 1;
      call *EMITRR* ("1B", 0, 0);
      call *FINDADDRESS* (*strl*);
      call *EMITRX* (*store*, 0, 0, *adreg, adrdisp*);
      call *FIXBFW* (*i, pp*);
   end *CHECK_STRING_OVERFLOW*;

/*   Expressions: */

CONDTOREG:
   procedure (*mp, cc*);
      declare (*mp, cc, j*) **fixed**;
      j = FINDAC;
      call *EMITRX*(*la, j*, 0, 0, 0);
      if *pp* < 4084 **then**
         call *BRANCH*(*cc, pp*+8);
      else
         call *BRANCH*(*cc, pp*+12);
      call *EMITRX*(*la, j*, 0, 0, 1);
      type(*mp*) = *accumulator*;
      reg(*mp*) = *j*;
      stillcond = cc;
   end *CONDTOREG*;

FORCEACCUMULATOR:
 procedure (*p*);
  declare *p* **fixed**;
  /* Force the operand at *p* into an accumulator. */
  declare (*r, sb, sd, tp, sfp*) **fixed**, *t1* **character**;
  count#force = *count#force* + 1;
  tp = *type*(*p*);
  if *tp* = *condition* **then call** *CONDTOREG* (*p, reg*(*p*));
  else if *tp* = *variable* **then**
   do;
    sb = *sybase*(*fixl*(*p*));   *sd* = *sydisp*(*fixl*(*p*));
    sfp = *sytype*(*fixl*(*p*));
    if *sfp* = *labeltype* | *sfp* = *char_proc_type* **then**
     do;
      call *CALLSUB*(*sb,sd,3,p*);
      if *length*(*syt*(*fixl*(*p*) + *cnt*(*p*) + 1)) = 0 **then**
       if *control*(*byte*(' N')) **then**
        output = ' ** Warning——not all parameters supplied.' ;
      if *sfp* = *char_proc_type* **then** *type*(*p*) = *descript*;
     end;
    else if *sfp* = *forwardtype* | *sfp* = *forwardcall* **then**
     do;
      call *CALLSUB_FORWARD*(*sb,sd,3,p*);
      sytype(*fixl*(*p*)) = *forwardcall*;
     end;
    else if *sfp* = *special* **then**
     do;
      call *EMITRX*("90", 1, 3, *dbr, io_save*);
      if *sd* = 6 **then**
       do; /* *input* */
       call *CHECK_STRING_OVERFLOW*;
       if *reg*(*p*) = 0 **then call** *EMITRR* ("1B", 2, 2);
       else if *reg*(*p*)¬=2 **then call** *EMITRR*("18", 2, *reg*(*p*));
       bases(*reg*(*p*)) = *avail*;
       call *FINDADDRESS* (*tsa*);
       call *EMITRX* (*load*, 0, 0, *adreg, adrdisp*);
       /* This is a pointer to bottom of free string area. */
       call *EMITRX* (*la*, 1, 0, 0, 4); /* 4 is read card */
       call *EMITRR* (*balr, brchreg, ioreg*); /* Monitor call. */
       /* Move free string area pointer. */
       call *EMITRX* (*store*, 1, 0, *adreg, adrdisp*);
       call *FINDADDRESS* (*strl*); /* Last computed string. */
       call *EMITRX* (*store*, 0, 0, *adreg, adrdisp*);
       reg(*p*) = 0; *type*(*p*) = *descript*;
      end;

```
      else if sd =  8 then
        call FILE_PSEUDO_ARRAY(p−2,p,0);
      else if sd >=  11 & sd <=  18 then
        do;
              /* trace, untrace, exit, time, date, etc.            */
              if sd =  15 then r =  1; else r =  0;
              if sd >  15 then
                  do;
                      if reg(p ) ¬=  0 then
                         call EMITRR ("18", 0, reg(p ) );
                      bases(reg(p ) ) =  avail;
                      if inx(p ) ¬=  2 then
                         call EMITRR ("18", 2, inx(p ) );
                      bases(inx(p ) ) =  avail;
                  end;
              /*  Set up monitor request code.  */
              call EMITRX(la,1,0,0,shl(sd−r,2)−32);
              /*  Monitor call.  */
              call EMITRR (balr, brchreg, ioreg );
              type(p ) =  accumulator;
              if r ¬=  0 then
                  call EMITRR ("18", 0, r );
              reg(p ) =  0;
        end;
      else call ERROR (' illegal use of ' || syt(fixl(p ) ));
      call EMITRX ("98", 1, 3, dbr, io_save );
  end;
else
  do;  /* Fetch the variable (all else has failed ).  */
    if sfp ¬=  bytetype then
        do;
            if inx(p ) ¬=  0 then
              do;
                if sfp =  halfword then
                   call EMITRR ("1A", inx(p ), inx(p ) );
                else
                   call EMITRX ("89", inx(p ), 0, 0, 2);
                /*  Shift index for word−type array.  */
                r =  inx(p );
              end;
            else r =  FINDAC;
            if sfp =  halfword then tp =  "48";  else tp =  load;
               call EMITRX(tp,r,inx(p ),sybase(fixl(p ) ),
            sydisp(fixl(p ) ) );
        end;
```

```
                else
                   do;
                      r =  FINDAC;
                      call EMITRR ("1B", r, r); /* clear r */
                         call EMITRX("43",r,inx(p),sybase(fixl(p)),
                      sydisp(fixl(p)));
                      /*  Insert character.  */
                      bases(inx(p)) =  avail;
                   end;
                if sfp =  chrtype then type(p) =  descript;
                   else type(p) =  accumulator;
                reg(p) =  r;
             end;
       end;
    else if tp =  constant then
       do;
          r,reg(p) =  FINDAC;
          /*  Fetch a constant into an accumulator.  */
          if fixv(p) =  0 then call EMITRR("1B", r, r);
          else if fixv(p) <  "1000" & fixv(p) >= 1 then
             call EMITRX(la, r, 0, 0, fixv(p));
             else
                do;
                   call EMITCONSTANT (fixv(p));
                   call EMITRX (load, r, 0, adreg, adrdisp);
                end;
          type(p) =  accumulator;
       end;
    else if tp =  chrtype then
       do;
          r,reg(p) =  FINDAC;
          type(p) =  descript;    t1 =  var(p);
          sd =  length(t1) −  1;
          if sd <  0 then
             call EMITRR("1B",r,r); /*  Clear  reg r, null string.  */
          else
             do;
                call FINDADDRESS (−dsp);
                call EMITDESC(shl(sd,24)+chp); /* Make up a descriptor. */
                do i =  0 to sd;
                   call EMITCHAR(byte(t1, i));
                end;
                call EMITRX (load, r, 0, adreg, adrdisp);
             end;
       end;
```

```
        else if tp ¬= accumulator then if tp ¬= descript then
            call ERROR (' FORCEACCUMULATOR failed ***' , 1);

    end FORCEACCUMULATOR;




FORCEDESCRIPT:
    procedure (p);
        /*  Get a descriptor for the operand p.  */

        declare p fixed;
        call FORCEACCUMULATOR (p);
        if type(p) ¬= descript then
            do;
                call EMITRX (store, reg(p), 0, dbr, strn);
                /*  Store in parameter location for number—to—decimal—string.  */
                bases(reg(p)) = avail;
                call CALLSUB(0,nmbrntry,3,p);
                /*  Assumes number—to—string is in the 1st page.  */
                type(p) = descript;
            end;
    end FORCEDESCRIPT;




GENSTORE:
    procedure (mp, sp);

        /*  Generate type conversion (if necessary) & storage code ——
            also handles output, byte and file on left of replace operator.  */

        declare (mp, sp, sfp, sb, sd) fixed;
        count # store = count # store + 1;
        if type(sp) = special then return;
        sb = sybase(fixl(mp));
        sd = sydisp(fixl(mp));
        sfp = sytype(fixl(mp));
        if sfp = special then
            do;
                if sd = 3 then        /*  Function byte on the left.  */
                    do;
                        call FORCEACCUMULATOR(sp);
                        call EMITRX("42",reg(sp),inx(mp),reg(mp),0);
                    end;
```

```
        else if sd = 7 then
            do;        /* output    */
                call EMITRX("90",1,3,dbr,io_save );
                target_register = 0;
                call FORCEDESCRIPT (sp );
                target_register = -1;
                if reg(sp ) ¬= 0 then call EMITRR ("18", 0, reg(sp ));
                if reg(mp ) = 0 then call EMITRR ("1B", 2, 2);
                else if reg(mp ) ¬= 2 then call EMITRR ("18", 2, reg(mp ));
                bases(reg(mp )) = avail;
                call EMITRX (la, 1, 0, 0, 8);   /* 8 = print code */
                call EMITRR (balr, brchreg, ioreg); /*  Monitor call */
                call EMITRX("98",1,3,dbr,io_save );
            end;
        else if sd = 8 then
            call FILE_PSEUDO_ARRAY(sp,mp,4);
        else call ERROR (' illegal use of '  ||  syt(fixl(mp )));
    end;
else
    do;
        call FORCEACCUMULATOR (sp );
        if type(sp ) ¬= special then
            do;
                if sfp = fixedtype & type(sp )= accumulator | sfp = chrtype then
                    do;
                        if sfp = chrtype then call FORCEDESCRIPT (sp );
                        /* Shift index for word array.  */
                        if inx(mp ) ¬= 0 then call EMITRX ("89", inx(mp ),0,0,2);
                        call EMITRX(store,reg(sp ),inx(mp ),sb,sd );
                    end;
                else if sfp = halfword & type(sp ) = accumulator then
                    do;
                        if inx(mp ) ¬=0 then call EMITRR ("1A",inx(mp ),inx(mp ));
                        call EMITRX ("40", reg(sp ), inx(mp ), sb, sd );
                    end;
                else if sfp = bytetype & type(sp ) = accumulator then
                    call EMITRX("42",reg(sp ),inx(mp ),sb,sd );  /* stc */
                else call ERROR(' assignment needs illegal type conversion' );
            end;
        end;
    bases(inx(mp )) = avail;
    bases(reg(sp )) = avail;
    call MOVESTACKS (sp, mp );

end GENSTORE;
```

STRINGCOMPARE:
   procedure;
      /* Generates the code to compare the strings at *sp* & *mp*. */
      declare (*i, j, k*) **fixed**;
      call *FORCEDESCRIPT*(*sp*); /* Get the descriptor for the second operand.*/
      i = 6 − *reg*(*mp*) − *reg*(*sp*);   /* Find the third register. */
      call *EMITRR* ("18", 0, *reg*(*mp*));   /* We can use 0 for scratch. */
      call *EMITRR* ("17", 0, *reg*(*sp*));   /* Exclusive or to compare. */
      call *EMITRX* ("8A", 0, 0, 0, 24);   /* Check high order 8 bits for zero. */
      if *reg*(*mpp*1) = 6 | *reg*(*mpp*1) = 8 **then**
         do;   /* If we only need to test equality, code is simpler. */
            k = *pp*;
            call *BRANCH* (6, 0);
         end;
      else
         do;
            j = *pp*;
            call *BRANCH* (8, 0);   /* Skip if equal length. */
            call *EMITRR* ("15", *reg*(*mp*), *reg*(*sp*));   /* Set condition code. */
            k = *pp*;   /* save for fixup */
            call *BRANCH* ("F", 0);   /* Branch around string compare code. */
            call *FIXBFW* (*j*, *pp*);
         end;
      if *bases*(*i*) ¬= *avail* **then call** *EMITRR* ("18", 0, *i*);   /* Save reg *i*. */
      call *EMITRR* ("18", *i*, *reg*(*mp*));
      call *EMITRX* ("88", *i*, 0, 0, 24);   /* Scale length for execute command. */
      call *EMITDATAWORD* ("D5000000" + *shl*(*reg*(*mp*), 12));
      call *EMITBYTE* (*shl*(*reg*(*sp*), 4));
      call *EMITBYTE* (0);
      call *FINDADDRESS* (*dp*−6);
      call *EMITRX* ("44", *i*, 0, *adreg*, *adrdisp*);
      if *bases*(*i*) ¬= *avail* **then call** *EMITRR* ("18", *i*, 0);   /* Restore reg *i*. */
      bases(*reg*(*sp*)) = *avail*;
      call *FIXBFW* (*k*, *pp*);   /* Bring other branch in here. */
  end *STRINGCOMPARE*;

SHOULDCOMMUTE:
   procedure bit(1);
     if *type*(*sp*) = *variable* **then**
       if *sytype*(*fixl*(*sp*)) = *fixedtype* **then return** *false*;
     if *type*(*mp*) = *constant* **then return** *true*;
     if *type*(*mp*) = *variable* **then**
       if *sytype*(*fixl*(*mp*)) = *fixedtype* **then return** *true*;
     return *false*;
   end;

ARITHEMIT:
   procedure (*op*);
       /* Emit an instruction for an infix operator -- connects *mp* & *sp*. */

       declare (*op*, *tp*, *t*1) **fixed**;
       count#arith = *count#arith* + 1;
       tp = 0;   /* Remember if commuted. */

       if *commutative*(*op*) **then**
             if *SHOULDCOMMUTE* **then**
                do;
                    tp = *mp*; *mp* = *sp*; *sp* = *tp*;
                end;
       call *FORCEACCUMULATOR* (*mp*); /* Get the left one into an accumulator. */

       /* *fixl*(*sp*) is garbage if *type* ¬= *variable*, we get 0C5 if we test it. */
       *t*1 = "0";
       if *type*(*sp*) = *variable* **then if** *sytype*(*fixl*(*sp*)) = *fixedtype* **then** *t*1 = "1";
       if *type*(*mp*) = *descript* **then**
          do;
              if *op* = *cmprr* **then call** *STRINGCOMPARE*;
              else call *ERROR* (' arithmetic with a string descriptor');
          end;
       else if *t*1 **then**
          do;   /* Operate directly from storage. */
              if *inx*(*sp*) ¬= 0 **then call** *EMITRX* ("89", *inx*(*sp*), 0, 0, 2);
              /* Shift to word indexing. */
              call *EMITRX*(*op*+64,*reg*(*mp*),*inx*(*sp*),*sybase*(*fixl*(*sp*)),
                sydisp(*fixl*(*sp*))));
              /* RR opcode + 64 = RX opcode. */
              bases(*inx*(*sp*)) = *avail*;
          end;
       else if *type*(*sp*) = *constant* **then**
          do;
              call *EMITCONSTANT* (*fixv*(*sp*));
              call *EMITRX* (*op*+64, *reg*(*mp*), 0, *adreg*, *adrdisp*);
          end;
       else
          do;
              call *FORCEACCUMULATOR* (*sp*);
              if *type*(*sp*) ¬= *accumulator* **then**
                 call *ERROR* (' arithmetic between string descriptors' , 1);
              call *EMITRR* (*op*, *reg*(*mp*), *reg*(*sp*));
              bases(*reg*(*sp*)) = *avail*;
          end;

```
if tp ¬= 0 then
    do;  /*  Commuted  */
        sp = mp;   mp = tp;
        call MOVESTACKS (sp, mp);
    end;
        /*  By the algorithm, type(mp) is already accumulator.  */
end ARITHEMIT;


BOOLBRANCH:
    procedure (sp, mp);
        /*  Generate a conditional branch for a do while or an if statement.  */

        declare (sp, mp, t1) fixed;
        t1 = "0";
        if type(sp) = variable then if sytype(fixl(sp)) = bytetype then t1 = "1";
        if stillcond ¬= 0 then
            do;
                bases(reg(sp)) = avail;
                    if pp < "1008" then pp = pp − 12; else pp = pp − 16;
                if control(byte(' E' )) then
                        output = x70 || '                       Back up code emitter' ;
                instruct(bc) = instruct(bc) − 1;   /*  Keep statistics accurate.  */
                instruct(la) = instruct(la) − 2;
                reg(sp) = stillcond;
            end;
        else if t1 then
            do;
                if inx(sp) ¬= 0 then
                    do;
                        call EMITRR("1A",inx(sp),sybase(fixl(sp)));
                        call EMITRX("91",0,1,inx(sp),sydisp(fixl(sp)));
                        /*  Test under mask.  */
                        bases(inx(sp)) = avail;
                    end;
                else call EMITRX("91",0,1,sybase(fixl(sp)),sydisp(fixl(sp)));
                        /*  Test under mask.  */
                reg(sp) = 8;
            end;
        else if type(sp) = constant then
            do;
                if fixv(sp) then
                    do;  fixl(mp) = 0;   return; end;
                else reg(sp) = 15;
            end;
```

```
        else if type(sp) ¬= condition then
            do;
                call FORCEACCUMULATOR (sp);
                call EMITRX ("54", reg(sp), 0, dbr, trueloc);
                        /*  Test least significant bit.  */
                bases(reg(sp)) = avail;
                reg(sp) = 8;
            end;
        fixl(mp) = pp;  /*  Save address for future fixup.  */
        call BRANCH (reg(sp), 0);  /*  reg(sp) has the cc to be tested for.  */
    end BOOLBRANCH;


SET_LIMIT:
    procedure;
        /*  Sets do loop limit for <iteration control>.  */

        if type(mpp1) = constant then
            call EMITCONSTANT(fixv(mpp1));
        else
            do;
                call FORCEACCUMULATOR(mpp1);
                call EMITDATAWORD(0);
                call FINDADDRESS(dp−4);
                call EMITRX(store,reg(mpp1),0,adreg,adrdisp);
                bases(reg(mpp1)) = avail;
            end;
        inx(mp) = adreg;
        fixv(mp) = adrdisp;
    end  SET_LIMIT;


DIVIDE_CODE:
    procedure;
        /*  Generates the code for division.  */

        target_register = 0;
        call FORCEACCUMULATOR(mp);
        target_register = −1;
        if reg(mp) ¬= 0 then
            do;
                call EMITRR("18",0,reg(mp));                /*  lr    0,reg(mp)  */
                bases(reg(mp)) = avail;
                reg(mp) = 0;
            end;
```

```
        if bases(1) = avail then
            do;
                /*  Must "smear"  the sign.  */
                call EMITRX("8E",0,0,0,32);              /*  srda  0,32        */
                bases(1) = accumulator;
                call ARITHEMIT("1D");                    /*  Divide  */
                reg(mp) = 1;                             /*  Result  */
            end;
        else
            call ERROR(' division or mod requires busy register' ,1);

    end  DIVIDE_CODE;


SHIFT_CODE:
    procedure (op);
        /*  Generates code for the built in functions  shl  and  shr.  */
        declare op bit (8);
        if cnt(mp) ¬= 2 then
            call ERROR(' shift requires two arguments' ,0);
        else if type(mpp1) = constant then
            do;
                if op = "89" & fixv(mpp1) = 1 then
                    call EMITRR ("1A", reg(mp), reg(mp));
                else call EMITRX (op, reg(mp), 0, 0, fixv(mpp1));
            end;
        else
            do;
                call FORCEACCUMULATOR(mpp1);
                call EMITRX(op, reg(mp), 0, reg(mpp1), 0);
                bases(reg(mpp1)) = avail;
            end;
        type(mp) = accumulator;
    end  SHIFT_CODE;



    /*                    Builtin functions:                      */


REGISTER_SETUP_CODE:
    procedure;
        call EMITRR("18",pbr,2);  /*  Set base.  */
        call EMITRR("18",dbr,3);
        call EMITRX(store,brchreg,0,dbr,rtnadr);
```

```
    call EMITCONSTANT (256);
    call EMITRX ("5B", 1, 0, adreg, adrdisp );
    limitword = dp;
    call EMITRX (store, 1, 0, dbr, dp );
    call ENTER (' freelimit' , fixedtype, dp, 0);
    call EMITDATAWORD (0);
    basedata = dp;
    dp = dp + 16;
    call EMITRX ("98", 4, dbr−1, dbr, dp );   /*  Load multiple   */
    do i = 4 to dbr−1;
        call EMITRR("1A",i,dbr );
    end;
    dp = dp + shl(dbr−4, 2);
  end REGISTER_SETUP_CODE;


RELOCATE_DESCRIPTORS_CODE:
  procedure;
      /*  Emit code to relocate descriptors to absolute addresses.  */

    call EMITRX(load,0,0,dbr,basedata + 8);
    call EMITRR("1A",0,dbr );
    call EMITRX(store,0,0,dbr,tsa );
    call EMITRX (store, 0, 0, dbr, dp );
    call ENTER (' freebase' , fixedtype, dp, 0);
    call EMITDATAWORD (0);
    call EMITRX("91",0,1,dbr,basedata + 12);
    k = pp;
    call BRANCH (1, 0);
    call EMITRX("96",0,1,dbr,basedata + 12);
    call EMITRX(load,1,0,dbr,basedata );
    call EMITRX (la,sbr,1,dbr,0);
    call EMITRX(load,2,0,dbr,basedata + 4);
    call EMITRR ("1A",2,dbr );
    j = pp;                              /*  Save destination for loop.  */
    call EMITRX (load,3,1,dbr,0);
    call EMITRR ("12",3,3);
    call BRANCH (8,pp + 10);             /*  Escape.  */
    call EMITRR ("1A",3,2);
    call EMITRX (store,3,1,dbr,0);
    call EMITRX (la,1,0,1,4);
    call EMITRX(cmpr,1,0,dbr,basedata + 4);
    call BRANCH (4,j );                  /*  Loop.  */
    call FIXBFW (k,pp );
    call BRANCH (15,0);      /*  Jump to first compiled code.  */
  end RELOCATE_DESCRIPTORS_CODE;
```

CATENATE_CODE:
  procedure;
        /*   Build a catenate subroutine.   */

        catentry = pp;
        call *CHECK_STRING_OVERFLOW*;
        call *EMITRX* (*load*,1,0,*a*1,*a*2);   /*   Load first descriptor.   */
        call *EMITRR* ("18", 3, 1);   /*   Copy into reg 3.   */
        call *EMITRX* ("5E", 3, 0, *b*1, *b*2);   /*   Combine descriptors.   */
        call *EMITRR* ("12", 1, 1);   /*   Test for null first operand.   */
        call *EMITRR* (*bcr*, 8, *brchreg*);   /*   Return with result in reg 3.   */
        call *EMITRR* (*cmprr*, 3, 1);   /*   Is second operand null?   */
        call *EMITRR* (*bcr*, 8, *brchreg*);   /*   Return with result in reg 3.   */
        call *FINDADDRESS* (*maskf*000);
        call *EMITRX* ("54", 3, 0, *adreg*, *adrdisp*);   /*   Mask out address.   */
        call *EMITRX* ("5E", 3, 0, *dbr*, *catconst*);   /*   Correct length of result.   */
        call *FINDADDRESS* (*mover*);   /*   Find move instruction.   */
        *t*1 = *adreg*;   *t*2 = *adrdisp*;
        call *EMITRR* ("18", 0, 3);   /*   Save length in reg 0.   */
        call *FINDADDRESS* (*tsa*);   /*   Find current top of str area.   */
        call *EMITRX* (*load*,2,0,*adreg*,*adrdisp*);
        call *FINDADDRESS* (*strl*);   /*   Last string made in string area.   */
        call *EMITRX* (*cmpr*, 1, 0, *adreg*, *adrdisp*);   /*   Skip move if at top.   */
        j = *pp*;
        call *BRANCH* (6, 0);   /*   Fake move.   */
        call *EMITRX* (*la*, 1, 0, 1, 0);
        call *EMITRR* ("16", 0, 1);
        k = *pp*;
        call *BRANCH* ("F", 0);
        call *FIXBFW* (*j*, *pp*);
        call *EMITRR* ("16",0,2);   /*   "or" in correct address.   */
        call *EMITRX* ("43",3,0,*a*1,*a*2);   /*   Insert length field.   */
        call *EMITRX* ("44",3,0,*t*1,*t*2);   /*   Execute the move.   */
        call *EMITRX* ("41",2,3,2,1);   /*   Update *tsa*.   */
        call *FIXBFW* (*k*, *pp*);
        call *EMITRX* (*load*,1,0,*b*1,*b*2);   /*   Load second descriptor.   */
        call *EMITRX* ("43", 3,0,*b*1,*b*2);   /*   Insert length field.   */
        call *EMITRX* ("44",3,0,*t*1,*t*2);   /*   Execute the move.   */
        call *EMITRX* ("41",2,3,2,1);   /*   Update *tsa*.   */
        call *EMITRX* (*store*, 0, 0, *adreg*, *adrdisp*);   /*   Store into *strl*.   */
        call *FINDADDRESS* (*tsa*);
        call *EMITRX* (*store*,2,0,*adreg*,*adrdisp*);   /*   Save top of string area.   */
        call *EMITRR* ("18", 3, 0);   /*   Result to reg 3.   */
        call *EMITRR* (*bcr*, 15, *brchreg*);   /*   Return.   */
    end *CATENATE_CODE*;

CONVERT_CODE:
   procedure;

   /*   The number−to−string conversion subroutine.   */

   nmbrntry = pp;
   call *CHECK_STRING_OVERFLOW*;   /*   Call *compactify*.   */
   call *EMITRX* (*load*, 3,0, *dbr, strn*);
   call *EMITRR* ("10",3,3);   /*   Set positive for convert.   */
   call *EMITRX* (*load*, 1,0,*dbr,tsa*);   /*   Free some string area.   */
   call *EMITRX*   (*la*,1,0,1,11);   /*   11 is the maximum number of digits
                                                             in a converted 32 bit integer.   */
   call *EMITRX* (*store*,1,0,*dbr,tsa*);
   call *EMITRX* (*la*,0,0,0,10);   /*   Base 10 for division.   */
   i = pp;
   call *EMITRR* ("06",1,0);   /*   Count the digit.   */
   call *EMITRR* ("1B",2,2);   /*   Clear register 2.   */
   call *EMITRR* ("1D",2,0);   /*   Divide by 10.   */
   call *EMITRX* (*la*,2,0,2,*byte*(' 0'));   /*   Add in the EBCDIC code.   */
   call *EMITRX* ("42",2,0,1,0);
   call *EMITRR* ("12",3,3);   /*   Test for zero.   */
   call *BRANCH* (6,*i*);   /*   Get next digit.   */
   call *EMITRX* (*load*,3,0,*dbr,strn*);
   call *EMITRR* ("12",3,3);   /*   Test for negative.   */

   'i = pp;
   call *BRANCH* (10,0);
   call *EMITRX* (*la*,2,0,0,*byte*(' −'));   /*   Minus sign.   */
   call *EMITRR* ("06",1,0);
   call *EMITRX* ("42",2,0,1,0);
   call *FIXBFW* (*i,pp*);
   call *EMITRX* (*load*,3,0,*dbr,tsa*);   /*   Make up result descriptor.   */
   call *EMITRR* ("1B",3,1);
   call *EMITRR* ("06",3,0);
   call *EMITRX* ("89",3,0,0,24);   /*   Shift length field left.   */
   call *EMITRR* ("1A",3,1);   /*   Add in address.   */
   call *FINDADDRESS* (*strl*);   /*   Update pointer to newest string.*/
   call *EMITRX* (*store*, 3, 0, *adreg, adrdisp*);
   call *EMITRR* (*bcr*,15,*brchreg*);   /*   Return.   */
   call *FIXBFW* (*catentry*−4, *pp*);

end *CONVERT_CODE*;

/*   Time and date: */

PRINT_TIME:
```
  procedure (message, t);
    declare message character, t fixed;
    message = message || t/360000 || ':' || t mod 360000 / 6000 || ':'
        || t mod 6000 / 100 || '.';
    t = t mod 100;  /* Decimal fraction. */
    if t < 10 then message = message || '0';
    output = message || t || '.';
  end PRINT_TIME;
```

PRINT_DATE_AND_TIME:
```
  procedure (message, d, t);
    declare message character, (d, t, year, day, m) fixed;
    declare month(11) character initial (' January', ' February', ' March',
        ' April', ' May', ' June', ' July', ' August', ' September', ' October',
        ' November', ' December' ),
      days(12) fixed initial (0, 31, 60, 91, 121, 152, 182, 213, 244, 274,
        305, 335, 366);
    year = d/1000 + 1900;
    day = d mod 1000;
    if (year & "3") ¬= 0 then if day > 59 then day = day + 1;/* ¬ leap year*/
    m = 1;
    do while day > days(m);  m = m + 1;  end;
    call PRINT_TIME(message || month(m-1) || x1 || day-days(m-1) || ','
        || year || '.  clock time = ', t);
  end PRINT_DATE_AND_TIME;
```

```
/*                           Initialization:                           */
```

INITIALIZATION:
```
  procedure;
    eject_page;
    call PRINT_DATE_AND_TIME (' XPL Compilation − "This Installation" −
    XCOM    III version of ', date_of_generation, time_of_generation );
    double_space;
    call PRINT_DATE_AND_TIME (' Today is ', date, time );
    double_space;
    do i = 1 to nt;
      s = v(i);
      if s = '<number>' then number = i;  else
      if s = '<identifier>' then ident = i;  else
      if s = '<string>' then string = i;  else
      if s = '/' then divide = i;  else
```

```
        if s = '_|_' then eofile = i;  else
        if s = 'declare' then stopit(i) = true;  else
        if s = 'procedure' then stopit(i) = true;   else
        if s = 'end' then stopit(i) = true;  else
        if s = 'do' then stopit(i) = true;  else
        if s = ';' then stopit(i) = true;  else
        if s = '|' then orsymbol = i; else
        if s = '||' then concatenate = i; else
        ;
    end;
    if ident = nt then reserved_limit = length(v(nt−1));
    else reserved_limit = length(v(nt));
    v(eofile) = 'eof';
    stopit(eofile) = true;
    chartype(byte(' ')) = 1;
    chartype(byte('''')) = 2;
    chartype(byte('"')) = 3;
    do i = 0 to 255;
        not_letter_or_digit(i) = true;
    end;
    do i = 0 to length(alphabet) − 1;
        j = byte(alphabet, i);
        tx(j) = i;
        not_letter_or_digit(j) = false;
        chartype(j) = 4;
    end;
    do i = 0 to 9;
        j = byte('0123456789', i);
        not_letter_or_digit(j) = false;
        chartype(j) = 5;
    end;
    do i = v_index(0) to v_index(1) − 1;
        j = byte(v(i));
        tx(j) = i;
        chartype(j) = 7;
    end;
    chartype(byte('|')) = 8;
    chartype(byte('/')) = 6;
    commutative("14") = true;
    commutative("16") = true;
    commutative("1A") = true;
    returned_type = fixedtype;              /*  Default return type.  */

    lastbase = dbr;  bases(lastbase) = 0;
    pp = 60;  /*  Offset code for control  record  (see LOADER).  */
```

```
dp = 0;      /*  Data origin.  */
dsp = 4;
chp = 1;
pplim, dplim, chplim = diskbytes;
    /*  Upper bound for emitter arrays.  */
pporg, dporg, chporg = 0;
    /*  Lower bound for emitter arrays.  */
curcblk, curdblk, cursblk = 0;
    /*  Current block occupying emitter arrays.  */
shortcfix, shortdfix, longcfix, longdfix = 0;
    /*  Statistical counters for fixups.  */
fcp = 0;   /*  Pointer into fixup array.  */
                /*  Initialize symbol table variables.  */
ndecsy ,procmark = 1;   parct = 0;
/*  Integers for branch addressing.  */
do i = 0 to programsize;   call EMITDATAWORD(shl(i,12) );  end;
```

```
/*  Warning, the following section of INITIALIZATION depends on
      the initialization of the builtin function and pseudo
      variable names and attributes in the symbol table arrays.
*/
sydisp(2) = dp;                              /*  monitor_link              */
dp = dp + 16;   /*  Reserve 4 words for communication with monitor.  */
maskf000 = dp;   call EMITDATAWORD("FF000000" );
io_save = dp;   dp = dp + 12;   /*  Register save for monitor calls.  */
```

```
/*  Set up the move template in data area.  */
```

```
mover = dp;
call EMITBYTE("D2" );   /* mvc */
call EMITBYTE(0);
call EMITBYTE("20" );
call EMITBYTE(0);
call EMITBYTE("10" );
call EMITBYTE(0);
call EMITDATAWORD(0);   tsa = dp−4;
sydisp(3) = dp;                              /*  time_of_generation        */
call EMITDATAWORD(time );
sydisp(4) =  dp;                             /*  date_of_generation        */
call EMITDATAWORD(date );
sydisp(5) = 0;                               /*  coreword                  */
sydisp(6) = 0;                               /*  corebyte                  */
sydisp(7) = tsa;                             /*  freepoint                 */
sydisp(8) = dsp;                             /*  descriptor                */
sydisp(9) = dp;                              /*  ndescript                 */
```

```
descl = dp;
call EMITDATAWORD (0);
a1, b1 = sbr;        /*   a1,a2 is the first parameter to ||,   */
a2 = dsp;            /*   b1,b2 is the second.   */
call EMITDESC (0);
b2 = dsp;
call EMITDESC (0);
strl = −dsp;  call EMITDESC(0);
strn = dp;  call EMITDATAWORD(0);
trueloc = dp;  call EMITDATAWORD(true );
comploc = dp;  call EMITDATAWORD("FFFFFFFF" );
catconst = dp;  call EMITDATAWORD ("1000000" );
rtnadr = dp;  call EMITDATAWORD (0);
ndecsy = 28;    /*   One beyond last function name.   */

call EMITDATAWORD (0);
sydisp(ndecsy ) = dp−4;              /*   compactify              */
string_recover = ndecsy;
call CLEARREGS;


/*          Emit code for builtin functions.                      */


call REGISTER_SETUP_CODE;

call RELOCATE_DESCRIPTORS_CODE;

call CATENATE_CODE;

call CONVERT_CODE;


mainloc = pp;
call CLEARREGS;
/*   First set up global variables controlling SCAN, then call it.   */
cp = 0;   text_limit = −1;
text, current_procedure = ' ' ;
call SCAN;


/*   Initialize the parse stack.   */
sp = 1;   parse_stack(sp ) = eofile;

end INITIALIZATION;
```

```
/*                    Symbol and statistics printout.                  */

SYMBOLDUMP:
  procedure;
      /* Lists the symbols in the procedure that has just been
         compiled if $S or $D is enabled
         (maintain parity on $S and $D ).
      */
      declare (lpm, i, j, k, l, m ) fixed;
      declare (buffer, blanks ) character;
      declare exchanges bit(1), sytsort(sytsize ) bit(16);

   OUTLINE:
      procedure (name, p ) character;
         declare name character, (p, b, d ) fixed;
         if sytype(p ) = labeltype | sytype(p ) = char_proc_type then
            do;
                b = pbr;
                d = shl(sybase(p ), 12) + sydisp(p );
            end;
         else
            do;
                b = sybase(p );
                d = sydisp(p );
            end;

         buffer = PAD (d || '( ' || b || ' ),', 11);
         return name || ': ' || typename(sytype(p )) || ' at ' || buffer ||
             ' declared on line ' || declared_on_line(p ) ||
             ' and referenced ' || sytco(p ) || ' times.' ;
      end  OUTLINE;


      if procmark <= ndecsy then
         do;
             double_space;
             output = 'Symbol  table   dump:' ;
             double_space;
             lpm = length(syt(procmark ) );
             l = 15;
             do i = procmark to ndecsy;
                if length(syt(i ) ) > l then
                    l = length(syt(i ) );
             end;
             if l > 70 then l = 70;
```

```
            blanks =  substr(x70, 0, l);

        do  i =  procmark to ndecsy;
            sytsort(i) =  i;
            k =  length(syt(i));
            if  k >  0 then
                if  k <  l then
                    do;
                        buffer =  substr(blanks,k);
                        syt(i) =  syt(i) || buffer;
                    end;
                else
                    do;
                        buffer =  substr (syt(i), 0, l);
                        syt(i) =  buffer;
                    end;
        end;


        exchanges =  true;
        k =  ndecsy − procmark;


        do while exchanges;
            exchanges =  false;
            do j =  0 to  k − 1;
                i =  ndecsy − j;
                l =  i − 1;
                if  syt(sytsort(l)) >  syt(sytsort(i)) then
                    do;
                        m =  sytsort(i);
                        sytsort(i) =  sytsort(l);
                        sytsort(l) =  m;
                        exchanges =  true;
                        k =  j;              /*  Record last swap.  */
                    end;
            end;
        end;


        i =  procmark;
        do while length(syt(sytsort(i))) =  0;
            i =  i + 1;                      /*  Ignore null names.  */
        end;
```

```
        do i = i to ndecsy;
           k = sytsort(i);
           output = OUTLINE(syt(k), k);

           k = k + 1;
           do while (length(syt(k)) = 0) & (k <= ndecsy);
              j = k - sytsort(i);
              output =
                 OUTLINE('   parameter  ' || j || substr(blanks, 14), k);
              k = k + 1;
           end;

        end;

        buffer = substr(syt(procmark), 0 , lpm);
        syt(procmark) = buffer;
        eject_page;
     end;

  end  SYMBOLDUMP;



DUMPIT:
  procedure;      /*  Dump out the compiled code & data areas.  */
     call SYMBOLDUMP;
     output = ' Macro definitions:' ;
     double_space;
     do i = 0 to top_macro;
        output = PAD(macro_name(i), 20) || '  literally: ' || macro_text(i);
     end;
     double_space;
     /*  Put out the entry count for important procedures.  */

     output = ' idcompares          = ' || idcompares;
     output = ' Symbol table size = ' || maxndecsy;
     output = ' Macro definitions = ' || top_macro + 1;
     output = ' Stacking decisions= ' || count#stack;
     output = ' SCAN              = ' || count#scan;
     output = ' EMITRR            = ' || count#rr;
     output = ' EMITRX            = ' || count#rx;
     output = ' FORCEACCUMULATOR  = ' || count#force;
     output = ' ARITHEMIT         = ' || count#arith;
     output = ' GENSTORE          = ' || count#store;
     output = ' FIXBFW            = ' || count#fixbfw;
```

```
output =  ' Fix data word       = '  ||  count # fixd;
output =  ' FIXCHW              = '  ||  count # fixchw;
output =  ' GETDATA             = '  ||  count # getd;
output =  ' GETCODE             = '  ||  count # getc;
output =  ' FINDADDRESS         = '  ||  count # find;
output =  ' Short code fixups = '  ||  shortcfix;
output =  ' Long code fixups  = '  ||  longcfix;
output =  ' Short data fixups = '  ||  shortdfix;
output =  ' Long data fixups  = '  ||  longdfix;
output =  ' Free string area  = '  ||  freelimit − freebase;
double_space;
output =  ' Register values (relative to R11):' ;

do i =  4 to 13;
    output =  'R'  ||  i ||  ' = '  ||  bases(i);
end;

output =  ' '; output =  ' Instruction frequencies:' ;
output =  ' ';

do i =  0 to 255;
    if instruct(i) ¬ =  0 then
        output =  substr(opnames,oper(i),4) ||  x4 ||  instruct(i);
end;

end DUMPIT;




STACK_DUMP:
    procedure;

        declare line character;
        line =  ' Partial parse to this point is: ' ;
        do i =  2 to sp;
            if length(line) >  105 then
                do;
                    output =  line;
                    line =  x4;
                end;
            line =  line ||  x1 ||  v(parse_stack(i) );
        end;
        output =  line;

    end STACK_DUMP;
```

```
/*                    The synthesis algorithm:                          */


SYNTHESIZE:
procedure(production_number);
   declare production_number fixed;


   /*  One statement for each production of the grammar.  */


do case production_number;
     ;        /*  Case 0 is a dummy, because we number productions from 1.  */

  /*  <program>   ::=  <statement list>      */
     do;   /*  Final code for submonitor interface & setup.  */
        if mp ¬= 2 then  /*  We didn' t get here legitimately.  */
           do;
                call ERROR (' eof at invalid point' , 1);
                call STACK_DUMP;
           end;
        do i = 1 to ndecsy;
           if sytype(i) = forwardtype | sytype(i) = forwardcall then
            if sytco(i) > 0 then
                call ERROR (' Undefined label or procedure: '  ||  syt(i), 1);
        end;
        call EMITRR ("1B", 3, 3);   /*  Return code of zero.  */
        call EMITRX(load, brchreg, 0, dbr, rtnadr);
        call EMITRR(bcr, "F", brchreg);  /*  Set up base registers.  */
        bases(sbr) = (dp + 3) & "FFFFFC";
        do i = 4 to dbr−1;
           call FIXWHOLEDATAWORD(basedata + shl(i,2), bases(i));
        end;
        call FIXWHOLEDATAWORD(descl, shr(dsp,2)−1);
        compiling = false;
     end;


  /*  <statement list> ::= <statement>      */
   ;
  /*  <statement list> ::= <statement list> <statement>       */
   ;
  /*  <statement> ::= <basic statement>      */
     do;
        call CLEARREGS;
        statement_count = statement_count + 1;
     end;
```

```
/*  < statement>  ::=  < if statement>       */
   call CLEARREGS;

/*  < basic statement>  ::=  < assignment> ;     */
   ;
/*  < basic statement>  ::=  < group> ;     */
   ;
/*  < basic statement>  ::=  < procedure definition> ;     */
   ;
/*  < basic statement>  ::=  < return statement> ;     */
   ;
/*  < basic statement>  ::=  < call statement> ;     */
   ;
/*  < basic statement>  ::=  < go to statement> ;     */
   ;
/*  < basic statement>  ::=  < declaration statement> ;     */
   ;

/*  < basic statement>  ::=  ;     */
   ;
/*  < basic statement>  ::=  < label definition>  < basic statement>     */
   ;
/*  < if statement>  ::=  < if clause>  < statement>     */
   call FIXBFW(fixl(mp), pp ); /* Fix the escape branch now that stmt is done.*/

/*  < if statement>  ::=  < if clause>  < true part>  < statement>     */
   do;  /* There are two branches to be filled in with addresses here.  */
      call FIXBFW(fixl(mpp1), pp ); /*  Escape from < true part>.  */
      call FIXBFW(fixl(mp ), fixv(mpp1) ); /*  Branch around < true part>.  */
   end;

/*  < if statement>  ::=  < label definition>  < if statement>     */
   ;

/*  < if clause>  ::=  if < expression>  then     */
   call BOOLBRANCH(mpp1, mp ); /*  Branch on false over < true part>.  */



   /*  < true part>  ::=  < basic statement>  else     */
   do;  /*  Save the program pointer & emit the conditional branch.  */
      fixl(mp ) = pp;
      call BRANCH("F", 0); /*  "F" means unconditional branch.  */
      fixv(mp ) = pp;
   end;
```

```
/*  <group> ::= <group head> <ending>       */
   do;   /*  Branch back to loop & fix escape jump.   */
      if inx(mp) = 1 | inx(mp) = 2 then
         do;  /*  Step or while loop fix up.   */
            call BRANCH("F", ppsave(mp) );
            call FIXBFW(fixl(mp), pp );
         end;
      else if   inx(mp) = 3 then
         do;   /*  Case group.  */
            /*  Justify to word boundary.   */
            dp = (dp + 3) & "FFFFFC";
            call FINDADDRESS(dp );
            call FIXCHW(fixl(mp)+2, shl(adreg,4)+shr(adrdisp,8), adrdisp );
            do i = ppsave(mp) to casep−1; call EMITDATAWORD(casestack(i)); end;
            casep = ppsave(mp) − 1;
            call FIXBFW(fixv(mp), pp );
         end;
      if length(var(sp)) > 0 then if var(mp−1) ¬= var(sp) then
         call ERROR (' end '  ||  var(sp)  ||  '   must match label on group' , 0);
   end;


/*  <group head> ::= do ;     */
   inx(mp) = 0;


/*  <group head> ::= do <step definition> ;     */
   do;
      call MOVESTACKS(mpp1, mp );
      inx(mp) = 1;  /*  1 denotes step.  */
   end;


/*  <group head> ::= do <while clause> ;     */
   do;
      ppsave(mp) = ppsave(mpp1);
      fixl(mp) = fixl(mpp1);
      inx(mp) = 2;  /*  2 denotes while */
   end;


/*  <group head> ::= do <case selector> ;     */
   do;
      call MOVESTACKS(mpp1, mp );
      inx(mp) = 3;  /*  3 denotes case  */
      information = information || ' Case 0.' ;
   end;
```

```
/*  <group head> ::= <group head> <statement>      */
  if  inx(mp) = 3 then
      do;  /*  Case group, must record statement addresses.  */
          call BRANCH ("F", fixv(mp));
      if casep >= caselimit then call ERROR (' too many cases' , 1);
          else casep = casep + 1;  casestack(casep) = pp;
      if bcd ¬= ' end' then
          information = information || 'Case '||casep–ppsave(mp)||period;
      end;


/* < step definition> ::=< variable>< replace>< expression>< iteration control>
        */
  do;  /*  Emit code for stepping do loops.  */
      call FORCEACCUMULATOR(mp+2);
      if inx(mp) ¬ = 0 then
          call ERROR (' subscripted do variable' , 0);
      stepk = pp;
      call BRANCH("F", 0);
      ppsave(mp) = pp;
      l = fixl(mp);
      adreg = sybase(l);
      adrdisp = sydisp(l);
      if sytype(l) = bytetype then
          do;
              call EMITRR("1B", reg(mp+2), reg(mp+2));
              call EMITRX ("43", reg(mp+2), 0, adreg, adrdisp);
          end;
      else if sytype(l) = halfword then
          call EMITRX ("48", reg(mp+2), 0, adreg, adrdisp);
      else
          call EMITRX (load, reg(mp+2), 0, adreg, adrdisp);
      call EMITRX ("5A", reg(mp+2), 0, reg(mp+3), fixl(mp+3));
      call FIXBFW(stepk, pp);
      if sytype(l) = bytetype then i =  "42";
      else if sytype(l) = halfword then i =  "40";
      else i = store;
      call EMITRX (i, reg(mp+2), 0, adreg, adrdisp);
      call EMITRX (cmpr, reg(mp+2), 0, inx(mp+3), fixv(mp+3));
      fixl(mp) = pp;
      call BRANCH("2", 0);
      bases(inx(mp)) = avail;
      bases(reg(mp+2)) = avail;
  end;
```

```
/*  <iteration control>  ::=  to <expression>       */
  do;
     reg(mp) =  dbr;
     fixl(mp) =  trueloc;   /*  Point at the constant one for step.   */
     call SET_LIMIT;
  end;


/*  <iteration control>  ::=  to <expression>  by <expression>       */
  do;
     if type(sp) =  constant then call EMITCONSTANT (fixv(sp));
     else
        do;
           call FORCEACCUMULATOR (sp);
           call EMITDATAWORD (0);
           call FINDADDRESS (dp−4);
           call EMITRX (store, reg(sp), 0, adreg, adrdisp);
           bases(reg(sp)) =  avail;
        end;
     reg(mp) =  adreg;
     fixl(mp) =  adrdisp;
     call SET_LIMIT;
  end;



/*  <while clause>  ::=  while <expression>       */
  call BOOLBRANCH(sp, mp);


/*  <case selector>  ::=  case <expression>       */
  do;
     call FORCEACCUMULATOR(sp);
     call EMITRX("89", reg(sp), 0, 0, 2);
     fixl(mp) =  pp;
     call EMITRX(load, reg(sp), reg(sp), 0, 0);
     call EMITRX(bc, "F", reg(sp), pbr, 0);
     bases(reg(sp)) =  avail;
     fixv(mp) =  pp;
     call BRANCH("F", 0);
     if casep >= caselimit then call ERROR (' too many cases' , 1);
     else casep =  casep + 1;
     casestack(casep) =  pp;
     ppsave(mp) =  casep;
  end;
```

```
/* <procedure definition>::=<procedure head><statement list><ending>      */
do; /*   Procedure is defined, restore symbol table.   */
   if length(var(sp)) > 0 then
      if substr(current_procedure, 1) ¬= var(sp) then
         call ERROR('procedure' || current_procedure || 'closed by end '||
            var(sp), 0);
   if control(byte(' S' )) then call SYMBOLDUMP;
   do i = procmark to ndecsy;
      if sytype(i) = forwardtype | sytype(i) = forwardcall then
      if sytco(i) > 0 then
         call ERROR (' undefined label or procedure: '  || syt(i), 1);
   end;

   do i = procmark + parct to  ndecsy + 1;
      syt(i) = x1;
   end;

   ndecsy = procmark + parct − 1;
   /*  Parameter address must be saved but names discarded.  */
   do i = procmark to ndecsy;
      if sytype(i) = 0 then
         do;
            call ERROR(' undeclared parameter:' || syt(i));
            sytype(i) = fixedtype;
            call EMITDATAWORD(0);
            call FINDADDRESS(dp−4);
            sybase(i) =  adreg;
            sydisp(i) =  adrdisp;
         end;
      syt(i) = ' ';
   end;

   current_procedure =  var(mp);
   procmark =  fixv(mp);   parct =  cnt(mp);
   returned_type =  type(mp) ;
   /*  Emit a gratuitous return.  */
   call FINDADDRESS(rtnadr);
   call EMITRX(load, brchreg, 0, adreg, adrdisp);
   call EMITRR(bcr, "F", brchreg);
   rtnadr =  ppsave(mp);
   call FIXBFW(fixl(mp), pp); /* Complete jump around procedure definition */

end;
```

```
/*  <procedure head> ::= <procedure name> ;    */
  do;  /*  Must point at first parameter even if nonexistent.  */
     /*  Save old parameter count.  */
     cnt(mp) = parct; parct = 0;
     /*  Save old procedure mark in symbol table.  */
     fixv(mp) = procmark;  procmark = ndecsy + 1;
     type(mp) = returned_type;
     returned_type = 0;
     call PROC_START;
  end;


/*  <procedure head> ::= <procedure name> <type> ;.   */
  do;
     cnt(mp) = parct;
     parct = 0;
     fixv(mp) = procmark;
     procmark = ndecsy + 1;
     type(mp) = returned_type;
     returned_type = type(sp−1);
     if returned_type = chrtype then
        sytype(fixl(mp)) = char_proc_type ;
     call PROC_START;
  end;

/*  <procedure head> ::= <procedure name> <parameter list> ;    */
  do;
     cnt(mp) = cnt(mpp1);  /* Save parameter count.  */
     fixv(mp) = fixv(mpp1);
     type(mp) = returned_type;
     returned_type = 0;
     call PROC_START;
  end;


/* <procedure head> ::= <procedure name> <parameter list> <type> ; */
  do;
     cnt(mp) = cnt(mpp1);
     fixv(mp) = fixv(mpp1);
     type(mp) = returned_type;
     returned_type = type(sp−1);
     if returned_type = chrtype then
        sytype(fixl(mp)) = char_proc_type ;
     call PROC_START;
  end;
```

```
/*  <procedure name>  ::=  <label definition>  procedure     */
   do;
       s =  current_procedure;
       current_procedure =  x1  ||  var(mp );
       var(mp ) =  s;
   end;


/*  <parameter list>  ::=  <parameter head>  <identifier>  )     */
   do;
       parct =  parct +  1;
       call  ENTER  (var(mpp1), 0, 0, 0);
   end;


/*  <parameter head>  ::=  (    */
   do;  /*  Point at the first parameter for symbol table.  */
       fixv(mp ) =  procmark;  procmark =  ndecsy +  1;
       cnt(mp ) =  parct;
       parct =  0;
   end;


/*  <parameter head>  ::=  <parameter head>  <identifier>  ,     */
   do;
       parct =  parct +  1;
       call  ENTER  (var(mpp1), 0, 0, 0);
   end;


/*  <ending>  ::=  end     */
   var(mp ) =  ' ';


/*  <ending>  ::=  end  <identifier>       */
   var(mp ) =  var(sp );


/*  <ending>  ::=  <label definition>  <ending>      */
   var(mp ) =  var(sp );


/*  <label definition>  ::=  <identifier>  :     */
   fixl(mp ) =  ENTER  (var(mp ), labeltype, pp, fixl(mp ) );



/*  <return statement>  ::=  return     */
   do;  /*  emit a return branch */
       call  FINDADDRESS(rtnadr );
       call  EMITRX(load,  brchreg,0,adreg,adrdisp );
       call  EMITRR(bcr,"F",brchreg );
   end;
```

```
/*   <return statement>  ::=  return  <expression>        */
   do;  /*  Emit a return branch and pass value in register 3.  */
      /* now force it into register 3 */
      target_register =  3;
      if returned_type  =  chrtype then
         call FORCEDESCRIPT(mpp1);
      else
         call FORCEACCUMULATOR(mpp1);
      target_register =  −1;
      if reg(mpp1) ¬ =  3 then call  EMITRR("18",3,reg(mpp1) );
      call FINDADDRESS(rtnadr );
      call EMITRX(load, brchreg, 0, adreg, adrdisp );
      call EMITRR(bcr, "F", brchreg );
      call CLEARREGS;
   end;


/*   <call statement>  ::=  call  <variable>        */
   do;
      call FORCEACCUMULATOR(sp );
      call CLEARREGS;
   end;


/*   <go to statement>  ::=  <go to>  <identifier>        */
   do;
      call ID_LOOKUP(sp );
      j =  fixl(sp );
      if j <  0 then              /*  1st ocurrence of the label.  */
         do;
            call EMITDATAWORD(0);        /*  Space for fixup.  */
            j =  ENTER (var(sp ), forwardtype, dp−4, fixl(sp ) );
            sytco(j ) =  1;
         end;
      if sytype(j ) =  labeltype then
         call BRANCH_BD("F",sybase(j ),sydisp(j ) );
      else if sytype(j ) =  forwardtype then
         do;
            call EMITRX(load,brchreg,0,sybase(j ),sydisp(j ) );
            call EMITRX(bc,"F",brchreg,pbr,0);
         end;
      else
         do;
            call ERROR(' target of go to is not a label' ,0);
            call EMITRX(bc,"F",0,sybase(j ),sydisp(j ) );
         end;
   end;
```

```
/*  < go to>  ::=  go to      */
   ;
/*  < go to>  ::=  goto       */
   ;
/*  < declaration statement>  ::=  declare < declaration element>      */
   ;

/* < declaration statement> ::= < declaration  statement> , < declaration element>
        */
   ;

/*  < declaration element>  ::=  < type declaration>      */
  do;
     if type(mp ) =  chrtype then
        dsp =  newdsp ;
     else
        do;
           dp =  newdp ;
           call CHECKBASES ;
        end;
  end;


/*   < declaration element>  ::=  < identifier> literally < string>       */
     ·if top_macro >= macro_limit then
        call ERROR(' macro table overflow' ,1);
      else
        do;
           top_macro = top_macro + 1;
           i = length(var(mp ) );
           j = macro_index(i );
           do l = 1 to top_macro − j;
              k = top_macro − l;
              macro_name(k+1) = macro_name(k );
              macro_text(k+1) = macro_text(k );
           end;
           macro_name(j ) = var(mp );
           macro_text(j ) = var(sp );
           do j = i to 255;
              macro_index(j ) = macro_index(j )+1;
           end;
        end;

/*  < type declaration>  ::=  < identifier specification> < type>      */
  call TDECLARE(0);
```

```
/*  <type declaration>  ::=  <bound head> <number>  ) <type>      */
    call  TDECLARE(fixv(mpp1) );


/*  <type declaration>  ::=  <type declaration>  <initial list>      */
    ;


/*  <type>  ::=  fixed      */
  type(mp ) =  fixedtype ;


/*  <type>  ::=  character      */
  type(mp ) =  chrtype ;


/*  <type>  ::=  label      */
  type(mp ) =  forwardtype ;


/*  <type>  ::=  <bit head>  <number>  )      */
    if  fixv(mpp1) <=  8  then  type(mp ) =  bytetype;
    else if  fixv(mpp1) <=  16  then  type(mp ) =  halfword;
    else if  fixv(mpp1) <=  32  then  type(mp ) =  fixedtype;
    else  type(mp ) =  chrtype;


/*  <bit head>  ::=  bit (     */
    ;


/*  <bound head>  ::=  <identifier specification>  (     */
    ;


/*  <identifier specification>  ::=  <identifier>      */
  do;
    inx(mp ) =  1;
    i =  fixl(mp );
    fixl(mp ) =  casep;
    if  casep >=  caselimit  then
       call  ERROR(dclrm,1);
    else
       casep =  casep +  1;
    casestack(casep ) =  ENTER (var(mp ), 0, 0, i );
  end;
```

```
/*  < identifier specification>  ::=  < identifier list> < identifier>  )      */
  do;
      inx(mp ) =  inx(mp ) +  1;
      if casep >=  caselimit then
          call ERROR(dclrm, 1);
      else
          casep =  casep +  1;
      casestack(casep ) =  ENTER  (var(mpp1), 0, 0, fixl(mpp1) );
  end;

/*  < identifier list>  ::=  (      */
  do;
      inx(mp ) =  0;
      fixl(mp ) =  casep;
  end;

/*  < identifier list>  ::=  < identifier list> < identifier> ,       */
  do;
      inx(mp ) =  inx(mp ) +  1;
      if casep >=  caselimit then
          call ERROR(dclrm, 1);
      else
          casep =  casep +  1;
      casestack(casep ) =  ENTER  (var(mpp1), 0, 0, fixl(mpp1) );
  end;

/*  < initial list>  ::=  < initial head> < constant>  )      */
  call SETINIT ;

/*  < initial head>  ::=  initial (     */
  if inx(mp−1) =  1 then
      itype =  type(mp−1);       /*  Information from  < type declaration>.  */
  else
      do;
          call ERROR(' initial may not be used with identifier list' ,0);
          itype =  0;
      end;


/*  < initial head>  ::=  < initial head> < constant> ,       */
  call SETINIT;

/*  < assignment>  ::=  < variable> < replace> < expression>       */
  call GENSTORE(mp,sp );
```

```
/*  <assignment> ::= <left part> <assignment>      */
   call GENSTORE(mp,sp);

/*  <replace> ::= =      */
   ;

/*  <left part> ::= <variable> ,      */
   ;

/*  <expression> ::= <logical factor>      */
     ;
/*  <expression> ::= <expression> | <logical factor>      */
   /* "16" = or, "56" = o */
   call ARITHEMIT("16");

/*  <logical factor> ::= <logical secondary>      */
     ;

/*  <logical factor> ::= <logical factor> & <logical secondary>      */
   /* "14" = nr, "54" = n */
   call ARITHEMIT("14");

/*  <logical secondary> ::= <logical primary>      */
   if type(mp) = condition then call CONDTOREG(mp, reg(mp));

/*  <logical secondary> ::= ¬ <logical primary>      */
   do;
      call MOVESTACKS (sp, mp);
      if type(mp) = condition then
         call CONDTOREG (mp, "E" − reg(mp));
      else
         do;
            call FORCEACCUMULATOR (mp);
            /* "57" = exclusive or */
            call EMITRX ("57", reg(mp), 0, dbr, comploc);
         end;
   end;

/*  <logical primary> ::= <string expression>      */
     ;

   /*              condition codes      mask
          0  operands equal    bit 8
          1  first operand lo bit 9
          2  first operand hi bit 10                          */
```

```
/* <logical primary>::=<string expression><relation><string expression> */
   do;
       call ARITHEMIT(cmprr);
       bases(reg(mp)) = avail;     reg(mp) = reg(mpp1);
       type(mp) = condition;
   end;

/*  <relation> ::= =     */
   reg(mp) = 6;

/*  <relation> ::= <     */
   reg(mp) = 10;

/*  <relation> ::= >     */
   reg(mp) = 12;

/*  <relation> ::= ¬ =     */
   reg(mp) = 8;

/*  <relation> ::= ¬ <     */
   reg(mp) = 4;

/*  <relation> ::= ¬ >     */
   reg(mp) = 2;

/*  <relation> ::= < =     */
   rcg(mp) - 2;

/*  <relation> ::= > =     */
   reg(mp) = 4;

/*  <string expression> ::= <arithmetic expression>     */
     ;

/* <string expression>::=<string expression>||<arithmetic expression> */
   do; /*   Catenate two strings.   */
       call FORCEDESCRIPT(mp);
       call EMITRX(store,reg(mp),0,a1,a2);
       bases(reg(mp)) = avail;
       call FORCEDESCRIPT(sp);
       call EMITRX(store,reg(sp),0,b1,b2);
       bases(reg(sp)) = avail;
       call CALLSUB(0,catentry,3,mp);     type(mp) = descript;
       /*   Assume the catenate routine is in the 1st 4096 bytes of program.   */
   end;
```

```
/*  <arithmetic expression>  ::=  <term>      */
    ;
/*  <arithmetic expression>  ::=  <arithmetic expression>  +  <term>      */
    /* "1A" = ar, "5A" = a  */
    call ARITHEMIT("1A");

/*  <arithmetic expression>  ::=  <arithmetic expression>  -  <term>      */
    /* "1B" = sr, "5B" = s */
    call ARITHEMIT("1B");

/*  <arithmetic expression>  ::=  +  <term>      */
    call MOVESTACKS(mpp1,mp);

/*  <arithmetic expression>  ::=  -  <term>      */
  do;
      call MOVESTACKS(mpp1, mp);
      if type(mp) = constant then fixv(mp) = - fixv(mp);
      else
          do;
              call FORCEACCUMULATOR(mp);
              call EMITRR("13", reg(mp), reg(mp));   /* lcr = complement */
          end;
  end;

/*  <term>  ::=  <primary>      */
    ;

/*  <term>  ::=  <term>  *  <primary>      */
  /* "1C" = mr, "5C" = m */
  do;
      call FORCEACCUMULATOR(mp);
      if reg(mp) = 1 then
          do;  /*  Multiply is funny on a System/360--sorry.  */
              reg(mp) = 0;
              call ARITHEMIT("1C");
              reg(mp) = 1;
          end;
      else
          do;
              call FORCEACCUMULATOR(sp);
              if reg(sp) = 1 then
                  do;
                      call EMITRR("1C",0,reg(mp));
                      bases(reg(mp)) = avail;    reg(mp) = 1;
                  end;
```

```
                    else if reg(mp ) + reg(sp ) = 5 then
                        do;   /* operands are in 2 & 3 */
                            call EMITRR("1C",2,2);
                            bases(2) = avail;
                            reg(mp ) = 3;
                        end;
                    else call ERROR (' multiply failed ***' , 1);
                end;
        end;


/*  < term>  ::= < term> / < primary>      */
    call DIVIDE_CODE;
    /*  Divide is even funnier than multiply.  */


/*  < term>  ::= < term> mod < primary>      */
    do;
        call DIVIDE_CODE;
        call EMITRR("18",1,0);                        /*  lr      1,0         */
    end;


/*  < primary>  ::= < constant>      */
        ;

/*  < primary>  ::= < variable>      */
        if fixv(mp ) = 3 then      /*  Finish off the function byte. */
            if cnt(mp ) = 1 then
                do;
                    if type(mp ) = chrtype then
                        do;
                            type(mp ) = constant;
                            fixv(mp ) = byte(var(mp ) );
                        end;
                    else
                        do;
                            i = FINDAC;
                            call EMITRR("1B",i,i );      /*  sr     i,i         */
                            call EMITRX("43",i,0,reg(mp ),0);
                                                         /*  ic                  */
                            bases(reg(mp ) ) = avail;
                            reg(mp ) = i;
                            type(mp ) = accumulator;
                        end;
                end;
```

```
          else if cnt(mp) = 2 then
             do;
                i = inx(mp);
                     call EMITRX("43",i,i,reg(mp),0);
                     bases(reg(mp)) = avail;
                     reg(mp) = i;
                type(mp) = accumulator;
             end;

/*  <primary> ::= ( <expression> )     */.
  call MOVESTACKS(mpp1, mp);




/*  <variable> ::= <identifier>     */
   do;        /*  Find the identifier in the symbol table.  */
     call ID_LOOKUP(mp);
     if fixl(mp) = −1 then
         call UNDECLARED_ID(mp);
   end;




/*  <variable> ::= <subscript head> <expression> )     */
   do;  /*  Either a procedure call or array or builtin function.  */
     cnt(mp) = cnt(mp) + 1;
     i = fixv(mp);

     if i < 6 then
     do case i;

        /*  Case  0.  */

        do;        /* subscript or call */
           call FORCEACCUMULATOR (mpp1);
           if sytype(fixl(mp)) = labeltype |
              sytype(fixl(mp)) = char_proc_type   then
              call STUFF_PARAMETER;
           else
              do;        /*  Subscripted variable.  */
                 if cnt(mp) > 1 then
                    call ERROR (' multiple subscripts not allowed' , 0);
                 inx(mp) = reg(mpp1);
              end;
        end;
```

```
/*   Case   1.   */



do;   /*   Builtin function: length   */
   call FORCEDESCRIPT (mpp1);
   call EMITRR ("12", reg(mpp1), reg(mpp1)); /* ltr to check for null*/
   call EMITRX ("88", reg(mpp1), 0, 0, 24);   /* Shift to character */
   i = pp;
   call BRANCH (8, 0);     /*  Don't increment length on null string.  */
   call EMITRX (la, reg(mpp1), 0, reg(mpp1), 1); /*Add 1, true length*/
   call FIXBFW (i, pp);   /*  Destination of null string jump.  */
   reg(mp) = reg(mpp1);   /*  Record containing accumulator.  */
   type(mp) = accumulator;
end;


/*   Case   2.   */



/*   Builtin function substr.   */
do;
   if cnt(mp) = 2 then
      do;
         if type(mpp1) = constant then
            do;
               call EMITCONSTANT (shl(fixv(mpp1), 24) − fixv(mpp1));
               call EMITRX ("5F", reg(mp), 0, adreg, adrdisp);
            end;
         else
            do;
               call FORCEACCUMULATOR (mpp1);
               call EMITRR ("1E", reg(mp), reg(mpp1)); /* alr base */
               call EMITRX ("89", reg(mpp1), 0, 0, 24);
               call EMITRR ("1F", reg(mp), reg(mpp1));
               bases(reg(mpp1)) = avail;
            end;
         i = pp;
         call BRANCH (1, 0);     /*  We may now have negative length. */
         call EMITRR ("1B", reg(mp), reg(mp)); /*  Null descriptor.  */
         call FIXBFW (i, pp);
      end;
   else
      do;             /*  Three arguments.  */
         call EMITRX (la, reg(mp), inx(mp), reg(mp), ppsave(mp));
         bases(inx(mp)) = avail;
```

```
        if type(mpp1) ¬= constant then
           do;
               call FORCEACCUMULATOR (mpp1);
               call EMITRX (la, reg(mpp1), 0, reg(mpp1), "FF");
                          /*  Decrement length by 1.  */
               call EMITRX ("89", reg(mpp1), 0, 0, 24);
               call EMITRR ("16",reg(mp),reg(mpp1));  /* Or into d.*/
               bases(reg(mpp1)) = avail;
           end;
        else
           do;
               call EMITCONSTANT (shl(fixv(mpp1)−1, 24));
               call EMITRX ("56", reg(mp), 0, adreg, adrdisp);
           end;
      end;
    type(mp) = descript;
end;


/*  Case  3.  */


do;      /*  Builtin function byte.  */
   if cnt(mp) = 1 then
      do;
         if type(mpp1) = chrtype then
            do;
               type(mp) = chrtype;
               var(mp) = var(mpp1);
            end;
         else
            do;
               call FORCEDESCRIPT(mpp1);
               if reg(mpp1) = 0 then
                  do;
                     reg(mp) = FINDAC;
                     call EMITRR("18",reg(mp),0);
                                     /*  lr    reg(mp),0  */
                  end;
               else
                  reg(mp) = reg(mpp1);
               type(mp) = descript;
               inx(mp) = 0;
            end;
       end;
```

```
        else if cnt(mp) = 2 then
            do;
                call FORCEACCUMULATOR(mpp1);
                inx(mp) = reg(mpp1);
            end;
        else
            call ERROR(' byte called with more than two arguments' ,0);
    end;

    /*  Case   4.  */


    call SHIFT_CODE("89" );          /*  sll  */

    /*  Case   5.  */


    call SHIFT_CODE("88" );          /*  srl  */
end;      /*  of case statement.  */

else if i = 10 then
    call EMIT_INLINE;
else if i = 19 then      /*  Builtin function addr.  */
    do;
        reg(mp) = FINDAC;
        call FORCE_ADDRESS(mpp1,reg(mp ) );
        type(mp) = accumulator;
    end;
else
    do;
        call FORCEACCUMULATOR (mpp1);
        if cnt(mp) = 1 then reg(mp) = reg(mpp1);
        else inx(mp) = reg(mpp1);
    end;

end;      /*  of production */


/*  <subscript head> ::= <identifier> (   */
do;
    call ID_LOOKUP(mp );
    if fixl(mp ) < 0 then
        call UNDECLARED_ID(mp );
end;
```

```
/*  <subscript head> ::= <subscript head> <expression> ,      */
   do;      /* Builtin function or procedure call.  */
      cnt(mp) = cnt(mp) + 1;

      if fixv(mp) = 0 then
         do;         /* ¬ built in function */
            call FORCEACCUMULATOR (mpp1);
            if sytype(fixl(mp)) = labeltype |
               sytype(fixl(mp)) = char_proc_type  then
               call STUFF_PARAMETER;
         end;

      else if fixv(mp) = 2 | fixv(mp) = 3 then
         do;         /* substr or byte */
            if cnt(mp) = 1 then
               do;
                  call FORCEDESCRIPT (mpp1);
                  if reg(mpp1) = 0 then
                     do;
                        reg(mp) = FINDAC;
                        call EMITRR ("18", reg(mp), 0);
                     end;
                  else reg(mp) = reg(mpp1);
               end;
            else if cnt(mp) = 2 then
               do;
                  if type(mpp1) = constant then ppsave(mp) = fixv(mpp1);
                  else
                     do;
                        call FORCEACCUMULATOR (mpp1);
                        inx(mp) = reg(mpp1);
                        ppsave(mp) = 0;
                     end;
               end;
            else call ERROR (' too many arguments to substr or byte' );
         end;

      else if fixv(mp) = 4 | fixv(mp) = 5 then
         do; /*  shr  or  shl  */
            call FORCEACCUMULATOR(mpp1);
            reg(mp) = reg(mpp1);
         end;

      else if fixv(mp) = 10 then
         call EMIT_INLINE;
```

```
        else if fixv(mp) >= 8 then
            do;        /* Some sort of submonitor call. */
                call FORCEACCUMULATOR (mpp1);
                if cnt(mp) = 1 then reg(mp) = reg(mpp1);
                else call ERROR (' too many arguments for ' || syt(fixl(mp)));
            end;
        else;         /* Reserved for other builtin functions. */
    end;

/*   <constant> ::= <string>        */
    type(mp) = chrtype;

/*   <constant> ::= <number>        */
    type(mp) = constant;

    end;  /* of case selection on production number. */
end SYNTHESIZE;



/*               Syntactic parsing functions:                              */


RIGHT_CONFLICT:
    procedure (left) bit(1);
        declare left fixed;
    /* This procedure is true if token is not a legal right context of left. */
        return ("C0" & shl(byte(c1(left)), shr(token,2)), shl(token,1)
            & "06")) = 0;
    end RIGHT_CONFLICT;


RECOVER:
    procedure;
        /* If this is the second successive call to RECOVER, discard one symbol. */
        if ¬ failsoft then call SCAN;
        failsoft = false;
        do while ¬ stopit(token);
            call SCAN;  /* To find something solid in the text, */
        end;
        do while RIGHT_CONFLICT (parse_stack(sp));
            if sp > 2 then sp = sp − 1;  /* and in the stack, */
            else call SCAN;  /* but don't go too far. */
        end;
        output = ' Resume:' || substr(pointer, text_limit + lb−cp + margin_chop + 7);
    end RECOVER;
```

STACKING:
```
    procedure bit(1);   /*  Stacking decision function.  */

        count#stack =  count#stack  +  1;
        do forever;     /*  Until return.  */
            do case shr(byte(c1(parse_stack(sp))),shr(token,2)),shl(3−token,1)&6)&3;

                /*  Case 0.  */

                do;    /*  Illegal symbol pair.  */
                    call ERROR('illegal symbol pair: ' || v(parse_stack(sp))||x1||
                        v(token), 1);
                    call STACK_DUMP;
                    call RECOVER;
                end;


                /*  Case 1.  */

                return true;      /*  Stack token.  */


                /*  Case 2.  */

                return false;      /*  Don't stack it yet.  */


                /*  Case 3.  */

                do;      /*  Must check triples.  */
                    j = shl(parse_stack(sp−1), 16) + shl(parse_stack(sp), 8) + token;
                    i = −1;  k = nc1triples + 1;   /*  Binary search of triples.  */
                    do while i + 1 < k;
                        l = shr(i+k, 1);
                        if c1triples(l) > j then k = l;
                        else if c1triples(l) < j then i = l;
                        else return true;   /*  It is a valid triple.  */
                    end;
                    return false;
                end;


            end;    /*  of do case.  */
        end;    /*  of do forever.  */

    end STACKING;
```

PR_OK:
  procedure(*prd*) **bit**(1);

  /* Decision procedure for context check of equal or imbedded right parts. */
  declare (*h*, *i*, *j*, *prd*) **fixed**;
  do case *context_case*(*prd*);

```
        /*  Case 0  —— no check required.  */

    return true;

        /*  Case 1  —— right context check.  */

    return ¬ RIGHT_CONFLICT (hdtb(prd));

        /*  Case 2  —— left context check.  */

    do;
        h =  hdtb(prd)  −  nt;
        i =  parse_stack(sp  −  prlength(prd));
        do j =  left_index(h−1) to  left_index(h)  −  1;
            if  left_context(j) =  i then return true;
        end;
        return false;
    end;

        /*  Case 3  —— check triples.  */

    do;
        h =  hdtb(prd)  −  nt;
        i =  shl(parse_stack(sp  −  prlength(prd)), 8)  +  token;
        do j =  triple_index(h−1) to  triple_index(h)  −  1;
            if  context_triple(j) =  i then return true;
        end;
        return false;
    end;

    end;  /*  of do case  */
  end PR_OK;
```

  /*   Analysis algorithm: */

```
REDUCE:
  procedure;
    declare (i, j, prd) fixed;
    /*  Pack stack top into one word.  */
    do i = sp − 4 to sp − 1;
      j = shl(j, 8) + parse_stack(i);
    end;
    do prd = pr_index(parse_stack(sp )−1) to pr_index(parse_stack(sp )) − 1;
      if (prmask(prlength(prd )) & j ) = prtb(prd ) then
        if PR_OK(prd ) then
          do;  /*  An allowed reduction.  */
            mp = sp − prlength(prd ) + 1; mpp1 = mp + 1;
            call SYNTHESIZE(prdtb(prd ));
            sp = mp;
            parse_stack(sp ) = hdtb(prd );
            return;
          end;
    end;
    /*  Look−up has failed, error condition.  */
    call ERROR(' no production is applicable' ,1);
    call STACK_DUMP;        failsoft = false;
    call RECOVER;
  end REDUCE;


COMPILATION_LOOP:
  procedure;
    compiling = true;
    do while compiling;    /*  Once around for each production (reduction ).  */
      do while STACKING;
        sp = sp + 1;
        if sp = stacksize then
          do;
            call ERROR (' stack overflow *** compilation aborted ***' , 2);
            return;    /*  Thus aborting compilation.  */
          end;
        parse_stack(sp ) = token;
        var(sp ) = bcd;
        fixv(sp ) = number_value;
        fixl(sp ) = card_count;
        ppsave(sp ) = pp;
        call SCAN;
      end;
      call REDUCE;
    end;        /*  of do while compiling.  */
  end COMPILATION_LOOP;
```

LOADER:
  procedure;

/* Write out a load file of compiled code and data.
    Assumes code on *file(codefile, j)*   *j* = 0 to *codemax*
    assumes data on   *file(datafile, j)*   *j* = 0 to *datamax*
    assumes strings on *file(stringfile,j)*
    output on *file(binaryfile, j)*   *j* = 0 to *codemax + datamax +* 1
    assumes that *binaryfile* = *codefile*.   */

/* Put some control information in the first 60 bytes of the
    first block of code. Consecutive words of this control
    information contain:

        1   # of bytes of program
        2   # of bytes of data
        3   # of blocks of program
        4   # of blocks of data
        5   # of bytes per block
        6   # of bytes actually filled in the last code block
        7   # of bytes actually filled in the last data block

    The file is formatted:

        1   *codemax +* 1 blocks of program
            (and control information at head of first block)
        2   *datamax +* 1 blocks of data and strings
*/

declare (*i, j*) **fixed**;
declare *blockcnt* **fixed**; /* Cumulative block counter during load. */

control(*byte*(' E')) = *false*;
eject_page;
dp = *bases*(*sbr*);
call *FIXWHOLEDATAWORD* (*basedata, dp*);
do *i* = 0 **to** *shr*(*dsp*,2);
   call *EMITDATAWORD* (*desc*(*i*));
end;
call *FIXWHOLEDATAWORD*(*basedata* + 4, *dp*);

/* Copy compiled character strings to the program data area. */
chporg = 0;
chplim = *diskbytes*;

```
file(stringfile,cursblk) = strings;      /*  Write out current block.  */
cursblk = 0;
strings = file(stringfile,cursblk);      /*  Read in first block.  */

do i = 0 to chp;
    if i >= chplim then
        do;
            cursblk = cursblk + 1;
            strings = file(stringfile,cursblk);   /*  Read in next block.  */
            chporg = chporg + diskbytes;
            chplim = chplim + diskbytes;
        end;
    call EMITBYTE(strings(i−chporg));
end;


call FIXWHOLEDATAWORD(basedata+8, dp);

call INSERT_CODE_FIXUPS;

code = file(codefile,0);               /*  Read in first code record.  */

codemax(1) = diskbytes*(codemax+1);
codemax(2) = diskbytes*(datamax+1);
codemax(3) = codemax + 1;
codemax(4) = datamax + 1;
codemax(5) = diskbytes;
if severe_errors > 0 then if ¬ control(byte(' Z' )) then
    do;
        code(60) = "07";
        code(61) = "FC";
        output = '#### Execution of this program will be inhibited.' ;
    end;
j = pp − codemax(1) + diskbytes;      /*  Portion actually used.  */
/*  Forces remainder to word boundary.  */
j = (j + 3) & "FFFFFC";
codemax(6) = j;
    /*  Portion of the last data record which was actually used.  */
codemax(7) = (dp − codemax(2) + diskbytes + 3) & "FFFFFC" ;


output = ' *  File control block  '  || codemax(1) || x4 ||
    codemax(2) || x4 || codemax(3) || x4 || codemax(4) || x4 ||
    codemax(5) || x4 || codemax(6) || x4 || codemax(7);

file(binaryfile,0) = code;    /*  Write first record to binary file.  */
```

```
     blockcnt = codemax + 1;
     file(datafile,curdblk) = data;   /*  Write out current data array.  */


     /*  Write out the compile data array.  */

     do j = 0 to datamax;
        data = file(datafile,j);
        file(binaryfile, blockcnt)  =  data ;
        blockcnt = blockcnt + 1;
     end;


     output = ' *  Load file written.' ;

  end LOADER;


PRINT_SUMMARY:
   procedure;
      declare i fixed;
      call PRINT_DATE_AND_TIME (' End of compilation ', date, time);
      output = '' ;
      output = card_count || ' cards containing ' || statement_count
         || ' statements were compiled.' ;
      if error_count = 0 then output = ' No errors were detected.' ;
      else if error_count > 1 then
         output = error_count || ' errors (' || severe_errors
            || ' severe ) were detected.' ;
      else if severe_errors = 1 then output = ' One severe error was detected.' ;
         else output = ' One error was detected.' ;
      if previous_error > 0 then
         output = ' The last detected error was on line ' || previous_error
            || period;
      output = pp || ' bytes of program, '|| dp-dsp-chp || 'of data, '|| dsp
         || ' of descriptors, ' || chp || ' of strings.  Total core requirement'
         || x1 || pp + dp || ' bytes.' ;
      if control(byte(' D' )) then call DUMPIT;
      double_space;
      clock(3) = time;
      do i = 1 to 3;   /*  Watch out for midnight.  */
         if clock(i) < clock(i-1) then clock(i) = clock(i) +  8640000;
      end;
      call PRINT_TIME (' Total time in compiler   ', clock(3) - clock(0));
      call PRINT_TIME (' Set up time              ', clock(1) - clock(0));
      call PRINT_TIME (' Actual compilation time  ', clock(2) - clock(1));
```

```
        call PRINT_TIME (' Post–compilation time      ', clock(3) − clock(2));
        if clock(2) > clock(1) then     /*   Watch out for clock being off.  */
        output = ' Compilation rate: '  ||  6000*card_count/(clock(2)−clock(1))
             || ' cards per minute.' ;
     end PRINT_SUMMARY;


MAIN_PROCEDURE:
   procedure;
        clock(0) = time;  /*  Keep track of time in execution.  */
        call INITIALIZATION;

        /*  clock(1) gets set in GETCARD.  */
        call COMPILATION_LOOP;

        clock(2) = time;
        call LOADER;

        /*  clock(3) gets set in PRINT_SUMMARY.  */
        call PRINT_SUMMARY;

     end MAIN_PROCEDURE;



call MAIN_PROCEDURE;
return severe_errors;

eof  eof  eof
```

Appendix 4

compactify

/*   compactify:

This source version of the procedure *compactify* is automatically inserted in front of each XPL program by XCOM. It is called to repack the string data area each time the area becomes full. */

```
compactify:
  procedure;
    declare (i, j, k, l, nd, tc, bc, delta) fixed;
    declare dx_size literally '500', dx(dx_size) bit(16);
    declare mask fixed initial ("FFFFFF"), lower_bound fixed, tried bit(1);
    /* First we must set the lower bound of the collectable area. */
    if lower_bound = 0 then lower_bound = freebase;
    do tried = 0 to 1;
        nd = -1;
        /* Find the collectable descriptors. */
        do i = 0 to ndescript;
            if (descriptor(i) & mask) >= lower_bound then
                do;
                    nd = nd + 1;
                    if nd > dx_size then
                        do;  /* We have too many potentially collectable strings.*/
                            output =
' *** Notice from compactify: Disasterous string overflow. Job abandoned. ***' ;
                            call exit;
                        end;
                    dx(nd) = i;
                end;
        end;
        /* Sort in ascending order. */
        k, l = nd;
        do while k <= l;
            l = -2;
            do i = 1 to k;
                l = i - 1;
                if (descriptor(dx(l)) & mask) > (descriptor (dx(i)) & mask) then
                    do;
                        j = dx(l); dx(l) = dx(i); dx(i) = j;
```

459

```
                           k =  l;
                       end;
               end;
       end;
       /* Move the active strings down. */
       freepoint =  lower_bound;
       tc, delta =  0;
       bc =  1;    /* Set up initial condition. */
       do  i =  0 to nd;
          j =  descriptor(dx(i));
          if (j & mask) − 1 > tc then
               do;
                   if delta > 0 then
                   do k = bc to tc;
                       corebyte(k−delta) =  corebyte(k);
                   end;
                   freepoint =  freepoint + tc − bc + 1;
                   bc = j & mask;
                   delta =  bc − freepoint;
               end;
          descriptor (dx(i)) = j − delta;
          l = (j & mask) + shr(j, 24);
          if tc < l then tc = l;
       end;
       do k =  bc to tc;
          corebyte(k−delta) =  corebyte(k);
       end;
       freepoint =  freepoint + tc − bc + 1;
       if shl(freelimit−freepoint, 4) < freelimit−freebase then
          lower_bound =  freebase;
       else
          do;
               lower_bound =  freepoint;
               return ;
          end;
       /* The hope is that we won't have to collect all strings every time. */
    end ;   /* of the do tried loop        */
    if freelimit−freepoint < 256 then
               do;
                   output =
' *** Notice from compactify:  Insufficient string space. Job abandoned. ***' ;
               call exit;    /* Force ABEND.   */
               end;


end compactify ;
```

Appendix 5

SKELETON

/*   SKELETON:

        The proto—compiler of the XPL system.

This version of SKELETON is a syntax checker for the following grammar:

<program>   ::=   <statement list>

<statement list>   ::=   <statement>
               | <statement list> <statement>

<statement>   ::=   <assignment> ;

<assignment>   ::=   <variable> = <expr>

<expr>   ::=   <arith expr>
      | <if clause> **then** <expr> **else** <expr>

<if clause>   ::=   **if** <boolean>

<boolean>   ::=   true
         | **false**
         | <expr> <relation> <expr>
         | <if clause> **then** <boolean> else <boolean>

<relation>   ::=   =
         | <
         | >

<arith expr>   ::=   <term>
           | <arith expr> + <term>
           | <arith expr> − <term>

<term>   ::=   <primary>
      | <term> * <primary>
      | <term> / <primary>

```
<primary>    ::=   <variable>
             |   <number>
             |   ( <expr> )

<variable>   ::=   <identifier>
             |   <variable> ( <expr> )
```
                                                                                    */
/*   First we initialize the global constants that depend upon the input
     grammar. The following cards are punched by ANALYZER: */

declare *nsy* **literally** ' 32' , *nt* **literally** ' 18' ;

declare *v*(*nsy*) **character initial** ('<Error: *token* = 0>' , ';' , '=' , '<' , '>' ,
     '+' , ' −' , ' *' , ' /' , ' (' , ')' , ' if' , '_|_' , ' then' , ' else' , ' true' ,
     'false', '<number>' , '<identifier>' , '<term>' , '<program>' , '<primary>' ,
     '<variable>' , '<relation>' , '<statement>' , '<if clause>' , '<assignment>' ,
     '<expr>' , '<statement list>' , '<arith expr>' ,
     '<boolean>' , ' else' , ' else');

declare *v_index*(12) **bit**(16) **initial** (1, 11, 12, 13, 16, 17, 17, 17, 18, 18,
     18, 18, 19);

declare *c1*(*nsy*) **bit**(38) **initial** (
     "(2) 00000 00000 00000 0000",
     "(2) 00000 00000 00200 0002",
     "(2) 00000 00003 03000 0033",
     "(2) 00000 00002 02000 0022",
     "(2) 00000 00002 02000 0022",
     "(2) 00000 00001 00000 0011",
     "(2) 00000 00001 00000 0011",
     "(2) 00000 00001 00000 0011",
     "(2) 00000 00001 00000 0011",
     "(2) 00000 00001 01000 0011",
     "(2) 02222 22222 20022 0000",
     "(2) 00000 00001 01000 1111",
     "(2) 00000 00000 00000 0001",
     "(2) 00000 00001 01000 1111",
     "(2) 00000 00002 02000 2222",
     "(2) 00000 00000 00022 0000",
     "(2) 00000 00000 00022 0000",
     "(2) 02222 22220 20022 0000",
     "(2) 02222 22222 20022 0000",
     "(2) 02222 22110 20022 0000",
     "(2) 00000 00000 00000 0000",
     "(2) 02222 22220 20022 0000",
     "(2) 02322 22221 20022 0000",
     "(2) 00000 00001 01000 0011",
     "(2) 00000 00000 00200 0002",
```
```

```
      "(2) 00000 00000 00010 0000",
      "(2) 01000 00000 00000 0000",
      "(2) 02333 00000 30023 0000",
      "(2) 00000 00000 00200 0001",
      "(2) 02222 11000 20022 0000",
      "(2) 00000 00000 00023 0000",
      "(2) 00000 00001 01000 0011",
      "(2) 00000 00001 01000 1111" );
```

declare *ncltriples* **literally** ' 17' ;

declare *cltriples*(*ncltriples*) **fixed initial** (596746, 727810, 727811, 727812,
792066, 858882, 858883, 858884, 858894, 859662, 1442313, 1442315, 1442321,
1442322, 1840642, 2104066, 2104067, 2104068);

declare *prtb*(28) **fixed initial** (0, 26, 0, 0, 0, 1444123, 2331, 0, 0, 0, 0, 0,
0, 7429, 7430, 0, 4871, 4872, 0, 0, 28, 0, 420289311, 5634, 6935, 0, 0,
420290080, 11);

declare *prdtb*(28) **bit**(8) **initial** (0, 4, 13, 14, 15, 26, 24, 0, 0, 9, 10, 23,
25, 17, 18, 16, 20, 21, 19, 22, 3, 2, 7, 5, 11, 1, 6, 12, 8);

declare *hdtb*(28) **bit**(8) **initial** (0, 24, 23, 23, 23, 22, 21, 31, 32, 30, 30,
21, 22, 29, 29, 29, 19, 19, 19, 21, 28, 28, 27, 26, 30, 20, 27, 30, 25);

declare *prlength*(28) **bit**(8) **initial** (0, 2, 1, 1, 1, 4, 3, 1, 1, 1, 1, 1, 1,
3, 3, 1, 3, 3, 1, 1, 2, 1, 5, 3, 3, 1, 1, 5, 2);

declare *context_case*(28) **bit**(8) **initial** (0, 0, 0, 0, 0, 0, 0, 2, 0, 0, 0, 0,
0, 0, 0, 0, 0, 0, 0, 0, 0, 0, 0, 0, 0, 0, 0, 0);

declare *left_context*(0) **bit**(8) **initial** (27);

declare *left_index*(14) **bit**(8) **initial** (0, 0, 0, 0, 0, 0, 0, 0, 0, 0, 0, 0, 0,
0, 1, 1);

declare *context_triple*(0) **fixed initial** (0);

declare *triple_index*(14) **bit**(8) **initial** (0, 0, 0, 0, 0, 0, 0, 0, 0, 0, 0, 0, 0,
0, 0, 1);

declare *pr_index*(32) **bit**(8) **initial** (1, 2, 3, 4, 5, 5, 5, 5, 5, 5, 7, 7, 7,
7, 9, 10, 11, 12, 13, 16, 16, 19, 20, 20, 22, 22, 22, 25, 26, 27, 29, 29,
29);

/*   End of cards punched by ANALYZER.   */

/*   Declarations for the scanner: */

/* *token* is the index into the vocabulary *v*( ) of the last symbol scanned,
   cp is the pointer to the last character scanned in the card image,
   bcd is the last symbol scanned (literal character string). */

declare (*token*, *cp*) **fixed**, *bcd* **character**;

/* Set up some convenient abbreviations for printer control. */

declare *eject_page* **literally** ' *output*(1) = *page*' ,
   page **character initial** (' 1'), *double* **character initial** (' 0'),

```
    double_space literally ' output(1) =  double' ,
    x70 character initial (

                                                                        ' );
```

/* Length of longest symbol in *v*, amount to be deleted from each card. */
declare (*reserved_limit, margin_chop*) **fixed**;

/* *chartype*( ) is used to distinguish classes of symbols in the scanner.
    tx( ) is a table used for translating from one character set to another.
    control( ) holds the value of the control toggles set in $ cards.
    not_letter_or_digit( ) is similiar to *chartype*( ) but used in scanning
    identifiers only.

    All are used by the scanner and *control*( ) is set there.
*/
declare (*chartype, tx*) (255) **bit**(8),
            (*control, not_letter_or_digit*)(255) **bit**(1);

/* *alphabet* consists of the symbols considered alphabetic in building
    identifiers.   */
declare *alphabet* **character initial** (
    '*ABCDEFGHIJKLMNOPQRSTUVWXYZabcdefghijklmnopqrstuvwxyz_$@#*');

/* *buffer* holds the latest card image,
    text holds the present state of the input text
    (not including the portions deleted by the scanner),
    text_limit stores the pointer to the end of *text*,
    card_count is incremented by one for every source card read,
    error_count tabulates the errors as they are detected,
    severe_errors tabulates those errors of fatal significance.
*/
declare (*buffer, text*) **character**,
    (*text_limit, card_count, error_count, severe_errors, previous_error*) **fixed**;

/* *number_value* contains the numeric value of the last constant scanned. */

declare *number_value* **fixed**;

/* Each of the following contains the index into *v*( ) of the corresponding
    symbol.   We ask: **if** *token = ident*   etc.   */
declare (*ident, number, divide, eofile*) **fixed**;

/* *stopit*( ) is a table of symbols which are allowed to terminate the error
  flush process. In general they are symbols of sufficient syntactic
  hierarchy that we expect to avoid attempting to start checking again
  right into another error—producing situation. The token stack is also
  flushed down to something acceptable to a *stopit*( ) symbol.
  failsoft is a bit which allows the parser one attempt at a gentle
  recovery. Then it takes a strong hand.   When there is real trouble
  compiling is set to false, thereby terminating parsing.
*/
declare *stopit* (*nt*) **bit**(1), (*failsoft, compiling*) **bit**(1);

declare *s* **character**; /* A temporary used various places */

/* The entries in *prmask*( ) are used to select out portions of coded
  productions and the stack top for comparison in the analysis algorithm. */
declare *prmask*(5) **fixed initial** (0, 0, "FF", "FFFF", "FFFFFF", "FFFFFFFF");

/* The proper substring of *pointer* is used to place an | under the point
  of detection of an error during checking. It marks the last character
  scanned. */
declare *pointer* **character initial** ('
                                        |');
declare *callcount*(20) **fixed**   /* Count the calls of important procedures. */
    initial(0,0,0,0,0,0,0,0,0,0,0,0,0,0,0,0,0,0,0,0);

/* Record the times of important points during checking. */
declare *clock*(5) **fixed**;

/* Commonly used strings */
declare *x*1 **character initial**(' '), *x*4 **character initial**('   ');
declare *period* **character initial** ('.');

declare (*i, j, k, l*) **fixed**;   /* Temporaries used throughout */

declare *true* **literally** ' 1', *false* **literally** ' 0', *forever* **literally** ' while 1' ;

/* The stacks declared below are used to drive the syntactic
  analysis algorithm and store information relevant to the interpretation
  of the text. The stacks are all pointed to by the stack pointer *sp*. */

declare *stacksize* **literally** ' 75' ; /* Size of stack */
declare *parse_stack* (*stacksize*) **bit**(8);
          /* Tokens of the partially parsed text */
declare *var* (*stacksize*) **character**;/* EBCDIC name of item */
declare *fixv* (*stacksize*) **fixed**;   /* Fixed (numeric) value */

```
/* sp points to the right end of the reducible string in the parse stack,
   mp points to the left end, and
   mpp1 = mp + 1.
*/


declare (sp, mp, mpp1) fixed;
```

```
/*                    P r o c e d u r e s :                        */
```

```
PAD:
   procedure (string, width) character;
      declare string character, (width, l) fixed;

      l = length(string);
      if l >= width then return string;
      else return string || substr(x70, 0, width−l);
   end PAD;

I_FORMAT:
   procedure (number, width) character;
      declare (number, width, l) fixed, string character;

      string = number;
      l = length(string);
      if l >= width then return string;
      else return substr(x70, 0, width−l) || string;
   end I_FORMAT;

ERROR:
   procedure(msg, severity);
      /* Prints and accounts for all error messages. */
      /* If severity is not supplied, 0 is assumed. */
      declare msg character, severity fixed;
      error_count = error_count + 1;
      /* If listing is suppressed, force printing of this line. */
      if ¬ control(byte(' L' )) then
         output = I_FORMAT (card_count, 4) || ' |' || buffer || ' |';
      output = substr(pointer, text_limit−cp+margin_chop);
      output = ' *** Error, ' || msg || '. ***';
```

```
   if error_count > 1 then
      output = ' *** Last previous error was detected on line '  ||
           previous_error || '. ***'  ;
   previous_error = card_count;
   if severity > 0 then
      if severe_errors > 25 then
         do;
            output = ' *** Too many severe errors, checking aborted. ***' ;
            compiling = false;
         end;
      else severe_errors = severe_errors + 1;
end ERROR;
```

```
/*                        Card image handling procedure:                    */
```

```
GET_CARD:
   procedure;
      /* Does all card reading and listing.                                 */

      declare i fixed, (temp, temp0, rest ) character, reading bit(1);
           buffer = input;
           if length(buffer ) = 0 then
               do; /* Signal for eof */
                   call ERROR ('eof missing or comment starting in column 1',1);
                   buffer = PAD (' /*' ' /* */ eof;end;eof' , 80);
               end;
           else card_count = card_count + 1;  /* Printed on listing. */
       if margin_chop > 0 then
          do; /* The margin control from dollar | */
             i = length(buffer ) − margin_chop;
             rest = substr(buffer, i);
             buffer = substr(buffer, 0, i );
          end;
       else rest = '' ;
       text = buffer;
       text_limit = length(text ) − 1;
       if control(byte(' M' )) then output = buffer;
       else if control(byte(' L' )) then
          output = I_FORMAT (card_count, 4) || ' |' || buffer || ' |' || rest;
       cp = 0;
   end GET_CARD;
```

```
/*                      The scanner procedures:                */


CHAR:
   procedure;
      /* Used for comments to avoid card boundary problems. */
      cp = cp + 1;
      if cp <= text_limit then return;
      call GET_CARD;
   end CHAR;



SCAN:
   procedure;
      declare (s1, s2) fixed;
      callcount(3) = callcount(3) + 1;
      failsoft = true;
      bcd = ' ' ;   number_value = 0;
      do forever;
         if cp > text_limit then call GET_CARD;
         else
            do; /* Discard last scanned value. */
               text_limit = text_limit - cp;
               text = substr(text, cp );
               cp = 0;
            end;
         /*   Branch on next character in text.                */
         do case chartype(byte(text ) );

            /*  Case 0  */

            /* Illegal characters fall here. */
            call ERROR (' illegal character: ' || substr(text, 0, 1) );

            /*  Case 1  */

            /*  Blank   */
            do;
               cp = 1;
               do while byte(text, cp ) = byte(' ' ) & cp <= text_limit;
                  cp = cp + 1;
               end;
               cp = cp - 1;
            end;
```

```
    /*   Case 2   */

;   /*   Not used in SKELETON (but used in XCOM ). */

    /*   Case 3   */

;   /*   Not used in SKELETON (but used in XCOM ). */

    /*   Case 4   */

do forever;   /* A letter:  identifiers and reserved words. */
   do cp = cp + 1 to text_limit;
      if not_letter_or_digit(byte(text, cp)) then
         do;   /* End of identifier  */
            if cp > 0 then bcd = bcd || substr(text, 0, cp);
            s1 = length(bcd);
            if s1 > 1 then if s1 <= reserved_limit then
               /* Check for reserved words */
               do i = v_index(s1−1) to v_index(s1) − 1;
                  if bcd = v(i) then
                     do;
                        token = i;    return;
                     end;
               end;
            /*   Reserved words exit higher: therefore <identifier> */
            token = ident;    return;
         end;
   end;
   /*  End of card   */
   bcd = bcd || text;
   call GET_CARD;       cp = −1;
end;

/*   Case 5   */
do;       /*  Digit:  a number. */
   token = number;
   do forever;
      do cp = cp to text_limit;
         s1 = byte(text, cp);
         if s1 < byte(' 0' ) then return;
         number_value = 10*number_value + s1 − byte(' 0' ) ;
      end;
      call GET_CARD;
   end;
end;
```

```
/*  Case 6  */

do;        /*  A "/":  may be divide or start of comment. */
   call CHAR;
   if byte(text, cp ) ¬= byte(' *' ) then
      do;
         token = divide;
         return;
      end;
   /* We have a comment. */
   s1, s2 = byte(' ' );
   do while s1 ¬= byte(' *' ) | s2 ¬= byte(' /' );
      if s1 = byte(' $' ) then
         do;  /* A control character  */
            control(s2) = ¬ control(s2);
            if s2 = byte(' T' ) then call trace;
            else if s2 = byte(' U' ) then call untrace;
            else if s2 = byte(' |' ) then
               if control(s2) then
                  margin_chop = text_limit − cp + 1;
               else
                  margin_chop = 0;
         end;
      s1 = s2;
      call CHAR;
      s2 = byte(text, cp );
   end;
end;

/*  Case 7  */
do;        /*  Special characters. */
   token = tx(byte(text ));
   cp = 1;
   return;
end;

/*  Case 8  */
;   /* Not used in SKELETON (but used in XCOM ). */

end;      /* of case on chartype. */

cp = cp + 1;   /* Advance scanner and resume search for token. */
end;

end SCAN;
```

```
/*                        Time  and  date:                              */
```

PRINT_TIME:
  procedure (*message*, *t*);
    declare *message* **character**, *t* **fixed**;
    message = *message* || *t*/360000 || ' :' || *t* **mod** 360000 / 6000 || ' :'
      || *t* **mod** 6000 / 100 || ' .' ;
    t = *t* **mod** 100;   /* Decimal fraction   */
    if *t* < 10 **then** *message* = *message* || ' 0' ;
    output = *message* || *t* || ' .' ;
  end *PRINT_TIME*;

PRINT_DATE_AND_TIME:
  procedure (*message*, *d*, *t*);
    declare *message* **character**, (*d*, *t*, *year*, *day*, *m*) **fixed**;
    declare *month*(11) **character initial** (' January' , ' February' , ' March' ,
      ' April' , ' May' , ' June' , ' July' , ' August' , ' September' , ' October' ,
      ' November' , ' December'),
    days(12) **fixed initial** (0, 31, 60, 91, 121, 152, 182, 213, 244, 274,
      305, 335, 366);
    year = *d*/1000 + 1900;
    day = *d* **mod** 1000;
    if (*year* & "3") ¬= 0 **then if** *day* > 59 **then** *day* = *day* + 1; /* ¬ leap year*/
    m = 1;
    do while *day* > *days*(*m*);   *m* = *m* + 1;   **end**;
    call *PRINT_TIME*(*message* || *month*(*m*−1) || *x*1 || *day*−*days*(*m*−1) || ' , '
      || *year* || ' . Clock time = ' , *t*);
  end *PRINT_DATE_AND_TIME*;


```
/*                        Initialization:                              */
```

INITIALIZATION:
  procedure;

    eject_page;
    call *PRINT_DATE_AND_TIME* (
      ' Syntax Check − "This Installation" − SKELETON III Version of ' ,
      date_of_generation, *time_of_generation*);
    double_space;
    call *PRINT_DATE_AND_TIME* (' Today is ' , *date*, *time*);
    double_space;

```
do i = 1 to nt;
    s = v(i);
    if s = '<number>' then number = i;   else
    if s = '<identifier>' then ident = i;   else
    if s = '/' then divide = i;   else
    if s = '_|_' then eofile = i;   else
    if s = ';' then stopit(i) = true;   else
    ;
end;
if ident = nt then reserved_limit = length(v(nt−1));
else reserved_limit = length(v(nt));
v(eofile) = ' eof' ;
stopit(eofile) = true;
chartype(byte(' ' )) = 1;
do i = 0 to 255;
    not_letter_or_digit(i) = true;
end;
do i = 0 to length(alphabet) − 1;
    j = byte(alphabet, i);
    not_letter_or_digit(j) = false;
    chartype(j) = 4;
end;
do i = 0 to 9;
    j = byte(' 0123456789' , i);
    not_letter_or_digit(j) = false;
    chartype(j) = 5;
end;
do i = v_index(0) to v_index(1) − 1;
    j = byte(v(i));
    tx(j) = i;
    chartype(j) = 7;
end;
chartype(byte(' /' )) = 6;

/* First set up global variables controlling SCAN, then call it. */
cp = 0;   text_limit = −1;
text = '' ;
control(byte(' L' )) = true;

call SCAN;

/* Initialize the parse stack. */
sp = 1;   parse_stack(sp) = eofile;

end INITIALIZATION;
```

DUMPIT:
  procedure;   /* Dump out the statistics collected during this run. */

    double_space;
    /* Put out the entry count for important procedures. */

    output = ' Stacking decisions= ' || *callcount*(1);
    output = ' SCAN   = ' || *callcount*(3);
    output = ' Free string area = ' || *freelimit* − *freebase*;
  end *DUMPIT*;

STACK_DUMP:
  procedure;
    declare *line* **character**;
    line = ' Partial parse to this point is: ' ;
    do *i* = 2 **to** *sp*;
      if *length*(*line*) > 105 **then**
        do;
          output = *line*;
          line = *x4*;
        end;
      line = *line* || *x1* || *v*(*parse_stack*(*i*));
    end;
    output = *line*;
  end *STACK_DUMP*;

  /*   The synthesis algorithm: */

SYNTHESIZE:
procedure(*production_number*);
  declare *production_number* **fixed**;

    /* This procedure is responsible for the semantics (code synthesis), if
    any, of the SKELETON compiler. Its argument is the number of the
    production which will be applied in the pending reduction. The global
    variables *mp* and *sp* point to the bounds in the stacks of the right part
    of this production.
    Normally, this procedure will take the form of a giant **case** statement
    on *production_number*. However, the syntax checker has semantics (the
    termination of checking) only for production 1.   */

```
/*  <program>   ::=   <statement list>     */

    if production_number = 1 then
    do;
        if mp ¬= 2 then   /* We didn' t get here legitimately. */
            do;
                call ERROR (' eof at invalid point' , 1);
                call STACK_DUMP;
            end;
        compiling = false;
    end;
end SYNTHESIZE;
```

```
/*                 Syntactic parsing functions :                    */
```

```
RIGHT_CONFLICT:
    procedure (left ) bit(1);
        declare left fixed;
        /* This procedure is true if token is an illegal right context of left. */
        return ("C0" & shl(byte(c1(left ), shr(token,2) ), shl(token,1)
            & "06" )) = 0;
    end RIGHT_CONFLICT;
```

```
RECOVER:
    procedure;
        /* If this is the second successive call to RECOVER, discard one symbol.*/
        if ¬ failsoft then call SCAN;
        failsoft = false;
        do while ¬ stopit(token );
            call SCAN;                        /* Find something solid in the text, */
        end;
        do while RIGHT_CONFLICT (parse_stack(sp ));
            if sp > 2 then sp = sp − 1;   /* and in the stack, */
            else call SCAN;               /* but don' t go too far. */
        end;
        output = ' Resume:'  ||  substr(pointer, text_limit−cp+margin_chop+7);
    end RECOVER;
```

STACKING:
  procedure bit(1);   /* Stacking decision function. */

    callcount(1) = *callcount*(1) + 1;
    do *forever*;   /* until return */
      do case *shr*(*byte*(*c*1(*parse_stack*(*sp*))),*shr*(*token*,2)),*shl*(3−*token*,1)&6)&3;

          /* Case 0 */
          do;   /* Illegal symbol pair. */
             call *ERROR*(' illegal symbol pair: ' || *v*(*parse_stack*(*sp*)) || *x*1 ||
               v(*token*), 1);
             call *STACK_DUMP*;
             call *RECOVER*;
          end;

          /* Case 1 */
          return *true*;   /* Stack *token*. */

          /* Case 2 */
          return *false*;   /* Don' t stack it yet. */

          /* Case 3 */
          do;   /* Must check triples. */
            j = *shl*(*parse_stack*(*sp*−1), 16) + *shl*(*parse_stack*(*sp*), 8) + *token*;
            i = −1; *k* = *ncl triples* + 1; /* Binary search of triples */
            do while *i* + 1 < *k*;
               l = *shr*(*i*+*k*, 1);
               if *c*1*triples*(*l*) > *j* **then** *k* = *l*;
               else if *c*1*triples*(*l*) < *j* **then** *i* = *l*;
               else return *true*; /* It is a valid triple. */
            end;
            return *false*;
          end;

      end;   /* of **do case** */
    end; /* of **do** *forever* */

end *STACKING*;

PR_OK:
  procedure(*prd*) **bit**(1);

    /* Decision procedure for context check of equal or imbedded right parts*/
    declare (*h, i, j, prd*) **fixed**;

    do case *context_case*(*prd*);

        /* Case 0 —— no check required. */

        return *true*;

        /* Case 1 —— right context check. */

        return ¬ *RIGHT_CONFLICT* (*hdtb*(*prd*));

        /* Case 2 —— left context check. */

        do;
            h = *hdtb*(*prd*) − *nt*;
            i = *parse_stack*(*sp* − *prlength*(*prd*));
            do *j* = *left_index*(*h*−1) **to** *left_index*(*h*) − 1;
                if *left_context*(*j*) = *i* **then return** *true*;
            end;
            return *false*;
        end;

        /* Case 3 —— check triples. */

        do;
            h = *hdtb*(*prd*) − *nt*;
            i = *shl*(*parse_stack*(*sp* − *prlength*(*prd*)), 8) + *token*;
            do *j* = *triple_index*(*h*−1) **to** *triple_index*(*h*) − 1;
                if *context_triple*(*j*) = *i* **then return** *true*;
            end;
            return *false*;
        end;

    end;   /* of **do case**   */

  end *PR_OK*;

    /*   Analysis algorithm :   */

REDUCE:
  procedure;
    declare (*i, j, prd*) **fixed**;
    /* First pack stack top into one word. */
    do *i* = *sp* − 4 **to** *sp* − 1;
      j = *shl*(*j*, 8) + *parse_stack*(*i*);
    end;
    do *prd* = *pr_index*(*parse_stack*(*sp*)−1) **to** *pr_index*(*parse_stack*(*sp*)) − 1;
      if (*prmask*(*prlength*(*prd*)) & *j*) = *prtb*(*prd*) **then**
        if *PR_OK*(*prd*) **then**
        do;   /* An allowed reduction */
          mp = *sp* − *prlength*(*prd*) + 1; *mpp1* = *mp* + 1;
          call *SYNTHESIZE*(*prdtb*(*prd*));
          sp = *mp*;
          parse_stack(*sp*) = *hdtb*(*prd*);
          return;
        end;
    end;
    /* Look up has failed, error condition. */
    call *ERROR*(' no production is applicable' ,1);
    call *STACK_DUMP*;
    failsoft = *false*;
    call *RECOVER*;
  end *REDUCE*;

COMPILATION_LOOP:
  procedure;
    compiling = *true*;
    do while *compiling*;   /* Once around for each production (reduction). */
      do while *STACKING*;
        sp = *sp* + 1;
        if *sp* = *stacksize* **then**
          do;
            call *ERROR* (' stack overflow *** checking aborted ***' , 2);
            return;   /* thus aborting checking */
          end;
        parse_stack(*sp*) = *token*;
        var(*sp*) = *bcd*;
        fixv(*sp*) = *number_value*;
        call *SCAN*;
      end;
      call *REDUCE*;
    end;   /* of **do while** *compiling* */
  end *COMPILATION_LOOP*;

```
PRINT_SUMMARY:
    procedure;
        declare i fixed;
        call PRINT_DATE_AND_TIME (' End of checking ', date, time);
        output = ' ';
        output = card_count || ' cards were checked.' ;
        if error_count = 0 then output = ' No errors were detected.' ;
        else if error_count > 1 then
            output = error_count || ' errors (' || severe_errors
                || ' severe ) were detected.' ;
        else if severe_errors = 1 then output = ' One severe error was detected.' ;
            else output = ' One error was detected.' ;
        if previous_error > 0 then
            output = ' The last detected error was on line ' || previous_error
                || period;
        if control(byte(' D' )) then call DUMPIT;
        double_space;
        clock(3) = time;
        do i = 1 to 3;    /* Watch out for midnight. */
            if clock(i) < clock(i−1) then clock(i) = clock(i) +  8640000;
        end;
        call PRINT_TIME (' Total time in checker     ', clock(3) − clock(0));
        call PRINT_TIME (' Set up time                ', clock(1) − clock(0));
        call PRINT_TIME (' Actual checking time       ', clock(2) − clock(1));
        call PRINT_TIME (' Clean−up time at end       ', clock(3) − clock(2));
        if clock(2) > clock(1) then    /* Watch out for clock being off. */
        output = ' Checking rate: ' || 6000*card_count/(clock(2)−clock(1))
            || ' cards per minute.' ;
    end PRINT_SUMMARY;

MAIN_PROCEDURE:
    procedure;
        clock(0) = time;  /* Keep track of time in execution. */
        call INITIALIZATION;
        clock(1) = time;
        call COMPILATION_LOOP;
        clock(2) = time;
        /* clock(3) gets set in PRINT_SUMMARY. */
        call PRINT_SUMMARY;
    end MAIN_PROCEDURE;

call MAIN_PROCEDURE;
return severe_errors;

eof
```

Appendix 6

ANALYZER

/* ANALYZER:

       The syntax analysis and table building program
       of the XPL system.

  This program builds tables directly acceptable for use in
    the compiler XCOM or the proto—compiler SKELETON.

Input to ANALYZER may be nearly "free format."
Cards with the character "$" in column 1 are treated as comment or control
   cards, and listed unchanged. The character in column 2 is the control
   character, as follows:
      L   complement listing mode,
      T   complement tracing mode,
      P   complement punching mode,
      O   complement line printer listing of computed "card output,"
      I   complement iterative improvement mode,
      EOG end of grammar; (another grammar follows).

Blank cards are ignored.
Productions are placed one to a card.
A token is
   any consecutive group of non—blank characters not beginning with a   "< "
     and followed by a blank,
  the character "<" followed by a blank,
  the character "<" followed by a non—blank character and then any
     string of blank or non—blank characters up to and including the
     next occurrence of the character ">".

If column 1 is non—blank, the first token on the card is taken to be the
   left part of the production; otherwise, the left part is taken to be
   the left part of the previous production.
The balance of the card (up to five tokens) is taken to be the right part.

Any symbol which does not occur as a left part is a terminal symbol.
Any symbol which occurs only as a left part is a goal symbol.
All productions with the same left part must be grouped.

Productions are reformatted for readability (including the insertion of
the meta–symbols ::= and |) before listing.
Extra blanks between tokens are not significant.

                                                                                    */

/* First come the global variable declarations: */

declare *v*(255) **character**, (*left_part, right_head*) (255) **bit**(8),
   production(255) **bit**(32), (*on_left, on_right*) (255) **bit**(1);
declare *index*(255) **bit**(8), (*ind, ind*1) (255) **bit**(16);
declare *sort*#(255) **fixed**, *ambiguous* **bit**(1);
declare (*nsy, npr, sp, cp, nt, level, goal_symbol*) **fixed**;
declare *control*(255) **bit**(1);
declare *true* **literally** ' 1', *false* **literally** ' 0' ;
declare *carriage* **literally** ' 1', *punch* **literally** ' 2', *disk* **literally** ' 3',
   page **character initial** (' 1'), *double* **character initial** (' 0'),
   eject_page **literally** ' *output*(1) = *page*',
   double_space **literally** ' *output*(1) = *double*' ;
declare *dollar* **literally** ' *byte*(' ' $' ')', *blank* **literally** ' *byte*(' ' ' ')' ;
declare *change* **bit**(1), *work*("4000") **bit**(8);
declare *head*(255) **fixed**, *tail*(255) **bit**(8);
declare *stacklimit* **literally** ' 200', *textlimit* **literally** ' 255',
   depth **literally** ' 255' ;   /*   must be at least 255   */
declare *stack*(*stacklimit*) **bit**(8), *text*(*textlimit*) **bit**(8),
   token_save(*depth*) **bit**(8), *token* **fixed**, *mp_save*(*depth*) **bit**(8), *mp* **fixed**,
   tp_save(*depth*) **bit**(8), *tp* **fixed**, *p_save*(*depth*) **bit**(8), *p* **fixed**;
declare *head_table*("2000") **bit**(8);
   declare *empty* **character initial**('

                                          ');   /* The image of a blank card   */
declare *half_line* **character initial** ('
                     '), *x*12 **character initial** ('   ');
declare *cardimage* **character**, *outcard* **character**, *s* **character**, *t* **character**;
declare (*netry, first_time, last_time, this_time*) **fixed**;
declare *count*(3) **fixed**;
declare *print*(3) **character initial** (' ', ' Y', ' N', ' #');
declare *dots* **character initial** (' ... ');
declare *value*(1) **fixed initial** (2, 1);
declare (*i, j, k, l, m*) **fixed**;
declare *error_count* **fixed**;
declare *terminator* **fixed**;
declare *maxnf*11 **literally** ' 5000', *maxntrip* **literally** ' 1000' ;
declare *f*11(*maxnf*11) **fixed**, *nf*11 **fixed**;
declare *triple*(*maxntrip*) **fixed**, *tv*(*maxntrip*) **bit**(2), *ntrip* **fixed**;
declare *stacking* **bit**(1) **initial** (*true*);   /* Controls batching of grammars   */
declare *maxtrouble* **literally** ' 50', *trouble*1(*maxtrouble*) **bit**(8),
   *trouble*2(*maxtrouble*) **bit**(8), *trouble_count* **fixed**;

```
declare (basic_nsy, basic_npr) fixed;
declare iteration_count fixed;


/* Now some data packing/unpacking procedures used below:   */

IS_HEAD:
  procedure (i, j) bit(1);
  /* This procedure decodes the packed head table.  True if v(j) is a head
     of v(i).   */
  /* We must simulate a double subscript for the array
     head_table(0:255, 0:255) bit(1).   */

  declare (i, j) fixed;
  return 1 & shr(head_table(shl(i,5) + shr(j,3) ), j & 7);
end IS_HEAD;

SET_HEAD:
  procedure (i, j);
  /* This procedure adds v(j) as a head of v(i) in head_table.   */

  declare (i, j, k, l) fixed;
  change = true;
  k = shl(i, 5) + shr(j, 3);
  l = shl(1, j & 7);
  head_table(k) = head_table(k) | l;
end SET_HEAD;

CLEAR_HEADS:
  procedure;
  declare i fixed;
  do i = 0 to "2000";
     head_table(i) = 0;
  end;
end CLEAR_HEADS;

GET:
  procedure (i, j) bit(2);
  declare (i, j) fixed;
  /* This procedure decodes a 2-bit entry in the work matrix.   */
  /* We must simulate a double subscript for the array
     work(0:255, 0:255) bit(2).   */

  return 3 & shr(work(shl(i,6) + shr(j,2) ), shl(j & 3, 1) );
end GET;
```

```
SET:
   procedure (i, j, val);
   /* This procedure or's a 2-bit val into the work matrix.   */

   declare (i, j, val) fixed;
   declare (k, l) fixed;
   k = shl(i, 6) + shr(j, 2);
   l = shl(val & 3, shl(j & 3, 1));
   work(k) = work(k) | l;
end SET;

CLEAR_WORK:
   procedure;
   declare i fixed;
   do i = 0 to "4000";
      work(i) = 0;
   end;
end CLEAR_WORK;

PACK:
   procedure (b1, b2, b3, b4) fixed;
   /* This procedure has the value of the 4 bytes packed into a 32-bit word. */

   declare (b1, b2, b3, b4) bit(8);
   return shl(b1,24) + shl(b2,16) + shl(b3,8) + b4;
end PACK;


ERROR:
   procedure (message);
      declare message character;
      output = ' *** Error, ' || message;
      error_count = error_count + 1;
   end ERROR;


ENTER:
   procedure (env, val);
   /* This procedure records together the 2-bit val's for each unique env.
         To assist table lookup, the env's are stored in ascending order.
         They are located by a binary search.   */

   declare (env, val, i, j, k) fixed;
   netry = netry + 1; /* Count entries vs. unique entries. */
   i = 0;   k = ntrip + 1;
```

```
   do while i + 1 < k; /* Binary look—up */
      j = shr(i+k,1);
      if triple(j) > env then k = j;
      else if triple(j) < env then i = j;
      else
         do;
            tv(j) = tv(j) | val;
            return;
         end;
   end;
   if ntrip >= maxntrip then
      do;
         call ERROR (' too many triples for table.' );
         ntrip = 0;
      end;
   do j = 0 to ntrip − k;  /* Make room in table for new entry. */
      i = ntrip − j;
      triple(i+1) = triple(i );
      tv(i+1) = tv(i );
   end;
   ntrip = ntrip + 1;
   triple(k ) = env;
   tv(k ) = val;


end ENTER;



ADD_TROUBLE:
   procedure (left, right );

      declare (left, right ) fixed;
      declare i fixed;

      if left > basic_nsy then return;
      if left = terminator then return;
      if trouble_count = maxtrouble then return;   /* Trouble enough  */
      do i = 1 to trouble_count;
         if trouble1(i) = left then if trouble2(i) = right then return;
      end;

      trouble_count = trouble_count + 1;
      trouble1(trouble_count ) = left;
      trouble2(trouble_count ) = right;

   end ADD_TROUBLE;
```

LINE_OUT:
   procedure (*number, line*);
   /* Number a line and print it. */
   declare *number* **fixed**, *line* **character**;
   declare *n* **character**;
   n = *number*; *number* = 6 − *length*(*n*);   /* 6 = margin */
   output = *substr*(*empty*, 0, *number*) || *n* || '   ' || *line*;
end *LINE_OUT*;

BUILD_CARD:
   procedure (*item*);
   /* Add *item* to *outcard* and punch if card boundary exceeded. */

   declare *item* **character**;
   if *length*(*item*) + *length*(*outcard*) >= 80 **then**
      do;
         if *control*(*byte*(' P')) **then** *output*(*punch*) = *outcard*;
         if *control*(*byte*(' O')) **then**
            output = ' −−− card output −−−|' || *outcard*;
         outcard = '   ' || *item*;
      end;
   else *outcard* = *outcard* || ' ' || *item*;
end *BUILD_CARD*;

   .
PUNCH_CARD:
   procedure (*item*);
   /* Punch *outcard* and *item*. */
   declare *item* **character**;
   call *BUILD_CARD* (*item*);
   if *control*(*byte*(' P')) **then** *output*(*punch*) = *outcard*;
   if *control*(*byte*(' O')) **then**
      output = ' −−− card output −−−|' || *outcard*;
   outcard = ' ';
end *PUNCH_CARD*;

PRINT_MATRIX:
   procedure (*title, source*);
   /* Print and label the matrix specified by *source* (*head_table* or *work*). */

   declare *title* **character**, *source* **fixed**;
   declare (*i, j, k, l, m, n, bot, top, margin_size, number_across, wide*) **fixed**,
      (*margin, line, waste, bar, pages*) **character**,
      digit(9) **character initial** (' 0' ,' 1' ,' 2' ,' 3' ,' 4' ,' 5' ,' 6' ,' 7' ,' 8' ,' 9'),
      number_high **literally** ' 48' ,
      gs **literally** ' 16' ;

```
if source = 1 then wide = nt;   else wide = nsy;
margin_size = 5;
do i = 1 to nsy;
    if length(v(i)) >= margin_size then margin_size = length(v(i)) + 1;
end;
margin = substr('
                ', 0, margin_size);
waste = margin || '              ';
number_across = (122 − margin_size)/(gs + 1)*gs;
do i = 0 to 3;
    count(i) = 0;
end;
m = 0;
i = (wide−1)/number_across + 1;
pages = ((nsy−1)/number_high + 1)*i;
do i = 0 to (wide−1)/number_across;
    bot = number_across*i + 1;
    top = number_across*(i+1);
    if top > wide then top = wide;
    bar = substr(waste, 1) || ' +';
    do l = bot to top;
        bar = bar || ' −';
        if l mod gs = 0 then bar = bar || ' +';
    end;
    if top mod gs ¬= 0 then bar = bar || ' +';
    do j = 0 to (nsy−1)/number_high;
        /*  Once per page of printout:  */
        eject_page;
        m = m + 1;
        output = title || ': page ' || m || ' of ' || pages;
        double_space;
        l = 100;
        do while l > 0;
            line = waste;
            do n = bot to top;
                if n < l then line = line || ' ';
                else line = line || digit(n/l mod 10);
                if n mod gs = 0 then line = line || ' ';
            end;
            output = line;
            l = l / 10;
        end;
        output = bar;
        n = number_high*(j+1);
        if n > nsy then n = nsy;
```

```
      do k =  number_high*j  +  1 to n;
          l =  length(v(k));
          line =  v(k) || substr(margin, l) || ' | ' ;
          do l =  bot to top;
              if source ¬= 0 then
                  do;
                      n = GET (k, l);
                      line =  line || print(n);
                      count(n) =  count(n) + 1;
                  end;
                else line =  line || print(IS_HEAD (k, l));
                  if l mod gs = 0 then line =  line || ' | ' ;
              end;
              if top mod gs ¬= 0 then line =  line || ' | ' ;
              call LINE_OUT (k, line);
              if k mod gs = 0 then
                  output =  bar;
          end;
          if k mod gs ¬= 1 then output =  bar;
      end;
  end;
  double_space;
  if source ¬= 0 then
      do;
          output =  ' Table entries summary:' ;
          do i = 0 to 3;
              call LINE_OUT (count(i), print(i));
          end;
      end;
end PRINT_MATRIX;

PRINT_TRIPLES:
  procedure (title);
  /* Format and print the (2,1) triples for C1. */

  declare title character, (i, j) fixed;
  if ntrip = 0 then
      do;
          double_space;
          output =  ' No triples required.' ;
          count(1) = 0;    /* so we don' t punch any.  */
          return;
      end;
  eject_page;
  output =  title || ' :' ;
```

```
    double_space;
    do i = 1 to 3;
        count(i ) = 0;
    end;
    do i = 1 to ntrip;
        j = triple(i );
        k = tv(i );
        if k = 3 then
            do;
                call ERROR (' stacking decision cannot be made with (2,1) context:' );
                call ADD_TROUBLE (shr(j, 16), shr(j, 8) & "FF" );
            end;
        call LINE_OUT (i, print(k ) || ' for ' || v(shr(j, 16) ) || ' ' ||
            v(shr(j, 8)&"FF" ) || ' ' || v(j&"FF." ) );
        count(k ) = count(k ) + 1;
    end;
    double_space;
    output = netry || ' entries for ' || ntrip || ' triples.' ;
    double_space;
    output = ' Table entries summary:' ;
    do i = 1 to 3;
        call LINE_OUT (count(i ), print(i ) );
    end;
end PRINT_TRIPLES;



BUILD_RIGHT_PART:
    procedure (p );
        declare (p, pr ) fixed;
        pr = production(p );
        t = ' ' ;
        do while pr ¬= 0;
            t = ' ' || v(pr&"FF" ) || t;
            pr = shr(pr, 8);
        end;
        t = v(right_head(p ) ) || t;
    end BUILD_RIGHT_PART;



OUTPUT_PRODUCTION:
    procedure (p );
        declare p fixed;
        call BUILD_RIGHT_PART (p );
        call LINE_OUT (p, v(left_part(p ) ) || '   ::=   ' || t );
    end OUTPUT_PRODUCTION;
```

PRINT_TIME:
  procedure;

   /* Output elapsed times. */

  declare (*i*, *j*) **fixed**, *t* **character**;
  double_space;
  this_time = *time*;
  i = *this_time* − *last_time*;
  j = *i* **mod** 100;
  i = *i* / 100;
  t = ' time used was ' || *i* || '.' ;
  if *j* < 10 **then** *t* = *t* || ' 0' ;
  output = *t* || *j* || ' seconds.' ;
  i = *this_time* − *first_time*;
  j = *i* **mod** 100;
  i = *i* / 100;
  t = ' total time is ' || *i* || '.' ;
  if *j* < 10 **then** *t* = *t* || ' 0' ;
  output = *t* || *j* || ' seconds.' ;
  last_time = *this_time*;

end *PRINT_TIME*;

LOOK_UP:
  procedure (*symbol*) **bit**(8);   /* Get index of *symbol* in *v*. */

  declare *symbol* **character**;
  declare *j* **fixed**;
  do *j* = 1 **to** *nsy*;
    if *v*(*j*) = *symbol* **then** **return** *j*;
  end;
  if *j* = 256 **then**
    do;
      call *ERROR* (' too many symbols.');
      j = 1;
    end;
  /* Add *symbol* to *v*. */
  nsy = *j*;
  v(*j*) = *symbol*;
  return *j*;
end *LOOK_UP*;

EXPAND:

```
procedure (f11, p);   /* Expand production p in the context of f11.  */
declare (f11, i, j, p, oldp) fixed;
/* oldp remembers argument p from previous call to save repeated effort. */
if p ¬= oldp then
    do;
        oldp = p;        sp = 2;
        stack(sp) = right_head(p);
        j = production(p);
        do while j ¬= 0; /* Unpack production into stack. */
            i = shr(j, 24);
            if i ¬= 0 then
                do;
                    sp = sp + 1;
                    stack(sp) = i;
                end;
            j = shl(j, 8);
        end;
    end;
stack(1) = shr(f11, 8) & "FF";   /* Left context */
stack(sp+1) = f11 & "FF";          /* Right context */
end EXPAND;
```

```
/*  Now the working procedures:  */
```

READ_GRAMMAR:

```
procedure;  /*  Read in and list a grammar.  */
declare (p, long) fixed;
```

SCAN:

```
procedure bit(8); /* Get a token from input card image.  */
declare lp fixed, left_bracket literally ' byte(' '<' ' )',
    right_bracket literally ' byte(' '>' ' )', stop fixed;
do cp = cp to long;
    if byte(cardimage,cp) ¬= blank then
        do;
            lp = cp; /* Mark left boundary of symbol. */
            if byte(cardimage,cp) = left_bracket & byte(cardimage,cp+1)
                ¬= blank then
                stop = right_bracket;
            else stop = blank;
            do cp = cp + 1 to long;
                if byte(cardimage, cp) = stop then go to delimit;
            end;
```

```
            if stop ¬= blank then
                do;
                    call ERROR (' unmatched bracket: <' );
                    cp = cp − 1;
                    do while byte(cardimage, cp ) = blank;   /* Error recovery */
                        cp = cp − 1;
                    end;
                end;
        delimit:
            if stop ¬= blank then cp = cp + 1; /* Pick up the ">". */
            t = substr(cardimage, lp, cp−lp );   /* Pick up the symbol. */
            return LOOK_UP (t );
        end;
    end;  /* End of card  */

    t = ' ' ;
    return 0;

end SCAN;




GET_CARD:
    procedure bit(1);   /* Read the next card.   */


    cp = 0;
    do while true;
        cardimage = input;   /* Get the card. */
        long = length(cardimage ) − 1;
        if long < 0 then
            do;     /* End of file detected.   */
                stacking = false;
                return false;
            end;
        if byte(cardimage ) = dollar then
            do;   /* Control card or comment. */
                if substr(cardimage, 1, 3) = ' EOG'  then return false;
                if control(byte(' L' )) then output = cardimage;
                control(byte(cardimage,1) ) = ¬ control(byte(cardimage,1) );
            end;
        else if cardimage ¬= empty then return true;
    end;

end GET_CARD;
```

SORT_V:
```
  procedure;   /* Sort the vocabulary.  */

  do i = 1 to nsy;
      /* Sort on:  1)  terminal vs. non−terminal,
                   2)  length of symbol,
                   3)  original order of occurrence.  */
      sort#(i) = shl(on_left(i), 16) | shl(length(v(i)), 8) | i;
  end;
  /* Bubble sort  */
  k, l = nsy;
  do while k <= l;
      l = 0;
      do i = 2 to k;
          l = i − 1;
          if sort#(l) > sort#(i) then
              do;
                  j = sort#(l);   sort#(l) = sort#(i);   sort#(i) = j;
                  t = v(l);   v(l) = v(i);   ·v(i) = t;
                  k = l;
              end;
      end;
  end;
  do i = 1 to nsy;  /* Build a table to locate the sorted symbols of v.  */
      index(sort#(i)&"FF") = i;
  end;
  nt = nsy;   /* Prepare to count non−terminal symbols.  */
  do while sort#(nt) > "10000";   nt = nt − 1;   end;
  /* Substitute new index numbers in productions.  */
  do i = 1 to npr;
      left_part(i) = index(left_part(i));
      j = index(right_head(i));
      on_right(j) = true;
      right_head(i) = j;
      l = production(i);
      do k = 0 to 3;
          j = index(shr(l,24));
          on_right(j) = true;
          l = shl(l,8) + j;
      end;
      production(i) = l;
  end;
  terminator = index(1);   /* Add "_|_"  to vocabulary.  */
  on_right(terminator) = true;
end SORT_V;
```

```
PRINT_DATE:
    procedure (message, d);
        declare message character, d fixed;
        declare month(11) character initial (' January', ' February', ' March',
            ' April', ' May', ' June', ' July', ' August', ' September', ' October',
            ' November', ' December' ), days(11) fixed initial (0, 31, 60, 91,
            121, 152, 182, 213, 244, 274, 305, 335);
        declare (year, day, m) fixed;

        year = d/1000 + 1900;
        day = d mod 1000;
        if (year & 3) ¬= 0 then if day > 59 then day = day + 1;
        m = 11;
        do while day <= days(m);   m = m - 1;   end;
        output = message || month(m) || '.' || day-days(m) || ', ' ||
            year || '.';
    end PRINT_DATE;


eject_page;
call PRINT_DATE (
' Grammar analysis  --  "This Installation"  --  ANALYZER version of ',
    date_of_generation );
double_space;
call PRINT_DATE (' Today is ', date );
double_space;
output = '                  P R O D U C T I O N S';
double_space;
control(byte(' L' )) = true;
v(0) = ' <Error: token = 0>';
nsy = 1;   v(1) = '_|_';
npr, error_count = 0;
do i = 0 to 255;  /* Clear on_left and on_right.  */
    on_left(i), on_right(i) = 0;
end;
do while GET_CARD;  /* (Watch the side effect.) */
    if npr = 255 then call ERROR (' too many productions.' );
    else npr = npr + 1;
    if byte(cardimage) = blank then left_part(npr) = left_part(npr-1);
    else
        do;
            i = SCAN;        /* Left part symbol */
            left_part(npr) = i;
            on_left(i) = true;
        end;
    i = SCAN; /* First symbol on the right */
```

```
if i = 0 then call ERROR (' empty right part.' );
right_head(npr) = i;
j, p = 0;
do j = 1 to 4;
   i = SCAN;
   if i ¬= 0 then
      p = shl(p, 8) + i;  /* Pack 4 to a word.  */
end;
if substr(cardimage, cp) ¬= substr(empty, cp) then
   call ERROR ('too many symbols in right part. Forced to discard  ' ||
      substr(cardimage, cp));
production(npr) = p;
if control(byte(' L' )) then
   do;  /* Unpack table and print production. */
      if left_part(npr) = left_part(npr−1) then
         do;
            i = length(v(left_part(npr)));
            cardimage = substr(empty, 0, i) || '     |   ';
         end;
      else
         do;
            output = '';
            cardimage = v(left_part(npr)) || '   ::=   ';
         end;
      call BUILD_RIGHT_PART (npr);
      call LINE_OUT (npr, cardimage || t);
   end;
if control(byte(' P' )) then
   do;  /* Unpack table and print XPL comment. */
      p = production(npr);
      outcard = '  /*  ' || v(left_part(npr)) || '  ::= ' ||
         v(right_head(npr));
      do k = 1 to 4;
         i = shr(p, shl(4−k, 3)) & "FF";
         if i ¬= 0 then call BUILD_CARD (v(i));
      end;
      call PUNCH_CARD ('    */' );
   end;
end;
call PRINT_TIME;
call SORT_V;
eject_page;
output = '    T E R M I N A L    S Y M B O L S
N O N T E R M I N A L S';
double_space;
```

```
     if nsy − nt > nt then l = nsy − nt;  else l = nt; /* l = number of lines */
     do i = 1 to l;  /* Print v: */
        if i > nt then cardimage = half_line;
        else
            do;  /* Terminal symbols */
                t = i;
                j = 5 − length(t);
                cardimage = substr(substr(empty, 0, j) || t || '    ' || v(i)
                    || half_line, 0, 66);
            end;
        k = i + nt;
        if k <= nsy then
            do;  /* Non−terminal symbols */
                t = k;
                j = 5 − length(t);
                cardimage = cardimage || substr(empty, 0, j) || t || '    '
                    || v(k);
            end;
        output = cardimage;
     end;

     double_space;
     goal_symbol = 0;
     do i = 1 to nsy;   /* Locate the goal symbol: */
        if ¬ on_right(i) then
            if goal_symbol = 0 then
                    do;
                        goal_symbol = i;
                        output = v(i) || ' is the goal symbol.' ;
                    end;
                else output = 'Another goal: ' || v(i) || ' (will not be used).' ;
     end;

     if goal_symbol = 0 then
        do;
            goal_symbol = left_part(1);
            output = 'No goal symbol found. ' || v(goal_symbol) ||
                ' used for goal symbol.' ;
        end;

     basic_nsy = nsy;
     basic_npr = npr;
     trouble_count = 0;

end READ_GRAMMAR;
```

```
IMPROVE_GRAMMAR:
    procedure;
        declare (t1, t2, s1, s2) fixed, change bit(1),
            internal bit(1), add_on character initial (' 0123456789abcdefghijkl' );
        eject_page;
        output = ' Grammar modification to attempt to resolve conflicts:' ;
        do i = 1 to basic_nsy;
            index(i) = 0;
        end;
        do i = 1 to trouble_count;   /* Step through problems:  */
            double_space;
            t1 = trouble1(i);    t2 = trouble2(i);
            do p = 1 to basic_npr;
                internal, change = false;
                s1 = right_head(p);
                m = production(p);
                do l = 1 to 4;   /* Step through right part.  */
                    s2 = shr(m, 24);
                    m = shl(m, 8) + s2;
                    if s2 ¬= 0 then
                        do;
                            if s1 = t1 & IS_HEAD (s2, t2) then
                                do;
                                    j, index(t1) = index(t1) + 1;
                                    if nsy < 255 then nsy = nsy + 1;
                                    else call ERROR (' too many symbols.' );
                                    s = substr(add_on, j, 1);
                                    v(nsy) = '<' || v(t1) || s || '>' ;
                                    if npr < 255 then npr = npr + 1;
                                    else call ERROR (' too many productions.' );
                                    left_part(npr) = nsy;       right_head(npr) = t1;
                                    production(npr) = 0;   change = true;
                                    call OUTPUT_PRODUCTION (npr);
                                    if internal then m = m & "FFFF00FF" | shl(nsy, 8);
                                    else right_head(p) = nsy;
                                end;
                            internal = true;   s1 = s2;
                        end;
                end;   /* of do l. */
                production(p) = m;
                if change then call OUTPUT_PRODUCTION (p);
            end;   /* of do p. */
        end;   /* of do i.  */
        trouble_count, error_count = 0;
    end IMPROVE_GRAMMAR;
```

COMPUTE_HEADS:

```
procedure;   /* Set up head symbol matrix.  */
call CLEAR_HEADS;
call CLEAR_WORK;
do i = 1 to npr;   /* First get immediate heads, */
   call SET_HEAD (left_part(i), right_head(i) );
end;
do while change;   /* then compute transitive completion. */
   change = false;
   do i = nt + 1 to nsy;
      do j = nt + 1 to nsy;
         if IS_HEAD (i, j) then
            do k = 1 to nsy;
               if IS_HEAD (j, k) then
                  if ¬ IS_HEAD (i, k) then
                     call SET_HEAD (i, k);   /* side effect on change */
            end;
      end;
   end;
end;
change = true;
if iteration_count = 1 then
   do;
      ambiguous = false;
      do i = 1 to npr;
         j = right_head(i);   k = production(i);
         do while k ¬= 0;   j = shr(k, 24);   k = shl(k, 8);   end;
         call SET (left_part(i), j, true );
      end;
      do while change;
         change = false;
         do i = nt + 1 to nsy;
            do j = nt + 1 to nsy;
               if GET (i, j) then
                  do k = 1 to nsy;
                     if GET (j, k) then if ¬ GET (i, k) then
                        do;
                           call SET (i, k, true );
                           change = true;
                        end;
                  end;
            end;
         end;
      end;
```

```
        do i = nt + 1 to nsy;
            if IS_HEAD (i, i) then if GET (i, i) then
                do;
                    ambiguous = true;
                    call ERROR (
' grammar is ambiguous.  It is left and right recursive in the symbol '
                        || v(i) );
                end;
            end;
        end;
    do i = 0 to nsy;    /* Finally, the reflexive transitive completion. */
        call SET_HEAD (i, i);
    end;
    call PRINT_MATRIX (' produced head symbols' , 0);
end COMPUTE_HEADS;
```

```
PRODUCE:
    procedure;   /* Run through the generation algorithm to compute F11. */
    declare maxlevel fixed, new bit(1);

NEVER_BEEN_HERE:
    procedure; /* Record the F11.  Return false if it is already in table.  */
    declare (new_f11, i, j, k, nf11p1) fixed;
    netry = netry + 1;
    new_f11 = PACK(0, stack(sp), stack(sp−1), token);
    i − 0;  k, nf11p1 = nf11 + 1;
    do while i + 1 < k; /* Binary look−up */
        j = shr(i+k,1);
        if f11(j) > new_f11 then k = j;
        else if f11(j) < new_f11 then i = j;
        else return false;   /* Found it */
    end;

    /* If we got here, we didn' t find it. */
    if nf11 >= maxnf11 then do;   call ERROR (' f11 overflow.' );   nf11 = 1; end;
    do j = 0 to nf11 − k;    /* Make room to insert new entry. */
        f11(nf11p1−j) = f11(nf11−j);
    end;
    nf11 = nf11p1;
    f11(k) = new_f11;
    return true;

end NEVER_BEEN_HERE;
```

```
ADD_ITEM:
    procedure (item);
    declare item character;
    if length(cardimage) + length(item) > 130 then
        do;
            output = cardimage;         cardimage = '        ';
        end;
    cardimage = cardimage || ' ' || item;
end ADD_ITEM;


PRINT_FORM:
    procedure; /* Print the current sentential form while tracing
                    the generating algorithm.   */
    cardimage = 'level ' || level || ': ';
    do i = 1 to sp;
        call ADD_ITEM (v(stack(i)));
    end;
    call ADD_ITEM (' | ');
    do i = 0 to tp - 1;
        call ADD_ITEM (v(text(tp−i)));
    end;
    output = cardimage;
end PRINT_FORM;


APPLY_PRODUCTION:
    procedure;  /* Perform one parse step (on stack and text) and recur.  */
        level = level + 1;  /* Simulate the effect of recursion.  */
        if level > maxlevel then if level > depth then
            do;   call ERROR (' level overflow.' );   level = 1;   end;
            else maxlevel = level;
        mp_save(level) = mp;         /* Save pointer to left part of production,*/
        mp = sp;
        tp_save(level) = tp;          /* save pointer into text, */
        p_save(level) = p;            /* save number of production to be applied,*/
        token_save(level) = token;/* save pointer into IS_HEAD array, */
        stack(sp) = right_head(p);/* and expand production into stack. */
        j = production(p);
        do while j ¬= 0;
            k = shr(j,24);   j = shl(j,8);
            if k ¬= 0 then
                if sp = stacklimit then call ERROR (' stack overflow.' );
                else do;   sp = sp + 1;   stack(sp) = k;   end;
        end;
        if control(byte(' T' )) then call PRINT_FORM;  /* Trace */
end APPLY_PRODUCTION;
```

DIS_APPLY:
  procedure;

 /* Undo the pseudo–recursion, reversing the effect of
  APPLY_PRODUCTION. */
 token = *token_save*(*level*);
 p = *p_save*(*level*);
 tp = *tp_save*(*level*);
 sp = *mp*;
 mp = *mp_save*(*level*);
 stack(*sp*) = *left_part*(*p*);
 level = *level* − 1;

end *DIS_APPLY*;

do *i* = 1 **to** *nsy*; *index*(*i*) = 0; **end**;
do *i* = 1 **to** *npr*;   /* Make sure productions are properly grouped. */
 j = *left_part*(*i*);
 if *j* ¬= *left_part*(*i*−1) **then**
  if *index*(*j*) = 0 **then**
   index(*j*) = *i*;
  else call *ERROR* (' productions separated for ' || *v*(*j*) ||
   '. Production ' || *i* || ' will be ignored.');
end;

left_part(*npr*+1) = 0; /* Flag end of table. */
/* Set initial sentential form to "_|_ <goal> _|_". */

tp = 0;
mp, *sp* = 1;
stack(0), *text*(0) = *terminator*;
stack(1) = *goal_symbol*;
netry, *nf*11, *level*, *maxlevel* = 0;

eject_page;
output = ' Sentential form production:' ;
double_space;

if *control*(*byte*(' T')) **then call** *PRINT_FORM*;

/* Now comes the basic algorithm for generating the tables: */

```
production_loop:
    do while sp >= mp;   /* Step through right part of production: */
        if stack(sp) > nt then    /* Only non-terminals can expand. */
            do;
                new = false;
                i = text(tp);
                do token = 1 to nt;    /* Step through terminal heads. */
                    if IS_HEAD (i, token) then
                        if NEVER_BEEN_HERE then new = true;
                end;

                if new then
                    do;   /* Expand stack(sp) with all applicable rules: */
                        p = index(stack(sp));
                        do while left_part(p) = stack(sp);
                            call APPLY_PRODUCTION;
                            go to production_loop;   /* Now down a level,  */


                    continue:                       /* and now back up a level.  */
                            p = p + 1;   /* Move on to next production. */
                        end;
                    end;
            end;


        if tp = textlimit then call ERROR (' text overflow.' );
        else tp = tp + 1;
        text(tp) = stack(sp);   /* Run the compiler backwards,  */
        sp = sp - 1;                    /* unstacking as we go. */


    end;

    /* Fully expanded at this level, */
    call DIS_APPLY;   /* so come up a level.  */

    if level >= 0 then go to continue;

    if control(byte(' T' )) then double_space;

    output = ' Fl1 has ' || nfl1 || ' elements.' ;
    output = ' The maximum depth of recursion was ' || maxlevel || ' levels.' ;
    output = netry || ' sentential forms were examined.' ;

end PRODUCE;
```

*INDEX_F*11:
  procedure;
  /* Build an index into *f*11 for each production. */
  declare (*y*, *yp*, *p*) **fixed**;
  do *i* = 1 **to** *npr*;
    ind(*i*) = 0;
    *ind*1(*i*) = −1;
  end;
  y, *yp* = 0;
  *f*11(*nf*11+1) = *shl*(*nsy*+1, 16); /* Boundary condition */
  do *i* = 1 **to** *nf*11+1; /* Check each *f*11. */
    if *f*11(*i*) >= *yp* **then**
      do;   /* *f*11 for a new left part */
        p = *index*(*y*);
        do while *left_part*(*p*) = *y*;   /* Record end for old left part. */
          *ind*1(*p*) = *i* − 1;
          p = *p* + 1;
        end;
        y = *shr*(*f*11(*i*), 16);   /* New left part */
        p = *index*(*y*);
        do while *left_part*(*p*) = *y*;   /* Record start for new left part. */
          ind(*p*) = *i*;
          p = *p* + 1;
        end;
        yp = *shl*(*y*+1, 16);   /* To compare with triple */
      end;
  end;
end *INDEX_F*11;

SORT_PRODUCTIONS:
  procedure;   /* Re−number the productions in an optimal order for C2. */
  do *i* = 1 **to** *npr*; *p_save*(*i*) = 0; **end**;
  p = 0;
  do *i* = 1 **to** *npr*;
    j = *right_head*(*i*); /* Convert 1 − 4 packing to 4 − 1 packing. */
    m = *production*(*i*);
    if *m* = 0 **then**
      do;
        m = *j*;
        j = 0;
        l = 7;
      end;
    else *l* = 6;
    tail(*i*) = *m* & "FF";
    m = *m* & "FFFFFF00";

```
    do while m ¬= 0;
        k = shr(m, 24);   m = shl(m, 8);
        if k ¬= 0 then
            do;
                j = shl(j, 8) + k;
                l = l - 1;
            end;
    end;
    head(i) = j;
    /* Sort on:  1)  tail symbol of right part,
                 2) length of right part,
                 3) number of f11' s.                    */
    sort#(i) = shl(tail(i), 23) + shl(l, 20) + ind1(i) - ind(i);
    index(i) = i;
  end;  /* of do i.  */
  /* Bubble sort  productions:  */
  k, l = npr;
  do while k <= l;
    l = -1;
    do i = 2 to k;
      l = i - 1;
      if sort#(l) > sort#(i) then
          do;
              j = sort#(l);   sort#(l) = sort#(i);   sort#(i) = j;
              j = index(l);   index(l) = index(i);   index(i) = j;
              k = l;
          end;
    end;
  end;
  index(npr+1) = 0;

end SORT_PRODUCTIONS;



COMPUTE_C1:
  procedure;
    declare (cx, ctrip, s1, s2, s3, tr, pr) fixed;

    call CLEAR_WORK;
    netry, ntrip, ctrip = 0;
    do cx = 0 to 2;          /* Repeat basic loop 3 times:
                                1) compute pairs,
                                2) compute triples for pair conflicts,
                                3) emit diagnostics for triple conflicts. */
```

```
   do p = 1 to npr;          /* Step through the productions:  */
     do i = ind(p) to ind1(p);     /* Step through the expansion triples:  */
       call EXPAND (f11(i), p);
       do j = 2 to sp;        /* Step through right part of production:  */
         k = value(j = sp);
         s1 = stack(j−1);
         s2 = stack(j);
         l = stack(j+1);
         do s3 = 1 to nt;        /* Step through the heads of stack(j+1):  */
           if IS_HEAD(l, s3) then
             do case cx;

                 /* case 0 −− enter pair.  */
                 call SET (s2, s3, k);

                 /* case 1 −− if pair conflict, then enter triple.  */
                 if GET (s2, s3) = 3 then
                   call ENTER (PACK (0, s1, s2, s3), k);

                 /* case 2 −− if triple conflict, emit diagnostic.  */
                 do;
                   tr = PACK (0, s1, s2, s3);
                   do m = 0 to ctrip;
                     if sort#(m) = tr then
                       call ENTER (PACK(m, p, stack(1), stack(sp+1)),
                         k);
                   end;
                 end;      /* of case 2.  */
             end;       /* of do case.  */
         end;      /* of do s3.  */
       end;       /* of do j.  */
     end;      /* of do i.  */
   end;    /* of do p.  */
   do case cx;  /* Clean up:  */

     /* case 0  */
     do;
       do i = 1 to nt;        /* Special relations for terminator:  */
         if IS_HEAD (goal_symbol, i) then
           call SET (terminator, i, value(true));
       end;
       call SET (goal_symbol, terminator, value(false));
       call PRINT_MATRIX (' C1 matrix for stacking decision' , 1);
       call PRINT_TIME;
     end;
```

```
/* case 1   */
do;
    call PRINT_TRIPLES (' C1 triples for stacking decision' );
    if count(3) = 0 | iteration_count > 1 then return;
    if ¬ control(byte(' I' )) then
        if control(byte(' P' )) | control(byte(' O' )) then return;
    call PRINT_TIME;
    do i = 1 to ntrip;
        if tv(i ) = 3 then
            do;
                sort#(ctrip ) =  triple(i );
                ctrip =  ctrip  + 1;
            end;
    end;
    ctrip =  ctrip  − 1;
    netry, ntrip =  0;
    double_space;
    output =  ' Analysis of (2,1) conflicts:' ;
end;

/* case 2   */
do;
    j = 1;
    do m = 0 to ctrip;   /* Step through conflicts:   */
        do k = 0 to 1;     /* Step through truth values:  */
            i =  sort#(m );
            output =  ' ' ;
            output =  '     The triple  ' || v(shr(i,16) ) || ' ' ||
                v(shr(i,8)&"FF" ) || ' ' || v(i&"FF" ) ||
                '  must have the value ' || print(value(k )) ||
                ' for' ;
            output =  ' ' ;
            l =  shl(m+1, 24);
            i =  j;
            s1 =  0;
            do while triple(i ) < l & i <=  ntrip;
                if (tv(i )&value(k )) ¬=  0 then
                    do;
                        tr =  triple(i );
                        p =  shr(tr, 16) & "FF";
                        if p ¬=  s1 then call OUTPUT_PRODUCTION (p );
                        s1 =  p;
                        output =  '              in the context  ' ||
                            v(shr(tr, 8)&"FF" ) || dots || v(tr&"FF" );
                    end;
```

```
                                    i = i + 1;
                              end;        /* of do while.  */
                         end;   /* of do k.  */
                         j = i;
                         output = ' ' ;
                    end;        /* of do m.  */
               end;
          end;        /* of do case.  */
     end;        /* of do cx.  */
end COMPUTE_C1;


COMPUTE_C2:
   procedure;
   /* Determine what (if any) context must be checked for each production
      to augment the "longest match" rule for the production selection
      function   C2.       */

      declare (ij, ik, tj, tk, pj, pk, jct, kct, jcl, jcr) fixed,
         proper bit(1);
      declare context_class(3) character initial (' either (0,1) or (1,0)' ,
         ' (0,1)' , ' (1,0)' , ' (1,1)' );

      eject_page;
      output = ' Context check for equal and embedded right parts:' ;
      do i = 1 to npr;   mp_save(i), p_save(i) = 0;   end;
      do j = 1 to npr − 1;
         ij − index(j );
         k = j + 1;
         ik = index(k );
         do while tail(ij ) = tail(ik );   /* Check all productions with */
            tj = head(ij );                    /* the same tail symbol.  */
            tk = head(ik );
            do while (tj & "FF" ) = (tk & "FF" ) & tj ¬= 0;
               tj = shr(tj, 8);   tk = shr(tk, 8);
            end;

            if tk = 0 then
               do;        /* Production ik is included in ij.  */
                  output = ' ' ;
                  output = '    There are ' || ind1(ij )−ind(ij )+1 ||
                     ' and ' || ind1(ik )−ind(ik )+1 ||
                     ' valid contexts, respectively, for' ;
                  call OUTPUT_PRODUCTION (ij );
                  call OUTPUT_PRODUCTION (ik );
                  proper = tj ¬= 0;  /* ik is a proper substring.  */
```

```
                        if proper then
                           do;
                               jcl = shl(tj & "FF", 8);
                               do i = 1 to nsy;
                                   on_right(i) = false;
                               end;
                           end;
                        else p_save(ij) = 1;   /* Remember that equal right parts
                                                      must be distinguished somehow  */
                        mp = 0;
                        do pj = ind(ij) to ind1(ij);
                           jct = f11(pj) & "FFFF";
                           jcr = jct & "00FF";
                           if proper then jct = jcl | jcr;
                           else jcl = jct & "FF00";

                           do pk = ind(ik) to ind1(ik);
                               kct = f11(pk) & "FFFF";
                               if kct = jct then
                                    do;
                                        if mp < 4 then call ERROR (
' these productions cannot be distinguished with (1,1) context.' );
                                        mp = mp | 4;
                                        if proper then
                                            do;
                                                if ¬ on_right(jcr) then
                                                    output = '      '  || v(left_part(ik)) ||
                                                         '  has  ' || v(shr(jcl, 8)) ||
                                                            dots || v(jcr) || '  as context and  '
|| v(jcr) || '  is valid right context for  ' || v(left_part(ij));
                                                    on_right(jcr) = true;
                                                end;
                                            else output =
'    They have equal right parts and the common context  '
                                                 || v(shr(jcl, 8)) || dots || v(jcr);
                                                call ADD_TROUBLE (shr(kct, 8), left_part(ik));
                                    end;

                               else if (kct & "FF00") = jcl then
                                    mp = mp | 1;   /* We can' t tell by left context. */
                               else if (kct & "00FF") = jcr then
                                    mp = mp | 2;   /* We can' t tell by right context. */
                           end;      /* of do pk.  */

                        end;    /* of do pj.  */
```

```
              if mp < 4 then
                 do;        /* Resolvable by context  */
                    if proper & (¬mp) then /* Context implicit in length  */
                       output = '    They can be resolved by length.' ;
                    else
                       do;
                          mp_save(ij) = mp_save(ij) | mp;
                          output = '    They can be resolved by ' ||
                             context_class(mp) || ' context.' ;
                       end;
                 end;
              end;        /* of tk = 0.  */
        k = k + 1;
        ik = index(k);
     end;        /* of do while.  */
  end;     /* of do j.  */


  eject_page;
  output = ' C2 production choice function:' ;
  tk = 0;
  do j = 1 to npr;
     ij = index(j);
     tj = tail(ij);
     if tj ¬= tk then
        do;
           tk = tj;
           double_space;
           output = '    ' || v(tj) ||
'   as stack top will cause productions to be checked in this order:' ;
        end;
     output = '' ;
     call OUTPUT_PRODUCTION (ij);
     do case mp_save(ij) & 3;
        /* case 0  */
        if p_save(ij) then go to case_1;  /* Equal right part must check */
        else output = '         There will be no context check.' ;

        /* case 1  */
     case_1:
        do;
           output =
'   (0,1) context will be checked.  Legal right context:' ;
           do i = 1 to nsy;  on_right(i) = false;  end;
           do pj = ind(ij) to ind1(ij);
              jcr = f11(pj) & "FF";
```

```
                      if ¬ on_right(jcr) then
                          do;
                              on_right(jcr) = true;
                              output = x12 || dots || v(jcr);
                          end;
                  end;
              end;


              /* case 2  */
              do;
                  output =
          (1,0) context will be checked.  Legal left context:' ;
                  do i = 1 to nsy;  on_left(i) = false;  end;
                  do pj = ind(ij) to ind1(ij);
                      jcl = shr(f11(pj) & "FF00", 8);
                      if ¬ on_left(jcl) then
                          do;
                              on_left(jcl) = true;
                              output = x12 || v(jcl) || dots;
                          end;
                  end;
              end;


              /* case 3  */
              do;
                  output =
                              (1,1) context will be checked.  Legal context:' ;
                  do pj = ind(ij) to ind1(ij);
                      output = x12 || v(shr(f11(pj) & "FF00", 8)) ||
                          dots || v(f11(pj) & "FF");
                  end;
              end;
          end;    /* of do case.  */
      end;  /* of do j.  */
  end COMPUTE_C2;

PUNCH_PRODUCTIONS:
  procedure;
  declare wide fixed;
  if ¬(control(byte(' P')) | control(byte(' O'))) then return;
  if control(byte(' O')) then eject_page;
  outcard = '   ';
  call PUNCH_CARD (' declare nsy literally ''' || nsy || ''', nt literally '''
      || nt || ''';' );
  call BUILD_CARD (' declare v(nsy) character initial (' );
```

```
do i = 0 to nsy;
   s = v(i);        t = '';
   l = length(s) − 1;
   do while byte(s, l) = blank;  l = l − 1;  end;
   if i > basic_nsy then
      do;         /* Created symbol:  adjust print name.  */
         l = l − 3;
         s = substr(s, 1);
      end;
   do j = 0 to l;
      if substr(s, j, 1) = '''' then t = t || '''''';
      else t = t || substr(s, j, 1);
   end;
   if i < nsy then call BUILD_CARD ('''' || t || ''',' );
   else call PUNCH_CARD ('''' || t || ''' );' );
end;
l = length(v(nt));
call BUILD_CARD (' declare v_index(' || l || ' ) bit(8) initial (' );
j = 1;

do i = 1 to l;
   call BUILD_CARD (j || ',' );
   do while length(v(j)) = i;  j = j + 1;  end;
end;

call PUNCH_CARD (nt+1 || ' );' );
if nt <= 15 then wide = 16;  /* Force long bit strings. */
else wide = nt;
i = 2*wide + 2;
call PUNCH_CARD (' declare c1(nsy) bit(' || i || ' ) initial (' );

do i = 0 to nsy;
   t = '    "(2)' ;
   do j = 0 to wide;
      if j mod 5 = 0 then
         do;
            call BUILD_CARD (t);
            t = '' ;
         end;
      t = t || GET (i, j);
   end;
   if i < nsy then call PUNCH_CARD (t || ' ",' );
   else call PUNCH_CARD (t || ' ");' );
end;
k = count(1) − 1;
```

```
if k < 0 then
   do;
      call PUNCH_CARD (' declare ncltriples literally ''0'';' );
      call PUNCH_CARD (' declare cltriples(0) fixed;' );
   end;
else
   do;
      call PUNCH_CARD (' declare ncltriples literally ''' || k || ''';' );
      call BUILD_CARD (' declare cltriples(ncltriples) fixed initial (' );
      j = 0;
      do i = 1 to ntrip;
         if tv(i) = 1 then
            do;
               if j = k then call PUNCH_CARD (triple(i) || ' );' );
               else call BUILD_CARD (triple(i) || ',' );
               j = j + 1;
            end;
      end;
   end;
call BUILD_CARD (' declare prtb(' || npr || ' ) fixed initial (0,' );
do i = 1 to npr − 1;
   call BUILD_CARD (head(index(i)) || ',' );
end;
call PUNCH_CARD (head(index(npr)) || ' );' );
call BUILD_CARD (' declare prdtb(' || npr || ' ) bit(8) initial (0,' );
do i = 1 to npr;
   l = index(i);
   if l > basic_npr then l = 0;
   if i < npr then call BUILD_CARD (l || ',' );
   else call PUNCH_CARD (l || ' );' );
end;
call BUILD_CARD (' declare hdtb(' || npr || ' ) bit(8) initial (0,' );
do i = 1 to npr − 1;
   call BUILD_CARD (left_part(index(i)) || ',' );
end;
call PUNCH_CARD (left_part(index(npr)) || ' );' );
call BUILD_CARD (' declare prlength(' || npr || ' ) bit(8) initial (0,' );
do i = 1 to npr;
   j = 1;    k = head(index(i));
   do while k ¬= 0;
      j = j + 1;    k = shr(k, 8);
   end;
   if i = npr then call PUNCH_CARD ( j || ' );' );
   else call BUILD_CARD (j || ',' );
end;
```

```
call BUILD_CARD (' declare context_case(' || npr || ' ) bit(8) initial (0,' );
do i = 1 to nsy;  tp_save(i) = 0;  end;
do i = 1 to npr;    /* Compute context case: */
   j = mp_save(index(i));   /* Set up in COMPUTE_C2, used here.   */
   k = left_part(index(i));
   do case j;
      /* case 0: can tell by either left or right context,
      use length to decide unless equal. */
      j = p_save(index(i));   /* Use the cheap test, if required.   */
      /* case 1: use C1 matrix for this one. */
      ;
      /* case 2:  need left context table. */
      tp_save(k) = tp_save(k) | 1;
      /* case 3:  need both left and right context. */
      tp_save(k) = tp_save(k) | 2;
   end;
   token_save(k) = index(i);
   if i = npr then call PUNCH_CARD (j || ' );' );
   else call BUILD_CARD (j || ',' );
end;
j = 0;    /* Construct context tables for C2: */
do i = nt + 1 to nsy;   /* Step through non-terminals: */
   sort#(i) = j;
   if tp_save(i) then
      do;
         k = token_save(i);    m = 0;
         do l = ind(k) to ind1(k);
            p = shr(f11(l), 8) & "FF";
            if p ¬= m then
               do;
                  work(j), m = p;
                  j = j + 1;  /* Count the number of entries. */
               end;
         end;
      end;
end;
if j = 0 then j = 1;  /* Assure non-negative upper bound for array. */
call BUILD_CARD (' declare left_context(' || j - 1 || ' ) bit(8) initial(' );
do i = 0 to j - 2;
   call BUILD_CARD (work(i) || ',' );
end;
call PUNCH_CARD (work(j-1) || ' );' );
if j > 255 then k = 16;   else k = 8;   /* j < 256 allows 8 bit packing. */
call BUILD_CARD (' declare left_index(' || nsy-nt || ' ) bit(' || k
   || ' ) initial (' );
```

```
      do i = nt + 1 to nsy;
         call BUILD_CARD (sort#(i) || ',' );
      end;
      call PUNCH_CARD (j || ' );' );
      j = 0;
      do i = nt + 1 to nsy;
         sort#(i) = j;   /* Record where each non-terminal starts. */
         if shr(tp_save(i), 1) then   /* We need both contexts. */
            do;
               k = token_save(i);
               do l = ind(k) to ind1(k);
                  triple(j) = f11(l) & "FFFF";   j = j + 1;
               end;
            end;
      end;
      if j = 0 then j = 1;   /* Assure non-negative upper bound for array. */
      call BUILD_CARD (' declare context_triple(' || j−1 || ' ) fixed initial (' );
      do i = 0 to j − 2;
         call BUILD_CARD (triple(i) || ',' );
      end;
      call PUNCH_CARD (triple(j−1) || ' );' );
      if j > 255 then k = 16;   else k = 8;   /* j < 256 allows 8 bit packing. */
      call BUILD_CARD (' declare triple_index(' || nsy−nt || ' ) bit(' || k
         || ' ) initial (' );
      do i = nt + 1 to nsy;   /* Punch marginal index table. */
         call BUILD_CARD (sort#(i) || ',' );
      end;
      call PUNCH_CARD (j || ' );' );
      do i = 0 to nsy;   p_save(i) = 0;   end;
      do i = 1 to npr;         /* Step through the productions: */
         p = tail(index(i));   /* Marginal index into production table */
         if p_save(p) = 0 then p_save(p) = i;
      end;
      p_save(nsy+1) = npr + 1;   /* Mark the end of the production table. */
      do j = 0 to nsy −1; /* Take care of symbols that never end a production: */
         i = nsy − j;
         if p_save(i) = 0 then p_save(i) = p_save(i+1);
      end;
      call BUILD_CARD (' declare pr_index(' || nsy || ' ) bit(8) initial (' );
      do i = 1 to nsy;
         call BUILD_CARD (p_save(i) || ',' );
      end;
      call PUNCH_CARD (npr+1 || ' );' );
      call PRINT_TIME;
   end PUNCH_PRODUCTIONS;
```

```
/* The actual execution of ANALYZER is controlled from this loop:  */

do while stacking;

    first_time, last_time = time;
    iteration_count, trouble_count = 1;

    do while trouble_count > 0;

        if iteration_count = 1 then call READ_GRAMMAR;
        else call IMPROVE_GRAMMAR;
        call PRINT_TIME;
        call COMPUTE_HEADS;
        call PRINT_TIME;

        if ¬ ambiguous then
            do;
                call PRODUCE;
                call PRINT_TIME;
                call INDEX_F11;
                call SORT_PRODUCTIONS;
                call COMPUTE_C1;
                call PRINT_TIME;
                call COMPUTE_C2;
                call PRINT_TIME;
                double_space;
            end;

        output = ' Analysis complete for iteration ' || iteration_count;
        if error_count = 0 then output = ' No errors were detected.' ;
        else if error_count = 1 then output = ' * One error was detected.' ;
        else if error_count <= 20 then
            output = substr(' ********************', 0, error_count) || ' ' ||
                error_count || ' errors were detected.' ;
        else output = ' ******************** ... ' || error_count ||
            ' errors were detected.' ;
        iteration_count = iteration_count + 1;
        if ambiguous | ¬ control(byte(' I' )) then trouble_count = 0;
    end;

    if ¬ ambiguous then call PUNCH_PRODUCTIONS;
    if control(byte(' P' )) then output = ' Punching complete.' ;
end;

eof
```

Exercise Evaluations

Exercises are not optional. Often they provide the motivation for further developments, or attempt to solidify key points which have just been made. They should be read and digested in much the same fashion as the rest of the text. In addition, serious students should expect to work most of them—the number will vary with the seriousness of the student and the time available.

The exercises vary in both difficulty and importance. To assist in the selection of those to be worked, we give a rough evaluation of the difficulty and importance factors for each exercise. These take the form "$C[d/i]$", where C is a category as follows:

T   Thought problem. These are sometimes tricky, but if carefully thought out, the amount of routine work should be minimal.

E   Exercises to be worked out. These can be solved by routine application of principles developed in the text.

P   Programming problem. The number of these which can be attempted will be controlled by the type and amount of computer access that is available. Classes may be divided into teams, or different problems assigned to different students.

d is a "logarithmic" difficulty estimate on a scale of 0 to 10. Points on this scale may be read as follows:

0   utterly trivial
2   easy
5   routine
8   challenging
10   term project.

Anyone who finds himself stumped by exercises rated 6 or less should certainly reread the preceding section(s); the exercises should not be particularly hard when the section is understood.

i is a "logarithmic" importance or payoff estimate, again on a scale of 10, to be read as follows:

0   completely optional
2   interesting
5   part of the development
8   key point, very worthwhile
10   vital to some readers.

Of course, the actual payoff will depend on the interests of particular readers.

Some evaluations are also followed by an asterisk. This denotes an exercise in which it is important that the reader understand *why* the question was asked. Whether he can solve the problem or not, the reader should reread the section if he does not comprehend the reason for posing the problem.

Exercise Evaluations

0. 1. 1	T	[8/8]*	
0. 2. 1	TP	[8/7]*	
0. 2. 2	T	[8/5]	Refer to Exercises 3.3.14-16 for hints.
0. 3. 1	EP	[5/5]	If you didn't write *any* programs for Exercise 0.2.1, pick some other programming assignment from this book for your evaluation.
1. 6. 1	T	[5/8]*	You should have quite a list.
1. 6. 2	T	[6/6]	"To each his suff'rings: all are men, condemnd alike to groan."†
2. 1. 1	T	[3/6]	
2. 2. 1	E	[2/5]	
2. 2. 2	E	[5/5]	Warning: One serious attempt at a grammar for English has 24,000 rules. Attempt only a modest improvement.
2. 2. 3	EP	[6/6]	
2. 2. 4	T	[5/6]	
2. 2. 5	E	[5/5]	
2. 2. 6	T	[4/6]	
2. 2. 7	T	[4/6]	
2. 2. 8	T	[4/6]	
2. 2. 9	T	[4/6]	
2. 2.10	E	[5/5]	
2. 2.11	E	[5/6]	
2. 3. 1	T	[4/6]	
2. 3. 2	T	[6/6]	It may help to change your answer to Exercise 2.3.1.
2. 3. 3	T	[6/7]	
2. 3. 4	T	[6/7]	
2. 3. 5	T	[5/5]	First determine $L(P_3)$ and $L(P_4)$.
2. 3. 6	E	[3/5]	
2. 3. 7	E	[6/5]	
2. 3. 8	E	[5/6]	
2. 3. 9	T	[6/6]	
2. 3.10	T	[5/6]	
2. 3.11	T	[6/6]	
2. 3.12	T	[6/6]	
2. 3.13	T	[7/4]	
2. 3.14	T	[6/4]	Use a single non-terminal for the cycle.

---

† From Thomas Gray, *On a Distant Prospect of Eton College.*

2. 3.15	T [5/4]	Hint: Look ahead to Section 5.1.
2. 3.16	T [6/4]	
3. 2. 1	E [3/6]	
3. 2. 2	EP[4/6]	
3. 2. 3	EP[4/6]	
3. 2. 4	EP[4/5]	
3. 2. 5	EP[4/5]	
3. 2. 6	T [5/5]	
3. 2. 7	T [5/5]	
3. 3. 1	E [4/6]	
3. 3. 2	T [5/7]	Find a tight bound.
3. 3. 3	T [5/5]	
3. 3. 4	T [5/5]	
3. 3. 5	T [5/5]	
3. 3. 6	EP[5/6]	
3. 3. 7	EP[5/6]	
3. 3. 8	T [5/6]	
3. 3. 9	EP[5/5]	
3. 3.10	EP[5/6]	
3. 3.11	EP[5/6]	
3. 3.12	EP[5/6]	
3. 3.13	T [4/7]*	
3. 3.14	TP[6/5]	
3. 3.15	EP[5/4]	
3. 3.16	T [7/5]	Try to prove something about "code density."
3. 4. 1	E [4/7]	
3. 4. 2	E [5/6]	
3. 4. 3	E [5/5]	
3. 4. 4	E [5/5]	
3. 4. 5	E [6/6]	
3. 4. 6	E [6/6]	
3. 4. 7	T [6/6]	
3. 4. 8	T [6/5]	Your grammar need not allow the translation of *all* assignments.
3. 4. 9	T [6/5]	Fully parenthesized expressions are easiest.
3. 4.10	EP[5/5]	
3. 5. 1	E [3/6]	
3. 5. 2	E [5/5]	
3. 5. 3	E [3/5]	
3. 5. 4	T [5/5]	
3. 5. 5	E [3/5]	
3. 5. 6	T [6/6]	
3. 5. 7	T [7/6]	Derive a contradiction from the assumption that the algorithm fails.
3. 5. 8	T [8/6]	

3. 5. 9   T [6/6]

4. 1. 1   T [2/6]   Recall Section 2.3.
4. 1. 2   T [5/6]
4. 1. 3   T [6/6]

4. 2. 1   E [4/5]
4. 2. 2   T [5/5]
4. 2. 3   E [6/6]
4. 2. 4   T [5/4]
4. 2. 5   E [3/5]
4. 2. 6   T [5/7]
4. 2. 7   E [6/6]
4. 2. 8   E [5/6]
4. 2. 9   T [8/8]
4. 2.10   T [7/7]
4. 2.11   T [7/7]   Derive a contradiction from the contrary assumption.
4. 2.12   T [6/8]   There is a simple condition.
4. 2.13   T [6/8]   Derive a contradiction from the contrary assumption.
4. 2.14   T [6/7]   What do "real compilers" do?

4. 3. 1   E [3/6]
4. 3. 2   T [6/7]   Derive a contradiction from the contrary assumption.
4. 3. 3   T [6/7]
4. 3. 4   T [6/6]
4. 3. 5   T [5/6]
4. 3. 6   T [5/7]

4. 4. 1   T [6/6]
4. 4. 2   T [4/6]
4. 4. 3   E [4/5]
4. 4. 4   E [4/5]
4. 4. 5   E [5/5]
4. 4. 6   E [5/5]
4. 4. 7   T [5/5]
4. 4. 8   T [6/6]
4. 4. 9   T [7/7]
4. 4.10   T [7/6]
4. 4.11   T [7/5]

5. 1. 1   T [4/6]
5. 1. 2   T [4/5]
5. 1. 3   T [5/5]
5. 1. 4   T [5/5]
5. 1. 5   T [5/5]
5. 1. 6   T [6/5]
5. 1. 7   T [5/6]
5. 1. 8   E [4/5]
5. 1. 9   E [5/5]

5. 1.10   T [6/6]
5. 1.11   T [5/6]
5. 1.12   T [5/5]

5. 2. 1   E [5/5]
5. 2. 2   T [6/5]
5. 2. 3   T [6/5]
5. 2. 4   E [5/5]   Think.
5. 2. 5   E [5/5]
5. 2. 6   E [5/6]
5. 2. 7   E [5/5]

5. 3. 1   E [6/6]
5. 3. 2   E [6/6]
5. 3. 3   T [8/8]

5. 4. 1   E [5/5]
5. 5. 1   T [9/7]

5. 6. 1   E [6/7]
5. 6. 2   E [7/7]
5. 6. 3   E [7/7]
5. 6. 4   T [6/4]
5. 6. 5   T [6/7]
5. 6. 6   T [8/7]
5. 6. 7   T [6/7]
5. 6. 8   T [6/6]

6.18. 1   P [3/5]
6.18. 2   TP[5/5]
6.18. 3   TP[4/4]
6.18. 4   P [3/4]
6.18. 5   TP[5/5]
6.18. 6   TP[6/5]
6.18. 7   TP[8/5]
6.18. 8   TP[7/5]
6.18. 9   P [3/4]
6.18.10   P [5/4]
6.18.11   P [4/4]
6.18.12   P [4/4]
6.18.13   P [4/5]
6.18.14   TP[6/6]
6.18.15   P [5/5]
6.18.16   TP[6/6]
6.18.17   T [5/5]
6.18.18   T [6/4]
6.18.19   T [5/5]   See [Minsky 1968]
6.18.20   P [5/5]
6.18.21   TP[5/6]

6.18.22   P [5/6]

7. 1. 1   T [5/7]
7. 1. 2   T [4/6]
7. 1. 3   E [5/6]
7. 2. 1   E [4/6]
7. 2. 2   E [5/5]
7. 2. 3   E [5/5]
7. 2. 4   E [6/6]
7. 2. 5   E [5/6]
7. 2. 6   E [5/6]
7. 2. 7   T [5/6]*
7. 2. 8   T [6/6]
7. 2. 9   T [6/6]

8. 2. 1   TP[7/6]
8. 4. 1   T [6/6]*
8. 4. 2   T [6/6]
8. 4. 3   P [9/9]
8. 5. 1   P [8/7]
8. 5. 2   P [7/8]
8. 5. 3   P [7/7]
8. 5. 4   T [7/7]
8. 5. 5   P [9/9]
8. 5. 6   T [6/6]
8. 7. 1   P [1/5]
8. 7. 2   TP[7/5]
8. 7. 3   T [8/7]
8. 7. 4   P [9/9]
8. 7. 5   T [6/6]
8. 8. 1   P [5/5]
8. 8. 2   P [5/5]
8. 8. 3   T [5/4]   What columns do card readers read ?
8. 8. 4   TP[5/6]
8. 8. 5   P [5/5]   Wiil program deck size grow ?
8. 9. 1   P [5/6]
8. 9. 2   TP[6/7]
8. 9. 3   T [7/7]
8. 9. 4   P [6/6]
8.10. 1   TP[7/6]   Handle string descriptors carefully.
8.10. 2   T [6/6]
8.10. 3   T [5/6]
8.11. 1   T [5/7]
8.11. 2   P [6/7]
8.11. 3   T [7/7]
8.11. 4   P [8/7]

8.11. 5   P [6/6]
8.11. 6   TP[7/6]
8.12. 1   T [6/7]
8.12. 2   TP[7/7]
8.12. 3   P [5/5]
8.12. 4   P [5/4]
8.13. 1   T [5/6]*

9. 6. 1   EP[5/6]   Recall Chapter 3.
9. 6. 2   EP[5/5]
9. 6. 3   EP[5/5]
9. 6. 4   TP[5/6]
9. 6. 5   EP[6/6]
9. 6. 6   TP[7/6]
9. 6. 7   TP[10/10]
9. 6. 8   TP[10/10]

A1.11.1. P [6/5]
A1.11.2. TP[4/4]
A1.11.3. TP[8/6]

Bibliography

[Bach 64] Bach, E., *An Introduction to Transformational Grammars*, New York: Holt, Rinehart & Winston, Inc. 1964.

[Bar-Hillel 64] Bar-Hillel, Y., *et al.*, "On Categorical and Phrase Structure Grammars," *Bulletin of the Research Council* (Israel), Sec. F, 9 (1960), 155.

[Bratman 61] Bratman, H., "An Alternate Form of the UNCOL Diagram," *Communications of the Association for Computing Machinery*, **4**, No. 3 (1961), 142.

[Chomsky 57] Chomsky, N., *Syntactic Structures*. The Hague: Mouton and Company, 1957.

[Chomsky 63] Chomsky, N., "Formal Properties of Grammars," in *Handbook of Mathematical Psychology*, II. New York: John Wiley & Sons, Inc. (1963), 323.

[Chomsky 65] Chomsky, N., *Aspects of the Theory of Syntax*. Cambridge, Mass.: M.I.T Press, 1965.

[De Remer 69] De Remer, F. L., *Practical Translators for LR(k) Languages*, Ph.D. dissertation, M.I.T. (September, 1969).

[Dijkstra 65] Dijkstra, E. W., "Cooperating Sequential Processes," *Report EWD123*, Mathematical Department, Technological University, Eindhoven, September 1965.

[Early 70] Early, J., "An Efficient Context-free Parsing Algorithm," *Communications of the Association for Computing Machinery*, **13**, No. 2 (1970), 94.

[Falkoff *et al.* 64] Falkoff, A. D., K. E. Iverson, and E. H. Sussenguth, "A Formal Description of System/360," *IBM System Journal*, **3**, No. 3 (1964), 198.

[Feldman and Gries 68] Feldman, J., and D. Gries, "Translator Writing Systems," *Communications of the Association for Computing Machinery*, **11**, No. 2 (February 1968), 77.

[Floyd 62] Floyd, R. W., "On Ambiguity in Phrase-structure Languages," *Communications of the Association for Computing Machinery*, **5** (1962), 526.

[Floyd 63] Floyd, R. W., "Syntactic Analysis and Operator Precedence," *Journal of the Association for Computing Machinery*, **10**, No. 3 (July 1963), 316.

[Floyd 64] Floyd, R. W., "Bounded Context Syntactic Analysis," *Communications of the Association for Computing Machinery*, **7**, No. 2 (February 1964), 62.

[Floyd 67] Floyd, R. W., "Assigning Meanings to Programs," *Proceedings of the Symposium in Applied Mathematics*, **19** (1967), 19.

[Ginsberg 66] Ginsberg, S., *The Mathematical Theory of Context-free Languages*. New York: McGraw-Hill Book Company, 1966.

[Hoare 64] Hoare, C.A.R., "Case Expressions," *Algol Bulletin*, **18** (October 1964), 20.

[IBM 6Xa] "Operating System/360, Concepts and Facilities," *Form C28-6535*, IBM Corporation (1965).

[IBM 6Xb] "IBM System/360 Operating System Job Control Language, *Form C28-6539*, IBM Corporation (1967).

[IBM 6Xc] "IBM System/360 Operating System Supervisor and Data Management Services," *Form C28-6646*, IBM Corporation (1967).

[IBM 6Xd] "IBM System/360 Operating System Supervisor and Data Management Macro-instructions," *Form C28-6647*, IBM Corporation (1967).

[IBM 6Xe] "IBM System/360 Operating System Assembler Language," *Form C28-6514*, IBM Corporation (1967).

[IBM 6Xf] "IBM System/360 Principles of Operation," *Form A22-6821*, IBM Corporation (1966).

[IBM 6Xg] "IBM System/360 PL/I Language Specifications," *Form Y33-6003*, IBM Corporation (1968).

[Illife 68] Illife, J. K., *Basic Machine Principles* (Computer Monograph Series) New York: American Elsevier, 1968.

[Iverson 62] Iverson, K. E., *A Programming Language*. New York: John Wiley & Sons, Inc., 1962.

[Knuth 65] Knuth, D. E., "On the Translation of Languages from Left to Right," *Information and Control*, **8** (1965), 607.

[Knuth 68] Knuth, D. E., private communication.

[Knuth 70] Knuth, D. E., *Sorting and Searching, The Art of Computer Programming*, III. Reading, Mass.: Addison-Wesley Publishing Co., Inc., 1970.

[Lowry and Medlock 69] Lowry, E. S., and C. W. Medlock, "Object Code Optimization," *Communications of the Association for Computing Machinery*, **12**, No. 1 (January 1969), 13.

[Lynch 68] Lynch, W. C., "A High Speed Parsing Algorithm For ICOR Grammars," *Report 1097*. Computing Center, Case Western Reserve University (1968), 13.

[McCarthy 65] McCarthy, J., P. Abrahams, D. Edwards, T. Hart, and M. Levin, *LISP 1.5 Programmer's Manual*. Cambridge, Mass.: M.I.T Press, 1965.

[McCarthy 67] McCarthy, J., and J. Painter, "Correctness of a Compiler for Arithmetic Expressions," *Proceedings of the Symposium in Applied Mathematics*, **19** (1967), 33.

[McKeeman 66] McKeeman, W. M., *An Approach to Computer Language Design*, Ph.D. dissertation, Stanford University, 1966.

[McKeeman 67] McKeeman, W. M., "Language Directed Computer Design," *Proceedings of the Fall Joint Computer Conference* (1967), 413.

[Minsky 67] Minsky, M., *Computation: Finite and Infinite Machines*. Englewood Cliffs, N. J.: Prentice-Hall, Inc., 1967.

[Naur 60] Naur, P., *et al.*, "Report on the Algorithmic Language ALGOL 60," *Communications of the Association for Computing Machinery*, **3** (1960), 299.

[Naur 63] Naur, P., *et al.*, "Revised Report on the Algorithmic Language ALGOL 60," *Communications of the Association for Computing Machinery*, **6**, No. 1 (January 1963), 1.

[Pierce 61] Pierce, J., *Symbols, Signals & Noise*. New York: Harper & Row, Publishers, 1961.

[Pohl 67] Pohl, I. (letter), *Communications of the Association for Computing Machinery*, **10**, No. 12 (December 1967), 757.

[Randell and Russell 64] Randell, B., and L. J. Russell, *Algol 60 Implementation*. New York: Academic Press, Inc., 1964.

[Shaw 64] Shaw, C. J., "More Instructions . . . Less Work," *Datamation*, **10**, No. 6 (June 1964), 34.

[Wirth 66] Wirth, N., and H. Weber, "Euler: A Generalization of Algol 60 and Its Formal Definition," *Communications of the Association for Computing Machinery*, **9**, Nos. 1 and 2 (January and February 1966), 1.

[Wortman 70] Wortman, D., *A Study of Language-Directed Machine Design*, Ph.D. dissertation, Stanford University, 1970.

Index